LEADERSHIP COMMUNICATION THEORY AND PRACTICE

Through the theorization of leadership from various communicative perspectives, this book offers a comprehensive, multi-perspectival framework and actionable insights for building responsible, relational, and inclusive leadership practices.

This book presents three distinct perspectives on how sub-disciplines in communication studies understand, utilize, and theorize the intersections between communication and leadership: (1) diversity, equity, inclusion, and access (DEIA), intercultural, and critical cultural approaches; (2) relational, discursive, and collective approaches; and (3) pedagogical and training approaches. Contributors showcase how communication theory assists in building more responsible, relational, dialogical, ethical, and meaningful leadership practices, using applied cases, scenarios, and leader profiles to demonstrate theoretical approaches in practical contexts. Each chapter features suggested further readings and questions to spark continued engagement with the issues presented.

This text is suited to advanced undergraduate and graduate students in leadership communication, organizational communication, and leadership studies within communication studies, business, psychology, higher education and administration, and military leadership programs.

Sandra L. Pensoneau-Conway is Professor of Communication Studies in the School of Communication Studies at Southern Illinois University, USA.

Nilanjana Bardhan is Professor of Public Relations and Intercultural Communication in the School of Communication Studies at Southern Illinois University, USA.

Sean M. Eddington is Associate Professor of Organizational Communication in the A.Q. Miller School of Media and Communication at Kansas State University, USA.

LEADERSHIP COMMUNICATION THEORY AND PRACTICE

An Advanced Introduction

Edited by Sandra L. Pensoneau-Conway, Nilanjana Bardhan, and Sean M. Eddington

Routledge
Taylor & Francis Group
NEW YORK AND LONDON

Designed cover image: © A.B. Art

First published 2027
by Routledge
605 Third Avenue, New York, NY 10158

and by Routledge
4 Park Square, Milton Park, Abingdon, Oxon, OX14 4RN

Routledge is an imprint of the Taylor & Francis Group, an informa business

ISBN: 978-1-032-91512-8 (hbk)
ISBN: 978-1-032-90228-9 (pbk)
ISBN: 978-1-003-56366-2 (ebk)

DOI: 10.4324/9781003563662

Typeset in Sabon
by KnowledgeWorks Global Ltd.

CONTENTS

CONTRIBUTORS

Ahmet Aksoy (Ph.D., Texas Tech University) is Assistant Professor of Communication in the Department of Communication and Media at Winona State University. His research examines how cultural identities are formed, expressed, and negotiated through communication practices within diverse social, institutional, and intercultural contexts, with emphasis on culture and meaning.

Amy Aldridge is a Vice Provost and Professor of Communication at Middle Tennessee State University. Her work centers on social justice, activism, identity, and leadership. She is published widely in books, journals, and editorials. Her forthcoming co-edited volume, *Reconciliation: The Final Step in Achieving Nonviolent Social Change*, is expected in 2026.

Mary Z. Ashlock is Professor in the Department of Communication at the University of Louisville. During Mary's tenure at the university, she has been named as Faculty Favorite, Distinguished Teaching Professor, and Faculty Mentor along with a National Communication Association Outstanding Tenured Teaching Award.

Nilanjana Bardhan is Professor of Intercultural Communication and Public Relations at Southern Illinois University Carbondale. Her scholarship focuses on identity/difference/culture, public relations, diversity and inclusion, leadership, globalization, and postcolonial theory. She has published several books, book chapters, and journal articles on these topics throughout her career.

David Barnhart, Ph.D., is a recent graduate of Kansas State University's Staley School of Leadership, where he earned his doctorate in Leadership Communication. His research interests center on co-constructed resilience and leadership practices.

Mac T. Benavides is Assistant Professor in the Staley School of Leadership at Kansas State University. As a community-engaged scholar, Mac's teaching, research, and practice center around global and domestic community-based learning, reciprocal partnerships in community-driven sustainable development, leadership education, and creating equitable learning environments at higher education institutions.

Timothy Betts (Ph.D., University of South Florida) is Assistant Professor at Texas Christian University. His research engages organizational communication theory to examine, critique, and reimagine how people organize economies. His interest in economic communication connects with issues of communicative resilience, antenarrative and computational research methods, online organizing, and policymaking.

William Brantley is President and Chief Learning Officer of Brantley Advanced Social Science Applications. A certified project manager, agile leader, business analyst, talent developer, and data scientist, he teaches at the University of Louisville and the University of Maryland, creates online courses, and authors books on leadership, strategy, and management.

Patrice M. Buzzanell (Ph.D., Purdue University) is Distinguished Professor at the University of South Florida and AAAS Fellow. Her research, teaching, engagement, and grants coalesce around career, work-life issues, resilience, feminisms/gender, ethics, and design.

Jayita Chakraborty M.B.A., M.A. (she/her), is a doctoral student and teaching assistant in the Department of Communication and Journalism at the University of New Mexico. Her research interests include health communication, strategic communication, and media.

Jamie Hong Chow, MA, is a Ph.D. Candidate in the Department of Political Science at the University of Western Ontario. Her research explores the intersection of gender and leadership, social cognition, personality traits, and political participation. She is Project Director at the Body Politics Lab.

Willow Craine is a Ph.D. student in the University of South Florida's Department of Communication. Her scholarship is committed to multi-level resilience theorizing in the contexts of marginalization, family, and career. Specifically, Willow's work seeks to understand how disruption is anticipated and navigated when organizing resilience in workplaces and communities.

Christine E. Crouse-Dick is Professor and Chair of Communication Arts at Bethel College. Her research explores identity, representation, leadership, and narrative-based learning. She is co-founder of the TRHT Campus Center, which fosters racial healing through narrative change, and the Slow Leadership Institute, which promotes compassionate, collaborative leadership and restorative justice.

Carolyn Cunningham is Professor of Communication and Leadership Studies at Gonzaga University. She teaches courses in women and leadership, digital storytelling, and social media analysis. Her research explores the intersections of gender and technology with a specific focus on girls and leadership.

Sean M. Eddington is Associate Professor of Organizational Communication at the A.Q. Miller School of Media and Communication at Kansas State University. His research addresses career communication, new media, resilience, and gendered organizing. He has published work in journals such as *Social Media + Society* and *Management Communication Quarterly*.

Chrys Egan is the Fulton School of Liberal Arts Associate Dean, Center for the Advancement of Faculty Excellence Interim Director, and Communication Professor at Salisbury University. She has 55 academic publications and 150+ conference presentations on communication, leadership, and culture. She earned local, state, national, and international awards.

Jennifer Martin Emami is Adjunct Professor for Southern New Hampshire University, teaching courses on Cultural Awareness. She is a substitute teacher, wife, and mom. Jennifer's expertise includes womanist pedagogy, social justice in the classroom, and managing difficult classroom conversations. She earned her Ph.D. in Multicultural Women's and Gender Studies.

Craig Engstrom, Ph.D., is Associate Professor of Business Communication and Director of the Center for Teaching Excellence at Southern Illinois University Carbondale. He is Certified Professional in Talent Development (CPTD) and is Microsoft Innovative Educator Trainer. He is a principal consultant at Communication@Work LLC.

Sharmila Pixy Ferris is Professor of Communication at William Paterson University of New Jersey and has taught at the University of Alberta and Royal Roads University, Canada. Her research examines identity, power, leadership, mentoring, and technology in higher education. She has published many articles and book chapters and ten books.

Amanda Friesen, Ph.D., is Canada Research Chair in Political Psychology, Associate Professor of Political Science, and Director of the Body Politics Lab at the University of Western Ontario, Canada. She also holds appointments in Psychology and Gender, Sexuality and Women's Studies and serves as Associate Editor of *Political Psychology*.

Janie M. H. Fritz (Ph.D., University of Wisconsin-Madison), is Professor and Chair of the Department of Communication and Rhetorical Studies at Duquesne University and studies organizational/interpersonal communication ethics, leadership, and religious communication. Her publications include *Professional Civility: Communicative Virtue at Work* and *Communication Ethics Literacy: Dialogue and Difference* (with Leeanne Bell McManus and Michael R. Kearney).

Ralph A. Gigliotti serves as Chief of Staff to President at Rutgers University, where he also holds several affiliated faculty appointments. His research and consulting interests explore topics related to leadership, crisis, strategy, team dynamics, and organizational communication. He has authored or edited ten books and over 50 peer-reviewed publications.

Jacy King Gross is a Communication Specialist focused on developing authentic voice and leadership through public speaking. She holds a master's degree in communication from Gonzaga University and teaches in the Los Angeles Community College District, specializing in performance-based pedagogy and professional communication training across educational, nonprofit, and corporate contexts.

Jenna Haugen, Ph.D., serves as Clinical Associate Professor of Management and Corporate Communication at UNC Kenan-Flagler Business School. Her research examines organizational communication, dissent, and persuasive communication. Her teaching emphasizes social responsibility, community-engaged learning, and the belief that business should serve as a force for good.

Lauren B. Hearit Klug (Ph.D., Purdue University) is Associate Professor of Management at Hope College in Holland, Michigan. Her research focuses on the intersection of economics and organizational communication. She is interested in how economic and political actors shape our perceptions about the performance of the economy during crises.

Rose Helens-Hart is Associate Professor at Fort Hays State University. She enjoys working with professionals through communication training and consulting and teaches courses in professional development and business and corporate communication.

Sovi Herring is a Ph.D. student in Rhetoric at Duquesne University whose work explores communication ethics, nonprofit leadership, and applied communication. Her scholarship appears in *Listening: Journal of Communication Ethics, Religion, and Culture*, The Forbes Funds *Tropman Report*, *Explorations in Media Ecology*, and others.

Amy N. Heuman is Professor of Communication Studies and Director of Women's and Gender Studies at Texas Tech University. Her research centers on negotiations and performances of identity as well as how community members utilize communication to mobilize for social change from interpretive, critical, and feminist perspectives.

John M. Hinck (Ph.D., University of San Diego) is Associate Professor of Leadership Studies and Director, VECTOR (the Center of Excellence for Learning Professionals) for Air University, US Air Force. His teaching and research span 40+ publications on leadership, leader development, coaching, communication, the Indo-Pacific Region, and teaching/learning.

Jen Jones is an international speaker and has published numerous journal articles and book chapters, as well as the book *A Research Agenda for Organizational Ethics* (2023). Her teaching and research integrate the humanities with contemporary issues in leadership and organizational ethics, illuminating insights from key philosophical figures.

Saya Kakim is a female international scholar specializing in interdisciplinary and participatory approaches to research. She earned her doctorate in leadership communication from Kansas State University. Kakim's research agenda includes questions about deliberative practices in the community and classroom, health communication, and health equity in rural and urban settings.

Brandon W. Kliewer, Ph.D., is Associate Professor of Civic and Organizational Leadership in Leadership Studies at the University of Tennessee,

Knoxville. Currently, he is serving as Interim Faculty Director of the Jones Center for Leadership and Service.

Stephen M. Kromka, Ph.D., is a tenured Associate Professor of Communication at the University of Tampa. His research spans instructional, interpersonal, and conflict communication, with a focus on teaching effectiveness, burnout, and applied pedagogy. He publishes widely and presents nationally on evidence-based effective communication practices.

Dorine Lawrence-Hughes, J.D., Ed.D., is the founder of Brazen Communication, a consulting company specializing in academic leadership development and coaching. She served as Assistant Dean for Undergraduate Education at the University of Michigan and as Clinical Associate Professor in the Annenberg School of Communication and Journalism at USC.

Jasmine R. Linabary (Ph.D., Purdue University) is Assistant Professor in the Department of Public and Applied Humanities and Director of the Co-Design Collaborative (Co-Lab) at the University of Arizona in Tucson, AZ, USA. Her research focuses on organizing for social change, new media, and feminist and participatory methodologies.

Sherri Lynch, Ph.D., is a scholar of Leadership Studies at Gonzaga University. She co-founded the Women Lead program, a program with a mission to educate and empower women, authored Gonzaga's Certificate in Women's Leadership, and teaches undergraduate, graduate, and professional leadership programs. Her research examines women's leadership and community-building.

Lauren Mackenzie has been a military educator for 16 years and currently leads the faculty development effort and *Military Scholarship of Teaching and Learning* program at Marine Corps University in Quantico, VA.

Kerry McCaig is Director of Academic Success Center at the US Air Force Academy. She holds a B.S. from Kansas State University, M.A. from University of Denver, and Ph.D. from Florida State University. She served as an administrator, academic advisor, NCAA coach, and faculty member for a variety of undergraduate- and graduate-level courses at six universities and three community colleges.

Shannon K. McManimon (Ph.D.) is Associate Professor and Program Director of the interdisciplinary Ethical Leadership Doctorate in Education at Viterbo University (La Crosse, WI). Her research has used narrative, arts-based, and participatory methods to study equity-focused teaching, learning, and leading in both informal and formal settings.

Dylan Medeiros is Learning and Development Specialist for HFA (an international Architecture/Engineering firm). His work is centered on group dynamics and interpersonal success in the workplace. He has previously been published in the *International Journal of Interactive Communication Systems and Technologies* (IJICST).

Diane M. Monahan holds a Ph.D. in Communication from Temple University, an M.A. from the University of Central Florida, and a B.A. in Psychology from Florida State University. She is Associate Vice President and Dean of Graduate Studies at Agnes Scott College and the author of *Making the Most of Your Communication Degree.*

Scott A. Myers (Ph.D., Kent State University, 1995) is Professor and Peggy Rardin McConnell Endowed Teaching Chair in the Department of Communication Studies at West Virginia University, where he teaches courses in organizational, instructional, and positive communication. His research interests center primarily on the student–instructor relationship in the college classroom.

Sandra L. Pensoneau-Conway is Professor of Communication Studies at Southern Illinois University Carbondale. Her research interests include critical communication pedagogy, identity, and automethods. Her work appears in outlets such as *Communication Education, Critical Education, Critical Interpersonal and Family Communication Pedagogy*, and *Handbook of Autoethnography*.

Sara Pitts earned her Ph.D. from West Virginia University. She teaches a variety of classes ranging from interpersonal to advanced public speaking. Her research focuses on student learning which is reflected in the way she interacts with her students in her classroom and in the academic advising office.

Kerry L. Priest is Professor in the Staley School of Leadership at Kansas State University. She studies leadership development, leadership pedagogy, and how groups collaborate to create change through collective, adaptive, and systems approaches to leadership. She seeks to help individuals and communities develop resilience to navigate complex challenges.

Evgeniya Pyatovskaya (Ph.D., University of South Florida) is Assistant Professor at Loyola Marymount University. Her research focuses on organizational communication, leadership, and resilience, and aims to bridge critical scholarship and social change.

Robyn Remke is Director of Higher Education at Templar International Group, a leading cyber security consultancy. Previously at Lancaster University, she co-created the Cyber Security Executive MBA and directed the full-time MBA. Her research spans leadership, communication, and gender equity in business education.

Brett W. Robertson, Ph.D., is Associate Professor in the College of Information and Communications and Associate Director of the Hazards Vulnerability and Resilience Institute at the University of South Carolina. His research explores disaster preparedness, risk communication, and access to critical information during emergencies, earning national recognition for scholarship and teaching.

C. Kyle Rudick is Full Professor at the University of Northern Iowa. His work focuses on communication, teaching, and learning in organizations within and beyond higher education. He has published over 50 articles in journals such as the *International Journal of Communication*, *Communication Education*, and *Communication Studies*.

Soham Sen is a doctoral student in the Department of Communication and Journalism at the University of New Mexico.

Stacy Smulowitz, Ph.D., ABC, is Chairperson and Associate Professor in the Department of Communication at The University of Scranton, Executive Director of the Eastern Communication Association, and has a freelance strategic communication consulting firm. Dr. Smulowitz's most recent book is *The Communication Solution: Leading Successful Change in Higher Education*.

Melissa F. Tindage (Ph.D., West Virginia University) is Associate Professor in the Department of Communication Studies at California State University, Northridge. Her current research centers on the role that social identities play in the communicative experiences of students of color.

Robin VanMeter is a dynamic inclusion leader based in Orlando, FL, bringing 15+ years of DEI expertise. With an MBA in Project Management and doctoral work in Organizational Psychology, she is dedicated to dismantling systemic barriers, championing equity, and driving meaningful, sustainable change in workplaces and beyond.

Lisa A. Waite, owner of Waite Communication and Executive Development, is a seasoned executive coach specializing in leadership, teams, and communication. She brings three decades of experience in higher education and is Communication Studies Professor at Kent State University, where she collaborates with organizations on professional development and leadership initiatives.

Kathleen Waldron, President Emerita of William Paterson University, led the institution to Hispanic-serving status from 2010 to 2018. She is Former Baruch College (CUNY) President and a Citibank international banking executive. Her most recent book, coauthored with Sharmila Pixy Ferris, is *The Future of Higher Education*.

Andrew Wefald, Ph.D., ACC, is Associate Professor in the Staley School of Leadership at Kansas State University. He is currently serving as Graduate Program Director of the Leadership Communication Doctoral Program at K-State.

Jessica M. Welsh is Assistant Professor of Business at Viterbo University in La Crosse, WI. She holds an M.S. in Communication Studies from South Dakota State University and an Ed.D. from the University of South Dakota. Her research focuses on organizational disclosures and policy.

Jeff Youngquist (Ph.D., Wayne State University) is Associate Professor at Oakland University in the Department of Communication, Journalism, and Public Relations. His research and writing explore leadership and communication, with a focus on ethics and leadership and also academic leadership.

FOREWORD

By Robyn Remke

Leadership is among the most enduring—and most contested—phenomena of scholarly and practitioner inquiry. Across disciplines, leadership has been theorized as a trait, behavior, style, skill, identity, and influence; operationalized through countless models and frameworks; and mobilized in service of organizational performance, social change, and even moral purpose.

With this in mind, I know what you are probably thinking: the last thing this world needs is another book about leadership. Library and bookstore shelves are packed with books about leaders, books exploring different styles and types of leadership, and countless "how-to" guides on practicing leadership. This is without even mentioning the millions of YouTube videos, podcasts, and social media posts devoted to the subject. Discussions, theories, and conversations on leadership are everywhere. Indeed, you may wonder—quite rightly—whether there is anything left to say about leadership. The answer to that question is, quite simply, yes. This volume extends these conversations in directions that are typically neglected, offering both necessary critique and practical frameworks for thinking more carefully and intelligently about leadership.

Within leadership literature, a persistent tension remains: leadership is frequently discussed as though it exists independently of the communicative processes through which it is enacted, interpreted, resisted, and transformed. Communication is often positioned as a talent leaders possess, a mechanism that enhances effectiveness, or a channel through which leadership messages are transmitted. Far less often is communication treated as the constitutive medium of leadership itself.

This edited volume steps into that gap. The editors and authors of this volume advance a multifaceted and persuasive argument that leadership does not, in fact, precede communication, nor is communication merely instrumental to leadership outcomes. Rather, leadership is an emergent, relational, and culturally situated phenomenon that comes into being through communication. Representing varied theoretical traditions, empirical contexts, and pedagogical environments, these authors demonstrate how leadership is not something individuals simply do or have; it is something that is continually accomplished with others through discourse, interaction, sensemaking, and collective practice.

Importantly, at a time when leadership is increasingly invoked to address global crises, institutional mistrust, and demands for equity and accountability, this reframing is not merely academic. It has significant implications for how leadership is studied, taught, and ultimately, practiced. The central contribution of this volume lies in making communication visible not as an adjunct to leadership, but as its very condition of possibility.

Reframing leadership through communication

One of the most important contributions of this volume is its sustained challenge to dominant leadership paradigms that continue to privilege individualism, universality, and decontextualized competence. Despite decades of critique, much leadership scholarship and practice remain anchored in assumptions that leadership resides primarily in individuals, that effectiveness can be generalized across contexts, and that power and culture are secondary considerations. These assumptions have shaped not only academic theory but also leadership development programs, professional training, and organizational expectations across industries.

The chapters in this volume collectively resist these tendencies by foregrounding leadership as communicative, relational, and ethically charged. Rather than asking what traits or competencies leaders should possess, the contributors ask how leadership is constituted through interaction; how power, identity, and difference shape who can lead and how; and how leadership practices are embedded within—and constrained by—social, cultural, and institutional contexts.

Section I lays the conceptual groundwork for this reorientation. Drawing on feminist, critical, and intercultural communication traditions, the chapters in this section challenge essentialist and individual-centered models of leadership. Leadership is theorized not as a fixed role or identity, but as a dynamic process that unfolds through communicative engagement. Feminist perspectives foreground care, resilience, and relational accountability, illustrating how leadership emerges through transparency, empathy, and collective sensemaking rather than heroic decision-making. Intersectional analyses further destabilize singular leadership narratives, demonstrating how leaders' communicative capacities are shaped by intersecting identities and structural conditions.

Notably, several chapters in this section offer pointed critiques of leadership frameworks that have gained considerable traction in both academic scholarship and practice. The interrogation of authentic leadership, for example, exposes the normative assumptions embedded in calls to "be oneself," highlighting how authenticity often privileges those whose identities already align with dominant expectations. From a communication perspective, such models obscure the performative, strategic, and relational dimensions of leadership while raising ethical concerns about inclusion and responsibility to others.

What unites these contributions is a shared insistence that leadership cannot be meaningfully understood apart from communication, nor responsibly practiced without attention to power, difference, and ethics. Communication is not merely how leadership is expressed; it is how leadership is constituted, contested, and transformed.

Advancing leadership as a relational and discursive accomplishment

Building on this critical foundation, Section II advances relational, discursive, and collective approaches to leadership communication. Here, leadership is examined not only in moments of formal authority or crisis but in the everyday interactions, narratives, and institutional practices through which organizing occurs. The chapters in this section collectively demonstrate that leadership emerges across multiple levels—interpersonal, organizational, institutional, and digital—and that communication is the connective tissue linking these domains.

A significant contribution of this section is its explicit integration of communication theory and leadership theory. Long-standing fragmentation between these bodies of scholarship has limited the explanatory power of both. By bringing foundational communication theories into conversation with leadership frameworks, the chapters show how leadership can be more richly understood as an interactional and sensemaking process. This integration is not merely conceptual; it is methodological and practical as well. The use of novel data sources illustrates how leadership communication can be studied empirically in situ, offering insights that are directly relevant to organizational practice.

Relational dynamics are a central concern throughout this section. Chapters examining privacy management, social cognition, and superior-subordinate exchanges illustrate how leadership is enacted through ongoing negotiations of boundaries, expectations, and meaning. Importantly, these analyses attend to the uneven distribution of communicative risk and scrutiny, particularly for leaders from historically marginalized groups. Leadership communication is shown to be inseparable from broader cultural evaluative frameworks that shape how warmth, competence, authority, and legitimacy are interpreted.

While we tend to study leadership communication from an interpersonal perspective, several of these authors extend the analysis of leadership communication to organizational and collective contexts. Leadership discourse is examined as it becomes sedimented in organizational practices such as sustainability reporting, leadership development programs, and digital infrastructures. These chapters underscore that leadership is not only enacted by individuals but also embedded in systems and technologies that shape what leadership can be and do.

The exploration of collective leadership in digitally mediated mutual aid organizing is particularly illustrative of this point. By centering collaboration, distributed agency, and post-heroic leadership, this chapter challenges traditional assumptions about authority and control. Leadership is shown to emerge through everyday communicative practices enabled by digital affordances, offering a compelling example of leadership as a collective accomplishment rather than a centralized role.

Taken together, the authors in Section II demonstrate that leadership is fundamentally relational and discursive. They move beyond abstract calls for collaboration or participation to show, in concrete terms, how leadership is communicatively accomplished across contexts characterized by complexity, uncertainty, and interdependence.

Leadership development as communicative practice

Section III extends the volume's core arguments into the domain of pedagogy, training, and leadership development. Too often, leadership education is treated as a technical exercise focused on skill acquisition or competency frameworks, with communication relegated to presentation skills or interpersonal effectiveness. The chapters in this section challenge such instrumental approaches by positioning leadership development as an ongoing, communicative, and ethical process.

Across educational, military, civic, and organizational contexts, the contributors demonstrate that leadership capacities are cultivated through intentional pedagogical design, experiential learning, and public engagement. Classrooms, training environments, and community partnerships are treated not as sites where leadership is merely taught, but as spaces where leadership is actively constituted through dialogue, reflection, and collective action.

Humanistic and relational foundations are foregrounded as essential correctives to narrow, performance-oriented models of leadership education. By centering dignity, relational responsibility, and whole-person engagement, these chapters call for a substantive reorientation of leadership curricula. Leadership education, they argue, should prepare individuals not only to manage organizations but to participate ethically and responsibly in complex social systems.

Several chapters emphasize feminist and critical pedagogies that mobilize students and trainees to engage with real-world challenges through communicative practice. Community-based research, dialogic engagement, and reflexive learning are presented as key mechanisms through which leadership capacities are developed. In these accounts, leadership learning is embodied, relational, and deeply contextual.

Ethics and inclusion are also central themes. The examination of DEI leadership pitfalls within servant leadership frameworks, for example, illustrates how well-intentioned approaches can reproduce harm when divorced from critical reflection and communicative accountability. By offering alternative models grounded in coalition-building and community engagement, these chapters provide educators and trainers with nuanced tools for cultivating ethical leadership.

Importantly, this section does not shy away from tensions. Chapters addressing authenticity, performance, and institutional expectations highlight the contradictions leaders and learners must navigate. Rather than resolving these tensions, the volume treats them as productive sites for critical engagement, reinforcing the idea that leadership development is not about eliminating complexity but learning to communicate responsibly within it.

Emergent communicative process

Taken together, this edited volume is distinctive in that it does not merely apply communication concepts to leadership, nor does it position communication as one variable among many contributing to leadership effectiveness; rather, it advances and consolidates a constitutive claim that leadership does not precede communication but instead emerges through communicative processes.

While this claim has appeared in fragmented form across the Communicative Constitution of Organization (CCO), relational leadership, and leadership-as-practice literatures, the present volume makes three substantive contributions. First, it systematically centers communication as an ontological condition rather than a managerial technique, theorizing leadership as relational rather than individual, emergent rather than positional, situated rather than universal, and ethical and political rather than neutral—a commitment sustained across theory, method, pedagogy, and practice rather than merely invoked. Second, the volume integrates critical, feminist, intercultural, and relational traditions that are sometimes treated in isolation, with chapters engaging one another around shared concerns of power, difference, legitimacy, voice, inclusion, and responsibility. This integrated approach acts as a scholarly intervention rather than a loosely assembled collection. Third, its structure is itself instructive: by moving from conceptual critique, to relational and institutional enactment, and finally to pedagogy and leadership development, the volume traces leadership communication across the full lifecycle from theory to practice to formation, positioning leadership education and training as central rather than ancillary to the field. The cumulative effect of this volume is a powerful response to many of the questions that drive our leadership inquiry.

As a result of these arguments, we understand that leadership failures cannot be reduced to deficits of character, competence, or vision alone. They are often failures of communication—failures of relationship, sensemaking, listening, and ethical engagement. Further, because communication is always situated—shaped by culture, power, history, and institutional structures—leadership effectiveness cannot be abstracted from context. To ignore these dimensions is to misunderstand leadership itself.

Perhaps most importantly, this volume suggests that the future of leadership lies not in more refined models of individual excellence, but in deeper attention to how leadership is collectively produced through communication under conditions of difference, uncertainty, and constraint. In a time marked by polarization, global crises, and growing demands for accountability, leadership as heroic individual action is increasingly inadequate. What is required instead are communicative practices that foster trust, inclusion, adaptability, and shared meaning.

A book for scholars and practitioners alike

Not surprisingly, this volume will be of interest to scholars of communication, leadership, organization studies, and related disciplines who seek theoretically robust and critically engaged approaches to leadership. It offers conceptual clarity, methodological innovation, and a coherent agenda for future research.

In addition, the book addresses concerns of interest to practitioners, educators, and trainers. Through rich cases and applied analyses, it provides diagnostic lenses for understanding leadership challenges without resorting to simplistic prescriptions and "how-to" guides. Practitioners are invited to reconsider not only how they lead but how leadership is being communicatively constructed within their organizations and communities.

In bringing together critique, theory, practice, and pedagogy, this volume invites us to reconsider how we engage with communication and leadership. It does not offer easy answers or universal solutions. Instead, it offers something far more valuable: a way of seeing leadership as it actually unfolds—in conversation, in relationship, and in collective action.

INTRODUCTION

Sandra L. Pensoneau-Conway, Nilanjana Bardhan, and Sean M. Eddington

Setting a context

Leadership is a highly popular area of interdisciplinary study and for good reasons. Its contours, complexities, and dynamics keep shifting with conjunctions and disjunctions occurring simultaneously in our fast-paced, hyper-digital, and interconnected world. The need for leadership (in terms of people, practices, and processes) equipped to navigate these fluid complexities is higher than ever before. This means how we study the subject also needs to keep pace with these tectonic shifts and provide heuristic pathways for knowledge building, praxis, and pedagogy. Relatedly, it is evident all around us that the rhetoric of leaders, and how such rhetoric impacts the leadership process, organizations/organizing, societies, and the entire world, has enormous consequences for one and all. Platforms for communication, especially digital ones, are proliferating, as are the opportunities and dangers for leadership communication. While many leaders are concerned with and communicate for the greater good, many powerful, self-serving leaders seem to get away with astonishing claims that normalize the unethical and the dangerous. Therefore, a laser-sharp focus on how leaders communicate and on the communicative constitution of leadership is essential.

It is usually assumed that a good leader is a good communicator (Barret, 2006; Fairhurst & Connaughton, 2014; Ruben & Gigliotti, 2017). But how well have we studied leadership primarily through the lens of communication? Not well enough. What kinds of theoretical and applied understandings do we have of this crucial relationship between communication

DOI: 10.4324/9781003563662-1

and leadership? Some, but more is needed. It is notable that neither the National Communication Association nor the International Communication Association, the two major professional organizations for communication studies, has divisions, interest groups, or caucuses dedicated to leadership communication. The work that has emerged resides mainly within the organizational communication arm of communication studies.

To explain this lack of focus on research at the intersection of leadership and communication theory, we need to consider how the structural locations of knowledge production and pedagogy influence epistemological directions. Leadership in Western academia has traditionally been studied and taught in disciplines such as management, psychology, organizational studies, and higher education. Thus, it is no surprise that the theoretical and pedagogical tenor of leadership studies skews towards these disciplines. There is good news, though. We have arrived at a point where the centrality of communication in the leadership process is being given due attention, and leadership communication scholarship is poised for rigorous growth. From a pedagogy perspective, more and more communication studies programs are including leadership communication courses in their curricula. But we continue to hear colleagues who teach these courses lament that there are not enough textbooks or other materials available to teach leadership primarily through the lens of communication. The idea for our edited volume grew out of this pressing need.

The extant work on leadership communication, conducted mostly by organizational communication scholars, has been shaped by the same paradigmatic shifts that have transformed organizational communication more broadly. As the field has moved beyond traditional managerial and corporate contexts to examine organizing in community groups, nonprofits, digital networks, and activist coalitions, meaningful opportunities have emerged to study leadership communication beyond the boundaries of brick-and-mortar organizations. According to Jian and Fairhurst (2025), editors of the recent handbook on organizational leadership communication, the various metatheoretical perspectives that undergird organizational leadership communication scholarship include the following: postpositivist perspectives (pre-1980s), interpretive and constructionist perspectives (1980s onward), critical perspectives (1990s onward), the communicative constitution of organization (or CCO) perspective (late 1990s onward), and the more recent (post 2000) dialogic and relational perspectives. These paradigmatic trends do not stand in isolation; instead, they generate productive tensions, debates, interparadigmatic conversations, and opportunities to further our knowledge of leadership communication. A notable change over the last few decades has been a shift away from "great man" theories of leadership and communication toward more collectivist approaches that view leadership as a complex, distributed communicative process that does not reside in a single heroic individual known as *the leader* (Bolden, 2011; Gill, 2011).

Although scholarship on leadership communication within organizational communication is valuable and provides a strong foundation, it taps only a portion of the broader body of communication theory. This volume, therefore, begins with general communication theory and brings together authors and perspectives from across the field. Contributors draw on intercultural and feminist approaches, critical communication pedagogy, relational, dialogic, and discursive perspectives, rhetorical and narrative work, constitutive perspectives, critical organizational and management communication, training and development, military studies, and digital communication and media theories, as well as activism and community engagement, globalization and communication, and intersectional perspectives grounded in diversity, equity, inclusion, and access (DEIA).

Each chapter connects the dots between specific communication theories and leadership theories and presents a case, scenario, or exemplar to demonstrate the connection/s. While some of the examples are within organizational contexts, others go beyond to showcase societal, political, and other supra-organizational contexts (e.g., the leadership case of New Zealand's former prime minister Jacinda Ardern, building leadership capacity in a semester-long community-based research project to combat food insecurity, and digital mutual aid organizing in response to the systemic and institutional breakdowns caused by the COVID-19 pandemic). Overall, the volume offers a rich dive into the intersections of communication and leadership theory, illustrated through applications that bring these theories to life.

Organization of the book

This book is organized into three sections: (1) DEIA, Intercultural, and Critical Approaches to Leadership and Communication; (2) Relational, Discursive, and Collective Approaches to Leadership and Communication; and (3) Pedagogical and Training Approaches to Leadership and Communication. We developed this structure to reflect our own areas of expertise as scholars and teachers. We appreciate the careful synopsis of and commentary on each section Dr. Robyn Remke has provided in the foreword to this collection.

Chapter 1 opens the first section of the book. Authors Pyatovskaya, Craine, and Buzzanell challenge traditional individual-centric approaches to leadership by stitching together leadership-as-practice (LAP) and feminist communication theory of resilience (FCTR)-as-design. They advocate for theorizing and practicing leadership as a more emergent and humane communicative process that works to bring about change for a more socially just world. In Chapter 2, Ferris and Waldron highlight the value of connecting the notion of intersectional identity and communication with leadership-as-medium and demonstrate how such inclusive leadership communication praxis can bring about desired organizational change. Next, in Chapter 3, author Youngquist challenges the assumptions and premises of the popular authentic leadership model. Using a critical and ethical communication perspective, he questions the positioning of the self (leader) in relation to others (followers and stakeholders) in this model and shows its tendency to cause more harm than good.

Chapter 4 draws directly upon intercultural communication theory. This chapter puts dominant group theory and co-cultural theory into conversation with leadership communication practices in the context of U.S. academia. Working through a DEIA lens, authors Aksoy, Heuman, Sen, and Chakraborty describe how identity, power, culture, and difference influence communication between leaders and organizational members in organizational life. Next, connecting the communicative practice of microaffirmations with a gendered approach to leadership, in Chapter 5, Lynch examines how those who identify as women work to build inclusive organizational cultures. Finally, in Chapter 6, Bardhan draws upon intercultural communication theory and critical dialectical leadership theory to offer a praxis model for leadership in a complex, contradictory, and paradox-filled intercultural world.

Section II opens with Chapter 7, by Brantley, Ashlock, and McCaig. The authors link communication to leadership outcomes in United States federal agencies through an analysis of data from the Federal Employee Viewpoint Survey. The authors show how transformational, ethical, and leader-member exchange (LMX) leadership theories are associated with improved employee satisfaction and trust, introduce a framework that aligns theory-driven index scores with "Best Places to Work" rankings, and outline a 12-month development program for agency leaders.

Turning to evolving workplace arrangements, Chapter 8 uses communication privacy management (CPM) theory and Heifetz's adaptive leadership model to examine remote and hybrid work. Welsh and colleagues center a case study of mandatory video check-ins to illustrate CPM components such as ownership, control, and turbulence, and they call on leaders to create "holding environments" that support co-constructed, privacy-respectful policies. Chapter 9 by Crouse-Dick, Friesen, and Chow, connects relational leadership theory with the stereotype content model to analyze the tension leaders face in projecting both warmth and competence. The chapter highlights how demographic factors, particularly for historically excluded groups, shape the strategic use of communication styles in managing these expectations.

Chapter 10 shifts to an existential view of leadership. Fritz, Jones, and Herring position leaders as "leaders-in-narrative" whose practice is formed through dialogue, empathy, and responsibility within shared stories. Drawing on Hazel Barnes's "mythodology" and Fisher's narrative paragraph, they critique prescriptive, "bad-faith" leadership and advance a form of "good faith" leadership that accepts uncertainty, fosters collective resilience, and centers ethical communication. In Chapter 11, Myers and colleagues integrate LMX with the Theory of Independent-Mindedness (TIM) to examine superior-subordinate dynamics in a minor league baseball organization. They argue that high-quality LMX relationships, coupled with TIM-guided communication marked by argumentativeness, low verbal aggressiveness, and an affirming style, can enhance performance, and they close by offering four concrete recommendations for improving dyadic communication.

The final three chapters extend these concerns into institutional and collective contexts. Chapter 12, by Engstrom, Helens-Hart, and Haugen, analyzes how environmental, social, and governance (ESG) leadership communication becomes institutionalized in the global restaurant sector. Using a textual analysis of CEO letters, they show how coercive, normative, mimetic, and discursive pressures generate relatively predictable sustainability rhetoric, finding that leaders primarily "define" ESG priorities and "construct" firm identities. At the same time, differentiation emerges through nuanced rhetorical tactics and boundary-spanning collaborations. In Chapter 13, Kliewer, Wefald, and Barnhart conceptualize leadership communication learning as a dialogic, socio-spatial-material process. They argue that sensemaking and meaning-making in communication are central to building leadership capacity in the face of complex adaptive challenges. Finally, Chapter 14, by Eddington and colleagues, investigates how digital affordances shape collective leadership in online mutual aid organizing during the early stages of the COVID-19 pandemic, using a CCO framework. Through a case study of a mutual aid organization, they show how leadership emerges through continuous, collaborative communicative practices, while also revealing coordination and accountability challenges that are characteristic of decentralized digital environments.

Chapter 15 opens the final section of this collection. Waite puts humanistic leadership in conversation with critical pedagogy to teach business leadership students the importance of seeing people in workplace settings as more than their workplace roles. In Chapter 16, authors Smulowitz, Gigliotti, Cunningham, Egan, and Lawrence-Hughes use two vignettes to underscore the relationship among distributed leadership, social construction, and the dynamics of change as they unfold in a higher education context. In Chapter 17, Rudick, Aldridge, VanMeter, Medeiros, and Emami develop a typology of four problematic diversity, equity and inclusion (DEI) related leader pitfalls: Guru, Corporatist, Legalistic, and Relationist. Their typology fosters the development of a set of ethics that inform Inclusive Servant Leadership, a key contribution of this chapter.

In Chapter 18, Mackenzie elucidates the development and delivery of a resilience and leadership course, grounded in Buzzanell's Communication Theory of Resilience. This approach establishes the utility of a communication perspective for military leadership training. In Chapter 19, Hinck keeps readers in a military context. He focuses on the communication of mission command in the U.S. Air Force leader development program. The teaching of mission command, a specific approach to conducting military operations, benefits from the intentional integration of communication and leadership theory. In Chapter 20, Gross identifies authenticity, as it intersects with classical rhetoric and narrative paradigm, as a core element of effective leadership. She offers a detailed exercise to help leaders articulate their purpose and cultivate self-awareness.

Chapter 21 illustrates the power of community-based research in an undergraduate Group Leadership class, as part of the Emporia At the Table (EAT) Initiative at Emporia State University. Author Linabary used feminist pedagogies and adaptive leadership to guide students in a semester-long project in collaboration with campus and community partners, all aimed at combating food insecurity. In Chapter 22, Priest, Eddington, Benavides, and Kakim present the work of two doctoral students as an entry into the impact of publicly engaged scholarship with a leadership program. In so doing, readers encounter the possibilities when the public good is centered in leadership education. Finally, in Chapter 23, Pensoneau-Conway combines Paulo Freire's radical leadership with Fassett and Warren's critical communication pedagogy. This combination manifests in the work of Rukia Rogers, founder of the Highlander School early childhood program in Atlanta, Georgia, who Pensoneau-Conway positions as an exemplar of contemporary radical educational leadership.

Conclusion

Our goal in crafting this compendium is to provide scholars, students, and practitioners with a robust resource for exploring the many intersections of communication and leadership theory. In addition to the chapters themselves, each author or author team provides suggested readings and questions for further engagement, which we imagine being taken up in classrooms, professional development programs, reading groups, and community spaces.

Collectively, the chapters in this collection demonstrate the breadth of communication-centered approaches to leadership. They address urgent issues, interrogate inherited assumptions, and propose creative interventions that range from interpersonal and organizational contexts to global, digital, and supra-organizational settings. Taken together, they show that leadership is not simply what leaders do, but what communication makes possible. We invite you to use these chapters as starting points for reimagining how leadership is studied, taught, and practiced in the complex worlds we inhabit.

References

Barrett, D. J. (2006). Strong communication skills a must for today's leaders. *Handbook of Business Strategy*, *7*(1), 385–390. https://doi.org/10.1108/10775730610619124

Bolden, R. (2011). Distributed leadership in organizations: A review of theory and research. *International Journal of Management Reviews*, *13*(3), 251–269. https://doi.org/10.1111/j.1468-2370.2011.00306.x

Fairhurst, G., & Connaughton, S. L. (2014). Leadership: A communicative perspective. *Leadership*, *10*(1), 7–35. https://doi.org/10.1177/1742715013509396

Gill, R. (2011). *Theory and practice of leadership* (2nd ed.). Sage.

Jian, G., & Fairhurst, G. (2025). Introduction. In G. Jian & G. Fairhurst (Eds.), *The Routledge handbook of organizational leadership communication* (pp. 1–16). Routledge.

Ruben, B. D., & Gigliotti, R. A. (2017). Communication: Sine qua non of organizational leadership theory and practice. *International Journal of Business Communication*, *54*(1), 12–30. https://doi.org/10.1177/2329488416675447

SECTION I

DEIA, Intercultural, and Critical Approaches to Leadership and Communication

1

FEMINIST COMMUNICATION THEORY OF RESILIENCE AS DESIGN FOR LEADERSHIP IN A CULTURALLY COMPLEX WORLD

Evgeniya Pyatovskaya, Willow Craine, and Patrice M. Buzzanell

Leaders in different kinds of organizations face complex challenges, paradoxes, and tensions that require diverse perspectives and membership (Eagly, 2018; Norander, 2019). Yet leadership studies still indicate preferences for white, male, able-bodied, and cis-gender leadership theories and contexts (Ladkin & Patrick, 2022) that reify heroic and charismatic characteristics, embody masculine logics of effectiveness, and focus on leaders who use their position to make unilateral decisions and are skeptical of collective leadership as "lethargic and bureaucratic" (Raelin, 2018, p. 59). We step away from trait-, behavior-, and tools-based approaches to leadership that focus on who leaders are, what they do, and how leaders and leadership can be used for specific outcomes. Instead, we tap into communicative, collective, and relational endeavors. Doing so enables us to align our conceptualization of leadership with a practice approach which studies leadership as it "emerges and unfolds through day-to-day experience" and does not pre-conceive the "occupants of leadership roles" (Raelin, 2017, p. 216). Instead of putting any one individual on a leadership pedestal, the practice approach to leadership requires that people engage diverse viewpoints (Raelin, 2018). Additionally, this approach admits the validity of data derived from noticing perspectives that are muted and the views of those who are usually excluded from participating (Raelin, 2017).

We begin with a few assumptions about what leadership is and what it means to practice leadership. Our first premise is that leadership is a collaborative and emergent process, rather than separate instances of individual heroism or collective exertion. Following Crevani et al. (2010), we understand *leadership* as "several people constructing in interactions a limited

DOI: 10.4324/9781003563662-3

space for action" (p. 82). These processes of construction are continuous, embedded into the everyday "muddling-through," tensional, and encompass human and non-human actors. Our second premise is that engaging in leadership means managing multiple threats to organizational stability and existence, advancing organizations' ability to fulfill their mission, and promoting employees' well-being—a constant "learning process punctuated and nourished by setbacks and disruptions" (Norander, 2019, p. 136). Resilience as a communicative process through which individuals "reintegrate from and engage in meaning-making about disruptive events to construct new normals" (Buzzanell, 2021, p. 45) is, therefore, central to leadership. The third premise encompasses leaders and our ability to recognize them outside of formal titles. We insist that "constellations" of leaders constantly change and shift—elevating some into positions of influence when exigencies demand these roles (see Buzzanell et al., 1997). These constellations can, at different times, encompass the more powerful and privileged members of an organization, while at other times draw from those without formal authority, as well as objects, documents, and other non-human participants (e.g., video-audio conferencing platforms) needed to practice leadership. Such collective re-constitution of leadership requires fluid adaptive-transformative capacities. In this regard, leadership as practice necessitates communicative resilience (Buzzanell, 2018, 2021). We contend that the key to knowing *leaders* is observing the enactment of leadership and resilience practices *in situ* and reflecting on *who* and *what* seem to contribute to them.

With these premises in mind, we put Leadership-as-Practice (LAP) in conversation with the Feminist Communication Theory of Resilience (FCTR)-as-design—an iteration of Communication Theory of Resilience (CTR) (Buzzanell, 2010, 2018). Combining FCTR-as-design and LAP creates space for imagining leadership that is collective, rooted in "relational networks" (Buzzanell, 2021, p. 46), conscious of society-wide "oppressions and structural disparities" (p. 46), and their impact on organizational members and issues that organizations face. LAP draws our attention away from individual leaders and toward *leadership practices*, which comprise "complex and continuous stream of actions" (Woods, 2016, p. 82). They can include formal/informal meetings, brainstorming, decision-making, and many other communication formats and stages of collaboration that are critical to design (Buzzanell et al., 2024). FCTR presupposes orientation to community and transformation and accounts for the perspectives and interests of individuals by focusing on their specific needs. It also emphasizes design by advocating for the importance of understanding the problem at hand and continuously iterating and refining prototypes to find effective solutions. As a design project, FCTR values critical empathy and acknowledges that failure is an integral part of design, embracing it as a learning opportunity that is essential for transformative change in both individual lives and institutional practices (Buzzanell, 2021).

We invite readers to imagine what it could be like to view leadership and resilience as continuous engagement and collaborative practice to appreciate diverse ways of being and leading. Further, we hope this approach will help create more humane organizational cultures and leaders, thereby encouraging the well-being of both communities and individuals—especially during disruptions.

In the following sections we describe in more detail (a) LAP and (b) CTR and FCTR, before (c) linking the two by portraying how taking a design perspective and using these communication and leadership theories can benefit analyses of extended examples and cases. Specifically, to connect FCTR-as-design and LAP, we offer cases and examples that speak to material and discursive processes of leadership through the lens of FCTR, suggesting how leaders can broaden their approaches to being effective in promoting and practicing resilience for the self, others, and organizations. Finally, we conclude by (d) summarizing and providing some practical applications for readers.

Leadership-as-Practice

For a long time, studies of leadership focused on individuals in formal authority positions in organizations (e.g., CEOs and executives) and on their traits, competences, and behaviors directed toward subordinates (e.g., authentic, servant, transformational, and discursive leadership models). This focus has been lately critiqued for its seeming neutrality that obscures its racial, gendered, class, and other biases (Ladkin, 2020; Ladkin & Patrick, 2022), romanticization of leadership (Collinson et al., 2018), and preoccupation with an individual as the sole source of leadership (Ospina et al., 2020). While people remain central to leadership, the past decade has seen a growing shift toward practice-based approaches that challenge the limitations of leader-centric models (Crevani et al., 2010; Endrissat & Von Arx, 2013; Raelin, 2017, 2018; Raelin et al., 2018).

Specifically, LAP emerged as an innovative "movement" (Raelin, 2017, p. 215) and "a way to think about leadership" (Raelin et al., 2018, p. 379) within leadership research and practice. LAP shifts our attention from leaders (individuals) to leadership (practice), emphasizing leadership's processual nature and its entangled relational, situational, discursive, and material character (Crevani et al., 2010). It is viewed not as an impetus for collective action but rather as its outcome: a process of "producing direction for organizing" that is emergent and co-constructed through collaborative agency (Crevani & Endrissat, 2016, p. 23) that is discernible in mundane day-to-day activities of organizations and their routines. Sergi (2016) offers a pointed question that guides research within the practice perspective on leadership: "How does leadership happens *in situ*?" (p. 111). This line of inquiry considers both human and non-human participants as agentic in producing leadership effects. In other words, material objects can contribute significantly to the practice of leadership or hamper its becoming (Case & Śliwa, 2020). For example, Sergi (2016), in her research on the development of a software project, demonstrated how various processes and communication that comprised the project's emergence benefited from the presence of objects, including multiple documents, emails, reports, and the like.

LAP emphasizes dialogue among participants who are committed to one another, open to others' ideas, and willing to adapt based on new perspectives (Raelin, 2017). As it stands, LAP attempts to transcend the disciplining power of hierarchy within organizations by focusing on leadership as both a collective and reflexive effort that "transforms the meanings of situations" (Simpson, 2016, p. 172). It allows us to "bring the other back in" (Raelin, 2016, p. 149) by rejecting the necessity for participants to hold and play any predetermined roles (e.g., leaders and followers) for leadership to take place. Overall, by inviting us to develop the awareness of others and their needs, promoting communal participation in leadership, individual and collective reflexivity, and dialogue, LAP may enable resistance to oppression and unjust social structures.

Taken together the premises of LAP allow us to recognize leadership in many of its possible forms, expressions, and contexts and open up possibilities of examining leadership from new vantage points untangled from its traditional conceptualizations. This different optic permits seeing *who is included* and *excluded* from the practice and addressing unjust exclusions through amending practices.

By privileging "the value of social interactions and connectedness" (Raelin, 2017, p. 217), leadership practice emerges in communication which plays a key role in leadership production. Yet, LAP undertheorizes communication as constitutive of leadership. In the following section, we outline CTR and its iteration—FCTR-as-design—before demonstrating how the latter can enrich current LAP theory and practice and deepen our understanding of leadership.

Communication Theory of Resilience and Feminist Communication Theory of Resilience

When individuals, communities, and organizations experience disruption or uncertainty, they may generate or maintain practices and behaviors that help recreate a sense of normalcy, stability, and transformation—what CTR refers to as resilience (Buzzanell, 2010). Placing a communication lens at the center of resilience, CTR moves away from ideals of endurance, coping, or trait-based capacities for survival; instead, the theory describes resilience as a dynamic process that unfolds over time and events through discursive and material resources (Buzzanell, 2018). Simply put, CTR is interested in how resilience is *practiced* rather than *possessed.*

Usually, CTR begins with a *trigger*—a disruption, ranging in scale from a rupture in everyday stability (e.g., job loss, illness, interpersonal conflict) to that which may appear embedded in the navigation of chronic disruptions (e.g., recessions, marginalized identity, infertility). In this way, triggers may be anticipated (Betts et al., 2022), routinely experienced (Siegenthaler et al., 2024), or entirely unexpected. Whether systemic or situational, instabilities set in motion communicative sensemaking processes that both renegotiate what normalcy looks like while transforming surrounding circumstances.

In responding to trigger events, CTR outlines five core processes that emerge through communication. *Crafting normalcy* refers to the routines, rituals, and stories that create *temporal* stability while communicatively balancing it with a hope of future change (Buzzanell, 2018). For example, in their study on rape crisis advocates, Biss and Barrett (2024) found that volunteers used their daily commute to create checklists that prepped them for difficult work, pray for victims, and release built-up emotions, thereby crafting a new normalcy in continuing advocacy efforts. *Affirming identity anchors* (Buzzanell, 2018) refers to making particularly meaningful markers of identity visible so others may acknowledge and affirm them in helping move through disruptive circumstances. Identity anchors can be situated in norms of gender, race, class, and ability, such as affirming "breadwinner" status in times of job loss (Buzzanell & Turner, 2003). For example, Gettings and Hall (2024) found that women beginning traditionally male careers leaned into and defied female stereotypes to both affirm their femininity and organizational belonging as advantageous.

Maintaining and utilizing communication networks, the third process, refers to the process of using disruptions to form valuable connections and resources for both present and future stability (Buzzanell, 2010). These networks could be friends and family, social media groups, disaster relief networks, and the like. *Foregrounding productive actions while legitimizing negative feelings*, the fourth process, refers to moments when people utilize their challenging emotions and feelings during a disruption as momentum forward (Buzzanell, 2018). For example, in their study of people living with autoimmune diseases, Siegenthaler et al. (2024) found that participants used the disappointment of reoccurring misdiagnoses or dismissals to continue in their diagnostic journey while critiquing medical institutions that downplayed their concerns. Finally, *putting alternative logics to work* refers to "the heart of feminist resilience" (Buzzanell, 2018, p. 52). Alternative logics include reframing a situation, coping through traditionally unexpected mediums (e.g., humor), and creating unconventional workarounds to move through disruption.

Just as CTR's five processes may appear dynamic, co-occurring, and temporally situated, they are also nested in adaptive-transformative tensions (Buzzanell, 2018). Following disruption, adaptation is often the immediate response in regaining a sense of stability; however, adaptation—traditionally associated with enduring or coping—often produces new/continuous disruptions, such that "people prepare for, continuously learn to enact, and engage strategically in resilience" (Buzzanell, 2018, p. 15).

CTR reveals that resilience and transformative capacities are struggled for and cultivated through disruptions; however, there is an urgent need to also acknowledge that some individuals do not have their best interests met by existing systems or by their mere adaptation; instead, their needs are better addressed through transformative change (Buzzanell, 2018). Therefore, it is crucial to center the transformative needs of those who experience both disruption and the impact of privilege—especially at intersections of race, gender, class, ability, nationality, and other marginalizing characteristics (Lillie & Sánchez Sánchez, 2022; Pyatovskaya, 2024; Scharp et al., 2021). Considering the theory's critical bent, CTR has been developed further to serve as a template in designing feminist resilience.

FCTR (Buzzanell, 2021) is aimed at understanding "how relationships between gender within intersectional configurations and resilience are co-constituted and politicized" (Buzzanell, 2021, p. 44) to disrupt adaptive tendencies that benefit unjust institutions and status quos. It brings attention to and engages voices that are habitually excluded from conversations about and theorization of resilience (Pyatovskaya & Buzzanell, 2023). In doing so, the intentional use of design processes is especially beneficial to centering the collective and relational in communicative resilience, while also addressing the epistemic and structural injustices that are often obscured by traditional "bouncing back" understandings of resilience. The consequential and beneficial nature of resilience is reimagined toward inclusive, productive, and transformative change.

Combining LAP and FCTR perspectives through this design lens creates a unique vantage point from which leadership can be studied and enacted. In what follows, we describe what it means to take a design perspective on leadership and resilience and offer a case study of former New Zealand prime minister Jacinda Ardern's leadership during the recent coronavirus pandemic to illustrate how leaders can expand their approaches to being effective in promoting and practicing resilience for the self, others, organizations, and communities.

Taking a design perspective

People engage in design every day. Design is a process whereby people grapple with a problem or need for innovation, discuss ideas and research possibilities, and develop possibilities for solutions that are then tested and retested for safety, feasibility, cost effectiveness, utility, and other qualities before finalizing these prototypes. These basics of design are embedded in variations of the Design Thinking model of Inspiration, Ideation, and Implementation (IDEO, n.d.). They also are essential in Human-Centered Design (HCD) that prioritizes human or potential user knowledge and interaction with the materialities of design, such as the artifacts, bodies, and places (Ashcraft et al., 2009) for such purposes as conflict reduction, leadership, diversity and inclusion, and client requests and interests (Buzzanell & Pyatovskaya, 2025; Buzzanell et al., 2023). We focus on how LAP acts as a process to facilitate adaptative-transformative resilience processes for outcomes such as the well-being, inclusion, and belongingness of people situated in politicized and cultural contexts. This situatedness means that the practices designed by and for leadership take into consideration the historical events and understandings that produce contemporary life as well as the ways in which powerful agents act to maintain and increase their hold on what everyday life and our futures look like.

In taking a design perspective, we see resilience as constantly changing, always and everywhere becoming, and embedded in and productive of sociomaterialities. FCTR positions feminist design at the forefront of engaging for social justice while acknowledging the risks, harms, backlashes, and resentments that can fuel the organizing of workplaces, online community sites, national and global politics, and other contexts (e.g., Eddington et al., 2025; see also Costanza-Chock, 2018). Rather than centering on one identity of people, such as gender, FCTR and LAP take an intersectional approach to bring whole people as both privileged and marginalized into the collaborative imagining, creating, testing, prototyping of communicative resilience (Costanza-Chock, 2018). Accountability—which means "those most affected by the outcomes should lead and own digital [and other] design processes and products"—and incorporation of new non-normative knowledge are centered (Costanza-Chock, 2018, p. 10; see also Das et al., 2023). Consistent with FCTR, accountability and new knowledge can be integrated through narratives to foster voice, agency, reflection, and ethics of care, which are developed through scenarios (Jones, 2016; Riley, 2013) and extended examples and cases. We now present one such case.

The case of Jacinda Ardern

The coronavirus pandemic that began in early 2020 was a major challenge to all areas of human life. Previous research has shown that in times of crisis and uncertainty, people often prefer heroic leaders who are prepared and want to act decisively, take charge, and call all the shots (Franco, 2016). However, approaches to leadership during the pandemic were diverse and did not solely revolve around heroism and charisma (Kars-Unluoglu et al., 2022; Sharma et al., 2021), including those of women leaders.

Women in formal leadership roles during the onset of COVID-19 demonstrated that alternative ways to lead in crises are not only possible but can also yield better outcomes for everyone involved. These leaders skillfully balanced agency and communion, decisiveness and humility, courage and care, while always working collaboratively with others. This approach challenged the persistent skepticism surrounding women's ability to lead in crises, countering the "think leader–think male" cliché (Ryan et al., 2011; Wilkinson & Male, 2025; Zheng et al., 2018).

One standout example of leadership during the pandemic was Jacinda Ardern, New Zealand's prime minister during the time. Her leadership has been described as compassionate, thoughtful, and adaptive (Le Fevre, 2021; Simpson et al., 2022). While these attributes are accurate, we also see Ardern's approach as embodying leadership intertwined with FCTR-as-design that fosters socially oriented and inclusive collective effort. In her approach, aimed at steering the nation through the utmost uncertainty of COVID-19, she adeptly integrated bits of normative and empathic leadership—usually perceived as opposites—through a repertoire of practices that enabled her to enact leadership with transformational potential. In what follows we highlight some of the examples of that approach.

From the beginning of the pandemic, Ardern encouraged a collaborative and situated response across New Zealand, emphasizing adaptability to the changing conditions of the pandemic. She highlighted New Zealand's unique geography and history of overcoming adversity, and the necessity for its relatively small population to work together with the government to curb the virus's spread (McGuire et al., 2020). Ardern stressed the importance of solidarity, framing leadership and resilience as communal endeavors. She referred to New Zealanders as a "team of 5 million," reassuring them that "if [they] work[ed] together, [they would] get through it" (Ardern, 2020), thus inviting all citizens to share the responsibility of minimizing the pandemic's impact.

To support the idea of one-ness in practice, Ardern announced that as a gesture of solidarity with New Zealanders facing unemployment or substantial pay cuts, every government minister, including the prime minister, along with public services executives, would take a 20% pay reduction for six months (Walls, 2022). By first discursively reimagining the nation as a team and then taking action to support this framing, Ardern leaned into the country's relative geographic isolation from the rest of the world and positioned this way of responding to the disruption as one of the salient *identity anchors* that stressed the need to stick together and allowed mobilization of citizens' support of anti-pandemic efforts. This discursive-material framing highlighted collective agency in leadership as the foundation for a successful and locale-specific response to the global healthcare crisis, easing the potential discomfort of facing competing demands of anti-pandemic measures. The continuous emphasis on collaboration, shared responsibility, and being in it together achieved its goal, fostering a shared sense of purpose among the citizens and leading to high national compliance with the state's proposed measures (Wilson, 2020).

In her numerous addresses to the nation, Ardern communicated that the *construction of the new normal* of the pandemic life was a complex and paradoxical process that rested on principles of community and required new learning and leaning into alternative ways of being together. First, she engaged with both sides of the contradiction that the word "community" encapsulated during the pandemic: community as the only way to fight against the virus—"if we work together, we will get through it" (Ardern, 2020), and community as the potential source of pandemic intensification—"make sure you stick to your bubble at home" (Ministry of Health – Manatū Hauora, 2020)—because if the transmission took off, a lot of people could die. Ardern's approach was rooted in embracing these contradictions while focusing on human-centered solutions. She advocated for necessary restrictions to curb the virus's spread, yet she also resisted overly harsh measures, allowing safe recreational activities even under strict lockdown. Her consistent message to "Stay strong. Be kind" and reassurance that "We are going to be okay" (New Zealand Parliament, 2020), together with practices that supported the veracity of these messages, helped build public trust and a sense of solidarity.

Ardern also relied on multiple agencies (schools, essential services, businesses) and those with relevant expertise (scientists, researchers, public health professionals) in developing and testing prototypes of solutions. This inclusive strategy, attentive to multiple voices, demonstrated an openness to diverse perspectives and a willingness to adapt rather than rigidly adhere to a single solution (Kars-Unluoglu et al., 2022; Wilson, 2020). By balancing the inevitability of the *new normal* with its contradictory nature and potentially life-saving aspects, Ardern promoted a vision of a safe and resilient society. She managed to instill a sense of comfort with these contradictions and limitations amidst the unavoidable disruptions of the pandemic, while simultaneously building collective resolve among New Zealanders to counteract the virus.

A notable practice was Ardern's use of Facebook Live sessions. In a series of live broadcasts, she complemented official briefings on the pandemic by sharing important information and answered citizens' questions in real time, without any preparation. During these sessions Ardern appeared as her mundane self, often wearing everyday clothing and communicating in a relaxed style. This practice helped lower the traditional barriers of hierarchy between the people and the government, solidifying a sense of togetherness as the nation worked together to combat the virus (Martin-Anatias, 2021; McGuire et al., 2020). Put differently, these live sessions served as vital channels of connection, creating and *maintaining a network* that linked the state with its citizens and encouraging collaborative discussions about the ongoing crisis. By actively soliciting questions and feedback from the public, Ardern demonstrated in practice the state's openness to new information and its willingness to collaborate with multiple others in shaping the next steps. This approach effectively placed the needs of the people at the forefront of planning for the future.

In Facebook Live sessions, Ardern often expressed empathy with the people of New Zealand and shared their feelings of frustration with quarantine and self-isolation protocols. She noted, "I know many people have been upset by that" (Sadler, 2020). However, she also stressed the importance of continuing these measures: "Keep doing what you are doing. Stay home if you're sick. Get tested quickly. Work and learn from home if you can" (New Zealand Parliament, 2020). As she provided updates on the status of anti-pandemic measures and outlined the next steps, Ardern *foregrounded action* while also recognizing the feelings of frustration with the challenges posed by the lockdown. The Facebook Live format helped build collective trust in the actions taken to combat the pandemic, highlighted the diverse voices and efforts involved in the nationwide resilience practices, and reinforced the idea that collective action was key to overcoming the crisis.

In keeping with the principles of FCTR-as-design, Ardern consistently prioritized people in her handling of the pandemic. Recognizing the adaptive and transformative nature of the national crisis response, she encouraged open communication grounded in the admission of limitations of existing solutions and the need for continuous adjustment of the strategy. Both her communication and practices reflected a key aspect of collective design-based approach to leadership in times of disruptions: acknowledging uncertainty and the value of diverse insights that can come from anyone and anywhere. Ardern's approach emphasized the need for citizens' active participation and the government's readiness to listen to them, promoting inclusivity in leadership and resilience practices. This approach fostered a sense of sharing in shaping New Zealand's response to the crisis.

Disclaimer to the case of Jacinda Ardern

Not all leadership and resilience efforts lead to positive outcomes for everyone. While Ardern's leadership received praise from some quarters, it was also perceived as highly controversial, particularly regarding its impact on the health and well-being of indigenous communities. The rhetoric of kindness and support fell short for those already experiencing social disparities before the pandemic. These disparities were exacerbated, highlighting "existing conditions of colonial inequality and injustice" (Barber & Naepi, 2020, p. 694).

FCTR-as-design emphasizes iteration and continuous improvement of solutions to better serve people and communities and allows us to embrace failure as an integral part of the process of exploration and experimentation, especially when we act in situations of uncertainty and ambiguity. Ardern faced criticism for implementing a uniform response to the pandemic and disregarding recommendations of Māori (indigenous community) medical experts (Alofaituli et al., 2022). This led to a lower vaccination rate among the Māori compared to other New Zealanders (Alofaituli et al., 2022) and exacerbated the pandemic's various inequities for them. Recognizing the failure to fully uphold the values of partnership and participation, acknowledging various experiences and contexts, and promoting mutual learning to develop new approaches to complex issues such as the pandemic, New Zealand established the Māori Health Authority in 2022 (Munford, 2021). This body aims to manage Māori health services and well-being in line with mātauranga Māori (Māori knowledge) (Curtis et al., 2022). The foundation of the Māori Health Authority represents an iteration and possibilities for transformation of the previous healthcare system design to tackle the persistent inequities in health outcomes for indigenous populations. Accepting failure as an opportunity to learn something new, therefore, allowed moving forward with the new knowledge at hand to ideate better prototypes, *strengthening social networks* between the country's communities, and increasing collaboration in addressing future disruptions.

Conclusion

In this chapter we explored the intersection of LAP and FCTR-as-design, revealing both the affordances and limitations of leadership as an everyday, communicative, collective, situated, and tension-filled practice. Traditional heroic and charismatic leadership, which seeks full control, often proves counterproductive, subjugating those who are already marginalized and/or oppressed to some illusory grand needs of the majority. Instead, by reacting to uncertainty, fear, and anxiety with improvisation, spontaneity, and reliance on communal prototyping and emergent knowledge, multiple participants of leadership practice might be able to co-create timely interventions that are not perfect, might have no clear vision of the future, but are open to constant change and adjustment to meet the changing needs of the community.

The intersection of LAP and FCTR-as-design points toward a more inclusive and collective approach to leadership and acknowledges that accessing both individual and collective wisdom may be challenging if communicative, ideological, and sociomaterial barriers to meaningful participation are not identified and addressed. In practice, this approach involves the following: (a) continuously engaging with ongoing conversations that surround us, taking on the responsibility for helping others develop their ideas, and creating opportunities for people to contribute these ideas and have them tested; (b) identifying and addressing sociomaterial obstacles that prevent certain individuals and/or groups from participation, and creating conditions for broader and more meaningful engagement. Additionally, it requires learning to take the perspectives of others by not comparing them in opposition but rather focusing on what is effective in each case and identifying transferrable elements.

While there is a tendency in leadership practice to include some people and exclude others, communication plays a pivotal role in addressing this issue and rethinking traditional approaches. FCTR-as-design encourages us to challenge our deeply seated and learned tendency to rely on those in formal positions to make decisions. It also emphasizes the dangers of recreating hierarchical leadership structures. In these systems, communication breakdowns often result in silenced voices and neglected vulnerabilities for the sake of achieving a "correct" management outcome. Instead, communication should be seen as a way of tapping into collective wisdom, where ideas and solutions can emerge from all members, regardless of their status. By fostering open and inclusive communication, we can explore unconventional solutions without fear of appearing vulnerable or incompetent. Ultimately, such efforts would help us better see where collective leadership and resilience might lead us on our journey to creating a better way to exist in our complex world.

Suggested further readings

Edwards, G., & Bolden, R. (2023). Why is collective leadership so elusive? *Leadership*, *19*(2), 167–182.

Fairhurst, G. T., Jackson, B., Foldy, E. G., & Ospina, S. M. (2020). Studying collective leadership: The road ahead. *Human Relations*, *73*(4), 598–614. https://doi.org/10.1177/0018726719898736

Ospina, S. M. (2018). Toward inclusive leadership scholarship: Inviting the excluded to theorize collective leadership. In B. Caroll, J. Firth & S. Wilson (Eds.), *After leadership* (pp. 147–156). Routledge. https://doi.org/10.4324/9781315110196

Randel, A. E., Galvin, B. M., Shore, L. M., Ehrhart, K. H., Chung, B. G., Dean, M. A., & Kedharnath, U. (2018). Inclusive leadership: Realizing positive outcomes through belongingness and being valued for uniqueness. *Human Resource Management Review*, *28*, 190–203. https://doi.org/10.1016/j.hrmr.2017.07.002
Roberson, Q., & Perry, J. L. (2022). Inclusive leadership in thought and action: A thematic analysis. *Group & Organization Management*, *47*(4), 755–778. https://doi.org/10.1177/10596011211013161
Salovaara, P., Vuori, J., & Collinson, D. L. (2024). Leaderless leadership in radically decentralized organizations. In D. Knights, Liu, H., Smolović-Jones, O. & S. Wilson (Eds.), *The Routledge critical companion to leadership studies* (pp. 148–159). Routledge.

Questions for further engagement

1 How can leaders effectively balance the need for decisive action with the principles of inclusive and collective decision-making as advocated by FCTR-as-design? Discuss using a specific example.
2 What specific strategies can be employed to identify and dismantle sociomaterial barriers that prevent meaningful participation in leadership processes, and how can these strategies be implemented in various organizational contexts? Can you think of specific examples?
3 In what ways can leaders cultivate a culture that embraces vulnerability and learning from failure, while still striving for effective and adaptable solutions in the face of complex challenges? Discuss using specific examples.

References

Alofaituli, B. T., Clegg, P., Mutu, M., Sullivan-Lee, A., Talagi, S., & Tupou, P. T. (2022). Polynesia in review: Issues and events, 1 July 2020 to 30 June 2021. *The Contemporary Pacific*, *34*(1), 167–225.
Ardern, J. (2020, March 25). [Facebook live broadcast] [Video]. Facebook. https://www.facebook.com/watch/live/?ref=watch_permalink&v=147109069954329
Ashcraft, K. L., Kuhn, T. R., & Cooren, F. (2009). Constitutional amendments: "Materializing" organizational communication. *Academy of Management Annals*, *3*(1), 1–64. https://doi.org/10.5465/19416520903047186
Barber, S., & Naepi, S. (2020). Sociology in a crisis: Covid-19 and the colonial politics of knowledge production in Aotearoa New Zealand. *Journal of Sociology*, *56*(4), 693–703. https://doi.org/10.1177/1440783320939679
Betts, T., Hintz, E. A., & Buzzanell, P. M. (2022). Emplotting anticipatory resilience: An antenarrative extension of the communication theory of resilience. *Communication Monographs*, *89*(2), 211–234. https://doi.org/10.1080/03637751.2021.1971272
Biss, D. C., & K. Barrett, A. (2024). Exploring resilience and meaningful work in rape crisis advocacy. *Women's Studies in Communication*, *47*(3), 317–341. https://doi.org/10.1080/07491409.2024.2366170

Buzzanell, P. M. (2010). Resilience: Talking, resisting, and imagining new normalcies into being. *Journal of Communication*, *60*(1), 1–14. https://doi.org/10.1111/j.1460-2466.2009.01469.x

Buzzanell, P. M. (2018). Organizing resilience as adaptive-transformational tensions. *Journal of Applied Communication Research*, *46*(1), 14–18. https://doi.org/10.1080/00909882.2018.1426711

Buzzanell, P. M. (2021). Designing feminist resilience. In S. Eckert, & I. Bachmann (Eds.), *Feminist communication and media scholarship: Theory, method, impact* (pp. 43–58). Routledge. http://dx.doi.org/10.4324/9781003102786

Buzzanell, P. M., Eddington, S., Pyatovskaya, E., & Mestrovich Seay, A. (2023). Design thinking and design communication for intercultural conflict management. In D. Busch (Ed.), *The Routledge handbook of intercultural mediation* (pp. 253–261). Routledge. https://doi.org/10.4324/9781003227441

Buzzanell, P. M., Ellingson, L., Silvio, C., Pasch, V., Dale, B., Mauro, G., Smith, E., Weir, N., & Martin, C. (1997). Leadership processes in alternative organizations: Invitational and dramaturgical leadership. *Communication Studies*, *48*(4), 285–310. https://doi.org/10.1080/10510979709368509

Buzzanell, P. M., Margulies, S., & Pyatovskaya, E. (2024). Clients' political considerations in establishing new trainings. In R. L. Jackson III & S. K. Camara (Eds.), *Communication training and development: Exploring the cutting edge* (3rd ed.). Kendall Hunt.

Buzzanell, P. M., & Pyatovskaya, E. (2025). Leadership communication and diversity, equity, and inclusion. In G. Jian, & G. Fairhurst (Eds.), *Routledge handbook of organizational leadership communication* (pp. 357–267). Routledge. https://doi.org/10.4324/9781003380115

Buzzanell, P. M., & Turner, L. H. (2003). Emotion work revealed by job loss discourse: Backgrounding-foregrounding of feelings, construction of normalcy, and (re) instituting of traditional masculinities. *Journal of Applied Communication Research*, *31*(1), 27–57. https://doi.org/10.1080/00909880305375

Case, P., & Śliwa, M. (2020). Leadership learning, power and practice in Laos: A leadership-as-practice perspective. *Management Learning*, *51*(5), 537–558. https://doi.org/10.1177/1350507620909967

Collinson, D., Smolović-Jones, O., & Grint, K. (2018). 'No more heroes': Critical perspectives on leadership romanticism. *Organization Studies*, *39*(11), 1625–1647. https://doi.org/10.1177/0170840617727784

Costanza-Chock, S. (2018). Design justice: Towards an intersectional feminist framework for design theory and practice. *Proceedings of the Design Research Society*. University of Limerick.

Crevani, L., & Endrissat, N. (2016). Mapping the leadership-as-practice terrain: Comparative elements. In J. A. Raelin (Ed.), *Leadership-as-practice: Theory and application* (pp. 21–49). Routledge. https://psycnet.apa.org/doi/10.4324/9781315684123

Crevani, L., Lindgren, M., & Packendorff, J. (2010). Leadership, not leaders: On the study of leadership as practices and interactions. *Scandinavian Journal of Management*, *26*(1), 77–86. https://doi.org/10.1016/j.scaman.2009.12.003

Curtis, E., Loring, B., Harris, R., McLeod, M., Mills, C., Scott, N., & Reid, P. (2022). *Māori Health Priorities: A report commissioned by the interim Māori Health Authority (iMHA) to inform development of the interim New Zealand Health Plan (iNZHP)*. Māori Health Authority.

Das, M., Roeder, G., Ostrowski, A. K., Yang, M. C., & Verma, A. (2023). What do we mean when we write about ethics, equity, and justice in engineering design? *Journal of Mechanical Design*, *145*(6), 061402. https://doi.org/10.1115/1.4057056

Eagly, A. H. (2018). Some leaders come from nowhere: Their success is uneven. *Journal of Social Issues*, *74*(1), 184–196. https://doi.org/10.1111/josi.12263
Eddington, S., Jarvis, C., Morrow, C., McGee, M., & Jordan, C. (2025). Navigating employee communication during times of backlash: An affordance perspective on online organizing. In S. Kim, P. M. Buzzanell, J-N. Kim, & A. Mazzei (Eds.), *Routledge handbook of employee communication and organizational process*. Routledge. https://doi.org/10.4324/9781003415619-33
Endrissat, N., & Von Arx, W. (2013). Leadership practices and context: Two sides of the same coin. *Leadership*, *9*(2), 278–304. https://doi.org/10.1177/1742715012468786
Franco, Z. E. (2016). Heroism in times of crisis: Understanding leadership during extreme events. In S. T. Allison, G. R. Goethals, & R. M. Cramer (Eds.), *Handbook of heroism and heroic leadership* (pp. 207–224). Routledge. https://doi.org/10.4324/9781315690100
Gettings, P. E., & Hall, E. D. (2024). Exploring the career resilience processes of women in the early stages of traditionally male careers. *Western Journal of Communication*, *88*(2), 259–283. https://doi.org/10.1080/10570314.2022.2132830
IDEO. (n.d.). https://www.designthinking.ideo.com/
Jones, N. (2016). Narrative inquiry in human-centered design: Examining silence and voice to promote social justice in design scenarios. *Journal of Technical Writing and Communication*, *46*(4), 471–492. https://doi.org/10.1177/0047281616653489
Kars-Unluoglu, S., Jarvis, C., & Gaggiotti, H. (2022). Unleading during a pandemic: Scrutinising leadership and its impact in a state of exception. *Leadership*, *18*(2), 277–297. https://doi.org/10.1177/17427150211063382
Ladkin, D. (2020). *Rethinking leadership: A new look at old questions* (2nd ed.). Edward Elgar. https://doi.org/10.4337/9781788119320
Ladkin, D., & Patrick, C. B. (2022). Whiteness in leadership theorizing: A critical analysis of race in Bass' transformational leadership theory. *Leadership*, *18*(2), 205–223.
Le Fevre, D. M. (2021). Leading through crisis: The adaptive leadership of Jacinda Ardern. In M. Raei, & H. T. Rasmussen (Eds.), *Adaptive leadership in a global economy* (pp. 165–179). Taylor & Francis.
Lillie, H. M., & Sánchez Sánchez, V. (2022). The impact of social and material resources on resilience communication at the intersection of race and gender. *Journal of Health Communication*, *27*(10), 706–716. https://doi.org/10.1080/10810730.2022.2153290
Martin-Anatias, N. (2021). New Zealand's success in tackling COVID-19: How Ardern's government effectively used social media and consistent messaging during the global pandemic. In J. C. Pollock, & D. A. Vakoch (Eds.), *COVID-19 in international media* (pp. 139–149). Routledge. https://doi.org/10.4324/9781003181705
McGuire, D., Cunningham, J. E., Reynolds, K., & Matthews-Smith, G. (2020). Beating the virus: An examination of the crisis communication approach taken by New Zealand Prime Minister Jacinda Ardern during the Covid-19 pandemic. *Human Resource Development International*, *23*(4), 361–379. https://doi.org/10.1080/13678868.2020.1779543
Ministry of Health – Manatū Hauora (2020, April 27). *COVID-19 (novel coronavirus) update – 27 April, 2020* [Video]. YouTube. https://www.youtube.com/watch?v=RJ5b8_JQeJM

Munford, R. (2021). Reflections from Aotearoa New Zealand: Stay home, stay safe, stay strong and be kind. *Qualitative Social Work*, *20*(1–2), 110–115. https://doi.org/10.1177/1473325020973203

New Zealand Parliament. (2020, April 28). Hansard Debates, 28 April 2020. *New Zealand Parliament.* https://www.parliament.nz/en/pb/hansard-debates/rhr/combined/HansD_20200428_20200428

Norander, S. (2019). Cultivating feminist reflexivity and resilience in leadership communication. In J. Cubbage (Ed.), *Developing women leaders in the academy through enhanced communication strategies* (pp. 131–150). Lexington.

Ospina, S. M., Foldy, E. G., Fairhurst, G. T., & Jackson, B. (2020). Collective dimensions of leadership: Connecting theory and method. *Human Relations*, *73*(4), 441–463. https://doi.org/10.1177/0018726719899714

Pyatovskaya, E. (2024). Zoom saved all of our lives: A case of non-profit resilient organizing during the COVID-19. In M. Nunes, & C. Ozog (Eds.), *'You're Muted:' Performance, precarity, and the logic of Zoom* (pp. 229–250). Bloomsbury.

Pyatovskaya, E., & Buzzanell, P. M. (2023). Integrating tenacious hope and feminism: Global necessity. *The Journal of Dialogic Ethics: Interfaith and Interhuman Perspectives*, 2(2), 137–155. https://doi.org/10.5840/jde20232211

Raelin, J. (2016). Imagine there are no leaders: Reframing leadership as collaborative agency. *Leadership*, *12*(2), 131–158. https://doi.org/10.1177/1742715014558076

Raelin, J. (2017). Leadership-as-practice: Theory and application—An editor's reflection. *Leadership*, *13*(2), 215–221. https://doi.org/10.1177/1742715017702273

Raelin, J. (2018). What are you afraid of: Collective leadership and its learning implications. *Management Learning*, *49*(1), 59–66. https://doi.org/10.1177/1350507617729974

Raelin, J., Kempster, S., Youngs, H., Carroll, B., & Jackson, B. (2018). Practicing leadership-as-practice in content and manner. *Leadership*, *14*(3), 371–383. https://doi.org/10.1177/1742715017752422

Riley, D. (2013). Hidden in plain view: Feminists doing engineering ethics, engineers doing feminist ethics. *Science and Engineering Ethics*, *19*, 189–206. https://doi.org/10.1007/s11948-011-9320-0

Ryan, M. K., Haslam, S. A., Hersby, M. D., & Bongiorno, R. (2011). Think crisis–think female: The glass cliff and contextual variation in the think manager–think male stereotype. *Journal of Applied Psychology*, *96*(3), 470–484. https://doi.org/10.1037/a0022133

Sadler, R. (2020, March 29). Coronavirus: Jacinda Ardern urges Kiwis to have a plan when returning from overseas. *Newshub*. https://www.newshub.co.nz/home/politics/2020/03/coronavirus-jacinda-ardern-urges-kiwis-to-have-a-plan-when-returning-from-overseas.html

Scharp, K. M., Geary, D. E., Wolfe, B. H., Wang, T. R., & Fesenmaier, M. A. (2021). Understanding the triggers and communicative processes that constitute resilience in the context of migration to the United States. *Communication Monographs*, *88*(4), 395–417. https://doi.org/10.1080/03637751.2020.1856395

Sergi, V. (2016). Who's leading the way? Investigating the contributions of materiality to leadership-as-practice. In J. Raelin (Ed.), *Leadership-as-practice: Theory and application* (pp. 110–131). Routledge. https://psycnet.apa.org/doi/10.4324/9781315684123

Sharma, G., Bartunek, J., Buzzanell, P. M., Carmine, S., Endres, C., Etter, M., Fairhurst, G., Hanh, T., Lê, P., Li, X., Pamphile, V., Pradies, C., Putnam, L. L.,

Rocheville, K., Schad, J., Sheep, M., & Keller, J. (2021). A paradox approach to societal tensions during the pandemic crisis. *Journal of Management Inquiry*, *30*(2), 121–137. https://doi.org/10.1177/1056492620986604

Siegenthaler, B., Worwood, J. V., & Craine, W. (2024). Patterns of disruptions: Complexities of discursive-embodied triggers and resilience responses of individuals with autoimmune diseases. *Communication Monographs*, *1*(22), 396–417. https://doi.org/10.1080/03637751.2023.2295461

Simpson, A. V., Rego, A., Berti, M., Clegg, S., & Pina e Cunha, M. (2022). Theorizing compassionate leadership from the case of Jacinda Ardern: Legitimacy, paradox and resource conservation. *Leadership*, *18*(3), 337–358. https://doi.org/10.1177/17427150211055291

Simpson, B. (2016). Where's the agency in leadership-as-practice? In J. A. Raelin (Ed.), *Leadership-as-practice: Theory and application* (pp. 159–177). Routledge. https://psycnet.apa.org/doi/10.4324/9781315684123

Walls, J. (2022, September 30). Covid 19 coronavirus: MPs' pay cuts finally in effect after Jacinda Ardern promised them three months ago. *New Zealand Herald*. https://www.nzherald.co.nz/nz/covid-19-coronavirus-mps-pay-cuts-finally-in-effect-after-jacinda-ardern-promised-them-three-months-ago/WDCQYJTS4UOTTA3AXLMKRPHKA4/

Wilkinson, J., & Male, T. (2025). Perceptions of women senior leaders in the UK Higher Education during the COVID-19 pandemic. *Educational Management Administration & Leadership*, *53*(1), 123–140. https://doi.org/10.1177/17411432221150079

Wilson, S. (2020). Pandemic leadership: Lessons from New Zealand's approach to COVID-19. *Leadership*, *16*(3), 279–293. https://doi.org/10.1177/1742715020929151

Woods, P. A. (2016). Democratic roots: Feeding the multiple dimensions of leadership-as-practice. In J. Raelin (Ed.), *Leadership-as-practice: Theory and application* (pp. 70–87). Routledge. https://psycnet.apa.org/doi/10.4324/9781315684123

Zheng, W., Kark, R., & Meister, A. L. (2018). Paradox versus dilemma mindset: A theory of how women leaders navigate the tensions between agency and communion. *The Leadership Quarterly*, *29*(5), 584–596. https://doi.org/10.1016/j.leaqua.2018.04.001

2

INTERSECTIONAL LEADERSHIP, LEADERSHIP-AS-MEDIUM, AND INSTITUTIONAL CHANGE

Sharmila Pixy Ferris and Kathleen Waldron

This chapter focuses on how intersectional leadership can achieve institutional change through the theoretical lens of leadership-as-medium. We start with a brief consideration of the meaning of leadership and move on to discuss Crenshaw's (1989, 1991) concept of intersectionality and Weick's (1978) theory of leadership-as-medium.

Intersectionality, as articulated by Crenshaw (1989, 1991), considers the social and cultural identity factors (such as race, gender, ethnicity, age, and immigrant status) that are woven into individuals' lives. Intersectionality is not diversity; it is a perspective that highlights how identity politics focusing on singular identity categories fails to capture how multiple social and cultural identities shape the lives of individuals. Weick's (1978) theory of leadership-as-medium (as related to Weick's classic theory of sensemaking, 1969) challenges traditional views of leadership and highlights the dynamic, fluid, and interactive nature of leadership, focusing on the role of leaders in helping individuals and organizations create meaning and adapt to changing conditions. Leadership is conceptualized as an interactional process where communication, particularly overt messaging, is crucial for facilitating organizational members' understanding of obstacles and achieving goals.

We draw upon the concept of intersectionality and Weick's (1978) theory of leadership-as-medium to examine how one leader effected creative institutional change in a real-world situation, drawing parallels in the way both concepts emphasize the complex, interconnected nature of individuals, leadership, and organizations. Specifically, we apply our theoretical framework to present the story of an Asian-born female leader who successfully managed organizational change at a U.S. university by leveraging

DOI: 10.4324/9781003563662-4

her intersectional skills to inform her use of object and action mediation (explained later) and engaged in interactional leadership and effective communication. This chapter thus provides an example of theory and practice, showing how leaders can effect successful institutional change.

Intersectionality and leadership-as-medium

Leadership is a complex concept, as is reflected in the variety, diversity, and extent of scholarly and popular definitions. In popular literature there are tens of thousands of books on leadership, as evidenced by a July 2024 search of Goodread's (n.d.) shelf on leadership which found 40,326 books. A much-cited meta-analysis of leadership literature by Kellerman (2012) found over 1500 definitions and 40 models of leadership. Several other meta-analyses over the decades (e.g., Borgmann et al., 2016; Eagly & Johnson, 1990; Jackson et al., 2013; Mackey et al., 2021) support Zheng et al.'s (2021) statement that there "is no universal meaning associated with the role of leader" (p. 1179). In this chapter we acknowledge the complexity of leadership and limit ourselves specifically to a consideration of leadership as successfully managing change, as informed by intersectionality. Leadership and change management are much studied perspectives (e.g., meta-analyses by Peng et al., 2021) as leaders undeniably manage change. All of us live and work in increasingly complex environments in which change is a norm, as the American Management Association (AMA) (2019) notes: "Change is no longer a force in the environment. It is the environment" (para 2).

Intersectionality

Understanding that leadership is hard to define, and influenced by many factors, including a leader's identity, we are particularly interested in identity characteristics of leaders who successfully manage change. In the U.S., leaders who bring their multiple social and cultural identities to their leadership face challenges that rarely affect the mainstream white male leader (Owen, 2020). By "identity characteristics" we do not mean those leadership characteristics espoused by classical theories such as personality and physical traits, nor do we mean behavioral traits such as charisma or relational skills. Instead, we are interested in identity factors that encompass *social and cultural identities* around factors including race, gender, ethnicity, age, sexual identity, immigrant status, physical ability, and other factors that individuals bring to their leadership roles. In leadership literature, such characteristics are commonly discussed in Diversity Equity and Inclusion (DEI) research (Harriott et al., 2023; Medvec et al., 2023) but our focus is on the ways that identity politics fail to capture the ways in which multiple social identities shape the lives of individuals. This concept was framed decades ago by Kimberlé Crenshaw and termed *intersectionality*. It recognizes that peoples' experiences are shaped by the interplay of multiple social factors creating something distinct from their constituent parts (Crenshaw, 1989, 1991). As Crenshaw explained it, social categorizations, such as race, class, gender, sexual orientation, disability, and other identities, are interconnected. These intersections create unique and complex experiences—of discrimination and privilege (see meta-analysis by Parker et al., 2020).

Intersectionality is different from other approaches to the study of race, gender, national origin, and other categories of difference as it presumes that individual identity/demographic categories are transformed into something new after intersecting. Gender is an important demographic as the U.S. population today has a higher percentage of women than men (50.52% female compared to 49.48% male) (Pew Research Center, 2023). Yet the same study indicates that women remain marginalized in the workplace as measured on key indicators of salary and leadership positions. Race and national origin/immigrant identities are equally important, as the U.S. today has a significant percentage of foreign-born residents, with about 15.8% of the population being foreign-born, i.e., categorized as "immigrants" (Pew Research Center, 2025). Such leaders labor under greater burdens (Pogrebna et al., 2024; Shapiro et al., 2010) making an understanding of intersectional leadership important.

Intersectional leadership, if better understood and supported, could potentially impact institutions in ways that substantially benefit society. In the corporate world 45% of Fortune 500 companies, including Apple, Tesla, and Alphabet, were founded by first- or second-generation immigrants (New American Economy Research Fund, 2019). Despite this, research on intersectionality and leadership remains scarce, although there is recent interest (e.g., Owen, 2020).

Leadership-as-medium

Leaders with intersectional experiences bring distinctive perspectives to their roles (Owen, 2020; Parker et al., 2020). Weick's (1978) theory of leadership-as-medium is particularly relevant to such leaders. Rooted in Weick's (1969) earlier sensemaking theory, which describes how individuals create meaning from collective experiences—especially in times of uncertainty or complexity—leadership-as-medium emphasizes the leader's role in shaping organizational understanding. Leaders act as sensemakers, helping organizations frame their experiences in ways that are both understandable and actionable. By giving structure and meaning to ambiguity, leaders serve as cognitive and social anchors, guiding others through complex and uncertain situations.

Weick (1978) identifies several ways in which leaders achieve effective leadership. One key role is mediating between an organization's actions and its performance, particularly by helping the organization manage and interpret information. Leaders do this through two main forms of mediation: action mediation and object mediation. Action mediation involves purposeful, behavioral actions that remove environmental obstacles. By taking direct action, leaders reduce uncertainty and facilitate smoother organizational functioning, helping their teams make sense of complex situations. Object mediation, on the other hand, focuses on the leader's interpretive role. Leaders analyze information from the environment and structure it to create reasonable and meaningful interpretations. This process helps others understand their context and act effectively within complex settings. In this view, leadership is an interactional, behavioral, and communicative process that helps manage organizational environments. Leaders not only facilitate members' understanding of obstacles but also take actions that enable the organization to achieve its goals. Communication is central to leadership-as-medium, with a strong emphasis on leaders' overt messaging. Weick also highlights communication skills as the ability to perform specific tasks competently.

Weick's theory of leader-as-medium (1978, hereafter cited without the date) provides the theoretical framework for this chapter. Challenging traditional views of leadership as a set of prescribed traits or behaviors, it highlights the dynamic, fluid, and interactive nature of leadership, focusing on the role of leaders in helping individuals and organizations create meaning and adapt to changing conditions.

We see leadership-as-medium as being closely aligned with intersectionality, with parallels in the way both concepts emphasize the complex, interconnected nature of individuals, leadership, and organizations. First, both concepts emphasize complexity and diversity. Intersectionality acknowledges the complexity of human identities and experiences. Weick's theory also highlights the complexity of organizations and the dynamic nature of leadership within them. Both ideas recognize that individuals and organizations are not monolithic but are shaped by multiple, interconnected factors. Second, both concepts accentuate the role of socialization and social categories. In Weick's theory, leaders serve as cognitive and social anchors, helping individuals make sense of their environment. Intersectionality recognizes that individuals' experiences are influenced by a combination of social and cultural categories, and their identities serve as anchors for their experiences. Third, Weick's theory underscores the importance of collective sensemaking in organizations, and intersectionality highlights that the collective experiences of diverse individuals are shaped by their multiple identities. Leaders, according to both views, must be sensitive to these intersecting identities and engage in inclusive and equitable sensemaking processes. Fourth, both views acknowledge the need for adaptive flexibility. From an intersectional perspective, leaders must adapt their approaches to account for the unique experiences and needs of individuals with various intersecting identities. Weick's theory also emphasizes adaptability in leadership to respond to changing circumstances. Finally, communication and social interaction are crucial in both theories. Intersectionality emphasizes the importance of listening to and amplifying the voices of those at the intersections of various identities. Relatedly, dialogue and communication are essential for sensemaking in the organizational workplace (Weick, 1978, 1995).

It is clear that Weick's theories of sensemaking (1969, 1995) and leadership-as-medium (1978) are highly relevant to intersectional leaders. Sensemaking is central to the human experience and the organizational workplace, while leadership is influenced by many factors, including a leader's identity. Leaders who bring their intersectional identities to their leadership face challenges that rarely impact mainstream and usually white male leaders, as we demonstrate in this chapter. In the context of change initiatives, leaders often serve as crucial cognitive anchors, helping individuals make sense of the changes and helping them adapt effectively. Weick's perspective (Weick, 1969, 1978) underscores the dynamic nature of leadership in facilitating collective sensemaking and embracing the uncertainties inherent in change management efforts.

To contextualize, change management is the structured approach of guiding individuals, teams, and organizations through a transition from a current state to a desired future state, often in response to evolving conditions, technological advancements, or internal shifts in strategy. It involves not only the logistical aspects of managing resources and timelines but also the critical human element, where emotions, perceptions, and cultural norms play a significant role in how individuals respond to change. Change management seeks to address resistance, foster adaptability, and ensure that all members of an organization are aligned toward common goals and are equipped to embrace the new reality (AMA, 2019; Peng et al., 2021).

In relation to leadership, change management highlights leaders' roles as facilitators of transition and adaptive capacity builders. Leaders are instrumental in bridging their organization's strategic objectives with the lived experiences of its people, providing a clear vision while empathetically addressing concerns and resistance. Weick's concept of leadership-as-medium aligns closely with change management, particularly in how leaders act as cognitive and social anchors, offering interpretive frameworks that help people make sense of uncertainty and complexity. By engaging in sensemaking, leaders help organizational members navigate the ambiguity inherent in change initiatives, guiding them in interpreting shifts and providing meaning to their roles and contributions. Effective leadership in change management is adaptive, communicative, and responsive, enabling organizations not only to meet immediate challenges but also to cultivate resilience and a proactive stance toward future changes.

Applying theory to a case involving intersectionality and leadership-as-medium

As humans, we create theories to make sense of the world around us. Theories serve as frameworks that help us interpret various phenomena, providing a structured way to understand complex realities. In the social sciences, theories go beyond mere explanation or understanding; by applying theories, social scientists can develop strategies to address societal issues and improve human interactions and organizations. In order to do so, however, students and scholars must test and validate theories through empirical research (Williams & Ferris, in press). Below, we explain how we conducted empirical research to apply intersectionality and leadership-as-medium to a real-life case, examining one leader's story.

Research design

To connect theory with practice by applying leadership-as-medium and intersectionality to the real-world actions of a leader effecting organizational change, we used a narrative design, following established scholarly tradition. Stories have been recognized by scholars as an effective way to define leadership in practice (Amado, 2019; Smith, 2019; Zheng et al., 2021). Stories have been universal to human cultures through the millennia and are important in organizational communication (Fisher, 1985, 1994). Fisher's scholarship theorizes that humans are storytellers and observers/interpreters of narratives; we understand complex information through narrative. Storytelling is a powerful tool for leaders to drive organizational change (Brown et al., 2004), with scholars such as Smith (2019) noting that leadership is "about weaving a story so compelling (as) to bring everyone along the journey" (p. 1). The leader whose story we analyze models effective intersectional leadership through sensemaking and application of strategies of leadership-as-medium. Her story illustrates the ways leadership-as-medium can be used effectively to achieve change management for all leaders, but especially for leaders who bring intersectionality to the ways in which they further organizational change and/or growth.

Procedures

In line with our narrative design, we used a semi-structured interview to qualitatively elicit one leader's story. Interviewing is a long-established qualitative method (Aspers & Corte, 2019; Treadwell & Davis, 2020) that "allows the researcher to explore a topic in a way that yields rich data impossible to obtain through surveys, document analysis, or observation" (Ortiz, 2003, p. 37) or other methods (Treadwell & Davis, 2020). We use a pseudonym to protect our interviewee's privacy. We refer to her henceforth as "Zhang Jing," "Dean Jing," and (since she identifies as a cis-female) use the gendered pronouns "she" or "her." Zhang Jing was selected along with others, using purposive convenience sampling, in a larger study of experienced academic leaders at a wide range of U.S. universities (Ferris & Waldron, 2021). Dean Jing is one of very few Asian female higher-level leaders at Research 1 universities in the U.S. She was contacted to invite her participation through a cold email through an Institutional Review Board approved process. The interview was conducted virtually, digitally recorded, and then transcribed and shared with Dean Jing. Subsequent to the interview, we communicated with her several times over the course of two years to expand on the original data.

For our initial analysis of the interview, we utilized Lanigan's technique of phenomenological description, reduction, and interpretation (Lanigan, 1977, 1988) to focus on Dean Jing's conscious experiences. Each of us separately analyzed the recording of the oral interview and the written transcript, being careful to avoid external presuppositions and to objectively examine Dean Jing's narrative. We then engaged in the second step, reduction, analyzing the narratives for essential themes, and the third step, interpretation, aiming to distill and describe the conscious experiences of the interviewees (Lanigan, 1977, 1988). After individual analysis we met to share our findings and cross check our interpretations.

For further analysis, we expanded on our initial findings by deductively analyzing the interviews using our theoretical framework, which incorporates the concepts of intersectional identity, sensemaking, and leadership-as-medium as detailed below.

An analysis of leading change through the lens of intersectionality and leadership-as-medium

Zhang Jing was a health care professional in Asia who emigrated to the U.S. as an adult to continue her education. After obtaining her doctoral degree in the United States, with a dissertation focusing on minority health promotion and health disparity research, Dr. Jing entered higher education as a faculty member. As a professor she supervised a program and then rapidly rose through the organizational ranks to become dean at a diverse, urban, public U.S. Research 1 University. The leadership story shared here occurred at that university. At a pivotal point during her first deanship, Dean Jing faced a critical moment of change affecting the future of her school, her faculty, and herself. Her university was experiencing financial difficulties due to lower state and federal assistance, while being led by new senior leaders. The university's new interim president and the new provost had called together the deans of all the colleges and schools to announce an academic reorganization after a recently completed analysis of the institution's enrollments, finances, and organizational structure. Specifically, among other changes at the university, this dean's school was to be merged with two other health-related schools to form a large new college. Notably, the decision was a surprise; the deans of the three schools slated for merger were not consulted before the announcement.

Dean Jing was faced with a significant unplanned institutional change (or an environmental obstacle) at her organization. While she understood the financial predicament of the university, she believed that subsuming her school into a combined college would lower the visibility of her programs, and of her faculty. The provost's public announcement of the proposed changes would, to most, have signaled a final decision. But not to Dean Jing. After conducting *object mediation* by putting a great deal of thought on how she could make sense of the information within the environment to arrive at reasonable *interpretation* that met her vision for her School of Nursing, Dean Jing decided in favor of *action mediation* through suggesting an alternative course of action that would remove the environmental obstacles. She spent substantial time considering the complex factors involved and then *communicated* directly with her senior leader, the university provost, making a persuasive case for a different course of action. Rather than merging her school into the new college, Dean Jing asked to remain independent and implement a new mission at her School of Nursing focusing on meeting the needs of the external community through academic-practice partnerships.

We believe that *intersectionality* played a role in Dean Jing's decision. Her identity as an *adult immigrant* who had left a career and family in Asia to pursue higher education in a Western country may have played a role in the way she initiated change. Classic and contemporary research shows that distinct cultural contexts and practices shape the processes of Asian ways of communication (Liu, 2024; Wu & Talhelm, 2024). People from East Asian societies often employ holistic thinking, which focuses on context and relationships and accepts contradictions and changes (Gudykunst, 2003; Gudykunst et al., 1996), as contrasted with the more individualistic thinking prevalent in Western cultures (Gudykunst et al., 1996;

Humphrey & Bliuc, 2022). As an immigrant from Asia who successfully adapted to Western ways of communication, Dean Jing demonstrated intersectionality by leveraging the positive aspects of collectivism as well as the positive aspects of individualism. *Collectivism* values group cohesion, prioritizing harmony and interdependence, often found in East Asian cultures. This perspective encourages decision-making that considers relationships and collective well-being (Gudykunst, 2003; Wu & Talhelm, 2024). *Individualism*, common in Western cultures, emphasizes personal autonomy and achievement, with decisions guided by individual goals rather than group concerns (Humphrey & Bliuc, 2022). In Dean Jing's case, her intersectional identity allowed her to balance these values: she leveraged collectivism to build respectful relationships while also taking an individualistic approach by asserting her views publicly, blending cultural strengths effectively. In essence, we feel that Dean Jing's intersectional *identity* as an Asian woman in the U.S. influenced the ways in which she respectfully challenged authority. She took a professional risk, knowing she was publicly disagreeing with her provost and president, and understood that if she did not convince them to accept her proposed course of action, she probably would have to seek new employment.

Having made sense of the environment and engaging in a *decision to act* to promote her own vision for her School of Nursing, Dean Jing was aware of the *action mediation* needed in sending a written communication to her provost to make her case. In both making the decision and mediating action by penning the persuasive memo, Dean Jing was practicing the type of effective *communication* that Weick stated was necessary for leaders-as-medium. In order to accomplish her communication task effectively, Dean Jing drew upon *gendered communication* skills (Belenky et al., 1986) honed by her experiences. She adeptly recognized the importance of context, experience, and relationships in the process of knowing and exercised her gendered skills of empathy, relational understanding, and contextual thinking in education and knowledge construction.

Dean Jing additionally leveraged her *intersectionality* utilizing collectivist communication skills, which are commonly perceived as *Asian* and *gendered* skills (Liu, 2024; Wu & Talhelm, 2024), in deciding to consult with some local health administrators whom she knew from the community outreach programs of her School of Nursing. Gendered collaboration by women emphasizes the importance of relationships and interconnectedness since women typically tend to develop their understanding through dialogue and cooperation with others (Belenky et al., 1986; Fletcher, 1999; Mavin & Yusupova, 2024). Dean Jing also drew upon her gendered (intersectional) communication strengths by remaining genuinely open to feedback and listening fully and actively. She listened mindfully to one administrator, in particular, who provided wise counsel, suggesting Dean Jing think big and think beyond her own institution. This colleague asked, "Can you imagine a school that becomes a complete partner with this community? Can you envision students and faculty developing practicums with local organizations beyond what already exists?" Here, in addition to leveraging skills that are associated with intersectionality, we also see Dean Jing practicing *object mediation* as she sought out additional information to make sense of her environment (Weick, 1995).

Dean Jing's actions had the felicitous result of the provost arranging a phone conference, at which time Dean Jing made her case for a separate school that would be actively involved in external/community systems. Dean Jing practiced the effective *communication* of leader-as-medium by conveying her own message clearly to foster understanding. By creating shared meanings and fostering a sense of collective purpose with her provost, she further practiced *sensemaking*. The meeting resulted in positive change, as the provost told Dean Jing he would not merge her school into the new college without opening the door to further discussion. He did make a proviso that faculty and community leaders would have to participate in the conversation. Dean Jing not only accepted this condition, but, drawing on collaborative practices commonly noted in Asian professional cultures (Morrison & Conaway, 2006; Wu & Talhelm, 2024), she recognized a real opportunity to practice *action mediation* and behavioral actions aimed at removing environmental obstacles. She considered her options for *managing change* effectively and made the decision to turn first to the largest donors to the school. She practiced *object mediation* and effective *communication* by explaining to the donors her vision of an independent unit within the university structure and demonstrated why that was important. The success of her strategies can be seen in that the donors would eventually contribute nearly $17 million toward a $60 million building project. Equally impactful, some donors agreed to make a public statement in support of Dean Jing's objectives, thus supporting her case for an independent school or college to the provost.

Dean Jing then continued to practice *sensemaking, action* and *object mediation,* and effective *communication* in turning to a different constituency: the relevant community leaders in the city. She emphasized to them the significant role her faculty and students already played in the city's essential services and underscored the potential for greater cooperation in the future. *Object mediation* called for a delicate balance here. On the one hand, Dean Jing knew that she did not want it to appear that she was criticizing the senior administrators' decision regarding restructuring as she did understand her university needed to cut costs and streamline.

On the other hand, she saw an opportunity to build better community services, with increased interaction and participation with her faculty and students, while reciprocally benefiting her school. Dean Jing communicated this so well, drawing upon her culturally unique, intersectional, and gendered ways of thinking and communicating (Belenky et al., 1986; Wu & Talhelm, 2024), that the community leaders agreed to meet with the provost to discuss her school. Here we see Dean Jing demonstrate not only a nuanced consideration of issues around *change management* but also engage in application of the *interactional processes* that Weick states leaders should use to facilitate organizational members' *understanding of obstacles* and achieve *actions that accomplish goals*.

Having engaged the community, Dean Jing needed to communicate with her faculty to persuade them to participate in the institutional change. She realized that without the support of the faculty and a commitment on their part to step up their community engagement, she would not be able to convince the provost and president. Indeed, the provost had told her he would reconsider his original position only after she consulted directly with the faculty. To convince faculty to participate actively in this initiative, Dean Jing played a central role in shaping collective understanding within an organization. She ensured that the faculty *understood* the purpose, goals, and benefits of participation and engaged in *open dialogue*, thus inspiring them to contribute to the success of her proposal. At a faculty meeting in which she outlined the steps she had taken to ensure the independent survival of her school, Dean Jing recalls telling the faculty that she had done her part, and that now it was their turn. Through these ways of sensemaking, she demonstrated how *interactional leadership* helps people in organizations manage their environment.

The outcome was all Dean Jing could have wished for, and it effectively demonstrated how the combined application of intersectional knowledge and leadership-as-medium can achieve creative institutional change. In a subsequent public communication, the provost announced that the university would continue to maintain a separate nursing school. Dean Jing was pleased that she had achieved a critical victory for her academic unit, but she did not stop there. *Action mediation* calls for ongoing behavioral actions aimed at removing environmental obstacles. Dean Jing swiftly followed up with a request that the restructuring be revised so that the school would become a college, thus achieving equity with the other colleges at the institution. This new college not only demonstrated the value placed on the discipline, faculty, students, and programs, but it also meant that the college would be more visible to students wishing to pursue the degree. Dean Jing continued to do what was necessary to achieve her vision and, later, she gained the approval of the State Board of Regents. Today, her college has a highly regarded online master's program, has introduced a doctoral program, and has an undergraduate degree that is one of the highest ranked programs in the region.

Conclusion

This leadership case study and story illustrates Crenshaw's (1989, 1991) theory of intersectionality and Weick's (1978) theory of leadership-as-medium in action, highlighting the skills of an Asian-born female leader through her intersectional lived experience. By practicing sensemaking, action and object mediation, effective communication, and interactional leadership, Dean Jing succeeded in fulfilling the goals of effective leadership. She made sense of the organizational environment and took actions to pursue desired goals, thereby helping the organization. Dean Jing's success at achieving institutional change is also indicative of the skills learned from negotiating multiple identities as an immigrant, Asian woman, and leader. She had the ability to tailor her communication to very different audiences while keeping on message. Her ability to engage external constituents was a particularly valuable skill which women and immigrants are often forced to practice while living in the United States where the dominant powers are white and male.

Particularly useful to leaders from diverse backgrounds, this chapter demonstrates the link between theory and practice. While this is just one leader's story, it specifically shows how the theory of leadership-as-medium and the intersectional view are linked to practice when it comes to communication skills and variety of ways leaders can effectively apply sensemaking and interactional leadership. This chapter also demonstrates how an established but underutilized scholarly tradition of storytelling can illustrate effective leadership in practice and add diversity to organizational communication and leadership theory by providing practical examples and lessons that everyone, but especially intersectional leaders, can apply in their lives.

Future scholarship could build on this exploration of intersectional leadership and leadership-as-medium by expanding empirical research on leaders from various intersectional backgrounds. A valuable next step would be to examine how intersectional leaders in diverse sectors, such as healthcare, education, and technology, apply Weick's concepts of sensemaking and mediation. Such research could investigate how these leaders' unique social and cultural identities influence their problem-solving approaches and communication strategies, particularly in high-stakes or crisis situations, providing deeper insights into the nuances of intersectional leadership styles (Owen, 2020; Parker et al., 2020).

Additionally, a comparative analysis of intersectional leaders in varying cultural and organizational contexts could reveal how diverse identities shape leadership approaches differently across cultures. Intercultural leadership scholarship is sparse, and more research on this topic could include exploring how intersectional leaders adapt communication and mediation strategies across collectivist and individualistic cultures, broadening understanding of how Weick's theory can apply in global contexts. Finally, integrating storytelling as a methodological tool for capturing the nuanced experiences of intersectional leaders, as this chapter demonstrates, would enrich leadership literature by bringing forward voices traditionally underrepresented in scholarship (Fisher, 1985; Prusak et al., 2004). This approach could inform not only theory but also practical training programs for developing effective, adaptable leaders across complex, multicultural environments.

Suggested further readings

Amado, A. P. (2019). *Stories our leaders tell: A collection and compilation of stories of leadership*. (Proquest # 27543620). [Doctoral Dissertation, Fielding Graduate University.] Proquest Dissertations and Theses Global.

Gottardello, D. (2023). The maze: Reflections on navigating intersectional identities in the workplace. *Gender, Work & Organization*, *35*(5), 1839–1854. https://doi.org/10.1111/gwao.13030

Sim, E., & Bierema, L. (2024). A systematic literature review of intersectional leadership in the workplace: The landscape and framework for future leadership research and practice to challenge interlocking systems of oppression. *Journal of Leadership & Organizational Studies*, *32*(1), 71–93. https://doi.org/10.1177/15480518241292214

Weick, K. E. (1969). *The social psychology of organizing* (1st ed.). Addison-Wesley.

Questions for further engagement

1 How does the concept of intersectional leadership differ from traditional views of leadership?
2 Why is it important to consider multiple social identities (e.g., race, gender, ethnicity, age, and immigrant status) in leadership roles? To illustrate your answer, please provide an example of how multiple social identities might intersect to shape a leader's experience and approach?
3 How does Weick's theory of leadership-as-medium challenge traditional views of leadership?
4 How can you, personally, apply the principles of intersectional leadership in the different organizational contexts of your own life?
5 In your own words, discuss the theoretical framework this chapter uses to address the complexities of identity politics, effective communication,

and organizational change. Try to support your answer with the principles of intersectional leadership, as illustrated by Weick's theory of leadership-as-medium, and the actions of the Asian-born female leader.

References

(AMA) American Management Association. (2019). *What's changed in change management?* https://www.amanet.org/articles/what-s-changed-in-change-management-/

Amado, A. P. (2019). *Stories our leaders tell: A collection and compilation of stories of leadership* (Proquest # 27543620). [Doctoral Dissertation, Fielding Graduate University.] Proquest Dissertations and Theses Global.

Aspers, P., & Corte, U. (2019). What is qualitative in qualitative research. *Qualitative.*

Belenky, M. F., Clinchy, B. M., Goldberger, N. R., & Tarule, J. M. (1986). *Women's ways of knowing: The development of self, voice, and mind.* Basic Books.

Borgmann, L., Rowold, J., & Bormann, K. C. (2016). Integrating leadership research: A meta-analytical test of Yukl's meta-categories of leadership. *Personnel Review*, *45*(6), 1340–1366. https://doi.org/10.1108/PR-07-2014-0145

Brown, J. S., Denning, S., Groh, K., & Prusak, L. (2004). *Storytelling in organizations: Why storytelling is transforming 21st century organizations and management.* Butterworth and Heinemann. https://doi.org/10.4324/9780080517834

Crenshaw, K. (1989). Demarginalizing the intersection of race and sex: A Black feminist critique of antidiscrimination doctrine, feminist theory, and antiracist politics. *University of Chicago Legal Forum*, *1*(8), 139–167. https://www.biscmi.org/wp-content/uploads/2020/11/K-Crenshaw-Demarginalizing-the-Intersection.pdf

Crenshaw, K. (1991). Mapping the margins: Intersectionality, identity politics, and violence against women of color. *Stanford Law Review*, *43*, 1241–1299. https://archive.org/details/mapping-the-margins-intersectionality-identity-politics-and-violence-against-women-of-color/page/1243/mode/2up

Eagly, A. H., & Johnson, B. T. (1990). Gender and leadership style: A meta-analysis. *Psychological Bulletin*, *108*(2), 233–256. https://doi.org/10.1037/0033-2909.108.2.233.

Ferris, S. P., & Waldron, K. (2021). *Higher education leadership: Pathways and insights*. Emerald Publishing. https://doi.org/10.1108/9781839822308

Fisher, W. R. (1985). The narrative paradigm: In the beginning. *Journal of Communication*, *35*(4), 74–89. https://doi.org/10.1111/j.1460-2466.1985.tb02974.x

Fisher, W. R. (1994). Narration as a human communication paradigm: The case of public moral argument. *Communication Monographs*, *51*, 1–20. https://doi.org/10.1080/03637758409390180

Fletcher, J. K. (1999). *Disappearing acts: Gender, power, and relational practice at work*. MIT Press. https://doi.org/10.7551/mitpress/2440.001.0001

Goodreads. (n.d.) *Leadership books*. https://www.goodreads.com/shelf/show/leadership

Gudykunst, W. B. (2003). *Cross cultural and intercultural communication*. Sage.

Gudykunst, W. B., Matsumoto, Y., Ting-Toomey, S., Nishida, T., Kim, K., & Heyman, S. (1996). The influence of cultural individualism-collectivism, self construals, and individual values on communication styles across cultures. *Human Communication Research*, 22, 510–543. https://doi.org/10.1111/j.1468-2958.1996.tb00377.x

Harriott, S. A., Tyson, J., & Powell, C. A. (2023). Breaking the mold: The power of transformational leadership and DEI in driving organizational change. In D. Roache (Ed.), *Transformational leadership styles for global leaders: Management and communication strategies* (pp. 391–413). IGI Global. https://doi.org/10.4018/979-8-3693-1380-0.ch024

Humphrey, A., & Bliuc, A.-M. (2022). Western individualism and the psychological wellbeing of young people: A systematic review of their associations. *Youth*, *2*(1), 1–11. https://doi.org/10.3390/youth2010001

Jackson, T. A., Meyer, J. P., & Wang, X.-H. (2013). Leadership, commitment, and culture: A meta-analysis. *Journal of Leadership and Organizational Studies*, *20*(1), 84–106. https://doi.org/10.1177/1548051812466919

Kellerman, B. (2012, August 10). *Cut off at the pass: The limits of leadership in the 21st century*. Brookings Institution. https://www.brookings.edu/wp-content/uploads/2016/06/0810_leadership_deficit_kellerman.pdf

Lanigan, R. L. (1977). *The phenomenology of human communication as a rhetorical ethic* [ED136314]. ERIC. https://eric.ed.gov/?id=ED136314

Lanigan, R. L. (1988). *Phenomenology of communication*. Duquesne University Press.

Liu, Y. (2024). Reviving the aspiration, fostering impactful research, and contributing to the sustainable development and societal impact at Asian business and management. *Asian Business Management*, *23*, 1–8. https://doi.org/10.1057/s41291-024-00262-9

Mackey, J. D., Parker Ellen, B., McAllister, C. P., & Alexander, K. C. (2021). The dark side of leadership: A systematic literature review and meta-analysis of destructive leadership research. *Journal of Business Research*, *132*, 705–718. https://doi.org/10.1016/j.jbusres.2020.10.037

Mavin, S., & Yusupova, M. (2024). Jostling discourses of competition: Women leaders self-positioning. *Organization Studies*, *45*(6), 801–823. https://doi.org/10.1177/01708406241236606

Medvec, B. R., Knight, S. W., & McLaughlin-Grayson, T. (2023). Cultivating leadership competency using virtual reality: DEI and anti-racism. *Journal of Interactive Learning Research*, *34*(3), 475–494. https://www.learntechlib.org/primary/p/222420/

Morrison, T., & Conaway, W. A. (2006). *Kiss, bow, or shake hands: The bestselling guide to doing business in more than 60 countries* (2nd ed.). Adams Media.

New American Economy Research Fund. (2019, July 2022). *Research report 'Fortune 500 in 2019: Top American companies and their immigrant roots.'* https://data.newamericaneconomy.org/en/fortune500-2019/

Ortiz, A. M. (2003). The ethnographic interview. In F. K. Stage & K. Manning (Eds.), *Research in the college context: Approaches and methods* (pp. 35–48). Brunner-Routledge. https://doi.org/10.4324/9781315740447

Owen, J. E. (2020). *We are the leaders we've been waiting for: Women and leadership development in college*. Routledge. https://doi.org/10.4324/9781003448631

Parker, P. D., Van Zanden, B., Marsh, H. W., Owen, K. B., Duineveld, J. J., & Noetel, M. (2020). The intersection of gender, social class, and cultural context: A meta-analysis. *Educational Psychology Review*, *32*, 197–228. https://doi.org/10.1007/s10648-019-09493-1

Peng, J., Li, M., Wang, Z., & Lin, Y. (2021). Transformational leadership and employees' reactions to organizational change: Evidence from a meta-analysis. *Journal of Applied Behavioral Science*, *57*(3), 369–397. https://doi.org/10.1177/0021886320920366

Pew Research Center. (2023, February 28). Gender gains and gaps in the US, ahead of Women's History Month. *Pew Research Center*. https://www.pewresearch.org/short-reads/2024/02/27/for-womens-history-month-a-look-at-gender-gains-and-gaps-in-the-us/

Pew Research Center. (2025, August 21). What the data says about immigrants in the U.S. *Pew Research Center*. https://www.pewresearch.org/short-reads/2025/08/21/key-findings-about-us-immigrants/#:~:text=Here's%20some%20information%20about%20the%20origins%20of,immigrants**%2014%20million%20unauthorized%20immigrants%20in%202023

Pogrebna, G., Angelopoulos, S., Motsi-Omoijiade, I., Kharlamov, A., & Tkachenko, N. (2024). The impact of intersectional racial and gender biases on minority female leadership over two centuries. *Scientific Reports*, *14*(1), 111. https://doi.org/10.1038/s41598-023-50392-x

Prusak, L., Groh, K., & Denning, S. (2004). *Storytelling in organizations: Why storytelling is transforming 21st century organizations*. Elsevier Butterworth-Heinemann. https://doi.org/10.4324/9780080517834

Shapiro, J. R., Leigh, J. M., & Penny, S. H. (2010). Developing diverse, collaborative leaders: An empirical program evaluation. *Journal of Leadership & Organizational Studies*, *17*(4), 370–379. https://doi.org/10.1177/1548051809355510

Smith, P. (2019). *The 10 great stories leaders tell*. Ignite Reads/SimpleTruths.

Treadwell, D., & Davis, A. (2020). *Introducing communication research* (4th ed.). Sage.

Weick, K. E. (1969). *The social psychology of organizing* (1st ed.). Addison-Wesley. https://doi.org/10.3917/mana.182.0189

Weick, K. E. (1978). The spines of leaders. In M. McCall & M. Lombardo (Eds.), *Leadership: Where else can we go?* (pp. 37–61). Duke University Press.

Weick, K. E. (1995). *Sensemaking in organizations* (1st ed.). Sage.

Williams, S., & Ferris, S. P. (in press). From theory to practice: Social media and misinformation. In G. Hummel & A. R. Hall (Eds.), *Perspectives on communication*. Kendall Hunt.

Wu, K., & Talhelm, T. (2024). Hide a dagger behind a smile: A review of how collectivistic cultures compete more than individualistic cultures. In S. M. Garcia, A. Tor, & A. J. Elliot (Eds.), *The Oxford handbook of the psychology of competition* (pp. 611–642). Oxford University Press. https://doi.org/10.1093/oxfordhb/9780190060800.001.0001

Zheng, W., Meister, A., & Caza, B. B. (2021). The stories that make us: Leaders' origin stories and temporal identity work. *Human Relations*, *74*(8), 1178–1210. https://doi.org/10.1177/0018726720909864

3

AUTHENTIC LEADERSHIP

A Step Backward from a Communication Perspective

Jeff Youngquist

The communication discipline seems surprisingly disinterested in the topic of leadership, or at least disinterested in addressing it explicitly and giving it the prominence of place that it needs in this age. Evidence of this can be found by reviewing the divisions of both the National Communication Association (NCA) and the International Communication Association (ICA). The NCA has 51 divisions and the ICA has 25 divisions and eight interest groups. None of the divisions or interest groups directly or explicitly address leadership. The words "leader" and "leadership" are completely lacking in the titles of all of these divisions and interest groups. A further review of the annual conference programs for these important disciplinary organizations will, predictably, reveal a similar dearth of panels, presentations, and papers that are clearly and directly related to leadership. This is a problem for the communication discipline.

Leadership is a topic of study that is arguably more important now than it has ever been. We need a better understanding of how leadership works and how leadership can be improved. The communication discipline is better positioned to contribute to this effort than any other discipline. Much of what a leader does involves communication, including important tasks like communicating with followers, building relationships, persuading stakeholders, shaping messages, and numerous other communication-related matters. Many different approaches to leadership have been proposed over time, especially in recent decades, but they are not all of equal value. In fact, some may cause more difficulties with leadership than they resolve. For instance, a transactional approach to leadership may be an effective way to accomplish a leader's goals in the short term but can

DOI: 10.4324/9781003563662-5

be highly problematic once instituted, especially if the leader's ability to provide material incentives becomes diminished.

In this chapter I am taking issue with an approach to leadership called authentic leadership. Authentic leadership, at its most basic level, is about being true to oneself. For many, there is something very appealing about the idea that being true to oneself will be adequate preparation for effective leadership. However, this is exactly what I contest in this chapter. I am not arguing against the authentic leadership perspective in its entirety. It has aspects that I find valuable and laudable. For instance, intense self-reflection and thinking about one's own values, thinking about why one thinks and feels the way one does, and pondering how one's behaviors are affected by these values would be beneficial to any prospective leader. However, some of the fundamental aspects of this leadership perspective, and some of its logic, are highly questionable and problematic.

In the sections that follow, a summary of authentic leadership is provided. This is followed by a critique of authentic leadership from an ethical perspective, a critical perspective, and, importantly, a communicative perspective. The chapter concludes with a brief discussion about leadership in general and provides suggestions regarding where leadership scholars and thinkers should go from here.

Overview of authentic leadership

This chapter critiques authentic leadership from a variety of perspectives. However, before this can be done, it is important to provide a basic overview of authentic leadership. This overview is by no means comprehensive, but the important, significant, and foundational aspects of this perspective on leadership are presented.

Authentic leadership is arguably not a theory in the formal sense (Einola & Alvesson, 2021), but more of an approach to leadership. The rapid increase in the popularity of authentic leadership has contributed to confusion because of competing definitions, conceptualizations, and methods of measurement. Dugan (2017) suggests that, more than any other leadership theory, scholars of authentic leadership "seem to blur the boundaries of statements based on evidence versus mere conjecture" (p. 264) and bluntly describes the body of literature regarding authentic leadership as "a mess" (p. 258). Nonetheless, an attempt is made in the following paragraphs to summarize some of the more prominent aspects of authentic leadership that seem to resonate with both academics and practitioners alike.

Bill George (2003) brought authentic leadership to the popular press and to the forefront of the corporate world with his influential book, *Authentic Leadership: Rediscovering the Secrets to Creating Lasting Value.*

However, authentic leadership had already been established as a bona fide perspective on leadership which various scholars had attempted to explore and expand upon. For example, Luthans and Avolio (2003) had already summarized existing work on authentic leadership and they defined the authentic leader as someone who "is true to him/herself" and is also "confident, hopeful, optimistic, resilient, transparent, moral/ethical, future-oriented, and gives priority to developing associates to be leaders" (p. 243).

Authentic leadership focuses heavily on self-awareness (McManus et al., 2018) and it emphasizes acting in alignment with one's values, being vulnerable, being open about one's weaknesses, but not being "fake" in one's relationships (Newman, 2019). Middlebrooks et al. (2020) describe authentic leadership as a leader's unique, honest, and ethical approach to leadership. Authentic leaders are original and unique and they "do not fake their leadership" (p. 416). What is meant by this is that authentic leaders do not copy other leaders' styles, or other leaders' approaches. They spend a lot of time and energy engaged in self-exploration and they deeply understand their own values, motivations, strengths, and weaknesses. Their actions are clearly connected to their own values, and they have a strong sense of purpose or mission.

At its core, authentic leadership involves being transparent and sincere. Authentic leaders must exhibit resiliency and be "beyond reproach in their moral/ethical conduct and decision-making" (Luthans & Avolio, 2003, p. 244). An authentic leader's primary motivation is to help the group, or the movement, or the team, or the organization. They do not embrace the leadership role for personal rewards or benefits to themselves (Middlebrooks et al., 2020).

Some scholars have attempted to distill authentic leadership down to its essential characteristics. Possibly the best summary of these essential elements, or core ideas, is provided by McManus et al. (2018). They describe authentic leadership as having four core ideas. One involves self-reflection which leads to increased *self-awareness*. This self-awareness gives leaders a strong sense of identity and direction. Authentic leaders also exhibit *balanced processing*. Balanced processing is simply being objective or unbiased in processing new ideas and recognizing that others may have valuable ideas that the leader does not have. Authentic leadership also requires that leaders have an *internalized moral perspective*. Authentic leaders must spend time reflecting on their own morals and values and, presumably, will evolve over time to a higher level of moral understanding where their personal morals and values are also positive morals and values, rather than negative ones. Last, authentic leadership requires *relational transparency*. Relational transparency involves acting "in a way that others perceive as personifying their beliefs" (p. 246).

Empirical research has attempted to show how the use of academic leadership can result in positive organizational outcomes. For instance, research has found a relationship between trust and perceptions of authentic leadership which then led to improved organizational performance (Clapp-Smith et al., 2009). Research has also shown a relationship between authentic leadership, job satisfaction, and work engagement (Giallonardo et al., 2010). Interestingly, research has also shown that leaders who embrace the collective interests of the group are then perceived as more authentic (Steffens et al., 2016).

Based on this overview, it may appear to the reader that authentic leadership is a straightforward and desirable approach to leadership that allows little room for criticism. However, I challenge the reader to look a bit more deeply into this theory and consider some of the potential problems and inconsistencies of this approach to leadership. The overall critique that begins in the following section starts with an ethical critique of authentic leadership and is followed by a critical critique and then a communicative critique. It must be emphasized though that this approach to leadership may still have aspects worth embracing as a leader. For instance, other approaches to leadership encourage an understanding of the self, like authentic leadership does. Taking the time to better understand one's own values, actions, and one's own self will undoubtedly help one to become a better leader.

Ethical critique

Before discussing ethics as it relates to authentic leadership, it is important to explore what ethics is about and also explore how ethics relates to leadership in general. Ethics has been an important topic since ancient times and much has been contested and argued. Nonetheless, some consistencies have emerged from centuries of contemplation and debate. One very regularly occurring component of discussions regarding ethics is the concern with the "other." The "other" could be defined as simply anyone beyond the self, but it could also be viewed as those beyond the immediate people that the self is interacting with. For instance, Arneson (2007), an established scholar of communication and ethics, defined ethics as something "that concerns judgements about 'goodness' and the quality of our communicative actions in the capacity to either harm or benefit others" (p. xii). Anderson (2007), another scholar of communication and ethics, states that "ethics exists to serve the community, to serve the polis" and "does not exist just to serve the source or the immediate receiver, but in a larger sense serves the whole polity" (p. 131). An ethical person is a thoughtful person who is considerate about the consequences of their choices and actions and how those consequences impact the "other."

Of course, there is much more to ethics than what was just briefly addressed. Yet understanding the importance of the "other" in discussions of ethics is necessary before discussing authentic leadership from an ethical perspective since the marginalization of the other in this approach is somewhat striking. The authentic leadership approach has appropriately been referred to as "leader-centric" (McManus et al., 2018, p. 246) and, at its most fundamental level, is based on the *self* and a leader's understanding of their personal values. Authentic leadership stresses personal integrity and self-awareness before all else. The logic of this perspective on leadership is that a leader's authenticity will cause followers to view them as being more ethical leaders, having more personal integrity, and being more trustworthy.

George (2010) describes the authentic leaders' personal values as their "moral compass" (p. 580) and states this moral compass provides them with a "deep sense of the right thing to do" (p. 580). George's vision of the authentic leader extends beyond simply having a strong moral compass but also indicates that an authentic leader must have integrity. He describes integrity as "not just the absence of lying, but of telling the whole truth, as painful as it may be" (p. 580). On the surface, this dogmatic vision of integrity and honesty is appealing in its simpleness. But a leader's life is anything but simple, and leaders will regularly encounter situations where any moral dogma will be challenged. George essentially presents the reader with a simple truth/falsehood dichotomy to make his point. This is a weak argument because "truth" and "falsehood" are rarely a simple dichotomy. Additionally, it is easy to visualize a leader being in a situation where expressing the complete and unfiltered truth could be very problematic. For those that struggle to see the problems with George's description of integrity, they will also probably find the idea of authentic leadership to be very appealing and self-validating.

Though understanding of the self is certainly important to all leaders, authentic leadership prioritizes this focus on the self probably more so than any other perspective on leadership. Think, for instance, of two common and contemporary approaches to leadership: transformational leadership and servant leadership. While an understanding of the self is still an important and useful component of both transformational and servant leadership, neither of these approaches *begins* with a focus on the self. Instead, the focus of these approaches to leadership is clearly more relational and connected to the "other," whether it's about serving the needs of others or working to transform the other and to help them achieve their potential. Though it has been argued that "authentic leadership has evolved to incorporate a distinctly ethical dimension" (McManus et al., 2018, p. 244), its core foundational premise is still primarily considering the "self." With that in mind, authentic leadership is arguably an ethically flawed approach to leadership. To be both ethical and effective, it is helpful for leadership to start with, and be based on, the "other," not the "self."

Critical critique

Authentic leadership can be critiqued from an ethical perspective at a fundamental level, and it can also be seen as significantly flawed when viewed from a critical perspective. The critical perspective prioritizes identifying the abuse of power by one person or group to oppress other peoples or groups. The critical perspective also strives to provide ways to liberate or free oppressed groups from this problematic power dynamic (Deetz, 2001).

Leadership inherently involves power, and because power is so easily abused, leaders should be very conscious about their own use or misuse of power. Authentic leadership is no exception. Authentic leadership is an understandably appealing approach to leadership, at least on the surface. It was developed and gained popularity in response to corrupt and self-serving leadership practices that were very visible and that deceived and negatively impacted many people. However, as Wilson (2016) indicates, authentic leadership is nothing new, and "through maintaining an account of the leaders as ones comprised only of praiseworthy and desirable attributes, offering a standard which followers are incited to replicate, authentic leadership discourse simply adds a new player to what is an old game" (p. 150).

Authentic leadership advises that leaders should discover and focus on their most authentic, or "true," selves (George, 2003). The assumption is that doing so will lead to better leaders and better leadership. This may be true in some cases, but this can just as easily be untrue in other cases. What is necessary for this to happen, and what is overlooked by advocates of authentic leadership, is that these authentic selves must align with leadership characteristics that are effective and that are desired by followers. In some cases, the opposite may happen. Focusing on the "true self" may bring into focus personal characteristics that do *not* align, at all, with effective leadership practices, or that do *not* align with what followers are looking for in a leader. So, in following along with the logic of authentic leadership, people will try to discover and highlight their true, or authentic, selves and the result will be that some people's true selves will align with and lead to effective leadership, while other people's true selves will highlight behaviors and ways of being that do *not* lead to effective leadership (Pfeffer, 2015). To take this argument a step further, those whose natural or authentic behaviors and selves happen to align with the necessary characteristics of a leader in a particular moment or context will then be much more likely to emerge as leaders and will inherently acquire power and influence. On the other hand, those whose natural or authentic selves do not lend themselves to "preferred" leadership traits could become subject to the power and influence of those who are perceived as "natural" leaders.

Two clear examples of the problem with this logic that underlies authentic leadership easily present themselves. First, traditional leadership behaviors have a long history of being intertwined with behaviors stereotypically associated with masculinity (Kolb, 1997). This connection between leadership behaviors and masculinity has changed and evolved over time, but it has not entirely gone away. In fact, some may argue they are on the rise again. So, it is much more likely that a male will potentially benefit from the connection between "authenticity" and leadership, and a female is much more likely to experience this problematically. Wilson (2016) elaborates on this further and explains that female leaders commonly exhibit behaviors that align with stereotypical expectations of female behavior, and this often conflicts with traditional ideas of what are effective or normative leadership behaviors, and this conflict can be problematic for a female leader's self-esteem. Pfeffer (2015) extended this idea when he indicated that females *would* need to become inauthentic to be successful as leaders if they otherwise exhibited stereotypical behaviors "such as eschewing competition, not negotiating as hard as men, not asking for promotions, and not trying to stand out" (pp. 96–97). In a second example, leadership always involves extensive communication with others. There is no way around this, and it aligns nicely with the behavioral characteristics of extroverts. Although there is no guarantee that an extrovert will actually be a good leader, we commonly think that extroverts are good candidates for leadership roles. An extrovert, therefore, would likely find some agreement with authentic leadership's core idea that embracing the true self will lead to better leadership. On the other hand, the communication with others that is required of nearly all leadership roles conflicts heavily with the characteristics of an introvert. Introverts would likely find that embracing their true selves would yield very little value in terms of effective leadership. Introverts are perfectly capable of being good leaders, but they typically must learn to exhibit behaviors that are contrary to what they consider to be their true selves (Spark & O'Connor, 2021). What this says about authentic leadership is that valuing the true self empowers some people and potentially disempowers or oppresses others. Those who must learn to act contrary to their true selves in order to be an effective leader risk being labeled inauthentic, or "fake," even though it may be the only way they can perform the behaviors perceived as necessary to be a leader.

Communicative critique

Thus far, an overview of authentic leadership has been provided and authentic leadership has been critiqued from both an ethical angle and a critical angle. In this section, the critique is completed by looking at how authentic leadership is flawed from a communicative perspective.

Leadership, from a communicative perspective, is strongly about performance and adaptation. Leadership is also a set of learned but constantly changing behaviors. The best (or most effective) leaders exhibit behaviors that are, for many, an unnatural set of communicative acts. If a leader embraces and exhibits their true self, or their natural state, they will unfortunately oftentimes exhibit behaviors that are ineffective in terms of leadership, or perhaps even counter-effective. As Pfeffer (2015) states quite clearly, "Leaders must be able to put on a show, to display energy and pay attention to others, regardless of how they may feel at that time" (p. 86). Pfeffer goes on to elaborate that leaders need to "act" like a leader and that this ability to act like a leader is essential to effective leadership. What this act entails can vary widely, but it is unlikely to conveniently and completely align with whatever someone considers to be their "true self." At the very least, leaders must regularly perform in such a manner that exudes and inspires confidence and that garners the support of followers. There are, of course, many situations where being authentic would be a better leadership strategy than being inauthentic. However, it is also quite evident that being *inauthentic* is a very regular part of being an effective leader, and in many instances, inauthenticity is absolutely essential to being an effective leader. As contradictory as that may seem, being inauthentic is not inherently bad, or inherently problematic, nor does it imply a deficiency in a leader's character.

The study of leadership and leadership development in the modern era has certainly evolved and changed, as has the perceived role of communication in leadership. Early studies of leadership attempted to identify consistent traits and characteristics of leaders but ultimately concluded that there were no such universal traits. The focus then moved to the leader's behaviors and styles without much regard for the role of followers. More currently, leadership studies have begun to focus more on the interplay of leaders and followers, the communication that happens between them, and the social construction of leadership (Gigliotti & Shankman, 2021). The social construction perspective of leadership sees leadership as the outcome of the interactions between social actors and moves away from more leader-centric approaches (Fairhurst & Grant, 2010).

Interestingly, as leadership studies move more toward an understanding of leadership as socially constructed, authenticity is nearly simultaneously gaining momentum as a concept that is essentially *not* socially constructed. Schwarz and Williams (2021) describe two paradigms that underlie these competing ideas: critical realism and social constructionism. Critical realism views identity and authenticity as things that are actual, stable, and consistent. Social constructionism, on the other hand, views identification and authentication as social processes and concepts that are constantly emerging and inextricably connected to endlessly changing cultures and contexts. There is no essential, fixed self (Calder-Dawe & Gavey, 2017) and communication is a central force in creating and shaping our evolving and changing identities and performances as leaders.

McCauley and Palus (2021) take this further and state that, from a constructionist perspective, "leadership is located in the relational processes and mutually constructed through communication, negotiation, and sense-making" (p. 2). Leadership, from this perspective, is viewed as a relational construct. The practices of leadership, from this perspective, are recognized to occur within the context of organizational members interacting (Fletcher, 2012). As the concept of leadership has developed, communication has become more and more of a central feature.

Leadership is also adaptive. Effective long-term leadership involves utilizing behaviors that are appropriate and effective in a given context or situation. But contexts and situations are constantly in a state of flux and the behaviors that will result in effective leadership in each new context or situation will also change. Leaders who desire to remain effective over time and across contexts must learn to identify these changes, identify which behaviors or actions will work best in the new context or situation, and then be able to act out those behaviors or actions (Youngquist, 2019). The small percentage of leaders whose "authenticity" happens to align with followers' expectations for leader-like behaviors will be successful, at least in the short term. The larger percentage of leaders whose "authenticity" does not happen to align with follower expectations of leader-like behaviors are either out of luck, or they will have to adapt and perform in such a manner that their behaviors do align with follower expectations of leader behaviors. And, of course, even for those leaders whose "authenticity" does align with the follower expectations for leaders, this alignment will falter over time as situations and contexts evolve. As Pfeffer (2015) states, "People need to grow, develop, and change, not get stuck in their temporarily authentic selves" (p. 95).

Leadership, in general, is communicative, performative, and adaptative, and leadership is also learned. The communicative behaviors that equate to effective leadership are natural to few (if any), but these behaviors can be learned, to varying degrees, by all. Leaders learn how to lead/communicate through trial and error, through reasoning and testing, through emulating others, through mentoring, through training and classes, and through numerous other means. Some learn early in their lives, and some learn later. We need to learn because we do not inherently know, and dogmatically embracing our "true selves" will reveal little that is valuable regarding leadership. Ongoing education, on the other hand, is crucial to the development of effective leaders.

Authentic leadership, unfortunately, moves against the idea that leadership is performative, adaptive, and learned. Authentic leadership asks leaders to identify, embrace, and show their "authentic" selves. The assumption is that this true self is stable and consistent and that embracing and exhibiting this essence will result in good leaders even as contexts and situations change around them. But, as was indicated previously, there is scholarship that argues convincingly that there is no "true" self that is consistent over time and that exists independent of context, culture, and social factors (Calder-Dawe & Gavey, 2017; Schwarz & Williams, 2021).

Johnson and Hackman (2018) describe authentic leadership as including self-awareness, balanced processing, internalized moral perspective, and relational transparency. When they discuss relational transparency, they describe it as "the presentation of the authentic self to others, openly expressing honest thoughts and feelings appropriate to the situation" (p. 135). This is a problematic component of authentic leadership. Many people will view "being authentic" as expressing what they think and feel without hesitation and without a "filter," so to speak. To adjust or shape one's communication based on the goals one is trying to achieve, or the relationship one is trying to shape, or the audience one is trying to reach, or the situation or context that one is trying to work with would seem to be insincere, or inauthentic. In fact, the Authentic Leadership Scale includes an item which states "Says exactly what he or she means" (Walumbwa et al., 2008). How is it possible to interpret this any other way than to "wear your heart on your sleeve" and say exactly what you are thinking without much concern for anything else? We all know people who express themselves like this, and these same people sometimes feel strongly that this is the right and best way to communicate; but it is also easy to see how problematic communicating like this can be for everyone, whether one is a "leader" or a "follower."

Bill George (2010) himself said that "Any prospective leader who buys into the necessity of attempting to emulate all of the characteristics of a leader is doomed" (p. 575). The advice he provides to prospective leaders is "simply to be themselves" (p. 575). George indicated that the one essential quality that a leader must exhibit is "to be your own person" (p. 575) and that "if we conform to a style that is not consistent with who we are, we will never become authentic leaders" (p. 575). There is much room for criticism in these simple and seemingly valuable bits of advice. First of all, how is it valuable to disregard the experiences, thoughts, and actions of successful leaders (including, presumably, George himself)? To advise prospective leaders to ignore the characteristics and behaviors of those historical leaders that have succeeded, and those that have failed, flies in the face of education itself. The advice to leaders to "be themselves" or "to be your own person" is equally flawed. What if "being yourself" doesn't work, or what if "being" something other than yourself will be more effective or more successful? What should a leader do who realizes that performing a persona that is different from their "authentic" self would be more effective? Should this leader continue to stubbornly be "authentic," or would it be better to embrace and perform a different persona in the hopes of achieving the desired goal? And what about leaders who are new to the role and have no idea what they are doing, or no idea what will work to be an effective leader? Just "be yourself"? Is that sufficient?

Application scenario

The following hypothetical scenario was developed to help the reader think through the problems that may arise if a leader sticks dogmatically to the principles of authentic leadership. The discussion questions that follow should aid with parsing out some of the complexities involved.

Scenario: Bjorn is a manager at an automotive plant in Detroit. He is an older white male, is a strong advocate of authentic leadership, and has been tasked with developing a leadership development seminar for some prospective managers. He intends to use the principles of authentic leadership as the framework for the seminar. Bjorn has a clear understanding of the values that drive him, and he has a great deal of confidence that these are the right values to embrace. He has strong opinions and does not hesitate to share his thoughts on anything. The seminar attendees include the following:

- Erik: A young white male with a strong drive to move up the corporate ladder. He is highly competitive and will not hesitate to do whatever is necessary to succeed. Bjorn is very fond of Erik because he reminds him of himself as a young man.
- Isabella: A young gay Hispanic female who is proud of her heritage. She is very quiet and part of the reason she chose her career as a statistician and data analyst is that it involves limited interaction with others.
- Yang: A middle-aged female who transferred to the company from China three years ago. She's a hard worker, and very smart, but she has struggled to adapt to U.S.-American culture. She has a strong tendency to defer to authority figures.

- Aaliyah: A black woman who grew up in urban Detroit to a poor family. She is a proud union member and embraces the principle of working together for the greater good. She still lives in Detroit and loves her community. The company is "just a job" to her.

Discussion questions:

- What difficulties will Bjorn encounter in trying to convince this group that embracing authentic leadership will help them to become strong leaders in this organization?
- Will being "authentic" work equally well for all four members of this group in developing them as leaders?
- To be a successful leader, will any of these group members have to do things that might be considered inauthentic to them?

Conclusion

Authentic leadership is a popular but problematic approach to leadership. The critique of authentic leadership included in this chapter approaches authentic leadership from an ethical perspective, from a critical perspective, and from a communicative perspective. Based on this critique of authentic leadership, we can identify some aspects of leadership in general that should be the focus of leadership practitioners and scholars alike. First, leadership should be about the "other." This "other" includes a leader's specific followers and also includes the people who are not the leader's followers, including other groups and humanity in general. Leadership is performative and constitutive and, therefore, inseparable from communication. Leadership, if anything, is a subset of the broader general concept of communication. The behaviors that are necessary for effective leadership are not inherent in any one person, and they must be learned. Because these behaviors must be learned, there is great value in providing education related to leadership. Last, leadership is adaptive. There is no single best way to approach leadership. Long-term leadership (sustainable leadership) demands that leaders adapt and change over time and from context to context. Conversely, a leader that enthusiastically and exclusively embraces only a single approach to leadership restricts their ability to adapt to the changing and dynamic world in which they, as leaders, are heavily involved.

Other scholars (Alvesson & Einola, 2022; Einola & Alvesson, 2021) have argued that leadership and authenticity should be treated as separate concepts because authenticity looks inward and leadership should look outward. As it is, authentic leadership looks mostly at who a leader is, and much less so at what a leader does. They note that authentic leadership is a very simple idea that is promoted as a "catch all" solution to many complicated problems, and the academic work connected to authentic leadership is suspicious in that it is overwhelmingly positive and largely devoid of any thoughtful critique. Alvesson and Einola suggest that academics should be more skeptical regarding authentic leadership and suggest that future research should explore what happens when managers who are attempting to be authentic tackle various dilemmas at work.

Alvesson and Einola (2022; Einola & Alvesson, 2021), however, do not entirely reject the importance of authenticity and integrity as related to leadership but stress that they need to be explored more thoroughly and more objectively. I, also, would suggest parsing authentic leadership in a search for both the useful and the problematic aspects of this theory. It seems important, to me, for a leader to engage in intense self-reflection, to understand their own values, and to look at how their behaviors do or do not align with their own values. However, that in itself will not make a good or effective leader. Leadership is much more complicated than that.

Suggested further readings

Alvesson, M., & Einola, K. (2019). Warning for excessive positivity: Authentic leadership and other traps of leadership studies. *The Leadership Quarterly*, *30*(4), 383–395. https://doi.org/10.1016/j.leaqua.2019.04.001

Ford, J., & Harding, N. (2011). The impossibility of the 'true self' of authentic leadership. *Leadership*, *7*(4), 463–479. https://doi-org.proxy.lib.siu.edu/10.1177/1742715011416894

Gardner, W. L., Karam, E. P., Alvesson, M., & Einola, K. (2021). Authentic leadership theory: The case for and against. *The Leadership Quarterly*, *32*(6), 1–25. https://doi.org/10.1016/j.leaqua.2021.101495

Nyberg, D., & Sveningsson, S. (2014). Paradoxes of authentic leadership: Leader identity struggles. *Leadership*, *10*(4), 437–455. https://doi-org.proxy.lib.siu.edu/10.1177/1742715013504425

Questions for further engagement

1 Authentic leadership prioritizes authenticity and understanding one's "true self," yet authentic leadership also identifies numerous specific values that authentic leaders should embrace. Does your "true self" align with these values? Is it a problem, in terms of your leadership, if they don't?

2 As a leader, have you ever had to engage in behaviors that did not align with what you consider to be your "true self"? Clearly, there are times when this can be a problem. However, are there also times where the better approach would be to act counter to what you consider to be your "true self"?

3 Do people who have a deep understanding of their own values and exhibit confidence in these personal values make better leaders? Or do people who understand that values change and evolve and exhibit uncertainty in their own values make better leaders? Or is it not that simple and are other variables also important in determining what makes a better leader?

References

Alvesson, M., & Einola, K. (2022). The gaslighting of authentic leadership 2.0. *Leadership, 18*(6), 814–831. https://doi.org/10.1177/17427150221125271

Anderson, K. E. (2007). A conversation about communication ethics with Kenneth E. Anderson. In P. Arneson (Ed.), *Exploring communication ethics: Interviews with influential scholars in the field* (pp. 131–142). Peter Lang. https://doi.org/10.1007/s11616-007-0220-x

Arneson, P. (2007). Introduction. In P. Arneson (Ed.), *Exploring communication ethics: Interviews with influential scholars in the field* (pp. xi–xxiii). Peter Lang. https://doi.org/10.1007/s11616-007-0220-x

Calder-Dawe, O., & Gavey, N. (2017). Authentic feminist? Authenticity and feminist identity in teenage feminists' talk. *British Journal of Social Psychology, 56*, 782–798. https://doi-org.proxy.lib.siu.edu/10.1111/bjso.12207

Clapp-Smith, R., Vogelgesang, G. R., & Avey, J. B. (2009). Authentic leadership and positive psychological capital: The mediating role of trust at the group level of analysis. *Journal of Leadership and Organizational Studies, 15*(3), 227–240. https://doi-org.proxy.lib.siu.edu/10.1177/1548051808326596

Deetz, S. (2001). Conceptual foundations. In F. M. Jablin & L. L. Putnam (Eds.), *The new handbook of organizational communication: Advances in theory, research, and methods* (pp. 3–46). Sage. https://doi.org/10.4135/9781412986243

Dugan, J. P. (2017). *Leadership theory: Cultivating critical perspectives*. Jossey-Bass.

Einola, K., & Alvesson, M. (2021). The perils of authentic leadership. *Leadership, 17*(4), 483–490. https://doi-org.proxy.lib.siu.edu/10.1177/17427150211004059

Fairhurst, G. T., & Grant, D. (2010). The social construction of leadership: A sailing guide. *Management Communication Quarterly, 24*(2), 171–210. https://doi-org.proxy.lib.siu.edu/10.1177/0893318909359697

Fletcher, J. K. (2012). The relational practice of leadership. In M. Uhl-Bien & S. M. Ospina (Eds.), *Advancing relational leadership research: A dialogue among perspectives* (pp. 83–106). Information Age Publishing.

George, B. (2003). *Authentic leadership: Rediscovering the secrets of creating lasting value*. Jossey-Bass.

George, B. (2010). Authentic leadership. In J. T. McMahon (Ed.), *Leadership classics* (pp. 574–583). Waveland Press. https://doi.org/10.1108/01437731011079682

Giallonardo, L. M., Wong, C. A., & Iwasiw, C. L. (2010). Authentic leadership of preceptors: Predictor of new graduate nurses' work engagement and job satisfaction. *Journal of Nursing Management, 18*, 993–1003. https://doi-org.proxy.lib.siu.edu/10.1111/j.1365-2834.2010.01126.x

Gigliotti, R. A., & Shankman, M. L. (2021). Assessing leadership: Historical roots and contemporary considerations. *New Directions for Student Leadership, 170*, 13–21. https://doi-org.proxy.lib.siu.edu/10.1002/yd.20438

Johnson, C. E., & Hackman, M. Z. (2018). *Leadership: A communication perspective* (7th ed.). Waveland Press.
Kolb, J. A. (1997). Are we still stereotyping leadership? A look at gender and other predictors of leader emergence. *Small Group Research*, *28*(3), 370–393. https://doi-org.proxy.lib.siu.edu/10.1177/1046496497283003
Luthans, F., & Avolio, B. (2003). Authentic leadership development. In K. S. Cameron, J. E. Dutton, & R. E. Quinn (Eds.), *Positive organizational scholarship: Foundations of a new discipline* (pp. 241–258). Berrett-Koehler Publishers.
McCauley, C. D., & Palus, C. J. (2021). Developing the theory and practice of leadership development: A relational view. *The Leadership Quarterly*, *32*(5), 1–15. https://doi.org/10.1016/j.leaqua.2020.101456
McManus, R. M., Ward, S. J., & Perry, A. K. (2018). *Ethical leadership: A primer*. Edward Elgar Publishing.
Middlebrooks, A., Allen, S. J., McNutt, M. S., & Morrison, J. L. (2020). *Discovering leadership: Designing your success*. Sage. https://doi.org/10.1002/jls.21670
Newman, A. (2019). *Building leadership character*. Sage. https://doi.org/10.4135/9781544343129
Pfeffer, J. (2015). *Leadership BS: Fixing workplaces and careers one truth at a time*. Harper-Business.
Schwarz, K. C., & Williams, J. P. (2021). Introduction to the social construction of identity and authenticity. In J. P. Williams & K. C. Schwarz (Eds.), *Studies on the social construction of identity and authenticity* (pp. 1–24). Taylor & Francis.
Spark, A., & O'Connor, P. J. (2021). State extraversion and emergent leadership: Do introverts emerge as leaders when they act like extraverts? *The Leadership Quarterly*, *32*(3), 1–13. https://doi.org/10.1016/j.leaqua.2020.101474
Steffens, N. K., Mols, F., Haslam, A., & Okimoto, T. G. (2016). True to what *We* stand for: Championing collective interests as a path to authentic leadership. *The Leadership Quarterly*, *27*, 726–744. https://doi.org/10.1016/j.leaqua.2016.04.004
Walumbwa, F. O., Avolio, B. J., Gardner, W. L., Wernsing, T. S., & Peterson, S. J. (2008). Authentic leadership: Development and validation of a theory-based measure. *Journal of Management*, *34*, 89–126. https://doi-org.proxy.lib.siu.edu/10.1177/0149206307308913
Wilson, S. (2016). *Thinking differently about leadership: A critical history of leadership studies*. Edward Elgar Publishing. https://doi.org/10.4337/9781784716790
Youngquist, J. (2019). Adaptability: A universal constant of effective academic leadership. *The Department Chair*, *30*(2), 9–10. https://doi-org.proxy.lib.siu.edu/10.1002/dch.30282

4

EMBRACING DIFFERENCE IN LEADERSHIP AND ORGANIZATIONAL LIFE

A Critical Intercultural Communication Perspective

Ahmet Aksoy, Amy N. Heuman, Soham Sen, and Jayita Chakraborty

"What difference means to us"

The first line of the article read, "Texas public universities, diversity, equity, and inclusion (DEI) offices likely to have six months left before they're banished" (McGee, 2023, para. 1). We placed our simmering cups of hot tea on our coffee tables, taking time to re-read the sentence published in *The Texas Tribune*. A sense of anxiety swept over us, as our minds drifted toward countless questions and a multitude of possibilities that could impact our futures in the "land of opportunity." Pacifying ourselves with small sips of tea, we continued reading, "Critics accuse DEI programs of pushing what they characterize as a left-wing ideology onto students and faculty and say that these programs prioritize social justice over merit and achievement" (McGee, 2023, para. 18). We found ourselves chuckling under our breaths, as we read this. Closing the tab and keeping our phones aside, we continued to sip on our tea while trying to understand the implications of such a law for people like us, critically minded people of various co-cultures with two of us also being international sojourners. Our minds slowly shifted toward the recent conversation we had between us as three emerging and one seasoned academician in a predominantly white institution (PWI) of higher education (i.e., within an organizational structure clearly marked by a dominant culture). At that time, we contemplated what our universities would look and feel like without institutional support for diversity, equity, inclusion, and accessibility (DEIA) efforts; what might our communicative strategies and performances look and feel like in the face of eroding and/or absent DEIA support and presence given the long history of DEIA in

DOI: 10.4324/9781003563662-6

organizational life throughout our lifetimes? Now, in this moment, those contemplations seemed to be even more imminently real.

To us, DEIA efforts hold our organizations and leadership accountable toward creating environments in which people of all cultural groups can feel welcomed, valued, and able to participate and contribute fully to the organization's mission. Based upon our experiences, we know that environments lacking in DEIA presence impact and constrain cultural group members' abilities to fully contribute and feel a sense of belonging within their organizations.

With the removal of DEIA programs and efforts in Texas institutions of higher education alongside our very real experiences navigating dominant structures in organizational workplaces—both academic and otherwise—we embrace the need for critical perspectives in leadership communication studies. Our contributions encourage a consideration of co-cultural and dominant group lenses as a means of better managing the dialectical tensions at play within institutional workplaces. While Co-Cultural Theory (CCT) examines the interactions co-cultural group members have with their dominant group counterparts, Dominant Group Theory (DGT) looks at these interactions through dominant group members' perspectives (Orbe, 1998; Razzante & Orbe, 2018). We utilize our own experiences within an educational workplace as a case in point before detailing CCT and DGT and their possibilities within leadership communication and organizational studies more fully.

Depending upon the cultural context, we are members of both co-cultural and dominant groups, and these shifting positionalities also inform the argument we make here. Three of us identify as emerging scholars or entry-level members of higher education organizational structures, with one of us being an untenured faculty member and a man of the Turkish American U.S. co-culture, while the other two of us identify as international sojourners, a man and a woman, from India working on our doctorate degrees. The fourth one of us identifies as a mentor/supervisor in mid-level academic leadership and as a seasoned member of the discipline's organizational structures. She is simultaneously a co-cultural member (i.e., working class, woman, outsider to the geographic region, a critical academician in a conservative, neoliberal institution) and a dominant group member (i.e., white, educated, cisgender). With our varying cultural positionalities, we have found ourselves utilizing a range of co-cultural and dominant group strategies to embrace DEIA within our workplaces. Moreover, we find that applying such critical lenses to leadership practices better assists us in navigating and managing today's complexities within organizational structures, particularly during this time of moral panic about DEIA (Hall et al., 1978).

Our institutional experiences as a case in point

We opted not to provide a traditional case study to illustrate the theories we are working with. Instead, we illustrate them through sharing our experience of coming together in an academic space and at a tier one research-intensive institution situated within one of the most conservative pockets of the state (and the U.S.). As such, it would be fair to assert that the cultural context within the institution is conservative and neoliberal and oftentimes colorblind ideologies are embedded within its institutional practices. Because the institution and city are tucked away in a region that is not close to other metro cities, the local government, institution, and daily practices tend to be somewhat isolated from larger social changes as compared to other cities of its size within the state and surrounding states. During the time-period that we worked together within this institution, we experienced shifts in departmental and upper administrative leadership, an external program review at the college level, external searches for members of leadership, and tenure-track and continuing appointment hires within our department and college. We found ourselves working to navigate the dominant structure overwhelmingly comprising white men at different levels of administration and within a college and department that was not reflective of the U.S. sociocultural landscape nor that of the region. For example, the institution where we worked together continues to comprise predominantly white (European descent) students even though it identifies as a Hispanic-serving institution (HSI). It enrolls just below 27% Hispanic students and 5.7% Black students yet it is situated in a majority-minority Hispanic/Latinx state and within a region that comprises an approximate 50/50 split between white and co-cultural populations with over 36.5% of its population identifying as Hispanic, 8% as Black/African American, 2.5% as Asian American, 2% as multiracial, and 1.5% as Indigenous/Native American (U.S. Census Bureau, 2025).

At times it was difficult to successfully negotiate the dominant structure and ascertain whether state institutional commitments to DEIA were simply paying lip service or more fully intending to embrace and support DEIA in meaningful ways. We often worked to protect ourselves first and foremost, with one of us—Amy—as mentor/supervisor working to make us visible without doing harm and/or putting us in harm's way. Amy often worked behind the scenes in subtle ways to promote us, open up spaces for us, and offer opportunities for us to thrive at a time when there were and are concerted attacks against us and/or people who look, act, and feel like us. As a seasoned member of the discipline and institution and a member of lower-level leadership, she also utilized her dominant group and leadership position to affirm us in conversations with her colleagues, our peers, and members of institutional leadership. She also communicated with us *and* about us in ways that served as a model for them as well. Simultaneously, Amy identifies as a co-cultural ally and some (operating with dominant ideologies) would probably say that she "pushed her agenda" to make us visible and, very importantly, to make the hierarchies visible to dominant group members. However, this was a delicate balance. To aggressively or even accommodatively (Orbe, 1998; Razzante & Orbe, 2018) call out and/or call attention to oppressive ideologies was a recipe for attacks upon us and upon her. It often led her to engage in a great amount of finessing and sacrifice of social status that also came with a substantial personal cost. Yet, she showed up for those like and different from herself, as well as for herself, daily. We, in turn, did the same for each other and for her as a means of promoting diversity of thought and experiences more reflective of the sociocultural landscape and where institutional members and applicants would be considered in equitable and inclusive ways. We—Ahmet, Soham, and Jayita—reciprocated our mentor/supervisor's attempts to position us for opportunities that would promote DEIA efforts reflective of our sociocultural landscape.

These efforts proved to be quite difficult as there were dominant group members who did not value experiences *with* and *of* difference and who would reinforce the status quo or dominant group perspectives and practices in subtle (i.e., nonassertive) and sometimes overt (i.e., aggressive) ways. Others would engage in communication that served as impediments to co-cultural group members and privileged dominant group members' status. However, our communicative strategies resulted in some success—with two of us being named assistant course directors, another one of us being invited to teach within the communication studies program and also receiving a National Endowment for the Humanities fellowship, and another one of us being named to tenure-track search committees and mid-level and upper-level leadership search committees.

But there were also times when we witnessed individuals engaged in behaviors, whether consciously or unconsciously, that did not align with DEIA practices. For example, we witnessed that leaders and/or applicants who could have truly made a structural difference were somehow discounted, ignored, or not given full consideration by certain dominant group members with social capital during position searches. Being part of a PWI structure, we have all been exposed to situations or privy to instances where marginalized group members have resorted to co-cultural strategies to find their foothold. We witnessed instances where searches for leadership and tenure-track faculty positions implicitly privileged white, cis-gender males over scholars of color or LGBTQIA+ members.

Protecting dominant territory was performed in various ways such as remaining neutrally silent, endorsing the status quo, practicing microaggressions, or dismissing co-cultural concerns (Razzante & Orbe, 2018). Dismissive attitudes on the part of particular dominant group members toward co-cultural scholars and their scholarship were at times painstakingly visible. The strategic absence and/or minimal participation of certain dominant group faculty members at research and leadership presentations was also apparent as was the shallow depth of probes and questions asked of such candidates. Moreover, the fact that these faculty members typically remained silent asking few to no questions about these scholars' work was blatantly evident.

We vividly recollect the consistent questioning and dismissal of our interests in critical work across a spectrum of specializations within the discipline from organizational to health communication to media studies and a particular disengagement with our critical intercultural communication research by numerous dominant group faculty members. We found that mid-level and upper-level college leadership and faculty would often remain neutrally silent or dismiss our concerns on the subject. They opted to also endorse the status quo of course offerings and this obstructed our abilities to fully engage with critical perspectives. We also found a pervading sentiment of white privilege amongst the graduate student community. These structures of power worked strategically to mute and muffle voices of color, most of whom had arrived in a distant land and were already overwhelmed with navigating a foreign space. Being up against this situation led us to co-culturally network with our mentor. She, in turn, opened up spaces for further co-cultural networking and allyship (Aksoy & Heuman, 2024; Razzante & Orbe, 2018) within the institution and also outside of it in the larger discipline so that we could be more wholly supported (Heuman & Labador, 2020; Heuman & Mitchell, 2022). Overall, we each recognized that the conservative, neoliberal tenor of the institution (i.e., context) somewhat narrowed our abilities (i.e., abilities and field of experience) regarding which co-cultural and/or dominant group strategies we could employ to effectively work against the dominant culture and the institutional structure.

Our experiences clearly highlight the importance of and need for co-cultural and dominant group approaches to the examinations and study of leadership from a dialectical and critical communication perspective. We now turn to a discussion of the history of DEIA and culture within leadership studies, a review of CCT and DGT, and then to how these combined lenses can assist us in thinking dialectically and more complexly about DEIA in leadership communication.

Historicizing DEIA

The concept of DEI (Loyd et al., 2013; Ramos et al., 2016), and more recently an added emphasis on accessibility, or DEIA, has been popular organizational topics for more than two decades. In fact, initial diversity training efforts in the United States started in the 1960s due to legislation and compliance. Title VII of the Civil Rights Act (1964) made it illegal for employers exceeding 15 employees to discriminate in hiring, termination, promotion, compensation, job training, or any other term, condition, or privilege of employment based on race, color, religion, sex, or national origin. This was followed by the development of the Equal Employment Opportunity Commission (EEOC). Such macro-level legal and policy changes made organizations realize the impact of demographic workforce changes on microelements like organizational functioning and competitiveness (Kuczynski, 1999). Studies in the 2000s have found two major categories of diversity ideologies prevalent in organizations: identity-blind and identity-conscious ideologies (Plaut et al., 2018). Identity-blind ideologies downplay demographic differences and promote the melting pot metaphor (Gleason, 1964), while identity-conscious ideologies emphasize differences and promote the salad bowl metaphor (Berray, 2019).

More recently, U.S. and global sociopolitical unrest in the time-period leading up to COVID-19 acted as a further catalyst for DEIA (Peiker, 2022) and DEIA efforts were no longer limited to the onboarding process of organizations (Bauer & Erdogan, 2011). Rather, initiatives evolved to focus on the post-onboarding stages like keeping track of how much inclusion or exclusion the employees were experiencing. Managing diversity became a more central concern of organizations and DEIA began referring to a systematic and planned commitment on the part of organizations to recruit and retain employees with diverse backgrounds and abilities (Peiker, 2022). Kumar and Malhotra (2022) posit that the same constituents (culture, gender, nationality, sexual orientation, physical abilities, social class, age, socioeconomic status, and religion) that are at the core of a diverse workforce are the underlying elements that constitute co-cultures within Orbe's (1998) CCT. Additionally, we argue that Razzante and Orbe's (2018) DGT provides further connections to DEIA for leaders and workplaces in that group members can either use communication to further assert or maintain dominance or to strive for equity, inclusion, and accessibility.

Now more than ever, DEIA initiatives continue to be of importance particularly in the face of scrutiny within our current sociopolitical landscape (Guynn & Fraser, 2023; Peiker, 2022). However, while organizational leaders are expected to foster diverse environments, leadership diversity itself remains limited. Currently, women are outnumbered 5–1 by their male counterparts, and people of color hold a small amount of leadership positions in corporate America (Guynn & Fraser, 2023). As a result, co-cultural group members must navigate organizational spaces dominated by mainly white males. At the same time, they rely on the agency and power these white male leaders have within their workspaces. From a leadership perspective, Javidan et al. (2010) note that leaders must be able to influence individuals inside and outside their organization and support employees from diverse cultural backgrounds to help achieve their organization's goals. Thus, a critical question for leadership and communication scholars becomes: *what is the communicative nature and power dynamics of leadership in intercultural organizational environments?*

With this, we turn to previous studies that have examined diversity and inclusion practices specifically in academic institutional settings, since these spaces align with our current workplace contexts and because some focus has been specifically given to these spaces in critical communication leadership studies. Using a CCT lens, Ruiz-Mesa (2022) investigated how chief diversity officers (CDOs) in higher education frame their work on campus and employ communicative practices in both formal and informal settings as a means of designing institutional policies and building campus support for their efforts. Similarly, Simmons et al. (2013) provide insight into the intercultural context of higher education in the U.S. from a relational dialectics point of view. Their research asserts that university leaders would benefit from acknowledging present dialectical tensions, especially the dialectics of Blackness-Whiteness and Integration-Segregation, and should strive to create programs that give voice to all cultural perspectives.

A dialectical perspective refers to a method of looking at a situation by concurrently considering conflicting or differing viewpoints (Martin & Nakayama, 1999). Through multiple viewpoints, Martin and Nakayama (1999) believed we might better understand the relationship between culture and communication. The use of CCT and DGT takes on a dialectical perspective through the examinations of both co-cultural group and dominant group members' communication and interactions with each other.

Culture in leadership studies

Prior to the above-outlined research, numerous studies have attempted to account for the dynamics of culture in leadership studies through, for example the application of Hofstede's (1984) cultural dimensions and the GLOBE (Global Leadership and Organizational Behavior Effectiveness) framework (House et al., 2002). Two distinct levels of analysis are present in the literature on the relationship between culture and leadership: (1) the relationship between organizational culture and leadership, and (2) the relationship between national culture and leadership (Javidan et al., 2010). The relationship between organizational culture and leadership suggests that leaders play a large role in shaping the culture of an organization, while the relationship between national culture and relationships refers to the leadership attitudes and behaviors shaped by an individual's experiences across cultures (Hofstede, 1984; Javidan et al., 2010).

Scholars have leaned toward the GLOBE dimensions to develop a theoretical framework that bridges relationships between leaders and organizational and societal cultural influence (Hofstede, 1984). The GLOBE framework pulls from Hofstede's cultural dimensions and extends this by identifying nine primary dimensions of outstanding leadership and six global leadership dimensions (Javidan et al., 2010). Through GLOBE, House et al. (2002) illustrated that cultural values and leadership attributes impact the ability an individual has toward influencing, motivating, and enabling others' contributions within an organization. GLOBE operationalized attributes and values (such as being charismatic, team-orientated, self-protective, participative, humane, and autonomous) as tools for eliciting and understanding the cultural behaviors of leaders in and across societies (House et al., 2002).

While the GLOBE cultural dimensions provide rich insight, they fail to address issues such as power, control, asymmetries, and inequalities between leaders and the diverse members within their cultural organizations. Moreover, what is missing is a more in-depth analysis of communicative interactions and interplays that connect communication, culture, and power. In other words, frameworks such as GLOBE promote a more psychological and positivist-rooted paradigm that paints broad brushstrokes through an internationally (i.e., country-level analysis) centered cultural lens without fully accounting for the diverse cultural groups that make up various multiracial societies. Collinson (2011) encouraged a Critical Leadership Studies (CLS) approach which takes a social constructionist perspective and focuses on the multiple discursive meanings that can occur in leadership dynamics. He also advocates for a dialectical perspective and suggests that such approaches assist with analyzing the nuanced power relations between leaders and followers because they facilitate "new ways of thinking about their complex, ambiguous and potentially contradictory interrelations" (p. 190). Given the constitutive nature of communication in shaping, maintaining, and perpetuating identities and social relations (Butler, 1990; Warren, 2003), we draw from critical intercultural frameworks that invite a constitutive and dialectical approach to better understand communication between leaders and constituents.

Leadership and Co-Cultural Theory

Within this section, we propose the integrated lenses of CCT (Orbe, 1998) and DGT (Razzante & Orbe, 2018) to support understandings of CLS scholarship which emphasizes the need for dialectical perspectives between leaders and followers. CCT examines the communicative strategies employed by co-cultures when interacting with dominant group members (Orbe, 1998). Orbe (1998) defines dominant group members as those who hold more power, privileges, and social status than other group members within a given society, while co-cultural individuals are people who are members of marginalized groups. It provides a framework for understanding the diverse communicative practices enacted by co-cultures. Within CLS, and as mentioned earlier, Collinson (2011) noted that dialectical perspectives can enhance the understanding of complex power relations between leaders and followers. For example, Collinson noted that dialectical perspectives invite us to examine how gendered and racialized bodies are shaped amongst leaders and their followers. Another example is how class inequalities and ethnicity can be influenced by organizational power and conflict (Collinson, 2011). CCT allows us to take a dialectical perspective, and it provides us with a lens for adequately examining the complexities of the process through which members of co-cultural groups negotiate, reinforce, and resist intercultural tensions with their leaders (and dominant group members) by utilizing various communication approaches and strategies, and by being aware of possible communication outcomes.

There are more than 30 communicative strategies within CCT (see Table 4.2). Over time, scholars have identified and compiled a composite of communicative strategies identified from the standpoint(s) of co-cultural members. These communicative strategies arise from influential factors experienced by co-cultures (Orbe, 1998). Based on these factors, members of co-cultures will utilize a communicative strategy toward orientations that can be assertive, aggressive, or nonassertive, and they encourage actions like assimilating with the dominant group, making accommodations with them, or breaking away from them (Orbe, 1998; Orbe & Roberts, 2012) (see Table 4.1). According to Orbe and Roberts (2012), nonassertive orientations involve subtle behaviors, whereas aggressive and assertive orientations pertain to vigorous and sometimes contentious communication practices.

Unlike the GLOBE framework which focuses on leadership perspectives, CCT can provide us with the discursive meanings that can occur in leadership communicative dynamics from a follower's and marginalized group member's perspective. At the same time, it can also provide insights into the dialectical perspectives of marginalized individuals in leadership roles. A study by Okesson (2023) found that CDOs at primarily white

TABLE 4.1 Co-cultural communication typologies

Nonassertive assimilation	*Assertive assimilation*	*Aggressive assimilation*
Averting controversy Emphasizing commonalities Developing positive face Censoring self Interrogating self* Checking yourself*** Remaining silent*** Journaling***	Extensive preparation Overcompensating Manipulating stereotypes Bargaining Rationalization**** Blending*****	Dissociating Mirroring Strategic distancing Ridiculing self Showing appreciation***
Nonassertive accommodation	*Assertive accommodation*	*Aggressive accommodation*
Increasing visibility Dispelling stereotypes	Communicating self Intragroup networking Utilizing liaisons Educating other Report incident to authorities**	Confronting Gaining advantage Speaking out***
Nonassertive separation	*Assertive separation*	*Aggressive separation*
Avoiding Maintaining barriers Leaving the situation*** Isolation***	Exemplifying strengths Co-cultural networking*****	Attacking Sabotaging others Intimidation***

Source: Strategies not originally conceptualized by Orbe (1998)
* Camara (2002)
** Camara and Orbe (2010)
*** Gates (2003)
**** Castle Bell et al. (2015)
***** Aksoy and Heuman (2024)

This table depicts various functions and strategies of co-cultural members, as they navigate assimilation, accommodation, and/or separation in ways that are nonassertive, assertive, and/or aggressive.

member institutions of the Council for Christian Colleges and Universities (CCCU) strategically utilize the communicative strategies in CCT when engaging with dominant group members at their institutions to achieve their diversity initiatives on their respective campus. These officers identified that emphasizing commonalities, averting controversy, extensive preparation, intragroup networking, increasing visibility, communicating self, educating others, and exemplifying strengths afforded them the ability to address diversity issues on their respective campuses (Okesson, 2023). These initial explorations of leadership through the lens of CCT open pathways for better understanding workplace power, leadership, and identity dynamics in all their dialectical complexities.

Utilizing Dominant Group Theory in leadership studies

Our introduction noted there has been little growth in diversity in leadership roles over the decades. According to Collinson (2011), the power dynamics between leaders and followers impact work environments. The dialectical viewpoints of leaders and their followers allow us to address the power, control, asymmetries, and inequalities lacking in mainstream leadership studies (Collinson, 2011). DGT, like CCT, can be useful here since it examines the dialectical tensions that emerge when majority group members in privileged positions within a society communicate with others (Razzante & Orbe, 2018). Like CCT, but from the opposite perspective, DGT examines the communicative strategies that arise from factors that can influence the communication of dominant group members with co-cultural group members such as their "communication approach, interactional outcome, field of experience, abilities, perceived costs and rewards, and situational context" (Razzante et al., 2018, p. 49). Depending on these factors, dominant group members could employ a communicative strategy with a particular orientation. Orientations are nonassertive, assertive, and aggressive and could result in three possible outcomes: (1) maintaining the status quo in terms of institutional racism, sexism, and other forms of oppression; (2) preventing the continuation of these structures through communication that challenges the prejudice and discrimination experienced by members of co-cultural groups on a daily basis; and (3) destroying the oppressive structures through the use of privilege to fight against institutional policies and practices that grant undeserved entitlements (Razzante & Orbe, 2018) (see Table 4.2).

Like CCT, DGT can be extremely valuable for examining the communicative behaviors between leaders and their followers, especially those who are members of co-cultural groups since the current culture of corporate America reflects the views and practices of the already privileged. Moreover, DGT supports the call from CLS to explore workplace power, dialectical complexities, and identity dynamics between leaders and followers (Collinson, 2011). For example, Razzante et al. (2018) have examined how dominant group members in the workplace can strategically use their positions to bring about organizational cultural changes. Their study demonstrated how dominant group members can use the communicative strategies of DGT to move toward more equitable, affirming, and bullying-free workplace environments (Razzante et al., 2018). Other research (Razzante, 2018) has also demonstrated how analyzing the intersection of CCT and DGT can help understand how marginalized administrators within

TABLE 4.2 Dominant group typologies

Nonassertive reinforcement	
Ignoring one's privilege	A lack of awareness of, or outright refusal to acknowledge, the societal privilege that comes with dominant group status.
Remaining neutrally silent	Recognition of oppression but not speaking out to avoid conflict.
Assertive reinforcement	
Redirection	Highlighting aspects of one's identity that reflect disadvantage, as a means to deemphasize one's own privilege.
Resisting group essentialism	Objections to criticisms by others that generalize majority group members into one large homogenous group.
Aggressive reinforcement	
Endorsing the status quo	Communicative messages that rationalize, support, and/or endorse existing ideologies, values, and oppressive institutions.
Dismissing co-cultural concerns	Communicative messages that regard co-cultural concerns as trivial, illegitimate, or outright false.
Victim blaming	Assigning responsibility to co-cultural groups to remove themselves from oppressed positions.
Microaggressions	Everyday exchanges that feature denigrating messages to others because of their co-cultural identities.
Nonassertive impediment	
Recognizing one's privilege	Verbal acknowledgments of one's own societal privilege that increase awareness for others.
Engaging in self-reflexivity	Ability and willingness to reflect on the consequences of individual thoughts and actions as dominant group members.
Assertive impediment	
Affirming co-cultural concerns	Acknowledging the legitimacy and magnitude of co-cultural issues and the realities of societal oppression.
Educating others	Drawing from one's own growth—cognitively, emotionally, spiritually, etc.—to facilitate growth in others.
Setting an example for others	Communicating in ways that can serve as a model for other dominant group members.

(*Continued*)

TABLE 4.2 (Continued)

Microaffirmations	Everyday exchanges that feature affirming messages to others because of their co-cultural identities *when considering* others' desire or wishes on how to be affirmed.
Aggressive impediment	
Confronting oppressive rhetoric	Explicitly naming, without regard to others, dominant group messages as ignorant, hurtful, and/or discriminatory to co-cultural group members.
Microaffirmations	Everyday exchanges that feature affirming messages to others because of their co-cultural identities *regardless of* others' desire or wishes on how to be affirmed.
Nonassertive dismantling	
Sacrificing self	Efforts to challenge institutionalized oppressions that come with significant personal cost.
Assertive dismantling	
Challenging oppressive ideologies	Questioning the legitimacy of policies that unfairly discriminate against co-cultural group members.
Identifying as co-cultural ally	Communicating in ways that challenge policies that negatively affect co-cultural group members.
Assuming responsibility for action	Assuming an action-orientated approach that utilizes one's own privilege to work against systems that foster that very privilege.
Aggressive dismantling	
Forcing	Pushing one's agenda to advocate for societal change with little to no regard for dominant group members' concerns.
Taking advantage of one's privileges	Using one's societal standing to challenge oppressive structures at the expense of co-cultural groups' agency.

Source: Razzante and Orbe (2018, pp. 363–364)

This table depicts various functions and strategies of dominant group members, as they navigate communication orientations that are nonassertive, assertive, and/or aggressive. These result in either maintaining the status quo (reinforcement), preventing structural continuation (impediment), or destroying oppressive structures (dismantling).

higher education leadership roles navigate their positions at PWIs. Both CCT and DGT can be utilized fruitfully in future critical intercultural leadership communication studies to understand the dialectical complexities that mark the communicative and DEIA practices of leaders and followers from the perspectives of dominant and co-cultural groups.

Conclusion

In conclusion, through our own positionalities and experiences, we have demonstrated how CCT and DGT can serve as particularly relevant lenses to better understand the dialectical perspectives at play within leadership at workplaces. We began our chapter referencing the banning of DEIA support within our own institutional settings where members of co-cultural groups struggled and faced moments of tension between their respective leaders and organizational structures. The American Association of University Professors (AAUP) (2023) gathered survey data from several key states impacted by such bans and their findings from Texas faculty respondents, the state where we resided, reported the following insights: (1) about 63% of respondents said they would not recommend out-of-state colleagues take positions in our state; and (2) 57% cited the state's political climate as their top reason for wanting to leave the region. Another 48% voiced concerns over their ability to engage in academic freedom. Students who support diversity initiatives say the pushback to these offices and programs will make it harder for college campuses to become more equitable and representative of the state's population (McGee, 2023). The AAUP (2023) press release notes that a failure to structurally support DEIA could "result in a significant exodus of faculty, challenges attracting academic talent, and an overall decline in the quality of higher education" (para. 10).

The implications of these recent anti-DEIA laws, especially within the institutional spaces of higher education in certain states, are dire. Policies which are emerging will make it even more difficult for leaders to effectively support and enhance DEIA within workplaces. As a result, leaders will need to be even more strategic in their communication practices to manage the dialectics between their constituents and the organization. For example, we may encounter more subtle communicative strategies employed by co-cultural group members and ally-oriented dominant group members alike to deal with policies that prohibit them from being more direct and assertive in their communication practices. Although we speak to our particular experiences with prohibitive DEIA policies, a CCT and DGT lens applies more broadly in prohibitive and in DEIA-supportive spaces. This is because such a lens can assist critical intercultural leadership communication scholars with analyzing how leaders and constituents interact dialectically and can promote future vision for more functional organizational settings. Future research may utilize the dialectical lens of CCT and DGT to examine perspectives of leaders and their constituents amongst/within numerous institutional settings not yet fully explored such as the media, health, business, science, technology, and engineering. Both

CCT and DGT address Collinson's (2011) call for dialectical perspectives between leaders and followers because these frameworks can offer examinations of difference in workspaces from multifaceted viewpoints and thus embrace the potential of DEIA going forward. Our chapter provides insight into this and a necessary direction in the future work of leadership and intercultural communication scholarship.

Suggested further readings

Barrett, D. (2014). *Leadership communication* (4th ed.). McGraw-Hill.

Gamble, T. K., & Gamble, M. W. (2012). *Leading with communication: A practical approach to leadership communication*. Sage Publications.

Herakova, L. L. (2012). Nursing masculinity: Male nurses' experiences through a co-cultural lens. *Howard Journal of Communications*, *23*(4), 332–350. https://doi.org/10.1080/10646175.2012.722822

Nohria, N., & Khurana, R. (Eds.). (2010). *Handbook of leadership theory and practice*. Harvard Business Press.

Razzante, R. J., & Al Balushi, A. W. (2023). Collaborative and inclusive leadership: Co-cultural calls for dominant group action. In B. J. Van Gilder, J. T. Austin, & J. S. Bruscella (Eds.), *Communication and organizational changemaking for diversity, equity, and inclusion: A case studies approach* (pp. 294–307). Routledge. https://doi.org/10.4324/9781003333746

Questions for further engagement

1. How might communicative practices leading toward accommodation serve members of co-cultural groups and the interactions they have with their organizational leaders? Can you think of a specific example or two?
2. How might DGT assist us in assessing the communicative practices of organizational leaders that either facilitate and support DEIA initiatives or hinder them? Can you think of any examples from personal experiences or cases you may have read about?
3. How might taking critical intercultural communication approaches help to foster equity, inclusion, and belonging amongst the interactions we have within organizational environments?
4. What communicative practices might organizational leaders implement to improve organizational life amongst their co-cultural group members? Can you think of any examples you have experienced or come across?
5. How might some of the communicative practices between dominant group members and co-cultural members be more beneficial for DEIA initiatives than others? Review both theories (DGT and CCT), associated practices, and communication orientations to elaborate.

References

Aksoy, A., & Heuman, A. N. (2024). "Being the needle in the haystack:" The addition of "blending" and "co-cultural networking" as practices to Orbe's (1998) co-cultural theory. *Journal of Intercultural Communication Research*, *53*(1–2), 63–80. https://doi.org/10.1080/17475759.2024.2399096

American Association of University Professors (AAUP). (2023, September 6). Large majority of Texas faculty express concern about higher education; more than a quarter consider leaving next year, survey finds [Press release]. https://aaup-utaustin.org/wp-content/uploads/2023/09/texas-faculty-survey-press-release-sept-2023.pdf

Bauer, T. N., & Erdogan, B. (2011). Organizational socialization: The effective onboarding of new employees. In S. Zedeck (Ed.), *APA handbook of industrial and organizational psychology, vol. 3. Maintaining, expanding, and contracting the organization* (pp. 51–64). American Psychological Association. https://doi.org/10.1037/12171-002

Berray, M. (2019). A critical literary review of the melting pot and salad bowl assimilation and integration theories. *Journal of Ethnic and Cultural Studies*, *6*(1), 142–151. https://doi.org/10.29333/ejecs/217

Butler, J. (1990). *Gender trouble: Feminism and the subversion of identity*. Routledge.

Camara, S. K. (2002). Ideological uncertainty: Exploring racism as a social issue in communication. *Journal of Intergroup Relations*, *29*, 16–38. https://scholarworks.calstate.edu/concern/publications/2n49t523h

Camara, S. K., & Orbe, M. P. (2010). Analyzing strategic responses to discriminatory acts: A co-cultural communicative investigation. *Journal of International and Intercultural Communication*, *3*(2), 83–113. https://doi.org/10.1080/17513051003611602

Castle Bell, G., Hopson, M. C., Weathers, M. R., & Ross, K. A. (2015). From "laying the foundations" to building the house: Extending Orbe's co-cultural theory to include "rationalization" as a formal strategy. *Communication Studies*, *66*(1), 1–2. https://doi.org/10.1080/10510974.2013.858053

Civil Rights Act. (1964). Civil Rights Act of 1964. *Title VII, Equal Employment Opportunities*. https://blowthetrumpet.org/documents/CivilRightsActLBJ_000.pdf

Collinson, D. (2011). Critical leadership studies. In A. Bryman (Ed.), *The Sage handbook of leadership* (pp. 181–194). Sage Publications.

Gates, D. (2003). Learning to play the game: An exploratory study of how African American women and men interact with others in organizations. *The Electronic Journal of Communication*, *12*(2–3), 1–20. https://www.researchgate.net/publication/336839370_LEARNING_TO_PLAY_THE_GAME_AN_EXPLORATORY_STUDY_OF_HOW_AFRICAN_AMERICAN_WOMEN_AND_MEN_INTERACT_WITH_OTHERS_IN_ORGANIZATIONS

Gleason, P. (1964). The melting pot: Symbol of fusion or confusion? *American Quarterly*, *16*(1), 20–46. https://www.jstor.org/stable/2710825

Guynn, J., & Fraser, J. (2023, March 16). Who has power in corporate America? Men do. New data shows women vastly outnumbered at top. *USA Today*. https://www.usatoday.com/in-depth/money/2023/03/16/men-run-corporate-america/11173762002/?gps-source=BRNMSVCPSPXXCORPORATEDIVERSITY&itm_source=usat&itm_medium=onsite-spike&itm_campaign=corporatediversity-storytellingstudio-n&itm_content=static

Hall, S., Critcher, C., Jefferson, T., & Roberts, B. (1978). *Policing the crisis: Mugging, the state, and law and order*. Macmillan.

Heuman, A. N., & Labador, M. A. (2020). Intercultural bridgework between mentor and mentee: Critical cultural feminists working in the margins. In C. R. Webber (Ed.), *Working in the margins* (pp. 97–120). Peter Lang. https://doi.org/10.3726/b14794

Heuman, A. N., & Mitchell, S. L. (2022). Co-creating home and community in inhospitable terrains through critical mentoring. In A. Atay & D. Trebing (Eds.), *Mentoring and communication: Theories and practices* (pp. 159–178). Peter Lang. https://doi.org/10.3726/b14792

Hofstede, G. (1984). Cultural dimensions in management and planning. *Asia Pacific Journal of Management*, *1*, 81–99. https://doi.org/10.1007/BF01733682

House, R., Javidan, M., Hanges, P., & Dorfman, P. (2002). Understanding cultures and implicit leadership theories across the globe: An introduction to project GLOBE. *Journal of World Business*, *37*(1), 3–10. https://doi.org/10.1016/S1090-9516(01)00069-4

Javidan, M., Dorfman, P. W., Howell, J. P., & Hanges, P. J. (2010). Leadership and cultural context. In N. Nohria & R. Khurana (Eds.), *Handbook of leadership theory and practice* (pp. 346–372). Harvard Business Press.

Kuczynski, S. (1999). If diversity, then higher profits. *HR Magazine*, *44*(13), 66–71.

Kumar, A., & Malhotra, I. (2022). Communication and diverse workplaces: A co-cultural perspective through organizational autoethnography. *Academy of Marketing Studies Journal*, *26*(5), 1–6. https://www.abacademies.org/articles/Communication-and-diverse-workplaces-a-co-cultural-1528-2678-26-5-246.pdf

Loyd, D. L., Wang, C. S., Phillips, K. W., & Lount, R. B., Jr. (2013). Social category diversity promotes premeeting elaboration: The role of relationship focus. *Organization Science*, *24*, 757–772. http://dx.doi.org/10.1287/orsc.1120.0761

Martin, J. N., & Nakayama, T. K. (1999). Thinking dialectically about culture and communication. *Communication Theory*, *9*(1), 1–25. http://dx.doi.org/10.1111/j.1468-2885.1999.tb00160.x

McGee, K. (2023, June 20). Texas lawmakers find consensus on bill banning diversity, equity and inclusion offices in public universities. *The Texas Tribune*. https://www.texastribune.org/2023/05/27/texas-university-diversity-equity-inclusion-dei-bill-conference/

Okesson, K. A. (2023). *In their own words: A co-cultural examination of the communication strategies of chief diversity officers in the CCCU* (Publication No: 979-8-3811-8640-6) [Doctoral dissertation, Regent University]. ProQuest.

Orbe, M. P. (1998). *Constructing co-cultural theory: An explication of culture, power, and communication.* Sage Publications. https://doi.org/10.4135/9781483345321

Orbe, M. P., & Roberts, T. L. (2012). Co-cultural theorizing: Foundations, applications & extensions. *Howard Journal of Communications*, *23*(4), 293–311. https://doi.org/10.1080/10646175.2012.722838

Peiker, S. (2022, August 18). Three diversity mistakes employers are still making in 2022 (and how to fix them). *Forbes*. https://www.forbes.com/sites/forbeshumanresourcescouncil/2022/08/18/three-diversity-mistakes-employers-are-still-making-in-2022-and-how-to-fix-them/

Plaut, V. C., Thomas, K. M., Hurd, K., & Romano, C. A. (2018). Do color blindness and multiculturalism remedy or foster discrimination and racism?

Current Directions in Psychological Science, 27(3), 200–206. https://doi.org/10.1177/0963721418766068

Ramos, M., Hewstone, M., Barreto, M., & Branscombe, N. R. (2016). The opportunities and challenges of diversity: Explaining its impact on individuals and groups. *European Journal of Social Psychology*, *46*, 793–806. http://dx.doi.org/10.1002/ejsp.2261

Razzante, R. J. (2018). Intersectional agencies: Navigating predominantly White institutions as an administrator of color. *Journal of International and Intercultural Communication*, *11*(4), 339–357. https://doi.org/10.1080/17513057.2018.1501082

Razzante, R. J., & Orbe, M. P. (2018). Two sides of the same coin: Conceptualizing dominant group theory in the context of co-cultural theory. *Communication Theory*, *28*(3), 354–375. http://dx.doi.org/10.1093/ct/qtx008

Razzante, R. J., Tracy, S. J., & Orbe, M. P. (2018). How dominant group members can transform workplace bullying. In *The Routledge handbook of communication and bullying* (pp. 46–56). Routledge. https://doi.org/10.4324/9781315148113

Ruiz-Mesa, K. (2022). 'We're talking about race!' Communicative practices of chief diversity officers. *Journal of Applied Communication Research*, *50*(3), 309–326. https://doi.org/10.1080/00909882.2022.2083432

Simmons, J., Lowery-Hart, R., Wahl, S. T., & McBride, M. C. (2013). Understanding the African-American student experience in higher education through a relational dialectics perspective. *Communication Education*, *62*(4), 376–394. https://doi.org/10.1080/03634523.2013.813631

U.S. Census Bureau. (2025). *Texas*. U.S. Department of Commerce. https://data.census.gov/profile/Texas?g=040XX00US48

Warren, J. T. (2003). *Performing purity: Whiteness, pedagogy, and the reconstitution of power*. Peter Lang.

5

LEADERSHIP AND BUILDING INCLUSIVE ORGANIZATIONAL CULTURES THROUGH MICROAFFIRMATIONS

Sherri Lynch

This chapter explores how those who identify as women create and build inclusive communities through the communication practice of microaffirmations. Microaffirmations are "gestures of inclusion and caring that help to reaffirm a person's value" (Rowe, 2008, p. 46). They can be a tool for building community and help make members of underrepresented identities such as women, people of color, and members of the LGBTQ+ community feel included in organizations. Systemic bias and discrimination have negatively impacted these groups over time, stalling diversity in organizations. Increasing the use of microaffirmations has the potential not only to help combat embedded unconscious biases but also to help build cultures of inclusion.

This chapter also seeks to better understand the communication practice of microaffirmations through the lens of social learning theory and the creation of leader identity. It seeks to understand the impact of gender on communication patterns, and the ways inclusive practices can impact organizational culture. Linking communication theories of gender (Tannen, 1995) and social learning theory (Bandura, 1969) to leadership identity (Ibarra, 2004), this chapter focuses on how microaffirmations can help build inclusive cultures which, in turn, can lead to increased personal and collective well-being in organizational life. I use findings from a qualitative study as evidence of this claim. A point to note here is that Tannen's genderlect theory has been aptly critiqued for essentializing gender and reinforcing gender binaries, and this is not the spirit in which I draw from her contributions. Instead, I emphasize that those who identify as women and men have been found to be socially and culturally conditioned over

DOI: 10.4324/9781003563662-7

time to communicate in particular ways and this is a relevant reality which aids my research. The chapter concludes with suggested practices that can be implemented to improve individual and organizational thriving.

Gender and communication

Let us begin with a brief introduction of the communication theory of genderlect, which is critical to a complete understanding of the communication styles of different genders. Introduced in the early 1990s, genderlect theory is tied to the assumption that men and women communicate differently and may even speak and listen in different cultural dialects (Tannen, 1995). The theory assesses the conversational styles of those who identify as men and those who identify as women through a humanistic and social scientific approach.

Genderlect theory posits that the use of language communicates ideas and negotiates relationships, and that lessons learned in childhood often carry over to the workplace (Tannen, 1995). In early life, those assigned as female often spend time talking with a single friend or in small groups. They learn to speak in ways that balance their own needs with the needs of the group (Tannen, 1995). This connects to leadership styles since women tend to be more collaborative and participatory when they take on leadership roles (Offermann & Foley, 2020). On average, research shows that women adopt a more democratic and relational style of leadership (Eagly & Johnson, 1990; van Engen & Willemsen, 2004). On the contrary, men tend to use language to negotiate status in a group and spend more time using language giving orders that raise status within the group (Tannen, 1995, p. 140). This use of language is reflected in leadership styles that can be more authoritarian.

How a worker accepts feedback or compliments others, how often a person apologizes and for what reasons, and numerous other factors of linguistic style impact how we are viewed and valued by our coworkers. These factors also contribute to how those who identify as women value themselves and their contributions in the workplace. As noted earlier, while Tannen (1995) approached genderlect theory from a binary perspective, her framework can be used as a lens to better understand how all genders communicate in the workplace. Recognizing speech patterns and linguistic styles across different groups and genders can allow the opportunity for organizations to create more inclusive cultures. For example, encouraging workers to state their preferred pronouns can contribute to a work culture where everyone feels welcomed. These differences and complex nuances affect the ways in which all genders communicate in the workplace. This is an important distinction which I will explore further as we look at social learning theory in the next section.

Social learning theory

Albert Bandura's (1969) social learning theory emphasizes the importance of observing, modeling, and imitating the behaviors, attitudes, and emotional reactions of others. The theory highlights the role of "observational learning, where individuals acquire knowledge, skills, attitudes, and beliefs by watching the actions of others and the consequences that follow, leading to the modeling and adoption of observed behaviors" (Bandura, 1969, p. 215). This process leads to the eventual adoption of observed behaviors, shaping how individuals navigate social and organizational contexts. Additionally, the theory is often used to address how people are motivated and can motivate others, how they perform, how they go about learning new skills, and how they self-regulate (Koutroubas & Galanakis, 2022). In the workplace, this theory is particularly useful for understanding how employees internalize cultural norms, leadership practices, and practices of communication. It sheds light on the way individuals – especially those from underrepresented groups, such as women – construct their professional identities through interaction with their organizational environment. Ibarra's (1999) research on identity construction introduced the concept of "provisional selves," illustrating how professionals try on different behaviors modeled by others to shape an individual leadership identity. In similar fashion, Ely et al. (2011) found that women participating in leadership development programs benefited from environments that modeled inclusive, relational leadership behaviors, enabling them to reconstruct unique leadership identities in alignment with their personal and professional values. These findings reinforce the argument that identity formation in the workplace is not static, but an evolving process shaped by social observation and feedback.

Social learning theory, therefore, offers a powerful lens for analyzing how workplace experiences are gendered, and how modeling inclusive behaviors – such as microaffirmations – can lead to broader behavioral and cultural change. For women in particular, environments that consistently model recognition, affirmation, and inclusivity provide the conditions for more robust identity development and leadership emergence. As such, social learning theory supports a deeper understanding of both the social construction of workplace experience and the systemic reinforcement or disruption of identity norms through organizational behavior.

Leader identity

Ibarra's (2004) research on identity creation speaks to working identity, described as "how we see ourselves in our professional roles, what we convey about ourselves to others, and ultimately, how we live our working lives" (p. 7). Throughout a lifetime, one's identity may shift, change, and be revised again and again with change resulting from both internal and external factors (Ibarra, 2004, p. 14). Combined with genderlect and social learning theory, leader identity theory can help us understand human behavior and conditions for human thriving for all genders in the workplace.

The formation of one's individual identity occurs over a lifetime, with intersections of many identities making the situation even more complex. Identity seeks to answer the "Who am I?" and "How am I unique?" questions of life. Arnett Jensen (2003) asserts that identity formation is most prominent during emerging adulthood and that impacts of globalization, such as access to international travel and the increased use of digital technologies, must be considered. Personal identity roles and where they intersect may affect one's identity formation, including multiple identities that are being formed throughout life, including cultural identity, professional identity, religious identity, gender identity, and others (Robinson, 2002). Environmental influences such as education, parenting, socioeconomic status, for example, greatly impact this process (Arnett Jensen, 2003). For this chapter, the focus is not on individual psychosocial identity, but on the process of forming a leader identity, especially in the modern workplace.

Development

For many leaders, lifelong learning and continuous development and refinement of skills can be a top priority. Leader identity refers to how one thinks of oneself as a leader (Day & Harrison, 2007). Bass (1990) described leader identity as influenced by peers, superiors, as well as family and friends, and emphasized how such influence "shape[s] one's subsequent performance as a leader" (p. 911).

The development of leader identity is not exclusive to organizational settings. Petriglieri et al. (2011) noted that the ability to develop one's leader identity is important in three areas: personal experiences of leading and following, making sense of one's life experiences as part of an identity, and making sense of emotions and the unconscious. The opportunity for leadership development is highly subjective and based on how one processes and interprets the experiences and events of their life. Therefore, self-awareness and being open to curiosity and exploration is crucial for leadership development. It is through self-awareness that one can come to identify areas of strength and developmental opportunities. This process is ongoing and ever-changing.

Lord and Hall's (2005) research indicated that there are three reasons for the critical nature of developing leader identity: leader identity creation offers structure around which new knowledge and skills can be developed, leader identity creation can become a source of motivation for a leader to seek new developmental opportunities, and leader identity can become a source from which others find inspiration and motivation. Further, as leaders develop expertise, they become more collaborative, and more reliant on their "principled understanding of situations and others, often in terms of values, emotions, and identities" (p. 594). As leaders develop and evolve in their identity, they often shift from individual identity, which differentiates self from others, to relational identity, which defines the self in terms of roles or relations, to collective identity, which defines the self in terms of collectives such as groups or organizations (Brewer & Gardner, 1996). This is an important distinction between individual and collective forces in one's learning.

Influences

One's gender identity, socioeconomic status, country of origin, and educational attainment influence early leader identity formation (Arnett Jensen, 2003). Later in life, when a person enters an organization, these factors continue to play a role, along with cultural factors such as how supportive an organization is to all genders, and the industry in which one chooses to work. Some scholars argue that the social identities in which one finds themself may play the greatest role in the formation of leader identity (Lord & Brown, 2003; van Knippenberg, 2011: van Knippenberg et al., 2004) and that group membership informs their responses to leadership (van Knippenberg, 2011). Internal and external forces are at play when influencing the formation and development of leader identity.

The impact of ascribed as well as avowed gender identities can play a major role in the formation of one's leader identity. Historically, leader positions have most often been held by males; thus, leader identity is most often referred to as male oriented. Even in relatively less patriarchal societies, men still dominate positions of public leadership (Wood & Eagly, 2002), perhaps suggesting the male desire to "lead and dominate others" (Eagly & Carli, 2004, p. 280). The suggestion of males, most often identifying as leaders, may lead women to question their own identity and acceptance as leaders. These influences are important to take into account in the development of leader identity over time.

Weaving together theories of gender and communication, social learning theory, and the development of leader identity, it becomes clear that the influence of leader identity is greatly impacted by the organizational settings in which women are situated. Understanding the communication patterns of those who identify as women, as well as social learning theory, the most widely used learning theory in the workplace to address and enhance adult learning (Gibson, 2004), is crucial for understanding the development of female leaders. The next section looks further into the importance of inclusive cultures, for personal and collective well-being.

Inclusive cultures

According to Woods (2002), "Inclusion describes the way an organization configures opportunity, interaction, communication, and decision-making to utilize the potential of its diversity" (p. 38). Certain practices, language, and behaviors influence the creation of inclusive cultures and increase feelings of belonging. Initiatives that focus on diversity and inclusion together allow for an open exchange of ideas and different perspectives (Prayson & Rowe, 2019). Inclusive cultures are those that create "an organizational environment that allows people with multiple backgrounds, mindsets and ways of thinking to work effectively together and to perform to their highest potential in order to achieve organizational objectives based on sound principles" (Pless & Maak, 2004, p. 130). Additionally, levels of inclusiveness at work can have direct impacts on employee happiness.

Organizational culture

A culture depends on a group having been formed, in which its members have shared and solved problems and invited new members (Schein, 1984); thus, organizations can be considered groups with organizational culture. Literature reveals that community building efforts and the formation of more communal relationships impact organizational culture. According to Thomas et al. (2019), "The foundation of a good culture is a safe and respectable workplace" (p. 12). Safe environments are those that are free from harassment, discrimination, and unfair bias toward disadvantaged groups or individuals. Such cultures can have longer-term benefits for employees, and attention to organizational culture is vital to employee health and well-being and for the longevity of thc organization.

Organizational cultures that are rigid yield fewer women in top leadership positions (Toh & Leonardelli, 2012), yet organizations with more females in executive positions are more profitable (Sandberg, 2013). Additionally, employees who understand the culture and know what to expect from their company are better equipped to make good decisions that align with the acceptable practices of the organization (Maurer, 2023). Thus, the inclusion of women as leaders becomes vital to attracting top talent, retaining employees, and creating strong workplace cultures. In addition to the human and employee well-being benefits of strong organizational culture, there is also evidence that there is a financial impact on cultures that include more women. When viewing communities under stress, such as a workplace, the vital role that networks of women play in holding families and communities together becomes clear (Taylor, 2002). Fondas and Sassalos (2000) found that having women on an organization's board of directors has a positive impact on performance.

Organizational health

There are many reasons why it would be important and beneficial to understand the ways women build community and create a sense of belonging. For an organization, understanding the phenomenon of how women build community could lead to higher productivity and employee satisfaction for all genders. Companies with higher employee satisfaction tend to engage their employees and attract new talent seeking employee-centered work environments (Frank et al., 2004).

A recent study of over 700 graduate students found that women with a close inner circle of women confidants were more likely to secure executive leadership positions (Uzzi, 2019). Additionally, a female CEO of an organization dedicated to gender equality in the workplace was recently quoted as saying, "A woman alone has power; collectively we have impact" (McGee, 2019, para. 1), pointing to the importance of women building community for the collective benefit of organizations and workers.

The impact of workplace behaviors

Building on the previous sections, this section covers workplace behaviors, including a specific communication practice, microaffirmations, that can aid in the development of strong organizational cultures.

Microaffirmations

A communicative phenomenon called a microaffirmation can be used to build community, both consciously and naturally. Though the term microaffirmation was first used and studied in the early 1970s, this phenomenon is still a highly under-researched one:

> Microaffirmations are gestures of inclusion and caring that help to reaffirm a person's value and help build strength and correct weakness ... Microaffirmations are apparently small acts, which are often ephemeral and hard to see, events that are public and private, often unconscious but very effective, which occur wherever people wish to help others to succeed.
>
> *(Rowe, 2008, p. 46)*

Microaffirmations are behaviors that create feelings of belonging and inclusion. They are important and useful as a means of focusing on positive experiences, in the hopes that these experiences will be replicated (Koch et al., 2022). One specific microaffirmation that has been studied is the simple act of head nodding. Research shows that women nod their heads more often (Helweg-Larsen et al., 2004), signaling agreement with the person speaking and thereby increasing likability and approachability (Osugi & Kawahara, 2018). Another more culturally specific example is that in predominantly white spaces, a simple head nod is an acknowledgment affirming the existence of fellow people of color to one another (Okwonga, 2014). The effects of microaffirmative behaviors in various contexts may lead to more positive workplaces, especially in more diverse spaces.

Cissna (1976) and others have studied the subject of interpersonal confirmation since the early 1970s, and it has even been labeled as being among "maybe the most pervasive and important aspects of interpersonal communication" (Cissna, 1976, p. 4). The philosophical grounding of this practice began as early as 1957, in the writings of Jewish theologian Martin Buber (1957), who cogently made the case that confirmation is an element of basic human communication. These early aspects of communication studies may have paved the way for further study in the area of microaffirmations. Examples of microaffirmations could include "tiny acts of opening doors to opportunity, gestures of inclusion and caring, and graceful acts of listening" (Rowe, 2008, p. 4). When applied in the workplace, microaffirmations foster inclusion and support for people who may feel unwelcome or invisible (Powell et al., 2013, p. 2). Though they can seem like natural and unintentional acts, it can be argued that, if linked to social learning theory, microaffirmations can be understood as a learned behavior and intentionally incorporated into patterns of behavior.

Microaggressions

Contrary to microaffirmations, the more well-known and better-researched workplace behavior is that of microaggressions: "Microaggressions are the brief everyday slights – verbal, nonverbal, environmental – whether intentional or not, that send negative or hostile messages toward marginalized groups" (Sue, 2017, p. 170). Microaggressions may be unconsciously delivered and often take the form of subtle slights, snubs, and questions about one's abilities and sense of belonging in the majority group (Solórzano, 2018; Sue et al., 2007). Common examples of microaggressions include being interrupted or spoken over at meetings, being deprived of acknowledgment for one's ideas, having others claim as their own someone else's ideas, having one's expertise, knowledge, or skills under-estimated, and being excluded from networks, groups, or activities (Solórzano, 2018; Sue et al., 2007). The impact of microaggressions on leader identity development can be great.

Communities that exist in the margins, such as religious minorities and people of color, are often the target of microaggressions and experience microinequities. Microaggressive behaviors can push marginalized populations further to the margins. However, while the use of microaffirmations is one method of eliminating various biases, it is necessary to point out there is a dark side. One study noted the disadvantage of microaffirmations, citing the "implicit assimilatory undertone of paternalistic tolerance that accepts the unquestioned retention of Whiteness as the dominant center" (Vass, 2018, p. 80). Highlighting the workplace as a male-dominated environment, the study alludes to how the use of microaffirmations continues to place current structures as dominant, rather than introduce new and different ways of being in a community. The results of this study do highlight possible dark sides of the practice. Thus, the use of microaffirmations has positive and perhaps probable negative aspects that must be kept in mind.

The practice of microaffirmations

Intentionally increasing the use of microaffirmations in the workplace can help combat unconscious bias (Sue et al., 2020). Encouraging positive interaction and inclusive workplaces is central to bystander training, which focuses on directly stopping workplace bias. Training goes beyond simply stating expectations of civility and includes the use of microaffirmations in all organizational groups, considering the "invisible work" of women, "particularly actions that foster collegiality and trust in groups" (Scully & Rowe, 2009, p. 4). Inclusive practices in an organization, such as the simple act of inviting others in, can foster a culture of mutual respect and connection with those who might otherwise feel like outsiders. Trained bystanders can prove to be allies in the workplace and work collectively in creating inclusive environments. Key players in an organization, such as leaders who encourage others to advance gender equity, are pivotal to the sustained usage of microaffirmations (Helitzer et al., 2017).

Microaffirmations can help women feel included in an organization when it comes to performance. Women, however, have also noted that often microaffirmations come in the form of a comment about one's physical appearance, further highlighting the tension between women and societal expectations of beauty. Thus, microaffirmations that are related to women's capabilities and not about their outward or physical appearance have the greatest ability to give females credibility and respect in workplace settings. When microaffirmations are abundant among and between all genders and relate to performance, behavior, and ability, they are likely to positively impact the development of leader identity and how a person sees themselves as a leader (Lynch, 2022). These intentional practices, if used appropriately, can be used to enhance individual and organizational thriving.

Exploratory research

To further delve into the relationship between microaffirmations, gender, organizational culture, and leader identity, I conducted a qualitative, phenomenological study of eight female leaders, with the intention of exploring the phenomenon of women building community. Qualitative inquiry covers a variety of approaches to research that focus on the *quality* of things rather than the *quantity* (Bazeley, 2013, p. 3). The phenomenological research approach explores in depth the lived experience of people and seeks to discover the commonality in the human experience, often referred to as the essence (Bloomberg & Volpe, 2019, p. 54). The essence is universal and worthy of understanding and exploration (Patton, 1990; van Manen, 2016).

One focus group was conducted that included eight participants, with seven participants continuing on to individual, semi-structured interviews. Table 5.1 displays demographic data submitted by participants. Blank cells are those wherein the participant chose not to answer.

Participants in the focus group and semi-structured individual interviews represent an array of industries and educational backgrounds, ranging from non-profit to aerospace, and educational journeys from high school diploma to doctoral degree. Types of organizations represented include academic institutions, banks and credit unions, a homeless and addiction recovery service, and a Fortune 100 airplane manufacturer. Four of the women (44%) identified themselves as doing all remote/virtual work. Two of the women (22%) self-identified as women of color.

I began each interview by asking the interviewee to describe her experience of being a woman in the workplace. As the conversations began, women spoke of the changes that have occurred in the workplace over the course of their careers, and the evolution of both them and of workplace culture. They talked about the challenges of being a woman in the workplace, including sexual harassment, microaggressions and bias from their male colleagues, and bullying from other females. The women were able to cite specific examples of being talked over, criticism for their emotions, or lack of emotions, and being the only female surrounded by male colleagues in very male environments. Many of the women alluded to the experience of not fitting in or feeling like they stood out in the workplace. "I just remember kind of always feeling like I don't I don't fit in anywhere because I'm not a guy...," said Participant Three. This factor of being

TABLE 5.1 Participant demographic data

Participant	*Education*	*Race/ ethnicity*	*Industry*	*Years in workforce*	*Years in leadership*
P1	Bachelor's degree	Hispanic	Agricultural lending	19	6
P2	Bachelor's degree	White	Banking	19	11
P3	Bachelor's degree	Caucasian	Homelessness and addiction recovery	25	5
P4	Master's degree	Caucasian	Consulting/ coaching	27	20
P5	Doctoral/Ph.D.		Academia/non-profit service	50	20
P6	Master's, pursuing doctoral degree	African American and Filipino	Academia – executive education	20	19
P7	Bachelor's degree	White	Banking	24	16
P8	Bachelor's degree		Aerospace engineering	28	15

This table presents demographic data of the study participants, including their participant number, education level, race/ethnicity, industry, years in workforce, and years in leadership.

isolated impacted the women in a variety of ways and all of them recognized the specific uniqueness of being female that they bring to their workplace experiences. These experiences impacted the development of their leader identity and how they have and continue to see themselves as leaders. Participant Six stated,

> I felt like when I was being bullied, I didn't feel like a leader. I felt powerless…it just permeated into my personal life, and I wasn't happy, and I wasn't in a good place, and I didn't feel like a leader anymore.

What has worked for many of these women in their work experience is the ability to be authentic and to show up as they are, rather than how they have been socially constructed to behave. To explore the phenomenon of building community, I prompted each interviewee to tell a story of a time that women created community within a workplace. The women spoke of support, intentionality, and empowerment, as well as relationships that extended beyond the professional roles they held. When asked about inclusion and the specific behaviors that build cultures that feel inclusive and create community, the women told stories of times that they felt included. They defined behaviors such as respect, support, curiosity, and safety in their stories. I recorded the following examples of inclusive practices that impacted participants:

> A safe space. To speak openly...share thoughts and ideas...trust that nobody is going to get shamed or put down.
>
> *(Participant Six)*

> I think the inquisitiveness about each other also brought that close vulnerability, and safety...everyone felt really safe in that environment.
>
> *(Participant Seven)*

> We created an environment where people feel comfortable, they feel that they will be heard. Building that relationship so that they feel like [they are in a] relatively safe place.
>
> *(Participant Five)*

When asked specifically what behaviors the women personally exhibit that create community, all eight women listed inclusive microaffirmative behaviors they practice. All eight women also noted the importance of seeing people as whole human beings, and not simply as an employee. The women also noted being intentional about building a relationship with each person in the community and making time to interact with each person. Some examples of microaffirmations from my research include the following:

> It's the little things of supporting or just sending a kind note to one another. It's intentionally doing things and it's actually a great way to build relationships and really kind of build allyships too.
>
> *(Participant Two)*

Participant Five said:

> I've definitely seen those kinds of things. I've seen people say later, "That point you've made at the meeting today, I think was so important." Or "Thank you for doing that" or a text message later or an email later after something's happened. Just little things like in Zoom now people are putting in chat, things like "thanks for being so brave," and "thanks for sharing that" and that to me is so little but those things are so kind.

This exploratory research underscores the powerful role microaffirmations play in shaping inclusive cultures and supporting women's leader identity development. Across diverse industries, backgrounds, and experiences, the women in this study described how intentional acts of recognition and respect helped them feel seen, valued, and cared for – especially in environments where they typically felt isolated or out of place. These affirming behaviors are tools for individual empowerment and can be foundational to community building and cultural transformation. Social learning is evident in the way these women modeled and mirrored inclusion, cultivating spaces that gave others permission to bring their full, authentic selves to work. Ultimately, leadership emerged from relational depth, care, and authenticity. As bell hooks (1995) wrote, "Beloved community is formed not by the eradication of difference but by its affirmation, by each of us claiming the identities and cultural legacies that shape who we are and how we live in the world" (p. 263). Through microaffirmations, these female leaders are not only affirming others but reshaping what leadership looks like from within.

Conclusion

This chapter has highlighted a gendered view of communication, the impact of social learning theory, and the formation of leader identity. This theoretical framework has been used to shed light on communication practices, specifically microaffirmative communication, that help build inclusive cultures in the workplace. Numerous studies have been conducted on female leaders, and the differences between male and female leadership. Fewer studies have been conducted on the conditions under which women thrive in organizational settings. What is even less understood are the natural tendencies that women exhibit that help build organizational cultures, and how these behaviors can be replicated to enhance organizational life for all genders. My exploratory research concluded that organizations and programs that are inclusive make women feel more valued as employees, that women thrive when they are part of a supportive community, and that microaffirmations are a tool that can be used to build community, create connections, and help women feel included in organizational life.

Future research on microaffirmations and the intersections across race, culture, and generational lines could offer insights into how these behaviors need to be adapted for diverse organizational contexts. Quantitative studies could enhance the value of microaffirmations by focusing on employee engagement and organizational climate, and the study of microaffirmations in the remote workplace could offer additional context. Creating workplaces that allow all genders to thrive can lead to individual and communal well-being. As this chapter has sought to demonstrate, by using intentional practices of microaffirmations, it is possible to create inclusive cultures for all.

Suggested further readings

Agrawal, R. (2018). *Belong: Find your people, create community, and live a more connected life*. Hachette.

Brown, B. (2018). *Dare to lead: Brave work. Touch conversations. Whole hearts*. Random House.

Cunningham, C. M., & Egan, C. (2024). Communication approaches to gender and leadership theory. In S. Madsen (Ed.), *Handbook of research on gender and leadership* (pp. 99–110). Edward Elgar Publishing. https://doi.org/10.4337/9781035306893

Field, E., Krivkovich, A., Kugele, S., & Yee, L. (2023, October). *Women in the workplace report 2023*. McKinsey & Co. https://www.mckinsey.com/featured-insights/diversity-and-inclusion/women-in-the-workplace#/

Stephens, J. P., Heaphy, E., & Dutton, J. E. (2011). High-quality connections. In K. S. Cameron & G. M. Spreitzer (Eds.), *The Oxford handbook of positive organizational scholarship* (pp. 385–399). Oxford University Press. https://doi.org/10.1093/oxfordhb/9780199734610.001.0001

Questions for further engagement

1 What are some examples of microaggressions/microaffirmations that you have experienced? Do you think they may have impacted your leadership development process in any way? Please elaborate.
2 Have you seen microaffirmations or microaggressions play a role in your workplace? Did they help or hinder in building inclusive cultures? Please explain.
3 How can organizations promote microaffirmations? What types of programs can organizations support that could aid in creating cultures that embrace microaffirming communication?
4 Is there a downside to microaffirmations? How can these behaviors be harmful in the workplace?
5 What role does gender play in creating inclusive organizational cultures? In what ways can gender be helpful or a hindrance?

References

Arnett Jensen, L. (2003). Coming of age in a multicultural world: Globalization and adolescent cultural identity formation. *Applied Developmental Science*, *7*(3), 189–196. https://doi-org.proxy.lib.siu.edu/10.1207/S1532480XADS0703_10

Bandura, A. (1969). Social-learning theory of identificatory processes. In D. A. Goslin (Ed.), *Handbook of socialization theory and research* (pp. 213–262). Rand McNally & Company.

Bass, B. M. (1990). From transactional to transformational leadership: Learning to share the vision. *Organizational Dynamics*, *18*(3), 19–31. https://doi.org/10.1016/0090-2616(90)90061-S

Bazeley, P. (2013). *Qualitative data analysis: Practical strategies*. Sage. https://doi.org/10.4135/9781036233808

Bloomberg, L. D., & Volpe, M. (2019). *Completing your qualitative dissertation: A roadmap from beginning to end*. Sage. https://doi.org/10.4135/9781452226613

Brewer, M. B., & Gardner, W. (1996). Who is this "We"? Levels of collective identity and self-representations. *Journal of Personality and Social Psychology, 71*(1), 83. https://psycnet.apa.org/doi/10.1037/0022-3514.71.1.83
Buber, M. (1957). Distance and relation. *Psychiatry*, *20*(2), 97.
Cissna, K. N. (1976, April). *Interpersonal confirmation: A review of current theory, measurement, and research* [Paper presentation]. Annual Meeting of the International Communication Association, Portland, OR.
Day, D. V., & Harrison, M. M. (2007). A multilevel, identity-based approach to leadership development. *Human Resource Management Review*, *17*(4), 360–373. https://doi.org/10.1016/j.hrmr.2007.08.007
Eagly, A., & Johnson, B. T. (1990, September). Gender and leadership style: A meta-analysis. *Psychology. Bulletin*, *108*(2), 233–256. https://doi.org/10.1037/0033-2909.108.2.233
Eagly, A. H., & Carli, L. L. (2001). Women and men as leaders. In J. Antonakis, A. T. Cianciolo, & R. J. Sternberg (Eds.), *The nature of leadership* (pp. 279–301). Sage. https://doi.org/10.4135/9781506395029
Ely, R. J., Ibarra, H., & Kolb, D. M. (2011). Taking gender into account: Theory and design for women's leadership development programs. *Academy of Management Learning & Education*, *10*(3), 474–493. https://doi.org/10.5465/amle.2010.0046
Fondas, N., & Sassalos, S. (2000). A different voice in the boardroom: How the presence of women directors affects board influence over management. *Global Focus*, *12*(2), 13–22.
Frank, F. D., Finnegan, R. P., & Taylor, C. R. (2004). The race for talent: Retaining and engaging workers in the 21st century. *Human Resource Planning*, *27*(3), 12–25.
Gibson, S. K. (2004). Social learning (cognitive) theory and implications for human resource development. *Advances in Developing Human Resources*, *6*(2), 193–210. https://doi.org/10.1177/1523422304263429
Helitzer, D. L., Newbill, S. L., Cardinali, G., Morahan, P. S., Chang, S., & Magrane, D. (2017). Changing the culture of academic medicine: Critical mass or critical actors? *Journal of Women's Health*, *26*(5), 540–548. https://doi-org.proxy.lib.siu.edu/10.1089/jwh.2016.6019
Helweg-Larsen, M., Cunningham, S. J., Carrico, A., & Pergram, A. M. (2004). To nod or not to nod: An observational study of nonverbal communication and status in female and male college students. *Psychology of Women Quarterly*, *28*(4), 358–361. https://doi-org.proxy.lib.siu.edu/10.1111/j.1471-6402.2004.00152.x
hooks, b. (1995). *Killing rage: Ending racism*. Henry Holt and Company.
Ibarra, H. (1999). Provisional selves: Experimenting with image and identity in professional adaptation. *Administrative Science Quarterly*, *44*(4), 764–791. https://doi.org/10.2307/2667055
Ibarra, H. (2004). *Working identity: Unconventional strategies for reinventing your career*. Harvard Business Press.
Koch, J. M., Knutson, D., Loche, L., Loche, R. W., III, Lee, H. S., & Federici, D. J. (2022). A qualitative inquiry of microaffirmation experiences among culturally diverse graduate students. *Current Psychology*, *41*(5), 2883–2895. https://doi.org/10.1007/s12144-020-00811-3
Koutroubas, V., & Galanakis, M. (2022). Bandura's social learning theory and its importance in the organizational psychology context. *Psychology*, *12*(6), 315–322. http://dx.doi.org/10.17265/2159-5542/2022.06.001
Lord, R. G., & Brown, D. J. (2003). *Leadership processes and follower self-identity*. Psychology Press. https://doi.org/10.4324/9781410608864

Lord, R. G., & Hall, R. J. (2005). Identity, deep structure and the development of leadership skill. *The Leadership Quarterly*, *16*(4), 591–615. https://doi.org/10.1016/j.leaqua.2005.06.003
Lynch, S. A. (2022). *The ways women build community: An exploratory descriptive qualitative research study* (Publication No. 29215647) (Doctoral dissertation, Gonzaga University). ProQuest Dissertations and Theses Global.
Maurer, R. (2023, December 21). Onboarding key to retaining, engaging talent. *SHRM*. https://www.shrm.org/topics-tools/news/talent-acquisition/onboarding-key-to-retaining-engaging-talent
McGee, J. C. (2019, August 22). *Growing the power of the pack – Why women should build stronger communities at work*. LinkedIn. https://www.linkedin.com/pulse/growing-power-pack-why-women-should-build-stronger-coppernoll-mcgee/
Offermann, L. R., & Foley, K. (2020, February 28). Is there a female leadership advantage? *Oxford Research Encyclopedia of Business and Management*. https://oxfordre.com/business/view/10.1093/acrefore/9780190224851.001.0001/acrefore-9780190224851-e-61
Okwonga, M. (2014, October 6). The nod: A subtle lowering of the head you give to another black person in an overwhelmingly white space. *Medium*. https://medium.com/matter/the-nod-a-subtle-lowering-of-the-head-to-another-black-person-in-an-overwhelmingly-white-place-e12bfa0f833f
Osugi, T., & Kawahara, J. I. (2018). Effects of head nodding and shaking motions on perceptions of likeability and approachability. *Perception*, *47*(1), 16–29. https://doi-org.proxy.lib.siu.edu/10.1177/0301006617733209
Patton, M. Q. (1990). *Qualitative evaluation and research methods* (2nd ed.). Sage Publications, Inc.
Petriglieri, G., Wood, J. D., & Petriglieri, J. L. (2011). Up close and personal: Building foundations for leaders' development through the personalization of management learning. *Academy of Management Learning & Education*, *10*(3), 430–450. https://doi.org/10.5465/amle.2010.0032
Pless, N., & Maak, T. (2004). Building an inclusive diversity culture: Principles, processes and practice. *Journal of Business Ethics*, *54*, 129–147. https://doi.org/10.1007/s10551-004-9465-8
Powell, C., Demetriou, C., & Fisher, A. (2013). Micro-affirmations in academic advising: Small acts, big impact. *The Mentor: An Academic Advising Journal*, *15*(1), 2. https://doi.org/10.26209/mj1561286
Prayson, R. A., & Rowe, J. J. (2019). LGBTQ inclusivity and language in the workplace. *Critical Values*, *12*(2), 28–30. https://doi-org.proxy.lib.siu.edu/10.1093/crival/vaz004
Robinson, T. L. (2002). The intersections of identity. In A. Garrod, J. V. Ward, T. L. Robinson, & R. Kilkenny (Eds.), *Souls looking back: Life stories of growing up black* (pp. 111–124). Routledge.
Rowe, M. (2008). Micro-affirmations and micro-inequities. *Journal of the International Ombudsman Association*, *1*(1), 45–48. http://oastats.mit.edu.proxy.lib.siu.edu/bitstream/handle/1721.1/156541/Rowe_2008_JN_micro-affirm-ineq.pdf?sequence=1&isAllowed=y
Sandberg, S. (2013). *Lean in: Women, work and the will to lead*. Random House.
Schein, E. H. (1984). Coming to a new awareness of organizational culture. *Sloan Management Review*, *25*(2), 3–16. https://www.researchgate.net/publication/284435496_Schein%27s_article_translated_to_Portuguese
Scully, M., & Rowe, M. (2009). Bystander training within organizations. *Journal of the International Ombudsman Association*, *2*(1), 1–9. https://hdl-handle-net.proxy.lib.siu.edu/1721.1/156545

Solórzano, D. G. (2018). Why racial microaggressions matter. In L. W. Perna (Ed.), *Taking it to the streets: The role of scholarship in advocacy and advocacy in scholarship* (pp. 92–99). Johns Hopkins University Press.

Sue, D. W. (2017). Microaggressions and "evidence" empirical or experiential reality? *Perspectives on Psychological Science*, *12*(1), 170–172. https://doi-org.proxy.lib.siu.edu/10.1177/1745691616664437

Sue, D. W., Calle, C. Z., Mendez, N., Alsaidi, S., & Glaeser, E. (2020). *Microintervention strategies: What you can do to disarm and dismantle individual and systemic racism and bias*. John Wiley & Sons.

Sue, D. W., Capodilupo, C. M., Torino, G. C., Bucceri, J. M., Holder, A., Nadal, K. L., & Esquilin, M. (2007). Racial microaggressions in everyday life: Implications for clinical practice. *American Psychologist*, *62*(4), 271. https://psycnet.apa.org/doi/10.1037/0003-066X.62.4.271

Tannen, D. (1995). The power of talk: Who gets heard and why. *Harvard Business Review*, *73*, 138. https://cla.middcreate.net/wp-content/uploads/tainacan-items/1018/4108/Tannen_PowerofTalk.pdf

Taylor, S. E. (2002). *The tending instinct: How nurturing is essential to who we are and how we live*. Macmillan.

Thomas, R., Cooper, M., Konar, E., Bohrer, A., Mohsenin, A., Yee, L., Krivkovich, A., Starikova, I., Huang, J., & Zanoschi, D. (2019). *Women in the workplace 2019*. McKinsey & Co. https://www.mckinsey.com/~/media/McKinsey/Featured%20Insights/Gender%20Equality/Women%20in%20the%20Workplace%202019/Women-in-the-workplace-2019.pdf

Toh, S. M., & Leonardelli, G. J. (2012). Cultural constraints on the emergence of women as leaders. *Journal of World Business*, *47*(4), 604–611. https://doi.org/10.1016/j.jwb.2012.01.013

Uzzi, B. (2019, February 25). Research: Men and women need different kinds of networks to succeed. *Harvard Business Review*. https://hbr.org/2019/02/research-men-and-women-need-different-kinds-of-networks-to-succeed

van Engen, M. L., & Willemsen, T. M. (2004). Sex and leadership styles: A meta-analysis of research published in the 1990s. *Psychological Reports*, *94*(1), 3–18. https://doi-org.proxy.lib.siu.edu/10.2466/pr0.94.1.3-18

van Knippenberg, D. (2011). Embodying who we are: Leader group prototypicality and leadership effectiveness. *The Leadership Quarterly*, 22(6), 1078–1091. https://doi.org/10.1016/j.leaqua.2011.09.004

van Knippenberg, D., van Knippenberg, B., De Cremer, D., & Hogg, M. A. (2004). Leadership, self, and identity: A review and research agenda. *The Leadership Quarterly*, *15*(6), 825–856. https://doi.org/10.1016/j.leaqua.2004.09.002

van Manen, M. (2016). *Phenomenology of practice: Meaning-giving methods in phenomenological research and writing*. Routledge. https://doi.org/10.4324/9781003228073

Vass, G. (2018). White microaffirmations in the classroom: Encounters with everyday race-making. In G. Vass, J. Maxwell, S. Rudolph, & K. Gulson (Eds.), *The relationality of race in education research* (pp. 72–84). Routledge. https://doi.org/10.4324/9781315144146

Woods, S. (2002). Creating inclusive organizations: Aligning systems with diversity. *Profiles in Diversity Journal*, 38–39. https://ecommons.cornell.edu/server/api/core/bitstreams/8917856e-9d63-46c1-90e2-2434e42cd32a/content

Wood, W., & Eagly, A. H. (2002). A cross-cultural analysis of the behavior of women and men: Implications for the origins of sex differences. *Psychological Bulletin*, *128*(5), 699. https://psycnet.apa.org/doi/10.1037/0033-2909.128.5.699

6

A CRITICAL DIALECTICAL PERSPECTIVE FOR INTERCULTURAL LEADERSHIP COMMUNICATION

Nilanjana Bardhan

Introduction

Leadership across cultural differences, while increasingly common in our global landscape, remains poorly understood and performed. And yet, the theoretical repertoire of intercultural communication scholarship, which offers a wealth of knowledge on communication across cultural differences, remains largely untapped in leadership studies. Conversely, intercultural communication scholarship has not paid much attention to the complexities of leading across cultural differences. This chapter builds conceptual bridges between relevant intercultural communication theory and leadership theory. It pays special attention to the concepts of diversity, equity, and inclusion (DEI) and foregrounds the critique that extant leadership scholarship displays a clear North American/Western bias (Dugan, 2017; Eagly & Chin, 2010).

The trajectory of leadership scholarship: A brief review

The study of leadership has a long history, and some popular lines of theorizing are as follows. The situational leadership body of work studies how situational factors impact leadership effectiveness (Northouse, 2022). Functional leadership studies the behaviors of leaders, the leader-follower relationship quality, and how these impact the productivity and satisfaction level of followers (e.g., leader-member exchange theory or LMX). The servant leadership style, developed in the 1970s by Robert Greenleaf, foregrounds followers and sees follower empowerment and development

DOI: 10.4324/9781003563662-8

as the primary mission. Inspired by James McGregor Burns's (1978) scholarship, the popular concept of transformational leadership (as opposed to transactional leadership wherein work is done for expected reward) focuses on change inspired by leaders who aim to appeal to the moral and intellectual needs of their followers. Other views include the notion of the authentic leader who is self-aware, performs with relational transparency (genuineness), engages in balanced processing, and has an internalized moral compass (Boekhorst, 2015; Cottrill et al., 2014). Scholarship on vision development, strategy, ethics, conflict management, leadership during crises, power, influence, leader development, and cultural intelligence has also been prevalent (Johnson & Hackman, 2018; Northouse, 2022; Yukl, 2020).

A leader-follower dualism and an individual-centric focus are evident in the above body of work, and a drawback of traditional leadership theories is their focus on influential acts of individuals (Burns, 2008; Fairhurst, 2001). These "great man" theories do not pay much attention to the phenomenon of leadership itself, which is a complex and dynamic process involving many interconnected stakeholders and contexts. The more recent "post-heroic" scholarship spotlights the relational and dialogic aspects of leadership and highlights the importance of leadership responsibility and accountability. Context, organizational culture, power, and stakeholders are being increasingly centered, and DEI have moved to the forefront. Further, emphasis is placed on the need to question dominant North American/Western theories and models of leadership that are assumed to be universal but are based on research that excludes the experiences of non-dominant identity leaders and employees and centers the experiences of the "power elite" (White, heterosexual, Protestant, Western male leader prototype) (Chin & Trimble, 2015; Dugan, 2017; Ensari & Riggio, 2021).

Relational, dialogic, and responsible leadership

While the study of relationships with regards to leadership is not new, the explicit focus on relationships is more recent. According to Uhl-Bien (2006), the relational approach "changes the focus from the individual to the collective dynamic" and investigates leadership as "an *outcome* of relational dynamics" (p. 662, emphasis added). Ospina and Uhl-Bien (2012) emphasize that a relational focus requires "viewing the invisible threads that connect actors engaged in leadership processes and relationships as part of the reality to be studied" (p. xx). Connected to relationality is the concept of dialogue. Gergen and Hersted (2016) emphasize the importance of moral accountability and dialogue and state that leaders should not allow power struggles to obstruct the potential of dialogue to generate new and creative meanings and relationships. They explain that dialogic scenarios can either sustain the status quo, generate enhanced organizational realities, or produce negative realities and relationships that harm the organization's health. Sugiyama et al. (2016) elaborate that leaders need to dialogically attend to identities and their intersections as they play out daily within organizations. Such social capital building involves embodied and co-created learning. Dialogical leaders transcend their egos without losing their leader identities (Bushe & Marshak, 2016) and this, according to Raelin (2016), can result in "collective agency" which does not extinguish the individual; rather, it merges the individual into a collective "we" embedded in a specific sociocultural context.

Responsible leadership scholarship combines social responsibility with relationality (Waldman, 2011). It shifts the focus from the individual as leader to leaders in relationship with stakeholders: "Responsible leadership is a specific frame of mind promoting a shift from purely economistic, positivist and self-centered mindset to a frame of thinking that has all the constituents and thus the common good in mind too" (Maak & Pless, 2006a, pp. 1–2). A responsible leader leads with "relational intelligence" (Maak & Pless, 2006b, p. 105), navigates multiple ideological perspectives as needed (Waldman, 2011), and is "a good *weaver* in the web of humanity" (Maak & Pless, 2006c, p. 50, emphasis in original).

Critical leadership studies

Critical leadership studies (CLS) is a more recent turn which emphasizes that power, while not the only focus, should be a fundamental consideration in leadership studies (Collinson, 2020); CLS is interventionist, aims to envision a better world, and should be continuously critical of itself to stay relevant (Chandler & Kirsch, 2018). Collinson (2017) writes that CLS's goal is to "examine workplace power and identity dynamics in all their asymmetrical, shifting, intersecting and contradictory forms" (p. 273). He elaborates that power is relational, produced in practice, and can be overt, covert, productive, oppressive, and dialectical.

The dialectical strand of CLS helps us grapple with the messiness and paradoxes of leadership in our complex world. In a comprehensive review and endorsement of the dialectical study of leadership, Fairhurst and Collinson (2023) write that dialectics is a "method of reasoning that searches for understanding through the clash of opposing arguments" (p. 485). Collinson (2005, 2020) argues that a dialectical perspective can problematize dichotomies and dualisms (e.g., leader-follower, powerful/powerless) that obstruct theorizing complex interplays of power in the everyday construction and performance of leadership.

Leadership communication scholarship

Leadership scholarship implicitly assumes that a successful leader, by definition, must be a good communicator (Barrett, 2006; Fairhurst & Connaughton, 2014; Ruben & Gigliotti, 2017). Despite this assumption, however, a communication theory lens on leadership is relatively recent. Johansson (2018) outlines three approaches to how communication is conceptualized in leadership scholarship: (1) communication as a tool/vehicle and linear process (sender-message-receiver, i.e., communication as transmission); (2) a focus on meaning production when leaders communicate with others; and (3) a focus on how communication constitutes leadership (interpretive/constitutive approaches). A skills and behavior focus dominates, with attention mainly paid to how leaders can be "effective" communicators rather than who they lead and the role of power. Along with the relational and dialogic turn in leadership scholarship, some communication scholars have delved into the second and third approaches (e.g., Barge & Fairhurst, 2008; Fairhurst & Putnam, 2004).

Fairhurst and Connaughton (2014) outline six value commitments of a communication-centered approach to leadership scholarship:

1 Leadership communication is both transmissional and meaning-centered.
2 Leadership (communication) is relational, neither leader nor follower centric.
3 Influential acts of organizing are the medium and outcome of leadership communication.
4 Leadership communication is inherently power-based, a site of contestation about the nature of leadership.
5 Leadership (communication) is a diverse, global phenomenon.
6 Leadership communication is alive with potential for reflexivity, moral accountability, and change (p. 8).

This approach highlights leaders' accountability and responsibility to others and to society and emphasizes that leaders do not speak/communicate/act alone.

Moving from theorizing leadership through a communication-centered to an intercultural and critical communication-centered lens requires us to consider the dialectical and contradictory plays of culture, identity, power, context, difference, and communication. The turbulent environments in which leaders practice today will get only more interculturally complex; therefore, the traditional view that leaders are (or should be) in full control of what they know, how they know, and how they think, communicate/act needs to be revised (Fairhurst & Connaughton, 2014).

Interculturality, DEI, and leadership scholarship: Need for a paradigm shift

According to Chin (2010), "Attention to diversity means paradigm shifts in our theories of leadership so as to make them inclusive; it means incorporating explanations of how dimensions of diversity shape our understanding of leadership" (p. 150). The concept of interculturality can be useful for this purpose. Briefly, interculturality refers to (usually asymmetrical) contact and interaction between different cultures/identity groups, and the state/condition wherein these differences intersect. It is

> an approach or framework for contact, dialogue and interaction between individuals and cultures that involve proactive exchange and bi-directional engagement involving both minority and majority groups. ... Its main purpose is the recognition, respect and acceptance of difference, as well as fostering deeper understanding of diverse perspectives and practices ... for engendering transformative (positive) change among individuals and by extension their communities.
>
> *(Elias & Mansouri, 2020, pp. 513, 514)*

Interculturality is anything but static.

It is harder to lead in more diverse environments than in more homogenous ones, yet leadership theory has not sufficiently grappled with this complexity (Chin & Trimble, 2015; Chrobot-Mason & Roberson, 2022; Chrobot-Mason et al., 2013; Ferdman, 2021). Research at the intersection of DEI, interculturality, and leadership is relatively recent (Chin, 2010; Chrobot-Mason et al., 2013), and we need new theories that centralize interculturality, DEI, social justice, accountability, dialogue, and intersectional relational complexities (Roberson & Perry, 2021).

Inclusion and leadership

While much theoretical heavy lifting still needs to be done on the relationship between leadership praxis and inclusion, one line of scholarly inquiry offers useful insights. Shore et al. (2011) applied Brewer's (1991) optimal distinctiveness theory to explain that people feel the need to be connected to groups through feelings of similarity, symbolic attachment, and belonging, and *simultaneously* also feel the need for uniqueness and individuation. They define inclusion "as the degree to which an employee perceives that he or she is an esteemed member of the work group through experiencing treatment that satisfies his or her needs for belongingness and uniqueness" (p. 1265). Depending on the context, one need may be greater than the other. This unique contribution highlights the need to balance opposite seeming (dialectical) feelings rather than focusing only on belonging, which can lead to glossing over important differences. Randel et al. (2018) further explored the belonging-uniqueness dialectic by weaving social identity theory with optimal distinctiveness theory. Several recent studies have followed in this direction (e.g., Mor Barak et al., 2021; Shore & Chung, 2022).

Inclusive leadership is anti-homogeneity, challenges what is accepted as normal, and addresses structural/cultural inequities in the workplace and in societies (Ferdman, 2021). Inclusive leaders avoid boxing people into simple identity categories, relate to them as intersectional beings, possess humility to recognize privilege, courage to make necessary changes to entrenched practices that maintain inequities, the ability to build accountability structures for themselves and others, address subtle discriminations, humanize all, constantly seek feedback, and build psychological safety and empowerment (Mor Barak et al., 2021; Nishii & Leroy, 2020; Roberson & Perry, 2021; Shore & Chung, 2022). Inclusive leadership is an active process that values people *because* of their differences and not *despite* their differences (Ferdman, 2021).

Interculturality and leadership scholarship

Leadership research has paid attention to understanding leadership styles in different national cultures since the 1980s; however, the focus on difference has been more "international" than "intercultural" or "interdifference." For example, the Global Leadership and Organizational Behavior Effectiveness (GLOBE) study has collected data from several countries over time and has distilled six leadership styles found worldwide (Barmeyer et al., 2021). While they provide valuable macro-level insights, a common assumption of such studies is that country is equal to culture, i.e., culture is conceptualized at the national level in a static manner. Culture and communication are complicated and fluid concepts that must be better understood by leaders at micro-, meso-, and macro levels.

Leadership scholars have borrowed from intercultural communication scholarship to understand how leaders can *competently* lead across cultural differences, and intercultural communication competence (ICC) scholarship has been tapped the most. According to Chen (1992), ICC is a process with three intertwined dimensions (cognitive, affective, and behavioral). Chen and Starosta (2012) emphasize the importance of intercultural sensitivity, empathy, and flexibility in attaining "intercultural adroitness." According to their model, self-concept, open-mindedness, a non-judgmental attitude, and social relaxation are necessary attributes of intercultural sensitivity; further, the ability to navigate interculturality and its resultant ambiguity and uncertainties is needed for attaining intercultural adroitness. Another stream of ICC research offers the integrated model of ICC (Arasaratnam, 2006) which highlights empathy, listening, experience, motivation, and positive attitude toward other cultures as significant variables that impact ICC.

The competency approach to intercultural leadership communication tends to position cultural differences as problems to overcome (e.g., a negative framing of difference), and intercultural leadership communication competence as a skill which combines knowledge about the "other" with an open attitude to understanding and connecting across differences that would otherwise pose obstacles. While there is nothing overtly problematic about this stance, such theorizing tends to be individualistic and leader-centric (Poprawski, 2009). Further, it does not account for the intertwined roles of identity, difference, and power inequities in the intercultural leadership communication process. Additionally, the larger social historical contexts at micro/meso/macro levels that generate and sustain systemic inequities do not get addressed because of the individualistic and acontextual focus of ICC research (Martin & Nakayama, 2014). And as Deardorff (2014) explains, what gets neglected is the attempt to theorize how individuals intersubjectively develop abilities to become intercultural thinkers and practitioners/leaders. To be clear, the concept of ICC itself is important and must not be abandoned; what we need are perspectives on competence which account for the dialectical complexities and nuances of interculturality.

A critical dialectical perspective for intercultural leadership communication

Martin and Nakayama (2014) suggest a critical dialectical approach to ICC as it "connects individual agency with larger, structural constraints [and] reveal[s] the complexities of culture" (p. 19). I meld their approach with critical leadership theory to offer an intercultural leadership communication perspective which highlights how leaders can develop critical ICC that is contextual, self-reflexive, and critically nuanced.

Difference and the space of the "inter"

How we conceptualize difference matters since difference is the modality through which diverse stakeholders in intercultural contexts communicate with each other. When cultural separateness is highlighted at the expense of interconnectedness, then cultures (and identities) are naturalized as bounded entities. This increases the possibility for stereotyping and exoticization of the cultural Other. The scope for imagining change, creativity, and growth through intercultural communication and mutual transformation is reduced (Sobré-Denton & Bardhan, 2013), and hierarchies and inequities that favor the already powerful remain unchanged.

The concept of interculturality, described earlier, offers another view – of *culture in action* across differences. The possibility of transformation comes into clearer focus because interculturality prioritizes challenging and changing dominant existing behaviors and cultural attitudes (Elias & Mansouri, 2020). Culture becomes a relational and active concept, and attention is on how we communicatively perform and navigate differences, *rather than just on the properties* (including communicative properties) of culture/identity (Appadurai, 1996). According to this view, *cultures are separate yet connected.* Interculturality lets us direct our conceptual attention to the in-between constitutive interfaces of culture where differences entangle, and intersubjective communicative performance unfolds (Langsdorf, 2008). *This is a space of possibility and interruption in how we navigate cultural differences in the face of received ideas about those differences.* According to Carrillo Rowe (2010), "The space of the inter into which we must insert ourselves in order to engage an/other is fraught, frightening, even as it brims with transformative possibilities" (p. 224). Communication at the intersection of differences could mutually transform meaning and give rise to new ways of seeing, thinking, and being in relation with cultural Others (Fisher, 2008; Langsdorf, 2008; Stewart, 2008).

Leadership is goal- and vision-oriented work which can benefit from thinking about difference and power in more nuanced ways. If we only theorize difference and power as oppositional, then we will be unable to theorize how people from different and uneven cultural backgrounds come together, communicate, relate, work, and accomplish goals in complex ways. A dialectical critical intercultural communication perspective lends itself to enabling such nuanced praxis.

A critical dialectical perspective

A dialectical lens entails negotiating the tensions between unitary opposites or contradictory seeming ideas. Unitary opposites are concepts that depend on each other for their meaning, e.g., leader-follower (Baxter & Montgomery, 1996). Hegel's work on dialectics posits that every concept (thesis) has its opposite (antithesis) and that people struggle to reach transcendent resolutions (synthesis). In everyday life people are enmeshed in managing tensions and interplays between opposite ideas which often mark our intercultural differences. Dialectics address the messiness of communication processes without assuming an end state (synthesis) and view interplay as indeterminate, involving ongoing dialogic interaction wherein individuals/entities engage in "simultaneous differentiation from yet fusion with one another" with the possibility of change (Baxter & Montgomery, 1996, p. 24). This perspective opens doors for nuanced treatments of the workings of power in the leadership process, especially at the micro everyday level of communicative interaction.

Leaders, by definition, exist only if there are followers, but this does not mean there is some kind of natural divide between them. Collinson (2006, 2020) writes that not enough attention has been paid to the power and influence of followers who are not necessarily always compliant but can be resistive and participate in dissent. Power and influence are complicated and context-specific. Drawing upon a Foucauldian view of power, Collinson (2020) explains, "The multiple identities, values and cultures of leaders and followers in various regions, societies and continents are likely to significantly shape leadership practices … Hence, future research could address the dialectical connections between cultures, contexts and power" (p. 15). He elaborates that power can be simultaneously oppressive and productive, overt and covert.

Bringing dialectics into intercultural communication, Martin and Nakayama (1999) explain that a dialectical perspective "recognizes and accepts as ordinary, the interdependent and complementary aspects of the seeming opposites" (p. 14), and that intercultural communication is well equipped to get at the dialectical tensions between cultures. Cultural difference is not necessarily perceived as a problem to be overcome but a reality that is charged with ambiguity, pregnant with possibility, and open to dialogue. They offer six dialectics: (1) cultural-individual dialectic, (2) personal/social-contextual dialectic, (3) differences-similarities dialectic, (4) static-dynamic dialectic, (5) present/future-history/past dialectic, and (6) privilege-disadvantage dialectic. Combining these with the dialectical leadership perspectives offered by Collinson (2006, 2020) and Shore et al. (2011), I present the following nine dialectics to develop a perspective for critical intercultural leadership communication: (1) cultural-individual dialectic, (2) differences-similarities dialectic, (3) belonging-uniqueness dialectic, (4) static-dynamic dialectic, (5) global-local dialectic, (6) present/future-history/past dialectic, (7) privilege-disadvantage dialectic, (8) control/consent-resistance/dissent dialectic, and (9) leader-follower dialectic. I utilize a hypothetical case of a transnational leader to demonstrate how each of these dialectics could come into play. Let's imagine this leader (mixed race, identifies as female, Spanish nationality) is the chief communications officer (CCO) of a West-based women's rights multinational non-profit organization (NGO) with operations spread across many parts of the world, especially the global South.

Cultural-individual dialectic

People are a dynamic mix of their unique individual characteristics, beliefs, and values and those that are more cultural (group level) in nature (Martin & Nakayama, 1999). This dialectic applies to both leaders and followers, who need to be mindful of these tensions in their everyday communication (both formal and informal) and use of language with cultural Others, i.e., they must be able to perceive the simultaneity of the individual and the cultural in themselves and others. For example, there might be a gender-oppression-related issue the aforementioned NGO may be engaged with in which clients and workers within their more collectivistically oriented locales disagree with those in more individualistically oriented locales on how to address it. However, there are individuals within both locales who may not completely agree with the others in their locale and lean toward the Other position. Our leader would be able to see this complexity, encourage dialogue, and position the issue in a way all involved feel they have been heard and received the opportunity to contribute to a solution. The leader would not force a top-down or simplistic binary (either/or) view.

Differences-similarities dialectic

Martin and Nakayama (1999) remind us, "There has been a tendency to overemphasize group differences in traditional intercultural communication research in a way that sets up false dichotomies and rigid expectations" (p. 16). No two people are completely different (i.e., cultural difference conceptualized as pure separation and opposition) or completely similar (i.e., the glossing over of important cultural differences). There are usually overlaps that are points of connection across differences. These connections, or spaces of the "inter," must be brought into focus so leaders can understand how they play out in their everyday communication within intercultural spaces. The dialogue encouraged by our leader in the gender-oppression example presented above could result in discoveries of connections between what initially seemed like oppositional positions. This could lead to creative solutions and new thinking about the issue in the space of the "inter."

Belonging-uniqueness dialectic

Shore et al. (2011) and others have demonstrated that to feel included within organizations, individuals need to feel like they belong (i.e., they are part of a superordinate organizational identity) as well as be recognized as unique (i.e., who they are as a mix of their individual, intersectional, and cultural identities). Leaders must communicate at all levels in ways that help construct a larger organizational identity that does not exclude anyone but at the same time does not lump everyone under one identity. They must emphasize that the diversity that members contribute is important and indispensable for creating the larger organizational identity. In keeping with our above scenario, the dialogue our leader encourages should strive to achieve a dialectical stance and emphasize how the superordinate identity of the organization and the unique, and maybe even contradictory seeming, cultural contributions of each locale are both necessary for the success and well-being of the entire organization and its work. Difference must be framed and communicated as an opportunity and not a problem to be overcome.

Static-dynamic dialectic

According to Martin and Nakayama (1999), "thinking about culture and cultural practices as both static and dynamic helps us navigate through a diverse world and develop new ways of understanding intercultural encounters" (p. 17). Some aspects of group culture endure, while others change over time, usually incrementally. This slow change over time, if one is not immersed in it, can surprise and seem contradictory. Leaders leading across diverse cultural spaces must recognize and incorporate this dialectic in their communicative interactions. Let's imagine that gift giving is perceived to be normal cultural practice, even in work contexts, in many locales around the globe where our hypothetical NGO has operations. However, global headquarters (Paris) leans toward discouraging gift giving in its policies. Our CCO could curate past practice for examples of how gift giving was successfully navigated in ways that respected context-specific cultural practices and simultaneously did not disregard global organizational policy. Reaching out to followers across cultures for such stories and then sharing them could spark creativity, dialogue, and self-reflexivity, empower followers across all locales, and generate intercultural communication and learning across the leader-follower dualism on how to navigate the static-dynamic dialectic on this issue (and possibly others) in mutually respectful ways.

Global-local dialectic

Intercultural communication, especially in transnational contexts, tends to occur at the nexus of the (perceived) global and the (perceived) local. The global tends to entail cultural values, beliefs, and practices that transcend regional/national borders. Local beliefs, values, and practices are more specific to a particular cultural place/space. The global and local are intertwined; anything considered global always has local roots, and something is considered global only because it has emerged as such through historic, discursive, and hegemonic plays of power. Keeping with the gift-giving scenario, if our hypothetical leader is unable to address the issue in nuanced ways, then this could lead to identity freezing on all sides and result in the imposition of dominant organizational practices and views, relational dissatisfaction, and possible dissent (which might be necessary). Similarly, followers who believe in gift giving must also understand the context and reasoning for the global policy. Without mutual intercultural understanding, the complexities of the oblique workings of power would not be comprehended and woven into communicative and relational praxis. What is perceived as global and what is considered local will remain dichotomized and the "inter" will remain elusive.

Present/future-history/past dialectic

Martin and Nakayama (1999) write that "we need to balance both an understanding of the past and the present. Also, the past is always seen through the lens of the present" (p. 17). Leadership communication must emphasize there is no capital "H" in history, and how the past is understood will pass through the kaleidoscope of multiple interpretations of all present intercultural actors involved. Simultaneously, how the future is envisioned (communicatively constructed) depends on how tensions between the past and the present are navigated, i.e., the visions collectively and communicatively built for the future must account for the past and be guided by the spirit of equity and the righting of past intercultural wrongs. For example, women's rights issues around the globe are diverse in nature and have myriad histories. Our leader must be knowledgeable about this matter and communicate and encourage dialogue and policies in ways that are simultaneously attentive to specific histories and practices and focus on communication/action for changing past wrongs in the future.

Privilege-disadvantage dialectic

Our intersectional identities are complex and contradictory, and no one is only privileged or only disadvantaged: "Individuals may be simultaneously privileged and disadvantaged, or privileged in some contexts and disadvantaged in others" (Martin & Nakayama, 1999, p. 18). This dialectic allows us to see that while power is usually associated with privilege, in some contexts it can be a disadvantage. Conversely, a disadvantaged aspect of one's identity could experience privilege in specific contexts. Collinson (2020) recommends a Foucauldian rather than Marxist view for theorizing power in relationship to leadership, stating that power is not just a possession because of one's title, identity, and/or sociocultural location; it is produced, exercised, and/or constrained through communication and interaction in context. Further, power is not always oppressive but can be empowering, productive, and deployed/shared for intercultural justice. Intercultural leadership communication must create awareness of the complex ways in which power works. Our leader could, through how she communicates and enables dialogue, share stories about how she is often but not always privileged as a White woman in a leadership role and encourage those avowing marginalized identities (e.g., women) to share stories about how they can sometimes experience privilege because of some aspects of their intersectional identities, e.g., higher social class, or shifting context (e.g., a U.S.-American woman working in a less economically privileged part of the world). In other words, leaders can encourage dialogue that helps interrupt the privilege/disadvantage binary.

Control/consent-resistance/dissent dialectic

This dialectic combines two dialectics suggested by Collinson (2005): control-resistance and consent-dissent. He writes, "Assuming that the interests of leaders and followers coalesce, orthodox leadership studies tend to see power and control as unproblematic forms of organizational authority whilst resistance is viewed as abnormal or irrational" (p. 1425). He argues such a narrow view underestimates the agency of followers who may have good reasons to resist. Control typically assumes consent and vice versa, and resistance typically assumes dissent and vice versa. Such assumptions ignore the fact that if sanctions and disciplinary actions are expected, then dissent may be subversive and disguised as consent. Collinson elucidates the complexities of this dialectic, stating that in some situations, leaders "may themselves be constrained by the very control systems they enact, and might even (subtly and indirectly) support employee resistance to control" (p. 1431).

Resistance/dissent, whether overt or covert, is an inherent aspect of leaders' interactions with others, especially in contexts where the cultural codes of communication involved may not align as expected. Combined with this, the control/consent-resistance/dissent dialectic emphasizes that leaders are not always in full control of meaning management and perceptions. For example, our leader may herself feel constrained by an organizational policy which favors West-centric understandings of feminism. She may have to shift gears between organizational well-being and what she perceives as Western bias in ways that allow for dissenting voices to be heard and unwelcome policies to be revised.

Leader-follower dialectic

The leader-follower dualism has been a central assumption throughout leadership scholarship. Learmonth and Morrell (2017) argue that any leadership scholarship "that uses leader and follower as a priori, universal categories will lack a certain potential for critique" (p. 267). According to Collinson (2020),

> Since asymmetrical power relations are always two-way, leaders will to some extent remain dependent on the led, while the latter retain a degree of autonomy and discretion. Accordingly, a dialectical approach recognizes that, while leaders' power is important and extensive, it may also be limited and constrained.
>
> *(p. 6)*

Therefore, while this dualism may be necessary to conduct leadership scholarship, the leader-follower relationship must also, simultaneously, be recognized as a dialectical one. For example, our leader may, while maintaining her leader identity, immerse herself into the collective "we" (Raelin, 2016) to interrupt this dualism so that dialogue about various forms of feminisms from around the globe is led by followers rather than constrained by leaders.

Conclusion

Intercultural communication theory can offer much to leadership communication knowledge and praxis in our deeply intercultural world. Therefore, in this chapter, I have woven together literature from leadership theory with relevant intercultural communication theory to build a critical dialectical perspective. This effort is in keeping with suggestions for needed research. Jian and Fairhurst (2025) recently emphasized that future leadership communication research should assume a new normal "where contradictions and paradoxes are the norm – where binaries coexist and form interdependencies, or shade into one another" (p. 12). However, while a dialectical perspective is gaining traction in the study of leadership and communication (Fairhurst & Collinson, 2023), there is a need to build on its intercultural dimensions. Connecting leadership and intercultural communication scholarship is a way forward in this direction.

From a praxis point of view, the perspective offered in this chapter could assist responsible, relational, and dialogic leaders to strive toward constructing inclusive climates and cultures of communication across asymmetrical differences in intercultural spaces. It could also serve as a springboard for developing related leadership communication perspectives, theories, and models. The nine combined dialectics presented are open to further fine tuning and development. Also, and following Martin and Nakayama (1999), I emphasize that they are not mutually exclusive and should not be treated as such. I further hope this perspective will assist in extending our scholarship beyond the constraints of West-centric and binaristic theorizing.

Suggested further readings

Fairhurst, G., Endres, C., & Jian, G. (2024). Leadership communication. In V. Miller, & M. S. Poole (Eds.), *Organizational communication theory and research* (pp. 127–148). De Gruyter Mouton.

Hino, K. (2019). Are leadership theories west-centric? In R.E. Riggio (Ed.), *What's wrong with leadership: Improving leadership research and practice* (pp. 138–149). Routledge. https://doi.org/10.4324/9781315163604

Jian, G., & Fairhurst, G. (Eds.). (2025). *The Routledge handbook of organizational leadership communication*. Routledge. https://doi.org/10.4324/9781003380115

Martin, J. N., & Nakayama, T. K. (2010). Intercultural communication and dialectics revisited. In R. T. Halualani, & T. K. Nakayama (Eds.), *Handbook of critical intercultural communication* (pp. 51–83). Wiley-Blackwell. https://doi.org/10.1002/9781119745426

Questions for further engagement

1 Think of another dialectic that could be added to the nine discussed in this chapter. Explain its praxiological value.
2 Is the form of intercultural leadership communication discussed in this chapter suitable for all contexts and types of leaders/leadership (e.g., corporate, political, and non-profit)? Explain your answer with examples.
3 If you were to further build on the intercultural leadership communication perspective described in this chapter, in what direction would you go and why? Provide theoretical and other rationales.

References

Appadurai, A. (1996). *Modernity at large: Cultural dimensions of globalization*. University of Minnesota Press.

Arasaratnam, L. A. (2006). Further testing of a new model of intercultural communication competence. *Communication Research Reports*, *23*(2), 93–99. https://doi.org/10.1080/08824090600668923

Barge, J. K., & Fairhurst, G. T. (2008). Living leadership: A systemic, constructionist approach. *Leadership*, 4, 227–251. https://doi.org/10.1177/1742715008092360

Barmeyer, C., Bausch, M., & Mayrhofer, U. (2021). *Constructive intercultural management: Integrating cultural differences successfully*. Edward Elgar Publishing.

Barrett, D. J. (2006). Strong communication skills a must for today's leaders. *Handbook of Business Strategy*, 7(1), 385–390. https://doi.org/10.1108/10775730610619124
Baxter, L., & Montgomery, B. (1996). *Relating: Dialogues and dialectics*. The Guilford Press.
Boekhorst, J. A. (2015). The role of authentic leadership in fostering workplace inclusion: A social information processing perspective. *Human Resource Management*, *54*(2), 241–264. https://doi.org/10.1002/hrm.21669
Brewer, M. B. (1991). The social self: On being the same and different at the same time. *Personality and Social Psychology Bulletin*, *17*(5), 475–448. https://web.mit.edu/curhan/www/docs/Articles/15341_Readings/Intergroup_Conflict/Brewer_1991_The_social_self.pdf
Burns, J. M. (1978). *Leadership*. Harper & Row.
Burns, J. M. (2008). Foreword. In R. E. Riggio, I. Chaleff, & J. Lipman-Blumen (Eds.), *The art of followership* (pp. xi–xii). Jossey-Bass.
Bushe, G. R., & Marshak, R. J. (2016). The dialogic mindset: Leading emergent change in a complex world. *Organization Development Journal*, *34*(1), 37–65. https://gervasebushe.ca/otherdocs/Dialogic_Mindset_ODJ.pdf
Carrillo Rowe, A. (2010). Entering the inter: Power lines in intercultural communication. In T. K. Nakayama, & R. T. Halualani (Eds.), *The handbook of critical intercultural communication* (pp. 216–226). Wiley-Blackwell. https://doi.org/10.1002/9781119745426
Chandler, J. L. S., & Kirsch, R. E. (2018). *Critical leadership theory*. Palgrave Macmillan. https://doi.org/10.1007/978-3-319-96472-0
Chen, G. M. (1992). A test of intercultural communication competence. *Intercultural Communication Studies*, 2, 63–82. https://digitalcommons.uri.edu/cgi/viewcontent.cgi?article=1014&context=com_facpubs
Chen, G. M., & Starosta, W. J. (2012). Intercultural communication competence: A synthesis. In B. Burleson (Ed.), *Communication yearbook 19* (pp. 353–383). Routledge. https://doi.org/10.4324/9780203856796
Chin, J. L. (2010). Introduction to the special issue on diversity and leadership. *American Psychologist*, *65*(3), 150–156. https://doi.org/10.1037/a0018716
Chin, J. L., & Trimble, J. E. (2015). *Diversity and leadership*. Sage. https://doi.org/10.4135/9781483368801
Chrobot-Mason, D., & Roberson, Q. (2022). Inclusive leadership. In P. G. Northouse (Ed.), *Leadership: Theory and practice* (9th ed., pp. 322–351). Sage.
Chrobot-Mason, D., Ruderman, M. N., & Nishii, L. H. (2013). Leadership in a diverse workplace. In Q. M. Roberson (Ed.), *The Oxford handbook of diversity and work* (pp. 315–340). Oxford University Press. https://doi.org/10.1093/oxfordhb/9780199736355.001.0001
Collinson, D. (2005). Dialectics of leadership. *Human Relations*, *58*(11), 1419–1442. https://doi.org/10.1177/0018726705060902
Collinson, D. (2006). Rethinking followership: A post-structuralist analysis of follower identities. *The Leadership Quarterly*, *17*(2), 179–189. https://doi.org/10.1016/j.leaqua.2005.12.005
Collinson, D. (2017). Critical leadership studies: A response to Learmonth and Morrell. *Leadership*, *13*(3), 272–284. https://doi.org/10.1177/1742715017694559
Collinson, D. L. (2020). 'Only connect!': Exploring the critical dialectical turn in leadership studies. *Organization Theory*, *1*, 1–22. https://doi.org/10.1177/2631787720913878
Cottrill, K., Lopez, P. D., & Hoffman, C. C. (2014). How authentic leadership and inclusion benefit organizations. *Equality, Diversity and Inclusion:*

An International Journal, *33*(3), 275–292. https://doi.org/10.1108/EDI-05-2012-0041
Deardorff, D. (2014, May). *Some thoughts on assessing intercultural competence.* University of Illinois and Indiana University, National Institute for Learning Outcomes Assessment (NILOA). https://scholar.google.com/citations?view_op=view_citation&hl=en&user=gbHB0skAAAAJ&cstart=20&pagesize=80&citation_for_view=gbHB0skAAAAJ:yD5IFk8b50cC
Dugan, J. P. (2017). *Leadership theory: Cultivating critical perspectives.* Jossey-Bass.
Eagly, A. H., & Chin, J. L. (2010). Diversity and leadership in a changing world. *American Psychologist*, *65*(3), 216–224. https://psycnet.apa.org/doi/10.1037/a0018957
Elias, A., & Mansouri, F. (2020). A systematic review of studies on interculturalism and intercultural dialogue. *Journal of Intercultural Studies*, *41*(4), 490–523. https://doi.org/10.1080/07256868.2020.1782861
Ensari, N., & Riggio, R. E. (2021). Exclusion of inclusion in leadership theories. In B. M. Ferdman, J. Prime, & R. E. Riggio (Eds.), *Inclusive leadership: Transforming diverse lives, workplaces, and societies* (pp. 25–38). Sage. https://doi.org/10.4324/9780429449673
Fairhurst, G. (2001). Dualisms in leadership research. In F. M. Jablin, & L. L. Putnam (Eds.), *The new handbook of organizational communication* (pp. 379–439). Sage. https://doi.org/10.4135/9781412986243
Fairhurst, G., & Collinson, D. (2023). Leadership dialectics. In D. Schedlitzki, M. Larsson, B. Carroll, M. Bligh, & O. Epitropaki (Eds.), *The SAGE handbook of leadership* (2nd ed., pp. 484–497). Sage. https://doi.org/10.4135/9781529781892
Fairhurst, G., & Connaughton, S. L. (2014). Leadership: A communicative perspective. *Leadership*, *10*(1), 7–35. https://doi.org/10.1177/1742715013509396
Fairhurst, G., & Putnam, L. L. (2004). Organizations as discursive constructions. *Communication Theory, (14)*, 5–26. https://doi.org/10.1111/j.1468-2885.2004.tb00301.x
Ferdman, B. M. (2021). Inclusive leadership: The fulcrum of inclusion. In B. M. Ferdman, J. Prime, & R. E. Riggio (Eds.), *Inclusive leadership: Transforming diverse lives, workplaces, and societies* (pp. 3–24). Sage. https://doi.org/10.4324/9780429449673
Fisher, W. (2008). Glimpses of hope: Rhetorical and dialogical discourse promoting cosmopolitanism. In K. G. Roberts, & R. Arnettt (Eds.), *Communication ethics: Between cosmopolitanism and provinciality* (pp. 47–68). Peter Lang.
Gergen, K. J., & Hersted, L. (2016). Developing leadership as dialogic practice. In J. A. Raelin (Ed.), *Leadership-as-practice: Theory and application* (pp. 178–197). Routledge.
Jian, G., & Fairhurst, G. (2025). Introduction. In G. Jian, & G. Fairhurst (Eds.), *The Routledge handbook of organizational leadership communication* (pp. 1–16). Routledge. https://doi.org/10.4324/9781003380115
Johansson, C. (2018). Leadership communication. In R. Heath, & W. Johansen (Eds.), *The international encyclopedia of strategic communication* (pp. 1–16). Wiley. https://doi.org/10.1002/9781119010722
Johnson, C. E., & Hackman, M. Z. (2018). *Leadership: A communication perspective* (7th ed.). Waveland Press, Inc.
Langsdorf, L. (2008). The reasonableness of bias. In K. G. Roberts, & R. Arnettt (Eds.), *Communication ethics: Between cosmopolitanism and provinciality* (pp. 241–261). Peter Lang.

Learmonth, M., & Morrell, K. (2017). Is critical leadership studies 'critical'? *Leadership*, *13*(3), 257–271. https://doi.org/10.1177/1742715016649722
Maak, T., & Pless, N. M. (2006a). Introduction. In T. Maak, & N. M. Pless (Eds.), *Responsible leadership* (pp. 1–13). Routledge.
Maak, T., & Pless, N. M. (2006b). Responsible leadership in a stakeholder society – A relational perspective. *Journal of Business Ethics*, *66*(1), 99–115. https://doi.org/10.1007/s10551-006-9047-z
Maak, T., & Pless, N. M. (2006c). Responsible leadership: A relational approach. In T. Maak, & N. M. Pless (Eds.), *Responsible leadership* (pp. 33–53). Routledge.
Martin, J., & Nakayama, T. (1999). Thinking dialectically about culture and communication. *Communication Theory*, *9*(1), 1–25. https://doi.org/10.1111/j.1468-2885.1999.tb00160.x
Martin, J., & Nakayama, T. (2014). Ethical issues in intercultural communication competence. In G.-M. Chen, & X. Dai (Eds.), *Intercultural communication competence: Conceptualization and its development in cultural contexts and interactions* (pp. 97–117). Cambridge Scholars Publishing.
Mor Barak, M. E., Luria, G., & Brimhall, K. C. (2021). What leaders say versus what they do: Inclusive leadership, policy-practice decoupling, and the anomaly of climate for inclusion. *Group & Organization Management*, *47*(4), 840–871. https://doi.org/10.1177/10596011211005916
Nishii, L. H., & Leroy, H. L. (2020). Inclusive leadership: Leaders as architects of inclusive workgroup climates. In B. M. Ferdman, J. Prime, & R. E. Riggio (Eds.), *Inclusive leadership: Transforming diverse lives, workplaces, and societies* (pp. 162–178). Sage. https://doi.org/10.4324/9780429449673
Northouse, P. G. (2022). *Leadership: Theory and practice* (9th ed.). Sage.
Ospina, S. M., & Uhl-Bien, M. (2012). Mapping the terrain: Convergence and divergence around relational leadership. In M. Uhl-Bien, & S. M. Ospina (Eds.), *Advancing relational leadership: A dialogue among perspectives* (pp. xix–xivii). Information Age Publishing, Inc.
Poprawski, M. (2009). Leadership. An intercultural approach. Alternate take .... *Journal of Intercultural Management*, *1*(1), 28–41. https://joim.pl/wp-content/uploads/2020/02/1-1-Leadership.-An-Intercultural-Approach....pdf
Raelin, J. A. (2016). Imagine there are no leaders: Reframing leadership as collaborative agency. *Leadership*, *12*(2), 131–158. https://doi.org/10.1177/1742715014558076
Randel, A. E., Galvin, B. M., Shore, L. M., Ehrhart, K. H., Chung, B. G., Dean, M. A., & Kedharnath, U. (2018). Inclusive leadership: Realizing positive outcomes through belongingness and being valued for uniqueness. *Human Resource Management Review*, *28*(2), 190–203. https://doi.org/10.1016/j.hrmr.2017.07.002
Roberson, Q., & Perry, J. L. (2021). Inclusive leadership in thought and action: A thematic analysis. *Group & Organization Management*, *47*(4), 755–778. https://doi.org/10.1177/10596011211013161
Ruben, B. D., & Gigliotti, R. A. (2017). Communication: Sine qua non of organizational leadership theory and practice. *International Journal of Business Communication*, *54*(1), 12–30. https://doi.org/10.1177/2329488416675447
Shore, L. M., Randel, A. E., Chung, B. G., Dean, M. A., Ehrhart, K. H., & Singh, G. (2011). Inclusion and diversity in work groups: A review and model for future research. *Journal of Management*, *37*, 1262–1289. https://doi.org/10.1177/0149206310385943
Shore, L., & Chung, B. G. (2022). Inclusive leadership: How leaders sustain or discourage work group inclusion. *Group & Organization Management*, *47*(4), 723–754. https://doi.org/10.1177/0149206310385943

Sobré-Denton, M., & Bardhan, N. (2013). *Cultivating cosmopolitanism for intercultural communication: Communicating as global citizens*. Routledge. https://doi.org/10.4324/9780203078150

Stewart, J. (2008). Cosmopolitan communication ethics understanding and action. In K. G. Roberts, & R. Arnettt (Eds.), *Communication ethics: Between cosmopolitanism and provinciality* (pp. 105–119). Peter Lang.

Sugiyama, K., Cavanagh, K. V., van Esch, C., Bilimoria, D., & Brown, C. (2016). Inclusive leadership development: Drawing from pedagogies of women's and general leadership development programs. *Journal of Management Education*, *40*(3), 253–292. https://doi.org/10.1177/1052562916632553

Uhl-Bien, M. (2006). Relational leadership theory: Exploring the social processes of leadership and organizing. *The Leadership Quarterly*, *17*(6), 654–676. https://doi.org/10.1016/j.leaqua.2006.10.007

Waldman, D. A. (2011). Moving forward with the concept of responsible leadership: Three caveats to guide theory and research. *Journal of Business Ethics*, *98*(1), 75–83. https://www.up.ac.za/media/shared/213/Articles%20on%20RL/Batch%203/waldman_2011_moving-forward-with-the-concept-responsible-leadership.zp143788.pdf

Yukl, G. (2020). *Leadership in organizations* (9th ed.). Pearson.

SECTION II

Relational, Discursive, and Collective Approaches to Leadership and Communication

7

INTEGRATING COMMUNICATION AND LEADERSHIP THEORIES FOR ENHANCED LEADERSHIP IN FEDERAL AGENCIES

William Brantley, Mary Z. Ashlock, and Kerry McCaig

In this chapter, we explain how communication theories and leadership phenomena can help understand and improve leadership success in organizational studies. We link key communication theories to major leadership theories and show how they work in practice. We also introduce a dataset, the Federal Employee Viewpoint Survey (FEVS), that can be used for studying communication and leadership in real-world situations. We end with an example of using these theories to help leaders improve their leadership skills and impact in their organizations. Furthermore, we argue that the FEVS datasets, which measure effective leadership communication in U.S. federal agencies, have valuable lessons for all organizations. One of the authors (Dr. Brantley) formerly worked in the U.S. federal government from 2008 to 2023. During that time, he was a policy analyst at the U.S. Office of Personnel Management (OPM) and a leadership development and coaching manager at the U.S. Patent and Trademark Office. He has extensive experience in testing the practical aspects of communication and leadership theories using the FEVS data.

Prior research into government leaders and communication effectiveness

Various studies show that government leaders who inspire and motivate their employees have a positive impact on trust, job satisfaction, and organizational effectiveness in the public sector. For example, Trottier et al. (2008) and Asencio (2016) reveal that federal employees favor transformational leaders over transactional ones, as they are more satisfied and

DOI: 10.4324/9781003563662-10

committed to their work. They also stress that transformational leaders who have a clear vision and create an inclusive environment are key to building trust among federal employees.

Ethical leadership

Ethical leadership can boost job satisfaction in the federal government, along with transformational leadership. Moon and Jung (2018) showed that employees are happier when they see their leaders as ethical and diverse. Ethical leaders are fair, honest, and caring, which builds trust and raises job satisfaction. Asencio's research backs this up, linking ethical leadership to better morale and performance. These studies imply that being ethical and having diverse leaders can make federal workers more satisfied.

Information technology's role in innovation leading to better leadership

Information technology (IT) has been seen as a key factor for improving federal management. Former Vice President of the United States, Al Gore (1994), pointed out how IT can help create flatter, wider, and faster organizations. These allow more local decisions with accountability. Gore urged federal executives to use IT to improve communication and employee empowerment. This fits with the Clinton administration's plan to reinvent government by making a better federal workforce.

Moreover, research such as Fernandez and Moldogaziev's (2013) work on employee innovation motivation, and the case study on the U.S. Department of Veterans Affairs (VA) emphasize the value of cultivating an innovative culture. Fernandez and Moldogaziev identified that managerial support, autonomy, and recognition are crucial factors for innovation among frontline employees. The VA case study showed that transformational leadership can greatly improve job satisfaction by creating a supportive work environment where employees feel appreciated. These results highlight the necessity for federal agencies to establish environments that support experimentation and acknowledge employee contributions to foster innovation.

The necessity for investing in leadership development

Research on government leadership shows the need for developing leadership styles that create trust, promote innovation, and improve job satisfaction. These goals are achieved by transformational and ethical leadership behaviors, as evidenced by studies from Asencio (2016), Moon and Jung (2018), and Trottier et al. (2008). These findings imply that federal agencies should invest in leadership development programs that foster transformational and ethical leadership skills and adopt technological innovations to make a more efficient and effective government.

The value of the Federal Employee Viewpoint Survey (FEVS) for leadership communication analysis

The FEVS, conducted annually by the OPM, assesses leadership communication and workplace climate in federal agencies. It measures employees' views on their work environment, leadership, job satisfaction, and organizational culture. The survey includes over 80 questions on key workplace dynamics, offering a comprehensive evaluation of leadership communication quality in government agencies.

Several features make the FEVS a valuable resource for understanding leadership communication:

- *Comprehensive*: The survey reviews leadership engagement and communication with employees.
- *Large Sample*: Responses from thousands of federal employees provide diverse workplace data.
- *Anonymous*: Employees give feedback without fear, ensuring reliable data on leadership.
- *Longitudinal*: Annual surveys track changes in leadership and workplace satisfaction over time.

Measuring leadership and communication quality with FEVS and Best Places to Work rankings

Federal agencies can use FEVS data to improve leadership communication, boosting employee motivation and organizational outcomes. Additionally, agencies should consult the *Best Places to Work in the Federal Government* rankings by the Partnership for Public Service (PPS), which uses FEVS data to assess leadership and workplace culture.

Essential elements of the Best Places to Work rankings consist of:

- *Employee Engagement Index*: This metric is derived from FEVS responses concerning job satisfaction, workplace inclusion, and motivation.
- *Leadership Effectiveness*: Evaluates the ability of senior leaders to communicate, inspire, and engage their workforce effectively.
- *Work-Life Balance*: Assesses employees' perceptions regarding work-life balance and the level of support provided by supervisors.
- *Innovation and Recognition*: Identifies agencies that promote innovation and recognize employee contributions.

By analyzing both FEVS data and PPS rankings, federal agencies can create strategies based on evidence to enhance communication between leadership and employee satisfaction.

Analysis of FEVS: Validity, benefits, and risk management

Researchers often utilize FEVS data to analyze trends in organizational behavior and leadership communication due to its cost-effectiveness and efficiency. The FEVS is considered a valid source for secondary research because of its rigorous data collection methodology, which ensures accuracy, reliability, and representativeness.

Validity of secondary analysis of the FEVS

The FEVS is a reliable tool for evaluating workplace culture and leadership in federal agencies. Its accuracy and reliability are ensured by the U.S. Office of Personnel Management's (2020) strict data collection protocols. The FEVS excels in its wide coverage and large sample size, gathering responses from employees in various federal agencies. This broad participation ensures the data accurately reflects the federal workforce, providing valuable insights into employee experiences and perceptions.

Since its annual implementation in 2010, the FEVS has provided longitudinal data that enables researchers and agency leaders to track changes in employee sentiment and workplace culture over time (Perry et al., 2006). This trend analysis helps organizations identify patterns and measure the impact of leadership initiatives on employee engagement and job satisfaction. Also, the FEVS shows strong construct validity, aligning with models of employee engagement, job satisfaction, and organizational commitment (Fernandez & Moldogaziev, 2013). This supports the survey's credibility for analyzing workplace dynamics and guiding improvements in federal agencies.

Managing risks in secondary analysis

Secondary analysis provides numerous benefits but requires researchers to address data integrity and ethical compliance challenges.

- Contextual Understanding: Analysts need to understand the sociopolitical context of data collection to avoid misinterpretation (Heaton, 2004).
- Data Quality and Integrity: Ensure the dataset is complete, accurate, and consistent for valid conclusions (Smith, 2008).

- Ethical Considerations: Maintain confidentiality and anonymity to prevent privacy breaches when using FEVS data (Broom et al., 2009).
- Addressing Measurement Error: Correct survey biases and inaccuracies with statistical methods like reliability testing and sensitivity analysis (Carmines & Zeller, 1979).

The FEVS is a valuable tool for assessing leadership communication in federal agencies. It offers extensive, large-scale, and longitudinal data suitable for both primary and secondary analysis. When combined with the Best Places to Work rankings, the FEVS can help identify both leadership strengths and areas needing improvement. To ensure meaningful insights from secondary research, analysts should focus on maintaining contextual understanding, data integrity, and adherence to ethical standards. Following these practices allows agencies and researchers to use the FEVS to support evidence-based improvements in leadership and organizational effectiveness.

Analyzing leadership and communication theories in the FEVS

The FEVS is an excellent tool for measuring how well leaders and communicators do their jobs in federal agencies. By using different theories of leadership and communication, such as Barnlund's (2008), Sullivan's (1988), Bass's (1985), Graen and Uhl-Bien's (1995), and Ethical Leadership Theory (Brown et al., 2005), we can understand how they affect how employees feel and work. This analysis shows what is important in leadership communication and gives useful ways to use these theories to improve leadership in federal agencies and other places. The following sections demonstrate how to conduct the analysis for each theory.

Barnlund's Transactional Model of Communication

To examine how communication works using Barnlund's Transactional Model of Communication with the FEVS, pay attention to questions that cover different facets of communication, such as two-way exchange, feedback, clarity, context awareness, and ongoing involvement. Here are the related questions from the 2023 FEVS:

1 *Two-Way Communication and Feedback*:

  - Q20: "The people I work with cooperate to get the job done."
  - Q49: "My supervisor listens to what I have to say."
  - Q50: "I feel encouraged to come up with new and better ways of doing things."

2 *Clarity and Understanding*:

- Q10: "My work unit is able to recruit people with the right skills."
- Q11: "I know what is expected of me on the job."
- Q30: "Employees have a feeling of personal empowerment with respect to work processes."
- Q31: "Employees are recognized for providing high-quality products and services."

3 *Context Sensitivity*:

- Q32: "Creativity and innovation are rewarded."
- Q33: "Pay raises depend on how well employees perform their jobs."
- Q58: "Managers promote communication among different work units (for example, about projects, goals, needed resources)."

4 *Continuous Communication*:

- Q34: "Policies and programs promote diversity in the workplace (for example, recruiting minorities and women, training in awareness of diversity issues, mentoring)."
- Q56: "Managers communicate the goals and priorities of the organization."

5 *Emotional and Relational Communication*:

- Q40: "I recommend my organization as a good place to work."
- Q41: "I believe the results of this survey will be used to make my agency a better place to work."
- Q47: "Supervisors in my work unit support employee development."

Analysis framework

As a way of examining communication patterns, use these questions and think about the following structure:

1. *Simultaneity*: Evaluate how well employees feel their communication with supervisors and colleagues is reciprocal.
2. *Interdependence*: Assess the mutual influence in communication, looking at cooperation and the effectiveness of two-way feedback.
3. *Multi-Dimensionality*: Consider whether communication addresses not just task-related information but also emotional and relational aspects.
4. *Continuous Process*: Examine the consistency and ongoing nature of communication efforts within the organization.
5. *Contextual Influence*: Analyze how well communication is tailored to different contexts and situations, ensuring relevance and sensitivity.

Example analysis questions

- How frequently do employees feel their input is listened to and acted upon by their supervisors?
- Are employees clear about their roles and expectations, and do they feel empowered in their work processes?
- How effectively do managers communicate organizational goals and promote inter-unit communication?
- Do employees feel recognized and rewarded for their contributions, indicating effective feedback mechanisms?

By systematically analyzing these FEVS questions, you can gain a comprehensive understanding of the communication dynamics within your organization based on Barnlund's Transactional Model of Communication.

Sullivan's Motivating Language Theory (MLT)

Use Sullivan's Motivating Language Theory with the FEVS to examine motivating language. Look at questions that measure the three kinds of motivating language: direction-giving, empathetic, and meaning-making. Here are the FEVS questions for each category:

1. *Direction-Giving Language*:
    - Q11: "I know what is expected of me on the job."
    - Q30: "Employees have a feeling of personal empowerment with respect to work processes."
    - Q56: "Managers communicate the goals and priorities of the organization."
    - Q68: "How satisfied are you with the information you receive from management on what's going on in your organization?"
2. *Empathetic Language*:
    - Q47: "Supervisors in my work unit support employee development."
    - Q48: "My supervisor listens to what I have to say."
    - Q49: "My supervisor treats me with respect."
    - Q51: "I have trust and confidence in my supervisor."
    - Q52: "Overall, how good a job do you feel is being done by your immediate supervisor?"
3. *Meaning-Making Language*:
    - Q4: "My work gives me a feeling of personal accomplishment."
    - Q12: "I know how my work relates to the agency's goals and priorities."

- Q17: "I recommend my organization as a good place to work."
- Q36: "Considering everything, how satisfied are you with your job?"
- Q38: "Considering everything, how satisfied are you with your organization?"

Analysis framework

To analyze motivating language with these questions, use this framework:

1. *Direction-Giving Language*: Evaluate how clearly and effectively leaders provide instructions, feedback, and communicate organizational goals.
2. *Empathetic Language*: Assess the level of care, concern, and respect shown by leaders toward employees and how well they support their development.
3. *Meaning-Making Language*: Determine how effectively leaders connect employees' work to broader organizational goals, providing a sense of purpose and accomplishment.

Example analysis questions

- Do employees feel they receive clear and actionable instructions from their leaders?
- How well do employees feel supported and respected by their supervisors?
- Do employees understand how their work contributes to the overall goals and success of the organization?

These FEVS questions can help you assess how well leadership communication matches Sullivan's Motivating Language Theory and find ways to improve it to increase employee motivation and engagement.

Transformational Leadership Theory

The key elements of transformational leadership in Bass' Transformational Leadership Theory are idealized influence, inspirational motivation, intellectual stimulation, and individualized consideration. To measure these elements with the FEVS, use these questions for each one:

1. *Idealized Influence*:
   - Q58: "My organization's senior leaders maintain high standards of honesty and integrity."
   - Q62: "I have a high level of respect for my organization's senior leaders."
   - Q61: "I hold my agency's senior leaders in high regard."

2 *Inspirational Motivation*:

- Q56: "Managers communicate the goals and priorities of the organization."
- Q60: "Overall, how good a job do you feel is being done by the manager directly above your immediate supervisor?"
- Q66: "How satisfied are you with the policies and practices of your senior leaders?"

3 *Intellectual Stimulation*:

- Q3: "I feel encouraged to come up with new and better ways of doing things."
- Q32: "Creativity and innovation are rewarded."
- Q30: "Employees have a feeling of personal empowerment with respect to work processes."

4 *Individualized Consideration*:

- Q47: "Supervisors in my work unit support employee development."
- Q48: "My supervisor listens to what I have to say."
- Q49: "My supervisor treats me with respect."
- Q51: "I have trust and confidence in my supervisor."

Analysis framework

Use this framework to guide your analysis of transformational leadership with these questions:

1 *Idealized Influence*: Assess how well leaders are perceived as ethical role models who inspire respect and admiration.
2 *Inspirational Motivation*: Evaluate the effectiveness of leaders in communicating a vision that motivates and inspires employees.
3 *Intellectual Stimulation*: Determine how well leaders encourage innovative thinking and empower employees to contribute new ideas.
4 *Individualized Consideration*: Measure the extent to which leaders provide individualized support and consider employees' personal development needs.

Example analysis questions

- Do employees perceive their leaders as ethical and respectable role models?
- How effectively do leaders communicate organizational goals and inspire employees?

- Are employees encouraged to think creatively and contribute innovative ideas?
- How well do leaders support and develop their employees on an individual basis?

These FEVS questions help you understand how leadership practices match Bass' Transformational Leadership Theory and find ways to improve leadership quality and employee involvement.

Leader–Member Exchange (LMX) Theory

Using Graen and Uhl-Bien's Leader–Member Exchange (LMX) Theory to examine LMX with the FEVS, pay attention to questions that measure how well leaders and their employees relate to each other, in terms of trust, respect, support, and communication. Here are the FEVS questions for each important part of LMX:

1. *Quality of Relationship*:
   - Q47: "Supervisors in my work unit support employee development."
   - Q48: "My supervisor listens to what I have to say."
   - Q49: "My supervisor treats me with respect."
   - Q51: "I have trust and confidence in my supervisor."
   - Q52: "Overall, how good a job do you feel is being done by your immediate supervisor?"
2. *In-Group and Out-Group Dynamics*:
   - Q29: "Promotions in my work unit are based on merit."
   - Q44: "Policies and programs promote diversity in the workplace (for example, recruiting minorities and women, training in awareness of diversity issues, mentoring)."
   - Q45: "My supervisor is committed to a workforce representative of all segments of society."
3. *Role-Making Process*:
   - Q3: "I feel encouraged to come up with new and better ways of doing things."
   - Q6: "I know what is expected of me on the job."
   - Q11: "My talents are used well in the workplace."
   - Q17: "I recommend my organization as a good place to work."

Analysis framework

To apply these questions to LMX analysis, use the following structure:

1 *Quality of Relationship*: Evaluate the level of trust, support, and respect between supervisors and employees.
2 *In-Group and Out-Group Dynamics*: Assess the fairness and equity in treatment and opportunities among team members.
3 *Role-Making Process*: Determine how well leaders involve employees in defining their roles and fostering an environment that encourages participation and innovation.

Example analysis questions

- How do employees perceive the level of support and respect from their supervisors?
- Are there any perceived disparities in treatment and opportunities among team members?
- How involved do employees feel in discussions and decisions that affect their roles and responsibilities?

By carefully examining these FEVS questions, you can get a holistic view of the quality of LMXs in your organization based on Graen and Uhl-Bien's LMX Theory and find opportunities to improve leader–follower relationships and overall organizational effectiveness.

Ethical Leadership Theory

To apply Ethical Leadership Theory to examine ethical leadership with the FEVS, concentrate on questions that measure leaders' ethical conduct, honesty, responsibility, and how they create an ethical work culture. Here are the related questions from the FEVS for each main component of ethical leadership:

1 *Ethical Behavior and Integrity*:

   - Q58: "My organization's senior leaders maintain high standards of honesty and integrity."
   - Q62: "I have a high level of respect for my organization's senior leaders."
   - Q66: "How satisfied are you with the policies and practices of your senior leaders?"

2 *Accountability and Responsibility*:

- Q17: "I recommend my organization as a good place to work."
- Q36: "Considering everything, how satisfied are you with your job?"
- Q38: "Considering everything, how satisfied are you with your organization?"

3 *Fairness and Justice*:

- Q29: "Promotions in my work unit are based on merit."
- Q44: "Policies and programs promote diversity in the workplace (for example, recruiting minorities and women, training in awareness of diversity issues, mentoring)."
- Q45: "My supervisor is committed to a workforce representative of all segments of society."

4 *Empathy and Concern for Employees*:

- Q47: "Supervisors in my work unit support employee development."
- Q48: "My supervisor listens to what I have to say."
- Q49: "My supervisor treats me with respect."

Analysis framework

Use this framework to think about ethical leadership with these questions:

1 *Ethical Behavior and Integrity*: Evaluate how consistently leaders demonstrate ethical behavior and maintain high standards of honesty and integrity.
2 *Accountability and Responsibility*: Assess the extent to which leaders hold themselves and their team members accountable for ethical behavior and organizational practices.
3 *Fairness and Justice*: Determine how fairly and impartially leaders make decisions and implement policies.
4 *Empathy and Concern for Employees*: Measure the level of care and concern leaders show for the well-being and development of their employees.

Example analysis questions

- Do employees perceive their leaders as ethical and trustworthy?
- How well do leaders promote and enforce ethical standards within the organization?

- Are leaders seen as fair and impartial in their decision-making processes?
- How effectively do leaders show concern for employees' well-being and development?

These FEVS questions can help you understand how well leadership practices match Ethical Leadership Theory and find ways to improve ethical behavior and integrity in your organization by analyzing them systematically.

The value of using leadership and communication theories to analyze FEVS data

We can learn a lot about how well leaders and employees communicate in organizations by using various leadership and communication theories to analyze FEVS data. These theories help us improve leadership quality, employee engagement, and organizational culture. Leaders can use this knowledge to build trust, inspire innovation, promote ethics, and support employee development, which leads to organizational success and employee satisfaction. These theories also help leaders deal with the complex challenges of modern organizational environments.

Comparison of the theories to the Partnership for Public Service's Best Places to Work in the Federal Government

The authors compared each theory index to an index calculated from the FEVS data to the PPS Best Places to Work in the Federal Government rankings to test the usefulness of the theories above. The authors hypothesized that higher scores for each theory index would correspond with higher rankings for federal agencies in the PPS Best Places to Work. Table 7.1 shows the Best Places to Work scores and the theory index scores for the top five large and midsize agencies. The reader can see, except for two cases, that higher rankings match the higher averages of the index scores. The rankings are percentages from some FEVS questions. The index scores are from 1 to 5, with 5 where participants agree the most or approve of an action taken by the agency.

The purpose of this exercise is to show how the elements of each of the theories can be analyzed to offer advice to the agency leadership. For instance, if an agency wants to measure how effectively leaders connect with organizational members, it can estimate the "Quality of Relationship" element of the LMX Theory. Evaluating several elements can provide a guide to help agencies enhance leadership and communication.

TABLE 7.1 Comparison of the leadership and communication theories calculated using FEVS and the Partnership for Public Service's Best Places to Work in the Federal Government scores

Agency	*Barnlund's Transactional Model of Communication index*	*Sullivan's Motivating Language Theory index*	*Transformational Leadership Theory index*	*Leader–Member Exchange Theory index*	*Ethical Leadership Theory index*	*Average of the index scores*	*PPS Best Places to Work in the Federal Government (large agencies; n = 17) (%)*	*PPS Best Places to Work in the Federal Government (midsize agencies; n = 26) (%)*
General Services Administration	4.126	4.138	4.051	4.040	3.945	4.060		84.5
Federal Energy Regulatory Commission	4.056	4.145	4.055	4.019	3.979	4.051		82.6
Environmental Protection Agency	3.833	3.893	3.775	3.804	3.659	3.793		77.9
Department of Energy	3.956	4.016	3.870	3.915	3.788	3.909		77.0
Small Business Administration	3.882	3.922	3.815	3.829	3.698	3.829		76.9
Department of Health and Human Services	3.877	3.945	3.820	3.854	3.732	3.846	75.2	
Department of Commerce	3.712	3.847	3.640	3.734	3.558	3.699	72.1	
Department of Transportation	3.714	3.798	3.602	3.697	3.516	3.665	70.9	
Department of the Treasury	3.672	3.757	3.578	3.648	3.477	3.626	68.4	
Department of the Interior	3.681	3.775	3.591	3.700	3.514	3.652	68.3	

Improving leadership in U.S. federal government agencies by connecting communication and leadership theories

Combining communication and leadership theories can help improve leadership outcomes in U.S. federal government agencies. By applying the knowledge from both areas, leaders can create more sophisticated and successful methods for motivating employees, encouraging innovation, and supporting ethical conduct. This comprehensive approach considers the challenges of leading a big, varied organization like the federal government, resulting in enhanced organizational effectiveness and employee happiness.

Integrated frameworks

How transactional communication and transformational leadership are related

Theory Connection: Barnlund's Transactional Model shows how communication is a dynamic, mutual process, while Transformational Leadership Theory concentrates on empowering and influencing followers. These theories imply that successful transformational leaders communicate both ways, pay attention to, and use employee feedback.

Practice: Federal leaders can use frequent feedback cycles to modify their vision and strategies, making sure they match employee needs and organizational goals.

Motivating language and ethical leadership

Theory Connection: Sullivan's Motivating Language Theory explains how leaders can use language to guide, connect, and give meaning. Ethical Leadership Theory stresses the importance of honesty and fairness. By using these theories together, leaders can convey ethical expectations clearly while also encouraging and empowering their employees.

Practice: Leaders can schedule frequent meetings to review ethical principles and acknowledge employees who demonstrate these values, strengthening a culture of integrity and motivation.

Leader–Member Exchange (LMX) and transactional communication

Theory Connection: LMX Theory emphasizes the role of high-quality relationships between leaders and followers, which depend on effective communication as explained by the Transactional Model. High-quality exchanges include ongoing, multi-faceted communication that creates trust and respect.

Practice: Leaders can adopt open-door policies and frequent individual meetings to strengthen relationships, making sure that employees feel listened to and appreciated.

A hypothetical scenario demonstrating how the integrated framework of communication and leadership theories can improve organizations

The following hypothetical scenario demonstrates how to use a combination of communication and leadership theories to improve organizational communication to bring about better employee engagement and productivity.

Scenario

Jane, the agency's director, seeks a smooth transition to remote work and satisfied workers. She applies a hybrid approach of communication and leadership theories.

Step-by-step application of the integrated framework

Initial communication

Jane starts with a town hall meeting, following Barnlund's Transactional Model. She introduces the new policy (language that gives direction) and clarifies its significance (language that creates meaning), making sure she also invites questions and feedback from the audience (simultaneity and interdependence).

Feedback and adaptation

After the town hall, Jane arranges smaller team meetings to collect specific feedback, using LMX Theory. In these meetings, she hears individual issues and ideas, building trust and respect.

Ethical considerations

Jane emphasizes ethical leadership by ensuring the policy is implemented fairly, addressing any concerns of favoritism or inequality. She uses empathetic language to show her support for employees who may face challenges adapting to the new policy.

Ongoing communication

Throughout the implementation, Jane maintains open communication channels, regularly updating employees on progress and any adjustments based on their feedback. This continuous process reflects Barnlund's principle of communication as ongoing and contextual.

Recognition and motivation

Jane praises and rewards teams and individuals who embrace the new policy, using transformational leadership to motivate others. She showcases these achievements in newsletters and meetings, connecting their efforts to the agency's wider goals.

Outcome

By applying communication and leadership theories, Jane effectively puts the new telework policy into practice with strong employee involvement and low disturbance. Employees feel listened to, valued, and inspired, resulting in a more unified and efficient organizational culture.

Discussion

A solid base for enhancing leadership in federal government agencies can be created by combining communication and leadership theories. These theories help leaders to gain a more complex understanding of how to communicate well with their teams, creating a culture of openness, trust, and mutual respect. Leaders can use concepts from Barnlund's Transactional Model, Sullivan's Motivating Language Theory, and Bass' Transformational Leadership Theory to design communication strategies that not only share information effectively but also encourage and motivate their employees. This comprehensive approach ensures that communication is not just about the exchange of information but also about forming strong relationships and creating a positive work environment.

As a practical example: Dr. Brantley revamped the U.S. Patent and Trademark Office's Supervisor Certificate Program from a command-and-control approach to a coaching and mentoring servant leadership model, using Barnlund's Transactional Model and Sullivan's Motivating Language Theory. Ratings for the program improved, with many participants informally expressing increased satisfaction with the new leadership style.

How lessons learned from the FEVS analysis can benefit organizations outside of the U.S. federal government

The FEVS analysis reveals useful insights that can improve communication and leadership in non-governmental organizations, too. Here are the main takeaways and their applications:

Comprehensive feedback mechanisms

The FEVS asks about different parts of the workplace, giving a broad view of how employees see things. Organizations can do surveys like the FEVS to get employee opinions on leadership, communication, job satisfaction, and organizational culture. Frequent and anonymous surveys can help find out what needs to get better and what is good, creating a culture of ongoing feedback and improvement.

Importance of effective leadership communication

FEVS questions show how important it is for leaders to communicate well with employees for their engagement and satisfaction, such as listening to them and explaining goals clearly. Organizations should coach leaders to improve their communication skills, making sure they listen to employees well, give clear instructions, and communicate organizational goals well. Leadership development programs can include training on Barnlund's Communication Model and Sullivan's Language Theory to boost two-way communication and motivational language.

Building trust and confidence

Trust and confidence in supervisors are key themes in the FEVS questions. Leaders need to establish strong, trust-based relationships with employees. Organizations should encourage a culture of trust by supporting transparency, integrity, and accountability in leadership. Leaders can use Graen and Uhl-Bien's LMX Theory to develop high-quality, trust-based relationships with their team members, improving organizational performance overall.

Ethical leadership and organizational culture

FEVS questions on ethical standards and integrity underscore the importance of ethical leadership in creating a positive organizational culture. Organizations should emphasize ethical leadership by integrating Ethical

Leadership Theory into their leadership practices. Leaders should model ethical behavior, promote ethical standards, and ensure fairness and justice in all organizational processes. This can be reinforced through ethics training programs and regular discussions on ethical dilemmas and best practices.

Employee engagement and motivation

Employee engagement and motivation, which the FEVS tracks, are tied to leadership quality and communication methods. Organizations should aim to improve employee engagement and motivation by using Bass' Transformational Leadership Theory. Leaders can influence and energize employees by sharing a clear vision, promoting creativity, and giving personalized support and development. Frequent appreciation of employee efforts and successes can also increase morale and engagement.

Data-driven decision making

The FEVS offers long-term data that enables trend analysis and informed decision-making. Organizations can use a data-driven method for leadership and communication by frequently gathering and examining employee feedback. This can assist in spotting trends, tackling new issues, and making informed decisions to enhance organizational practices. Data analysis tools and technologies can be used to obtain deeper insights and design specific interventions.

Continuous improvement and adaptation

The FEVS shows how vital it is to keep assessing and improving leadership and organizational practices. Organizations should make continuous improvement a habit by updating their leadership and communication strategies based on employee feedback. This can include forming cross-functional teams to review feedback, plan actions, and track progress. Being flexible and responsive to employee needs and concerns can boost organizational resilience and adaptability.

Using the insights gained from the FEVS, organizations can improve their communication and leadership methods, resulting in better employee engagement, satisfaction, and organizational performance. Incorporating communication and leadership ideas into daily practices can build a more vibrant, ethical, and driven workplace, supporting overall success and reaching organizational objectives.

Conclusion

Leaders can communicate better to be more effective, ethical, and motivational, which can boost a more loyal and efficient workforce. Communication skills help in setting clear goals, giving feedback, and recognizing employee achievements. For example, ethical communication makes leaders act as mentors, promoting honesty, integrity, and fairness in the organization. Furthermore, motivational communication, based on Sullivan's Motivating Language Theory, helps leaders bond with their employees on a deeper level, creating a sense of purpose and belonging. By combining these elements, leaders can create a work environment where employees feel valued, understood, and motivated to do their best.

The following section presents a practical example of a leadership development program based on this research that federal agencies can implement.

An example of a leadership development program incorporating insights from FEVS data analysis through the application of leadership and communication theories

A 12-month leadership program for federal agencies combines communication and leadership theories with data from the FEVS. Targeted at mid-level and senior leaders, it aims to enhance leadership communication, trust, ethical leadership, transformational leadership, and data-driven improvement. Phase one develops self-awareness and communication skills using Barnlund's Transactional Model and Sullivan's Motivating Language Theory. Phase two emphasizes trust-building and ethics, applying LMX Theory and Ethical Leadership Theory for fairness and accountability.

The third phase emphasizes transformational leadership and an innovation culture, applying Bass' Transformational Leadership Theory to inspire, motivate, and empower employees. Leaders engage in innovation challenges, recognition programs, and psychological safety workshops to encourage creativity and collaboration. In the final phase, participants utilize FEVS data for decision-making, sustain leadership excellence, and implement long-term leadership strategies. They develop leadership improvement roadmaps, peer learning groups, and leadership scorecards to track progress and ensure sustainable change. The program aligns with Best Places to Work rankings, helping agencies measure leadership success and implement data-driven improvements.

This program aims to boost employee engagement, improve leadership communication, enhance ethical leadership, and encourage innovation in federal agencies. By incorporating coaching, mentorship, and AI-driven learning, agencies can develop a high-performance leadership culture that evolves with public service demands. Focusing on trust, communication, and transformational leadership, this initiative improves FEVS scores and ensures federal agencies become more adaptive, employee-centric, and mission-driven.

Benefits from combining leadership and communication theories

This approach is vital for managing large, varied organizations effectively. Federal agencies, with their different and diverse staff, require leaders who can cope with complex organizational issues and address diverse employee needs. The combination of communication and leadership theories equips leaders with the skills to handle these issues well. It enables them to identify and solve the unique problems of different groups in the organization, so that all staff feel valued and supported. This approach also allows leaders to adapt their communication strategies for different contexts and situations, making them more flexible and effective in their roles.

Communication and leadership theories work better together to benefit organizations and employees. Leaders who communicate well, ethically, and inspirationally enhance employee engagement, satisfaction, and commitment. Employees trust their leaders more, work harder, and remain faithful to the organization. This boosts organizational performance, leading to better service, efficiency, and culture. With this integrated approach, organizations can build powerful leadership teams that can guide their organizations to success and reach their goals.

Suggested further readings

Brown, B. (2018). *Dare to lead: Brave work. Tough conversations. Whole hearts.* Random House.

Garcia, H. F. (2012). *The power of communication: Skills to build trust, inspire loyalty, and lead effectively.* FT Press.

Goleman, D., Boyatzis, R., & McKee, A. (2013). *Primal leadership: Unleashing the power of emotional intelligence.* Harvard Business Review Press.

Kotter, J. P. (2012). *Leading change.* Harvard Business Review Press.

Lencioni, P. (2002). *The five dysfunctions of a team: A leadership fable.* Jossey-Bass.

Questions for further engagement

1 What methods can organizations employ to incorporate theories of communication and leadership to tackle the problems associated with employee engagement and satisfaction?

2 Could you identify ethical challenges that might confront senior leaders, and discuss how they could use the principles of Ethical Leadership Theory to resolve such situations?

3 How can federal agencies leverage insights from the FEVS to cultivate an environment that encourages innovation and creativity in their workforce?
4 What are the ways in which LMX Theory can be utilized to enhance the dynamics between supervisors and teams that work remotely or are spread across various locations?
5 What are the potential difficulties in merging theories of communication and leadership within a multifaceted and diverse organization, and what are the strategies to surmount these hurdles?
6 How can the FEVS or similar surveys help pinpoint opportunities to enhance leadership communication, and what steps can be implemented in response to the insights gained from survey results?
7 How can organizations foster an environment that encourages ongoing enhancement and innovation, drawing on leadership and communication theoretical insights?

References

Asencio, H. (2016). Leadership, trust, and job satisfaction in the public sector: A study of US federal employees. *International Review of Public Administration*, *21*(3), 250–267. https://doi.org/10.1080/12294659.2016.1237342

Barnlund, D. C. (2008). A transactional model of communication. In *Communication theory* (2nd ed., pp. 47–57). Transaction Publishers.

Bass, B. M. (1985). *Leadership and performance beyond expectations*. Free Press.

Broom, A., Cheshire, L., & Emmison, M. (2009). Qualitative researchers' understandings of their practice and the implications for data archiving and sharing. *Sociology*, *43*(6), 1163–1180. https://doi.org/10.1177/0038038509345704

Brown, M. E., Treviño, L. K., & Harrison, D. A. (2005). Ethical leadership: A social learning perspective for construct development and testing. *Organizational Behavior and Human Decision Processes*, *97*(2), 117–134. https://doi.org/10.1016/j.obhdp.2005.03.002

Carmines, E. G., & Zeller, R. A. (1979). *Reliability and validity assessment*. SAGE Publications. https://doi.org/10.4135/9781412985642

Fernandez, S., & Moldogaziev, T. (2013). Using employee empowerment to encourage innovative behavior in the public sector. *Journal of Public Administration Research and Theory*, *23*(1), 155–187. https://doi.org/10.1093/jopart/mus008

Gore, A. (1994). The new job of the federal executive. *Public Administration Review*, *54*(4), 317–321. https://doi.org/10.2307/977378

Graen, G., & Uhl-Bien, M. (1995). Relationship-based approach to leadership: Development of leader-member exchange (LMX) theory of leadership over 25 years: Applying a multi-level multi-domain perspective. *Leadership Quarterly*, *6*(2), 219–247. https://doi.org/10.1016/1048-9843(95)90036-5

Heaton, J. (2004). *Reworking qualitative data*. SAGE Publications. https://doi.org/10.4135/9781849209878

Moon, K., & Jung, C. (2018). Management representativeness, ethical leadership, and employee job satisfaction in the U.S. federal government. *Public Personnel Management*, *47*(3), 265–286.

Perry, J. L., Mesch, D., & Paarlberg, L. (2006). Motivating employees in a new governance era: The performance paradigm revisited. *Public Administration Review*, *66*(4), 505–514. https://doi.org/10.1111/j.1540-6210.2006.00611.x

Smith, E. (2008). *Using secondary data in educational and social research*. McGraw-Hill Education.

Sullivan, J. (1988). Three roles of language in motivation theory. *Academy of Management Review*, *13*(1), 104–115. https://doi.org/10.5465/amr.1988.4306798

Trottier, T., Van Wart, M., & Wang, X. (2008). Reinforcing the need for more sophistication in leadership studies in the government sector. *Public Administration Review*, *68*(6), 1172–1174.

U.S. Office of Personnel Management. (2020). Federal employee viewpoint survey: Technical report. Retrieved from https://www.opm.gov/fevs/reports/technical-reports/

8

ACCIDENTALLY VISIBLE AND UNMUTED

Communication Privacy Management and Adaptive Leadership in Evolving Workplaces

Jessica M. Welsh, Shannon K. McManimon, and Diane M. Monahan

A viral (half a million likes) June 2024 video by TikToker Laura (verified) highlighted concerns about remote work. In the video, a supervisor questions employees about their location, stating they must not work from home as their background is different. The supervisor says, "You need to have permission to work somewhere other than home when you're remote," and "I would like you to inform me of your location should you not be at home." The employee replies, "Is there a policy about remote work locations that I am not aware of?" and "Now, you're just sounding like my mother, toodaloo."

Employee attitudes toward remote work have evolved significantly since COVID-19. Before the COVID-19 pandemic, remote work was relatively uncommon, with only about 6% of employed Americans primarily working from home in 2019 (U.S. Bureau of Labor Statistics, 2020). The pandemic necessitated a swift transition to remote work where possible, leading to a substantial increase in its prevalence. By May 2020, approximately 35% of the workforce was working remotely (Brynjolfsson et al., 2020).

The pandemic significantly transformed the U.S. workplace, with a lasting impact on employee preferences and expectations. About 41% of those with remote-capable jobs work from home all or most of the time (Pew Research Center, 2023). Most remote workers prefer working from home due to reduced commute times, improved flexibility, the ability to focus on tasks without distractions, and better work–life balance (Pew Research Center, 2022, 2023). Research also suggests that remote work can

DOI: 10.4324/9781003563662-11

enhance productivity, with studies indicating that industries with a higher percentage of remote workers experienced productivity gains during the pandemic (U.S. Bureau of Labor Statistics, 2023).

Despite worker preferences, major companies are implementing return-to-office mandates, reversing the hybrid and remote work policies adopted during the pandemic. High-profile corporations such as Amazon, AT&T, JPMorgan, Goldman Sachs, Apple, and Google have announced requirements for employees to return to the office for varying numbers of days per week (Business Insider, 2025). This has led to tensions between employees and employers, as many workers have grown accustomed to remote work's flexibility and autonomy.

Workplaces continue to adjust to the changing terrain of remote work and its implications. For instance, many employees might be unaware that private chats on organizational video calls are available to their employer. Not being intimately familiar with technologies has left many workers accidentally visible and unmuted in ways that may be embarrassing and violate privacy. Navigating remote work policies, changing technologies, and the shifting privacy boundaries resulting from the blurring of home, work, and other settings is an ongoing adaptive challenge.

Communication Privacy Management (CPM) Theory provides a framework for understanding how individuals manage and disclose private information. It emphasizes the dialectical tension between the need for privacy and disclosure in personal and professional interactions. Unlike self-disclosure, which is about the self (Cozby, 1973), private information can be about the self or others (e.g., disclosing a family's private information; Petronio, 2002). Petronio (2002) asserted that individuals establish, adhere to, and renegotiate mutually agreed-upon privacy rules through coordination. Adaptive leadership, theorized by Heifetz (1994), explores adapting to changing circumstances. Leaders create holding environments to aid people in making change (Heifetz, 1994). How and when to disclose and withhold information is part of this process. Thus, to create holding environments to keep followers engaged and supported requires managing the boundaries around communication privacy. Turbulence may ensue as workers adopt new values and behaviors. Finding solutions that meet the needs of all organizational members is an adaptive challenge that requires discussion and change in the beliefs and values of organizations and individuals.

This chapter explores this negotiation. First, we describe the theories of adaptive leadership and CPM. Second, we link the two theories through analysis and a case study. Finally, we provide questions for further thought and additional readings.

Adaptive leadership

Adaptive leadership is an innovative, interactive, iterative practice that engages "people to make progress on the adaptive problems they face" (Heifetz, 1994, p. 187). This practical approach to leadership necessitates adapting to changing circumstances (often across multiple levels) while navigating conflict, managing stress, and clarifying and addressing (potentially competing) values, perspectives, and beliefs. Organizations with more fluid patterns of identities and relationships can adapt more effectively (DeRue, 2011). Those with formal or informal authority can practice adaptive leadership; those without formal authority often have more space for creativity and are closer to stakeholders, enabling capacity for adaptive leadership (Heifetz, 1994). In complex adaptive systems, leadership can—and should—emerge from anywhere and everywhere and is both individual and collective, residing in the processes and innovation.

Adaptive leadership requires a culture of learning and creativity made possible through emergent processes, new networks, and new information flows; these adaptations are necessary in a world of complex adaptive systems that are interconnected, interdependent, uncertain, and continuously changing (Heifetz, 1994; Northouse, 2022; Uhl-Bien & Arena, 2017). Change is responsive to (shared) local contexts and needs, often emerging as network interactions link people together to learn and creatively solve problems. In contrast to a proclivity to respond to chaos through re-entrenching order and hierarchy, "adaptive responses resist the pull to order and capitalize on the collective intelligence of groups and networks" (Uhl-Bien & Arena, 2017, p. 10). Adaptive leadership necessitates speaking the unspeakable (naming the elephants in the room), sharing responsibility, expecting independent judgment, developing leadership capacity broadly, and institutionalizing reflection and learning processes (Heifetz et al., 2009).

Technical and adaptive challenges

The adaptive leadership model distinguishes between two types of challenges leaders and organizations face: technical and adaptive (Heifetz, 1994). Technical challenges can be solved (although not necessarily quickly or easily) using current knowledge and practices. In contrast, adaptive challenges, which are often systemic, do not have ready solutions. Instead, solutions rely on emergence in adaptive spaces (physical, virtual, temporal, and/or communal) that must be built on trust, support, and psychological safety (Uhl-Bien & Arena, 2018). Change often entails loss and uncertainty as normative beliefs, values, or working methods are challenged. Addressing this loss (personal, identity, organizational, economic, communal, etc.) may necessitate adopting new values and behaviors; working from a stance of adaptive leadership means acting as a guide in the process.

Practicing adaptive leadership

Whether holding formal or informal authority (or both), those practicing adaptive leadership can use the following strategies to enable collective work toward change on adaptive challenges. Before action, a problem must be diagnosed: diagnosis is the "single most important skill and most undervalued capacity for exercising adaptive leadership" (Heifetz et al., 2009, p. 19). Diagnosis may involve multiple interpretations and subsequent interventions and adjustments.

Practicing adaptive leadership means brokering bridges between different perspectives as adaptive work utilizes "the collective intelligence of employees at all levels, who need to use one another as resources, often across boundaries, and learn their way to those solutions" (Heifetz & Laurie, 1997, p. 124). Effective adaptive work requires a sense of group cohesion. In this trusting and psychologically safe environment, people can test and iterate ideas (and where failure may be part of the process). Learning and risk-taking are central, as is recognizing and working with, not against, the tensions of diverse ideas (e.g., Uhl-Bien & Arena, 2018). Adaptive leaders (who work from varying positions of authority) create a trusting "holding environment" to help modulate stresses provoked by change. They work across boundaries, knowing the need for cooperation; they orchestrate rather than stifle conflict. Indeed, conflict tensions can be motivating, pressuring systems to change and generating a "search for novelty through exploration, experimentation, learning and growth" (Uhl-Bien, 2021, p. 146). Adaptive leadership also protects the voices of leadership who do not have authority (e.g., people who point out contradictions or ask difficult questions) (Heifetz, 1994) and reminds people of an organization's values.

Those with formal leadership positions can enable the emergence of adaptive responses through fostering information flows centered around "common need, purpose or perspectives" (Uhl-Bien & Arena, 2017, p. 11). They pace and sequence the flow of information and direct attention where necessary, framing issues; they recognize that decisions must be made at different speeds depending on urgency and the amount of change required.

Heifetz and colleagues (Heifetz, 1994; Heifetz & Laurie, 1997; Heifetz & Linsky, 2017; Heifetz et al., 2009) have outlined essential practices for adaptive leadership. Adaptive leadership requires processes of (a) getting on the balcony (seeing with a bird's-eye view), (b) regulating distress, (c) directing attention, and (d) mobilizing people to address the issue. Adaptive leadership involves asking difficult questions, encouraging people to reconsider their expectations, and examining conflicting ideas, values, and needs. Adaptive leaders think politically and listen intently, working with networks of people, including those who are opposed to change and those who are uncommitted. An adaptive leader "gives the work back to the people" so that solutions can emerge.

Adaptive work may provoke distress and thus resistance, avoidance, or denial as the equilibrium or the status quo is disturbed. Those exercising leadership may be blamed when people feel uncomfortable, uncertain, or distressed. As Heifetz (1994) wrote, adaptive leadership is hard work:

> Rather than fulfilling the expectation for answers, one provides questions; rather than protecting people from outside threat, one lets people feel the threat in order to stimulate adaption; instead of orienting people to their current roles, one disorients people so that new role relationships develop; rather than quelling conflict, one generates it; instead of maintaining norms, one challenges them.
>
> *(p. 126)*

Because of the distress associated with addressing adaptive challenges, those exercising adaptive leadership may face marginalization, attack, or attempts to divert attention from the issue (Heifetz & Linsky, 2017). Thus, adaptive leaders must be able "to tolerate uncertainty, frustration, and pain" (Heifetz & Laurie, 1997, p. 128).

Communication Privacy Management Theory

CPM Theory provides a framework for understanding how individuals manage private information: how, where, and why people choose to disclose private information (Petronio, 1991, 2002). It emphasizes the dialectical tension between the need for privacy and the need for disclosure in personal and professional interactions. Disclosing private information carries risk to the owner of information and to the discloser of the information; the latter may or may not be the primary owner of the information (Petronio, 2002). The difference between CPM and other communication theories on disclosure is that the communicative act of disclosing can be done by the owner of the information or a variety of co-owners.

CPM was originally developed as an interpersonal theory for face-to-face communication; however, as communication technology has advanced, CPM has been applied to online communication. Because of the unique nature of online settings, private communication is managed differently based on the context (Child et al., 2012). CPM has three main components: privacy ownership, control, and turbulence (Petronio, 2002). Each raises specific concerns.

Privacy ownership

When interacting with others, we disclose private information. Revealing personal information is a self-disclosure in which we own the information (Petronio, 2002). However, when others are aware of private information, they are now co-owners of the private information.

Private information is coordinated by metaphorical *privacy boundaries* (Petronio, 2002). Depending on the information, privacy boundaries are maintained individually and collectively. Boundaries continuously evolve as information is revealed or concealed from individuals or collectives. Petronio (2002) theorized that boundaries change throughout an individual's lifespan: when we are young, we are dependent on others; as we mature, we own more private information and revert to depending on others, which decreases the private information we hold.

In online contexts, revealing private information creates co-ownership with those networked to you (Frampton & Child, 2013). For instance, Frampton and Child (2013) pointed out that the initial use of Facebook was to connect with friends and family; however, co-workers connecting raised the question of potential ramifications of disclosing private information on the social media site with employers.

Privacy control

When revealing private information, we want to maintain control over how the information is revealed to others. We assume the right for personal private information to be shared at our discretion; however, in organizations, employers have the right to private employee information if it impacts their job performance. Additionally, U.S. citizens hold a right to a reasonable expectation of privacy related to personal property that one owns and protects against unlawful search and seizure tactics by government entities (U.S. Constitution Fourth Amendment). With collectively owned information, co-owners share responsibility for managing who has access to the information (Petronio, 2002).

In online settings, control of who has access to private information depends on the context. For social media, the owner of a social media page can set boundaries for access to their online posts through privacy settings (Frampton & Child, 2013). In the workplace, online information is owned by the organization for which an employee works (Petronio, 2002).

The boundaries between private and public are blurred within the online sphere in an organizational office (Petronio, 2002).

Privacy turbulence

Privacy turbulence occurs when misunderstandings or a lack of coordination between privacy rules and boundaries cause privacy management to fail. Disclosing potentially private information in public spaces, oversharing of private information, or accidentally disclosing third-party information are all examples of privacy turbulence (Petronio, 2002). Petronio (2002) identifies six types of boundary turbulence: "(a) intentional rule violations, (b) boundary rule mistakes, (c) fuzzy boundaries, (d) dissimilar boundary orientation, (e) boundary definition predicaments, and (f) privacy dilemmas" (p. 177). Some of these are particularly relevant to the evolving landscape of remote work.

Boundary rule breakdowns occur when constructed privacy rules are violated unintentionally through judgment lapses or inattention (Petronio, 2002). Many times, boundary rule mistakes are considered miscommunication. For example, in an online Zoom call, a co-worker asks another participant how their job search is going without realizing that other members are unaware that the individual is looking for new employment. The lapse in judgment by the co-owner of the information may create tension about the privacy boundary.

Fuzzy boundaries occur when ownership of information is unclear (Petronio, 2002). When information is collectively owned, individuals may differ in how they reveal information and to whom, creating ambiguity about who knows the potentially private information. One person may deem the information private, whereas another in the collective may view it as public information. The result is potential deception in concealing information from one party or another.

Dissimilar boundary orientation can occur when individuals differ in how they treat boundary rules due to socialization (Petronio, 2002). Culture and socialization have direct impacts on boundary orientation. How the culture chooses to disclose information in organizational settings impacts the boundary orientation. Everyone within the organization impacts how boundary rules are constructed.

Privacy dilemmas are complex because they exemplify the multiple privacy boundaries that must be regulated (Petronio, 2002). "Boundaries become turbulent when individuals are put into binds where the solutions are problematic" (Petronio, 2002, p. 200). In organizations, individuals may have to balance multiple relationships and privacy boundaries when choosing what to disclose and withhold.

In a hypothetical scenario, Danae was hired for a job, and their co-worker friended them on Facebook.[1] Danae accepted, allowing the co-worker to see that Danae had shared their sexual orientation. During small talk before their next meeting, the co-worker (who was now a co-owner of Danae's information due to friending on social media) outed them by bringing it up in front of many team members disclosed in the workplace; however, Danae expected that the information shared on their social media would not be shared within the workplace created turbulence through a boundary rule breakdown This example highlights the tenets of CPM: privacy ownership, control, and turbulence in the workplace and online.

Linking adaptive leadership and CPM theories

Of course, concern over privacy and policies of online workplace communication had been the topic of lawsuits, academic studies, and conversation before the COVID-19 pandemic (Indiparambil, 2019; Katsabian, 2019; Rogers, 2000). Yet the pandemic drastically altered the landscape of office work, prompting a widespread shift to remote work during which organizations had to restructure the idea of work and faced dilemmas about privacy. As workers and organizations continue to navigate changes wrought by remote work and technological innovations, the losses they face include privacy, control, autonomy, and previous ways of working. These changes challenge individual and collective beliefs and values. Leaders must be able to delineate between adaptive and technical challenges pertaining to conflicts surrounding privacy management.

Additionally, in organizational settings, employee–employer relationships impact the limits of privacy within the workplace. Petronio (2002) theorized that individuals have a set of rules that govern how they share private information and boundaries that vary across contexts and people. Employees are expected to share private information with their employer, and employers have the right to monitor employees' online workplace communication (Chory et al., 2016). Employers' level of monitoring of online workplace communication impacts employee trust and sense of justice within an organization (Chory et al., 2016).

In the remote work landscape, complications arise around privacy management and leadership approaches to remote work policies. A 2024 *Harvard Business Review* article reviewed leaders' struggles to craft policy that meets the competing needs of wanting employees back in the office to build a sense of community and employees' requests for flexibility. Some organizations that have kept remote work have resorted to using software to monitor employees who work from different locations. Corporations' "big brothering" over employees creates privacy turbulence within an organization, leading to renegotiation of boundary rules. Adaptive leadership practices can help. Heifetz (1994) encouraged leaders to "get on the balcony" and view the challenge from a broader perspective to understand where there may be technical challenges they can address, such as, in this context, clarifying language surrounding fuzzy boundaries or where the challenges are adaptive. They need to encourage space for engaging in productive conflict to surface new ideas on addressing the evolving work environment in the era of remote work.

In the evolving workplace, CPM and the need for adaptive leadership in practice is wide-ranging, including (a) information ownership and disclosure, (b) privacy boundaries in digital spaces (as more traditional boundaries are blurred), (c) control and co-ownership of information with employers, (d) development of privacy rules, (e) boundary coordination, and (f) managing boundary turbulence. Examples of privacy violations include (but are not limited to) involuntary background exposure; unauthorized recording of meetings or sharing of those recordings; surveillance and monitoring software (e.g., geo-location tracking and attention-tracking software); forced participation in video calls (e.g., requiring cameras to be on); and a lack of data security measures.

Turbulence in CPM comes from a lack of clear solutions and violating the constructed privacy boundary rules (Petronio, 2002). The turbulence felt with the violation of privacy boundary rules requires leaders to use adaptive leadership practices such as (a) getting on the balcony, (b) regulating distress, (c) directing attention, and (d) mobilizing people to address the issue (Heifetz, 1994; Heifetz & Laurie, 1997). For instance, employees often believe they own their personal information and have the right to control its disclosure during remote work and video conferencing. To respect this, organizations must seek feedback on online practices and consent before sharing or recording private information. Policies or practices around tools such as virtual backgrounds and how recordings are shared or utilized must be developed, updated, and communicated with employee participation. Organizations often address these online concerns through technical solutions; however, these challenges are adaptive, as they involve changing norms and values and are highly emotional for many people. Leaders working from an adaptive leadership perspective must consider multiple perspectives, carefully balancing a need for security with respect for employee privacy, ensuring that monitoring tools are appropriately configured and transparent.

Addressing these concerns requires protecting voices from below by listening and creating a holding environment that allows creative solutions to emerge, potentially from unexpected places and networks. Through listening, leaders will have to manage the boundary turbulence of communication privacy and navigate conflicts that arise from remote working. Leaders must "get on the balcony" to understand policy implications for all involved. Clear communication is crucial to maintaining trust. Continuous feedback and open dialogue with employees about privacy concerns and potential solutions can be used to support and adjust boundaries as needed. Ongoing education, particularly with IT staff and employees on data privacy and security practices, must be part of these processes so that all can co-construct and clearly understand boundaries. Organizations can foster a more secure and respectful remote working environment by working with employees on developing remote work policies that address privacy concerns.

Case study: Remote work and video calls

TechInnovate Inc. is a hypothetical California-based company that merged nine months ago with three other companies worldwide. Now, most of its 500 employees work remotely worldwide. Recently, TechInnovate announced that team leaders must begin a mandatory, one-on-one daily video conference check-in with each team member to monitor employee productivity and maintain team cohesion. The HR policy required employees to have cameras on during these meetings with their team leader and record meetings in case headquarters wanted to see them.

Lara manages a team of ten employees, spread across three continents and time zones, in the sales division. She had been working over the previous seven months to build trust among her new team, create a holding environment where they could innovate and learn together, and understand their ways of working and local cultural norms. She was flexible and accommodating to the needs of her team members. She understood that the merger and their new team structure created a lot of distress. Lara held candid conversations with each team member, asking them to share their experiences and opinions about the new structure and merger. She assured her team members that she would hold the information in confidence. It was important that Lara demonstrated her trustworthiness to the latest team and wanted to help them adapt to the changes. She also knew that the tools and resources available to her in California might not be accessible to all her team members. She had learned, for instance, that one team member lived in a remote area in Norway, and using video frequently rendered his system unstable. Another, sensing the environment of trust, confided in Lara that because of time zone differences, she often took calls outside her home to avoid waking family members.

When Lara saw the new mandatory daily video check-in policy, she immediately sent calendar invites to team members for the following week.

She emailed her team about the new policy. The new policy's camera requirement directly challenged her leadership practice; however, as it was stressed as important for morale, she was inclined to enforce it. Human Resources' email about the policy change stated that employees see each other face-to-face when working onsite, so it is not unreasonable to see employees during check-in.

When team member Fatima's camera was off during their next call, Lara requested that she turn it on. Fatima responded, "I'm uncomfortable with this, and don't understand the new policy requirement." Lara apologized for the abrupt change but again asked Fatima to turn on her camera. Fatima did so, and Lara saw Fatima's two young children playing in the background. Lara could see a pile of bills on the dining room table where Fatima was working. In a follow-up conversation, Lara told Fatima that even though she was remote, she should have childcare. Fatima profusely apologized, saying that her babysitter fell ill, and she could not make other arrangements on short notice. Fatima pleaded, "Please do not fire me; this was unfortunate." Lara could see that Fatima was embarrassed by her messy home.

Right after this check-in, another team member, Kasper, messaged her, sharing in confidence that this new daily requirement would conflict with his familial commitment to take his mother-in-law to her dialysis appointments, and asked if his call could be rescheduled for a time in the morning to keep his afternoons to do work from the dialysis center. Lara had trouble finding a new time with her full meeting schedule as she tried to accommodate each team member on top of her own scheduled meetings. Additionally, Lara was not aware of any policies on restrictions on where team members worked remotely.

During Lara's next one-on-one video call with Fatima, she noticed a change in their interaction. Fatima answered her check-in questions briefly and spoke only of her productivity. Lara was happy to hear that Fatima was achieving company goals, but ended the call feeling as though her relationship with Fatima had changed. When Lara scheduled Kasper for their video call, Lara asked if he was at his work computer. He disclosed that, since he was at the dialysis center with his mother-in-law and it was after working hours, he had downloaded the video software and logged in through his personal device. Lara wondered what the privacy boundaries were for logging in through a personal device. Each team member's unique situation weighed on Lara's mind.

The next week, Lara was conflicted as she videoed into a management meeting with the 30 other team leaders. Before the call, she had met with her full team and listened to their concerns. When the vice president (VP) started the call, another manager immediately brought up his team's privacy concerns regarding the new check-in policy. The VP said the policy was created to increase morale and boost team productivity and asked for examples of problems. Lara thought carefully about whether to raise her team members' concerns as she was now a co-owner of this information; instead, she asked who had been consulted in creating the new policy. The VP was quiet but then said, "I do not think we consulted anyone as it was a business decision." Lara suggested that various employees from various levels be brought together to discuss and potentially revise the policy. She envisioned bringing together members of her sales team and employees from technology support, human resources, and information management to create a new information flow and build on their differing perspectives. She knew she would have to foster psychological safety and deliberately surface the tensions between their perspectives, focusing on their shared needs in a complex and changing situation. Importantly, they would need to resist the need to jump to a technical solution; the needs of the organization and its workers were more complex than could be fixed through a few statements in a handbook policy. The VP said, "Great idea! Let me know what you find out!"

TechInnovate Inc.'s experience highlights the importance of balancing productivity and privacy in remote work settings. By proactively addressing privacy concerns, companies can ensure a positive and secure remote working environment for their employees. This case underscores the need for clear policies, employee training, communication, and robust technical measures to protect employee privacy in remote work and video conferencing.

Questions on case study

1. What privacy boundaries were or might be violated in this scenario?
2. If you were Lara, how would you handle the boundary violation of seeing Fatima's children and home in the background? What is the impact of violating the privacy boundary of a home environment by exposing it in a video call?
3. What adaptive leadership practices might help TechInnovate establish, adhere to, and renegotiate mutually agreed-upon privacy rules that can be flexible for a complex work environment?
4. In revising policy, what should be transparent about information ownership and disclosure, particularly regarding video calls?
5. In the case study, what appear to be technical challenges? What appear to be adaptive challenges?
6. In what ways did leaders in different positions at TechInnovate practice adaptive leadership or not?
7. In what ways might Lara (and others) motivate employees to innovate and respond adaptively to their new organization?

8 If you were the VP, how might you create a holding environment to navigate a policy change? What losses and distress might employees be facing? What beliefs and values may need to change?
9 What creative ways might maintain team cohesion and ensure that TechInnovate's goals are being met?

Conclusion

Today's computer-mediated workplace communication requires adaptive leadership in addressing privacy ownership, privacy control, and boundary turbulence about remote work communications' when, where, and how. As with the Great Resignation, employers will need to adapt remote work policies to renegotiate privacy boundaries by protecting employees' voices, listening to their needs for flexibility, and helping them regulate distress and tolerate uncertainty. Adaptive leadership practices help workplaces identify evolving privacy challenges accompanying remote work and technological use by providing an environment of trust where the work of navigating these challenges is returned to the people. Utilizing adaptive leadership practices—fostering creativity, embracing change, naming elephants in the room, listening to multiple perspectives, sharing responsibility, encouraging the exercise of independent judgment, and promoting leadership capacity and learning—to address privacy concerns with remote work would render irrelevant videos like the one that opened this chapter.

CPM and adaptive leadership provide a valuable lens for navigating privacy concerns in remote work. Evolving technology will introduce new ways for workers to be "accidentally visible and unmuted." By recognizing the importance of information ownership, flexible privacy boundaries, and the need for coordinated privacy rules, organizations can better manage the challenges of protecting employee privacy in a digital work environment.

Acknowledgment: We thank the theorists who helped us develop this chapter. We particularly appreciate Dr. Sandra Petronio (1949–2024) and her lifelong work on the development of CPM Theory.

Suggested further readings

Grant, H., Carlier, G., & Giampietro, F. (2024). Using data to design your hybrid work policies. *Harvard Business Review*. https://hbr.org/2024/05/using-data-to-design-your-hybrid-work-policies
Heifetz, R. A. (1994). *Leadership without easy answers*. Harvard University Press. https://doi.org/10.2307/j.ctv1pncrt0
Petronio, S. (1991). Communication boundary management: A theoretical model of managing disclosure of private information between married couples.

Communication Theory, *1*(4), 311–335. https://doi.org/10.1111/j.1468-2885.1991.tb00023.x
Petronio, S. (2002). *Boundaries of privacy: Dialectics of disclosure*. SUNY Press.
Ramalingham, B., Nabarro, D., Oqubay, A., Carnall, D.R., & Wild, L. (2020, September 11). 5 principles to guide adaptive leadership. https://hbr.org/2024/05/using-data-to-design-your-hybrid-work-policies
Smith, S. A., & Brunner, S. R. (2017). To reveal or conceal: Using communication privacy management theory to understand disclosures in the workplace. *Management Communication Quarterly*, *31*(3), 429–446. https://doi.org/10.1177/0893318917692896
Uhl-Bien, M. (2021). Complexity leadership and followership: Changed leadership in a changed world. *Journal of Change Management*, *21*(2), 144–162. https://doi.org/10.1080/14697017.2021.1917490
Watkins Allen, M., Coopman, S. J., Hart, J. L., & Walker, K. L. (2007). Workplace surveillance and managing privacy boundaries. *Management Communication Quarterly*, *21*(2), 172–200. https://doi.org/10.1177/0893318907306033

Questions for further engagement

1 What are the social and ethical implications of workplace communication monitoring?
2 How will the rise in AI-assisted technology impact communication privacy and create adaptive challenges?
3 How might understanding the changes prompted by AI and remote working as adaptive challenges enable workplaces to more effectively address them?
4 What losses do people and organizations face as they navigate evolving technologies and working landscapes?
5 Unlike self-disclosure, which is about the self, private information can be about the self or others. How is private information regulated differently than self-disclosure in the workplace? How does technology, such as video conferencing, increase the complexity of maintaining control of private information?

Note

1 A hypothetical example is used throughout this section of the chapter to demonstrate CPM in action within the context of mediated communication.

References

Brynjolfsson, E., Horton, J. J., Ozimek, A., Rock, D., Sharma, G., & TuYe, H.-Y. (2020). *COVID-19 and remote work: An early look at US data*. National Bureau of Economic Research. https://doi.org/10.3386/w27344
Business Insider. (2025). *The list of major companies requiring employees to return to the office, from JPMorgan to Amazon*. https://www.businessinsider.com/companies-requiring-return-to-office-rto-mandate

Child, J. T., Haridakis, P. M., & Petronio, S. (2012). Blogging privacy rule orientations, privacy management, and content deletion practices: The variability of online privacy management activity at different stages of social media use. *Computers in Human Behavior*, *28*, 1859–1872.

Chory, R. M., Vela, L. E., & Avtgis, T. A. (2016). Organizational surveillance of computer-mediated workplace communication: Employee privacy concerns and responses. *Employee Responsibility and Rights Journal*, *28*, 23–43. https://doi.org/10.1007/s10672-015-9267-4

Cozby, P. C. (1973). Self-disclosure: A literature review. *Psychological Bulletin*, *79*, 73–91. https://doi.org/10.1037/h0033950

DeRue, D. S. (2011). Adaptive leadership theory: Leading and following as a complex adaptive process. *Research in Organizational Behavior*, *31*, 125–150. https://doi.org/10.1016/j.riob.2011.09.007

Frampton, B. D., & Child, J. T. (2013). Friend or not to friend: Coworker Facebook friend request as an application of communication privacy management theory. *Computers in Human Behavior*, *29*, 2257–2264. http://dx.doi.org/10.1016/j.chb.2013.05.006

Heifetz, R. A. (1994). *Leadership without easy answers*. Harvard University Press. https://doi.org/10.2307/j.ctv1pncrt0

Heifetz, R. A., Grashow, A., & Linksy, M. (2009). *The practice of adaptive leadership: Tools and tactics for changing your organization and the world*. Harvard Business Press.

Heifetz, R. A., & Laurie, D. L. (1997). The work of leadership. *Harvard Business Review*, *75*, 124–134.

Heiftez, R., & Linsky, M. (2017). *Leadership on the line: Staying alive through the dangers of change*. Harvard Business Review Press.

Indiparambil, J. J. (2019). Privacy and beyond: Socio-ethical concerns of "on-the-job" surveillance. *Asian Journal of Business Ethics*, *8*(1), 73–105. https://doi.org/10.1007/s13520-019-00089-0

Katsabian, T. (2019). Employees' privacy in the internet age. *Berkeley Journal of Employment and Labor Law*, *40*(2), 203–255. https://www.jstor.org/stable/26795244

Northouse, P. G. (2022). *Leadership: Theory & practice* (9th ed.). SAGE Publications.

Petronio, S. (1991). Communication boundary management: A theoretical model of managing disclosure of private information between married couples. *Communication Theory*, *1*(4), 311–335. https://doi.org/10.1111/j.1468-2885.1991.tb00023.x

Petronio, S. S. (2002). *Boundaries of privacy: Dialectics of disclosure*. State University of New York Press.

Pew Research Center. (2022, February 16). *COVID-19 pandemic continues to reshape work in America*. https://www.pewresearch.org/social-trends/2022/02/16/covid-19-pandemic-continues-to-reshape-work-in-america/

Pew Research Center. (2023, March 30). *About a third of U.S. workers who can work from home do so all the time*. https://www.pewresearch.org/short-reads/2023/03/30/about-a-third-of-us-workers-who-can-work-from-home-do-so-all-the-time/

Rogers, A. (2000). You got mail but your employer does too: Electronic communication and privacy in the 21st century workplace. *Journal of Technology Law & Privacy*, *5*(1), 3.

Uhl-Bien, M. (2021). Complexity leadership and followership: Changed leadership in a changed world. *Journal of Change Management*, *21*(2), 144–162. https://doi.org/10.1080/14697017.2021.1917490

Uhl-Bien, M., & Arena, M. (2017). Complexity leadership: Enabling people and organizations for adaptability. *Organizational Dynamics*, *46*, 9–20. http://dx.doi.org/10.1016/j.orgdyn.2016.12.001

Uhl-Bien, M., & Arena, M. (2018). Leadership for organizational adaptability: A theoretical synthesis and integrative framework. *The Leadership Quarterly*, *29*, 89–104. https://doi.org/10.1016/j.leaqua.2017.12.009

U.S. Bureau of Labor Statistics. (2020). American Time Use Survey—2019 Results. https://www.bls.gov/news.release/archives/atus_06252020.htm

U.S. Bureau of Labor Statistics. (2023). The rise in remote work since the pandemic and its impact on productivity. https://www.bls.gov/opub/btn/volume-13/remote-work-productivity.htm

9

RELATIONAL STYLES AND SOCIAL COGNITION IN LEADERSHIP COMMUNICATION

Balancing Warmth and Competence

Christine E. Crouse-Dick, Amanda Friesen, and Jamie Hong Chow

Relational approaches have become increasingly prevalent in leadership studies (Fairhurst & Uhl-Bien, 2012; Men, 2014; Uhl-Bien, 2006). These perspectives conceptualize leadership as a communicative process grounded in relationships and interactions between leaders and followers, rather than isolated traits or behaviors (Gittell, 2016). Scholars have investigated how high-quality leader–follower relationships, marked by mutual trust and respect, contribute to effective leadership and positive outcomes like employee satisfaction and performance (Drescher et al., 2014; Men & Stacks, 2013). However, less attention has focused on tensions leaders face in balancing communication styles, which can be particularly challenging for leaders from historically excluded groups.

Through an interdisciplinary integration of communication, leadership, and psychological theories of interpersonal relationships, we offer a new approach to understanding the perceived efficacy of leader communication styles. Using the Stereotype Content Model (SCM) from social psychology (Fiske et al., 2007), we examine how tensions between warmth and competence emerge within leadership contexts and scenarios.

This chapter unfolds in three sections. First, we provide an overview of relational approaches to leadership and their contribution to contemporary leadership studies. Second, we examine intersections of communication and relational leadership. Finally, we introduce social cognition frameworks, presenting our novel application of the SCM to relational leadership communication and explaining how this integration advances understanding of leadership effectiveness. Throughout, we note how leaders must balance competing demands for warmth and competence in their

DOI: 10.4324/9781003563662-12

communication. We especially consider challenges faced by leaders from historically excluded groups. By bridging diverse theoretical perspectives, we offer scholars and practitioners new insights into the complex dynamics of relational leadership communication.

Relational approaches to leadership

Relational approaches to leadership challenge paternalistic, ego-centric assumptions inherent in "heroic leader" models. Relational theories conceptualize leadership not as power possessed by those in formal positions, but as a multi-directional phenomenon emerging through dynamic exchanges between leaders and followers working toward mutual and organizational goals.

Scholarship examining relational approaches largely aligns with either an entity perspective (focusing on individual traits, behaviors, and actions within group processes) or a socio-constructionist perspective (viewing leadership as a process that is co-constructed through social relationships and emergent practices). We suggest that understanding social cognition – how individuals perceive others' motivations and goals – may be important in this co-creative leadership model.

While entity and constructionist perspectives highlight different aspects of how leadership is understood, experienced, and enacted, Uhl-Bien and Ospina (2012) assert these approaches are not mutually exclusive; together they offer a "multi-paradigmatic" approach that reveals the constitutive power of relationships in shaping leadership processes (p. xv). Integrating these perspectives creates a nuanced framework for understanding how leadership communication transcends traditional boundaries of individual traits and relational processes. Collectively, relational approaches characterize leadership as follows:

1. *Process-oriented and socially constructed.* Leadership unfolds through ongoing interactions and relationships that emerge through language, shared experiences, and collective meaning-making (Uhl-Bien, 2006, p. 655).
2. *Co-created and distributed.* Leadership involves leaders and followers mutually shaping each other through conversations, developing an intersubjective sense of reality, identity, and purpose, while collectively responding to organizational demands (Cunliffe & Eriksen, 2011, p. 1431).
3. *Contextual.* Leadership manifests based on specific situations, relationships, and cultural expectations, embedded within social networks and organizational structures (Uhl-Bien, 2006, p. 662).

4 *Empathy-driven.* Leadership cultivates high-quality interpersonal connections through emotional intelligence, mutual understanding, and trust, achieved by actively comprehending and addressing others' needs and perspectives (Cropanzano et al., 2017; Cunliffe & Eriksen, 2011; Jian, 2022; Sadri et al., 2011).
5 *Ethical.* Leadership upholds mutual benefit, voice, dignity, and social responsibility for all stakeholders, drawing upon frameworks with an ethic of care and integrity (Cunliffe & Eriksen, 2011, p. 1438; Jian, 2022).

The "relational turn" marks a significant shift from "Great Man" theories, guiding leadership concepts away from top-down approaches toward reciprocal-influence models. This pivot emphasizes greater collaboration and flattened hierarchies, giving rise to numerous influential relational theories. Eight stand out for their focus on interpersonal and emotional dimensions of effective leadership, with the first four primarily aligning with entity perspectives and the remaining four reflecting social constructionist views.

Entity approaches

Leader–Member Exchange (LMX) theory (Graen & Uhl-Bien, 1995) examines relational quality between leaders and followers and asserts that leaders develop differentiated relationships with subordinates, ranging from high-quality (in-group) to low-quality (out-group).

Authentic Leadership (Walumbwa et al., 2008) focuses on leader genuineness and ethical behavior, emphasizing self-awareness, relational transparency, feedback responsiveness, and internalized moral perspective to yield greater trust and motivation in subordinates.

Servant Leadership (Sendjaya & Sarros, 2002) prioritizes the leader's altruistic role in serving others, emphasizing strong relationships, ethical behavior, active empathy, and investment in followers' growth and well-being.

Transformational Leadership (Bass & Riggio, 2006) theorizes that leaders can inspire followers to achieve higher performance through four behaviors (inspirational motivation, idealized influence, intellectual stimulation, and individualized consideration).

Social constructionist approaches

The ***Relational Leadership Model*** (Komives et al., 2013) conceives of leadership as a relational process emphasizing inclusion, empowerment, purposefulness, and ethical behavior for positive change.

The ***Relational Constructionist Approach*** (Hosking, 2011) views leadership as meaning-making through social interactions, recognizing multiple realities and emphasizing ongoing processes of relating and power negotiation.

Distributed Leadership (Spillane, 2006) conceptualizes leadership as a dynamic practice dispersed across multiple individuals and organizational levels through leader–follower-contextual interactions that influence others' motivation, knowledge, affect, and practices within an organization.

The ***Social Network Approach to Leadership*** (Balkundi & Kilduff, 2006) examines how network structure influences leadership opportunities through patterns of interaction, information flow, and strategic positioning.

While these eight approaches (amongst others) offer diverse perspectives on relational leadership, their effectiveness ultimately hinges on communication processes. The study of leadership communication provides important insights into how relational dynamics unfold in practice.

Communication and relational leadership

Relational aspects of leadership have been a focus of communication scholarship since the mid-twentieth century (Redding, 1972). The study of relational communication, pioneered by scholars like Watzlawick et al. (1967), provided groundwork for understanding communication as a process that defines relationships. This foundation prompted research on specific relational communication styles in leadership contexts (Fairhurst & Chandler, 1989).

Burgoon's Interpersonal Adaptation Theory (IAT) further advanced the field by providing a framework for understanding how, when, and why people coordinate verbal and nonverbal styles with communication partners (Burgoon et al., 1995) – a concept relevant to leader–follower dynamics. This attunement of communication styles has since been linked to leadership effectiveness, especially in dynamic and diverse organizational environments (Madlock, 2008).

In leadership communication literature, "communication" refers to how leaders interact with and influence others both verbally (e.g., through speeches, conversations, reports, emails) and nonverbally (e.g., through body language, facial expressions, tone). However, the study of communication and leadership extends beyond mere information transfer; it examines how leaders use communicative practices to build relationships, create shared meanings, shape organizational culture, and achieve goals. Communication-centered relational leadership scholarship investigates how communicative styles, efforts, and tendencies impact leadership relationships and processes. These studies explore the influence of various communication aspects on the formation, quality, and maintenance of relationships in leadership contexts, as well as the collaborative, co-created development of leadership itself. Such scholarship examines dialogic communication (Barge & Fairhurst, 2008), inclusivity and participation (Uhl-Bien & Ospina, 2012), empathy (Jian, 2022), sense-making and sense-giving (Cunliffe & Eriksen, 2011), feedback (Mikkelson et al., 2019), nonverbal communication (Fairhurst & Connaughton, 2014), and social capital development (McCallum & O'Connell, 2009). These and other communication-related phenomena are treated as interrelated, interdependent practices.

The quality of leader–follower relationships carries significance for organizational health, tone, efficacy, and outcomes. Aggarwal et al. (2020) note high-quality leader–follower connections are associated with "a higher level of information exchange, trust, competence, commitment, role clarity, greater job satisfaction, and lower job stress," whereas low-quality leader–follower relationships are attributed to "a low level of interaction, limited support, formal relations, counterproductive behavior, psychological withdrawal behavior, employee turnover, lower level of job satisfaction, and higher job stress" (Aggarwal et al., 2020).

Research suggests individuals with well-functioning relationships tend to respond better to stressful events, experiencing less negative impact on their overall well-being. In organizations where leaders prioritize the building and maintenance of healthy relationships, employees demonstrate greater resilience in the face of workplace stress. They tend to handle challenges, invest in their own well-being, and perform effectively, despite demanding situations. This increased resilience benefits not only individual employees but also contributes to a more positive and productive organizational culture (Gittell, 2016). However, this process is not a simple equation of "effective leadership communication" yielding "employee satisfaction and institutional success." Leader/Messenger identity may carry more weight than the message itself, thereby highlighting the intricate psychological dynamics at play in these exchanges.

Scholars from many disciplines study leadership using a range of theories, paradigms, and methods. As often occurs in academic research, this work can become siloed within respective fields, where similar theories may flourish but rarely inform each other. As critical communication scholars and political psychologists, we approach leadership questions through our disciplinary lenses, yet in early conversations about our research, common interests and questions began to emerge.

Communication studies often conceptualize leadership as a relational and discursive phenomenon, investigating how leadership is enacted and negotiated through communication processes across diverse contexts and configurations, from dyads to large organizations. In contrast, psychologists view leaders and followers as individuals with distinct traits who engage in social cognition – a set of processes by which we try to understand others' motivations and capabilities to better inform our own actions. By integrating qualitative approaches with scientific findings from social cognition research, we can develop a more comprehensive understanding of leadership perception. Our interdisciplinary approach allows us to explore why and how leaders are perceived in particular ways and to identify potential challenges and opportunities that may emerge when new leadership styles are adopted. This multi-paradigmatic application allows leadership communication to be understood as a complex, dynamic interaction through which social cognition mediates leaders' choices.

In our application to leadership communication, tensions may emerge as leaders balance relational communication (which centers on cultivating interpersonal warmth) with top-down messages that attempt to project competence in line with organizational hierarchies. There may be fundamental trade-offs for leaders when emphasizing warmth-linked behaviors (compassion, empathy) versus competence-signaling actions (decisiveness, assertiveness). The SCM (Fiske et al., 2007) outlines how prejudice emerges toward different groups.

Building upon this framework, we suggest leaders from historically marginalized and oppressed backgrounds may face more severe penalties if perceived to have an imbalance of warmth and competence. For example, women and Black, Indigenous, and People of Color (BIPOC) leaders in the U.S. and Canada who communicate kindness and approachability may be seen as less capable, while those focused strictly on displaying competence risk harming social bonds. Understanding how warmth and competence are perceived requires a deeper look at social cognition. By integrating relational perspectives with an individual-focused social cognition approach, we develop a more comprehensive understanding of leadership perception that acknowledges both structural and interpersonal dynamics. The SCM provides a framework for exploring these multifaceted dimensions of leadership communication.

Applying the Stereotype Content Model to leadership communication

Replicated across 47 countries, the SCM posits that in all human interactions, we measure others along two dimensions: warmth and competence

(Fiske et al., 2007; Nicolas et al., 2021). In evaluating others, we try to anticipate their intentions and motivations to guide our actions and responses within an interaction. Meaning, we generally want to know "who is on my side (friend)? And who is not (foe)?" (Nicolas et al., 2021, p. 393). Warmth refers to the perceived intent of an individual and involves traits like friendliness and trustworthiness; competence refers to a person's perceived abilities and skills (Fiske et al., 2007). The warmth–competence framework highlights tensions in leadership communication across theoretical approaches. For instance, Transformational Leadership (Bass & Riggio, 2006) includes components that reflect this duality – "intellectual stimulation" (competence) focuses on developing capabilities, while "individualized consideration" (warmth) emphasizes relationship-building. Similarly, Authentic Leadership (Walumbwa et al., 2008) attempts to balance demonstrating expertise with fostering genuine interpersonal trust. Generally applied to groups in society and the emergence of prestige and prejudice, the SCM helps us understand social cognition between any number of individuals, including leaders and those they lead. Relationships are challenged because "virtually all interpersonal relationships are competitive-cooperative, or some amalgamation of the two; and every person we encounter is of higher, lower, or equal status relative to the self" (Russell & Fiske, 2008, p. 1193).

Understanding, changing, or even leveling hierarchies can be a defining dimension of relational leadership styles. Similarly, in the SCM, competence operates with status to create a "vertical dimension" of "capability and assertiveness" (Fiske & Bai, 2020, p. 216). Alternatively, the horizontal dimension of warmth and communality signals an actor's intent or motivation – will they be trustworthy or moral? Fiske and Bai (2020) suggest the horizontal nature is key as warmth and sociability often involve levels of reciprocity, much like the goals of relational leadership. Both Distributed Leadership (Spillane, 2006) and the Social Network Approach (Balkundi & Kilduff, 2006) directly address these hierarchical tensions through their reconceptualization of leadership as dispersed across organizational networks, thereby creating multiple avenues for competence demonstration while maintaining cooperative relationships.

When cooperation is at the center of these relationships, we perceive others as warm, whereas competition leads us to cold evaluations (Russell & Fiske, 2008).

Leadership inherently sets apart one or some individuals from the broader group. While the value of collaborative approaches is made clear in leadership scholarship, it remains that a completely decentralized, horizontal leadership relationship or style is nearly impossible. This arrangement would resemble a direct democracy with all decisions made by group consensus. For leaders to lead effectively, there must be a certain level of deference, respect, and, indeed, status afforded to the position and person. This necessary distinction between leaders and followers underscores the fundamental nature of leadership as a position of elevated responsibility and influence.

Given that leaders hold power through various means – be it money, resources, or the ability to hire or fire – relying on a vertical understanding of competence will always offer some level of effectiveness. But status or respect does not exist in a vacuum; verticality assumes there are others in subordinate positions. When leaders introduce warmth to temper this verticality, it is unclear if this will undergird or undermine respect and status. In fact, there is substantial evidence that individuals struggle to attribute both high warmth and high competence to particular groups simultaneously. On average, people generally respond positively to individuals exhibiting both warmth and competence (Fiske et al., 2015), but it can be difficult to perceive warmth from people who hold power and status (Fiske & Bai, 2020). Furthermore, individuals may manipulate their own presentation to counteract these stereotypes, including "playing dumb to be likable, or being mean to seem smart," particularly in social interactions with mixed status (Fiske et al., 2021, p. 398).

In hierarchical workplace settings, those with lower status tend to emphasize their competence in communication, whereas leaders with high status may focus on conveying warmth. This is because competence is often assumed to be associated with elevated status (Fiske et al., 2015). When asked to imagine interacting with a fellow employee of higher status, individuals reported wanting to emphasize their personal traits related to competence, whereas, if asked to interact with a lower status coworker, there was a focus on conveying warmth (Swencionis & Fiske, 2016). These contrasting communication tendencies present specific challenges for LMX (Graen & Uhl-Bien, 1995) practices, as the development of high-quality relationships may be complicated when leaders and followers emphasize different dimensions based on their hierarchical positions. Similarly, individuals often exhibit a positivity bias when evaluating others. Rather than expressing stereotypes or negative appraisals directly, we may omit unfavorable information and instead offer positive comments. This creates a pattern of innuendo: when an individual's warmth or likability is emphasized, we may assume they are less capable. Conversely, when a person's competence is a primary focus, it may suggest they are not particularly warm or sociable (Fiske et al., 2015).

In modern leadership environments, warmth is valued and can be necessary for advancement. Research shows that a leader's demonstrations of empathic concern for their employees are typically associated with a lower potential for career derailment (Gentry et al., 2015). For example, when bosses and employees rate a leader high on items like "Is sensitive to signs of overwork in others," they also report these leaders as less likely to miss promotions due to problems with interpersonal relationships and meeting organizational goals (Gentry et al., 2015). While this effect is mainly observed in women, likely due to societal expectations and rewards for empathy, warmth-infused communication can provide career benefits across genders. Furthermore, a meta-analysis demonstrates that leader traits affect (displays of positive or negative emotions) correlate with a variety of leadership measures. The positive relationship between positive leader affect and effective leadership appears to operate through Transformational Leadership practices ("i.e., possess a vision, pay attention to unique needs of followers, challenge followers to think in unconventional ways, and inspire followers to put forth effort") (Joseph et al., 2015, p. 570).

Leaders who convey emotions generally increase perceived closeness with others. Notably, displays of positive emotions lead to higher ratings of both warmth and competence (Ludwig et al., 2022). This emotional expression proves more impactful than merely sharing personal facts about oneself. Of particular significance for leaders attempting to implement relational leadership in their day-to-day actions, this finding suggests that expressing warmth, rather than simply engaging in small talk, is more effective. Such emphasis on authentic emotional expression aligns with both Servant Leadership (Sendjaya & Sarros, 2002) and the Relational Leadership Model (Komives et al., 2013). These genuine displays, rather than superficial relationship-building activities, may more effectively balance warmth with maintained competence in leadership interactions.

Conveying competence while generating warmth through relational leadership practices often presents a significant challenge for leaders. Although the status and prestige of a higher position signal a certain level of competence, leaders who are not liked may find their perceived competence undermined by those they lead. Rather than suggesting an optimum level of capability and likeability in one's communication strategies, it may be more useful for leaders to consider situational deployments of particular messaging styles.

For example, individuals evaluate groups differently based on their goals, whether relational or structural (Nicolas et al., 2022). Applied to leadership communication, it is possible that leaders emphasizing warmth in their messaging would be effective when the goal is team building, whereas a focus upon competence and ability may be better received if certain productivity goals are in play. Such situational approaches align with several relational leadership theories: LMX (Graen & Uhl-Bien, 1995) acknowledges these trade-offs through differentiated relationships; Authentic

Leadership (Walumbwa et al., 2008) balances competence with genuine connection; and the Relational Leadership Model (Komives et al., 2013) offers communication strategies that adjust to context. Furthermore, social identity and ingroup/outgroup dynamics influence how people present themselves and evaluate others in terms of warmth and competence. For instance, Black Americans might emphasize competence when speaking with white Americans (outgroup), but prioritize warmth when communicating with other Black Americans (ingroup) (Fiske et al., 2015).

Dupree et al. (2021) explore intersections of Race–Status Associations (RSAs) across a series of studies, examining perceptions of low status for Black Americans and high status for white Americans across types of jobs, ranking of these groups among other groups, and high/low-status attributes associated with these groups. Their findings show individuals who were more likely to assign high-status jobs to white Americans and low-status jobs to Black Americans also held hierarchy-maintaining beliefs, including social dominance, denial of white privilege, and support for meritocracy (Dupree et al., 2021). Consequently, merely seeing a white or Black face can initiate a series of assumptions about competence and status in the workplace. These persistent stereotypes can lead to different self-presentation strategies: higher status and white individuals generally seek to warm their image and downplay competence, whereas Black Americans and lower status individuals tend to lower their warmth in order to emphasize their competence (Swencionis et al., 2017). Yet, there is some evidence that race and ethnicity do not always impact performance expectations for leaders (Anderson et al., 2019).

Theoretical frameworks like the Relational Constructionist Approach (Hosking, 2011) offer guidance for addressing communication challenges by emphasizing leadership as co-constructed through language and dialogue, creating space for contextually appropriate expressions of both warmth and competence based on organizational goals. Yet, implementing such frameworks poses particular challenges for leaders adopting relational or Transformational Leadership styles, especially across demographic groups. White managers or leaders may more easily shift to relational styles to convey warmth without risking their perceived competence. In contrast, leaders from underrepresented groups (e.g., women or BIPOC Americans) who attempt relational communication may overemphasize warmth and risk a loss of esteem. We often see this dynamic in higher education, where men and white professors more easily ask students to call them by their first names, and women and BIPOC faculty often require a formal address to maintain a level of deference they may not otherwise be afforded.

Furthermore, Black Americans are stereotyped as having moderate warmth and low competence, while white Americans are stereotyped as having high competence and low warmth (Bergsieker et al., 2012; Dupree et al., 2021; Zou & Cheryan, 2017). As such, in interracial interactions, Black and Latinx Americans try to navigate their low-competence or low-status stereotypes by aiming to be respected. Similarly, white Americans try to navigate their unfriendly or cold stereotype by aiming to be liked (Bergsieker et al., 2010). These unique impression management goals arising from individuals who want to counter their stereotypes can shape their specific communication styles in their interactions with others.

To illustrate, Dupree and Fiske (2019) find white liberals reference competence less when speaking to a mostly minority (as opposed to mostly white) audience in order to appear less high-status, a stereotype reversal goal. While this impression management tactic might be motivated by innocent intentions, it can also come across as patronizing and condescending in white–minority interactions (Dupree & Fiske, 2019). Analyzing 250,000 Congressional remarks and 1 million tweets of white, Black, and Latinx politicians, Dupree (2021) finds that when Black and Latinx Americans interact with majority white audiences, their communication strategy tends to feature a competence upshift reflecting the pursuit of a stereotype reversal goal. Furthermore, Black and Latinx conservatives made references to high power more than Black and Latinx liberals when speaking to their mostly white peers (Dupree, 2021). These findings provide further evidence that individuals use distinct communication styles when responding to unique impression management goals arising out of interracial contexts.

Adopting a strategic communication style in interracial settings can be important for impression management when internalized stereotypes may lead to self-inhibiting behavior that can hinder positive interracial interaction. White and Black Americans can underestimate racial outgroup members' willingness to engage in interracial contact (Shelton & Richeson, 2005), possibly out of fear of rejection, but they may also think racial outgroup individuals do not engage in interracial contact due to lack of interest (Swencionis et al., 2017). These findings can be applied to interracial contact in the workplace, such that white, Black, and Latinx leaders may misperceive what their colleagues think of them. Thus, carefully utilizing a communication style that is specific to the interaction context can help resolve some of these invisible stereotype tensions.

More than race and ethnicity, the choice of communication style can also be influenced by gender. While women tend to talk more about people, reflecting their stereotype as high warmth-low competence, men talk more about objects, reflecting their stereotype as high competence-low warmth (Otterbacher et al., 2017). Women in the workforce, especially those who are in leadership roles or in male-dominated professions, may be expected to conform to masculine norms of professional behavior. Other work has found that women managers displayed counter-stereotypical behavior by referencing numbers more and emotions less when providing criticism to employees, a stereotypically masculine behavior (Mulac et al., 2000). This counter-stereotypical behavior performed by women managers arises out of a need to pursue impression management goals by attempting to increase their perceived competence and lower their perceived warmth. Thus, the intersection of race/ethnicity and gender, among other socially salient identities, can produce unique impression management goals that call for strategic communication styles to either play into or guard against stereotypes. The mixed pattern of evidence about leadership styles and leader demographics calls for an intersectional approach in our theories, studies, and applications of leader communication.

These intersectional challenges directly impact leadership communication across theoretical frameworks. Servant Leadership's (Sendjaya & Sarros, 2002) emphasis on empathy must be balanced with competence demonstration, particularly for women and BIPOC leaders who already face competence stereotypes (Rosette et al., 2008; Sy et al., 2010). The Relational Constructionist Approach (Hosking, 2011) and Distributed Leadership (Spillane, 2006) offer potential solutions by decentralizing authority and creating avenues for demonstrating competence, thereby addressing what Swencionis et al. (2017) identify as different self-presentation needs across demographic groups. These communication challenges underscore why approaches like the Social Network Approach to Leadership (Balkundi & Kilduff, 2006) must consider how network positioning influences warmth–competence perceptions across diverse organizational contexts. Our chapter primarily highlights the intersectional challenges of race/ethnicity and gender in adopting new leadership styles. Further attention should be paid to how culture, religion, dis/ability, and other identities can influence these relationships.

We caution against broad recommendations for leaders to adopt relational leadership strategies universally. While relational leadership is often perceived as a progressive and beneficial approach, we challenge assumptions that its application and practice will yield uniform, positive results for all leaders. The effectiveness of relational leadership may vary depending on factors such as organizational culture, team dynamics, individual leadership styles, leader–follower demographics and diversity, and leader–follower expectations and preferences. Further research is needed to identify contexts and conditions under which relational leadership is most effective and to develop tailored implementation strategies for diverse leadership scenarios.

Case study: Relational leadership meets reality

The following hypothetical case illustrates relational leadership tensions in practice.

At 29, Priya is the youngest branch manager in her bank's regional network. As a first-generation South Asian Canadian who earned her finance degree and MBA locally, Priya thought she was ready for anything. Then she attended a leadership workshop that changed everything. The training session encouraged managers to employ "relational leadership" strategies by building personal connections with employees, sharing vulnerabilities, and flattening hierarchies in decision-making. During break-out discussions, other managers – predominantly white Canadians over 40 – shared success stories about times they had employed relational approaches. They described how employees responded positively when they mentioned their kids' soccer games, openly discussed work challenges, and involved staff in major decisions.

"Sounds amazing," Priya thought. But she left the training with some hesitations.

First, she questioned whether she could "relate on a personal level." During team meetings, she considered sharing about caring for her aging parents or her younger brother's university struggles, but she wondered if, in her attempt to seem both competent and relatable, this might actually reinforce stereotypes about South Asian family obligations. Second, when she tried mentioning her weekend plans with friends, the response felt tepid compared to the warm reactions her colleagues received when discussing their children. Finally, a bigger challenge came when Priya attempted to initiate collaborative decision-making. During a staff meeting about updating customer service protocols, she opened the floor for input instead of simply announcing the new policies. What happened next caught her off guard. Several employees (most older than she) essentially took over the meeting. They dismissed her proposed changes and advocated for "the way we've always done things." Later, outside the conference room, she overheard, "She seems nice, but I'm not sure she knows what she's doing. A strong manager would just tell us what to do."

Priya felt stuck. When she tried to be warm and collaborative, people seemed to question her competence. When she was direct and commanding, she felt inauthentic. Moreover, Priya watched her white male counterparts successfully use the exact collaborative approaches that seemed to backfire for her. Now, six months later, Priya must lead her branch through the implementation of new digital services. She is wondering whether she should employ a traditional top-down approach, try collaboration again, or attempt to find some middle ground. As she prepares for next week's all-staff meeting, she wonders: Is relational leadership possible for her, or are these approaches only effective for leaders who fit a certain profile?

Suggested further readings

Crouse-Dick, C. E., Wilson, S., & Buller, R. E. (2025). The slow leadership framework: A decolonizing, humanizing approach to leadership. *Feminist Pedagogy, 1*(6). https://digitalcommons.calpoly.edu/feministpedagogy/vol6/iss1/7

Dupree, C. H. (2024). Words of a leader: The importance of intersectionality for understanding women leaders' use of dominant language and how others receive it. *Administrative Science Quarterly, 69*(2), 271–323. https://doi.org/10.1177/00018392231223142

Yzerbyt, V., Koch, A., Brambilla, M., Ellemers, N., Fiske, S. T., & Nicolas, G. (2025). Dimensions of stereotypes about groups. *Current Directions in Psychological Science, 34*(6), 365–372. https://doi.org/10.1177/09637214251345489

Questions for discussion

1 Considering the empathy-driven nature of relational leadership, what communication-related challenges might leaders from underrepresented groups face when trying to convey warmth to their employees? How might these challenges reflect broader systemic issues?

2 When Priya acts collaboratively, people question her competence. When she's directive, she feels inauthentic. How could she navigate this tension?

3 Relational leadership assumes employees prefer empathetic and non-hierarchical communication from leaders. Is this always the case? De scribe an organizational scenario where communication emphasizing competence might be preferred over warmth. How might leaders effectively balance these communication styles?

References

Aggarwal, A., Chand, P. K., Jhamb, D., & Mittal, A. (2020). Leader–member exchange, work engagement, and psychological withdrawal behavior: The mediating role of psychological empowerment. *Frontiers in Psychology, 11*. https://doi.org/10.3389/fpsyg.2020.00423

Anderson, A. J., Ahmad, A. S., King, E. B., & Gilrane, V. (2019). Subtle and overt behaviors toward ethnic minority leaders and the moderating role of competence. *Journal of Leadership & Organizational Studies, 26*(3), 372–388. https://doi.org/10.1177/1548051819859289

Balkundi, P., & Kilduff, M. (2006). The ties that lead: A social network approach to leadership. *The Leadership Quarterly, 17*(4), 419–439. https://doi.org/10.1016/j.leaqua.2006.01.001

Barge, J. K., & Fairhurst, G. T. (2008). Living leadership: A systemic constructionist approach. *Leadership, 4*(3), 227–251. https://doi.org/10.1177/1742715008092360

Bass, B. M., & Riggio, R. E. (2006). *Transformational leadership* (2nd ed.). Lawrence Erlbaum Associates Publishers. https://doi.org/10.4324/9781410617095

Bergsieker, H. B., Leslie, L. M., Constantine, V. S., & Fiske, S. T. (2012). Stereotyping by omission: Eliminate the negative, accentuate the positive. *Journal of Personality and Social Psychology*, *102*(6), 1214. https://doi.org/10.1037/a0027717

Bergsieker, H. B., Shelton, J. N., & Richeson, J. A. (2010). To be liked versus respected: Divergent goals in interracial interactions. *Journal of Personality and Social Psychology*, *99*(2), 248.

Burgoon, J. K., Stern, L. A., & Dillman, L. (1995). *Interpersonal adaptation: Dyadic interaction patterns*. Cambridge University Press. https://psycnet.apa.org/doi/10.1017/CBO9780511720314

Cunliffe, A. L., & Eriksen, M. (2011). Relational leadership. *Human Relations*, *64*(11), 1425–1449. https://doi.org/10.1177/0018726711418388

Cropanzano, R., Dasborough, M. T., & Weiss, H. (2017). Affective events and the development of leaders-member exchange. *Academy of Management Review*, *42*(2), 233–258. https://doi.org/10.5465/amr.2014.0384

Drescher, M. A., Korsgaard, M. A., Welpe, I. M., Picot, A., & Wigand, R. T. (2014). The dynamics of shared leadership: Building trust and enhancing performance. *Journal of Applied Psychology*, *99*(5), 771–783.

Dupree, C. H. (2021). Black and Latinx conservatives upshift competence relative to liberals in mostly white settings. *Nature Human Behaviour*, *5*(12), 1652–1662. https://doi.org/10.1038/s41562-021-01167-9

Dupree, C. H., & Fiske, S. T. (2019). Self-presentation in interracial settings: The competence downshift by white liberals. *Journal of Personality and Social Psychology*, *117*(3), 579.

Dupree, C. H., Torrez, B., Obioha, O., & Fiske, S. T. (2021). Race–status associations: Distinct effects of three novel measures among white and black perceivers. *Journal of Personality and Social Psychology*, *120*(3), 601.

Fairhurst, G. T., & Chandler, T. A. (1989). Social structure in leader-member interaction. *Communication Monographs*, *56*(3), 215–239. https://doi.org/10.1080/03637758909390261

Fairhurst, G. T., & Connaughton, S. L. (2014). Leadership: A communicative perspective. *Leadership*, *10*(1), 7–35. https://doi.org/10.1177/1742715013509396

Fairhurst, G. T., & Uhl-Bien, M. (2012). Organizational discourse analysis (ODA): Examining leadership as a relational process. *The Leadership Quarterly*, *23*(6), 1043–1062. https://doi.org/10.1016/j.leaqua.2012.10.005

Fiske, S. T., & Bai, X. (2020). Vertical and horizontal inequality are status and power differences: Applications to stereotyping by competence and warmth. *Current Opinion in Psychology*, *33*, 216–221. https://doi.org/10.1016/j.copsyc.2019.09.014

Fiske, S. T., Bergsieker, H., Constantine, V., Dupree, C., Holoien, D. S., Kervyn, N., & Swencionis, J. (2015). Talking up and talking down: The power of positive speaking. *Journal of Social Issues*, *71*(4), 834–846. https://doi.org/10.1111/josi.12152

Fiske, S. T., Cuddy, A. J., & Glick, P. (2007). Universal dimensions of social cognition: Warmth and competence. *Trends in Cognitive Sciences*, *11*(2), 77–83.

Fiske, S. T., Nicholas, G., & Bai, X. (2021). The stereotype content model: How we make sense of individuals and groups. In P. Van Lange, E. T. Higgins, & A. E. Kruglanski (Eds.), *Social psychology: Handbook of basic principles* (pp. 392–410). Guilford Press.

Gentry, W. A., Clark, M. A., Young, S. F., Cullen, K. L., & Zimmerman, L. (2015). How displaying empathic concern may differentially predict career derailment potential for women and men leaders in Australia. *The Leadership Quarterly*, *26*(4), 641–653. https://doi.org/10.1016/j.leaqua.2015.05.003

Gittell, J. H. (2016). Rethinking autonomy: Relationships as a source of resilience in a changing healthcare system. *Health Services Research*, *51*(5), 1701–1705. https://doi.org/10.1111/1475-6773.12578

Graen, G. B., & Uhl-Bien, M. (1995). Relationship-based approach to leadership: Development of leader–member exchange (LMX) theory of leadership over 25 years: Applying a multi-level multi-domain perspective. *Leadership Quarterly*, *6*(2), 219–247. https://doi.org/10.1016/1048-9843(95)90036-5

Hosking, D. M. (2011). Telling tales of relations: Appreciating relational constructionism. *Organization Studies*, *32*(1), 47–65. https://doi.org/10.1177/0170840610394296

Jian, G. (2022). From empathic leader to empathic leadership practice: An extension to relational leadership theory. *Human Relations*, *75*(5), 931–955. https://doi.org/10.1177/0018726721998450

Joseph, D. L., Dhanani, L. Y., Shen, W., McHugh, B. C., & McCord, M. A. (2015). Is a happy leader a good leader? A meta-analytic investigation of leader trait affect and leadership. *The Leadership Quarterly*, *26*(4), 557–576. https://doi.org/10.1016/j.leaqua.2015.04.001

Komives, S. R., Lucas, N., & McMahon, T. R. (2013). *Exploring leadership: For college students who want to make a difference* (3rd ed.). Jossey-Bass.

Ludwig, V. U., Berry, B., Cai, J. Y., Chen, N. M., Crone, D. L., & Platt, M. L. (2022). The impact of disclosing emotions on ratings of interpersonal closeness, warmth, competence, and leadership ability. *Frontiers in Psychology*, *13*, 989826. https://doi.org/10.3389/fpsyg.2022.989826

Madlock, P. E. (2008). The link between leadership style, communicator competence, and employee satisfaction. *The Journal of Business Communication*, *45*(1), 61–78. https://doi.org/10.1177/0021943607309351

McCallum, S., & O'Connell, D. (2009). Social capital and leadership development: Building stronger leadership through enhanced relational skills. *Leadership & Organization Development Journal*, *30*(2), 152–166. https://doi.org/10.1108/01437730910935756

Men, L. R. (2014). Strategic internal communication: Transformational leadership, communication channels, and employee satisfaction. *Management Communication Quarterly*, *28*(2), 264–284. https://doi.org/10.1177/0893318914524536

Men, L. R., & Stacks, D. (2013). The impact of leadership style and employee empowerment on perceived organizational reputation. *Journal of Communication Management*, *17*(2), 171–192. https://doi.org/10.1108/13632541311318765

Mikkelson, A. C., Sloan, D., & Hesse, C. (2019). Relational communication messages and leadership styles in supervisor/employee relationships. *International Journal of Business Communication*, *56*(4), 586–604. https://doi.org/10.1177/2329488416687267

Mulac, A., Seibold, D. R., & Farris, J. L. (2000). Female and male managers' and professionals' criticism giving: Differences in language use and effects. *Journal of Language and Social Psychology*, *19*(4), 389–415. https://doi.org/10.1177/0261927X00019004001

Nicolas, G., Bai, X., & Fiske, S. T. (2021). Comprehensive stereotype content dictionaries using a semi-automated method. *European Journal of Social Psychology*, *51*(1), 178–196. https://doi.org/10.1002/ejsp.2724

Nicolas, G., Fiske, S. T., Koch, A., Imhoff, R., Unkelbach, C., Terache, J., & Yzerbyt, V. (2022). Relational versus structural goals prioritize different social information. *Journal of Personality and Social Psychology, 122*(4), 659. https://psycnet.apa.org/doi/10.1037/pspi0000366

Otterbacher, J., Bates, J., & Clough, P. (2017, May). Competent men and warm women: Gender stereotypes and backlash in image search results. In *Proceedings of the 2017 chi conference on human factors in computing systems* (pp. 6620–6631).

Redding, W. C. (1972). *Communication within the organization: An interpretive review of theory and research*. Industrial Communication Council.

Rosette, A. S., Leonardelli, G. J., & Phillips, K. W. (2008). The white standard: Racial bias in leader categorization. *Journal of Applied Psychology, 93*(4), 758.

Russell, A. M. T., & Fiske, S. T. (2008). It's all relative: Competition and status drive interpersonal perception. *European Journal of Social Psychology, 38*(7), 1193–1201. https://doi.org/10.1002/ejsp.539

Sadri, G., Weber, T. J., & Gentry, W. A. (2011). Empathic emotion and leadership performance: An empirical analysis across 38 countries. *The Leadership Quarterly, 22*(5), 818–830. https://doi.org/10.1016/j.leaqua.2011.07.005

Sendjaya, S., & Sarros, J. C. (2002). Servant leadership: Its origin, development, and application in organizations. *Journal of Leadership & Organizational Studies, 9*(2), 57–64. https://doi.org/10.1177/107179190200900205

Shelton, J. N., & Richeson, J. A. (2005). Intergroup contact and pluralistic ignorance. *Journal of Personality and Social Psychology, 88*(1), 91. https://psycnet.apa.org/doi/10.1037/0022-3514.88.1.91

Spillane, J. P. (2006). *Distributed leadership*. Jossey-Bass.

Swencionis, J. K., Dupree, C. H., & Fiske, S. T. (2017). Warmth-competence tradeoffs in impression management across race and social-class divides. *Journal of Social Issues, 73*(1), 175–191. https://doi.org/10.1111/josi.12210

Swencionis, J. K., & Fiske, S. T. (2016). Promote up, ingratiate down: Status comparisons drive warmth-competence tradeoffs in impression management. *Journal of Experimental Social Psychology, 64*, 27–34. https://doi.org/10.1016/j.jesp.2016.01.004

Sy, T., Shore, L. M., Strauss, J., Shore, T. H., Tram, S., Whiteley, P., & Ikeda-Muromachi, K. (2010). Leadership perceptions as a function of race-occupation fit: The case of Asian Americans. *Journal of Applied Psychology, 95*(5), 902–919. https://doi.org/10.1037/a0019501

Uhl-Bien, M. (2006). Relational leadership theory: Exploring the social processes of leadership and organizing. *The Leadership Quarterly, 17*(6), 654–676. https://doi.org/10.1016/j.leaqua.2006.10.007

Uhl-Bien, M., & Ospina, S. M. (Eds.) (2012). *Advancing relational leadership research: A dialogue among perspectives*. Information Age Publishing.

Walumbwa, F. O., Avolio, B. J., Gardner, W. L., Wernsing, T. S., & Peterson, S. J. (2008). Authentic leadership: Development and validation of a theory-based measure. *Journal of Management, 34*(1), 89–126. https://doi.org/10.1177/0149206307308913

Watzlawick, P., Bavelas, J. B., & Jackson, D. D. (1967). *Pragmatics of human communication: A study of interactional patterns, pathologies, and paradoxes*. W. W. Norton & Company.

Zou, L. X., & Cheryan, S. (2017). Two axes of subordination: A new model of racial position. *Journal of Personality and Social Psychology, 112*(5), 696. https://psycnet.apa.org/doi/10.1037/pspa0000080

10

LEADERSHIP MYTHODOLOGY, NARRATIVE, AND COMMUNICATION ETHICS

Engaging the Other

Janie M. H. Fritz, Jen Jones, and Sovi Herring

Introduction

Existential approaches to leadership have gained traction over the last two decades (Agarwal & Malloy, 2000; Ashman, 2007; Ashman & Lawler, 2008; Ashman & Winstanley, 2006; Botha & Freeman, 2023; Fritz, 2023; Lawler, 2005; Lawler & Ashman, 2012; Thompson, 2024; Tomkins, 2024). Existentialism offers no convenient prescriptions that theorists yearn for but provides, in its complexity, a truer reflection of human life, which is knotted, ragged, and unpredictable. From an existentialist perspective, humans and human relations are always in a state of becoming. Attempting to capture one's being and pin it down is futile because each moment of existence offers new possibilities for change. Existentialism calls for deliberate choices and taking responsibility for these choices. Yet, one's being is always amid histories, cultures, stories, and communities with others that situate one's being in the world, which we argue is vital to deeper human engagement and worthy of further exploration. Accordingly, this chapter illuminates how leadership and communication are situated within narratives; we conceptualize existential being-in the-world as leader-in-narrative. Jones (2023a) advocates for this view, proposing the idea of "*myth*odology," grounded in the philosophy of American existentialist Hazel Barnes. Jones's approach to *myth*odology finds its theoretical and methodological substance in a commitment to narrative embraced by existentialist authors.

This understanding of narrative is given communicative purchase through the work of Arnett (1987), who identified Fisher's (1984) narrative paradigm as an approach to communication ethics with implications

DOI: 10.4324/9781003563662-13

for philosophy of communication as a meaning-making endeavor (Arnett & Holba, 2012). This chapter brings a communication ethics approach to narrative into conversation with a *myth*odological understanding of existential leadership, drawing on foundational work in these areas and proposing new avenues for research. We explicate Barnes's existential leadership "*myth*odology" (Jones, 2020, 2023a), review Fisher's narrative paradigm as an approach to communication ethics, and demonstrate how these areas of study speak to each other in the practice of leadership through human communicative engagement with others through dialogue, empathy, and communicative practices that promote resilience.

Rethinking leadership: An existentialist approach

Jones (2023b) argues that existential philosophy, literature, and art are more fitting lenses for a post-modern moment calling for critical thinking within existential encounters than prescriptive, normative theories. Ladkin (2006) also advocates for such an approach, positing deontology and utilitarianism as insufficient to help organizational leaders resolve ethical issues and offering a Heideggerian notion of dwelling to guide leaders' engagement with others amid human encounters. More recently, Simone de Beauvoir's existentialist perspective has elucidated leaders' ethical decision-making (Botha & Freeman, 2023) and moral agency (Botha, 2023). Thus, existentialist leadership attends to an intersectional dynamic that is ever-changing and radically different in each emergent moment, which is why de Beauvoir calls attention to ambiguity and Camus to the absurd in these encounters. There is no prescription for leading, contrary to normative theories.

Leadership scholars often propose pre-packaged plans to offer an audience eager to employ the latest theory, yet we argue that this approach is an act of bad faith. Arnett et al. (2007) reference the cliché that the path to hell is paved with good intentions, which was taken seriously by Sartre (1946). Regardless of the anxiety produced by living amid human encounters, dwelling with others (Ladkin, 2006) while doing our best to find a fitting response (Schrag, 2003) within existential moments is leading in good faith. Yet, despite our best efforts, as Barnes (1974b) observes, "counterfinality" may emerge—a result contrary to our expectations, which is always possible because the future is unknown. Therefore, leaders ought to be hopeful but not optimistic—a term connected to a false sense of deterministic certainty (Arnett, 2022) and considered potentially problematic in political leadership (e.g., Eddington, 2024).

Viewed phenomenologically, leadership is an embodied perceptual process existing in relationality as a socially constructed phenomenon rather than within a single leader as a cognitive construct. Ladkin's (2013) phenomenologically grounded work supports our emphasis on narrative in existential leadership. She cites Merleau-Ponty's philosophy of persons as perceiving bodies who always interpret their surroundings, where others and objects in the world have meaning grounded in the perceiver's lived experience. Two people observing the same object will gather differing meanings or understandings depending on each person's narrative ground or interpretive horizon (Fritz et al., 2023). Existential leadership involves consciousness of one's own embodied experience and awareness of others' embodied experience.

Phenomenology, an underutilized approach to leadership studies, offers an exceptionally fitting lens to open understanding. Scholars may undervalue this interpretive approach because it lacks quantifiable data. Instead, phenomenological scholars find themselves in the "mud" (Buber, 1975, p. 277) of human existence, or what communication and organizational scholars (Arnett, 1981; Bradbury & Lichtenstein, 2000) have identified as the primacy of the "between." Ladkin (2013) argues that "these invisible aspects" play a significant yet unsung role in the co-creation of communal experience (p. 330). While leaders can never truly see from another's perspective and should resist attempts to psychologize others, they should recognize the sacred ground upon which each human stands. Garnering a greater understanding of this "situational dimension" (Gordon, 1997, p. 70) of systems, structures, culture, stories, and histories supports a leader's engagement with others.

"Being" is often associated with the subjectivity of existential phenomenology (e.g., Stewart & Mickunas, 1974). Yet, this subjectivity is only one part of the dynamic relation to "the world"; "being-in-the-world" must always be held together. "Being" does not exist in a vacuum, and "the world" exists because we are in it.[1] Being and the world are mutually informing; the world shapes one's being while one's being shapes the world. To show that existentialism is not focused on individual subjectivity alone, Sartre (2007) states that in choosing for ourselves, we choose for humankind, and also writes,

> It is then that his freedom will become conscious of itself and will reveal itself as its own possibilities, it will apprehend by and in anguish that they are possibilities only on the ground of the possibility of other possibilities.
>
> *(Sartre, 1943, p. 797)*

Thus, the ground upon which we stand and the conversation that began ages ago that we have now joined is central to existence. For centuries, literature invited people to consider such dynamics in others' stories and, at the same time, contemplate their own lived experiences and shape their being-in-the-world. Therefore, we build upon Jones (2023a, 2023b) and Fritz (2023) to further an understanding of existential leadership and communication grounded in myth and narrative.

Grounding an existentialist approach in myth and narrative

Mythodology as existential narrative ground for leadership and communication

While existentialism emerged in the twentieth century and only recently joined the scholarly discussion in leadership studies, Barnes (1974a) argued that ancient playwrights employed existentialism. She illuminates how, in writing the *Hippolytus*, Euripides challenged the bad faith of people who blamed the gods for their misdeeds rather than living in good faith by taking responsibility for their actions. Barnes finds parallels within today's context when people engage in bad faith by blaming external forces, such as fate, or "essential" psychological factors for their flawed practices, faults, and failures. Indeed, some of these sources take their names from ancient myths, such as the Oedipus complex of Freudian fame. Hence, whether essence finds its provenance with the gods or in an inherent trait, the ancient playwrights and modern existentialists agree in denying its primacy, arguing that existence, and the question of what one should do with one's existence, precedes essence. Euripides challenged cultural norms with implicit messaging in his plays, urging audiences toward reflection and action through the power of story. Similarly, the existentialist philosophers turned to literature to convey their ideas.

Sartre produced a prolific amount of literary work and was eventually offered the Nobel Peace Prize in literature, which he refused to accept. For Sartre, literature was not merely fanciful fiction; it provided the liberating possibility of transforming people, organizations, and societies. Although ideas were conveyed implicitly in story form instead of explicitly in philosophical writing, Sartre was convinced that what he termed "engaged literature" is more potent in reaching people's consciousness. Barnes (1959, 1960, 1974b) writes extensively about engaged literature, while Jones (2020) interprets and analyzes Kafka's short story *The Metamorphosis* to critique and enhance understanding of caring leadership. Jones (2023a) later articulates this approach to studying organizations and leadership as *myth*odology, an alternative to social science methodology, contributing to a better balance between qualitative scholarship and quantitative research in leadership studies.

*Myth*odology calls for framing literature in situations rather than characters. A literature of situations is an existential account where characters are free to act and make choices, choosing their existence. Conversely, a literature of characters rests in psychology, where characters are determined by inherent traits, the past, or external circumstances, leading to inevitable actions. Characters in a literature of situations exist within ambiguity. In discovering or remaking choices for themselves in choosing their existence, the "fictional character becomes part of [readers'] experience of the real world and therefore modifies their experience in the world" (Jones, 2023a, p. 8). Hence, literature touches readers' particular experiences in the world rather than making a universal claim.

From this perspective, literature does not purport to account for or know what something *is*; rather, literature is always a "literature of possibility" (Barnes, 1959). Myths suggest, rather than define or fix, meaning. Myths may point to universal truths, such as Platonic ideas, yet they are interpreted repeatedly, speaking uniquely to the reader and the historical moment. For example, the relationship between anonymity and ethical action appears in Plato's "Ring of Gyges," where a ring offers the wearer invisibility. Rather than arriving at a definitive answer, the ancient story invites continued interpretation and questioning, as seen in contemporary tales such as Tolkien's *The Lord of the Rings* and Rowling's *Harry Potter*.

Contemporary scholar Michael Urick displays his commitment to this perspective through books uniting leadership and literature (e.g., Tong & Urick, 2023; Urick, 2021). *Myth*odology shows that myths remain alive, speaking new meaning into existence. Myths such as these and many more spanning millennia offer opportunities for new leadership insights. Myth's rhetorical nature supports or challenges culturally held beliefs in the form of narrative, whose fidelity (Fisher, 1984, 1985) an audience determines. As such, the idea of *myth*odology responds to the public domain's requirement (Arendt, 1998) to keep the conversation going for others to follow, question, accept, or reject ideas in the public sphere (Arnett, 2007).

Extending mytho*dology with Fisher's narrative paradigm*

Building upon this existential foundation of *myth*odology, we identify Fisher's narrative paradigm as a communicative framework that deepens understanding of leadership practices undertaken in good faith as an embodiment of narrative fidelity. Narrative offers a persuasive approach that operates enthymematically through shared commitment to a common center (Arnett, 1986; Buber, 1958b). Fisher's (1984) narrative paradigm offers a framework for understanding ethical communicative practice within an existentialist approach to leadership grounded in story-centered guidance (Arnett & Arneson, 1999), sounding the existentialist sensibility in a rhetorical key.

Extending Fisher's seminal work, scholars have explored narratives' implications as a central mode of human interaction and ethical reasoning (e.g., Arnett, 1987; Fritz et al., 2023). Arnett (1987) posited a narrative approach to communication ethics, following MacIntyre (1981), whose work inspired Fisher. Narratives begin as speech acts, move into stories, and then gather public adherence, becoming a framework for ethical decision-making and action (Arnett & Arneson, 1999). This approach to Fisher's work highlights the importance of overarching meaning structures in communication ethics, carrying implications for the context of leadership and existential philosophy, and resonates with an existential understanding of a literature of situations in which leaders make choices through responsive action. A central assumption of the narrative paradigm, that humans are storytelling creatures, does not negate the anti-essentialist stance of the existentialists; narrative as a suggesting, pointing guide provides ground for action and meaning within which persons enact their existence through freely chosen practices reflecting that narrative (e.g., Fritz, 2023).

Fisher (1984) defines narration as a theory of symbolic action, encompassing words and deeds possessing sequence and meaning for those involved in their creation, interpretation, or lived experience. Central to Fisher's understanding is the acknowledgment of narrative as a fundamental mode of human communication, bridging the argumentative or persuasive and the literary or aesthetic realms of rhetoric. This synthesis of human symbolic experience beyond information transmission highlights the importance of meaning emerging from the narrative nature of human interactions, emphasizing the significance of stories in shaping perceptions, beliefs, and ethical judgments in communicative contexts. The narrative paradigm's flexibility points to human responsiveness to context and emergent possibilities posited by existential philosophy and given shape by story-informed structures that protect and promote a given sense of the good (Fritz et al., 2023).

By embracing storytelling's intersubjective nature as it builds community and a shared understanding of the world, Fisher's narrative paradigm and *mytho*dology challenge rationalistic approaches to ethics and communication, offering a more comprehensive understanding of the human experience and ethical reasoning. Through their interdisciplinary approach and shared emphasis on engaged literature and a story-laden sense of the good, Fisher's narrative paradigm and *mytho*dology converge to enrich our understanding of communication ethics and organizational practices. Accordingly, leadership grounded in narrative provides a "gestalt" to drive foreground action (Arnett et al., 2018), inviting responses to ever-changing, unique existential encounters rather than following a predetermined behavioral script.

Thus, we shift the focus from narrative as individual stories to narrative as shared, intersubjective understandings of the world, consistent with the existentialists' understanding of narrative as a carrier of conceptual content in embodied form. Narrative is the nurturing ground for thoughts, words, and actions comprising human existence. A grounded understanding of communication is pivotal in contemplating leadership, and communication takes its meaning from narratives within which humans are embedded.

Existential communication: Leadership-in-narrative

Jaspers (1973), an early existentialist, first used the term "existential communication," asserting that "a human being's greatest achievement in this world is communication of one personality with another one" (p. 71). Through an existentialist lens, Ashman and Lawler (2008) observe that rather than viewing communication as a skill within leadership, the opposite may be true—"leadership might be considered as an aspect of communication" or "*is* communication" (p. 253). They acknowledge leadership's typical conceptualization as an instrumental means to an end, such as motivating and inspiring followers. However, communicative participants have an existential choice, which may involve engaging the existential "no." In this manner, "followers" grant themselves empowerment rather than being granted empowerment from a leader (p. 259). Existentialism reorients the traditional leader–follower hierarchy, which may, despite good intentions, become a totalizing relationship. This shift emphasizes the dynamic nature of ethical discourse within leadership, a field guided by ethics and (inter)subjective judgment that traditional understandings of rationality exclude. For example, Fritz (2023) explores the role of narrative in Flannery O'Connor's short story "The Lame Shall Enter First," offering existential leadership lessons from this cautionary tale.

Ashman and Lawler (2008) call attention to the situatedness of communicative interaction, often ignored in the leadership literature. Interpersonal relations exist within unique contexts, which makes leader–member exchange as an orienting principle (e.g., Graen & Uhl-Bien, 1995) not only totalizing but unrealistic in its homogenizing of "leader" and "member" roles. An existentialist view of communication transcends instrumental exchange, embracing situated encounters, engagement, and relationships with others central to one's becoming (Arnett, 2003). Hence, leadership may be newly conceived as intersubjective being-in-the-world where "leaders are inter-personally engaged with the world…as a dynamic process rather than a linear relationship" (Ashman & Lawler, 2008, p. 259). Leadership becomes a self–other communicative relation rather than a leader–follower exchange. The self–other relation implies no hierarchy or material reciprocity and honors the alterity of self and other.

Leadership in-the-world is contrary to a typical leader-centric approach. Leaders do not psychologize others in a manipulative manner to fashion them in a sought-after image, a type of professional interpersonal colonization (Fritz, 2023). Instead, through indirect communication, leaders attend to the situatedness of existence, inviting others to explore their being within narrative. Garrett (2012) points in this direction, calling for a Kierkegaardian revolution in the communication field. Ashman and Lawler (2008), in their advocacy of indirect leadership communication, state Kierkegaard's goal as "not to instruct [readers], but to emancipate them; to put them in touch with their own subjectivity and to emphasize the freedom through which to explore their own faith and sense of *Being*" (p. 264).

Leaders enact such existential leadership invitationally by living out an organizational mission and offering participants places of contribution. Although employees may not create the mission, they enact choices to become co-creators of an ongoing narrative responsive to new historical moments. For instance, for remote work, leaders may consider employees' particular skills and interests (e.g., Kane et al., 2021) invitationally, rather than applying a general policy indiscriminately. This grounded understanding of leadership and communication offers engagement with others through dialogue, empathy, and communicative practices, fostering resilience.

Dialogue

When applied in the realm of leadership, *myth*odology as narrative invites all to participate in shared leadership where each brings a unique perspective to a common center uniting diversity around a compelling project (Arnett, 1986). From this approach, leadership is de-centered, nonagentic, and nonhierarchical; it is a shared experience akin to a view of leadership that honors positionality (Ladkin, 2021). Ashman and Lawler (2008) turn to Buber's (1958a) *I-Thou* of dialogic encounter that honors the subjectivity of self and other. They view leader–follower exchange as *I-It* experiences that impoverish others through lack of attentive presence. Moreover, they cite Arnett and Arneson (1999), who, in interpreting Buber's (2002) *Between Man and Man*, argue that existential development and growth are found *in the between*. Insight that neither party could have anticipated emerges in dialogue.

Existentialist bad faith attempts to rise above and detach from unique subjectivities, narratives, and the between, always at play within interpersonal encounters. Imagine a human resources training asking leaders to role-play anticipated difficult conversations with employees using a prescriptive behavioral technique to gain compliance. In doing so, employees become objects to be manipulated rather than sacred subjects with existential dignity. While meeting employees without a preconceived prescription may elicit anxiety, attentive listening and allowing the encounter to reveal the unexpected may offer a better resolution to the conflict and strengthen the relationship (see Fritz et al., 2023). Thus, the leader practices good faith, garnering respect from the employee—a respect that cannot be demanded, only invited.

Empathy

Existential philosophy observes radical alterity, or plurality, among people. No one possesses the same experience as another. People cannot see themselves outside their existence, and no one can see inside another's. Phenomenologist Edith Stein (1989) wrestled with this issue, which Jones (2018) explores in relation to leadership. Stein depicts one's being as "here," and another's as "there," where every moment in life walks us into a new "here" as others experience the same movement. Stein calls us to be deliberate, dedicated to encountering experiences that provide glimpses into others' theres, opening an empathic relationship. However, empathy is not the feeling of a shared experience. Stein encourages us to empathize by feeling with another without sharing in a similar experience. Thus, from a phenomenological perspective, empathy is recognizing and allowing grace for another's narrative ground—a sacred space that each person embodies uniquely. Leaders would benefit from this phenomenological texturing of inclusion, a word that risks banality if applied without attentiveness to theoretical grounding.

Existentialism involves a temporal state of being and becoming, so knowing one's existence is impossible despite scientific research's attempts to capture it. Levinas (1969) insists that the Other always exceeds one's ability to know or contain the Other. Thus, existential leadership contradicts transformational leadership because to transform followers, a leader must understand what needs to be transformed, which is an impossibility and an act of hubris and interpersonal colonization (Fritz et al., 2023). Existential leadership de-centers, resituating leaders with others on the same plane of human existence, where others are "let be" and where the only thing known about them is that they are complex, storied beings with multiple narrative intersections on their life journeys, which are radically different from our own.

Resilience

Narratives shape our understanding of ethical reasoning, fostering resilience, the ability to continue in the face of adversity (Luthar, 2006). Resilience is often cultivated and expressed through storytelling, as evidenced by Viktor Frankl (1963), who explores the transformative power of narrative in overcoming trauma and hardship. Frankl's approach to narrative is closer to an existentialist understanding of a literature of situations than to a literature of characters. As people confront challenges and setbacks, they turn to storytelling, looking to larger narratives or narrative remnants (Arnett & Arneson, 1999) to make sense of their lives. Through crafting narratives, human beings weave together their experiences, finding meaning amid turmoil and charting a path forward.

Communicative approaches to resilience (e.g., Buzzanell, 2018a, 2018b; Buzzanell & Houston, 2018; Eddington, 2024; Houston, 2018; Okamoto, 2020) echo concerns of existentialism, focusing not, as Buzzanell (2018b) notes, "on traits or characteristics but on how resilience is constituted through storytelling, messages, routines, ... and other means" (p. 16), emphasizing communicative existence over essence. Although communicative resilience research focuses on personal narratives, narratives that carry public agreement provide additional focus for those gathered around a common purpose. Publicly agreed-upon narratives create what we could understand as collective resilience, akin to community resilience (e.g., Houston, 2018) and narrative resilience (Okamoto, 2020), with particular emphasis on the importance of place.

Leaders who protect and promote an organizational mission as an agreed-upon narrative background invite collective resilience through living out the mission through their practices, a way of walking the talk (e.g., Fritz et al., 2013). Yet, organizational leaders must resist instilling cult-like adherence to mission, whereby members lose subjectivity in a narrative of bad faith (Tomkins, 2023). Leaders who foster meaningful institutional homes (Arnett, 1992) invite participation in larger projects. They engage in good faith by finding places for others to flourish and welcoming hopes for distinctive contributions. From a communication ethics perspective, persons construct their particular positions within larger narratives that call them but that they did not create; in this sense, freely chosen participation within a larger story-guided framework creates a very different kind of "character," one not determined by the imperatives of a narrative but given traction by possibilities for meaning that create coherence rather than chaos in the face of the unexpected and the unwanted (Fritz, 2023). Opportunities for flourishing growth may risk employee relocation internally or organizational exit, but leading in good faith includes a willingness to take that risk.

Barnes (1964a) recognizes that without guiding narratives, human beings can experience a state of anxiety, absurdity, nausea, and guilt—common existentialist themes, which Arnett (1994) coined as existential homelessness. Barnes (1964b) writes the following:

> By his acts he inscribes himself in a world which he can never fully control, which distorts and disappoints his projects, which he cannot comprehend any more than he can understand himself. Each person is a self-creation, but chance furnishes most of the material out of which he must make himself. In short, man is absurd, but he does not always find his situation laughable.
>
> *(p. 125)*

Thus, as Levinas (1990) argues, freedom is difficult, especially in horrific situations such as the camps of World War II that he and Frankl experienced or the infinite task of Camus's Sisyphus. Still, existentialism offers a resilient way forward. Good faith constitutes the courage to embrace suffering in varying ways to find meaning and purpose in life.

Conclusion: Toward ethical leadership communication practice

This chapter opened with a discussion of *myth*odology and the narrative paradigm to emphasize the salience of story in literature and life that shapes, rather than determines, human existence. Existential leadership and communication build upon this ground, which calls for attentiveness to and mindfulness of people's impact on the world and others. Existentialist literature, such as that of Kafka (Tomkins, 2024) and O'Connor (Fritz, 2023), leaves readers with anxiety and despair by illuminating characters living in bad faith, but these stories can help leaders think critically about their existence, accept responsibility and accountability, strive to live in good faith, and recognize that outcomes and the future are uncertain. We also see, in these writers, glimpses of existential leadership in their uplifting of literature as a form of indirect communication, moving beyond the "essence" of ideas to show how they appear and are worked out in existence itself, demonstrating narrative fidelity through *myth*odology in their writings.

Ethical existential leaders who invite others to participate in an organizational narrative make possible joint responsiveness to changing moments. In the face of developments such as virtual work, the emergence of AI, and changes in the political environment, good faith requires trust in employees while not abandoning responsibility for leadership that honors organizational commitments. Paradox literature (e.g., Fairhurst & Putnam, 2024) provides creative resources for leadership when conditions are uncertain, contradictory, and complex, and crisis communication research shows us leaders of good faith who reframe crisis as opportunity (Seeger & Ulmer, 2001). Rather than assigning blame to outside forces for failures or for the event itself, such leaders press on, "bounc[ing] forward" (Houston, 2018, p. 19) to meet the moment.

Seeger and Sellnow (2016) focus on crisis narratives featuring leaders who acted in either bad faith or good faith. Blame narratives place responsibility for failure on persons inside or outside the organization (through, for example, scapegoating). Such stories limit insights from examination of "complex, often recurring series of events preceding crises" (p. 68). From an existentialist perspective, blame narratives are acts of bad faith because they fail to vest accountability in one's own leadership choices. Eddington's (2024) analysis of the communication efforts of someone in a political leadership role early in the COVID-19 pandemic reveals a focus on the economy rather than on human stories, which compromised the effectiveness of this figure's resilience narratives and "hurt the American people" (p. 215). In this case, bad faith rests in a failure to recognize human lives as of supreme worth and a negation of responsibility to provide comfort and hope to the suffering.

This existentialist view of leadership and communication contradicts the literature's widespread "explain and predict" models. *Myth*odology and narrative provide an alternative to the rational world paradigm. While scholars will continue searching for the perfect theory to dissolve dysfunction in communication, leadership, and organizational processes, existential leadership, paired with communication theory, reveals this striving as a bad-faith effort. Existential leadership through narrative, by way of *myth*odology, offers understanding, rather than definitive answers, in negotiating complex human life interwoven with ethical communicative practices of guiding narratives, which provide possibilities for resilience, hope, and empathy, resources for communicating and leading in good faith as best we can.

Case study: October Sky

The film *October Sky* (Johnston, 1999) provides a case study of *myth*odology, connecting narrative and existential leadership. Set in the 1950s during the space race between the United States and the USSR, this true story features Homer Hickam, a high school student from Coalwood, West Virginia. The young men of this community are destined to work in the mines unless they secure football scholarships to West Virginia University, and Homer, desperate to escape his ostensibly pre-ordained fate, is no football player.

Homer's life changes when he sees the USSR's *Sputnik* travel across the *October Sky*. The story unfolds as Homer and three friends pursue the unlikely dream of constructing a rocket that will actually fly. Miss Riley, their teacher, supports their choice and ensuing efforts. The high school principal opposes their project and warns Miss Riley not to give the young men false hopes. Homer's father thinks the pursuit of space exploration is foolish, expecting Homer to follow in his footsteps as a mine foreman—the only right path to support the town of Coalwood.

Miss Riley embodies an existential leader within a narrative of education and science to which the Rocket Boys (the nickname Homer, Quentin, Roy Lee, and Odell are given by fellow students) are drawn. However, despite her hopes for their success, Miss Riley respects Homer's ability to choose. When he withdraws from high school to work in the mine after his father is injured in an accident, Miss Riley tells Homer that she will be proud of him, regardless of his choice, offering an existential reason for why she has encouraged his project—she believes he made other plans. Homer's dad and the high school principal, on the other hand, lead in bad faith through the attempted colonization of Homer's future. The principal later throws his support behind the Rocket Boys' project, however, and even Homer's dad finally realizes that Homer's success is Coalwood's success.

Miss Riley's existential leadership provides freedom for Homer's choice to respond to the apparent end of his rocket-building dream. The Rocket Boys all enter professions reflecting their existential choices after placing first in the National Science Fair in Indianapolis and securing academic scholarships. Throughout the film, *myth*odology unfolds through communicative practices embodying existential leadership through narrative, moving implicit theory into explicit practice.

Suggested further readings

Arnett, R. C. (2005). *Dialogic confession: Bonhoeffer's rhetoric of responsibility*. Southern Illinois University Press.

Ladkin, D. (2020). *Rethinking leadership: A new look at old questions* (2nd ed.). Edward Elgar. https://doi.org/10.4337/9781788119320

Tomkins, L., & Eatough, V. (2013). The feel of experience: Phenomenological ideas for organizational research. *Qualitative Research in Organizations and Management*, *8*(3), 258–275. https://doi.org/10.1108/QROM-04-2012-1060

Questions for further engagement

1 Discuss how organizational culture and individual well-being are mutually cultivated and nourished through the lens of this chapter.

2 Watch the film *October Sky*. (a) Identify instances of communication that illustrate leading in good faith and in bad faith. (b) Consider Homer Hickam as an existential leader. How did his three friends support his leadership role?

Note

1 The conception of "the world" is what is phenomenologically experienced by humans as "the life world." While the natural world exists, humans cannot know it outside of their subjective experience.

References

Agarwal, J., & Malloy, D. C. (2000). The role of existentialism in ethical business decision-making. *Business Ethics: A European Review*, *9*, 143–154. https://doi.org/10.1111/1467-8608.00185

Arendt, H. (1998). *The human condition*. University of Chicago Press. https://doi.org/10.1017/S0003055400121628

Arnett, R. C. (1981). Toward a phenomenological dialogue. *The Western Journal of Speech Communication*, *45*, 201–212. https://doi.org/10.1080/10570318109374043

Arnett, R. C. (1986). *Communication and community: Implications of Martin Buber's dialogue*. Southern Illinois University Press.

Arnett, R. C. (1987). The status of communication ethics scholarship in speech communication journals from 1915 to 1985. *Central States Journal*, *38*, 44–61. https://doi.org/10.1080/10510978709368229

Arnett, R. C. (1992). *Dialogic education: Conversation about ideas and between persons*. Southern Illinois University Press.

Arnett, R. C. (1994). Existential homelessness: A contemporary case for dialogue. In R. Anderson, K. N. Cissna, & R. C. Arnett (Eds.), *The reach of dialogue: Confirmation, voice, and community* (pp. 229–246). Hampton Press, Inc.

Arnett, R. C. (2003). The responsive "I": Levinas's derivative argument. *Argumentation and advocacy*, *40*(1), 39–50. https://doi.org/10.1080/00028533.2003.11821596

Arnett, R. C. (2007). Interpretive inquiry as qualitative communication research. *Qualitative Research Reports in Communication*, *8*, 29–35. https://doi.org/10.1080/17459430701617887

Arnett, R. C. (2022). *Communication ethics and tenacious hope: Implications of the Scottish Enlightenment*. Southern Illinois University Press.

Arnett, R. C., & Arneson, P. (1999). *Dialogic civility in a cynical age: Community, hope, and interpersonal relationships*. State University of New York Press.

Arnett, R. C., Bell McManus, L., & McKendree, A. G. (2018). *Conflict between persons: The origins of leadership* (2nd ed.). Kendall Hunt.

Arnett, R. C., Fritz, J. H., & Holba, A. (2007). The rhetorical turn to Otherness: Otherwise than humanism. *Cosmos and History: The Journal of Natural and Social Philosophy*, *3*, 115–133.

Arnett, R. C., & Holba, A. M. (2012). *An overture to philosophy of communication: The carrier of meaning*. Peter Lang.

Ashman, I. (2007). Existentialism and leadership: A response to John Lawler with some further thoughts. *Leadership*, *3*, 91–106.

Ashman, I., & Lawler, J. (2008). Existential communication and leadership. *Leadership*, *4*, 253–269. https://doi.org/10.1177/1742715008092361

Ashman, I., & Winstanley, D. (2006). Business ethics and existentialism. *Business Ethics: A European Review*, *15*(3), 218–233. https://doi.org/10.1111/j.1467-8608.2006.00445.x

Barnes, H. E. (1959). *Humanistic existentialism: The literature of possibility*. University of Nebraska Press.

Barnes, H. E. (1960). *The Hippolytus of drama and myth*. University of Nebraska Press.
Barnes, H. E. (1964a). Greek tragicomedy. *The Classical Journal*, *60*, 125–131. https://www.jstor.org/stable/3295060
Barnes, H. E. (1964b). Schopenhauer, evangelist of pessimism. In A. Schopenhauer (Eds.), *The pessimist's handbook: A collection of popular essays* (pp. vii–xxxi). University of Nebraska Press.
Barnes, H. E. (1974a). *The meddling gods: Four essays on classical themes*. University of Nebraska Press.
Barnes, H. E. (1974b). *Sartre*. Quartet Books.
Botha, H. (2023). On bolstering the experience of moral agency: Simone de Beauvoir and ethical decision-making in organizations. In J. Jones (Ed.), *A research agenda for organizational ethics* (pp. 17–30). Edward Elgar. https://doi.org/10.4337/9781800884205
Botha, H., & Freeman, R. E. (2023). Existentialist perspectives on the problem and prevention of moral disengagement. *Journal of Business Ethics*, *185*, 499–511. https://doi.org/10.1007/s10551-022-05130-0
Bradbury, H., & Lichtenstein, B. M. B. (2000). Rationality in organizational research: Exploring the 'spaces between'. *Organization Science*, *11*, 551–564. https://doi.org/10.1287/orsc.11.5.551.15203
Buber, M. (1958a). *I and Thou*. Scribner Classics.
Buber, M. (1958b). What is common to all. *The Review of Metaphysics*, *11*(3), 359–379.
Buber, M. (1975). *Tales of the Hasidim*. Schocken Books.
Buber, M. (2002). *Between man and man*. Routledge (Original work published 1947). https://doi.org/10.4324/9780203220092
Buzzanell, P. M. (2018a). Communication theory of resilience: Enacting adaptive-transformative processes when families experience loss and disruption. In D. Braithwaite, E. Suter, & K. Floyd (Eds.), *Engaging theories in family communication* (2nd ed., pp. 98–109). Routledge. https://doi.org/10.4135/9781452204420
Buzzanell, P. M. (2018b). Organizing resilience as adaptive-transformational tensions. *Journal of Applied Communication Research*, *46*, 14–18. https://doi.org/10.1080/00909882.2018.1426711
Buzzanell, P. M., & Houston, J. B. (2018). Communication and resilience: multi-level applications and insights – A Journal of Applied Communication Research forum. *Journal of Applied Communication Research*, *46*, 1–4. https://doi.org/10.1080/00909882.2017.1412086
Eddington, S. M. (2024). Fact or fiction? The discursive framing of narrative resilience using Trump's COVID-19 presidential talk. In R. X. Browning (Ed.), *Power and politics in the media: The year in C-SPAN archives research, Volume 9* (pp. 199–221). Purdue University Press.
Fairhurst, G. T., & Putnam, L. (Eds.) (2024). *Performing organizational paradoxes*. Routledge. https://doi.org/10.4324/9781003014010
Fisher, W. R. (1984). Narration as a human communication paradigm: The case of public moral argument. *Communication Monographs*, *51*, 1–22. https://doi.org/10.1080/03637758409390180
Fisher, W. R. (1985). The narrative paradigm: An elaboration. *Communication Monographs*, *52*, 347–367. https://doi.org/10.1080/03637758509376117
Frankl, V. E. (1963). *Man's search for meaning: An introduction to logotherapy* (I. Lasch, Trans.). Pocket Books (Original work published in 1959).
Fritz, J. M. H. (2023). Ethical existential leadership lessons from Flannery O'Connor's "The Lame Shall Enter First." In J. Jones (Ed.), *A research*

agenda for organizational ethics (pp. 135–147). Edward Elgar. https://doi.org/10.4337/9781800884205

Fritz, J. M. H., Bell McManus, L. M., & Kearney, M. R. (2023). *Communication ethics literacy: Dialogue and difference* (3rd ed.). Kendall Hunt. https://doi.org/10.4135/9781452204048

Fritz, J. M. H., O'Neil, N. B., Popp, A. M., Williams, C. D., & Arnett, R. C. (2013). The influence of supervisory behavioral integrity on intent to comply with organizational ethical standards and organizational commitment. *Journal of Business Ethics*, *114*, 251–263. https://doi.org/10.1007/s10551-012-1345-z

Garrett, E. (2012). The essential secret of indirect communication. *Review of Communication*, *12*, 331–345. https://doi.org/10.1080/15358593.2012.683804

Gordon, L. (1997). Existential dynamics of theorizing black invisibility. In L. Gordon (Ed.), *Existence in black: An anthology of black existential philosophy* (pp. 69–79). Routledge.

Graen, G. B., & Uhl-Bien, M. (1995). Relationship-based approach to leadership: Development of a leader-member exchange (LMX) theory of leadership over 25 years—Applying a multi-level multi-domain perspective. *Leadership Quarterly*, *6*, 219–247. https://doi.org/10.1016/1048-9843(95)90036-5

Houston, J. B. (2018). Community resilience and communication: dynamic interconnections between and among individuals, families, and organizations. *Journal of Applied Communication Research*, *46*, 19–22. https://doi.org/10.1080/00909882.2018.1426704

Jaspers, K. (1973) *Way to wisdom*. Yale University Press. https://doi.org/10.5840/schoolman195330236

Johnston, J. (Director) (1999). *October sky* [Film]. Universal Pictures.

Jones, J. (2018). Empathic leadership: Saint Edith Stein's phenomenological perspective. In B. J. Denison (Ed.), *Women, religion, and leadership: Female saints as unexpected leaders* (pp. 155–177). Routledge.

Jones, J. (2020). A metamorphosis for leaders: Caring in good faith. In L. Tomkins (Ed.), *Paradox and power in caring leadership: Critical and philosophical reflections* (pp. 109–120). Edward Elgar. https://doi.org/10.4337/9781788975506

Jones, J. (2023a). Expanding horizons: *Myth*odology for interpretive scholarship. In J. Jones (Ed.), *A research agenda for organizational ethics* (pp. 3–17). Edward Elgar. https://doi.org/10.4337/9781800884205

Jones, J. (2023b). Preface. In J. Jones (Ed.), *A research agenda for organizational ethics* (pp. xvii–xxiii). Edward Elgar. https://doi.org/10.4337/9781800884205

Kane, G. C., Nanda, R., Phillips, A., & Copulsky, J. (2021). Redesigning the post-pandemic workplace: Work as we know it is forever changed by COVID-19. Now is the time for managers to envision the office that employees will return to. *MIT Sloan Management Review*, *62*(3), 12–14.

Ladkin, D. (2006). When deontology and utilitarianism aren't enough: How Heidegger's notion of "dwelling" might help organizational leaders resolve ethical issues. *Journal of Business Ethics*, *65*, 87–98. https://doi.org/10.1007/s10551-006-0019-0

Ladkin, D. (2013). From perception to flesh: A phenomenological account of the felt experience of leadership. *Leadership*, *9*, 320–334. https://doi.org/10.1177/1742715013485854

Ladkin, D. (2021). Problematizing authentic leadership: How the experience of minoritized people highlights the impossibility of leading from one's "true self." *Leadership*, *17*, 1–7. https://doi.org/10.1177/1742715021999586

Lawler, J. (2005). The essence of leadership? Existentialism and leadership. *Leadership*, *1*, 215–231. https://doi.org/10.1177/1742715005051860

Lawler, J., & Ashman, I. (2012). Theorizing leadership authenticity: A Sartrean perspective. *Leadership*, *8*, 327–344. https://doi.org/10.1177/1742715012444685
Levinas, E. (1969). *Totality and infinity: An essay on exteriority*. Duquesne University Press.
Levinas, E. (1990). *Difficult freedom: Essays on Judaism*. Johns Hopkins University Press.
Luthar, S. S. (2006). Resilience in development: A synthesis of research across five decades. In D. Cicchetti & D. J. Cohen (Eds.), *Developmental psychopathology: Risk, disorder, and adaptation* (pp. 739–795). Wiley. https://doi.org/10.1002/9780470939406
MacIntyre, A. (1981). *After virtue: A study in moral theory*. University of Notre Dame Press. https://doi.org/10.2307/jj.21995806
Okamoto, K. E. (2020). 'As resilient as an ironweed': Narrative resilience in nonprofit organizing. *Journal of Applied Communication Research*, *48*, 618–636. https://doi.org/10.1080/00909882.2020.1820552
Sartre, J.-P. (1943). *Being and nothingness: A phenomenological essay on ontology*. Washington Square Press.
Sartre, J.-P. (1946). *No exit and three other plays*. Vintage Books.
Sartre, J.-P. (2007). *Existentialism is a humanism*. Yale University Press (Original work published 1956). https://doi.org/10.2307/j.ctv15vwkgx
Schrag, C. O. (2003). *Communicative praxis and the space of subjectivity*. Purdue University Press.
Seeger, M. W., & Sellnow, T. L. (2016). *Narratives of crisis: Telling stories of ruin and renewal*. Stanford University Press. https://doi.org/10.1177/0001839216679614
Seeger, M. W., & Ulmer, R. R. (2001). Virtuous responses to organizational crisis: Aaron Feuerstein and Milt Cole. *Journal of Business Ethics*, *31*, 69–76. https://doi.org/10.1023/A:1010759319845
Stein, E. (1989). *On the problem of empathy* (W. Stein, Trans.). ICS Publications.
Stewart, D., & Mickunas, A. (1974). *Exploring phenomenology: A guide to the field and its literature*. American Library Association.
Thompson, N. (2024). *Authentic leadership revisited: An existentialist approach*. Edward Elgar. https://doi.org/10.4337/9781035340224
Tong, N., & Urick, M. J. (2023). *Bend the knee: Seize the throne: Leadership lessons from the seven kingdoms*. Emerald. https://doi.org/10.1108/9781802626476
Tomkins, L. (2023). The ethics of faith and suspicion: Reflections with the philosophy of Ricœur and the fiction of le Carré. In J. Jones (Ed.), *A research agenda for organizational ethics* (pp. 59–72). Edward Elgar. https://doi.org/10.4337/9781800884205
Tomkins, L. (2024). *Franz Kafka and the truths of leadership*. Edward Elgar. https://doi.org/10.4337/9781800379244
Urick, M. J. (2021). *A manager's guide to using the force: Leadership lessons from a galaxy far far away*. Emerald. https://doi.org/10.1108/9781800712300

11

LEADER-MEMBER EXCHANGE THEORY, THEORY OF INDEPENDENT-MINDEDNESS, AND SUPERIOR-SUBORDINATE RELATIONSHIPS

Scott A. Myers, Melissa F. Tindage, Stephen M. Kromka, and Sara Pitts

The superior-subordinate relationship is the most common workplace relationship in which most organizational employees will participate. It is a role-based, interpersonal relationship (Horan et al., 2021) between two coworkers where one coworker (i.e., the superior) (a) formally outranks the other coworker (i.e., the subordinate) by either organizational role or title and (b) both directs and evaluates the other coworker's task performance (Jablin, 1979; Sias, 2009). To facilitate functional superior-subordinate communication, it is recommended that superiors establish high-quality, communicative exchanges with their subordinates and create an autonomous and culturally aligned workplace environment in which they communicatively encourage their subordinates to be actively involved in decision-making.

Two theories—Leader-Member Exchange (LMX) Theory and the Theory of Independent-Mindedness (TIM), which center on superior-subordinate relationships—offer a unique perspective through which this recommendation can be made. LMX is a leadership theory based on the communicative exchanges between superiors and subordinates that result in differential quality relationships (Omilion-Hodges & Ptacek, 2021). In contrast, the TIM is a communication theory that explains how the link between superior-subordinate communication and employee involvement in active workplace decision-making is affected by the congruity that exists between an organization and the larger culture in which it is located (Avtgis & Rancer, 2024). Because leadership serves as one function of the superior-subordinate relationship and often is conveyed through how superiors choose to communicate with their subordinates (Sias, 2009),

DOI: 10.4324/9781003563662-14

it is necessary to consider how both the quality of superior-subordinate exchanges, as explained by LMX, and the emphasis on workplace autonomy and cultural alignment, as explored by TIM, are key to developing a deeper understanding of how superior-subordinate relationships can function effectively.

To reach this end, this chapter contains three sections. The first two sections conceptualize and explain LMX and the TIM, respectively. The third section bridges LMX and the TIM through a case study of three employees of the Raucous Raccoons, a minor-league baseball team. The chapter concludes with identifying four suggestions for improving communication in the superior-subordinate dyad, as well as additional readings and questions for further engagement.

Leader-Member Exchange (LMX) Theory

Developed initially as Vertical Dyad Linkage theory (Dansereau et al., 1975) and influenced by Role Theory (Graen, 1976), LMX has evolved from the study of how multiple subordinates view the same supervisor through the lenses of trust, respect, and obligation to how superior-subordinate relationships develop and affect employee, workgroup, and organizational performance (Graen & Uhl-Bien, 1995; Omilion-Hodges & Ptacek, 2021). LMX is considered to be a relational, communication-based leadership theory (Baker & Omilion-Hodges, 2013) that emphasizes the mutual exchange of material and social resources between superiors and subordinates, rather than the hierarchical relationship that exists between the two (Manata & Grubb, 2022), which then deems the relationship as either high-quality or low-quality (Omilion-Hodges et al., 2016; Sias & Shin, 2020). In a high-quality exchange relationship (i.e., leadership exchange, also known as an "in-group" relationship), superior-subordinate relationships are characterized by open communication and mutual trust, respect, and support; in a low-quality exchange relationship (i.e., supervisory exchange, also known as an "out-group" relationship), superior-subordinate relationships are characterized by less open communication and lower amounts of trust and support (Graen et al., 1982; Sias & Shin, 2020).

Historically, researchers have examined the differences between superiors and subordinates in high-quality and low-quality exchanges. Subordinates in high-quality relationships are perceived and treated more favorably by their superiors than subordinates who are perceived and treated by their superiors in low-quality relationships. As noted in several research summaries of the LMX literature (Graen & Uhl-Bien, 1995; Myers, 2006; Omilion-Hodges & Ptacek, 2021), subordinates in high-quality superior relationships are considered to be more productive, are rated higher in job performance, are granted greater role autonomy, and receive greater preferential treatment (e.g., challenging and engaging work assignments, mentoring, leadership development, and access to organizational resources) from their superiors than subordinates in low-quality superior relationships. They also report higher levels of commitment, job motivation, organizational identification, and satisfaction with their workplace, position within the organization, and superiors (Bakar et al., 2010; Lloyd et al., 2017; Sollitto et al., 2016). Conversely, subordinates in low-quality superior relationships feel less supported, receive more mundane work tasks, and are given either few or no opportunities for career development and advancement (Omilion-Hodges & Ptacek, 2021).

These exchanges are differentiated further by the quantity and quality of communication between superiors and subordinates (Sias, 2005). For example, subordinates in high-quality superior relationships typically discuss a myriad of work-related topics—their job performance, their work and personal problems, and ways to improve their performance—amidst playful banter, humor, teasing, and casual conversation while simultaneously engaging in more frequent amounts of communication (Bakar et al., 2010; Dienesch & Liden, 1986; Graen et al., 1982). High-quality superior-subordinate relationships also retain a person-centered communication focus (e.g., emphasizes autonomy, reflection, and perspective-taking) rather than a position-centered communication focus (e.g., emphasizes rules, commands, and authority; Fix & Sias, 2006) and, as Omilion-Hodges and Baker (2017) reported, are characterized by positive communication exchanges in which superiors solicit professional advice and feedback from, seek workplace collaboration with, offer development opportunities to, and express liking, support, and respect toward subordinates. Conversely, Fairhurst (1993) found that low-quality superior-subordinate relationships are characterized by polarizing communication exchanges in which superiors create a power distance between themselves and their subordinates by monitoring their work performance, engaging in face-threatening acts and conflict, or playing power games.

In sum, the strength of LMX is in explaining how superiors develop differential, hierarchical relationships with their subordinates, revealed through the communicative quality of their exchanges (Jian et al., 2014; Omilion-Hodges et al., 2016). Complementing this focus is the TIM, which identifies the communication traits that, when displayed proficiently by superiors and subordinates, lead to greater employee autonomy and involvement in organizational decision-making (Avtgis & Rancer, 2007). Therefore, while LMX emphasizes relational quality, the TIM offers a broader view that includes the role of individual autonomy and cultural alignment in shaping the communication patterns of superiors and subordinates.

Theory of Independent-Mindedness (TIM)

Developed as a corporatist theory (Infante et al., 2017) intended to reflect the cultural assumptions of the United States within U.S. organizations (Avtgis & Chory, 2010), the TIM is based on Infante's (1987; cited in Avtgis & Rancer, 2007) position that an organization's cultural norms and values should mirror the cultural norms and values of the larger culture in which it is located (Sollitto & Cranmer, 2019). The theory "assumes that the more an organization's culture is congruent with the larger culture within which it operates, the more satisfaction and contentment will be exhibited by its members regarding communication practices and feelings of self-worth" (Avtgis & Rancer, 2024, pp. 2–3). When congruity exists between an organization's culture and the larger culture in which it is embedded, organizational employees assume that their workplace relationships (e.g., superior-subordinate, peer, work friends, work spouse) are governed by the same relational expectancies and interaction norms as non-workplace relationships (Avtgis & Rancer, 2024).

Within the United States, however, cultural incongruities often exist between the larger American culture and its for-profit corporations in that individual (i.e., employee) needs for autonomy, self-expression, voice, freedom of speech, and the right to challenge authority—all of which are reflective of an individualistic culture—often are at odds with an organization's demands for its workers to conform, comply, or behave in a subservient manner (Avtgis & Chory, 2010; Avtgis & Rancer, 2024). In the U.S. workplace, these incongruities surface in the communication exchanges in the superior-subordinate relationship, which not only can negatively influence both the quality and the quantity of superior-subordinate communication but also highlight the status and power differentials that typically exist between superiors and subordinates in most organizations (Avtgis & Chory, 2010). For instance, a superior may ask their subordinate to complete a report to their preferred specifications, but it is not what the client has requested. The subordinate perceives they have the right to challenge the superior's request. However, the superior does not appreciate being challenged. This cultural incongruity between the superior's and subordinate's beliefs can result in strife within their relationship, wherein a low-quality communicative relationship materializes.

Rather than ignoring these cultural incongruities, the TIM proposes that differences in superior-subordinate relational quality, status, and power should be recognized and emphasized through superior-subordinate communication exchanges (Infante et al., 2017; Rancer & Avtgis, 2014) as a way to facilitate employee's active involvement in organizational decision-making (Avtgis & Rancer, 2007) and heighten employee satisfaction, commitment, and identification (Gorden & Infante, 1987). To do so, the TIM posits that superiors and subordinates embody three communication traits—argumentativeness, verbal aggressiveness, and affirming communicator style—as a way to foster independent-mindedness in superior-subordinate communication (Avtgis & Chory, 2010). That is, superiors and subordinates who are encouraged to engage in position-centered arguments (i.e., argumentativeness) while minimizing personal attacks or conflict (i.e., verbal aggressiveness) and adopting an affirming communicator style create a workplace communication climate that "facilitates the generally uncompromising desire for freedom of speech by individuals in American society" (Infante & Gorden, 1987, p. 74) and nurtures "free speech and affirmation of the individuals' self-worth" (Infante & Gorden, 1991, p. 295), which should then result in greater worker productivity (Gorden & Infante, 1987). For instance, a subordinate may ask their superior if they can work from home on Fridays because other work teams do. However, the superior may prefer that their team work together in person because they believe the subordinate will not be as diligent in finishing their work at home. The superior can use position-centered arguments that are delivered in an affirming style and do not personally attack the subordinate when discussing the issue to positively impact the quality of further communication between the superior and subordinate.

Argumentativeness and verbal aggressiveness

Argumentativeness and verbal aggressiveness are rooted in Infante's (1986, 1987) model of aggressive communication. Infante (1986) posited that interpersonal communication exists on an aggressive-nonaggressive continuum in that aggressive behavior "involves [an] attack, physical and/or symbolic in order, minimally to dominate and perhaps damage, or maximally, to defeat and perhaps destroy the locus of attack" (p. 1). Aggressive communication is constructive when it facilitates communication satisfaction and increases empathy, intimacy, and understanding between relational partners but is destructive when it results in dissatisfaction, makes one relational partner feel less favorable about themselves, or decreases relational quality (Infante, 1987).

Two traits—argumentativeness and verbal aggressiveness—form the core of an individual's use of aggressive communication in interpersonal relationships (Infante, 1986, 1987). Argumentativeness is a communication trait in which individuals can advocate for their position on a given topic while being able to verbally attack or refute other individuals' positions on the same topic (Infante & Rancer, 1982). In contrast, verbal aggressiveness is a communication trait in which individuals can attack the self-concept of other individuals instead of the individual's position on a given topic (Infante & Wigley, 1986). These verbally aggressive attacks can center on an individual's competence, character, background, or physical appearance, as well as emerge in the form of ridicule, threats, cursing, teasing, nonverbal emblems, or malediction (Infante, 1987; Infante et al., 1990, 1992).

Highly argumentative and lowly argumentative individuals differ in their perceptions of engaging in argumentativeness and their predispositions toward argumentativeness. Highly argumentative individuals—as compared to lowly argumentative individuals—exert a greater willingness and motivation to argue, express more interest in arguing, consider arguing to be an enjoyable activity, display greater argumentative skill when arguing, view arguing as a learning experience, and associate arguing with pragmatic outcomes (Infante, 1981; Infante et al., 1992; Rancer & Infante, 1985; Rancer et al., 1985; Rancer et al., 1992). Highly argumentative individuals also engage in greater advocacy and refutation (Infante & Rancer, 1993) and prefer counterarguing over bolstering (Wigley et al., 2021).

Similar differences exist between highly verbally aggressive individuals and lowly verbally aggressive individuals. Highly verbally aggressive individuals believe that their use of verbally aggressive messages is more justified, consider verbally aggressive messages to be less hurtful, and use verbally aggressive messages as a way to appear tough, express disdain toward or be mean to a relational partner, or as a result of a rational discussion turning into a fight more so than lowly verbally aggressive individuals (Infante et al., 1992; Martin et al., 1996). Highly verbally aggressive individuals also attack a person's competence, background, and physical appearance and engage in teasing, swearing, ridicule, and nonverbal emblems more frequently than lowly verbally aggressive individuals (Infante et al., 1992).

Affirming communicator style

Communicator style is a pervasive form of self-presentation revealed through an individual's unique use of verbal and nonverbal communication behaviors with their conversational partners (Myers, 2009). Broadly defined as "the signals that are provided to help process, interpret, filter, or understand meaning" (Norton, 1983, p. 47), communicator style indicates the extent to which a conversational partner should take a message

(Norton, 1978). Communicator style then becomes associated with an individual, establishing boundaries for how message content should and should not be interpreted (Norton, 1983).

Three attributes—relaxed, friendly, and attentive—comprise the affirming communicator style (Infante & Gorden, 1989). Individuals who communicate using the *relaxed* attribute appear to be calm, composed, and free of anxiety when interacting with a conversational partner; individuals who communicate using the *friendly* attribute recognize and confirm their partner's presence during their interactions; and individuals who communicate using the *attentive* attribute appear responsive and express interest in listening to a partner (Myers, 2009; Norton, 1983). By adopting an affirming communicator style, superiors and subordinates can communicate together to indicate respect and value for and toward each other (Avtgis & Rancer, 2007).

TIM research findings

Within the organization, researchers consistently have found support for the TIM (Avtgis & Rancer, 2007, 2024). From the workplace superior's perspective, superiors who were satisfied with their subordinates' job performance commented on the subordinates' quality of work, dependability, and interpersonal skills (Gorden et al., 1988). They also rated them higher in argumentativeness, lower in verbal aggressiveness, higher in affirming style, and as possessing a constructive disagreement style than superiors who were dissatisfied with their subordinates' job performance (Gorden et al., 1988; Infante & Gorden, 1989). Concomitantly, superiors who viewed their subordinates as verbally aggressive viewed them as less friendly, attentive, and relaxed (Infante & Gorden, 1987).

From the workplace subordinate perspective, subordinates with superiors who were perceived as highly argumentative and affirming reported higher levels of organizational commitment, satisfaction with their superiors, and satisfaction with their work than subordinates with superiors who were perceived as lowly argumentative and non-affirming (Infante & Gorden, 1991). Superiors who were perceived as high in argumentativeness and low in verbal aggressiveness had subordinates who perceived them as effective upward communicators, were satisfied with both their relationships with their superiors and their own careers, believed their employee rights were respected, and reported higher levels of organizational assimilation (Gorden & Infante, 1987; Infante & Gorden, 1985; Sollitto & Cranmer, 2019), whereas superiors who were perceived as low in argumentativeness and high in verbal aggressiveness had subordinates who viewed them as inattentive, unfriendly, and less relaxed (Infante &

Gorden, 1987). Subordinates reported being satisfied (a) with their superiors, their careers, and their tasks when their superiors encouraged them to argue about workplace issues, even if the subordinates categorized themselves as low argumentativeness (Gorden et al., 1988) and (b) with their superiors when they considered them to be friendly, attentive, and relaxed (Edge & Williams, 1994).

Case study: Put me in, coach!

Exploring the joint influence of LMX and the TIM on superior-subordinate communication offers a unique perspective on how employees' communication behaviors, traits, and styles can converge with the quality of the superior-subordinate relationship. Although different, LMX and the TIM provide complementary explanations to several aspects of superior-subordinate communication, including addressing the power differentials between superiors and subordinates regarding effective and collaborative decision-making. Power differentials are considered inequalities between individuals that result from status (Waldron, 2003) and, although inherent to the superior-subordinate relationship, can negatively influence the quality of the relationship (Fairhurst, 1993) as well as foster perceptions of cultural incongruities between the workplace and U.S. culture (Avtgis & Chory, 2010).

However, as suggested by both LMX and the TIM, these power differentials can be lessened when superiors and subordinates make adjustments to their communication, namely by focusing on the communicative quality of the relationships. This case study illustrates how communication interactions between superiors and subordinates shape the quality of their workplace relationship. Through the interactions between coworkers Patty and Marty and their supervisor, Ollie, the dynamic tensions between LMX and the TIM highlight the importance of effective leadership communication.

Organization and background

The Raucous Raccoons is a Minor League Baseball Team. Their marketing team is responsible for increasing box office ticket sales, creating promotions, and drawing crowds to watch the Raucous Raccoons play. The team is composed of five people. Ollie is the operations manager and supervisor. Patty works on creating promotions, and Marty focuses on social media marketing. There is also the box office coordinator and office assistant. All employees report to Ollie. Together, they are in charge of making sure the team has fans in the stands.

Operations manager Ollie and Promotions employee Patty have kids on the same community soccer team. Because of this, they tend to see each other out of the office three nights a week at their kids' soccer practices and on Saturday afternoons at soccer games. Their kids often carpool together to the practices and they sit with each other at the games. These frequent encounters have allowed Ollie and Patty to talk more and become close friends, in part because these frequent encounters consist of open communication and reflect the development of mutual trust, respect, and support. Conversely, marketing employee Marty, who does not have kids and likes to spend his out-of-office time hiking in the mountains with limited access to his phone and emails, is less talkative with Ollie. Given the circumstances, Patty has cultivated a high-quality exchange relationship with Ollie, while Marty's more distant, professional relationship with Ollie is reminiscent of a low-quality exchange relationship. Moreover, Ollie and Patty have informal conversations about work during the soccer games. In contrast, Marty only has the chance to communicate marketing ideas to Ollie during work hours, thus allowing Patty to become more actively involved in organizational decision-making.

The situation

In their weekly Monday team meeting, Ollie tasks Patty and Marty with brainstorming ideas for a new advertising campaign to bring in new audiences and increase ticket sales. They are given a week to develop ideas and present their pitches the following week during their standing team meeting. Both of them work all week on their pitches. The weekend arrives. As usual, Patty sits by Ollie during the Saturday afternoon soccer game. Ollie casually asks how her pitch is going. Patty delivers her pitch right there in the bleachers without thinking.

Ollie listens to Patty's idea and, conveying a highly verbally aggressive predisposition, says, "Patty, that's not a terrible idea for once. We still have some details to work out, but Marty can work on those."

Ollie continues to think on it and adds, "Honestly, your half-baked idea is probably better than anything Marty could come up with since he doesn't have the same vision for the team as we do."

Patty proudly says, "Thanks, boss! You're totally right about this!"

During their Monday team meeting, Marty arrives ready for the pitch. However, Ollie and Patty are already chatting about Patty's idea in the conference room. Patty sees Marty arrive and welcomes him in a somewhat affirming yet verbally aggressive style, saying, "Marty! We are glad you finally joined us. Sit down so we can bring you up to speed!"

Then, continuing in a verbally aggressive vein and highlighting the power differential between himself and Patty and Marty, Ollie says, "Patty delivered a workable idea to me on Saturday. With some tweaks I made yesterday, I think it can be highly effective, so that is the direction we will take."

Marty is disappointed. He researched his idea all week and compiled statistics to support his pitch. When his pitch was rejected before he could present it, he felt frustrated and needed to voice his concerns. Ollie's dismissal of Marty's pitch reinforces the lack of trust, support, and role autonomy typically associated with the low-quality superior-subordinate exchange relationship.

Marty speaks up in the meeting, employing a highly argumentative stance, saying, "Listen, I worked all week creating a thoughtful marketing pitch. I would appreciate the opportunity to share it with you."

Capitalizing on her high-quality exchange relationship with Ollie, Patty retorts, "You should be happy I did all the challenging work. Ollie sees the vision I pitched, and now all you have to do is the menial tasks."

Ollie then interjects,

> This is not a competition; we're a team. Patty is right this time, though. She knew what I was looking for in a campaign, so let's all get on board and support this idea. Besides, we must start this campaign before ticket sales open next month, so I don't want to waste more time.

Marty reacts by combining his highly argumentative stance with a highly affirming stance and says, "I'm sure Patty's idea is fine. Patty is a competent member of this team. *But* I would have appreciated it if my idea had been heard so that we could make an informed decision with all the facts."

Patty defensively responds, "Yeah, thanks! My idea is great! And it aligns with Ollie's vision to increase revenue at the ballpark."

Still visibly flustered, but refraining from speaking in a verbally aggressive manner, Marty continues to think about it and says,

> But if you just would look at my pitch, you would see that my idea has been successful in other ballparks, bringing up ticket sales by 10% each time it was implemented. I would appreciate it if you would consider hearing this idea. It's not democratic for all of our ideas not to at least be heard and considered before a decision is made.

Ollie solemnly responds, focusing on position-centered communication, "Marty, I am not interested in democracy this morning. This is my decision as the operations manager."

Suggestions for improving superior-subordinate communication

Superiors concerned with creating a workplace environment in which their subordinates are committed to, satisfied with, and productive within the organization should strive to engage in high-quality communicative interactions with their subordinates. To reach this end, we offer four suggestions for workplace superiors and subordinates to consider as a way to improve their communication.

The first suggestion is that because it is not uncommon for subordinates to hold expectations for, or impressions of, how their superiors exemplify effective leadership, superiors would be well-advised to reflect on how their interpersonal communicative behaviors and traits, in concert with their personality dispositions and supervisory behaviors, contribute to these expectations and impressions. One way in which superiors can enhance their perceived leadership ability is to become aware of and embrace the prototypical attributes of leadership (Vogel & Werkmeister, 2021), which include *achievement orientation* (e.g., assertive, confident, handles stress), *kind-heartedness* (e.g., kind, affectionate, compassionate), *progressiveness* (e.g., future-oriented, innovative, creative), *righteousness* (e.g., impartial, unselfish), and *rule abidance* (e.g., rule-oriented, loyal). Superiors who communicate with their subordinates in a manner that conveys these attributes likely will be able to enhance the efficiency, coordination, and accuracy associated with high-quality communicative exchanges (e.g., Jian et al., 2014).

The second suggestion is that for employees to achieve a state of independent-mindedness, workplaces should offer training and development sessions targeted at increasing worker argumentativeness, decreasing worker verbal aggressiveness, and increasing worker affirming communicator (Avtgis, 2023). These sessions should focus on employees learning how to (a) make the distinction between constructive and destructive communication (Rancer & Avtgis, 2014) as well as (b) argue constructively, (c) distinguish verbal aggression from argument, and (d) develop a presentational style that centers on validating, rather than dominating, the relational partner (Infante, 1988, 1995). Doing so would enhance both the task and relational competencies needed for functional workplace communication.

The third suggestion is that to facilitate high-quality communicative superior-subordinate exchanges characterized by argumentative and affirming, but not verbally aggressive, behaviors and messages, superiors should encourage their subordinates to engage in upward dissent. Upward dissent occurs when subordinates are able to articulate "disagreement or contradictory opinions about organizational practices, policies, or opinions" (Kassing, 1998, p. 183) to their supervisors under the premise that this articulation will be perceived as constructive and therefore not subject to retaliation (Kassing, 1997, 1998). Subordinates who are encouraged by their superiors to engage in upward dissent likely will feel empowered not only to strive toward high-quality communicative exchanges with their superiors but also to perceive that their input is vital for organizational decision-making, thereby increasing their involvement in day-to-day organizational tasks.

The fourth suggestion is that for the superior-subordinate relationship to sustain itself, superiors and subordinates must make a conscious effort to engage in relationship maintenance. Waldron (1991; Waldron & Sanderson, 2011) discovered that subordinates in high-quality LMXs use *personal* (i.e., communicating informally and engagingly with a focus on personal rather than task-related content), *contractual* (i.e., conforming to formal and informal role and relationship requirements and expectations), and *direct* (i.e., addressing and resolving relational injustices) relationship maintenance strategies more frequently, and *regulative* (i.e., engaging in impression management) maintenance strategies less regularly, than subordinates in low-quality LMXs. Superiors and subordinates should consider how these maintenance strategies can improve the communicative functionality of their relationships.

Conclusion

The purpose of this chapter was to propose how two theories—LMX and the TIM—offer a unique perspective to explore how relationships and communication traits work together to improve supervisor-subordinate relationships and subsequent workplace outcomes. Superiors who strive to develop high-quality communication relationships with their subordinates while adopting a highly argumentative and highly affirming communication style should find themselves well-suited to exhibit a leadership style to which subordinates respond positively. Doing so produces strong opportunities to foster positive and productive relationships between superiors and subordinates, which could prove worthwhile as organizations and their members face contemporary challenges such as declines in employee engagement and wellbeing, the emerging role that artificial intelligence continues to play in daily work life, and the challenges associated with moving employees from a face-to-face to a hybrid teamwork model (Wigert & Pendell, 2024).

Suggested further readings

Limon, M. S., & La France, B. H. (2005). Communication traits and leadership emergence: Examining the impact of argumentativeness, communication apprehension, and verbal aggressiveness in work groups. *Southern Communication Journal*, *70*(2), 123–133. https://doi.org/10.1080/10417940509373318

Manata, B. (2023). Examining the relationship between leader-member exchange (LMX) and subordinate achievement goal achievements. *Communication Studies*, *75*(3), 243–264.

Mikkelson, A. C., York, J. A., & Arritola, J. (2015). Communication competence, leadership behaviors, and employee outcomes in supervisor-employee relationships. *Business and Professional Communication Quarterly*, *78*(3), 336–354. https://doi.org/10.1177/2329490615588542

Minkin, R. (2023, November 13). *Most American workers say their boss is capable, confident, and fair*. Pew Research Center. https://www.pewresearch.org/short-reads/2023/11/13/most-american-workers-say-their-boss-is-capable-confident-and-fair/

Villaume, W. A., & Bodie, G. D. (2007). Discovering the listener within us: The impact of trait-like personality variables and communicator styles on preferences for listening style. *International Journal of Listening*, *21*(2), 102–123. https://doi.org/10.1080/10904010701302006

Questions for further engagement

1 After reviewing the case study, consider how the communication exchanges among Ollie, Patty, and Marty further reflect the LMX research findings obtained on the differences that exist between superiors and subordinates in high-quality and low-quality exchanges. Using these findings as a guide, identify several examples of how Ollie communicates differentially with both Patty and Marty. Similarly, what are some examples of how Patty and Marty might view their relationship with Ollie?

2 Manata (2023) found that subordinate orientation toward workplace tasks is associated with LMX superior-subordinate relationships. He discovered that subordinates who possess a mastery orientation (i.e., show an interest in learning the organizational material and content) perform better in high-quality relationships whereas subordinates who possess a performance-approach orientation (i.e., show a desire to outperform their peers) perform worse. Based on your workplace experience, what are some additional subordinate attitudes or orientations toward workplace performance that might affect the quality of the LMX superior-subordinate relationship?

3 In the case study, to what extent could the outcome of the situation differ had Ollie, Patty, and Marty embodied the levels of argumentativeness, verbal aggressiveness, and affirming communicator style needed to foster independent-mindedness?

4 Villaume and Bodie (2007) reported that individuals who possess different listening styles (i.e., people, action, content, time) vary in their levels of argumentative, verbally aggressive, and affirming communicator style behaviors. From either a workplace superior's or subordinate's perspective, how essential is listening to creating a high-quality communication relationship? How might listening contribute to worker involvement in organizational decision-making and heighten employee workplace satisfaction, commitment, and identification?
5 Applying the chapter content to the case study, what recommendations could be made to Ollie on how to improve their leadership ability? How could these improvements potentially affect how Patty and Marty communicate with both Ollie and each other?

References

Avtgis, T. A. (2023). Training and development in argumentative and aggressive communication: Contributions of Dr. Andrew S. Rancer. *Business and Professional Communication Quarterly*, *86*(1), 109–1163. https://doi.org/10.1177/23294906231152529

Avtgis, T. A., & Chory, R. M. (2010). The dark side of organizational life: Aggressive expression in the workplace. In T. A. Avtgis, & A. S. Rancer (Eds.), *Arguments, aggression, and conflict: New directions in theory and research* (pp. 285–304). Routledge. https://doi.org/10.4324/9780203855423

Avtgis, T. A., & Rancer, A. S. (2007). The Theory of Independent-Mindedness: An organizational theory for individualistic cultures. In M. B. Hinner (Ed.), *The role of communication in business transactions and relationships* (pp. 183–201). Peter Lang.

Avtgis, T. A., & Rancer, A. S. (2024). The theory of independent-mindedness: Three decades of research on organizational communication effectiveness. *Business and Professional Communication Quarterly*, *87*(40), 670–683. https://doi.org/10.1177/23294906221144765

Bakar, H. A., Dilbeck, K. E., & McCroskey, J. C. (2010). Mediating role of supervisory communication practices on relations between leader-member exchange and perceived employee commitment to workgroup. *Communication Monographs*, 77(4), 637–656. https://10.1080/03637751.2010.499104

Baker, C. R., & Omilion-Hodges, L. M. (2013). The effect of leader-member exchange differentiation within work units on coworker exchange and organizational citizenship behaviors. *Communication Research Reports*, *30*(4), 313–322. https://doi.org/10.1080/08824096.2013.837387

Dansereau, F., Graen, G., & Haga, W. J. (1975). A vertical dyad linkage approach to leadership within formal organizations. *Organizational Behavior and Human Performance*, *13*(1), 46–78. https://doi.org/10.1016/0030-5073(75)90005-7

Dienesch, R. M., & Liden, R. C. (1986). Leader-member exchange model of leadership: A critique and further development. *Academy of Management Review*, *11*(3), 618–634. https://doi.org/10.5465/AMR.1986.4306242

Edge, H. A., & Williams, M. L. (1994). Affirming communicator style of supervisor and subordinate use of upward influence tactics: An analysis of nonmanagerial and managerial employees. *Communication Research Reports*, *11*(2), 201–208. https://doi.org/10.1080/08824099409359958

Fairhurst, G. T. (1993). The leader-member exchange patterns of women leaders in industry: A discourse analysis. *Communication Monographs*, *60*(4), 321–351. https://doi.org/10.1080/03637759309376316

Fix, B., & Sias, P. M. (2006). Person-centered communication, leader-member exchange, and employee job satisfaction. *Communication Research Reports*, *23*(1), 35–44. https://doi.org/10.1080/17464090500535855

Gorden, W. I., & Infante, D. A. (1987). Employee rights: Content, argumentativeness, verbal aggressiveness, and career satisfaction. In C. A. B. Osigweh (Ed.), *Communicating employee responsibilities and rights: A modern management mandate* (pp. 149–163). Quorum Books.

Gorden, W. I., Infante, D. A., & Graham, E. E. (1988). Corporate conditions conducive to employee voice: A subordinate perspective. *Employee Responsibilities and Rights Journal*, *1*(2), 101–111. https://doi.org/10.1007/BF01385038

Gorden, W. I., Infante, D. A., & Izzo, J. (1988). Variations in voice pertaining to dissatisfaction/satisfaction with subordinates. *Management Communication Quarterly*, *2*(1), 6–22. https://doi.org/10.1177/0893318988002001002

Graen, G. (1976). Role-making processes within complex organizations. In M. D. Dunnette (Ed.), *Handbook of industrial and organizational psychology* (pp. 1201–1245). Rand McNally.

Graen, G. B., Liden, R. C., & Hoel, W. (1982). Role of leadership in the employee withdrawal process. *Journal of Applied Psychology*, *67*(6), 868–872. https://doi.org/10.1037/0021-9010.67.6.868

Graen, G. B., & Uhl-Bien, M. (1995). Relationship-based approach to leadership: Development of leader-member exchange (LMX) theory of leadership over 25 years: Applying a multi-level multi-domain perspective. *Leadership Quarterly*, *6*(2), 291–247. https://doi.org/10.1016/1048-9843(95)90036-5

Horan, S. M., Chory, R. M., Craw, E. S., & Jones, H. E. (2021). Blended work/life relationships: Organizational communication involving workplace peers, friends, and lovers. *Communication Research Trends*, *40*(2), 3–47. https://scholarcommons.scu.edu/crt/vol40/iss2/1?utm_source=scholarcommons.scu.edu%2Fcrt%2Fvol40%2Fiss2%2F1&utm_medium=PDF&utm_campaign=PDFCoverPages

Infante, D. A. (1981). Trait argumentativeness as a predictor of communicative behavior in situations requiring argument. *Central States Speech Journal*, *32*(4), 265–272. https://doi.org/10.1080/10510978109368105

Infante, D. A. (1986, April 30–May 3). *A conceptualization of aggressive communication*. [Paper presentation.] Eastern Communication Association 77th Annual Meeting, Atlantic City, NJ, United States.

Infante, D. A. (1987). Aggressiveness. In J. C. McCroskey & J. A. Daly (Eds.), *Personality and interpersonal communication* (pp. 157–192). Sage.

Infante, D. A. (1988). *Arguing constructively*. Waveland Press.

Infante, D. A. (1995). Teaching students to understand and control verbal aggression. *Communication Education*, *44*(1), 51–63.

Infante, D. A., & Gorden, W. I. (1985). Superiors' argumentativeness and verbal aggressiveness as predictors of subordinates' satisfaction. *Human Communication Research*, *12*(1), 117–125. https://doi.org/10.1111/j.1468-2958.1985.tb00069.x

Infante, D. A., & Gorden, W. I. (1987). Superior and subordinate profiles: Implications for independent-mindedness and upward effectiveness. *Central States Speech Journal*, *38*(1), 73–80. https://doi.org/10.1080/10510978709368232

Infante, D. A., & Gorden, W. I. (1989). Argumentativeness and affirming communicator style as predictors of satisfaction/dissatisfaction with subordinates. *Communication Quarterly*, *37*(2), 81–90. https://doi.org/10.1080/01463378909385529

Infante, D. A., & Gorden, W. I. (1991). How employees see the boss: Test of an argumentative and affirming model of supervisors' communicative behavior. *Western Journal of Speech Communication*, *55*(3), 294–304. https://doi.org/10.1080/10570319109374386

Infante, D. A., & Rancer, A. S. (1982). A conceptualization and measure of argumentativeness. *Journal of Personality Assessment*, *46*(1), 72–80. https://doi.org/10.1207/s15327752jpa4601_13

Infante, D. A., & Rancer, A. S. (1993). Relations between argumentative motivation, and advocacy and refutation on controversial issues. *Communication Quarterly*, *41*(4), 415–426. https://doi.org/10.1080/01463379309369902

Infante, D. A., Rancer, A. S., Avtgis, T. A., & MacGeorge, E. L. (2017). *Contemporary communication theory* (2nd ed.). Kendall Hunt.

Infante, D. A., Riddle, B. L., Horvath, C. L., & Tumlin, S. A. (1992). Verbal aggressiveness: Messages and reasons. *Communication Quarterly*, *40*(2), 116–126. https://doi.org/10.1080/01463379209369827

Infante, D. A., Sabourin, T. C., Rudd, J. E., & Shannon, E. A. (1990). Verbal aggression in violent and nonviolent marital disputes. *Communication Quarterly*, *38*(4), 361–371. https://doi.org/10.1080/01463379009369773

Infante, D. A., & Wigley, C. J., III. (1986). Verbal aggressiveness: An interpersonal model and measure. *Communication Monographs*, *53*(1), 61–69. https://doi.org/10.1080/03637758609376126

Jablin, F. M. (1979). Superior-subordinate communication: The state of the art. *Psychological Bulletin*, *86*(6), 1201–1222. https://doi.org/10.1037/0033-2909.86.6.1201

Jian, G., Shi, X., & Dalisay, F. (2014). Leader-member conversational quality: Scale development and validation through three studies. *Management Communication Quarterly*, *28*(3), 375–403. https://doi.org/10.1177/0893318914533201

Kassing, J. W. (1997). Articulating, antagonizing, and displacing: A model of employee dissent. *Communication Studies*, *48*(4), 311–332. https://doi.org/10.1080/10510979709368510

Kassing, J. W. (1998). Development and validation of the organizational dissent scale. *Management Communication Quarterly*, *12*(2), 183–229. https://doi.org/0893318998122002

Lloyd, K. J., Boer, D., & Voelpel, S. C. (2017). From listening to leading: Toward an understanding of supervisory listening within the framework of leader-member exchange theory. *International Journal of Business Communication*, *54*(4), 431–451. https://doi.org/10.1177/2329488415572778

Manata, B. (2023). Examining the relationship between leader-member exchange (LMX) and subordinate achievement goal achievements. *Communication Studies*, *75*(3), 243–264.

Manata, B., & Grubb, S. (2022). Conceptualizing leader-member exchange as a second-order construct. *Frontiers in Psychology*, *13*, 1–13. https://doi.org/10.3389/fpsyg.2022.953860

Martin, M. M., Anderson, C. M., & Horvath, C. L. (1996). Feelings about verbal aggression: Justifications for sending and hurt from receiving verbally aggressive messages. *Communication Research Reports*,*13*(1), 19–26. https://doi.org/10.1080/08824099609362066

Myers, S. A. (2006). Using leader-member exchange theory to explain students' motives to communicate. *Communication Quarterly*, *54*(3), 293–304. https://doi.org/10.1080/01463370600878008
Myers, S. A. (2009). Style, communicator. In S. W. Littlejohn, & K. A. Foss (Eds.), *Encyclopedia of communication theory* (pp. 941–942). Sage. https://doi.org/10.4135/9781412959384.n367
Norton, R. (1983). *Communicator style: Theory, applications, and measures*. Sage.
Norton, R. W. (1978). Foundation of a communicator style construct. *Human Communication Research*, *4*(2), 99–112. https://doi.org/10.1111/j.1468-2958.1978.tb00600.x
Omilion-Hodges, L. M., & Baker, C. R. (2017). Communicating leader-member relationship quality: The development of leader communication exchange scales to measure relationship building and maintenance through the exchange of communication-based goods. *International Journal of Business Communication*, *54*(2), 115–145.
Omilion-Hodges, L. M., & Ptacek, J. K. (2021). *Leader-member exchange and organizational communication: Facilitating a healthy work environment*. Palgrave Macmillan.
Omilion-Hodges, L. M., Ptacek, J. K., & Zerilli, D. H. (2016). A comprehensive review and communication research agenda of the contextualized workgroup: The evolution and future of leader-member exchange, coworker exchange, and team-member exchange. *Annals of the International Communication Association*, *40*(1), 343–377. https://doi.org/10.1080/23808985.2015.11735265
Rancer, A. S., & Avtgis, T. A. (2014). Aggressive communication in the organization. In *Argumentative and aggressive communication: Theory, research, and application* (2nd ed., pp. 101–116). Peter Lang.
Rancer, A. S., Baukus, R. A., & Infante, D. A. (1985). Relations between argumentativeness and belief structures about arguing. *Communication Education*, *34*(1), 37–47.
Rancer, A. S., & Infante, D. A. (1985). Relations between motivation to argue and the argumentativeness of adversaries. *Communication Quarterly*, *33*(3), 209–218. https://doi.org/10.1080/01463378509369599
Rancer, A. S., Kosberg, R. L., & Baukus, R. A. (1992). Beliefs about arguing as predictors of trait argumentativeness: Implications for training in argument and conflict management. *Communication Education*, *41*(4), 375–387. https://doi.org/10.1080/036345
Sias, P. M. (2005). Workplace relationship quality and employee information experiences. *Communication Studies*, *56*(4), 375–395. https://10.1080/10510970500319450
Sias, P. M. (2009). *Organizing relationships: Traditional and emerging perspectives on workplace relationships*. Sage. https://doi.org/10.4135/9781452204031
Sias, P. M., & Shin, Y. (2020). Workplace relationships. In A. M. Nicotera (Ed.), *Origins and traditions of organizational communication: A comprehensive introduction to the field* (pp. 187–206). Routledge. https://doi.org/10.4324/9780203703625
Sollitto, M., & Cranmer, G. A. (2019). The relationship between aggressive communication traits and organizational assimilation. *International Journal of Business Communication*, *56*(2), 278–296. https://doi.org/10.1177/2329488415613339
Sollitto, M., Martin, M. M., Dusic, S., Gibbons, K. E., & Wagenhouser, A. (2016). Assessing the superior-subordinate relationship involving part-time employees. *International Journal of Business Communication*, *53*(1), 74–96.

Villaume, W. A., & Bodie, G. D. (2007). Discovering the listener within us: The impact of trait-like personality variables and communicator styles on preferences for listening style. *International Journal of Listening*, *21*(2), 102–123. https://doi.org/10.1080/10904010701302006

Vogel, R., & Werkmeister, L. (2021). What is public about public leadership? Exploring implicit public leadership theories. *Journal of Public Administration Research and Theory*, *31*(1), 166–183. https://doi.org/10.1093/jopart/muaa024

Waldron, V. R. (1991). Achieving communication goals in superior-subordinate relationships: The multi-functionality of upward maintenance tactics. *Communication Monographs*, *58*(3), 289–306. https://doi.org/10.1080/03637759109376231

Waldron, V. R. (2003). Relationship maintenance in organizational settings. In D. J. Canary, & M. Dainton (Eds.), *Maintaining relationships through communication: Relational, contextual, and cultural variations* (pp. 163–184). Erlbaum. https://doi.org/10.4324/9781410606990

Waldron, V. R., & Sanderson, J. (2011). The role of subjective threat in upward influence situations. *Communication Quarterly*, *59*(2), 239–254.

Wigert, B., & Pendell, R. (2024, December 16). *7 workplace challenges for 2025*. GALLUP. https://www.gallup.com/workplace/654329/workplace-challenges-2025.aspx

Wigley, C. J., III, McCroskey, L. L., & Rancer, A. S. (2021). Trait argumentativeness as a correlate of bolster and counterargue tendencies in a resistance to persuasion research. *Communication Research Reports*, *38*(1), 12–22. https://doi.org/10.1080/08824096.2020.1867091

12

SERVING UP SUSTAINABILITY

Institutionalized Leadership Communication in the Restaurant Industry

Craig Engstrom, Rose Helens-Hart, and Jenna Haugen

Introduction

Let's begin this chapter with an illustrative quiz. Imagine a major restaurant chain CEO writing an annual letter introducing their company's sustainability practices. Various stakeholders, including shareholders, franchisees, and journalists, will read the letter. From the choices below, which claim are they likely to make?

A "Planet: We're making strides in our sustainable sourcing practices and in our restaurant operations, including food donation, recycling, and energy and water conservation."
B "Planet: We remain focused on driving climate action, helping to protect natural resources, reducing waste, and transitioning to more sustainable packaging."
C "Planet: We aim to maximize profits by leveraging the planet's resources. Our commitment to shareholder value supersedes environmental conservation."
D Both A and B are reasonable choices.

The correct answer is "D"—obviously. Greg Creed, the then-CEO of Yum! Brands, penned option A in its *2017 Global Citizenship & Sustainability Report* (p. 5). Chris Kempczinski wrote option B in the *McDonald's Corporation 2022–23 Impact Report* (p. 5). A skeptic might suggest that option C is truthful; however, no CEO would deliberately place shareholder value over the environment given the public relations

DOI: 10.4324/9781003563662-15

nightmare that would unfold. But why are these two executives' statements so similar? An institutional theory perspective of leadership communication offers one explanation: they feel a social pressure to share similar ideas, in similarly rhetorical ways, to retain their organization's legitimacy. If they do not appropriately express a commitment to environmental sustainability, they will lose credibility. So, they copy each other. In organizational communication theory, we call this type of communication institutionalized.

Leaders' communication practices in the environmental, social, and governance (ESG) sphere (broadly called sustainability) are institutionalized, which means this communication drives actual decision-making practices. For example, saying you are committed to the environment makes one committed to positive practices. However, practices may also become so institutionalized that leaders are constrained in what they can legitimately say, write, or do. Presenting a radical vision or a drastic departure from acceptable practices, like the claim that a restaurant group will become carbon net-zero within two years, would undermine their authority as leaders. Thus, as Guthey et al. (2022) suggest, leadership often becomes a game of legitimizing communication within multiple stakeholder groups.

In this chapter, we present a model and research application of how leadership communication is institutionalized in the context of ESG reporting within the restaurant industry. We textually analyze real-world examples of ESG-related leadership communication by integrating institutional theory with leadership theories. Our findings and discussion showcase the complexities and implications of ESG communication on organizational practices and stakeholder perceptions.

We begin by presenting a theoretical framework for institutionalized leadership communication, focused on ESG communication. We then use this framework to analyze global restaurant groups' CEO letters from annual sustainability reports. This analysis demonstrates how to identify institutionalized ESG communication in practice. Finally, we discuss the practical application of our findings for leaders, communication scholars, and communication consultants.

The institutionalized practice of leaders' communication

This section provides an abridged overview of the key concepts in institutional theory. We have prepared an illustrative model highlighting how key concepts interact to assist readers with how we use institutional theory to analyze leaders' ESG communication, which we posit is highly institutionalized.

The organizational theory of institutions, which articulated that organizations comprise ceremonial, taken-for-granted practices, emerged in scholarship in the late 1970s (see Meyer & Rowan, 1977) and expanded through the 1980s to include an explanation of why most formal organizational structures are *isomorphic*—i.e., look alike in form and practices (see DiMaggio & Powell, 1983). For example, higher education institutions within the United States tend to have the same departments, units, activities, terminology, timelines, etc. This is because they are highly institutionalized due to three types of isomorphic pressures: coercive, normative, and mimetic.

Coercive isomorphism results from pressures exerted on organizations by other organizations upon which they depend or by cultural expectations in the society within which organizations function. This type often involves legal and formal regulations. For example, external regulatory requirements and stakeholder expectations that compel organizations to adopt specific ESG practices and communication styles would result in more leaders following the same practices merely to comply.

Normative isomorphism stems from professionalization within a field and drives a consensus on acceptable communication practices. It involves the collective struggle of members of an occupation to define the conditions and methods of their work, to control "the production of producers," and thus to define standards of practice and professional behavior. For example, ESG practices and standards are codified by coursework in business schools, standards set by consulting groups (e.g., EY, KPMG), and investment firms (e.g., Blackrock). See, for example, KPMG's (2022) *ESG Leadership*.

Mimetic isomorphism occurs as organizations model other organizations they see as successful or legitimate. This mechanism is especially prevalent under conditions of uncertainty, where organizations imitate models considered more legitimate or successful. Mimetic pressures prompt organizations to imitate successful peers, resulting in similar communication styles and messages. For example, if a leading fast-casual restaurant group (i.e., benchmark organization) pursues partnerships with a large nonprofit organization and advertises this relationship, other restaurant groups would form a similar partnership to obtain the benefits of a partnership, even if leaders of these organizations are unsure what the benefits include. Miming organizations assume the benchmark organization has insight.

By the early 2000s, scholars expanded beyond the focus on pressures and taken-for-granted practices to study how *legitimacy*, "a crucial element in the creation and survival of new [and existing] organizational forms" (Suddaby & Greenwood, 2005, p. 37), is rhetorically acquired, maintained, and lost. Lammers and Barbour (2006) imported these ideas into the field of organizational communication by proposing five propositions of an institutional theory of organizational communication (p. 367):

- Proposition 1. Communication sustains institutions.
- Proposition 2. Communication aligns organizations with institutions.
- Proposition 3. Institutions operate and organize through formal communication.
- Proposition 4. The success of boundary-spanning communication depends on the presence of institutions.
- Proposition 5. Institutional hierarchy is manifested in organizing.

Alongside Lammers and Barbour's work, leadership and entrepreneurship scholars emphasized that while institutions stem from taken-for-granted practices, actors retain agency to shape and transform them. Lawrence and Suddaby (2006) defined this institutional work as active-processual-rhetorical practices such as advocating, defining, vesting, constructing identities, mimicking, and educating. For instance, a leader promoting legislative action engages in advocacy that may trigger coercive pressures on industry organizations to conform in specific ways.

Building on these theorists' work, Engstrom (2010) identified *discursive pressure* as a distinct isomorphic pressure, rooted in the rhetorically recursive relationship between institutions and practices. These pressures stem from cultural forces like media sentiment, influencing organizations to adjust practices in response to public narratives about ESG. Institutional norms are produced and reproduced through rhetorical elements such as language and symbols. Unlike mimetic pressures, which arise internally, discursive pressures originate in broader societal narratives, shaping how organizations frame their rhetoric. For example, a CEO might discursively reframe their ESG messaging—through word choice, metaphors, stories, analogies, symbols, visuals, and appeals to shared values—in response to media criticism of greenwashing, emphasizing transparency to align with public expectations and reduce reputational risk.

Today, research in organizational institutionalism remains strong and continues to highlight the ways rhetoric and communication logics affect professions, institutions, and institutional practices (see Cornelissen et al., 2015; Simonsson & Heide, 2021), including in the fields of leadership (e.g., Raffaelli & Glynn, 2015) and ESG (e.g., Weder, 2023).

A model of institutionalized ESG communication

Drawing on institutional theory and institutional work, we developed a model to illustrate the intricate, recursive relationship between

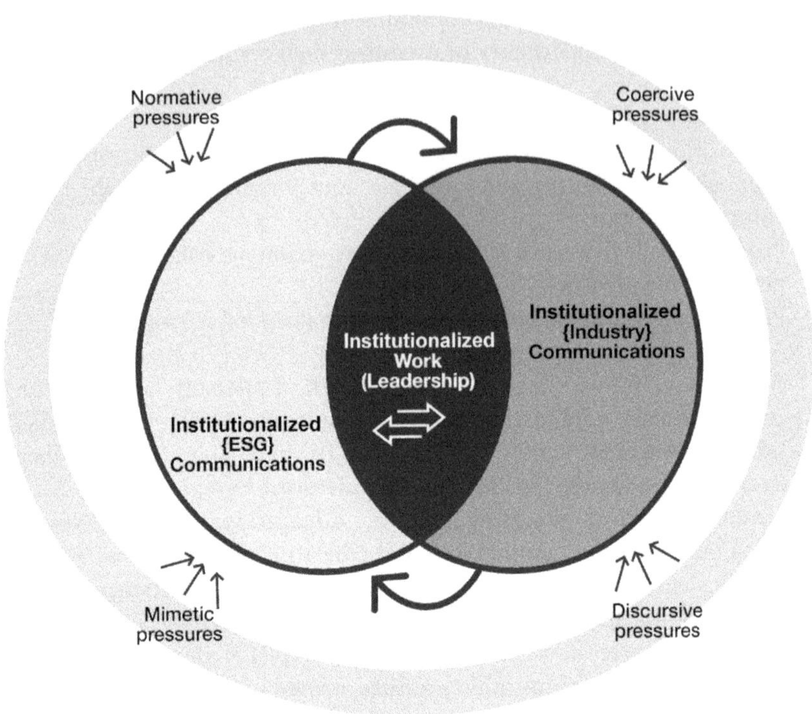

FIGURE 12.1 Illustration of institutional theory concepts in the context of ESG-related communication

institutional work, leadership communication, and institutionalized ESG practices, which guided the formation of our research questions (see Figure 12.1).

At the model's core is "Institutional Work," performed explicitly by leadership through "Institutionalized ESG Communication." This center represents leaders' communicative practices that create and reinforce organizational commitments to ESG goals as they intersect with cultural/discursive communication logic and industry or professional communication logic. Established industry norms and societal expectations shape and constrain institutionalized communication. Surrounding the core are four primary institutional pressures influencing leadership communication: normative, coercive, mimetic (DiMaggio & Powell, 1983), and discursive (Engstrom, 2010).

Institutional theory would suggest that these pressures, interacting with leadership communication, will produce "Institutionalized {Industry} Communication." This means organizations in the same industry, like

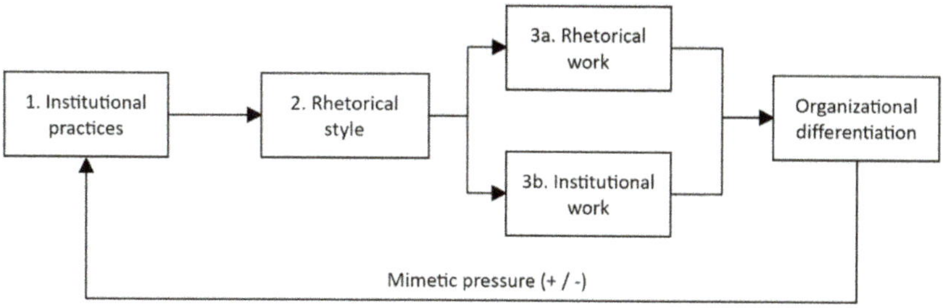

FIGURE 12.2 Research focus: Leadership style, institutional work, and organizational differentiation

the restaurant industry, will exhibit similar, predictable communication patterns. As a result, leaders' communication will be highly formulaic as "Institutionalized {ESG} Communication." We have placed concepts like {Leadership} and {ESG} in brackets because the literature suggests other forms of communication, like {Sports} communication, form distinct institutional practices. Forms of communication become standardized and constrained by isomorphic pressures, reflecting institutional norms shaped through "Institutional Work."

To capture the role of leadership communication in institutional work and how organizations develop differentiated practices, we illustrate a process grounded in the assumption that a leader's rhetorical style shapes both rhetorical and institutional work, which together influence organizational differentiators (see Figure 12.2). We begin with the premise that (1) practices within the restaurant industry—such as CEO letters in sustainability reports—are highly institutionalized. CEOs exhibit different (2) leadership styles, which moderate their (3a) rhetorical practices and (3b) institutional work. We show these dimensions are closely intertwined and 3a and 3b are differentiators, such as partnership choices and rhetorical strategies (e.g., word choice, analogies). Over time and under the influence of mimetic pressures, 3a and 3b reinforce (+) or shift (−) ESG engagement and reporting across the industry.

Research questions

Our goal is not to predict the adoption of specific language choices in the future but to address two broad research questions. These questions aim to assist leaders and communication practitioners, such as public relations and corporate communication professionals, by improving their abilities to expect and adapt to the constraints of institutionalized communication. We hope this chapter will inspire ideas for future research.

RQ1: What patterns of institutional work, such as defining or identity construction, are commonly employed in leaders' annual sustainability report letters within the restaurant industry?

RQ2: How do CEOs employ differentiation tactics in their letters introducing annual reports focusing on sustainability to distinguish their organizations from competitors within the same industry?

Research method

Institutional operations are often enacted through formal communication channels, which include documented policies, official announcements, and formal reporting. This formalization of communication solidifies the institution's norms and practices, making them more stable and resistant to arbitrary change. Examining formal communication helps with understanding institutional practices.

We selected the restaurant industry to investigate the institutionalized nature of ESG communication because of the industry's significant global environmental and social impacts. We utilized a 2024 list (Reiff, 2024) of the largest international restaurant companies to guide our selection of a group of successful peer firms. Then we analyzed executives' letters introducing annual reports on ESG practices and sustainability.

We chose four peer companies: Darden Brands International (DBI), McDonald's, Restaurant Brands International (RBI), and Yum! Brands (Yum!). Each uses the franchise model, is global, and has five years of recent publicly available annual reports addressing ESG criteria, including an introductory letter from company leadership. Table 12.1 lists the documents used for analysis and their publication dates.

We uploaded the CEO letters into Dedoose, a collaborative data analysis program, allowing us to generate and share a codebook during independent qualitative coding. We began analysis with preliminary codes generated through our literature review of institutional communication (e.g., identity construction, mimicry, education) and leadership communication (e.g., appealing to a shared purpose, goal setting, long-term strategy articulation). We included codes related to rhetorical strategy (e.g., types of appeals, language and style, and text structure), best practices in leadership communication (e.g., appeal to shared experiences and values), and ESG issues (e.g., animal welfare, food safety, and carbon footprint). As we independently coded letters for their rhetorical moves and content, we added, refined, and discussed additional codes as necessary.

TABLE 12.1 Texts used for analysis

Company	*Document title*	*In-text reference*
Yum! Brands	2017 Global Citizenship & Sustainability Report; Letter from Greg Creed, CEO	Creed, 2017 GCSR
–	2018 Global Citizenship & Sustainability Progress Update; Letter from Greg Creed, CEO	Creed, 2018, GCSPU
–	2019 (2020, 2021, 2022) Global Citizenship & Sustainability Report; Letter from David Gibbs, CEO	Gibbs, 2019 (or 2020, 2021, 2022), GCSPU
Darden Brands International	2019 (2020, 2021) Letter to Shareholders from Eugene Lee, President and CEO	Lee, 2019 (or 2020, 2021), Letter to Shareholders
–	2022 (2023) Letter to Shareholders from Eugene Lee, Executive Chairman; Rick Cardenas, President and CEO	Lee and Cardenas, 2022 (or 2023), Letter to shareholders
Restaurant Brands International	2016 (2017) Sustainability Report; Letter from Daniel Schwartz, CEO	Schwarts, 2016 (or 2017), SR
–	2020 (2021) Restaurant Brands for Good Report; Jose Cil, CEO	Cil, 2020 (or 2021), RBGR
–	2022 Restaurant Brands for Good Report; Josh Kobza, CEO	Kobza, 2022, RBGR
McDonald's	2019–2020 (2020–2021, 2021–2022, 2022–2023) Purpose and Impact Summary Report; Letter from Chris Kempczinski, President and CEO	Kempczinski, 2019–2020 (or 2020–2021, 2022–2023), PISR

Identifies the texts we used in our analysis, organized by company, document title, and in-text reference.

We identified themes in descriptive codes by observing textual data's recurrence, repetition, and forcefulness (Lindlof & Taylor, 2017). Through these themes, institutionalized patterns became apparent. We met regularly to discuss codes and our independent analysis (Giesen & Roeser, 2020) to agree on the most common and compelling themes, similarities, and differences among the letters. We determined that while there were rhetorical differences among the letters, each conformed to predictable patterns in form, content, and purpose, which provided us with compelling evidence of institutionalized ESG leadership communication. The following sections detail our findings and discuss the implications of institutionalized leadership communication in the ESG domain.

Analysis and discussion

As we compared the CEO letters, patterns of institutional work emerged. Our codes coalesced to demonstrate that CEOs' primary efforts in their leadership communication focused on two types of institutional work: *defining* and *constructing identities*. In this section, we provide examples of these forms of institutional work to demonstrate the institutionalized nature of ESG communication within CEO letters that introduce annual reports discussing sustainability. We first demonstrate how CEOs similarly defined ESG priorities for the restaurant industry, then compare how each constructed firm identity (and differentiated themselves) in the field.

Defining ESG in the restaurant industry

In the past 25 years, we have seen increased coercive, discursive, and normative isomorphic pressure on businesses to engage in sustainable practices. Public discourse and global initiatives promoting socially responsible and sustainable business practices have generated both legal and cultural ESG expectations for companies (e.g., the UN Global Compact, the United Nations Sustainable Development Goals). Consumer preferences have shifted to companies that articulate ESG claims (Frey et al., 2023). In response, businesses have launched initiatives and changed practices to improve their sustainability and communicate these improvements. This activity creates normative and mimetic pressure to conform. In addition to declaring their sustainable practices through marketing and advertising, companies can engage in clear and transparent reporting of their activities through voluntarily adopted frameworks such as the Global Reporting Initiative. Reporting is a form of institutionalized (and strategic) communication that provides stakeholders with financial and nonfinancial information (Uyar, 2016) that can serve as evidence of sustainable progress and institutional work.

External pressures shape and constrain which stakeholders consider the ESG activities legitimate for restaurant groups. CEO letters provided rhetorical evidence of government regulations (coercive isomorphism), industry standards (normative isomorphism), and consumer demands and preferences (discursive isomorphism) shaping their ESG choices and actions. The external pressures of government regulations and consumer demands were especially prominent in letters during the height of the COVID-19 pandemic. Companies responded to evolving public health regulations while seeking to satisfy core consumer needs and preferences. Cultural expectations of conscious capitalism and social responsibility for global firms pushed CEOs to address environmental, animal welfare, and health issues, defining ESG in the restaurant industry.

The rhetorical work of *defining* creates and sustains institutions by constructing rule systems that confer status or identity, define membership boundaries, and generate status hierarchies within a field (Fox-Wolfgramm et al., 1998). We coded content in CEO letters as *defining* when content provided and explained the *rule systems* in the context of ESG in the restaurant industry. This type of work allowed a reader to understand the ESG system in which the firm operated and assess whether a firm belonged within that system. In addition, *defining* constructed criteria for evaluating the firm's prestige within that system.

Planet, people, food

Each CEO letter we analyzed identified similar top environmental and social issues to define their industry's priorities. Environmental concerns include environmentally sustainable sourcing, waste, and reducing carbon emissions. Socially, supporting the labor force and communities in which firms operated were top issues. Diversity, development, and the safety of workers, along with nutritional improvements, food safety, and animal welfare, were regularly identified as areas where the restaurant industry could do the *most good*.

The restaurant industry significantly impacts the environment, from agricultural natural resource use to packaging waste. As such, CEOs prioritize sustainable environmental practices. Darden's 2020 shareholder letter from Eugene Lee of Darden includes the following: "We view conservation efforts at our restaurants as the first line of action in managing climate risks and resource volatility" (p. 4). McDonald's Kempczinski wrote,

> We are working with our suppliers to scale practices that make agriculture not just more sustainable, but also regenerative. It's not enough to just do less damage to our planet. We need to do *more good*. That's why we remain focused on driving climate action, helping to protect natural resources, reducing waste and transitioning to more sustainable packaging.
>
> *(2022–2023, PISR, p. 6)*

In addition to the restaurant industry's environmental impact, it is a significant employer. In Darden's 2021 shareholder letter, Eugene Lee highlighted the social pillar of ESG by directly acknowledging the restaurant industry is in a special position to improve the lives of workers: "Helping others realize their potential and achieve their dreams is one of the things that makes our industry special, and that's why a central tenet of our approach to team member development is a commitment to promoting from within" (p. 2). Centering employees in the story of the firm's success was common. Leaders frequently acknowledged the importance of supporting and developing employees to improve their lives, indicating normative pressures in industry human resource management.

The report letters we collected spanned the start of the COVID-19 pandemic and its endemic transition. All CEOs discussed how the pandemic affected the firm and posed new challenges for sustainability. CEOs commonly addressed stripping operations and efforts down, which assisted in identifying their core sustainability concerns. Yum!'s CEO, David Gibbs, wrote, "The last two years have presented one of the most challenging environments that the world, along with Yum!, have navigated: year two of a global pandemic, associated supply chain disruptions and persistent labor shortages" (2021, GCSPU, p. 4). Gibbs' focus on supply chains and labor was a significant concern echoed by other CEOs and was prioritized as an ESG concern—how products could be sourced sustainably and how staff could be retained.

In reference to food, CEOs similarly discussed nutritional progress made to improve healthy eating options and responsible portions. Darden President and Chief Executive Officer Eugene Lee wrote in the 2020 Shareholder Letter,

> We know great food starts with quality ingredients that are sustainably sourced. That is why we created our Food Principles in 2016, to outline our commitment to our guests in the areas of sustainable sourcing, nutritional discourse, food safety and animal welfare.
>
> *(p. 5)*

Focusing on nutritional information and dietary options responds to institutional pressures such as consumer preferences (normative, discursive pressure) and government legislation (coercive pressure).

As a result of this analysis, we expect leaders of global restaurant groups attempting to signal their legitimacy and professional belonging within ESG spaces will feel isomorphic pressure to address the Planet, People, and Food in their communication. Through the institutional work of *defining*, leaders identify themselves as institutional insiders and lay the foundation for constructing their firm identity. CEOs' work to define ESG in the restaurant industry operates in tandem with the *institutional work of constructing the firm's identity*. Their letters simultaneously *define* the system and then *position their firm within it*.

Constructing firm identities

Constructing identities is a form of institutional work that establishes the relationship between an actor and the field in which that actor operates (Lawrence & Suddaby, 2006). Generally, CEOs constructed their firms as moral actors highlighting successes and values-based goals corresponding with their ESG efforts. Each asserted their active participation in ESG, their unique position or leadership in these areas, and was motivated and grounded in firm and industry values to *do good* in the areas of people (labor and communities), food (nutrition, safety, animal welfare), and the environment (waste, carbon footprint, sustainable suppliers).

We purposefully selected some of the largest restaurant groups in the world for analysis because of their peer relationships and potential influence on environmental and social systems. As anticipated, each CEO addressed the magnitude of their firm's potential influence. According to the CEOs, firm size created an ethical obligation to participate in sustainable practices. For example, McDonald's CEO Chris Kempczinski mentions his firm's global presence when introducing McDonald's environmental activities (2022–2023, PISR), "As a leading global brand, we've embraced the opportunity to take action to respond to climate change, ..." (p. 5). Jose Cil, CEO of RBI, wrote,

> ...we must remain vigilant in doing what's right with integrity and heart and being a part of the solution that we, our guests, employees, franchisees and partners believe in. We have a real opportunity to implement local changes that make global impacts.
>
> *(2021, RBGR, p. 2)*

Greg Creed, CEO of Yum!, wrote in his letter, "...we are leveraging our scale to help address key societal issues" (2018, GCSPU, p. 1). Each CEO statement makes the Spiderman-esque pledge to leverage their company's *great power* with *great responsibility*. With a global presence, restaurant groups' impacts are great, and sustainability efforts are complex.

Consider the similar value-focused prose in the following excerpts. In his 2020 letter, RBI's Jose Cil wrote in the context of the COVID-19 pandemic, "we took the opportunity for our brands to become a force for good in the communities that we live and work" (p. 2). In 2021, David Gibbs of Yum!, wrote, "...we are actively embedding ESG considerations into our business strategy and adopting responsible business practices that resonate with our values" (p. 4). Darden's CEO Rick Cardenas and Executive Chairman Eugene Lee wrote, "At Darden, we continue to work together in pursuit of our higher purpose—to Nourish and Delight Everyone We Serve" (2023,

Letter to shareholders, p. 4). McDonald's Kempczinski wrote, "Our values guide us always to put our customers and people first, and ensure we open our doors to everyone. They guide us to do the right thing, be good neighbors and give back to our communities" (2019–2020, PISR, p. 3). The noted repetition of terms such as *doing good*, *purpose*, *serving*, and *values,* coupled with figurative and emotive language, crafts an ethical, compassionate, and humanized persona for firms. However, suppose each CEO follows the discursive and mimetic pressures to claim their ESG efforts are value-driven. In that case, they must also find ways to differentiate themselves to attract investors and inspire organizational and customer loyalty.

Given the institutional work of *defining*, these firms' ESG efforts were expected to revolve around a similar set of issues (Planet, People, Food). Still, our analysis suggests it is standard for these issues to be addressed through a value lens in addition to a financial lens. This tactic signals the authenticity of ESG efforts, which are integrated into the values and identity of a brand and not simply an add-on (Mazutis & Slawinski, 2015). With isomorphic pressures guiding CEOs to discuss the same issues and similarly tie them to their corporate values, further effort is needed to distinguish their firms from others in the same field. *Differentiating* is an essential part of identity construction. CEOs attempted differentiation in their letters by discursively detailing their firms' ESG successes, the uniqueness of their corporate values, and their connection to credible partners.

Differentiation through ESG success

Darden Executive Chairman Eugene Lee and President and CEO Rick Cardenas distinguished their firm's identity through its successes in 2019, "We also continue on our journey toward our aspirational goal of sending zero waste to landfills. We have more than doubled our diversion rate over the past 10 years…" (Letter to Shareholders, p. 8). Then, in 2023, they wrote about the firm's leadership in the industry by noting, "…several of our brands ranked number one among major casual dining brands in key measurement categories throughout the year within Technomic's industry tracking tool" (Letter to shareholders, p. 6). RBI's Josh Kobza wrote, "we're also honoured to be named to the Dow Jones Sustainability Index for the first time, a recognition that underscores our dedication to sustainability and motivates us to continue reaching new heights" (2022, RBGR, p. 2). Chris Kempczinski of McDonald's wrote in his 2020–2021 report, "I am proud to share that as of the end of last year, we have substantially achieved all of our 2020 Responsible Sourcing Goals" (PISR, p. 2). Each of these statements differentiates and further develops the firm's identity by noting specific ESG successes and unique goals.

Differentiation through corporate values

Measurable success is an important aspect of the ESG approach. However, CEOs also relied upon discussing their corporate values. Chris Kempczinski wrote in his 2021–2022 letter, "This past year showed us what makes McDonald's unique, once again. Guided by our core values, we've experienced first-hand how our focused actions—both big and small—can translate into meaningful experiences for our customers..." (PISR, p. 2). Darden's letters consistently mentioned valuing inclusion as a distinguishing factor for the firm with statements such as "We're proud of our team members and how they exemplify our value of inclusion, which is evident in our comparison to the industry" (Lee, 2020, Letter to shareholders, p. 2).

Values were also expressed through rhetorical approaches to differentiate their firms. CEOs named their ESG strategies or used repetitive language to describe the values supporting their ESG frameworks. For example, CEO of Yum!, David Gibbs, wrote,

> ...Yum! Brands' Good Growth strategy, also known as our "Recipe for Good Growth," is transformative in its potential—and it guides us in every aspect of what we do. This strategy is grounded in the idea that our business will only endure if our brands are inclusive, sustainable and reflective of evolving employee, franchisee and other stakeholder needs.
>
> *(2022, GCSPU, p. 5)*

Although CEOs termed their ESG efforts and frameworks differently, such as Yum!'s *Recipe for Good*, and RBI's *Brands for Good*, each firm consistently emphasized "good" and "service" for People, Food, and Planet across the years sampled. Rhetorical patterns fought to differentiate but struggled in their uniqueness, further evidence of the strength of the institutionalization of, specifically, the industry's memetic pressures. Yum!'s 2017 sustainability report details their "Recipe for Good," which included the ingredients of "Food, People, Planet." In 2019, RBI created their "Restaurant Brands for Good" framework, which contains "food, planet, people and communities." McDonald's consistently addressed "Our Planet," "Food Quality & Sourcing," "Jobs, Inclusion & Empowerment," and "Community Connection" in its "Purpose and Impact Summary" reports. DBI's terminology for its framework was less consistent than the other firms, but it always addressed the same general categories as the other firms. The final three DBI reports apply the consistent phrasing of "serving our..." to discuss hunger relief efforts in communities where they operate food sourcing, employee development, inclusivity, and environmental impacts.

Differentiation through boundary spanning

Boundary-spanning communication occurs when interactions cross organizational boundaries, helping diffuse institutional norms and practices across domains. This process is essential for building institutional coherence and incorporating diverse perspectives. Showcasing effective boundary-spanning efforts illustrates how firms collaborate and innovate within the constraints of institutional norms. Our model and findings underscore the significance of these interactions in sustaining institutional legitimacy. This aligns with prior research (Raffaelli & Glynn, 2015) and, as reflected in our data, often yields multiple benefits, such as gaining social responsibility credentials through strategic partnerships with organizations perceived as pro-social, pro-environment, and so on.

CEOs further differentiated their brand identities from one another through boundary-spanning prose referencing ESG partners. Chris Kempczinski of McDonald's mentions in his 2020–2021 letter that suppliers are a part of their "three-legged stool" (PISR, p. 2). Each CEO letter and subsequent sustainability report highlighted partnerships with organizations to fight hunger, educational programs, and animal welfare.

In his letter, Yum!'s David Gibbs wrote, "We also joined the OneTen coalition, uniting with other U.S. businesses in advancing equity and career opportunity for underrepresented people of color" (2020, GCSPU, p. 4).

Chris Kempczinski of McDonald's wrote, "That's why we continuously look to experts across industry to help us identify tangible and scalable solutions—from academics to farmers and ranchers, government officials and nonprofit organizations" (2020–2021, PISR, p. 2). Each report further detailed partnerships and alliances with charities, nonprofits, and other guiding bodies in the ESG space.

Future research could examine the effect of weak and strong ties and the risks associated with perceptions of linkages with other organizations. Collaborations across industries provide promising opportunities to blend long-standing corporate values and practices with partners that may be more innovative and nimbler in ESG spaces.

Practical implications

From an institutional theory perspective, leaders are compelled to provide a firm's vision and uphold its image, protect it, and ensure others see it as legitimate (Meyer & Rowan, 1977). By defining the ESG landscape for the restaurant industry and constructing firm identities within it, the CEO letters we analyzed demonstrate how institutionalized communication assists CEOs in accomplishing their duty.

Referring to our model (Figure 12.1), the norms of ESG reporting are shaped by coercive, normative, mimetic, and discursive pressures, creating a standardized communication pattern across the industry. We began our analysis assuming that CEOs were strategic communicators, making intentional choices about the content of their letters and introducing sustainability reports. Thus, the consistent emphasis on similar issues related to people (labor and communities), food (nutrition, safety, animal welfare), and the environment (waste, carbon footprint, sustainable suppliers) in CEO letters demonstrates a convergence of priorities. With the CEOs identifying their firms' similar impacts on the environment and society, it is reasonable to assume they recognized and responded to the same pressures pushing them to address these issues.

This analysis has practical communication implications for leadership. Given the tension arising from the need to differentiate within institutional settings, leaders must thoroughly understand institutional pressures and norms to effectively balance conformity and differentiation. They should leverage this understanding to employ various rhetorical devices, thereby developing clear, consistent, and compelling ESG messaging.

Institutional work is somewhat constrained in mature industries because of long-standing norms and the dominance of established firms; however, we identified specific uses of rhetorical devices, evidence in the form of data from standardized performance measures, and boundary-spanning communication strategies that can subtly differentiate firm identities.

Using pathos (emotional appeal) and metaphor in a highly constrained communication environment can help leaders distinguish their messages. These rhetorical devices can make communication more engaging and memorable, fostering a stronger connection with the audience. Understanding their use provides insights into how leaders can navigate institutional constraints to convey their vision effectively, as leaders demonstrated in our analysis.

In addition, providing ESG data in strategic places would further assist in firm differentiation. This is consistent with earlier research on institutional work (Suddaby & Greenwood, 2005). Except for Darden, which produced a consistent stakeholder letter addressing ESG for each year sampled, the rest of the firms increasingly used a highly visual report style that provided a humanizing narrative to ESG efforts. We saw Yum! move to provide data appendices to focus the body of the report on more engaging narratives, and we estimate others will do so because of mimetic isomorphism.

Finally, we recommend making boundary-spanning communication more deliberate and specific, so stakeholders recognize it as an effective tactic for firm identity differentiation. Leaders can clarify the distinct value of a collaboration by clearly defining roles, expectations, and desired outcomes, helping to project a more precise and impactful image of the partnership.

Executive leaders and communication practitioners, especially those in social media and public relations, should be trained in rhetoric, persuasion, and organizational or institutional theory to better support their work within their industries. These courses enhance their ability to successfully communicate in highly institutionalized environments, avoiding costly mistakes that might come with poor word choice. We recommend that students and professionals revisit or take courses in literary techniques or constructions of figures of speech. We recommend the book *Rhetorical Style: The Use of Language in Persuasion*, by Jeanne Fahnestock. Future studies may look specifically at what rhetorical strategies as rhetorical work can be formulated to assist leaders with differentiation strategies to help shift organizational structure or to understand how communication enhances legitimacy or constrains innovation.

Conclusion

In this chapter, we used an institutional theory perspective on leadership communication to analyze executives' letters in annual sustainability reports. We provided a comprehensive framework for understanding how leaders' communication is a product of and a contributor to institutional norms.

So, let's imagine two CEOs from competing restaurant chains are preparing their annual ESG reports. Both emphasize sustainability and employee well-being, using similar language and statistics commonly seen in the industry. However, one CEO incorporates a metaphor comparing their company to a "family table" where everyone has a seat. At the same time, the other uses a metaphor of a "community garden" to highlight growth and collaboration.

What lesson was learned from our study? Both CEOs conform to mimetic isomorphism by using similar industry-standard themes but differentiate through unique metaphors to reflect their company identity. It's subtle, but these subtleties will determine organizations' identity, reinforcing the importance of communication in leadership.

A communication perspective of institutional theory illuminates that leaders may not be as influential as we popularly believe; rather, their leadership success entails adhering to institutional norms (doing what appears legitimate, which means following trends); the real differentiator of their leadership style is in the nuances of their rhetorical communication style.

This chapter underscores the importance of understanding the intricate relationship between leadership communication and institutional norms.

By integrating institutional theory with rhetorical scholarship, we provided a perspective on how leaders' communication reflects institutional practices. The case study of global restaurant groups illustrates how these dynamics manifest in texts, offering valuable insights for communication practitioners and researchers.

Communication is fundamental in sustaining institutions by continuously reinforcing established practices and beliefs (see Figure 12.2). Leadership communication is not merely a reflection of individual leaders' characteristics but is deeply embedded in institutional contexts. Expected communication ensures coherence and continuity over time; subtle change comes about through rhetorical efforts embedded in institutional work. Understanding this will hopefully motivate leaders and communication professionals to craft messages that are effective, authentic, and uphold institutional values while promoting necessary changes in communication. This institutional work may be one of leaders' primary—and perhaps sacred—roles in highly institutionalized industries. The following discussion questions are designed to explore these themes and their implications further.

Suggested further readings

Aggerholm, H.K., & Thomsen, C. (2024). Strategic communication in contexts of high sustainability pressure: Balancing purposefulness, transparency and participation in pursuit of organizational legitimacy. *Journal of Communication Management*, *28*(1), 58–73. https://doi.org/10.1108/JCOM-12-2022-0131

Berger, P.L. & Luckmann, T. (1991). *The social construction of reality: A treatise in the sociology of knowledge*. Penguin Books (Original work published 1966).

Helens-Hart, R., Haugen, J., & Reuss, L. (2025). "It's not an add-on; it's one of our big bets": Shifting discourse from CSR to ESG. *International Journal of Business Communication*, Advance online publication. https://doi.org/10.1177/23294884251374621

Lammers, J. C., & Barbour, J. B. (2006). An institutional theory of organizational communication. *Communication Theory*, *16*, 356–377. https://doi.org/10.1111/j.1468-2885.2006.00274.x

Questions for further engagement

1 How does leadership communication reflect and shape institutional norms, especially in the context of ESG initiatives?

2 From an institutional theory perspective, why do leaders struggle to make meaningful organizational changes around concepts of ESG and other topics like access, diversity, equity, and inclusion?

3 What communication strategies might leaders use to meaningfully change institutionalized practices?

4 How do the theories presented in this chapter disrupt traditional thinking about leadership? Do you agree or disagree leadership success can

be a result of communication and texts, institutional practices, and taken-for-granted assumptions?

5 How can an institutional theory approach to organizational communication provide new insights into the relationship between leadership communication and organizational practices in industries?
6 In what ways can the findings from this chapter be applied to practices in public relations or other communication fields, such as media or persuasion, to achieve more effective and impactful ESG messaging?

References

Cornelissen, J. P., Durand, R., Fiss, P. C., Lammers, J. C., & Vaara, E. (2015). Putting communication front and center in institutional theory and analysis. *Academy of Management Review*, *40*(1), 10–27. https://doi.org/10.5465/amr.2014.0381

DiMaggio, P. J., & Powell, W. W. (1983). The iron cage revisited: Institutional isomorphism and collective rationality in organization fields. *American Sociological Review*, *48*(2), 147–160. https://www.jstor.org/stable/2095101

Engstrom, C. (2010). Rhetorical criticism as a method for examining cultural pressures on organizational form. *Qualitative Research in Organizations and Management*, *5*(3), 259–279. https://doi.org/10.1108/17465641011089872

Fox-Wolfgramm, S. J., Boal, K. B., & Hunt, J. G. (J.). (1998). Organizational adaptation to institutional change: A comparative study of first-order change in prospector and defender banks. *Administrative Science Quarterly*, *43*(1), 87–126. https://doi.org/10.2307/2393592

Frey, S., Bar Am, J., Doshi, V., Malik, A., & Nobel, S. (2023, February 6). *Consumers care about sustainability—And back it up with their wallets*. McKinsey & Company. https://www.mckinsey.com/industries/consumer-packaged-goods/our-insights/consumers-care-about-sustainability-and-back-it-up-with-their-wallets#/

Giesen, L., & Roeser, A. (2020). Structuring a team-based approach to coding qualitative data. *International Journal of Qualitative Methods*, *19*. https://doi.org/10.1177/1609406920968700

Guthey, E., Ferry, N. C., & Remke, R. (2022). Taking leadership fashions seriously as a vehicle for leadership learning. *Management Learning*, *53*(3), 397–416. https://doi.org/10.1177/13505076211009674

KPMG. (2022, June 29). *ESG leadership: How to be a facilitator of sustainability transformation*. Retrieved from https://kpmg.com/kpmg-us/content/dam/kpmg/pdf/2022/esg-leadership.pdf

Lammers, J. C., & Barbour, J. B. (2006). An institutional theory of organizational communication. *Communication Theory*, *16*, 356–377. https://doi.org/10.1111/j.1468-2885.2006.00274.x

Lawrence, T. B., & Suddaby, R. (2006). Institutions and institutional work. In S. R. Clegg, C. Hardy, T. B. Lawrence, & W. R. Nord (Eds.), *The Sage handbook of organization studies* (pp. 215–254). Sage. https://doi.org/10.4135/9781848608030.n7

Lindlof, T. R., & Taylor, B. C. (2017). *Qualitative communication research methods*. SAGE Publications, Inc.

Mazutis, D.D., & Slawinski, N. (2015). Reconnecting business and society: Perceptions of authenticity in corporate social responsibility. *Journal of Business Ethics*, *131*(1), 137–150. https://doi.org/10.1007/s10551-014-2253-1
Meyer, J. W., & Rowan, B. (1977). Institutionalized organizations: Formal structure as myth and ceremony. *The American Journal of Sociology*, *83*(2), 340–363. https://doi.org/10.1086/226550
Raffaelli, R., & Glynn, M. A. (2015). What's so institutional about leadership? Leadership mechanisms of value infusion. *Research in the Sociology of Organizations*, *44*, 283–316. https://doi.org/10.1108/S0733-558X20150000044011
Reiff, N. (2024, June 25). *10 biggest restaurant companies*. Investopedia. https://www.investopedia.com/articles/markets/012516/worlds-top-10-restaurant-companies-mcdsbux.asp
Simonsson, C., & Heide, M. (2021). Developing a communicative logic – The key to communication professionalism. *International Journal of Strategic Communication*, *15*(3), 253–273. https://doi.org/10.1080/1553118X.2021.1906682
Suddaby, R., & Greenwood, R. (2005). Rhetorical strategies of legitimacy. *Administrative Science Quarterly*, *50*(1), 35–67. https://doi.org/10.2189/asqu.2005.50.1.35
Uyar, A. (2016). Evolution of corporate reporting and emerging trends. *Journal of Corporate Accounting & Finance*, *27*(4): 27–30. https://doi.org/10.1002/jcaf.22157
Weder, F. (2023). Cultivation of sustainability in a discourse of change: Perspectives on communication for sustainability as new "norm" and principle of action in socio-ecological transformation processes. *Journal of Language & Politics*, *22*(5), 577–600. https://doi.org/10.1075/jlp.22122.wed

13

THE DIALOGIC SPECTRUM OF LEADERSHIP-AS-PRACTICE DEVELOPMENT

Brandon W. Kliewer, Andrew Wefald, and David Barnhart

A connection between the underlying assumptions of Leadership-as-Practice (LAP) and leadership communication learning exists. LAP defines leadership as a "socio-spatial process of accomplishing direction" (Alvehus & Crevani, 2022, p. 4). Processual ontologies of leadership, like LAP, consider the source of leadership to be the dialogic and socio-spatial-material interaction that emerges between groups of people (Drath et al., 2008; Raelin et al., 2018).

Scholar-practitioners have advanced forms of Leadership-as-Practice Development (LaPD) as one strategy to increase system capacity to confront complex adaptive system (CAS) challenges (Denyer & James, 2016; Heifetz et al., 2009; Marion & Uhl-Bien, 2001; Uhl-Bien & Arena, 2017; Uhl-Bien et al., 2007, p. 299). CAS challenges require forms of leadership capable of accounting for richly emergent, self-organizing, and interactive dynamics that co-produce new patterns of action and modes of operating (Heifetz, 1994; Plowman et al., 2007; Uhl-Bien et al., 2007). LAPD is an approach to leadership communication learning that attempts to account for CAS challenges.

LAPD includes a focus on ensuring that dialogic and socio-material conditions support "adaptive space" (Fairhurst & Connaughton, 2014; Fairhurst & Uhl-Bien, 2012; Schulze & Pinkow, 2020; Wilhoit, 2016) and often includes trained facilitators capable of giving, holding, and creating adaptive space (Kliewer, 2023). Typically, trained coaches/consultants use LAPD to focus leadership learning on making sense of group dynamics and patterns of action (Engeström et al., 1996; Goppell & Ray, 2015; Lichtenstein, 2014; Robinson & Renshaw, 2023; Swart, 2015).

DOI: 10.4324/9781003563662-16

Denyer and James (2016) offered the Collaborative Leadership Learning Group (CLLG) as a model of work-based LaPD. Our chapter extends approaches to LAPD that exist across what we call "The Dialogic Spectrum of Leadership-as-Practice Development." These LAPD experiences exist across a dialogic spectrum of leadership communication before, in, and after practice. This chapter situates LAPD within specific dialogic processes that support leadership learning and can be leveraged to simultaneously make progress on CAS challenges.

The chapter is divided into three sections. The first situates LAP within a processual ontology of leadership, and its connection to leadership communication learning. The second connects LAP to leadership communication theory. The third introduces the dialogic spectrum of LaPD. Broader implications are highlighted.

Leadership-as-practice development: Contemporary approaches to leadership communication

Leadership communication involves sense-making and creating shared meaning that allows for accomplishing leadership work (Fairhurst & Connaughton, 2014). Leadership activity is accomplished through intersubjective meaning and interactions that exist at the level of the collective or groups (Engeström & Sannino, 2010; Lektorsky, 2009). Typically, processual accounts of leadership learning require increasing capacity to make sense and meaning of group dynamics and patterns of action (Foldy et al., 2008; Gergen & Hersted, 2016; Goppell & Ray, 2015; Humphreys et al., 2012; Lim et al., 2021; Maitlis & Christianson, 2014; Pye, 2005).

Leadership learning, from the processual perspective, requires interaction between groups of people in a community (Lektorsky, 2009; Russell, 2009; Taylor, 2009). By situating leadership learning within specific dialogic interactions, the methods of teaching and leadership learning become necessary for co-creating leadership communication knowledge (Blackler, 2009; Foot, 2001, 2014). The collective and community context situates and offers specific meaning to various leadership communication processes.

LAPD and leadership communication

Leadership communication capacity is centered on an ability to influence discursive and socio-spatial-material interactions to "turn" group dynamics and patterns. Learning how to sense-make and meaning-make group dynamics, as represented through dialogic and socio-spatial-material interactions, is key to increasing leadership capacity through the lens of LAP (Craig, 2005; Wilhoit, 2016). LAP and a stream of leadership communication theory start from the assumption that civic and organizational leadership result from social construction. Socially constructed understandings of leadership and leadership learning tend to de-center leaders and followers to see how meaning is co-created more generally between people, space, place, and objects (Fairhurst & Connaughton, 2014; Fairhurst & Grant, 2010). Furthermore, social constructionist approaches to leadership can simultaneously reproduce existing structures of power while simultaneously including efforts to re-configure power, identity, and systems (Alvehus & Klitmøller, 2024; Śliwa & Case, 2024; Wilhoit, 2016).

Leadership communication learning becomes central to LAPD. Processual approaches to leadership learning depart from traditional leader development (Day, 2000; Day et al., 2014). Leader development is generally focused on developing the "…traits, styles, actions, and competencies of the individuals who have been formally assigned leadership roles or have the potential to become leaders" (Denyer & James, 2016, p. 263). Leadership development sharply departs from leader development. Instead of focusing on "the leader" or "leader-centered entities," LAPD focuses on how leadership work is accomplished through the interaction between people, systems, space, place, and material objects. The processual assumptions of leadership development elevate the need to learn and develop leadership communication capacity across an entire civic or organizational context.

The dialogic spectrum of leadership-as-practice development: Examples across the spectrum

Denyer and James (2016) offered the CLLG as a container that included these LAPD elements and advanced learning appropriate for processual ontologies of leadership. Building on the elements of CLLGs detailed previously, our chapter extends leadership communication learning across what we call "The Dialogic Spectrum LaPD." In addition to the four elements associated with CLLGs, outlined by Denyer and James (2016), our dialogic spectrum of LAPD recognizes a broader range of leadership communication processes that include the following nuances: (a) situated within a real-world leadership community/challenge context, (b) leadership learning is situated at the level of groups and/or includes sense-/meaning-making of group dynamics and patterns of action, and (c) the leadership learning and development also includes a focus on actual leadership work. For more information and details regarding CLLGs, we encourage readers to revisit Denyer and James (2016).

The dialogic spectrum of LAPD extends leadership learning across a range of leadership communication processes and practices. The four elements of LAPD initially described by Denyer and James (2016), highlighted through CLLGs, are still core to the spectrum. However, in addition to the original elements of LAPD described by Denyer and James (2016), we suggest that the fundamental aspects of LAPD can be understood as varying in degree to which (a) they are situated within real-world leadership communication challenge, (b) leadership learning is connected to making sense and meaning of group dynamics and patterns of action, and (c) the leadership learning is simultaneously connected to making progress on a real-world, work-based leadership challenge. Readers will notice that CLLGs, coaching, and simulation-based learning include all three elements. The degree to which they include each element varies.

Broadening real-world contexts

CLLGs sit squarely in the dialogic spectrum of LAPD by including all core elements of LaPD. Typically, a trained facilitator, either internal or external to the group, creates conditions to make sense and meaning of group dynamics and patterns of action. In this context, the trained facilitator is working with a group of people that are attempting to develop leadership capacity while simultaneously making progress on a real-world complex adaptive leadership challenge. Simulations and leadership coaching are removed from context to varying degrees. However, both leadership communication learning practices exist on the dialogic spectrum of LAPD in the sense that they are still tethered, in some way, to a real-world leadership challenge.

Group dynamics: Noticing process and practice through leadership communication learning

The group dynamics and patterns of action are situated directly in a real-world, work-based leadership challenge in CLLGs. Although removed from specific real-time group dynamics, simulations and leadership coaching work to develop capacity in individuals and groups to make sense and make meaning of group dynamics and patterns of action they might come across in related real-world leadership work. The dialogic spectrum of LAPD accounts for developmental readiness. In some cases, participants might need additional support to make the most of CLLGs. Simulations and leadership coaching provide a developmentally appropriate leadership communication opportunity to prepare groups of people for leadership work.

Progress on complex adaptive leadership challenge

Across the dialogic spectrum of LaPD, leadership communication learning is concerned with directly progressing on complex adaptive leadership challenges. CLLGs established the standard for LaPD. Leadership communication learning in CLLGs is connected to a real-world complex adaptive challenge. Leadership communication learning is tailored simultaneously to increase capacity to progress on the in-the-moment leadership challenges. Again, simulations and leadership coaching are defined in relation to complex adaptive leadership challenges but are framed in ways that attempt to meet leadership communication learners' developmental needs.

The following section describes the dialogic spectrum of LAPD and offers two examples from across the spectrum: simulations and individual/group coaching. Again, we encourage readers to revisit Denyer and James (2016) for a complete and detailed explanation of leadership communication processes associated with CLLGs. Each example in this chapter will describe and provide a specific example of how the leadership communication process and practice are implemented across the dialogic spectrum of LAPD (Table 13.1).

TABLE 13.1 Additional elements of the dialogic spectrum of LaPD

	Situated in real-world complex leadership communication/ adaptive leadership challenge context (context)	*Learning connected to collective group dynamics and patterns of action (collective/ group-level learning and/or sense-making)*	*Making progress on real work, work-based adaptive leadership challenges (learning directly connected to making progress on leadership challenge)*
CLLGS – Leadership learning in the flow of practice	X	X	X
Simulations – Leadership learning about practice	X	X	
Individual/group coaching – Leadership learning before or after practice		X	X

This table identifies the features (context, collective/group-level learning and/or sense-making, and learning directly connected to making progress on leadership challenge) associated with three different types of activities in LaPD: CLLGS, simulations, and individual/group coaching.

The dialogic spectrum of LAPD recognizes that the elements present in CLLGs can also appear, to varying degrees, in other approaches to leadership communication learning. Simulation-based leadership learning and leadership coaching occur across the dialogic spectrum of LaPD. The following section details how simulation-based practices and leadership coaching can be positioned along the dialogic spectrum of LAPD by highlighting their relationship to a real-world context. Additionally, we will emphasize the unique contributions of simulation-based learning and coaching to the dialogic spectrum of LaPD.

Simulation-based learning: Role-play

Simulation-based leadership learning is one approach to leadership development on the dialogic spectrum of LaPD. "Simulation-based learning approaches aim to imitate a system, entity, phenomenon, or process" (Lean et al., 2006, p. 228). Simulations facilitate experimentation by generating fictitious scenarios that replicate real-world outcomes, serving as consequences for behaviors (Lean et al., 2006). Feinstein et al. (2002) identified three specific types of simulation-based learning: computer simulation, gaming, and role-play. We offer the simulation-based learning approach of role-play as an LAPD experience within the dialogic spectrum of LaPD.

Role-playing allows participants to immerse themselves in a learning environment by taking on the perspective of characters in specific scenarios. Temporarily accepting a perspective fosters individual and group agency through social interactions in a safe environment (Feinstein et al., 2002; Lasley, 2022). As a simulation-based learning approach, role-play stands out from other simulation methods due to its focus on social interactions (Iftach & Shapira-Lishchinsky, 2023). Role-play provides a dynamic environment that allows participants to explore and practice different leadership and interpersonal interactions (Feinstein et al., 2002) needed to collectively pursue solutions to leadership challenges (Lasley, 2022). As one will begin to understand, role-playing's ability to facilitate collective creativity and leadership capacity makes it an appropriate LAPD experience aptly suited to addressing contemporary civic and organizational leadership challenges. In this section, we outline how role-play is situated within the dialogic spectrum of LaPD.

Denyer and James (2016) emphasize that "LAPD is deeply embedded and originates out of the context and the challenges that people in the organization face *collectively*" (p. 266, emphasis in the original). Role-play supports collective leadership development by immersing participants in real-world scenarios shaped by group dynamics and shared challenges. For instance, Iftach and Shapira-Lishchinsky (2023) asked middle-level educational leaders to present actual leadership dilemmas, which were then briefly simulated and recorded in a role-play setting. This co-action space allowed participants to explore alternative strategies collaboratively. Facilitated debriefs following each session – supported by video/audio recordings – enabled deeper analysis of the effects of group dynamics and patterns of action associated with overcoming leadership challenges.

Role-play scenarios place the participants "in the context of ongoing action" (Gergen & Hersted, 2016, p. 189). Situating role-play within the dialogic spectrum of LAPD demonstrates a significant benefit to leadership communication learning, as the learning method can be used to simulate actual work scenarios with authentic organizational processes and highlight the understanding of group dynamics that impact leadership practice where the participants of the simulated role-playing session are the actual ones entwined in the work-based leadership challenge. Participants can explore innovative and transformational ways of collectively learning to enact leadership processes and advance a leadership practice essential to navigating CAS challenges within these simulated environments.

Role-play is a relational, simulation-based learning method that enables participants to engage with each other by offering a "collaborative learning environment" where participants can explore collective group dynamics and experiment with various patterns of action to understand their different impacts on the organization as the group strives to address leadership challenges (Gergen & Hersted, 2016, p. 189). In the simulation, participants converge around a leadership challenge, engaging in experimental organizing driven by sense-making. Here, sense-making is understood as a key element of the group organizing process (Weick et al., 2005), which "leads to actionable intersubjectivity constructed through language" (Sandberg & Tsoukas, 2014, p. S9). However, this is not always a smooth process and may take multiple leadership development role-playing sessions to appropriately foreground specific group dynamics and action patterns that need further promotion or change.

As participants experience surprises while navigating complex situations (Schön, 1983), role-play allows for an interpersonal improvisational response (Feinstein et al., 2002). Improvisation within the context of a role-play simulation is a relational effort that can lead to collective learning through reflective practices (Morrow et al., 2025; Schön, 1983; Yanow & Tsoukas, 2009). Often, facilitators (at times simultaneously operating as a coach) are used during and/or after the role-playing exercise to help participants reflect and make sense of collective group dynamics and patterns of action leading to individual and group-level learning (Gergen & Hersted, 2016; Lasley, 2024). The aim of employing role-playing as a LAPD experience is to serve as a collective learning and sense-making tool that can be used at the group level and even potentially at the system level.

It is important to note that simulations are not entirely situated within a work-based learning activity (Raelin, 2020). This is because a simulation occurs with partial separation from the organization's actual work. Role-play provides a developmentally appropriate context that, while partially detached from lived experiences, helps move learners toward addressing real-world leadership challenges. But how does role-play help organizations progress in real-world leadership challenges if it is partially separated from lived experiences?

Role-play can accomplish this by (re)creating leadership challenges within an organizational context and group dynamics and positioning participants in these real-world challenges, where they can practice different dialogue and actions to comprehend the varying consequences of each (Allen, 2008; Shapira-Lishchinsky, 2020). The simulation's distinct yet analogous nature to real life is sufficiently detached enough from the actual context to reduce the negative consequences of failure, thereby encouraging participants to take chances and act creatively when exploring the different processes and practices associated with the context of the simulation scenario at hand (Hunsaker, 2007; Salas et al., 2009).

Role-play creates a dynamic environment for interpersonal improvisation (Feinstein et al., 2002), where participant agency shapes the flow of practice and the outcome of the simulated scenario (Morrow et al., 2025; Raelin, 2019). It positions leadership development as a collective, in-the-moment practice (Chia & Holt, 2006). Improvisation and experimentation allow leadership communication to shift between established discourse and more exploratory "hypothetical talk" (Kliewer, 2024), fostering creativity and innovation. For example, participants can prioritize "what-if" dialogue over traditional "this is how it has always been" discourse. Through these exchanges, participants use "conversational choice points" (Gergen & Hersted, 2016) to co-create generative scenarios in which collective action and creativity lead to achieving desired outcomes.

Role-play as a simulation-based learning approach provides a space and place to relationally interact in dialogic processes to explore collaborative and innovative ways of overcoming adaptive challenges. Likewise, role-playing allows participants to break away from dominant ways of thinking and "view reality as a dynamic process, in which they have agency to create a new way of being in the world" (Lasley, 2022, p. 74). Breaking away from the traditional discourse of leadership provides the environment for the collective creativity and transformation required to confront these adaptive challenges (Bolden & Gosling, 2006; Lasley, 2022). The crucial aspect of these leadership communication processes, employed during role-playing within a simulation-based learning framework on the dialogic spectrum of practice, is their ability to foster communal environments.

As previously discussed, the success of role-play in addressing civic and organizational leadership challenges hinges on the participants' collective capacity to understand group dynamics, patterns of action, and intervention strategies. At this juncture, the dialogic spectrum element of coaching can intercede to help foreground meaningful practices that address real-world leadership challenges. The subsequent section will explore coaching in the dialogic spectrum of LAPD and its connections to CLLGs and simulations.

Individual and group-level leadership coaching

Coaching has become a worldwide practice that helps people reach their goals, improve their leadership capacities, and solve challenges. Coaching has been defined as "…partnering with clients in a thought-provoking and creative process that inspires them to maximize their personal and professional potential" [International Coach Federation (ICF), 2024]. Coaches focus on the client and focus the coaching conversation on their clients' leadership challenges. Leadership coaching sessions help clients analyze their problems from multiple perspectives. By avoiding advice, the leadership coaching process gives clients the agency and self-efficacy to solve their work challenges.

Coaching serves several functions in organizations. It is used as a leadership development tool, an intervention to improve poor performance, a reward for rising stars in an organization, an interpersonal conflict resolution process, a group development tool, and a management and leadership tool/style/practice. Usually, clients are focused on navigating challenges in their job to create lasting changes in behaviors or ways of thinking, i.e., a developmental process (van Nieuwerburgh, 2020).

Most coaching happens outside a real-world context. Since most coaching focuses on individual development, it may not touch on learning directly related to progressing on collective leadership challenges (Brown & Grant, 2010). However, even coaching focused on individual development often touches on what is happening in everyday practices as clients work through group dynamics, organizational work issues, and interpersonal challenges. The variables that make a difference are the coach's training, experience, and focus, what the client (individual or organization) wants, and how the coaching is structured and framed. Situating coaching along the spectrum of practice takes intentionality from all parties (coach, client, and organization).

Coaching is adjacent to real-world learning and is still connected to circumstances of everyday work context; it is about the everyday work context and activities. Practices adjacent to actual work activities are essential because they allow space for critical reflection and idea generation to be implemented in practice. Further, organizations increasingly support their managers' coaching training (Grant, 2007). Organizations wanting their managers to be more coach-like are becoming more popular (McCarthy & Milner, 2013; Milner et al., 2018). According to Robinson and Renshaw (2023), being more coach-like in conversations is a managerial practice. When a manager coaches their subordinates at work, it's situated in a real-world context and involves real-world learning. When colleagues and peers coach each other, it is also in real-world contexts.

As more people in organizations are trained in coach-like behaviors, coaching becomes an actual workplace practice involving real-world learning. Managers, leaders, peers, and colleagues may engage in coaching or coach-like behaviors within their work contexts. An extension of this is the coaching style of leadership, an approach where people are trained in the methods and principles of coaching to exercise leadership with their colleagues (Karlsen & Berg, 2020). This is another example of coaching involving real-world learning and practice.

Individual coaching sessions help people make sense of collective group dynamics and patterns of action (often their patterns and sometimes their colleagues' patterns) and how those patterns affect the group. Coaching can also be focused on group dynamics and collective practices, although this may require a coach with specialized training and/or knowledge. The degree to which coaching is supported by an organization and the number of people in the organization receiving coaching all affect how the learning happening in those coaching sessions is connected to collective group dynamics and patterns of action. In these ways, coaching is directly connected to collective group dynamics and patterns of action.

Group and systems coaching offer innovative approaches to collective development and facilitating working through group and organizational dynamics (Britton, 2015; Brown & Grant, 2010; Fullan & Knight, 2011; Pierce, 2024). Systems coaching is an example of coaching focused on identifying systemic patterns and organizational dynamics, and working to change those systems (Fullan & Knight, 2011; Pierce, 2024). This approach to coaching directly involves collective dynamics and learning. When coaching is combined with shared goals and social and organizational support, it creates the conditions for collective leadership to emerge (Raelin, 2011). Group coaching facilitates the collective wisdom of people through shared experiences, social contagion, interpersonal learning, and modeling. This approach to coaching helps people be more accountable to shared objectives; they often get better at conflict resolution and make more substantial commitments to collective challenges (Kets de Vries, 2014).

With the prevalence of coaching training in organizations, coaching in work contexts can happen when one colleague coaches another or when a person, in a formal leadership role, with some coaching training, uses that training with their colleagues, adopting a coaching style of leadership (Berg & Karlsen, 2016). If only one person in an organization receives coaching, the net effect on the collective may be minimal. However, as more people become more coach-like, there may be a collective effect (i.e., a culture of coaching) that helps the organization make progress on its real-world challenges (Shams & Steffensmeier, 2023; Shams et al., 2022).

Coaching allows people to engage in reflective practice (Schön, 1983). Utilizing coaching as a space to reflect on and process what happens in CLLGs and simulations is one way coaching supplements them. One of the goals of a coach is to facilitate reflexive agency (Oliver, 2010). Coaching offers a structure for sense-making and meaning-making of experience by facilitating reflexivity necessary for leadership action. With organizational support and coordination, coaching can supplement CLLGs, simulations, and other forms of action learning that might align with the dialogic spectrum of LaPD.

Coaching also provides opportunities to prepare for and reflect on the work in CLLGs and simulations. Coaches focused on these practices help team members through contested interactions where groups are working to solve their own problems (Raelin & Robinson, 2022). These coaching sessions should focus on what happens in the CLLGs and simulations, reflect on what happened, and work on engaging in the following group activities. Coaching can help navigate conflict productively by allowing individuals to work through tensions, explore ways to navigate conflict, and support the collective progress on challenges and goals (Raelin & Robinson, 2022). When coaching, CLLGs, and simulations are coordinated and focused, they provide robust collective learning processes. We suggest coaching sessions focused on the CLLG/simulation before and after to facilitate the pre- and post-CLLG/simulation learning (Kliewer & Wefald, 2025). Coaching, CLLGs, and simulations work well together because they help individuals navigate and challenge organizational systems through differing levels of practice.

Since coaching can happen in, out, and adjacent to everyday work activities, we consider it to align with the dialogic spectrum of LaPD. Coaching is an important part of and supplement to practice development and has been framed as an essential component of LAPD, facilitating collectives' leaderful capacity (Raelin, 2017). Coaching can also supplement other collective approaches to developing collective leaderful capacities such as CLLGs and simulations. Coaching involves working with people immersed in practice, and it can help them learn and group using their own experiences to progress on work and organizational challenges (Raelin, 2020). Over time, coaching can also affect cultural norms through the development of collective practices (Raelin, 2011).

CLLGs, simulations, and coaching practices create containers for "leaderful coaching" (Raelin, 2011). Coaches working with people immersed in their own leadership practice are helping create the conditions that allow for co-created learning through emergent and situated leadership activity. Coaching provides a lens for team members to make sense of and assign meaning to their leadership challenges and make progress on civic and organizational leadership challenges, i.e., practice-based learning (Raelin, 2011). Coaches can leverage the CLLG, simulation containers, and action learning strategies more generally to support the collective in making sense of group dynamics, productive conflict, competing perspectives and interpretations, and leadership work in ways that tie leadership learning to solving a specific leadership challenge confronting the group (Raelin, 2017; Raelin & Robinson, 2022).

Conclusion

Recognizing leadership communication across the dialogic spectrum of LAPD creates new opportunities to advance innovative approaches to leadership communication learning capable of making progress on real-world challenges. Meeting leadership learners where they are at, in terms of their leadership capacity, also creates opportunity for new approaches to leadership and leadership learning knowledge creation (Engreström & Sannino, 2010), or design-based research (Cole et al., 2018); these broadly understood approaches to "interventionist social science" attempt to connect leadership learning and development to processes and practice that create material change in civic and organizational contexts (Engreström et al., 1996). The future of leadership communication research in CAS will require unique theoretical frameworks, methodological approaches, and strategies to connect new knowledge to contextual practice.

Short case study

A national research lab is strengthening safety protocols, an effort requiring shared responsibility and cross-system collaboration. To address this, a CLLG is formed to navigate this specific organizational challenge. Intentional facilitation is key to generating meaningful outcomes. Consider:

what types of leadership coaching questions would help diagnose leadership challenges? How would a leader coach hold the group together when there is disagreement?

Suggested further reading

Alvehus, J., & Klitmoller, A. (2024). Leadership, power, and politics. In D. Knight, H. Liu, O. Smolović-Jones, & S. Wilson (Eds.), *The Routledge critical companion to leadership studies* (pp. 67–79). Routledge. https://doi.org/10.4324/9781003363125

Śliwa, M., & Case, P. (2024). Leadership-as-practice. In D. Knights, H. Liu, O. Smolović-Jones, & S. Wilson (Eds.), *The Routledge critical companion to leadership studies* (pp. 160–171). Routledge. https://doi.org/10.4324/9781003363125-15

References

Allen, S. J. (2008). Simulations as a source of learning: Using *starpower* to teach ethical leadership and management. *Journal of Leadership Education*, 7(1), 140–149. https://doi.org/10.12806/V7/I1/AB3

Alvehus, J., & Crevani, L. (2022). Micro-ethnography: Towards an approach for attending to the multimodality of leadership. *Journal of Change Management*, 22(1), 1–21. https://doi.org/10.1080/14697017.2022.2081245

Alvehus, J., & Klitmøller, A. (2024). Leadership, power, and politics. In D. Knight, H. Liu, O. Smolović-Jones, & S. Wilson (Eds.), *The Routledge critical companion to leadership studies* (pp. 67–79). Routledge. https://doi.org/10.4324/9781003363125

Berg, M. E., & Karlsen, J. T. (2016). A study of coaching leadership style practice in projects. *Management Research Review*, *39*(9), 1122–1142. https://doi.org/10.1108/MRR-07-2015-0157

Blackler, F. (2009). Cultural-historical activity theory and organization studies. In A. Sannino, H. Daniels, & K. Gutierrez (Eds.), *Learning and expanding with activity theory* (pp. 19–39). Cambridge Press.

Bolden, R., & Gosling, J. (2006). Leadership competencies: Time to change the tune? *Leadership*, 2(2), 147–163. https://doi.org/10.1177/1742715006062932

Britton, J. J. (2015). Expanding the coaching conversation: Group and team coaching. *Industrial and Commercial Training*, 47(3), 116–120. https://doi.org/10.1108/ICT-10-2014-0070

Brown, S. W., & Grant, A. M. (2010). From GROW to GROUP: Theoretical issues and a practical model for organizational group coaching. *Coaching: An International Journal of Theory, Research, and Practice*, *3*(1), 30–45. https://doi.org/10.1080/17521880903559697

Chia, R., & Holt, R. (2006). Strategy as practical coping: A Heideggerian perspective. *Organization Studies*, 27(5), 635–655. https://doi.org/10.1177/0170840606064102

Cole, M., Penuel, W. R., & O'Neill, D. K. (Eds.). (2018). *Cultural-historical activity theory: Approaches to design-based research*. Routledge.

Craig, R. J. (2005). *Communication as a practice*. In G. Shepard, J. St. John, & T. Striphass (Eds.), *Communication as...: Perspectives on Theory* (pp. 38–47). SAGE. https://doi.org/10.4135/9781483329055

Day, D. V. (2000). Leadership development: A review in context. *The Leadership Quarterly*, *11*(4), 581–613. https://doi.org/10.1016/S1048-9843(00)00061-8
Day, D. V., Fleenor, J. W., Atwater, L. E., Sturm, R. E., & McKee, R. A. (2014). Advances in leader and leadership development: A review of 25 years of research and theory. *The Leadership Quarterly*, *25*(1), 63–82. https://doi.org/10.1016/j.leaqua.2013.11.004
Denyer, D., & James, K. J. (2016). Doing leadership-as-practice development. In J. A. Raelin (Ed.), *Leadership-as-practice: Theory and application* (pp. 262–284). Routledge.
Drath, W. H., McCauley, C. D., Palus, C. J., Van Velsor, E., O'Connor, P. M., & McGuire, J. B. (2008). Direction, alignment, commitment: Toward a more integrative ontology of leadership. *The Leadership Quarterly*, *19*(6), 635–653. https://doi.org/10.1016/j.leaqua.2008.09.003
Engeström, Y., & Sannino, A. (2010). Studies of expansive learning: Foundations, findings, and future challenges. *Educational Research Review*, *5*, 1–24. https://doi.org/10.1016/j.edurev.2009.12.002
Engeström, Y., Virkkunen, J., Helle, M., Pihlaja, J., & Poikela, R. (1996). The change laboratory as a tool for transforming work. *Lifelong Learning in Europe*, *1*(2), 10–17.
Fairhurst, G. T., & Connaughton, S. (2014). Leadership: A communicative perspective. *Leadership*, *10*(1), 7–35. https://doi.org/10.1177/1742715013509396
Fairhurst, G. T., & Grant, D. (2010). The social construction of leadership: A sailing guide. *Management Communication Quarterly*, *24*(2), 171–210. https://doi.org/10.1177/0893318909359697
Fairhurst, G. T., & Uhl-Bien, M. (2012). Organizational discourse analysis (ODA): Examining leadership as a relational process, *The Leadership Quarterly*, *23*(6), 1043–1062. https://doi.org/10.1016/j.leaqua.2012.10.005
Feinstein, A. H., Mann, S., & Corsun, D. L. (2002). Charting the experiential territory: Clarifying definitions and uses of computer simulation, games, and role play. *Journal of Management Development*, *21*(10), 732–744. https://doi.org/10.1108/02621710210448011
Foldy, E. G., Goldman, L., & Ospina, S. (2008). Sensegiving and the role of cognitive shifts in the work of leadership. *The Leadership Quarterly*, *48*(1), 514–529. https://doi.org/10.1016/j.leaqua.2008.07.004
Foot, K. A. (2001). Cultural-historical activity theory as practice theory: Illuminating the development of conflict monitoring network. *Communication Theory*, *11*(1), 56–83. https://doi.org/10.1111/j.1468-2885.2001.tb00233.x
Foot, K. A. (2014). Cultural-historical activity theory: Exploring a theory to inform practice and research. *Journal of Human Behavior in the Social Environment*, *24*(3), 329–347. https://doi.org/10.1080/10911359.2013.831011
Fullan, M., & Knight, J. (2011). Coaches as system leaders. *Educational Leadership*, *69*(2), 50–53.
Gergen, K. J., & Hersted, L. (2016). Developing leadership as dialogic practice. In J. A. Raelin (Ed.), *Leadership-as-practice: Theory and practice* (pp. 178–198). Routledge.
Goppell, J., & Ray, K. W. (2015). Dialogic process consultation: Working live. In G. R. Bushe & R. J. Marshak (Eds.), *Dialogic organization development: The theory and practice of transformational change* (pp. 371–391). Berret-Koehler Publishers, Inc.
Grant, A. M. (2007). Enhancing coaching skills and emotional intelligence through training. *Industrial and Commercial Training*, *39*(5), 257–266. https://doi.org/10.1108/00197850710761945

Heifetz, R. A. (1994). *Leadership without easy answers*. Harvard University Press. https://doi.org/10.2307/j.ctv1pncrt0

Heifetz, R. A., Linsky, M., & Grashow, A. (2009). *The practice of adaptive leadership: Tools and tactics for changing your organization and the world* (1st ed.). Harvard Business Press.

Humphreys, M., Ucbasaran, D., & Lockett, A. (2012). Sensemaking and sensegiving stories of jazz leadership. *Human Relations*, *65*(1), 41–62. https://doi.org/10.1177/0018726711424320

Hunsaker, P. L. (2007). Using social simulations to assess and train potential leaders to make effective decisions in turbulent environments. *Career Development International*, *12*(4), 341–360. https://10.1108/13620430710756744

Iftach, G., & Shapira-Lishchinsky, O. (2023). Exploring middle-level school leadership styles through role-play simulations. *Journal of Educational Administration*, *61*(2), 108–125. https://doi.org/10.1108/JEA-01-2022-0015

International Coach Federation. (2024). *All things coaching*. https://coachingfederation.org/about

Karlsen, J. T., & Berg, M. E. (2020). Coaching leadership style: A learning process. *International Journal of Knowledge and Learning*, *13*(4), 356–368. https://doi.org/10.1504/IJKL.2020.111143

Kets de Vries, M. F. (2014). The group coaching conundrum. *International Journal of Evidence Based Coaching and Mentoring*, *12*(1), 79–91. https://doi.org/10.2139/ssrn.2063730

Kliewer, B. W. (2023). Collective sensemaking: Training the leadership-as-practice development trainer for adult leadership learning. *Adult Learning*, *35*(4), 228–238. https://doi.org/10.1177/10451595231205551

Kliewer, B. W. (2024). Sending the right signals: A theoretical model to understand how interpretive leadership capacity advances cross-sector collaboration. *Journal of Nonprofit Education and Leadership*, *14*(3), 23–46. https://doi.org/10.18666/JNEL-2024-12046

Kliewer, B. W., & Wefald, A. (2025). Leadership-as-practice development coaching: Work-based leadership learning and development practice in civic and organizational leadership contexts. *Adult Learning*, *36*(4), 280–287. https://doi.org/10.1177/10451595251345254

Lasley, J. (2022). Role-playing games in leadership learning. In J. D. Egan & J. N. Banter (Eds.), *New directions for student leadership: No. 174. Games in leadership learning* (pp. 73–87). Wiley. https://doi.org/10.1002/yd.20501

Lasley, J. (2024). Role-playing games as a new adventure for leadership-as-practice: Forming a leadership framework around collective creativity and development. *Journal of Leadership Studies*, *17*(4), 47–55. https://doi.org/10.1002/jls.21876

Lean, J., Moizer, J., Towler, M., & Abby, C. (2006). Simulations and games: Use and barriers in higher education. *Active Learning in Higher Education*, *7*(3), 227–242. https://doi.org/10.1177/1469787406069056

Lektorsky, V. A. (2009). Mediation as a means of collective activity. In A. Sannino, H. Daniels & K. D. Gutiérrez (Eds.), *Learning and expanding with activity theory* (pp. 75–88). Cambridge University Press.

Lichtenstein, B. (2014). *Generative emergence: A new discipline of organizational, entrepreneurial, and social innovation*. Oxford University Press. https://doi.org/10.1093/acprof:oso/9780199933594.001.0001

Lim, S., Brower, R. S., & Berlan, D. G. (2021). Interpretative leadership skill in meaning-making by nonprofit leaders. *Nonprofit Management & Leadership*, *32*, 307–328. https://doi.org/10.1002/nml.21477

Maitlis, S., & Christianson, M. K. (2014). Sensemaking in organizations: Taking stock and moving forward. *The Academy of Management Annals*, *8*(1), 57–125. https://doi.org/10.5465/19416520.2014.873177
Marion, R., & Uhl-Bien, M. (2001). Leadership in complex organizations. *The Leadership Quarterly*, *12*, 389–418. https://doi.org/10.1016/S1048-9843(01)00092-3
McCarthy, G., & Milner, J. (2013). Managerial coaching: Challenges, opportunities and training. *Journal of Management Development*, *32*(7), 768–779. https://doi.org/10.1108/JMD-11-2011-0113
Milner, J., McCarthy, G., & Milner, T. (2018). Training for the coaching leader: How organizations can support managers. *Journal of Management Development*, *37*(2), 188–200. https://doi.org/10.1108/JMD-04-2017-0135
Morrow, C. J., Barnhart, D. P., Wefald, A. J., & Smith, A. A. (2025). In situ – Leadership as practice development and improvisational theatre: Practicing interpersonal and social dynamics through improv to develop collective leadership capacity. *Journal of Change Management*, *25*(1), 31–40. https://doi.org/10.1080/14697017.2025.2453142
Oliver, C. (2010). Reflexive coaching: Linking meaning and action in the leadership system. In S. Palmer & A. McDowall (Eds.), *The coaching relationship* (pp. 119–138). Routledge.
Pierce, J. D. (2024). Translating systems coaching research to practice. *TEACHING Exceptional Children*, *57*(4), 276–285. https://doi.org/10.1177/00400599241231751
Plowman, D. A., Solansky, S., Beck, T. E., Baker, L., Kulkarni, M., & Travis, D. V. (2007). The role of leadership in emergent, self-organization. *The Leadership Quarterly*, *18*(4), 341–356. https://doi.org/10.1016/j.leaqua.2007.04.004
Pye, A. (2005). Leadership and organizing: Sensemaking in action. *Leadership*, *1*(1), 31–49. https://doi.org/10.1177/1742715005049349 (Original work published 2005)
Raelin, J. A. (2011). From leadership-as-practice to leaderful practice. *Leadership*, *7*(2), 195–211. https://doi.org/10.1177/1742715010394808
Raelin, J. A. (2017). Leadership-as-practice: Theory and application—An editor's reflection. *Leadership*, *13*(2), 215–221. https://doi.org/10.1177/1742715017702273
Raelin, J. A. (2019). Toward a methodology for studying leadership-as-practice. *Leadership*, *16*(4), 480–508. https://doi.org/10.1177/1742715019882831
Raelin, J. A. (2020). Not leader development – Leadership-as-practice development. *Training Magazine*. https://ssrn.com/abstract=3565950
Raelin, J. A., Kempster, S., Youngs, H., Carroll, B., & Jackson, B. (2018). Practicing leadership-as-practice in content and manner. *Leadership*, *14*(3), 371–383. https://doi.org/10.1177/1742715017752422
Raelin, J. A., & Robinson, J. L. (2022). Update of leadership-as-practice "practice theory": Featuring Joe Raelin interviewed by Jenny Robinson. *Leadership*, *18*(5), 1–12. https://doi.org/10.1177/17427150221100594
Robinson, J., & Renshaw, P. (2023). Aligning the ontologies of leadership and coaching using leadership-as-practice. *Philosophy of Coaching: An International Journal*, *8*(8), 4–20. http://dx.doi.org/10.22316/poc/08.1.02
Russell, D. R. (2009). Uses of activity theory in written communication. In A. Sannino, H. Daniels, & K. D. Gutiérrez (Eds.), *Learning and expanding with activity theory* (pp. 53–75). Cambridge University Press.
Salas, E., Wildman, J. L., & Piccolo, R. F. (2009). Using simulation-based training to enhance management education. *Academy of Management Learning & Education*, *8*(4), 559–573. https://doi.org/10.5465/amle.8.4.zqr559

Sandberg, J., & Tsoukas, H. (2014). Making sense of the sensemaking perspective: Its constituents, limitations, and opportunities for further development. *Journal of Organizational Behavior*, *36*(1), 6–32. https://doi.org/10.1002/job.1937

Schön, D. A. (1983). *The reflective practitioner: How professionals think in action*. Basic Books.

Schulze, J. H., & Pinkow, F. (2020). Leadership for organizational adaptability: How enabling leaders create adaptive space. *Administrative Sciences*, *10*(3), 37. https://doi.org/10.3390/admsci10030037

Shapira-Lishchinsky, O. (2020). Proposing a new model for long-term learning among mid-level school leaders: Toward enhancing organizational learning via simulation training. *International Journal of Educational Management*, *34*(9), 1375–1386. https://doi.org/10.1108/IJEM-08-2019-0296

Shams, K., & Steffensmeier, T. (2023). *Pathways to develop leadership: 2023 impact study*. The KLC Press.

Shams, K., Steffensmeier, T., Dailey, S. R., & Mauricio, D. (2022). *Your leadership edge: Impact report*. Third Floor Research, Kansas Leadership Center. https://kansasleadershipcenter.org/third-floor-research/your-leadership-edge-impact-report/

Śliwa, M., & Case, P. (2024). Leadership-as-practice. In D. Knight, H. Liu, O. Smolović-Jones, & S. Wilson (Eds.), *The Routledge critical companion to leadership studies* (pp. 160–171). Routledge. https://doi.org/10.4324/9781003363125-15

Swart, C. (2015). Coaching from a dialogic organization development paradigm. In G. R. Bushe & R. J. Marshak (Eds.), *Dialogic organization development: The theory and practice of transformational change* (pp. 349–371). Berret-Koehler Publishers, Inc.

Taylor, J. R. (2009). The communicative construction of community. In A. Sannino, H. Daniels & K. D. Gutiérrez (Eds.), *Learning and expanding with activity theory* (pp. 228–240). Cambridge University Press.

Uhl-Bien, M., & Arena, M. (2017). Complexity leadership: Enabling people and organizations for adaptability. *Organizational Dynamics*, *46*(1), 9–20. https://doi.org/10.1016/j.orgdyn.2016.12.001

Uhl-Bien, M., Marion, R., & McKelvey, B. (2007). Complexity leadership theory: Shifting leadership from the industrial age to the knowledge era. *The Leadership Quarterly*, *18*(4), 298–318. https://doi.org/10.1016/j.leaqua.2007.04.002

van Nieuwerburgh, C. (2020). *An introduction to coaching skills: A practical guide*. Sage.

Weick, K. E., Sutcliffe, K. M., & Obstfeld, D. (2005). Organizing and the process of sensemaking. *Organization Science*, *16*(4), 409–421. https://doi.org/10.1287/orsc.1050.0133

Wilhoit, E. (2016). Organizational space and place beyond container or construction: Exploring workspace in the communicative constitution of organizations. *Annals of the International Communication Association*, *40*(1), 247–275. https://doi.org/10.1080/23808985.2015.11735262

Yanow, D., & Tsoukas, H. (2009). What is reflection-in-action? A phenomenological account. *Journal of Management Studies*, *46*(8), 1339–1364. https://doi.org/10.1111/j.1467-6486.2009.00859.x

14

LEVERAGING DIGITAL AFFORDANCES FOR COLLECTIVE LEADERSHIP

Insights from Mutual Aid Organizing

Sean M. Eddington, Lauren B. Hearit Klug, Timothy Betts, and Brett W. Robertson

The outbreak of COVID-19 triggered widespread instability, revealing the precarious nature of various social structures, including housing, medical, financial, and social safety net systems. As governments globally sought to curb the virus through shutdowns and stay-at-home orders, these measures simultaneously created harsh economic realities, including job losses, supply chain disruptions, and market volatility (Carlsson-Szlezak et al., 2020). The pandemic's impact was particularly severe on women and vulnerable communities. In the U.S., for example, women lost 140,000 jobs in December 2020 alone (Kurtz, 2021), while shelter-in-place orders exacerbated pre-existing caregiving burdens that disproportionately affected women as schools and daycare centers closed (Chotiner, 2020). Although governments attempted to alleviate some of these challenges through relief efforts, their effectiveness was limited by the pre-pandemic shortcomings of existing economic and political systems (Lindau et al., 2021).

Local communities organized support networks in response to systemic social and economic limitations. They coordinated relief efforts to respond at the neighborhood level and serve more at-risk groups, including the immunocompromised, incarcerated individuals, and workers who lost their jobs (Diavolo, 2020, para. 8). First popularized by Kropotkin (2021), mutual aid theory emphasizes cooperation over competition, with support and care seen as essential for social evolution and development. Mutual aid involves the voluntary sharing of resources, efforts, and assistance to promote mutual support, solidarity, and empowerment through communicative practices that constitute collective organizational responses.

DOI: 10.4324/9781003563662-17

The prevalence of mutual aid networks has increased throughout the COVID-19 pandemic, primarily due to digital infrastructures, or affordances, that facilitate visibility, mobilization, and volunteer coordination (Tiratelli & Kaye, 2020). For example, Mutual Aid Disaster Relief (n.d.) engages over 10,500 followers daily through Instagram. Pond and Lewis (2017) highlight the success of networked movements, arguing that online social movements can efficiently and accessibly communicate and mobilize across various contexts. By leveraging the affordances of socially mediated environments as communicative agents, activists can mobilize and amplify their messages, creating unique opportunities for engagement (Bennett & Segerberg, 2012; Cammaerts, 2019; Eddington, 2018). Networked movements, such as mutual aid organizations (MAOs), "create relationships and motivate prosocial behaviors that ultimately benefit society" through ongoing communicative accomplishments (Taylor & Kent, 2014, p. 76). This is significant because social movements often aim for transformation and change through communicatively constituted organizing processes (Eddington, 2018). However, scholars have called for further research on the online organization of social movements as digital spaces continue to evolve (Cammaerts, 2008, 2021). Thus, MAO practices and organizing can be viewed as collective leadership (CL), with shared responsibilities and decentralized decision-making processes that foster effective community-driven responses.

Using the context of online MAO organizing, this chapter surveys the scholarship on collective and networked leadership through a communicative constitution lens (for a review of recent CCO theorizing, see Brummans et al., 2024). Employing a constitutive (e.g., organizing) lens offers both conceptual and practical insights into how social movements are communicatively organized online, with a particular focus on how the affordances of online spaces facilitate the constitution of leadership communication. An affordance approach is helpful because it highlights how online social movements organize, constitute, and enact change through networked, pluralistic leadership. This leadership communication emerges in everyday posts, memes, and engagement in collective, networked movements (Jackson et al., 2020; Jarvis & Eddington, 2021). These activities foster engagement, visibility, and collective action, enabling social movements to mobilize quickly and efficiently through coordinated and distributed communicative practices.

Conceptualizing collective leadership

While CL has gained increasing attention in leadership and organizational studies, much of the literature continues to frame leadership as a structural or behavioral phenomenon (e.g., Contractor et al., 2012; Fairhurst et al.,

2020). Despite attempts to explore the structural and functional dimensions of CL, Carroll and colleagues (2019) noted that a persistent challenge in discussions of CL lies in the assumption that leadership is a discrete, nameable entity, or something that can be allocated or parceled out across an organization, as when a leadership team opts to engage others by distributing responsibility for action. In contrast, a communicative constitution of organizing (CCO) perspective shifts the focus from what leadership is to how leadership occurs. CCO highlights that leadership, identity, and organizing are not fixed entities but are continuously constituted through communicative practices (Brummans et al., 2024). This view offers valuable insight into how CL emerges, stabilizes, and evolves, particularly in decentralized or digitally mediated contexts such as mutual aid organizing.

Scholars have increasingly explored how CL is enacted through communication in nontraditional and networked settings. Yet as leadership becomes more mediated by digital platforms, understanding it as a communicatively constituted practice becomes even more essential for scholars, practitioners, and students alike. Ospina et al. (2020) pose a necessary challenge for CL research: to take seriously questions of what, where, and how CL is communicatively organized—that is, (1) what constitutes a "collective," (2) where CL exists (e.g., groups, teams, organizations, or social movements), and (3) how CL is enacted. From a CCO perspective, these are fundamentally communicative concerns: leadership is not merely distributed or located but enacted through the very interactions that constitute identity, authority, and collective action.

For the sake of this chapter, we build upon Yammarino et al.'s (2012) definition of *collectivist* leadership as a social process involving "multiple individuals assuming (and perhaps divesting themselves) of leadership roles over time in both formal and informal relationships" (p. 382) to advance a definition that foregrounds a coalitional understanding of leadership. Thus, our guiding conceptualization of CL is the following:

> Collective leadership is a collaborative process whereby individuals, regardless of their positions, share decision-making, influence, and responsibility to achieve common goals through ongoing interactions that constitute relationships, context, and emergent practices.

In short, this definition emphasizes three principles of CL in networked and online settings that help understand the impact and importance of mutual aid organizing. These three principles—collaboration, mutuality, and post-heroism—form the basis for the following discussion, in which we further explore each principle and its significance as a form of communication in networked and online contexts, particularly within mutual aid organizing.

Collaboration

Our definition first recognizes the importance of collaborative and relational bonds between individuals. These bonds go beyond simple transactions and foster reciprocal transformation. From a CCO perspective, these interactions co-orient, helping to build shared understanding and shape the organization. Carroll and Simpson's study of online discussions among managers participating in a leadership development program (2012) highlighted the role of online forums in creating a space for collective understanding of collaborative processes and sensemaking, offering an innovative, communicative framework of sociality (or the movements between and within multiple/differing perspectives) that can bolster and support collective, collaborative processes and relational leadership practices. Relatedly, drawing from Indigenous cultural practices that highlight the importance of collaborative processes and relational bonds in leadership, Rosile and colleagues (2019) advance an ensemble leadership theory that moves beyond the individual/group dualisms that exist in Eurocentric leadership theorizing,

> Indigenous peoples may see the self as the same as the tribe, just as holons each incorporate the whole system within each part. This less-important concept of the "self" or the "individual" contributes to the high importance placed on relationship and respect…within indigenous cultures.
> *(p. 13)*

An ensemble approach to collaboration shifts the focus from individual leaders to creating collective, relational bonds that include both human and nonhuman entities (e.g., the natural and material environments).

These entities act as agents within the leadership process, emphasizing that leadership is co-created through collective communication and action. These relational configurations align with CCO's understanding of actorhood as distributed and emergent through communication, not fixed roles. Sklaveniti (2020) described that ensemble leadership is not a fixed attribute of individuals but emerges through shared efforts and is deeply situated in the ongoing, dynamic process of "becoming." This approach recognizes that leadership is fluid and evolves as environments, relationships, and individuals change within the collective. As these elements shift, so does the nature of leadership, communication, and collaboration.

Mutuality

Our definition of CL highlights the role of mutuality within the leadership process, recognizing the role of influence on relationships and shaping common goals and decision-making processes. Similarly, Tourish (2014) framed leadership as a fluid and co-constructed process that mutually constitutes roles (e.g., leaders and followers), highlighting their entangled and knotted nature. For example, in a discussion of the bankruptcy of the U.S. financial firm Enron, Tourish highlighted the complicity and lack of dissent of Enron's workers (dubbed "Enronians") as a contributing factor for enabling the fraudulent behaviors of senior leaders: "When the organization crashed so did the reputations, livelihoods and liberties of its leaders—again, the identities and fates of leaders and followers were co-constructed and destructively intertwined" (pp. 86–87). This fluidity illustrates that roles such as "leader" or "follower" are not fixed in advance but are continuously co-created through ongoing communicative interactions. Thus, as Quick (2017) argued, mutuality affords "dynamic movement in who is leading [and following] at any given time" (p. 3).

Integrating relationships and nonhuman entities into the leadership process, the concept of mutuality—the reciprocal, interdependent, and mutually constitutive nature of these interactions—offers an innovative way to understand CL. For example, in their study of Māori leaders in New Zealand, Kelly and Nicholson (2022) drew upon Indigenous leadership frameworks to introduce the concept of ancestral leadership "in which place and community are intimately tied and inextricably linked, describing intergenerational leadership ethics that provide a system of accountability through reciprocal obligations to people, place and cosmology" (p. 141). More specifically, Kelly and Nicholson's study showcases how ancestral legacies inform contemporary leadership and are transmitted throughout time, place, and community, wherein the integration of spiritual, cultural, and practical leadership dimensions in ancestral leadership reflects a holistic perspective that aligns with CL's emphasis on mutuality. Their work shows how ancestral legacies shape contemporary leadership, integrating spiritual, cultural, and practical dimensions. This holistic perspective aligns with CL's focus on mutuality, shifting from an individual-centered view to one that embraces co-creative, adaptive leadership in harmony with its environment.

Post-heroic perspectives

Building from collaboration and mutuality, the final component of our definition advances a post-heroic perspective of leadership that moves away from the individual conceptualization of leadership as a "Great Man" toward communal goals and responsibilities, empowerment, and collective and distributed action (Raelin, 2016; Škerlavaj, 2022). According to Fletcher (2004), post-heroism offers a new understanding of the significance of relationships and relational interactions, along with a revised perspective on development and success.

Post-heroic leadership is characterized by its participatory and collective approach, where sensemaking emerges from group interactions, much like the improvisation of a jazz band. These sensemaking episodes lie at the heart of the organization, reflecting how conversation and text interact to shape structure (Brummans et al., 2024). Harrison (2017) argued that post-heroic perspectives are akin to a jazz band's improvisation, in which they adapt, create, and transform uncertainty and unpredictability into a coherent piece of art. Central to post-heroic approaches is the view that leadership is constituted through interactions, democratic and participatory practices, and sensemaking among groups, rather than residing in a singular figure. Put differently, Harrison's metaphor illustrates leadership as a dynamic, collective process that is adept at addressing modern societal challenges through participatory practices rather than relying on a single leader.

The 2017 Women's March exemplifies post-heroic leadership by promoting intersectional and democratic engagement. For example, Just and Muhr's (2019) study of the 2017 Women's March highlighted the transformative potential of post-heroic leadership in centering intersectional leadership that involves diverse voices, perspectives, and identities within leadership processes. Just and Muhr's analysis of the Women's March suggests that similar social movements provide alternative frameworks for organizing, illustrating how post-heroic leadership fosters collective agency, democratic participation, and "daring discussions" (p. 13). Despite the success of the Women's March, their study also highlights how the organizers of the protest grappled with challenges and shifting power dynamics, and they cautioned researchers to go beyond simply critiquing heroic perspectives:

> While this collective leadership narrative is an attractive alternative to the Great Man story that currently dominates leadership narratives, it runs the risk of post-heroic blindness to its own narrative veil... The potential of and for positive change lies in continuing to branch out and open up, to always explore new intersections and their various paths. Together we rise, but only if we keep pulling apart.
>
> *(p. 18)*

Their reflection emphasizes continually expanding and questioning leadership practices to ensure ongoing growth and inclusivity.

The concept of CL, which prioritizes collaboration, mutuality, and post-heroic practices, offers a flexible framework for analyzing leadership within dynamic, non-hierarchical contexts. While still developing in practice, these principles provide an essential foundation for understanding how leadership is distributed and enacted across networks. With the increasing shift toward digital environments, the study of CL must adapt to examine how these principles are actualized within online spaces, particularly in mutual aid organizations. The subsequent section will explore how online platforms facilitate CL and mutual aid organizing, addressing the emerging challenges of coordinating decentralized actions in virtual settings.

CCO and affordance perspectives

An increasing body of literature within leadership studies has begun to acknowledge the organizing and transformative capacity of communication (see, for review, Fairhurst & Connaughton, 2014). As Schoeneborn et al. (2019) articulate, the primary objective of the CCO framework is to position communication "as the main force that creates, generates, and sustains—constitutes—what we consider to be organization and organizing practices" (p. 476). In the realm of online organizing, Dobusch and Schoeneborn's (2015) study of the hacktivist collective Anonymous illustrates how fluid and dynamic processes shape collectives. Through strategic speech acts and networked protests, these collectives achieve *organizationality*.

Organizationality

This concept of organizationality is defined by three critical criteria for evaluating the "organization-ness" of loosely formed collectives: (1) interdependent decision-making episodes, where decisions are made collectively; (2) decisions made on behalf of a group or collective entity; and (3) collective identity anchors that hold the group together (Dobusch & Schoeneborn, 2015; Smith, 2022, 2023, 2024; Wilhoit & Kisselburgh, 2015). A key challenge in analyzing fluid collective organizing—especially online—is that "in digitally networked protests...membership and leadership are often undefined, few...people expect representatives to speak for the protests" (Poon, 2024, p. 394). This challenge is exemplified by Smith's (insert year) study of the subreddit community, /r/WallStreetBets, which achieved a form of organizationality while illustrating how loosely organized collectives can involve fluid levels of actorhood (the ability of individuals to take on roles within the group), latent forms of coordination (unspoken or informal ways of organizing actions), and tensions between organizing and appearing unorganized. The community also leveraged cultural elements such as memes and shared language to facilitate implicit communication, all without relying on formal organizational structures.

In the absence of formal and routinized organizational structures, how does CL emerge in loosely organized digital contexts? That is, how does the context facilitate or hinder the potential for CL? While digital platforms provide unique affordances, such as low barriers to entry and real-time communication, which enable rapid mobilization and collective decision-making, the lack of clear leadership structures can create challenges in accountability and coordination. For the purposes of this chapter, we adopt an affordance perspective—understanding affordances as the possibilities for communication and action that digital platforms provide to users—to highlight how they simultaneously shape the opportunities and limitations of CL in online movements. We focus on mutual aid organizations and the unique ways in which these affordances influence their organizational dynamics.

Organizing affordances

Affordances refer to potential uses and actions embedded within information and communication technologies, shaping technological, social, or communicative practices (for a review, see Rice et al., 2017). An affordance perspective recognizes how the materiality of an object both invites and constrains specific uses (Zammuto et al., 2007). Emerging from the interplay between the physical features of technological tools and the communication practices they facilitate (McVeigh-Schultz & Baym, 2015), affordances are relational, shaped by both the object and its social context. Zammuto et al. (2007) emphasized that discussing complex technologies without considering their social context is as incomplete as referring to a "door handle without discussing the people opening the open doors" (p. 753).

An affordance perspective offers valuable insights into how the technical, social, and communicative features of social media platforms shape user interactions and foster community building and organizational dynamics. Leonardi and Vaast's (2017) review of social media affordances encouraged researchers to examine how the features of these platforms influence communication processes, such as leadership. Affordances on social media can foster both community building and organizational dynamics (e.g., Eddington, 2018; Eddington et al., 2025; Poon, 2024; Treem & Leonardi, 2013). These affordances—ranging from communicative to technical—shape user interactions in various ways (Bucher & Helmond, 2018; Leonardi & Vaast, 2017; Rice et al., 2017). Additionally, user perceptions influence affordances, as individual understandings of a platform's capabilities can lead to varied usage (Rice et al., 2017). Affordances may be realized (e.g., upvotes on Reddit that rank content; hashtags creating spaces for community; Albu & Etter, 2016), perceived (e.g., (pseudo)anonymity or retweet-based engagement on Twitter/X;

Eddington, 2018), or emerge from the material and spatial features of communication tools (Wilhoit, 2017). Ultimately, by understanding how affordances facilitate user interactions and organizational dynamics, researchers can better grasp how individuals and collectives mobilize social change efforts through viral campaigns and hashtag activism (Eddington, 2018).

The technological affordances of platforms like Telegram and Twitter/X can significantly influence communication practices and leadership dynamics, as demonstrated by the organizing efforts during the Anti-Extradition Law Amendment Bill (Anti-ELAB) protests in Hong Kong. In Poon's (2024) study, Telegram was examined as a critical tool for Anti-ELAB organizing, particularly in the use of interactive polls during airport protests. Poon identified authorship affordances—such as anonymity, hyper-temporality, and affective communication—that shaped collective decision-making in politically contentious contexts. Similarly, Poon and Kohlberger (2022) analyzed Twitter/X's technological affordances, focusing on how they influenced leadership dynamics in the same protests. Their study highlighted the sociomaterial interplay between leadership and organizing in a "leaderless" movement, asserting that "just because a movement is leaderless, it is not leadership-less" (p. 670). These examples illustrate how Telegram and Twitter/X's affordances shape communication and leadership practices, emphasizing the value of an affordance perspective in understanding both digital organizing and CL processes. Building on these insights, examining mutual aid organizing online further illustrates how digital affordances enable decentralized leadership and collaborative decision-making in community-based efforts.

Midwest action for others: Collective leadership and online affordances in action

In the following section, we shift focus back to the context of mutual aid organizing, offering an integrative case study of a fictional mutual aid organization, Midwest Action for Others (D'Enbeau et al., 2010). This case is based on real mutual aid organizations and their experiences, with names, details, and circumstances altered to protect the privacy of groups and individuals involved. An integrative case analysis "creates imaginary places and spaces for discussions fraught with real issues and situated in everyday materialities" (Eddington & Buzzanell, 2019). By presenting a fictional narrative inspired by the real-life experiences of mutual aid organizers and their online organizing efforts, this illustrative case explores the leadership communication opportunities that emerge through CL and organizing in digital spaces.

Mutual aid organizations: A primer

Mutual aid is a form of solidarity-based support where communities unite to help those in need, with mutual aid organizations working to reshape systems into more equitable structures that benefit local communities. These organizations have gained popularity as diverse community members collaborate through regional networks, particularly focusing on marginalized and minoritized groups, to enact systemic change (Diavolo, 2020). Mutual aid operates by voluntarily sharing resources, efforts, and assistance for mutual benefit. This form of political engagement centers on collective responsibility through mutual care and the creation of alternative social relations. It moves beyond symbolic action or institutional advocacy, emphasizing materially grounded practices that foster survivability through relational and communicative labor (Spade, 2020). The concept of mutual aid highlights the importance of cooperation over competition. As Spade (2020) explains, "mutual aid projects are becoming an even more essential strategy for supporting survival, building new infrastructure, and mobilizing large numbers of people to work and fight for a new world" (p. 147). The COVID-19 pandemic further catalyzed the growth of mutual aid networks, which have successfully leveraged social media to boost visibility, mobilize resources, and coordinate volunteer efforts (Gordon, 2024; Maris et al., 2024; Swann, 2023; Tiratelli & Kaye, 2020; Zamponi, 2023).

Midwest action for others

The Pickney Valley neighborhood, located just two miles from a large midwestern city, has a complex history shaped by the city's redlining policies of the 1920s and 1930s. For decades, it served as a racial and socioeconomic dividing line. However, following the 1968 ban on redlining, the city invested in the community, transforming Pickney Valley into a thriving, multicultural neighborhood. The residents were a diverse mix of young professionals, working-class families, college students, and retirees, creating a community known for care and collaboration.

When COVID-19 struck, the city, like many others, was unprepared for the pandemic's widespread effects. Food banks faced severe shortages, healthcare systems were overwhelmed, and vulnerable groups, including low-income families and older adults, struggled to access basic needs. In response, the residents of Pickney Valley decided to take matters into their own hands by creating the Midwest Action for Others, a mutual aid organization that was communicatively constituted through initial online interactions, especially posts and conversations that solidified shared goals, norms, and collective identity.

Patrice Yoder, a public administration professional and long-time Pickney Valley resident, was inspired to start Midwest Action for Others after seeing a Facebook post in the neighborhood group asking if anyone was interested in forming a mutual aid organization. Patrice seized the opportunity, eager to create a community-driven space where marginalized and vulnerable residents could get the support they needed without feeling shame. Her goal was clear: to foster a safe and inclusive environment for mutual aid, especially for those affected by systemic inequities. Leveraging the fact that many Pickney Valley residents were already active on Facebook, Patrice started the Midwest Action for Others Facebook group to organize efforts. Although nervous about how people might respond, she took the first step by encouraging people to request help anonymously through her, reducing the vulnerability of publicly asking for assistance. Early requests focused on basic needs—food supplies, rent money, and transportation to grocery stores or doctor's appointments. To her surprise, the community quickly rallied, and soon the group was thriving, with neighbors stepping up to support one another.

As the Midwest Action for Others Facebook group gained momentum, word spread beyond Pickney Valley. The group's posts went viral, reaching residents across the city. Other communities began forming mutual aid groups but often used the Midwest Action for Others group as their primary organizing hub due to its success and visibility. Faced with the rapid growth, Patrice realized that she couldn't manage Midwest Action for Others' expanding operations alone. She and her core group of volunteers began branching out to other social media platforms to recruit volunteers and donations. However, as the demands on Midwest Action for Others increased, so did internal tensions. Managing the group's complexity online—particularly with diverse and growing needs—required new strategies for leadership, coordination, and communication.

Online affordances of various platforms, particularly Discord, became crucial. These affordances function as constitutive mechanisms; platform features, such as chat rooms, polls, and channels, become the "texts" through which organization emerges. Midwest Action for Others created specific chat groups on Discord to coordinate key tasks like food delivery, healthcare, and mental health support. This shift enabled volunteers to onboard quickly, and the fluidity of leadership roles allowed decisions to be made collectively in real time. For instance, during a tornado outbreak in the summer of 2020, the food delivery team became overwhelmed, and other volunteers from the mental health and healthcare groups immediately stepped in to help distribute food. This example of CL illustrates how Midwest Action for Others's flexible structure enabled members to adapt quickly to shifting community needs.

Midwest Action for Others' success stemmed from its emphasis on CL, a process constituted through communication in which members co-create meaning, norms, and leadership roles via their digital exchanges, where responsibilities were shared among members rather than centralized under one individual. This leadership style emphasized collaboration, mutuality, and decentralized decision-making, which was critical for Midwest Action for Others' ability to address the community's evolving needs during the pandemic. Midwest Action for Others' volunteers worked across platforms and functions, building relational bonds. Each team took responsibility for different aspects of the organization, whether managing social media, coordinating food deliveries, or organizing healthcare efforts. Leadership was fluid, with members stepping up to lead in their areas of expertise. This shared leadership enabled Midwest Action for Others to be more inclusive and adaptable. Finally, Midwest Action for Others adopted a post-heroic approach, where leadership was not tied to a single individual. This approach ensured that everyone, regardless of their role, had a voice in decision-making processes.

However, CL at Midwest Action for Others was not without challenges. As the organization grew, tensions arose, especially around social media strategy, which revealed ongoing negotiations of organizational boundaries and actorhood. In one instance, a volunteer promoted a community kitchen event, but another removed the post, arguing it did not "increase engagement." These moments highlighted the relational and communicative difficulties of balancing decentralized decision-making with accountability in digital spaces. As Midwest Action for Others expanded, coordinating efforts and maintaining consistent communication became more challenging without formal leadership structures. Volunteers struggled with organizing tasks, documenting requests, and staying engaged, especially as the pandemic continued into 2021 and burnout increased.

To address these challenges, Midwest Action for Others adopted more structured tools for collaboration and coordination, including shared calendars, task management apps, and formalized decision-making via Discord polls. This integration of flexible and structured practices allowed Midwest Action for Others to sustain its community-driven ethos while enhancing operational efficiency. Despite growing pains, Midwest Action for Others remained committed to its core principles of CL. Every member, from food delivery volunteers to social media managers, bears responsibility for the organization's functioning. This collective model fostered resilience and adaptability in the face of ongoing uncertainty. Midwest Action for Others' experience illustrates how online affordances—the features of digital platforms—can enable CL in mutual aid contexts. Platforms like Facebook and Discord allowed Midwest Action for Others to scale operations, respond to shifting community needs, and sustain volunteer engagement, all while preserving a decentralized and inclusive leadership model. Through CL and intentional use of digital tools, Midwest Action for Others built a resilient mutual aid network that demonstrates the transformative potential of community organizing in times of crisis.

Concluding thoughts

This chapter illustrates how digital affordances shape the communicative constitution of CL within mutual aid organizations (MAOs), particularly during times of crisis, such as the COVID-19 pandemic. Online platforms enable communities to quickly organize and distribute responsibility through decentralized, participatory processes rooted in mutuality, collaboration, and post-heroic leadership. These fluid, relational structures make leadership more inclusive and responsive; however, they also introduce challenges related to coordination and accountability as organizations grow.

In the case of Midwest Action for Others, leadership was not simply supported by communication—it was created through it. From outreach posts to real-time Discord exchanges, communicative practices defined who led, how decisions were made, and what the organization became. These interactions enacted organizationality by generating shared identities, norms, and responsibilities. While this communicative flexibility enabled Midwest Action for Others to respond and adapt in real time, it also made sustained coherence more difficult. Concepts from the CCO perspective, including actorhood, authoritative texts, and the relationship between text and conversation, were continually negotiated through everyday communication within a deliberately decentralized leadership structure.

Suggested further readings

Fairhurst, G. T., Jackson, B., Foldy, E. G., & Ospina, S. M. (2020). Studying collective leadership: The road ahead. *Human Relations*, *73*(4), 598–614. https://doi.org/10.1177/0018726719898736

Gordon, C. (2024). Learning mutual aid: Food justice, public pedagogy, and community fridge organizing online. *Journal of Applied Communication Research*, *52*(2), 158–178. https://doi.org/10.1080/00909882.2024.2327417

Maris, E., Caplan, R., & Thach, H. (2024). Taking back and giving back on TikTok: Algorithmic mutual aid in the platform economy. *New Media & Society*. https://doi.org/10.1177/14614448241238396

Ospina, S., & Foldy, E. (2010). Building bridges from the margins: The work of leadership in social change organizations. *The Leadership Quarterly*, *21*(2), 292–307. https://doi.org/10.1016/j.leaqua.2010.01.008

Spade, D. (2020). Solidarity not charity: Mutual aid for mobilization and survival. *Social Text*, *38*(1), 131–151. https://doi.org/10.1215/01642472-7971139

Questions for further engagement

1. The chapter outlines three communicative principles of collective leadership: collaboration, mutuality, and post-heroism. How do these principles shape leadership in digital mutual aid spaces? Can you identify examples where these were enacted or challenged through online communication in social movements or grassroots organizing?
2. As digital communication technologies evolve, what new affordances might mutual aid organizations adopt to strengthen collective leadership and community resilience? How could these tools help address current challenges related to burnout, coordination, or decision-making?
3. How do collaboration, mutuality, and post-heroic leadership, understood as communicative practices, challenge traditional hierarchical models of leadership, especially during crises like the COVID-19 pandemic? How might these principles apply to other decentralized social movements or community organizations?
4. What are the potential long-term effects of relying on digital affordances for organizing mutual aid? Can digital tools enhance the sustainability and resilience of these organizations, or do they create new risks related to leadership, participation, and communication?

References

Albu, O. B., & Etter, M. (2016). Hypertextuality and social media: A study of the constitutive and paradoxical implications of organizational Twitter use. *Management Communication Quarterly*, *30*(1), 5–31. https://doi.org/10.1177/0893318915601161

Bennett, W. L., & Segerberg, A. (2012). The logic of connective action: Digital media and the personalization of contentious politics. *Information, Communication & Society*, *15*(5), 739–768. https://doi.org/10.1080/1369118X.2012.670661

Brummans, B., Cooren, F., Dion, F., & Vásquez, C. (2024). Emerging trends and topics on the communicative constitution of organizations. In V. D. Miller & M. S. Poole (Eds.), *Organizational communication theory and research* (pp. 27–44). Walter de Gruyter GmbH & Co KG.

Bucher, T., & Helmond, A. (2018). The affordances of social media platforms. In J. Burgess, A. Marwick, T. Poell (Eds.), *The SAGE handbook of social media* (pp. 233–254). SAGE. https://doi.org/10.4135/9781473984066

Cammaerts, B. (2008). Critiques on the participatory potentials of web 2.0. *Communication, Culture & Critique*, *1*, 358–377. https://doi.org/10.1111/j.1753-9137.2008.00028.x

Cammaerts, B. (2019). A genealogy of communicative affordances and activist self-mediation practices. In H. Stephansen & R. Treré (Eds.), *Citizen media and practice: Currents, connections, challenges* (pp. 98–112). Routledge. https://doi.org/10.4324/9781351247375

Cammaerts, B. (2021). The new-new social movements: Are social media changing the ontology of social movements? *Mobilization: An International Quarterly*, *26*(3), 343–358. https://doi.org/10.17813/1086-671X-26-3-343

Carlsson-Szlezak, P., Reeves, M., & Swartz, P. (2020). What coronavirus could mean for the global economy. *Harvard Business Review*, *3*, 1–10. https://sea-connect.com/assets/img/uploads/pdf/d64d0f0c50f2154a135870b035c89700.pdf

Carroll, B., & Simpson, B. (2012). Capturing sociality in the movement between frames: An illustration from leadership development. *Human Relations*, *65*(10), 1283–1309. https://doi.org/10.1177/0018726712451185

Carroll, B., Taylor, S., & Ford, J. (2019). *Leadership: Contemporary critical perspectives*. SAGE.

Chotiner, I. (2020). The interwoven threads of inequality and health. *The New Yorker*. https://www.newyorker.com/news/q-and-a/the-coronavirus-and-the-interwoven-threads-of-inequality-and-health

Contractor, N. S., DeChurch, L. A., Carson, J., Carter, D. R., & Keegan, B. (2012). The topology of collective leadership. *The Leadership Quarterly*, *23*(6), 994–1011. https://doi.org/10.1016/j.leaqua.2012.10.010

D'Enbeau, S., Buzzanell, P. M., & Duckworth, J. (2010). Problematizing classed identities in fatherhood: Development of integrative case studies for analysis and praxis. *Qualitative Inquiry*, *16*(9), 709–720. https://doi.org/10.1177/1077800410374183

Diavolo, L. (2020). People are helping each other fight coronavirus. *Teen Vogue*. https://www.teenvogue.com/story/people-fighting-coronavirus-mutual-aid-efforts-help-each-other.

Dobusch, L., & Schoeneborn, D. (2015). Fluidity, identity, and organizationality: The communicative constitution of Anonymous. *Journal of Management Studies*, *52*(8), 1005–1035. https://doi.org/10.1111/joms.12139

Eddington, S., & Buzzanell, P. M. (2019). Tensions within bullying and career resilience in higher education. In R. West & C. Beck (Eds.), *The Routledge handbook of bullying, and communication* (pp. 164–172). Routledge. https://doi.org/10.4324/9781315148113

Eddington, S. M. (2018). The communicative constitution of hate organizations online: A semantic network analysis of "make America great again". *Social Media + Society*, *4*(3). https://doi.org/10.1177/2056305118790763

Eddington, S. M., Jarvis, C. M., Morrow, C., McGhee, M., & Jordan, C. R. (2025). Navigating backlash: An affordance perspective to online organizing. In S. Kim, P. M. Buzzanell, J-N. Kim, & A. Mazzei (Eds.). *The Routledge handbook of employee communication and organizational process* (pp. 302–311). Routledge. https://doi.org/10.4324/9781003415619

Fairhurst, G. T., & Connaughton, S. L. (2014). Leadership: A communicative perspective. *Leadership*, *10*(1), 7–35. https://doi.org/10.1177/1742715013509396

Fairhurst, G. T., Jackson, B., Foldy, E. G., & Ospina, S. M. (2020). Studying collective leadership: The road ahead. *Human Relations*, *73*(4), 598–614. https://doi.org/10.1177/0018726719898736

Fletcher, J. K. (2004). The paradox of postheroic leadership: An essay on gender, power, and transformational change. *The Leadership Quarterly*, *15*(5), 647–661. https://doi.org/10.1016/j.leaqua.2004.07.004

Gordon, C. (2024). Learning mutual aid: Food justice public pedagogy and community fridge organizing online. *Journal of Applied Communication Research*, *52*(2), 158–178. https://doi.org/10.1080/00909882.2024.2327417

Harrison, R. T. (2017). Leadership, leadership development and all that jazz. *Leadership*, *13*(1), 81–99. https://doi.org/10.1177/1742715016681120

Jackson, S. J., Bailey, M., & Welles, B. F. (2020). *#HashtagActivism: Networks of race and gender justice*. MIT Press. https://doi.org/10.7551/mitpress/10858.001.0001

Jarvis, C. M., & Eddington, S. M. (2021). Disentangling antifeminist paradoxes: Alternative organizing in antifeminist online spaces. *Management Communication Quarterly*, *35*(1), 96–126. https://doi.org/10.1177/0893318920972649

Just, S. N., & Muhr, S. L. (2019). "Together we rise": Collaboration and contestation as narrative drivers of the Women's March. *Leadership*, *15*(2), 245–267. https://doi.org/10.1177/1742715018809497

Kelly, D., & Nicholson, A. (2022). Ancestral leadership: Place-based intergenerational leadership. *Leadership*, *18*(1), 140–161. https://doi.org/10.1177/17427150211024038

Kropotkin, P. (2021). *Mutual aid: A factor of evolution*. Black Rose Books. (Original work published 1903)

Kurtz, A. (2021). The US economy lost 140,000 jobs in December. All of them were held by women. *CNN Business*. https://www.cnn.com/2021/01/08/economy/women-job-losses-pandemic/index.html

Leonardi, P. M., & Vaast, E. (2017). Social media and their affordances for organizing: A review and agenda for research. *Academy of Management Annals*, *11*(1), 150–188. https://doi.org/10.5465/annals.2015.0144

Lindau, S. T., Makelarski, J. A., Boyd, K., Doyle, K. E., Haider, S., Kumar, S., Lee, N. K., Pinkerton, E., Tobin, M., Vu, M., Wroblewski, K. E., & Lengyel, E. (2021). Change in health-related socioeconomic risk factors and mental health during the early phase of the covid-19 pandemic: A national survey of U.S. women. *Journal of Women's Health*, *30*(4), 502–513. https://doi.org/10.1089/jwh.2020.8879

Maris, E., Caplan, R., & Thach, H. (2024). Taking back and giving back on TikTok: Algorithmic mutual aid in the platform economy. *New Media & Society*, *27*(7), 4071–4089. https://doi.org/10.1177/14614448241238396

McVeigh-Schultz, J., & Baym, N. K. (2015). Thinking of you: Vernacular affordance in the context of the microsocial relationship app, couple. *Social Media + Society*, *1*(2). https://doi.org/10.1177/2056305115604649

Mutual Aid Disaster Relief [@mutualaiddisasterrelief]. (n.d.). Retrieved October 3, 2024 from https://www.instagram.com/mutualaiddisasterrelief/

Ospina, S. M., Foldy, E. G., Fairhurst, G. T., & Jackson, B. (2020). Collective dimensions of leadership: Connecting theory and method. *Human Relations*, *73*(4), 441–463. https://doi.org/10.1177/0018726719899714

Pond, P., & Lewis, J. (2017). Riots and Twitter: Connective politics, social media and framing discourses in the digital public sphere. *Information, Communication & Society*, *22*(2), 213–231. https://doi.org/10.1080/1369118X.2017.1366539

Poon, M. (2024). Achieving organizationality through authorship affordances—A communicative episode of Telegram polling from 2019 Hong Kong. *Social Movement Studies*, *23*(3), 391–412. https://doi.org/10.1080/14742837.2023.2296868

Poon, M., & Kohlberger, M. (2022). Twitter as a leadership actor—A communication as constitutive of organizing perspective on a 'leaderless' social movement. *Leadership*, *18*(5), 656–679. https://doi.org/10.1177/17427150221107271

Quick, K. S. (2017). Locating and building collective leadership and impact. *Leadership*, *13*(4), 445–471. https://doi.org/10.1177/1742715015605348

Raelin, J. A. (2016). Imagine there are no leaders: Reframing leadership as collaborative agency. *Leadership*, *12*(2), 131–158. https://doi.org/10.1177/1742715014558076

Rice, R. E., Evans, S. K., Pearce, K. E., Sivunen, A., Vitak, J., & Treem, J. W. (2017). Organizational media affordances: Operationalization and associations with media use: Organizational media affordances. *Journal of Communication*, *67*(1), 106–130. https://doi.org/10.1111/jcom.12273

Rosile, G. A., M Boje, D., & Claw, C. M. (2019). Ensemble leadership theory: Collectivist, relational, and heterarchical roots from indigenous contexts. *Leadership*, *14*(3), 307–328. https://doi.org/10.1177/1742715016652933

Schoeneborn, D., Kuhn, T. R., & Kärreman, D. (2019). The communicative constitution of organization, organizing, and organizationality. *Organization Studies*, *40*(4), 475–496. https://doi.org/10.1177/0170840618782284

Škerlavaj, M. (2022). *Post-heroic leadership: Context, process and outcomes*. Springer International Publishing. https://doi.org/10.1007/978-3-030-90820-1

Sklaveniti, C. (2020). Moments that connect: Turning points and the becoming of leadership. *Human Relations*, *73*(4), 544–571. https://doi.org/10.1177/0018726719895812

Smith, W. R. (2022). On relationality and organizationality: Degrees of durability, materiality, and communicatively constituting a fluid social collective. *Organization Studies*, *43*(11), 1815–1837. https://doi.org/10.1177/01708406211035497

Smith, W. R. (2023). "We like the stock!": Partial organizing, latency, and communicative contestations of actorhood in r/WallStreetBets. *Western Journal of Communication*, *88*(4), 861–886. https://doi.org/10.1080/10570314.2023.2231404

Smith, W. R. (2024). "No dig, no ride": The communicative constitution and consequences of imperfect authoritative texts in fluid collective organizing. *Management Communication Quarterly*, *38*(1), 147–170. https://doi.org/10.1177/08933189231173076

Spade, D. (2020). Solidarity not charity: Mutual aid for mobilization and survival. *Social Text*, *38*(1), 131–151. https://doi.org/10.1215/01642472-7971139

Swann, T. (2023). 'Anarchist technologies': Anarchism, cybernetics and mutual aid in community responses to the COVID-19 crisis. *Organization*, *30*(1), 193–209. https://doi.org/10.1177/13505084221090632

Taylor, M. L., & Kent, M. (2014). The value of social media for pushing activist organizations social agendas: Implications for public relations theory and practice. *Quarterly Review of Business Disciplines*, *1*, 76–87.

Tiratelli, L., & Kaye, S. (2020). Communities vs. coronavirus: The rise of mutual aid. https://www.newlocal.org.uk/publications/communities-vs-coronavirus-the-rise-of-mutual-aid/

Tourish, D. (2014). Leadership, more or less? A processual, communication perspective on the role of agency in leadership theory. *Leadership*, *10*(1), 79–98. https://doi.org/10.1177/1742715013509030

Treem, J. W., & Leonardi, P. M. (2013). Social media use in organizations: Exploring the affordances of visibility, editability, persistence, and association. *Annals of the International Communication Association*, *36*(1), 143–189. https://doi.org/10.1080/23808985.2013.11679130

Wilhoit, E. D. (2017). Affordances as material communication: How the spatial environment communicates to organize cyclists in Copenhagen, Denmark. *Western Journal of Communication*, *82*(2), 217–237. https://doi.org/10.1080/10570314.2017.1306098

Wilhoit, E. D., & Kisselburgh, L. G. (2015). Collective action without organization: The material constitution of bike commuters as collective. *Organization Studies*, *36*(5), 573–592. https://doi.org/10.1177/0170840614556916

Yammarino, F. J., Salas, E., Serban, A., Shirreffs, K., & Shuffler, M. L. (2012). Collectivistic leadership approaches: Putting the "we" in leadership science and practice. *Industrial and Organizational Psychology*, *5*(4), 382–402. https://doi.org/10.1111/j.1754-9434.2012.01467.x

Zammuto, R. F., Griffith, T. L., Majchrzak, A., Dougherty, D. J., & Faraj, S. (2007). Information technology and the changing fabric of organization. *Organization Science*, *18*(5), 749–762. https://doi.org/10.1287/orsc.1070.0307

Zamponi, L. (2023). Mutual aid and solidarity politics in times of emergency: Direct social action and temporality in Italy during the COVID-19 pandemic. *Social Movement Studies*, *23*(6), 756–776. https://doi.org/10.1080/14742837.2023.2204426

SECTION III

Pedagogical and Training Approaches to Leadership and Communication

15

HUMANISTIC LEADERSHIP

Transforming Business through Communication Education

Lisa A. Waite

Roadmap/introduction

This chapter explores the synergy between relational communication theory and humanistic leadership in transforming business education. As economic volatility and cultural shifts reshape business practices, alternative leadership approaches become necessary to mitigate a widespread decline in employee well-being and engagement (Ahn et al., 2011). Emphasizing relational qualities like caring and reflective listening (Tirmizi et al., 2023), the humanistic model assumes that human potential can be enhanced through business education (Pirson & Amann, 2011). However, insufficient studies consider the intersection of relational and humanistic approaches in business leadership education from a communication lens.

The quest for greater humanistic leadership topics in business education curriculum challenges traditional hierarchical norms by prioritizing employee well-being and fostering workplace harmony through relational competencies (Popper, 2004). Driven by empathy, inclusivity, and collaboration, it addresses modern demands for agility and diversity. Literature highlights this shift from leader-centered to people-centered leadership, emphasizing emotional and relational intelligence for transformational results (Chapman & Sisodia, 2015; Fletcher & Thornton, 2023; Pirson, 2017). The holistic approach aligns with the United Nations principles for responsible management education, emphasizing ethical reasoning and global endorsement (Secretariat, 2024a).

Relational communication principles enhance leadership education by encouraging critical reflection and ethical decision-making (Holt et al.,

DOI: 10.4324/9781003563662-19

2017; Secretariat, 2024b). Moral and narrative leadership further develop shared organizational values and empathy-driven strategies. Wellinghoff (2024) notes that sustainable leadership rooted in humanistic frameworks is vital amid a global "polycrisis." Institutions like Fordham University's Center for Humanistic Management exemplify integrating empathy and social responsibility into business education (Fordham University, 2023).

Amid rising rates of employee disengagement and stress, Gallup (2023) reveals that only one in four employees feel cared for, while nine out of ten would trade pay for meaningful work (Achor et al., 2018). Relational leadership addresses these challenges by fostering trust and connection, which is critical for combating workplace dissatisfaction and burnout (Brooks & Winfrey, 2023). This human-centric approach develops leaders equipped to navigate evolving societal needs in business environments where individuals thrive. This paradigm fosters visibility, value, and collaboration, underscoring the essential role of relational skills in education and practice (Chapman, 2024).

This chapter demonstrates how relational communication theory and humanistic leadership principles can reshape business education to address contemporary challenges. I first examine how the current state of business education argues for a shift toward more humanistic approaches. I explore the principles of humanistic leadership and its potential to transform organizational cultures, principles that emphasize employee well-being and relational competencies that foster innovation and collaboration. The role of relational communication theory in developing humanistic leadership skills highlights its importance in preparing future leaders for dynamic business environments. To illustrate these concepts in practice, I present a case study of Barry-Wehmiller, a manufacturing company that exemplifies humanistic leadership principles. This case demonstrates how relational communication and humanistic leadership can be applied in real-world business contexts. Finally, I propose critical questions and practical recommendations for integrating humanistic and relational principles into business education curricula, aiming to equip future leaders with the skills necessary to create more sustainable, inclusive, and people-centric organizations.

Humanistic leadership

Humanistic leadership recognizes people as the heartbeat of successful organizations, aiming for employees to thrive, not just survive. Unlike traditional economic models, it views individuals as the purpose, not merely resources or means to an end. The goal is human advancement over wealth creation (Pirson, 2017). While humanism is not innate, its qualities—empathy, reflective listening, trust, empowerment, inclusivity, and collaboration—can be developed through education and experience. These traits highlight the multifaceted nature of humanistic leadership and its essential communication skills.

Within the existing literature, Pirson and Amann (2011) successfully pinpoint the convergence between relational communication ideology and humanistic leadership:

> In short, humanistic management is the pursuit of strategies and practices that seek to create sustainable human well-being. This management structure derives its legitimacy from preserving human dignity in business by submitting its practices to societal critique. By engaging in an open dialogue about the criteria to assess managerial success, corporate decision-makers realize that the value proposition of business is ultimately to serve people rather than to make money only.
>
> *(p. 6)*

Humanistic leadership redefines business success by addressing global challenges and prioritizing people and the planet. Amann et al. (2011) advocate for leadership that inspires collective good over money, power, and status. Stewart (2024) emphasizes that leadership should be accessible to all, urging business schools to reform how leadership is taught.

Bass and Avolio (1990) argue that transformational leaders inspire innovation and motivation, more effectively than those relying on rewards and punishments. Transforming a me-centric mindset into a we-centric one fosters other-centeredness through interpersonal relationships. This "one-anothering" emphasizes employee well-being over shareholder value (Chapman & Sisodia, 2015) by creating workplaces that offer meaning, purpose, and respect for individual needs (Mackey et al., 2013). Humanistic leadership seeks to benefit all humanity, starting with relational perspectives in leadership communication. The Humanistic Leadership Academy, co-founded by Michael Pirson, launched in 2022 with a manifesto and programs to revolutionize business education, inspiring stakeholders to embody humanistic principles and drive transformative change. Their vision establishes this priority:

> Our vision is a global economy that protects human dignity and promotes human well-being in an economic system in which all stakeholders are equally respected so that market mechanisms are applied to maximize societal benefits rather than individual profits; an economy in which economic rationality is applied as a means rather than an end in itself.
>
> *(Pirson et al., 2018)*

Sisodia and Geib (2019) argue that empathy is humanity's strongest instinct, driving our success as a species. While traditional leadership assumes humans are motivated by scarcity, separation, and competition, they advocate for a new theory of "human" leadership rooted in selflessness, caring, sharing, trust, and community-building (p. 33). They highlight our ability to reshape social structures for the greater good. Mackey et al. (2013) suggest that business and capitalism are evolving toward more conscious practices. Brown (2018) underscores vulnerability as a core leadership trait, describing "daring" leaders who prioritize openness, authenticity, and transparency. These qualities foster trust, connection, and belonging within teams. Similarly, Rogers (2008) recognizes empathetic understanding and candid communication as key to building trust and sees them as central to humanistic leadership.

Relational communication theory

Relational communication theory embraces the idea that positive relationships are based on open communication and collaboration. Individual behaviors and self-awareness are primary features of this theory. In its infancy, Ruesch and Bateson (1951) proposed a "new order of communication" (p. 209) with a refreshed outlook on communication and relationships. It further identified interactive communication patterns among varied relationships in the outcomes of these patterns. This theory provided a practical understanding of how communication behaviors influence relationships (Rogers, 2008).

Relational communication theory supports humanistic leadership in business education by emphasizing leaders' understanding and connection with team members on a personal level, valuing individuals within an organizational context. As a crucial wake-up call, it promotes honest dialogue, active listening, and a supportive work environment. Integrating these theories enhances students' communication skills for empathetic leadership focused on team well-being. Hicks's (2018) insight on leading with care highlights how our treatment of others influences their lives and social roles, urging leaders to foster empathy and trust through ethical decisions.

A communication-driven approach to leadership

The link between humanistic leadership and relational communication theory considers how leaders structure their leadership style of interactions and relationships with employees. This often includes individual mentorship and deeper collaboration with teams. Wallace (2020) emphasizes creating a positive work environment and extended culture by building personal connections and motivating employees to genuinely *want* to work for their leaders. This aspect is crucial in the context of relational communication theory.

Hobson (2024) reminds us that high performance is never a solo effort. The business world benefits from expanding success metrics defined by results and achievements to include the synergy that leads to these outcomes. A culture of fear and competition established by an ego-driven leader often leaves employees feeling diminished and invisible. This may result in less creativity, innovation, and morale. In a modern context, proficient leaders elevate the quality of relationships within organizations through a commitment to the holistic well-being of employees, making each feel valued.

As humanistic leadership aspires to empower the workforce through positive and collaborative relationships, business education and graduate faculty play a crucial role in highlighting the tangible benefits of communication skills to students who are poised to become tomorrow's leaders (Garcia-Chitiva & Correa, 2023). For instance, the common term "soft skills" (relational competencies) should be replaced by "human skills." They are often scrutinized as less relevant and more easily acquired than "hard" skills such as technical expertise (Fletcher & Thornton, 2023). While denotation may consider "soft" as *weak or easy*, the reality is that relational versatility, including competence in building trust, displaying empathy, endorsing resilience, and practicing reflective listening, requires practice beyond the simplistic connotation. Although specialized knowledge or proficiency is undoubtedly valuable, humanistic principles reach their full potential and are best realized in an environment where effective communication, teamwork, and leadership (human skills) are present. Reframing the terminology reflects a more accurate appreciation for the profound impact these skills have on nurturing relationships in a business setting, cultivating a positive organizational culture, and ultimately driving success. There is hope on the curricular horizon where students are slowly recognizing the need to sharpen their humanistic awareness. One example is the course *Leading with Mindfulness and Compassion* offered at the Stanford Graduate School of Business, which is consistently waitlisted (Weiss, 2019), and *The Power of One: A New Culture of Leadership* offered as a senior-level communication seminar course at Kent State University's Stark campus (Waite, 2022).

Transforming business through human-centric practices

Bob Chapman, CEO of Barry-Wehmiller, is widely recognized for his dedicated approach to leadership rooted in care, empathy, and people-centered values. Chapman transformed Barry-Wehmiller from a struggling manufacturing company into a thriving global operation by rejecting traditional leadership in favor of "Truly Human Leadership" (Chapman & Sisodia, 2015). At the heart of this philosophy is a profound personal belief in treating employees as family, recognizing their intrinsic value, and fostering a culture of trust and respect.

Chapman's implementation of Truly Human Leadership focuses on listening to employees as individuals, creating environments where everyone feels heard and appreciated. A key example is Barry-Wehmiller's "listening training" sessions where leaders are taught the importance of active and reflective listening. Efforts enhance emotional connections within teams, fostering collaboration and mutual understanding. By prioritizing "people over profit," Chapman has consistently demonstrated that nurturing people leads to sustainable business success (Sinek, 2019, p. 12).

Additionally, Chapman's emphasis on employee well-being challenges conventional views of productivity. For instance, his decision to avoid layoffs during an economic downturn highlights his commitment to valuing human dignity over cost-cutting measures. Instead, he has implemented innovative solutions, such as shared sacrifice, to ensure financial stability without undermining employee trust (Chapman & Sisodia, 2015). Under his leadership, Barry-Wehmiller became a model for how organizations can align profitability with purpose (Buss, 2020).

Analysis: Relational communication theory and humanistic leadership in action

Chapman's leadership model aligns closely with relational communication theory by emphasizing the importance of dialogue, empathy, and mutual respect in fostering meaningful interpersonal connections. Identifying listening as a core leadership competency, Chapman operationalizes relational communication principles, treating conversations as opportunities for shared meaning and cultivating trust. His focus on listening training underscores the importance of reflective listening in reducing workplace conflict and fostering deeper relational bonds—a cornerstone of relational communication theory (Holt et al., 2017). Additionally, Chapman draws a connection between fundamental communication principles and their applicability to humanistic leadership, as highlighted in his popular TEDx Talk (2016, September 12). Applied to a higher-ed curriculum, these examples serve as diverse avenues for engagement, ensuring that students and aspiring leaders can implement these principles personally and professionally.

From a humanistic leadership perspective, Chapman's practices exemplify a shift from hierarchical, leader-centered models to people-centered frameworks. His approach reinforces the belief that organizations thrive when individuals feel visible, valued, and empowered. This reflects the humanistic principle of prioritizing dignity and ethical decision-making over purely financial concerns and aligns with the leadership aspects of humanistic models (Pirson, 2017).

Conversely, Chapman's ideology reveals some challenging critiques of humanistic leadership, such as being overly idealistic. For example, Monds and Liu (2024) find that Chapman's philosophy and its reliance on faith-based principles when applied in diverse, secular settings, may impose limitations. An emphasis on religious principles for instance could be perceived as exclusionary in multicultural or non-religious contexts, limiting its effectiveness and inclusivity. Additionally, the "workplace as family" concept has faced criticism in broader business discourse (Luna, 2021).

Barry-Wehmiller's financial turnaround and sustained profitability demonstrate that relational and humanistic approaches are both ethically and economically achievable. At its core, business is about relationships. In this regard, relational communication theory is the mechanism that broadcasts humanistic leadership through the airwaves of an organization where everyone plays a part in creating a strong and thriving network.

While relational communication theory and humanistic leaders provide valuable insights for teaching more effective leadership, it's crucial to acknowledge that challenges persist in practical applications beyond the classroom. One instance lies in the experience of American Airlines, which, despite embracing Chapman's principles, continues to grapple with issues such as contract disputes and traditional labor challenges, underscoring the complexity of reshaping organizational dynamics through leadership. Barry-Wehmiller Institute partner Matthew Whiat notes that navigating cultural shifts and operational improvements is challenging among an extensive workforce of 130,000 people (Buss, 2020). In short, if the leadership principles of a lone CEO in manufacturing can resonate with thousands of global business leaders, there is certainly optimism for a higher education business curriculum.

Global instability, such as the 2008 financial crisis, is one catalyst of a managerial trust deficit. This financial downfall resulted in part from the judgment of decision-makers who attended traditional business schools (George, 2008). Pirson, et al. (2011) hold business and management education programs accountable as "silent partners" contributing to a negative impact on business and society. This strengthens the justification for reforming higher education and MBA programs away from traditional leadership subjects and attitudes to a humanistic (relational) business curriculum. While virtually all academic programs can reap these rewards, embracing a humanistic approach with specific attention to communication modules has the potential to address and resolve social problems, making a meaningful contribution to the well-being of both business and the world at large. These learning modules require more than mere acknowledgment; instead, they become the very core of the business education experience.

The vision for humanizing business education is making its way beyond the halls of academia and into modern corporate universities where caring for the "whole" employee is a foundational business principle. In practice, Barry-Wehmiller University Training Center hosted a leadership event that imparted four "commitments" from the Humanistic Leadership Academy (n.d.) framing their effort:

> First, to transform business education for holistic learning experiences that nurture competent, courageous, caring leaders driving positive change. Second, to foster connections with self, others, nature, and beyond, encouraging others to do the same. Third, to uphold human dignity, freedom, and success models that benefit all. Lastly, to implement practices supporting healthy ecosystems and flourishing life, ensuring positive, measurable impacts and shared prosperity.

Teaching tactics to engage students in relational communication theory and applying humanistic practices to leadership involves challenging conventional strategies. One approach is using the *Be, Know, Do* model, which integrates character development (being), knowledge (knowing), and action (doing) into a framework for business education (Chapman, 2013). Adapted from the US Army's leadership principles, this model emphasizes self-awareness, leadership principles, and practical application. It encourages students to question power structures, organizational norms, and societal values (The Association of the United States Army, n.d.). This holistic approach promotes creativity, ethical decision-making, and sustainability in leadership education, guiding students through critical dialogue and self-reflection.

Leino and Mullola (2014) stress the importance of teaching humanistic leadership in business education. Character and temperament, though non-academic, significantly impact academic outcomes. By integrating humanistic leadership with relational communication theory, this approach emphasizes understanding others' perspectives and creating shared realities in teaching and content examination. Faculty and students can apply these principles to drive change through experiential opportunities (e.g., internships, fellowships, job shadowing) and classroom exercises. Ultimately, by embedding humanistic leadership principles and relational communication theory into the core of business curricula, educators can cultivate a new generation of leaders who prioritize ethical practices, meaningful connections, and a commitment to the well-being of individuals and society, reshaping the future of organizational culture and success.

Conclusion

Humanistic leadership and relational communication theory are essential in leadership literature, emphasizing their undervaluation in business education and modern leadership. There is momentum to reorient business education and cultivate humanistic leaders who can influence a like-minded workforce (Chapman, 2022). Alternative business frameworks are evolving, yet business education faces the ongoing challenge of shifting traditional programs toward more humanistic leadership. Gosling and Grodecki (2020) urge stakeholders to adopt relational communication principles, guiding students to innovate, view challenges differently, and enter their future confidently. For those dedicated to improving business education, several recommendations may lead to positive change. First, it is critical to include communication theory courses in business programs to give students a deeper insight into how communication influences leadership. Second, include exercises encouraging students to apply communication skills in real business situations like role-playing or collaborative projects. These help students build the interpersonal skills essential for effective leadership. Addressing these gaps in business education helps prepare future leaders to navigate the complexities of the professional world and establish a more positive impact.

Scholars and practitioners must engage in ongoing dialogue, research, and experimentation to develop leaders who focus on empathy, collaboration, and ethical decision-making. This integration signifies a revival of leaders who excel in business while enriching society (Amann et al., 2011, p. 8). Grounding business education in core human principles can foster workplaces that not only thrive but also inspire profound societal transformation, shaping a future where leadership and humanity coexist.

Suggested further readings

Abdelgaffar, H. A. (2021). A review of responsible management education: Practices, outcomes and challenges. *The Journal of Management Development*, *40*(9/10), 613–638. https://doi.org/10.1108/JMD-03-2020-0087

Anderson, M. (2017). Transformational leadership in education: A review of existing literature. *International Social Science Review*, *93*(1), 1–13. https://www.jstor.org/stable/90012919

California Department of Education. (n.d.) *Culturally sustaining pedagogy—Educator excellence*. https://www.cde.ca.gov/pd/ee/culturallysustainingped.asp

Care, E., Kim, H., Vista, A., & Anderson, K. (2018). *Educational systems alignment for 21st century skills* (p. 40). Brookings Institution. https://www.brookings.edu/wp-content/uploads/2018/11/Education-system-alignment-for-21st-century-skills-012819.pdf

Dugan, J., & Komives, S. (2007). *Developing leadership capacity in college students: Findings from a national study*. Multi-Institutional Study of Leadership/National Clearinghouse for Leadership Programs. https://www.researchgate.net/publication/237536892_Developing_Leadership_Capacity_In_College_Students_Findings_From_a_National_Study

Hennig, A., & Schiller, L. (2021). The soft overcomes the hard: Inspirations for leadership in the twenty-first century from Daoism. In J. Marques (Ed.), *Innovative leadership in times of compelling changes: Management, change, strategy, and positive leadership* (pp. 99–115). Springer International Publishing. https://doi.org/10.1007/978-3-030-67258-4_7

Holt, S., Marques, J., Hu, J., & Wood, A. (2017). Cultivating empathy: New perspectives on educating business leaders. *The Journal of Values-Based Leadership*, *10*(1), Article 3. https://doi.org/10.22543/0733.101.1173

Johns Hopkins Carey Business School. (May 22, 2023). *What can 50 years of leadership communication research tell us?* https://carey.jhu.edu/articles/50-years-leadership-communication-research

Muff, K., Liechti, A., & Dyllick, T. (2020). How to apply responsible leadership theory in practice: A competency tool to collaborate on the sustainable development goals. *Corporate Social-Responsibility and Environmental Management*, *27*(5), 2254–2274. https://doi.org/10.1002/csr.1962

Shields, C. M. (2017). *Transformative leadership in education: Equitable and socially just change in an uncertain and complex world*. Routledge. https://doi.org/10.4324/9781315207148

Vera, D., Samba, C., Kong, D. T., & Maldonado, T. (2020). Resilience as thriving: The role of positive leadership practices. *Organizational Dynamics*, *50*(2), 1–8. https://doi.org/10.1016/j.orgdyn.2020.100784

Waddock, S. (2016) Developing humanistic leadership education. *Humanistic Management Journal*, *1*, 57–73. https://doi.org/10.1007/s41463-016-0003-5

Questions for further engagement

As organizations contemplate the transition from traditional leadership styles to humanistic principles, several questions are worthy of extended study.

1. How does this shift impact the established hierarchical structures and authority dynamics within the organization?
2. What challenges might emerge in terms of employee adaptation and the integration of humanistic values into existing organizational cultures?
3. How can leaders effectively measure and assess the success of the transition from traditional leadership practices, ensuring that humanistic principles are genuinely enhancing employee well-being and organizational outcomes?

These questions invite thoughtful consideration of the implications and potential obstacles to a humanistic leadership approach. They potentially foster a more empathetic, inclusive, and sustainable organizational culture that secures the well-being of individuals within the workplace.

References

Achor, S., Reece, A., Rosen Kellerman, G., & Robichaux, A. (November, 2018). 9 out of 10 people are willing to earn less money to do more-meaningful work. *Harvard Business Review*. https://hbr.org/2018/11/9-out-of-10-people-are-willing-to-earn-less-money-to-do-more-meaningful-work

Alm, M. J., Ettner, L. W., & Loupin, A. (2011). From classical to contemporary leadership challenges. *Journal of Leadership Studies*, *5*, 6–22. https://doi.org/10.1002/jls.20201

Amann, W., Pirson, M., Dierksmeier, C., Kimakowitz, E., Spitzeck, H., & Von Kimakowitz, E. (Eds.). (2011). *Business schools under fire: Humanistic management education as the way forward*. Palgrave Macmillan.

Bass, B. M., & Avolio, B. J. (1990). The implications of transactional and transformational leadership for individual, team, and organizational development. *Research in Organizational Change and Development*, *4*(1), 231–272.

Brooks, A., & Winfrey, O. (2023). *Build the life you want: The art and science of getting happier*. Penguin.

Brown, B. (2018). *Dare to lead: Brave work. tough conversations. Whole hearts*. Penguin.

Buss, D. (2020, Jan/Feb) Love your people. *Chief Executive Magazine*, *1*, 1–6. https://chiefexecutive.net/welcome-to-the-leadership-by-caring-revolution/

Chapman, B. (2013, July 10). *Is your leadership due for a checkup?* Barry Wehmiller. https://www.barrywehmiller.com/post/blog/2020/03/05/is-your-leadership-due-for-a-checkup

Chapman, R. (2022, March 30). *Bringing humanity to business education*. Barry-Wehmiller Blog. https://www.barrywehmiller.com/post/blog/2022/03/29/bringing-humanity-to-business-education

Chapman, R. (2024, March 20). *Creating a more caring world: Teaching human skills in primary and secondary education*. Barry-Wehmiller Blog. https://www.barrywehmiller.com/post/blog/2024/03/19/creating-a-more-caring-world—teaching-human-skills-in-primary-and-secondary-education

Chapman, R., & Sisodia, R. (2015). *Everybody matters: The extraordinary power of caring for your people like family*. Penguin.

Fletcher, S., & Thornton, K. R. V. (2023). The top 10 soft skills in business today compared to 2012. *Business and Professional Communication Quarterly*, *86*(4), 411–426. https://doi.org/10.1177/23294906221148453

Fordham University. (2023). *Social innovation at the Gabelli School of Business*. https://www.fordham.edu/gabelli-school-of-business/about/social-innovation-at-the-gabelli-school-of-business/

Gallup. (2023). *State of the Global Workplace report*. Gallup Workplace. https://www.gallup.com/workplace/349484/state-of-the-global-workplace.aspx

Garcia-Chitiva, M. P., & Correa, J. C. (2023). Soft skills centrality in graduate studies offerings. *Studies in Higher Education*, *49*(6), 956–980. https://doi.org/10.1080/03075079.2023.2254799

George, B. (2008, November 19). Failed leadership caused the financial crisis. U.S. News and World Report. https://www.usnews.com/opinion/articles/2008/11/19/failed-leadership-caused-the-financial-crisis

Gosling, J., & Grodecki, A. (2020). Competences for responsible management (and leadership) education and practice. In D. C. Moosmayer, O. Laasch, C. Parkes, & K. G. Brown (Eds.), *Competences for responsible management (and leadership) education and practice* (pp. 245–264). Sage Publications. https://doi.org/10.4135/9781526477187.n16

Hicks, D. (2018). *Leading with dignity: How to create a culture that brings out the best in people.* Yale University Press. https://www.jstor.org/stable/j.ctvqc6gvg

Hobson, N. (2024, March) Jamie Lee Curtis's brilliant 2023 Oscar acceptance speech should be required reading for anyone leading a team. *INC. Magazine.* https://www.inc.com/nick-hobson/13amie-lee-curtiss-brilliant-oscar-acceptance-speech-should-be-required-reading-for-anyone-leading-a-team.html

Holt, S., Marques, J., Hu, J., & Wood, A. (2017). Cultivating empathy: New perspectives on educating business leaders. *The Journal of Values-Based Leadership*, *10*(1), 1–2. https://doi.org/10.22543/0733.101.1173

Humanistic Leadership Academy. (n.d.). *Manifesto commitments.* https://humanisticleadershipacademy.org/manifesto/

Leino, M., & Mullola, S. (2014). Temperament-conscious humanistic pedagogy. *Psychology*, *5*(7), pp. 753–761. https://doi:10.4236/psych.2014.57086

Luna, J. (October, 2021). The toxic effects of branding your workplace a "family." *Harvard Business Review*, October 27, 2021. https://hbr.org/2021/10/the-toxic-effects-of-branding-your-workplace-a-family

Mackey, J., Sisodia, R., & George, B. (2013). *Conscious capitalism: Liberating the heroic spirit of business.* Harvard Business Review Press.

Monds, C., & Liu, L. A. (2024). Faith, family, and firm: A case study of Bob Chapman. In P. Fu (Ed.), *Humanistic leadership practices: Exemplary cases from different cultures* (pp. 15–38). Springer Verlag. https://doi.org/10.1007/978-3-031-34366-7_2

Pirson, M. (2017, February 18). Developing humanistic management practice. *Gabelli School of Business, Fordham University, Research Paper* (1–24). https://ssrn.com/abstract=2916461

Pirson, M., & Amann, W. (2011, March 10). Humanistic management education: Concluding observations and suggestions. *Fordham University Schools of Business Research Paper*. http://dx.doi.org/10.2139/ssrn.1730383

Pirson, M., Bachani, J., & Blomme, D. R. J. (2018). *Humanistic management: Social entrepreneurship and mindfulness, volume II: Foundations, cases, and exercises*. Business Expert Press.

Pirson, M., Dierksmeier, C., Von Kimakowitz, E., & Spitzeck, H. (Eds.). (2011). *Business schools under fire: Humanistic management education as the way forward*. Palgrave Macmillan. https://doi.org/10.1007/978-3-030-22767-8_249

Popper, M. (2004). Leadership as relationship. *Journal for the Theory of Social Behavior*, *34*(2), 107–125. https://doi.org/10.1111/j.0021-8308.2004.00238.x

Rogers, L. (2008). Relational communication theory: A systemic-interactional approach to interpersonal relationships. In L. A. Baxter & D. O. Braithwaite (Eds.), *Relational communication theory: A systemic-interactional approach to interpersonal relationships* (pp. 335–348). SAGE Publications. https://doi.org/10.4135/9781483329529.n25

Ruesch, J., & Bateson, G. (1951). *Communication, the social matrix of psychiatry.* Norton & Company. https://archive.org/stream/communicationsoc00inrues/communicationsoc00inrues_djvu.txt

Secretariat. (2024a, March 18). *2023 PRME annual report* (p. 32). https://d30mzt1bxg5llt.cloudfront.net/public/uploads/PDFs/2023-PRME-Annual-Report.pdf
Secretariat. (2024b, January 31). *The PRME i5 playbook for pedagogical development: Transforming business education with impactful methods.* https://i5.unprme.org/resources/
Sinek, S. (2019). *The infinite game*. Penguin Random House.
Sisodia, R., & Geib, M. (2019). *The healing organization: Awakening the conscience of business to help save the world.* Harper Collins.
Stewart, B. (Executive Producer). (2024, March 8). *A transformative partnership for teaching leadership in business education* [Audio podcast episode]. Barry Wehmiller. https://www.barrywehmiller.com/post/podcast/2024/03/07/podcast--a-transformative-partnership-for-teaching-leadership-in-business-education
TEDx Talks. (2016, Sept. 12). *The insanity of leadership* [Video]. YouTube. https://youtube.com/watch?v=zaP9bxq525E
The Association of the United States Army. (n.d.). *Be, know, and do.* https://www.ausa.org/be-know-and-do
Tirmizi, S., Williams, K., & Tirmizi, S. (2023). More human, not less: Global relevance of values-based leadership. *Humanistic Management Journal*, *8*(1), 13–28. https://doi.org/10.1007/s41463-023-00142-y
Wallace, N. (2020). Conscious leadership: Moving to an intentional focus for a thriving workplace culture. *Leader to Leader*, *97*, 53–57. https://doi.org/10.1002/ltl.20512
Waite, L. (2022). *The power of one: A new culture of leadership* [Seminar course]. Kent State University at Stark. https://keys.kent.edu/ePROD/bwlkffcs.P_AdvUnsecureGetCrse
Weiss, L. (2019, January 28). *Viewpoint: The case for soft skills.* Society for Human Resource Management. https://www.shrm.org/topics-tools/news/organizational-employee-development/viewpoint-case-soft-skills
Wellinghoff, B. (2024, Apr. 29). *The power of humanistic leadership in practice.* [YouTube presentation]. International Humanistic Management Association. https://www.ignited.global/ihma/blog/power-humanistic-leadership-practice

16

SOCIAL CONSTRUCTION OF LEADERSHIP AND CHANGE

Cases from Higher Education

Stacy Smulowitz, Ralph A. Gigliotti, Carolyn Cunningham, Chrys Egan, and Dorine Lawrence-Hughes

Introduction

Leadership and communication are intricately connected. Leadership is made possible through communication. As detailed in this and other chapters in this book, leadership and communication often result from shared, distributed, and collective processes. Rather than view leadership as being isolated to the influence of the individual at the top of an organization's hierarchy, leadership is enacted and accomplished through collaborative interactions among leaders and followers within a particular context. As leaders, followers, and the contexts in which they are embedded intersect, leadership and communication are socially constructed, which shapes how individuals make meaning.

The social construction of meaning adds to the richness of our shared experiences. Individuals may have different views of similar phenomena because of the unique perspectives, paradigms, and lived experiences they bring to a particular situation—and by coming together, individuals can develop a more holistic understanding of an issue or matter of strategic concern. However, these individualized and interpretive lenses may also result in a perceived lack of trust in the other, an incomplete or inadequate view of the complexities of any given situation, or a limited desire to develop a shared understanding.

Within the context of higher education, the nexus of leadership and communication remains a ripe area for scholarly inquiry. One aspect, for example, is shared governance, where different groups of people like students, faculty, staff, and administrators might share different levels of

DOI: 10.4324/9781003563662-20

decision-making authority and responsibility. There are varied expectations regarding the role and purpose of higher education among a wide array of stakeholders. In addition, there are internal and external pressures for continuous change and innovation in higher education. These higher education dynamics create a unique space for leadership and communication analysis. This chapter explores the nexus of leadership and communication within a markedly distributed higher education ecosystem. This context creates a space to explore the interplay of norms, expectations, and traditions associated with shared governance; various approaches to change leadership to influence organizational direction or advance a particular agenda; and broader organizational and environmental pressures that influence institutional practices and strategies.

As well-documented in the change literature, the success or failure of change efforts rests on the shoulders of leaders (Kotter, 2012; Kotter & Heskett, 1992). Leaders establish the vision and goals for the change effort, provide resources to support the change, and help to champion the change as an organizational priority. Within the context of higher education and other organizations, leadership is a shared and distributed process that requires involvement, investment, and support from multiple groups to accomplish change. The success of change efforts must also take account of the unique culture and history of the organization and the experiences with similar change in the past.

The co-construction of reality with others in the organization plays an important role in how organizational stakeholders may perceive the success or failure of change efforts (Berger & Luckmann, 1967; Steigenberger, 2015). Oftentimes, this act of co-construction is shared in the communication environment as individuals discuss their feelings and thoughts about the change, build coalitions to advance or stall the change, and ultimately accept or resist the change (Lewis, 2006; Ruben & Gigliotti, 2019). These perceptions further impact organizational members' attitudes about future change efforts (Lewis, 2006).

We use higher education as the focal organizational context for this chapter because it is familiar to many readers and it offers a useful illustration of a complex system with multiple stakeholders who embody different perspectives. Theory-informed considerations are relevant for those seeking to study and engage in leadership across different types of organizations in addition to higher education.

We seek to explore leadership communication considerations in higher education, with a unique focus on issues related to distributed leadership, social construction, and the dynamics of change. We introduce two vignettes, situated in the context of higher education, to illustrate the ways in which these theoretical concepts may help to analyze the dynamics of leadership communication. Finally, it is our hope that the exploratory themes introduced in this chapter may help readers as they further engage in the study and practice of leadership communication across organizational contexts.

Current considerations of higher education

Colleges and universities are organizations with a mission to advance scholarship and educate students in the campus culture they create while remaining financially viable. Three important considerations for understanding higher education as an organization include a focus on mission (a university's reason for existence, their objectives, and who they are designed to serve), business model (generating enough funds to support that mission), and culture (who the members are, what they value, and how they operate) (Hess, 2021, p. 75). Consider your own college or university's mission, business model, and culture. Some of these points will be found on institutional websites, reports, and promotional materials, while other aspects are subtler and experienced in-person, like the "feel" of a campus.

Each institution of higher education manages its own unique challenges, yet as of the writing of this chapter, there are multiple difficulties and pressures facing colleges and universities across the United States. Many campuses are managing a complex combination of declining public confidence in the value of higher education, lingering educational impacts resulting from the pandemic and lockdown, and an "enrollment cliff" with fewer traditional college-age students. These factors and others have led to overall declining college enrollments and financial hardships for individuals, families, universities, and communities. In addition, students who attend college increasingly need academic accommodations for different learning needs and styles and more robust wellness and mental health support. This means that even if a campus is serving fewer students than previously, these students likely require more services and expect increased individual attention, which requires additional resources, time, and expertise. It is not surprising that stakeholders such as faculty and staff report feeling "burnout" by the increasing volume of work, stress, and expectations. Added to these factors are the growing presence of artificial intelligence (AI) in education and work, battles over the role of diversity and equity in higher education, campus protests generating international media attention, and a divisive political environment (Clark et al., 2024; Mitchell, 2024; Muscanell, 2024).

Simultaneously, there may be tensions within an institution related to shared governance, where multiple stakeholder groups participate in the decision-making process, thereby amplifying the unique role of the university's board, administration, faculty, staff, and students in sharing leadership to manage change, provide direction, and advance the institution. Complicating the decision-making process is the fact that high-ranking administrative leadership positions, such as presidents, vice presidents/provosts, and deans, have increasingly high turnover, with some leaders leaving these positions every few years. This can be especially problematic as each new administrator launches initiatives to "leave their mark" on the institution but soon moves on, leaving some projects incomplete or unsupported—and leaving the faculty and staff who remain with feelings of distrust or even apathy. Moreover, faculty and staff, some who have served the university for decades, may barely recognize the institution they once knew due to shifting institutional priorities and the impact these initiatives have on organizational culture. Further, campus employees may be advocating for or utilizing unions or shared governance groups—like a faculty senate, staff council, or student government association, or other collective representation—to address issues like compensation, labor expectations, legal rights and freedoms, diversity and inclusion, safety, and other crucial work issues. Faculty, in particular, are navigating shifting tenure (job security) and promotion models in an increasingly litigious climate. As new cohorts of students enter the university, they bring different ideas, opportunities, and issues that universities may not have considered before. Compounding these institutional challenges, campus members may be resistant to or hostile toward change, even when that change is inevitable. Layered upon these issues, all members of the campus community are accountable to higher institutional authorities like a governing board, board of trustees, or board of regents, who both shape and respond to the larger political and educational environment. Clearly, higher education is facing a perfect storm of changes that demand effective leadership and communication. Thus, higher education is an exemplary context in which to consider the nexus of leadership, communication, and change.

Underlying theoretical concepts

Leadership communication

Complex internal and external challenges facing higher education illustrate why skillful communication and leadership are vital to any organization and its members. Addressing these issues requires the ability to navigate change leadership, distributed power, and stakeholder perceptions through thoughtful, strategic communication. To more fully explore the dynamics of leadership and communication in advancing change in higher education, it is helpful to establish a shared understanding of some central concepts related to communication theory and change leadership theory.

Communication is recognized as a "process of making sense out of the world and sharing that sense with others by creating meaning through the use of verbal and nonverbal messages" (Beebe et al., 2020), involving the co-construction of meaning among individuals (Ruben & Stewart, 2006; Thayer, 1968, 1979). The formal study of communication explores the dynamics of meaning-making in dyads, groups, teams, and organizations. Traditional views of communication often imply a linear process whereby a sender transmits a message to a receiver, who in turn translates, interprets, and acts on that message (Ruben & Gigliotti, 2016). More nuanced views of this communication process explore more fully why the message sent may not equal the message received, and they focus directly on the ways in which communicators are embedded within a system of multiple messages, interpretations, and environmental factors that may complicate a shared understanding (Ruben & Gigliotti, 2016). If leadership is understood to be a process of social influence, communication serves a critical role in helping to shape how individuals influence how others think, feel, or behave. The Capacious Model of Leadership Identities Construction is particularly helpful for understanding the relationship between communication and influence. This model conceptualizes four essential influences on successful communication and leadership: (1) purpose and calling—why a person is inspired or chosen to lead, (2) self-identities—our answers to who we are, (3) social identities—how we and others shape our self-concept through group associations, and (4) relationships—personal and professional connections with others that help define our leadership (Egan et al., 2017). As such, enacting one's leadership through social influence is not limited to the most senior individual in the organization or the most powerful person based on organizational hierarchy; rather, as we see manifested in matrixed organizations, decentralized organizations, or organizations that rely upon the systems and structures of shared governance, such as colleges and universities, influence efforts are distributed, plural, or shared. Drawing upon Spillane's (2012) writing, Denis et al. (2023) differentiate distributed leadership as fundamentally relational in both formal and informal leadership roles. Distributed leadership differs from shared leadership in that leadership is held not only by designated leaders within the organization but also by many individuals who do not necessarily hold formal leadership roles. The practice of distributed leadership is constituted and shaped by continuous interactions between leaders and followers, and attention is paid to both the context in which leadership is enacted and the expression of joint agency (Gronn, 2002, 2003).

Certainly, within the context of colleges and universities, shared governance allows for multiple individuals and collective bodies to come together and shape the work of the organization. Leadership at the "top" still matters, and individuals with formal leadership roles in higher education—including presidents, vice presidents, and deans—possess a great deal of influence in shaping the work of the institution. As it relates to the progress of organizational change, their ability to deliver messages that resonate with the needs, expectations, and goals of members of the community will often impact the success or failure of the change effort (Gigliotti & Ruben, 2025; Ruben & Gigliotti, 2019). As Fairhurst (2009) suggests, "Even if leadership actors cannot always control events, they are still viewed as having the ability to control the context under which events are seen" (p. 1608). Often organizational members look to leaders to "tell the story" and "personify" the institutional vision (Mitchell & King, 2018, p. 56).

Communication-centered views of leadership often highlight the useful writing on sensemaking, making sense of an environment, and sensegiving, shaping how others form meaning. Social influence hinges upon this communicative interplay among leaders, followers, and the contexts in which leadership occurs. Both leaders and followers are involved in sensemaking and sensegiving activities that occur when attempting to manage meaning. Leaders and followers make sense of extracted cues in the environment, and through communication, they influence how these phenomena are understood by others. Recipients of these messages, in turn, play a role in co-constructing the meaning of these events and situations that are subject to multiple interpretations. Both sensemaking and sensegiving endeavors are impacted by the contexts in which these activities are embedded.

In short, leadership is a process of social influence that is made possible through communication. Communication itself, involving the exchange of symbols that are subject to multiple interpretations, allows for the potential creation and cultivation of shared meaning. This meaning-making process—both the making of sense based on the interpretation and creation of symbolic cues and the sharing of these cues with others—reflects the unique paradigms, perspectives, and assumptions of those involved in the communication situation. Finally, at the intersection of self, other, and context, leadership is both relationally and collectively called into existence—and these patterns are often reinforced through the systems and structures of shared governance. Our attempt to engage in shared meaning-making, which is fundamental to the success of organizational change efforts, can present a challenge given one's unique positional (e.g., vice president, professor, student) and disciplinary (e.g., chemistry, communication, marketing) orientation and the different mental models that converge in organizational endeavors.

Change leadership

A key task of those engaged in leadership is the need to initiate and manage change. In response to many of the higher education challenges detailed at the outset of this chapter, change leadership—to inspire and influence others during transition—remains an important expectation for those seeking to engage in social influence in colleges and universities. Leadership, trust, and belief in someone's reliability are critical to the success of any change effort and take time to develop. For leaders seeking to build trust and facilitate successful organizational change efforts, it is especially important that they understand their own and others' worldviews, involve stakeholders in the decision-making process, provide relevant information to others to reduce uncertainty, and provide stakeholders with an opportunity to share their voice and to monitor the communication environment (Smulowitz, 2021).

A thorough understanding of the leaders' worldview and a willingness to understand stakeholders' worldviews is always the first step to any successful change effort. Worldview is a compilation of experiences, assumptions, values, and perceptions. These experiences shape our "beliefs, actions, meanings and reality" and create our "rules for how things 'ought to' or 'should be'" (Smulowitz, 2021, p. 34). As leaders evaluate their own worldviews, they should also consider the worldviews of stakeholders. Comparing worldviews is often an eye-opening experience because many times they are quite different. Starting here will provide leaders with an idea of the details they need to include in their communication, information, and sensegiving about the change effort. The failure to understand the unique differences of others may result in communication challenges.

In developing a change implementation plan, leaders should also build in time to include stakeholders in decision-making. Often the leader has a sophisticated high-level view of the implications of the change effort. However, stakeholders who are "in the trenches" will provide a clearer picture of the implications of certain decisions and may be able to provide an easier way to accomplish the same goal. Done right, being involved in the decision-making early in the process also can help stakeholders to feel more invested in a positive outcome for the change effort. These stakeholders should be formally and informally encouraged to share their voice with others who may not be as engaged in the change process.

Despite the very best of leadership intentions, resistance to change, ranging from apathy to hesitation to outright opposition, may impede the progress and direction of the change effort. Within the context of higher education, there is a conventional view that colleges and universities are slow to change, with some describing an inevitable resistance to change (Rosenberg, 2023). As Balderston (1995) describes, "the expectation of permanence imparts more deliberateness to the university's attitude toward change than is true of many other organizations, for which the rule is: change or die" (p. 91). Many leaders view stakeholder resistance as solely a means to derail the effort. In reality, stakeholders often resist for several reasons, including concerns about job security or status, worries about the potential failure of the change, distrust of the long-term viability of the change, negative past experience with change, or the existence of personality conflicts or bad will toward the organization. In many instances, the leader's lack of communication effectiveness or lack of monitoring of the communication environment may cause the resistance (Smulowitz, 2021). Whatever the cause, leaders should take the opportunity presented by resistance to carefully listen to stakeholders, make corrective messaging about the change effort, and make improvements to the change effort based on stakeholder feedback. Often stakeholders know long before the leader that changes are necessary. In fact, they can often tell leaders what changes need to be made and how to improve. Leaders can reduce resistance from the start of the change effort implementation by using effective communication practices, involving stakeholders in the process early, sharing their vision, monitoring the communication environment, and providing resources, support, and feedback.

Finally, the narratives or stories that leaders choose to tell about what happened, or what to believe about what happened, serve an important purpose. As Hollihan and Baaske (2022) note, common stories "serve an important formative purpose" both for the people who choose to tell and believe them and for the culture that comes to accept them (p. 27). Successfully initiating change in higher education requires that leaders acknowledge the common stories or narratives seemingly embedded within higher education culture and consider invoking alternative narratives to help make sense of change. These common stories that individuals are often socialized to accept and repeat include inherent faculty distrust of administration, difficulty of collaboration due to departmental and even disciplinary silos, and the false narratives and assumptions that may form based on individuals who serve in different roles across the institution. These stories, accurate or not, can reaffirm the cultural values of the institution, all the while impeding the pace and progress of change. As we explore these various theoretical considerations, colleges and universities present a complex ecosystem of multiple stakeholders that make the communication surrounding change challenging. For these reasons, as Fortunato et al. (2017) write,

> Competent leadership requires an understanding of the unique and complex nature of internal and external stakeholder groups, their modes of interacting and the influence they have on another, and the communication skill to understand and interact effectively with these groups.
>
> *(p. 207)*

Based on these considerations of leadership and communication, we offer two vignettes, or short case studies, about hypothetical, yet realistic, higher education situations. We draw on our recent experiences working in higher education during change leadership efforts to illustrate how change efforts are influenced by the co-construction of reality with different stakeholders in the organization. Here, we emphasize the dynamics between external pressures facing the higher education landscape, and internal communication and leadership responses to these pressures to address how to improve future systemic change efforts. Further, we reflect on how these pressures and resulting internal strife affect the student population and how students can draw upon these lessons learned in their future careers. The first scenario examines changes primarily within the institution and how those changes are managed by multiple stakeholders. The second scenario reflects global politics on campus and the presence of different worldviews. As you read each, consider the key concepts and how people use communication and leadership during each of these unique change efforts.

Vignette #1: No confidence

At a private liberal arts college, a new provost (senior vice president for academic affairs) was hired to lead change in an environment where there were declining enrollments, budget shortfalls, and high turnover at the administrative level. In their first two years, the provost hired two new deans, launched another dean search that resulted from a resignation, and was preparing to launch a fourth dean search for a dean whose term ended. While building the leadership team was a priority, so was developing a new strategic plan that would guide decision-making and priorities. The provost believed that enrollments in new programs would be the answer to the current situation and thus, in their first year, invited faculty and staff to envision what these new programs might look like. Interdisciplinary faculty and staff working groups proposed new institutes like humanities, technology, sustainability, and health, plus new graduate and undergraduate programs. The pace of change was overwhelming, as documented in their shared online teams' sites. While some people were excited to contribute to these initiatives, others were wary.

The provost's approach to distributed leadership was intended to engage members at all levels of the university. This bottom-up approach seemed to come from a place of goodwill. Faculty had difficulty discerning the provost's motives because they received no explanation for why this process was chosen, how the final programs would be selected, and what results faculty could expect. Leaders often have so many high-priority items to attend to that they forget to provide necessary details to their constituents. Often the lack of details creates gaps that lead to incorrect or incomplete messaging, which then become significant topics of discussion for the constituents who are trying to make sense of the change effort. Further, the provost is new to the university and faculty have not yet been able to determine if they trust the leader's direction.

As a result, there was dissent and pushback from faculty who were already overburdened with teaching, research, and administrative duties. Faculty were critical of the provost for relying on unpaid labor to drive the strategic planning process. Much of this dissent, pushback, and criticism resulted from a series of formal (faculty union meetings) and informal (water cooler talk) opportunities for faculty to discuss the provost's approach and management style, often led by faculty who are considered social influencers. Through these formal and informal moments, sensemaking and co-construction of reality occurred. To that end, there was resistance to change.

Traditionally we think that leaders possess authority and power and therefore impose their ideas on constituents (or followers). Often, there are others in the organization who demonstrate similar or more social influence on constituents. In this instance, the faculty may be viewed as dominant agents or social influencers. When constituents have opportunities in these formal and informal moments to discuss the change effort and thus co-create their reality, the constituents make a crucial decision (albeit mostly unconsciously) as to whether they will go along with the leader's influence or resist (Ruben & Gigliotti, 2019). This decision is made on several levels. One of these levels is whether the leader's messaging resonates and connects with constituents' beliefs, prior experiences, worldview, and sensemaking with others (Ruben & Gigliotti, 2019).

Ironically, the provost launched a well-being and burnout lunch series in their second year. The ineffective change leadership efforts led to burnout. Budget cuts resulted in faculty and staff bearing the brunt of labor, sometimes in interesting ways, such as a dean asking faculty to either agree to water or adopt a plant from the hallways in the science center because there weren't enough resources.

One tension that emerged during this time was that new administrators were unfamiliar with established organizational culture, resulting in a lack of trust between faculty, staff, and administrators. Given the pace of change and the economic realities of the university, many established formal processes were not followed. Many people believed that these processes, while cumbersome, were important to maintain academic integrity and transparency. As a result, a distrust narrative circulated among faculty on internal listservs and in shared governance groups about the provost's overreach. The organizational culture was one in which faculty already had a healthy amount of skepticism in the administration. With the pace of change, many were threatened that their jobs would be at risk and that the university was being reduced to a profit-making corporation. Even though some of the accusations about the provost's overreach were simply not true, once the narrative was floated, it was difficult to correct. Faculty were concerned that shared governance decision-making was violated and there was a whisper campaign to hold a vote of "no confidence." While no-confidence votes hold limited power, they can play an important public relations role in drawing attention to perceived misbehaviors or transgressions from leadership. No-confidence votes can lead to action, including apologies, backtracking, or resignations (Zahneis, 2023). This process of sensemaking was directly related to the communication interplay between leaders and followers, leading to the erosion of goodwill and trust.

Meanwhile, students are watching. Students are much more in tune with internal organizational happenings than most faculty and administrators realize. Students can tell that faculty workload during the semester is heavy. They see their faculty carrying the emotional, organizational, and physical workload and stress, which erodes faculty bandwidth. Students can feel their faculty burning out and struggling with institutional demands, compounded with the new demands of student well-being and lack of academic preparedness. Students are frustrated when their classes are canceled or moved. And, they are concerned when administration asks them to recruit students from other programs. As a result, the institution's students, staff, faculty, and administrators are struggling, doing the best they can, trying to adapt to change, and worrying about one another.

This "No Confidence" vignette illustrates that successful organizations prioritize people and understand organizational culture. Change is happening at this university, and some of that change may be inevitable in response to the circumstances. However, thoughtful, strategic change leadership ensures that everyone understands the vision and the steps needed from each member to get there. When leaders communicate clear and appropriate levels of details to the groups impacted, individuals can better engage in sensemaking to understand and co-construct shared reality.

Careful distributed leadership allows the members to be autonomous, capable, and accountable to accomplish their work. Distributing too much or too little information and responsibility can cause members to create a distrust narrative, where they express no confidence in the leadership. Negatively impacted stakeholders may resist, reject, or even sabotage the change. There will always be complex external pressures on organizations. Skilled leaders and communicators manage the communication and leadership responses to address these pressures.

Vignette #1 questions for consideration

1. This vignette indicates that to address declining enrollment, the university created new majors. Imagine being a student in a new major that your university designed to attract more students like you. However, the new major has not been marketed well to prospective students, so there are very few students who are majoring in this new program. As a result, some of the key courses you need have low enrollment and are in danger of being canceled. This concerns you because the main reason you chose this university is for this new major. The administration asks for your advice on using "leadership as social influence" to inform students about this new major and to persuade them to join it. What suggestions would you give to help?
2. Consider a situation where using distributed leadership at your university would be a useful way to engage multiple stakeholders (students, faculty, staff, families, community, etc.) in shared decision-making. Give an example where it might be best for the leader to decide alone, or with a few key people, due to time or circumstance. How should leaders navigate this balance between involving everyone or acting alone?
3. In this scenario, faculty felt that the approach to decision-making and information sharing by the administration were out of balance. The administration sometimes left out vital information about strategic planning, while at the same time expected faculty to engage in tasks unrelated to their profession. As a result, the faculty voted "no confidence" in the leadership. This vote has no legal standing but is a public way to announce that faculty do not support the leaders. Is this public announcement of no confidence in the leadership a helpful or harmful step to resolving issues between faculty and administrators? How does a public vote of no confidence align with this chapter's lessons about communication and leadership?
4. We cannot overstate the importance of understanding and being sensitive to dynamics of leading change. Change agents must consider the nuances of the people and culture to determine the most successful way

to communicate change and influence attitudes and behaviors. Give an example of when you have seen leaders successfully use dynamics of leading change to get something accomplished with the support of those involved? What did the leaders do well in this situation?

5 Experienced leaders can anticipate sources of resistance so they can address it in advance. In this scenario, what could the provost have done to prepare for resistance and potentially avoid a vote of no confidence?
6 The scenario ends with negative impacts on students. Not marketing the new major to students results in low enrollment and the possibility of key courses being canceled. Additionally, feel the stress level of their faculty who are overworked and concerned about the students' well-being. How could the university practice meaningful stakeholder engagement in the co-construction of change to protect the mental and physical health of students and employees during these stressful times?

Vignette #2: Campus activism and individual rights

For the past several months, Latonian University, known for its diverse and international student and faculty population, has navigated a landscape of student protests, faculty discontent, graduate student unionization, and extraordinary engagement of its donors and trustee board. While much of this unrest is the result of current international conflicts, the campus discontent mirrors the nation's larger ongoing discussions around the value of higher education, faculty and graduate student contracts and compensation, the presence of unions advocating for campus employees, and the higher levels of "activist" engagement by campus members, politicians, donors, and university trustees.

Prior to the academic year, the university held a shared leadership meeting to plan for dealing with growing political and social tensions on campus. Invited to attend this meeting were executive university leaders, academic deans, department chairs, and other faculty and staff representatives. After much contemplation and consideration with the university general counsel, the provost reiterated to all faculty the importance of maintaining their own subjective political neutrality in the classroom. Faculty were reminded that they are free to discuss current events by making direct, relevant connections to course content, but that they should not force their opinions on students nor should their personal perspectives impact students' grades. The provost reaffirmed the belief that higher education is an ideal environment to help students engage in critical thinking and contribute to the co-construction of meaning, by educating students about the world, culture, and historical contexts so they can shape their own informed views. The legal and ethical balance of campus freedom of speech, institutional inclusion, and civic rights of individuals offers a challenging example of social influence, concerning who influences whom, how, and to what extent. The university aimed to be proactive in planning for the complex dynamics of leading change in higher education, and how these actions might be interpreted on and off campus. Some of the faculty worried this policy might have a "chilling effect," pressuring them to censor their legitimate free expression.

Deeply affected by ongoing global conflicts, teaching Professor Harper Bloomfield began to modify her chemistry lectures to allow time for classroom discussion about the science of war. Professor Bloomfield initially lectured on the chemistry of modern warfare, but as time went on, she felt ethically responsible to share her views on several global conflicts. Of concern to some students, Professor Bloomfield named particular countries as engaging in "genocide," even though students in the class had identified themselves as being from those cultures. She dismissed one class early and offered the students extra credit to participate with her in protest activities at a campus encampment constructed by student and community activists. So far, the encampment and protests have remained safe and legal, although the situation is growing increasingly tense and verbally combative with counter-protests, police presence, and media coverage.

One of Professor Bloomfield's students, Viktoriya Ivanov, complained to Professor Bloomfield that her latest class periods seemed to be off topic for a chemistry course and biased toward particular political perspectives. Professor Bloomfield replied that Viktoriya did not have to attend the protests or earn the extra credit. Another of Professor Bloomfield's students, Jacob Kauffman, informed his parents that he believed the professor's views were discriminatory and dangerous toward their culture. Consequently, Jacob's parents emailed letters to the department chair, dean, and provost accusing campus leadership of failing to ensure the safety of all students in the classroom and on campus. Excerpts of Kauffman's letter were also published in the opinion section of the online student newspaper, available for anyone to read. Some community members, alumni, and donors shared the Kauffman's online letter on social media to criticize the university and to threaten rescinding their university donations. The department chair met with Professor Bloomfield to remind her of the university's classroom code of conduct that contained a warning against grading practices that could be viewed as biased or even unethical. Professor Bloomfield also was warned against shifting her class content away from the official course catalog description. These varying perspectives of the professor, students, parents, administrators, and readers of the school newspaper illustrate sensemaking and sensegiving.

Professor Bloomfield's interpretation of these warnings from her supervisors is that her academic freedom as a faculty member and her freedom of speech as a US citizen were being curtailed. Believing she was anticipating and addressing sources of resistance, Professor Bloomfield complained to her students that she was being unfairly reprimanded for her political beliefs due to the comments of certain students in the class. She advocated that her students should contact her faculty union representatives to complain about this mistreatment. Professor Bloomfield explained to the students that this advocacy on her behalf was an example of meaningful stakeholder engagement in the co-construction of change. Some of her students were not sure this was an appropriate request for a teacher to make of her students while she was still responsible for assigning their course grades.

After consultation with the university human resources department and with the general counsel's office, the department chair and the dean decided against renewing Professor Bloomfield's teaching contract. Technically, this means that the university did not "fire" Professor Bloomfield, because she was on an annual contract that had to be renewed each year if the university wanted her to return. However, Professor Bloomfield interpreted this non-renewal as a direct attack on her personal and professional rights. While some of Professor Bloomfield's students are pleased with her removal from the classroom, the campus protestors and community activists supporting the encampments believe Professor Bloomfield was targeted for her political beliefs. Moreover, after hearing about her non-renewal, faculty members are now split with some supporting the decision to remove Professor Bloomfield, and others expressing trepidation about the university's commitment to academic freedom and free speech. Professor Bloomfield is working with the faculty union to officially object to this non-renewal as a form of retaliation and to be reinstated as a chemistry instructor.

This vignette illustrates that individual campus and community stakeholders will hold varying views, depending on their vantage point as a provost, dean, department chair, teaching faculty, student, general counsel, union representative, human resources representative, family member, community member, donor, activist, identity group member, journalist, or other stakeholder.

Vignette #2 questions for consideration

1 The essence of this vignette rests on the balance of multiple rights and responsibilities, which is especially challenging to manage at a diverse university with the public watching and judging. Explain where you see positive or negative examples of leadership and social influence in this case study. What lessons do you take away about how organizations

can address the needs of the majority and the minority? How can organizations identify and address the needs of internal members and external stakeholders?

2 Consider the types of leadership displayed by people in this case. Explain if the university administration (provost, general counsel, dean, chair) demonstrated shared leadership with the faculty. Explain if Professor Bloomfield demonstrated shared leadership with her students. What impact did these leadership choices have on the outcomes?
3 Perspective matters: It may be that someone's perception of reality matters more than the reality itself. Give a few examples of different perspectives or sensemaking by individuals in this scenario. What might these individuals communicate to one another to successfully share their perspectives with others and to understand alternate points of view?
4 This case examines the dynamics of leading change in a sometimes-charged sociopolitical environment on and off campus. We might appreciate the university's attempt to prepare in advance for some campus changes as a result of how ongoing international wars could impact campus members. How could the university have engaged multiple stakeholders more meaningfully in the change process? Do you believe the outcomes would be different?
5 Strategic communication requires anticipating and addressing potential sources of resistance. One way to do that is to anticipate a few possible objections and either revise your approach or prepare a thoughtful reply about decisions to help people understand. How might you revise the policy or reply to faculty claiming it is their right to share unsolicited, personal views in any classroom? How could you revise the policy or reply to students who want more political activism in all classrooms?
6 A key takeaway from this chapter is that co-construction of change involving meaningful stakeholder engagement helps people feel "buy-in," where they believe in the process and the outcomes. If your university solicited your recommendations on how to get multiple campus and community members to participate in a process to balance campus freedom, rights, responsibility, inclusion, safety, respect, and expression, what would you suggest?

Conclusions and recommendations

Leadership and communication are intertwined. Leadership is made possible through communication, and we see leadership and followership interactions come alive through instances of successful communication. The nexus of communication and leadership lends itself toward shared, distributed, and collective processes in how we engage as stakeholders. Therefore, we socially construct meaning together in contexts, including sometimes disagreeing on these meanings, as a result of the presence of different worldviews. Often using narratives and stories, we engage in sensemaking and sensegiving to help ourselves and others understand what is happening. Successful leadership requires trust, which is built over time. Even the best planned change may be met with resistance, which is why effective leaders anticipate objections and include stakeholders in the process. Communication and leadership are complex, interdependent processes.

Because higher education is a multilayered organization and a system familiar to most readers, this chapter uses this lens to illustrate the dynamics of change leadership and the various successes and pitfalls that one might encounter. The theoretical concepts introduced and applied throughout this chapter can provide guidance when considering the nexus of leadership communication in organizational contexts.

Suggestions for further reading

Egan, C., Shollen, S. L., Campbell, C., Longman, K., Fisher, K., Fox-Kirk, W., & Neilson, B. (2017). Capacious model of leadership identities construction. In J. Storberg-Walker (Ed.), *Theorizing women & leadership: New insights and contributions from multiple perspectives* (pp. 121–140). Information Age Publishing.

Fairhurst, G. T. (2009). Considering context in discursive leadership research. *Human Relations*, *62*, 1607–1633. https://doi.org/10.1177/0018726709346379

Fortunato, J. A., Gigliotti, R. A., & Ruben, B. D. (2017). Racial incidents at the University of Missouri: The value of leadership communication and stakeholder relationships. *International Journal of Business Communication*, *54*(2), 199–209. https://doi.org/10.1177/2329488416687056

Gigliotti, R. A., & Ruben, B. D. (2025). Leadership communication and social influence. In G. Jian & G. Fairhurst (Eds.), *Routledge handbook of organizational leadership communication*. Routledge. https://doi.org/10.4324/9781003380115

Ruben, B. D., & Gigliotti, R. A. (2016). Leadership as social influence: An expanded view of leadership communication theory and practice. *Journal of Leadership & Organizational Studies*, *23*(4), 467–479. https://doi.org/10.1177/1548051816641876

Ruben, B. D., & Gigliotti, R. A. (2019). *Leadership, communication, and social influence: A theory of resonance, activation, and cultivation*. Emerald Publishing. https://doi.org/10.1108/9781838671181

Smulowitz, S. (2021). *The communication solution: Leading successful change in higher education*. Rowman & Littlefield.

References

Balderston, F. E. (1995). *Managing today's university* (2nd ed.). Jossey-Bass.

Berger, P. L., & Luckmann, T. (1967). *The social construction of reality: A treatise in the sociology of knowledge*. Doubleday.

Beebe, S. A., Beebe, S. J., & Redmond, M. V. (2020). *Interpersonal communication: Relating to others*. Pearson.

Clark, C., Cluver, M., Fishman, T., & Kunkel, D. (2024, April 19). *2024 higher education trends*. Deloitte Center for Government Insights. https://www.deloitte.com/us/en/insights/industry/articles-on-higher-education/latest-trends-in-higher-education.html

Denis, J., Côté, N., & Côté-Boileau, E. (2023). Pluralism in studies on plural leadership: Analysis and perspectives. In D. Schedlitzki, M. Larsson, B. Carroll, M. C. Bligh, & O. Epitropaki (Eds.), *The SAGE handbook of leadership* (2nd ed, pp. 3–15). Sage. https://doi.org/10.4135/9781529781892

Egan, C., Shollen, S. L., Campbell, C., Longman, K., Fisher, K., Fox-Kirk, W., & Neilson, B. (2017). Capacious model of leadership identities construction. In J. Storberg-Walker (Ed.), *Theorizing women & leadership: New insights and contributions from multiple perspectives* (pp. 121–140). Information Age Publishing.

Fairhurst, G. T. (2009). Considering context in discursive leadership research. *Human Relations*, *62*, 1607–1633. https://doi.org/10.1177/0018726709346379

Fortunato, J. A., Gigliotti, R. A., & Ruben, B. D. (2017). Racial incidents at the University of Missouri: The value of leadership communication and stakeholder relationships. *International Journal of Business Communication*, *54*(2), 199–209. https://doi.org/10.1177/2329488416687056

Gigliotti, R. A., & Ruben, B. D. (2025). Leadership communication and social influence. In G. Jian & G. Fairhurst (Eds.), *Routledge handbook of organizational leadership communication*. Routledge. https://doi.org/10.4324/9781003380115

Gronn, P. (2002). Distributed leadership as a unit of analysis. *Leadership Quarterly*, *13*(4), 432–451. https://doi.org/10.1016/S1048-9843(02)00120-0

Gronn, P. (2003). *The new work of educational leaders: Changing leadership practice in an era of school reform*. Sage. https://doi.org/10.4135/9781446216347

Hess, M. (2021). *A leadership guide for women in higher education*. Johns Hopkins University Press.

Hollihan, T. A., & Baaske, K. T. (2022). *Arguments and arguing: The products and process of human decision-making*. Waveland Press.

Kotter, J. P. (2012). *Leading change*. Harvard Business Review Press.

Kotter, J. P., & Heskett, J. L. (1992). *Corporate culture and performance*. The Free Press.

Lewis, L. K. (2006). Employee perspectives on implementation communication as predictors of perceptions of success and resistance. *Western Journal of Communication*, *70*(1), 23–46. https://doi.org/10.1080/10570310500506631

Mitchell, B. (2024, February 14). Higher education faces hurdles in 2024. *Forbes*. https://www.forbes.com/sites/forbesbusinesscouncil/2024/02/14/higher-education-faces-hurdles-in-2024/?sh=2fb921ad48da

Mitchell, B. C., & King, W. J. (2018). *How to run a college: A practical guide for trustees, faculty, administrators, and policymakers*. Johns Hopkins University Press.

Muscanell, N. (2024, January 8). 2024 higher education trend watch. *Educause*. https://www.educause.edu/ecar/research-publications/higher-education-trend-watch/2024#:~:text=Colleges%20and%20universities%20continue%20to,increaseng%20security%20and%20privacy%20threats

Rosenberg, B. (2023). *"Whatever it is, I'm against it": Resistance to change in higher education*. Harvard Education Press.

Ruben, B. D., & Gigliotti, R. A. (2016). Leadership as social influence: An expanded view of leadership communication theory and practice. *Journal of Leadership & Organizational Studies*, *23*(4), 467–479. https://doi.org/10.1177/1548051816641876

Ruben, B. D., & Gigliotti, R. A. (2019). *Leadership, communication, and social influence: A theory of resonance, activation, and cultivation*. Emerald Publishing. https://doi.org/10.1108/9781838671181

Ruben, B. D., & Stewart, L. P. (2006). *Communication and human behavior* (5th ed.). Pearson Education.

Smulowitz, S. (2021). *The communication solution: Leading successful change in higher education*. Rowman & Littlefield.

Spillane, J. P. (2012). *Distributed leadership*. Wiley.

Steigenberger, N. (2015). Emotions in sensemaking: A change management perspective. *Journal of Organizational Change Management*, *28*(3), 432–451. https://doi.org/10.1108/JOCM-05-2014-0095

Thayer, L. (1968). *Communication and communication systems*. Irwin.

Thayer, L. (1979). Communication: Sine qua non of the behavioral sciences. In R. W. Budd & B. D. Ruben (Eds.), *Interdisciplinary approaches to human communication* (pp. 7–31). Hayden Book Company, Inc.

Zahneis, M. (2023, September 29). Why higher ed is seeing a spate of high-profile no-confidence votes. *Chronicle of Higher Education*. https://www.chronicle.com/article/why-higher-ed-is-seeing-a-spate-of-high-profile-no-confidence-votes

17

MORAL MAP OF DEI LEADERSHIP PITFALLS

Developing Inclusive Servant Leadership

C. Kyle Rudick, Amy Aldridge, Robin VanMeter, Dylan Medeiros, and Jennifer Martin Emami

Workplace initiatives created to address discrimination related to race, ethnicity, gender, religion, sexuality, age, and dis/ability go by a variety of names and acronyms, such as inclusion, diversity, equity, and accessibility (IDEA); justice, equity, diversity, and inclusion (JEDI); and diversity, equity, inclusion, and belonging (DEIB). However, perhaps the most used moniker, and the one used throughout this chapter, is diversity, equity, and inclusion (DEI). DEI initiatives are an outgrowth of the Civil Rights and Women's Rights movements of the 1960s and 1970s, which sought to reduce prejudice in the workplace and comply with federal and state laws concerning discrimination (Mease, 2016; Zheng, 2022). Half a century later, DEI spending increased dramatically in the aftermath of the 2020 police killing of George Floyd, Black Lives Matter activism, and consumer pressure to be socially conscious (Butler, 2023). DEI initiatives have ballooned into a multi-billion-dollar industry (McKinsey & Company, 2020; Williams & Dolkas, 2022), employing firms, consultants, and workshop presenters who promise to radically enhance organizational performance.

Although the tide seemed to be toward evermore investment in DEI, many companies have recently begun to shed their DEI goals. For example, 2024 has seen a number of high-profile corporations (e.g., John Deere, Tractor Supply Co., Google, and Meta) abandon DEI initiatives due to the growing conservative backlash against so-called woke training. Other companies such as Comcast, Goldman Sachs, and Bank of America have recently changed their women and minority-based programs to be open to men and White people, at the behest of conservative advocacy and shareholder groups. The Trump administration has issued a variety of executive

DOI: 10.4324/9781003563662-21

orders to ban DEI as it relates to government training, grants, and programs while also using government resources to target DEI-friendly corporations, non-profits, and organizations (MacLellen, 2025). Clearly, anti-DEI efforts from right-wing activists, judges, business leaders, and government officials are beginning to add up to a much bleaker landscape for traditionally marginalized groups.

We come to this project in the nexus of these considerations. As communication scholars and practitioners who promote DEI, we recognize that this work will be promoted, pursued, and protected to the extent that organizational leadership believes in it. That is, organizations need leaders that are morally attuned to DEI; otherwise, organizations will be characterized by shallow or superficial commitments that will quickly fold in the face of right-wing anti-DEI backlash. Therefore, we utilize Servant Leadership Theory (SLT) to articulate the value for, and pitfalls of, DEI as a leadership attribute in organizations (Frick & Spears, 1996; Greenleaf, 1977; Spears, 1998). We first review SLT, noting both its lack of emphasis on DEI and the importance of DEI integration. As servant leaders attempt to navigate DEI, we recognize its implementation is often characterized by challenges. Therefore, we detail a moral map of the ethical pitfalls of DEI leadership communication (Conquergood, 1985; Warren & Hytten, 2004). The map is a 2×2 box populated by four problematic DEI leader pitfalls: Guru, Corporatist, Legalistic, and Relationist. Within each of the four pitfalls lie both challenges that must be overcome and the seeds of potential for integrating DEI into servant leadership (see Figure 17.1). Thus, in the middle of the table, we propose inclusive servant leadership (ISL) as

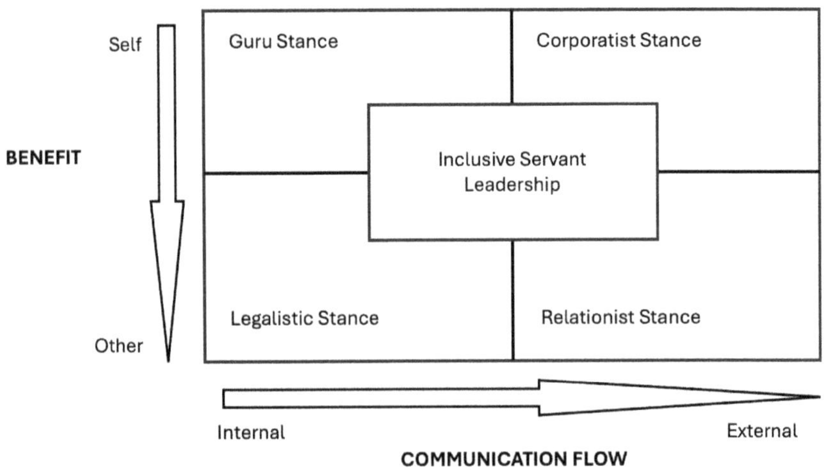

FIGURE 17.1 Moral map of Inclusive Servant Leadership

the point that articulates the push-pull of the various tendencies toward ethical DEI practices.

Servant leadership and DEI

Greenleaf's (1977) oft-quoted paragraph, "The Servant-Leader is servant first.... Then conscious choice brings one to aspire to lead" (p. 13) can be found in textbooks, web blogs, and university business and leadership courses. These sources paint a picture of servant leaders as heroic individuals, who put on (or are bestowed) the mantle of leadership through their moral clarity and generosity. These leaders, in turn, create organizational cultures characterized by positive affect, leading to organizational productivity. Empirical research has relied on these assumptions, associating servant leadership with a variety of organizationally important outcomes, such as turnover (e.g., Babakusa et al., 2010) and organizational identification (Zhao et al., 2016). Said differently, servant leadership is viewed as a way for leaders to promote collaboration, empathy, or awareness in service of an organization's productivity. This reading of Greenleaf's work (distinctly individualist and organizationally inward facing) is unsurprising given the U.S. context of leadership scholarship (see Bardhan & Gower, 2022).

Due to this approach, much of the scholarship on SLT does not seriously connect to DEI. As late as 2016, Gotsis and Grimani noted, "Servant leadership might be of particular interest to the endeavor of nurturing inclusiveness climates, yet there is scant research decisively moving to this direction" (p. 986, see also Eva et al., 2019). Perhaps what is missing from the vast majority of these writings is the second part of Greenleaf's (1977) quote:

> The difference manifests itself in the care taken by the servant—first to make sure that other people's highest-priority needs are being served. The best test, and the most difficult to administer, is: Do those served grow as a person? Do they, while being served, become healthier, wider, freer, more autonomous, more likely themselves to become servants? *And, what is the effect on the least privileged in society; will they benefit or, at least, not be further deprived?*
>
> *(p. 13, emphasis added)*

In other words, we see in Greenleaf's writings a pressing need to engage in leadership as a communal (and communicative) phenomenon—one that emerges within an organization, but whose effects and considerations may be far beyond it. Greenleaf's work, although it starts with the individual (i.e., making a "conscious choice"), is necessarily other-oriented. That is, "Contrary to other leadership approaches that primarily aim to advance the organizational bottom line in both financial or non-financial terms, servant leadership focuses on followers' growth in multiple areas, such as their psychological wellbeing, emotional maturity, and ethical wisdom" (Eva et al., 2019, p. 114). Due to this other-orientation, SLT is ripe for scholars to begin articulating the ways that DEI is a primary and specific concern for a servant leader.

Although Greenleaf never wrote a definitive articulation of what servant leadership entailed, subsequent writers have offered some parameters to its study. Eva et al. (2019), in their meta-analysis of SLT research, conceptualized servant leadership as "an (1) other-oriented approach to leadership (2) manifested through one-on-one prioritizing of follower individual needs and interests, (3) and outward reorienting of their concern for self towards concern for others within the organization and the larger community" (p. 114). Their definition emphasizes the leader's role in building connections with others both within and outside the organization. Additionally, Spears (1998) distilled ten characteristics of SLT: listening, empathy, healing, awareness, persuasion, conceptualization, foresight, stewardship, commitment to the growth of people, and building community. Important to this list is the belief that both the leader (self) and members (others) benefit from the implementation of SLT. For example, in practicing an ethic of healing with others, servant leaders will also, themselves, find healing from others in their relationships.

Although some may believe that the ethics that animate SLT naturally encompass DEI concerns, we believe that in the absence of a formal commitment, organizational leaders will minimize, overlook, ignore, or denigrate DEI issues when they conflict with bottom-line thinking. The fact that the majority of writings about SLT ignore DEI as a specific concern, and/or truncate Greenleaf's writings on the subject, is proof that (left to their own devices) those in C-suites, managerial roles, or who write about leadership (e.g., typically White, middle/upper class males) will minimize the specificity and importance of DEI in its practice. Given the current climate of anti-DEI backlash, it is all the more important that leaders boldly and forcibly articulate its value beyond organizational outcomes.

To extend SLT, we address common pitfalls in integrating DEI into leadership communicative practices. Drawing on Conquergood (1985) and Warren and Hytten (2004), we provide a moral map that details the ethical pitfalls of DEI leadership communication. Along the X-axis, the moral map is characterized by an emphasis on *Communication Flow*. As Eva et al. (2019) noted, communication and listening are primary considerations for the servant leader, who needs to navigate both the individual, group, organization, and those beyond it. Thus, along this axis leadership about DEI is anchored at the extremes where it is understood as something that should either be kept private (i.e., *Internal Communication Flow*) or whose value is only realized when communicated about to others (i.e., *External Communication Flow*). The Y-axis is distinguished by a focus on *Benefit*, where the extremes represent a view that DEI leadership either benefits the *Self* or *Other*. That is, an overemphasis on the self-results in self-centeredness and selfishness, whereas an overemphasis on the other can lead to a loss of self or self-worth. Spears (1998) wrote about the importance of servant leadership as benefiting both the self and other as an ongoing tension. By mapping these leader pitfalls, we articulate how negotiating the tensions between Internal/External Communication Flow and Self/Other Benefit results in Inclusive Servant Leadership, which occupies the center of the model.

Moral map of DEI leaders' pitfalls

The guru leader pitfall

The Guru Leader Pitfall in DEI overemphasizes personal growth, fulfillment, and individualization (i.e., *Self Benefit*). That is, utterances in this vein often position DEI as an individualistic concern, one whose execution is linked to feeling that a leader is a good person, self-actualized, and/or well-read because of their pursuit of DEI knowledge (or, conversely, failure to do so makes one wrong, evil, or ignorant). Guru Leaders often narrate DEI as a personal journey, where the belief that one is comfortable with cultural Others, reads materials about DEI, or engages in introspective practices (e.g., implicit bias training) indexes to moral progress.

Additionally, Guru Leaders prioritize *Internal Communication* by their emphasis on DEI as located in the individual's mental or moral reasoning rather than in dialogue with others. This overemphasis can lead to the belief that a leader does not need to listen to others in the organization as long as one has "done the homework" to be a good person. Ultimately, these types of statements perpetuate the notion that leadership that embodies the role of a self-actualized, enlightened individual is the best way to address organizational or systemic discrimination.

A consequence of this type of leader pitfall is how difference is understood. The Guru Leader characterizes social difference (e.g., gender, race, or sexuality) as an immutable "fact" that simply "is," which an enlightened person tolerates. For example, we recall one DEI business consultant at a workshop who stated, "We're all diverse in some way. Maybe you went to this school or college instead of that one. Maybe you wear a bowtie and someone else doesn't. It doesn't matter. We're all different." The Guru Leader fails to realize and communicate a language for how difference is made meaningful, an analysis of power, or who the dominant/marginalized groups are in a socio-political context (see Grimes, 2002). Guru Leaders often eschew naming power and, as a result, make it appear as if such statements are gauche, rude, or out-of-bounds. In other words, Guru Leaders conflate naming power with being confrontational because they believe such actions are an intrusion on an individual's personal journey toward enlightenment (i.e., one that should be largely pleasurable and self-directed).

The Guru Leader Pitfall is problematic due to its overreliance on *Self Benefit* and *Internal Communication Flow*. Guru Leaders offer a truncated understanding of self-actualization that over-privileges individualism and downplays the role of structure and context in humans' ability to find fulfillment. However, the Guru *does* challenge leaders to learn, grow, and develop their DEI ethics. As Frick and Spears (1996) noted, Greenleaf's theory may have started with the individual, but his thinking evolved over the decades to recognize how institutions mediate individual choices and virtues. Servant leaders recognize that values must be known, shared, and accepted by all members; that such values will be imperfectly and unevenly practiced; and that disconnection from others often leads to dogmatism. An understanding of DEI in leadership necessitates ongoing education, dialogue, and intercultural competence. These ethics, in turn, point away from the extremes and move toward the ISL model.

The corporatist leader pitfall

The Corporatist Leader Pitfall is well documented in writings about the business case for diversity. Here, we conceptualize it at the extremes of *Self Benefit* and *External Communication Flow*. As *Self Benefit,* Corporatist Leaders will often speak about DEI as benefiting the sponsoring organization because employees become maximally efficient in their jobs. A workforce that is DEI savvy is happy, collaborative, and productive which results in increased profit, bonuses, raises, or job opportunities (Williams & Dolkas, 2022). The value of DEI is discussed in instrumental terms, and its practice is an investment that should produce better value for the organization (and, where applicable, shareholders) (see Georgeac & Rattan, 2023).

Additionally, Corporatist Leaders often emphasize *External Communication Flow*. They speak about the value of DEI in marketing to potential new clients/consumers, obtaining new employees, and wooing new shareholders. For example, one of the authors remember listening to a DEI presenter at a business conference who said, "Who wouldn't want to work at our business? We have two different kinds of rice and two different kinds of beans in our cafeteria because we know how to feed people the food from their culture." The conflation between food and DEI, and the idea that commodified forms of culture recruit talent, is the hallmark example of this type of pitfall. Corporatist Leaders often do not focus on addressing systemic violence or discrimination against oppressed people; rather, they direct DEI efforts to reduce negative perceptions (e.g., the lack of racial representation on an organization's board) that may reduce consumers' confidence or affect toward the organization. As a result, diversity is framed as a "problem" that is forever "addressed," "worked on," or "prioritized" because discrimination results in unhappy workers which negatively affects the bottom line.

Corporatist Leaders's talk about DEI is often devoid of any analysis of power and often describes difference in terms of natural human variation (e.g., "everyone is different racially, ethnically, sexually, etc."). However, different from Gurus, difference is rhetorically constructed as a barrier to a maximally efficient workforce. Therefore, Corporatist Leaders believe that difference should be ignored, downplayed, or addressed in superficial ways (e.g., commodified forms of culture) rather than explored as sites of meaning and growth. Central to this ethic is the belief that discriminatory behaviors, indeed even talking about difference, can be reduced or eliminated through economic self-interest. That is, Corporatist Leaders work with others based on the assumption that DEI concerns will be met if it is economically beneficial to do so (e.g., disciplining/firing workers who say or do things that violate DEI insofar as those actions also threaten their profit motives).

Past research has found that when discussed as an investment toward profit-centered goals, DEI practices are often characterized by low-cost, one-off, and low-budget training programs (Bezrukova et al., 2016). Despite its weaknesses, the Corporatist Leader Pitfall does point toward important insights for ISL. Specifically, the notion that DEI goals are only actualized to the extent that leaders understand their worth and invest in them is a powerful rebuke to the Guru Leader Pitfall, which remains largely psychological and directionless. ISL recognizes that DEI leadership must be understood as a material investment with a material consequence, promoting the idea that its practice should have tangible and assessable results with its application (Williams, 2021; Zheng, 2022).

The legalistic leader pitfall

The Legalistic Leader approaches DEI as compliance to rules, laws, or regulations. Whereas the Corporatist Leader frames DEI as *Self Benefit* (i.e., doing DEI brings rewards to organizational members), the Legalistic

Leader relies on *Other Benefit* (i.e., DEI concerns are created to protect recognized minorities). That is, Legalistic Leaders recognize that failure to protect minorities (e.g., condoning or not addressing sexist communication on the job) can potentially result in bad public relations/litigation; however, when discussing DEI concerns, their emphasis on compliance is framed as an *Other Benefit* in that the rules, laws, or regulations that guide conduct (e.g., sexual harassment laws) are set in place protect legally protected organizational members (e.g., female workers).

The Legalistic Leader also relies on *Internal Communication Flow* in their approach to DEI. They do not tout DEI initiatives or outreach to prospective employees or consumers; rather, DEI is pursued only as a set of internal structuring guidelines (even if those structures were created externally, such as a law). For example, one author recalls going through training for hiring, where the human resources director stated, "It's important that if you have a video call for the initial interview that you turn the camera off. This is to make sure that we are not discriminating against people due to their appearance or identity." When asked how that process would make sense given that the application materials make it easy to find candidates through an Internet search and that the candidates would eventually have an on-campus interview, the director replied, "That doesn't matter. This is what we must do in order to make sure we are in compliance with hiring laws." It is telling that a process rife with opportunities for discrimination and workarounds was not viewed as a problem as long as the specific legal standard for DEI was met. As a result of this approach, non-organizational members may have little or no idea of how an organization treats DEI concerns until they are hired or otherwise on-boarded. Additionally, this Legalistic approach minimizes DEI as a leader concern for those who are not legally recognized as being "in charge" of DEI (e.g., human resources director or Chief Director of Diversity). Legalistic Leaders are therefore often invested with some type of institutional authority, limiting others' abilities to advocate or even talk about difference since they are not in the correct position (organizationally) to do so.

Because DEI is understood as a way to protect minorities through legal compliance, Legalistic Leaders often attempt to minimize or eliminate any non-essential communication about difference. That is, they often engage in discourses such as race-evasive rhetoric because simply "noticing" or "talking" about difference increases the likelihood someone will say or do something "wrong," harm a protected member, lead the organization to harm an organizational member, and (ultimately) create a public relations nightmare or litigation. When difference is discussed, it is couched in terminology that is officially sanctioned, which guides leaders to want precision and clarity about identity and its relation to legal compliance. As a result, Legalistic

Leaders often downplay or ignore the fluidity of identity (especially if it is not addressed in law), identities not enumerated in law, or identities that are specifically targeted or underserved by the law (e.g., trans workers) because compliance (even immoral compliance) is the most important goal.

The problem with Legalistic Leaders is that they often address DEI concerns with organizational members as mandatory or punitive. That is, they do not see DEI as having any positive aspect; rather, it is about ensuring those who are vulnerable (i.e., minorities) are not targeted for fear of repercussions. If there are no consequences for discrimination, then the Legalistic Leader will do nothing to protect those organizational members from that group and, in fact, may be motivated to do harm to those people in their pursuit of compliance. Although Greenleaf understood servant leaders as structured by institutional rules and culture, he was adamant that servant leadership was grounded in an ethic of deep care for others. Servant leaders do not promote DEI because a failure to do so may get them punished; rather, they see it as a way to ensure that organizational members flourish and realize their potential. In taking these insights, we argue that ISL is not limited to only protecting the vulnerable but also in theorizing how to ensure they thrive.

The relationist leader pitfall

The Relationist Leader interacts with others at the intersections of *Other Benefit* and *External Communication Flow*. As *Other Benefit*, leaders conceptualize the lack of DEI as threats to connection, relationships, and familial/friend bonds. Leaders may recount personal stories, anecdotes, or statistics about depression, lost friendships, or suicide as evidence that members need to do the "heart work" of DEI. They initiate self-disclosure about their struggles, worries, and desire for connection (and exhort others to do so as well) in the hope that doing so will provide the foundation to build DEI support networks. Through their overemphasis, they may not notice the actual needs of marginalized groups; instead, they prioritize emotional connection above all other concerns. Relationist Leaders may believe the absence of conflict or disagreement equates to a well-functioning organization (instead of marginalized members not feeling supported enough to discuss their problems). Additionally, they may try to address marginalized members' problems as socio-emotional rather than as material. For example, if a marginalized member is targeted by discriminatory behavior, the Relationist Leader may focus more on making sure that member feels validated, supported, or nurtured rather than addressing the source of the discriminatory act.

Additionally, Relationist Leaders' communication about DEI often emphasizes *External Communication Flow*. Leaders encourage others to go into their organizations and talk to coworkers and colleagues, specifically those who they identified as being a part of marginalized groups. Central to this ethic is the belief that marginalized people lack (and desire) contact with members of the dominant group and that those in the dominant group gain new knowledge and empathy through those interactions. Little attention is given to whether or not marginalized people want to interact with others in the organization about their feelings, experiences, or problems. Rather, their status as a marginalized person is proof enough that they are in relational pain and therefore it is the duty of organizational members to engage in supportive communication.

Although Relationist Leaders acknowledge difference, they often approach it with a very shallow analysis of power. They frame the struggles of marginalized people as problems of equity but couch them as gaps (i.e., education, achievement, or healthcare) between groups (e.g., disparities in suicidal ideation between cis and trans youth). For example, we remember one business leader who said,

> I know that it's not easy to change hearts and minds, but I want to believe the tide is turning and people are learning to accept others. I know I wasn't where I am now 15 years ago. I didn't really know anything about trans people or their issues, especially as it related to healthcare. And, when our son, who was assigned female at birth, showed signs of depression, I just chalked it up to normal teenage angst. But, they tried to take their own life when they were just 13 because they didn't feel like they could be their authentic self with us [their parents] and that was giving them so much anxiety that they felt like they couldn't take it anymore. Now that they've come out, we've been able to reforge those family bonds that we thought were broken.

Marginalized groups are discussed as subjects of pity, remorse, and charity whose poor outcomes are a result of people not caring for others enough to support equitable treatment. Importantly, there is often no analysis of how those from dominant groups enjoyed privileges or exercised power precisely because they accessed goods, services, and rewards at a level made possible through exploitation.

Although Relationist Leaders overemphasize the *Other Benefit/External Communication Flow*, it does hold some promise for ISL. Specifically, the acknowledgment that DEI is accomplished by connecting to others reminds us that leaders do the work of DEI *with* others rather than *for* them. We build on this insight for ISL, recognizing that DEI leadership must be connected to a broader community if it is to be effective within or beyond the organization.

Three ethics for inclusive servant leadership

We have outlined four problematic pitfalls for DEI leadership: Guru, Corporatist, Legalistic, and Relationist. Each of these pitfall's issues lies in its overemphasis on the quadrant it inhabits along the axes of *Self/Other Benefit* and *Internal/External Communication Flow*. If leaders are to realize their potential to change organizations and society, however, they must push past these dominant frames. At the same time, each pitfall holds the seeds for actualizing DEI goals if leaders can reside in the liminal, uncertain, and ethically fraught space of the push-pull dialectic between the X and Y axes (Conquergood, 1985; Warren & Hytten, 2004). In doing so, leaders can move past oppositional, dichotomous thinking that produces "a binary either/or epistemology and praxis that structures our perceptions, politics, and actions through a resistant energy" (Keating, 2013, p. 2) and move toward ISL.

The primary benefit of ISL is that it pulls from the recognizable patterns of speech from the four pitfalls while rearticulating them toward more liberatory goals. As such, it seeks to meet participants "where they are" by not articulating a leadership pitfall that is completely untethered to their everyday lives or practices; rather, its foundation is a difference within the repetition of DEI practices (Butler, 1990; Warren, 2008). Here, we address three ethics of the inclusive servant leader, building on its previously articulated commitments to explicitly radicalize it toward equity and justice.

Inclusive self-actualization

This ethic recognizes that leaders must develop members' full selves while also creating structures that support growth. As Gotsis and Grimani (2016) argued, servant leadership in inclusive organizations recognizes and affirms members' curiosity, autonomy, and wellbeing while identifying how policies, norms, and/or laws can curtail their health, freedom, and capabilities. Inclusive servant leaders should challenge themselves to articulate how organizational life can be a fulfilling experience—not necessarily fun or easy–but one that recognizes that we are more fully human when organizational structures enable us to be our best selves. In doing so, the first step in ISL is to help participants identify the ways that organizations' culture and practices shape, promote, or constrain DEI goals.

Inclusive servant leaders welcome task forces that are positioned and empowered to do an honest and transparent assessment of needs. Extant research provides some areas where these groups can start their fact-finding and begin developing policies that support organizational members. For example, Dobbin and Kalev (2022) found that policies such as flextime, parental leave, and childcare referral programs had positive correlations with diversity of management for men and women of all racial/ethnic groups except White men. Although the myth is that women who earn less drop out of the workforce so their higher earning partner can maintain an unencumbered professional life, a recent report from Institute for Fiscal Studies (2021) found that even when mothers earned more than fathers, they are more likely to drop out of the workforce than their lower-paid partner (see also Perriton, 2009). These insights recognize that, for many women, the ability to articulate and pursue their full potential (inside and outside of the organization) requires institutional structures that support them.

It is alarming that positions such as Chief Diversity Officer, and the practices that animate those positions, are being cut when recent research shows that they are among the most effective tools for challenging discrimination (Dobbin & Kalev, 2022). These positions should be separate from the Legalistic- and Corporate-stance imagination that often constrain HR departments (Minor, 2021), otherwise DEI policies will most likely be ineffective. Rather, these positions should be trained to, and train others toward, jointly identify issues that face organizational members and develop shared practices toward addressing those concerns. Most importantly, inclusive servant leaders should be found throughout the organization—not just in explicitly named positions. Otherwise, organizational members may not feel invested in DEI since it is not their "job" to care about it.

Inclusive dialogic politics

This ethic recognizes the interconnectedness of all, fosters authentic relationships among employees, and promotes the idea that inclusive servant leaders should work toward coalition building and shared goals of transformation (see Greenleaf, 1977). This approach encourages the idea that inclusive servant leaders must promote a clear sense of moral vision for themselves and others to intervene into oppression–even if it does not benefit the self (Spears, 1998). Absent a shared social vision for an organizational culture that supports DEI, organizational members are likely to return to ingrained habits, beliefs, and dispositions–ones often mired in oppressive framing (e.g., "this is the way we've always done this"). Inclusive servant leaders promote opportunities for shared introspection that combat insularity, orthodoxy, and loyalty tests (Smucker, 2017). As such, they should help members develop a shared vision for their organization's DEI mission and then promote practices that create ongoing, sustainable relationships toward a coalitional politic that fulfills DEI goals.

Organizations, in developing training about conflict management and resolution, must develop organizational members' capacities to identify and navigate the inevitability of conflict. One of the most pernicious myths about diversity is that "difference" itself is the issue and that practices should be implemented that downplay, eliminate, or ignore it (Allen, 2023). However, it is important that leaders do not promote the idea that it is identity, cultural, or linguistic differences that cause conflict; rather, it is how organizational relationships are developed and maintained that predict organizational success in navigating DEI. Ayoko and Konrad (2012) found that conflict in diverse teams was inversely related to leader behaviors that fostered relationships among team members and communicated a shared vision or goal. Leaders should not couch DEI in terms that ascribe moral (un)worth of members due to their adherence to some preconceived standard; rather, they must promote a shared vision for change and give participants the tools to pursue it.

Inclusive servant leaders should develop shared norms and rules about how to pursue conflict management. First, leaders must be able to identify conflict in their teams. Because conflict is negatively valenced in society, many people believe that disagreement will always be explicit, obvious, or acrimonious. However, research shows that, especially as it relates to marginalized-dominant group interactions, individuals may not voice conflict for fear of reprimand or retribution (Orbe & Roberts, 2012). As such, it is important that leaders recognize that silence is not consent to the organizational culture; rather, silence may indicate burn-out, separation, or self-protection from conflict trauma (Roloff, 2009). Second, after identifying conflict, steps must be taken to manage or resolve conflict; disagreements that are not addressed will fester and result in organizational exit or disidentification (Nicotera & Jameson, 2021). Steps such as encouraging open communication that emphasizes reciprocal self-disclosure, empathetic listening, avoiding negative assumptions about the other, information seeking about each other and the issue, taking responsibility for harm caused, framing the conflict as a problem-solving mediator, and/or obtaining a mediator all show promising results in managing/resolving conflict (Nicotera & Jameson, 2021). Leaders cannot afford to characterize DEI simply in terms of conflict prevention due to fear of bad PR or litigation (although, certainly such results are desirable); rather, they must help participants recognize DEI is an ongoing communicative negotiation. Organizations that retain toxic employees often do so out of a misguided sense that their organizational benefit outweighs their harms, but research shows that workplace bullies' detriments outweigh any perceived benefits (Namie & Namie, 2009).

The way to ensure inclusive servant leaders can oversee conflict management practices is to make sure that all members feel a sense of ownership in the issue as an organizational norm. Research has found that organizations that promoted collaboration across groups (e.g., mentoring) or empowered organizational members on DEI task forces had some of the best outcomes related to increasing diversity in management positions (Dobbin & Kalev, 2022; McCarty Kilian et al., 2005). In other words, creating structured opportunities for networking reduced stereotypes and increased organizational transformation. Leaders who oversee these types of programs must develop clear expectations and rewards for their implementation and success. Otherwise, simply putting people from various groups together on committees or projects (i.e., mix-and-stir politics) are not only ineffective but can create backlash (Pettigrew & Tropp, 2006).

Transformational community impact

The final ethic that characterizes ISL is the recognition that DEI work inside the organization must be connected to DEI work outside of it as well. Inclusive servant leaders push beyond the context of their organization and develop an organizational culture that is a catalyst for social change in its (global) community. Keeping DEI in-house ensures it will be, at best, a bird in a gilded cage. At worst, it positions organizations as lone islands, making it easier for reactionary forces to target them when they step out of line with repressive politics. DEI work is not complete until the rules, policies, and procedures that keep people oppressed change at a systemic level, and that change will not occur until direct action is taken.

One of the primary barriers to this type of ethic is the way that shareholder capitalism constrains many organizations' ability to pursue goals that are not profit-oriented (Deetz, 1992). Furthermore, actions such as addressing hunger, poverty, or discrimination can be seen as a direct threat to the societal dominance of those who are from traditionally dominant groups, such as those at the intersections of White, cishet, able-bodied males (i.e., the organizational leaders or owners). That is, these problems are not inevitable or intrinsic to human nature but are the outcomes of policies that concentrate wealth and power from the many into the hands of the few. Organizational members who call for change, such as just wages, an end to patriarchy, or environmental justice are sidelined in favor of union busting (e.g., Starbucks, Amazon), pinkwashing (e.g., the National Football League), or greenwashing initiatives (e.g., ExxonMobil).

Inclusive servant leaders work with others to identify areas for community partnerships and incentivize involvement in social justice movements. Although organizations who incorporate social justice in their training are rare (and research demonstrating their effectiveness even rarer), growing research shows that a moral case for DEI is more effective than traditional forms of DEI training (Bowman Williams & Cox, 2022; Dobbin & Kalev, 2022). ISL arises out of and is led by community membership instead of management prerogative. This ensures that community impact initiatives are true to the local communities and that transformational change is practiced both within and beyond the organizational context.

Conclusion

Investment in DEI may have stalled, but we do not see it as a retreat. Instead, it signals a pause to breathe and reflect upon our collective practices and ascertain what direction leaders can push for a stronger ethic of DEI in their organizations than has been done in the past. Our proposal is not the "only" or "correct" way to be an inclusive leader; rather, we understand its strengths as being rooted in current understanding of DEI while pushing past them to create true, lasting, and positive change. Leaders must balance self-reflection and structural analysis, material needs and organizational control, moral clarity and pragmatic politics, and relationship building and activism. It is not easy, nor do we believe there is a current form of leadership that perfectly negotiates these tensions. Rather, ISL is a goal, a reminder, and a reprimand to do DEI better for the sake of ourselves, our organizations, and our communities.

Suggested further readings

Auger-Domínguez, D. (2024). *Inclusion revolution: The essential guide to dismantling racial inequity in the workplace*. Wiley.

Jenkins, N. (2023). *The inclusive organization: Real solutions, impactful change, and meaningful diversity*. Wiley.

Smith, T., & Kirby, A. (2021). *Neurodiversity at work: Drive innovation, performance and productivity with a neurodiverse workforce*. Kogan Page. https://doi.org/10.1111/peps.12566

Questions for further engagement

1 How can inclusive servant leadership reframe power, authority, and decision-making in ways that advance equity rather than reproduce existing hierarchies?
2 How can servant leadership move organizations from performative DEI efforts toward community, structural, and cultural transformation?
3 How might inclusive servant leadership require leaders to accept personal risk, discomfort, or loss of privilege in order to meaningfully advance inclusion and belonging?

References

Allen, B. J. (2023). *Difference matters: Communicating social identity*. Waveland Press.

Ayoko, O. B., & Konrad, A. M. (2012). Leaders' transformational, conflict, and emotion management behaviors in culturally diverse workgroups. *Equality, Diversity and Inclusion*, *31*(8), 694–724. https://doi.org/10.1108/02610151211277581

Babakusa, E., Yavas, U., & Ashill, N. J. (2010), Service worker burnout and turnover intentions: roles of person-job fit, servant leadership, and customer

orientation. *Services Marketing Quarterly*, *32*(1), 17–31. https://doi.org/10.1080/15332969.2011.533091
Bardhan, N., & Gower, K. (2022). *The role of leadership in building inclusive diversity in public relations*. Routledge. https://doi.org/10.4324/9781003170020
Bezrukova, K., Spell, C. S., Perry, J. L., & Jehn, K. A. (2016). A meta-analytical integration of over 40 years of research on diversity training evaluation. *Psychological Bulletin*, *142*(11), 1227–1274. https://doi.org/10.1037/bul0000067
Bowman Williams, J., & Cox, J. M. (2022). The new principle-practice gap: The disconnect between diversity beliefs and actions in the workplace. *Sociology of Race and Ethnicity*, *8*(2), 301–314. https://doi.org/10.1177/23326492221078293
Butler, J. (1990). *Gender trouble: Feminism and the subversion of identity*. Routledge. https://doi.org/10.4324/9780203824979
Butler, K. (2023). Big tech layoffs are hitting diversity and inclusion jobs hard. *Bloomberg*. Retrieved from https://www.bloomberg.com/news/articles/2023-01-24/tech-layoffs-are-hitting-diversity-and-inclusion-jobs-hard?leadSource=uverify%20wall
Conquergood, D. (1985). Performing as a moral act: Ethical dimensions of the ethnography of performance. *Literature in Performance*, *5*(2), 1–13. https://doi.org/10.1080/10462938509391578
Deetz, S. A. (1992). *Democracy in an age of corporate colonization: Developments in communication and the politics of everyday life*. SUNY.
Dobbin, F., & Kalev, A. (2022). *Getting to diversity: What works and what doesn't*. Harvard University Press. https://doi.org/10.2307/j.ctv2t46rd6
Eva, N., Robin, M., Sendjaya, S., van Dierendonck, D., Liden, R. C. (2019). Servant leadership: A systematic review and call for future research. *The Leadership Quarterly*, *30*(1), 111–132. https://doi.org/10.1016/j.leaqua.2018.07.004
Frick, D. M., & Spears, L. C. (Eds.). (1996). *On becoming a servant-leader: The private writings of Robert K. Greenleaf*. Jossey-Bassey.
Georgeac, O. A. M., & Rattan, A. (2023). The business case for diversity backfires: Detrimental effects of organizations' instrumental diversity rhetoric for underrepresented group members' sense of belonging. *Journal of Personality and Social Psychology*, *124*(1), 69–108. https://doi.org/10.1037/pspi0000394
Gotsis, G., & Grimani, K. (2016). The role of servant leadership in fostering inclusive organizations. *Journal of Management Development*, *35*(8), 985–1010. https://doi.org/10.1108/JMD-07-2015-0095
Greenleaf, R. K. (1977). *Servant leadership: A journey into the nature of legitimate power and greatness*. Paulist Press.
Grimes, D. S. (2002). Challenging the status quo? Whiteness in the diversity management literature. *Management Communication Quarterly*, *15*(3), 381–409. https://doi.org/10.1177/0893318902153003
Institute for Fiscal Studies. (2021, March 12). *The careers and time use of mothers and fathers*. https://ifs.org.uk/publications/careers-and-time-use-mothers-and-fathers
Keating, A. L. (2013). *Transformation now! Toward a post-oppositional politics of change*. University of Illinois Press. https://doi.org/10.5406/illinois/9780252037849.001.0001
MacLellen, L. (2025, February 1). Can Trump kill DEI? What business leaders need to know according to a top constitutional lawyer. *Fortune*. https://fortune.com/2025/01/24/donald-trump-dei-executive-orders-constitutional-lawyer-explains/

Mease, J. J. (2016). Embracing discursive paradox: Consultants navigating the constitutive tensions of diversity work. *Management Communication Quarterly*, *30*(1), 59–83. https://doi.org/10.1177/0893318915604239

McCarty Kilian, C., Hukai, D., & McCarty, C. E. (2005). Building diversity in the pipeline to corporate leadership. *The Journal of Management Development*, *24*(2), 155–168. https://doi.org/10.1108/02621710510579518

McKinsey & Company. (2020, June 23). *Understanding organizational barriers to a more inclusive workplace*. https://www.mckinsey.com/capabilities/people-and-organizational-performance/our-insights/understanding-organizational-barriers-to-a-more-inclusive-workplace

Minor, M. (2021). *Here's the bottom line reason why companies need a chief diversity officer*. Forbes. https://www.forbes.com/sites/mariaminor/2021/05/03/heres-the-bottom-line-reason-why-companies-need-a-chief-diversity-officer/?sh=42c33fa87bc3

Namie, G., & Namie, R. (2009). *The bully at work: What you can do to stop the hurt and reclaim your dignity on the job*. Sourcebooks.

Nicotera, A. M., & Jameson, J. K. (2021). Conflict in organizations and organizing. *Oxford Research Encyclopedia of Communication*. https://doi.org/10.1093/acrefore/9780190228613.013.1275

Orbe, M. P., & Roberts, T. L. (2012). Co-cultural theorizing: Foundations, applications & extensions. *The Howard Journal of Communications*, *23*(4), 293–311. https://doi.org/10.1080/10646175.2012.722838

Perriton, L. (2009). "We don't want complaining women!" A critical analysis of the business case for diversity. *Management Communication Quarterly*, *23*(2), 218–243. https://doi.org/10.1177/0893318909343122

Pettigrew, T. F., & Tropp, L. R. (2006). A meta-analytic test of intergroup contact theory. *Journal of Personality and Social Psychology*, *90*(5), 751–783. https://doi.org/10.1037/0022-3514.90.5.751

Roloff, M. E. (2009). Links between conflict management research and practice. *Journal of Applied Communication Research*, *37*(4), 339–348. https://doi.org/10.1080/00909880903233200

Smucker, J. M. (2017). *Hegemony how-to: A roadmap for radicals*. AK Press.

Spears, L. C. (1998). Introduction. In L. C. Spears (Ed.), *The power of servant leadership* (pp. 1–15). Berret-Koehler.

Warren, J. T. (2008). Performing difference: Repetition in context. *Journal of International and Intercultural Communication*, *1*(4), 290–308.

Warren, J. T., & Hytten, K. (2004). The faces of whiteness: Pitfalls and the critical democrat. *Communication Education*, *53*(4), 321–339.

Williams, J. (2021). We need real metrics, not heartfelt conversations, to tackle workplace diversity. *Fortune*. https://fortune.com/2021/12/07/metrics-diversity-inclusion-workplace-careers-joan-williams

Williams, J. C., & Dolkas, J. (2022). Data driven diversity. *Harvard Business Review*. https://hbr.org/2022/03/data-driven-diversity

Zhao, C., Liu, Y., & Gao, Z. (2016). An identification perspective of servant leadership's effects. *Journal of Managerial Psychology*, *31*(5), 898–913. https://doi.org/10.1108/JMP-08-2014-0250

Zheng, L. (2022). *DEI deconstructed: Your no-nonsense guide to doing the work and doing it right*. Berrett-Koehler Publishers.

18

THE INTEGRATION OF RELATIONAL RESILIENCE INTO A LEADERSHIP COMMUNICATION COURSE FOR MILITARY STUDENTS

Lauren Mackenzie

Introduction

The goal of this chapter is to describe the development and delivery of a ten-session relational resilience course offered to military students at Marine Corps University in Quantico, VA. The seminar provides graduate-level military students from across all branches of service with an opportunity to examine *social* resilience and the role of relationship maintenance in the resilience process. While the overlap between resilience and relationship maintenance is becoming more pronounced (e.g., the *Social Fitness*[1] element of the USMC resilience program), this is still a relatively understudied domain of resilience in the military. This chapter will offer a case study describing how the new "Resilience and Leadership Communication" course makes relational research relevant and applicable to student veterans and active-duty servicemembers.

In recent years, there has been an increased emphasis on building resilience among security professionals. For example, each branch of service has its own resilience office (to include the *Office of Force Resiliency*); the Department of Defense community has opportunities to participate in various forms of resilience training; and there are a wide variety of books, podcasts, and videos dedicated to the various components of resilience. Although each branch of service approaches resilience slightly differently, and the ways in which resilience is framed and trained in the military continue to evolve (Knust et al., 2025), it is typically characterized as the ability to bounce back after setbacks (Reivich & Shatte, 2002). A core assumption of the current Resilience and Leadership Communication

DOI: 10.4324/9781003563662-22

course, however, borrows from Buzzanell's (2010) premise that resilience is *constituted in and through communicative processes*. Unlike the ways in which resilience is studied by psychologists, a communication approach proposes that resilience doesn't reside in the individual but rather in dialogue and narrative. Further, Buzzanell's *Communication Theory of Resilience* (CTR) contends that individuals *talk resilience into being* and helps explain how people *use* communication to create a new normal in their lives after disruption, loss, and trauma.

I am a communication faculty member in the Leadership Department of the Command and Staff College at Marine Corps University and piloted this course after conducting in-depth interviews with Marines devoted to difficult conversations – specifically, relationship repair and end-of-life communication. The findings are woven into the core themes of the class, such as, (1) communication skills for relational well-being, (2) social resilience: connections as a stress management resource, and (3) resilience and leadership: the role of difficult conversations.

This chapter will describe how CTR was integrated into this 2024 pilot course by offering a summary of how the theory was (1) introduced, (2) integrated into an infographic small-group assignment, and (3) reviewed using an in-seminar scenario activity. Drawing from both Cross et al.'s (2021) research devoted to *Resilience as a Team Sport* and a pedagogical approach drawn from the military scholarship of teaching and learning,[2] this chapter offers an illustration of how a communication perspective on resilience can add value to a leadership course for military students.

Theory

The Communication Theory of Resilience helps explain *how individuals talk resilience into being*. The goal of the theory is to "understand and explain how people utilize discursive and material resources to constitute the new normal of their lives after disruption, loss, trauma, and disaster" (Buzzanell, 2018, p. 100). Resilience is theorized as adaptive-transformative processes triggered by loss and involving five subprocesses (Buzzanell, 2010): crafting a new normalcy, affirming or anchoring important identities during difficult times, using and/or maintaining salient communication networks, putting alternative logics to work, and foregrounding productive action while backgrounding unproductive behaviors or negative feelings.

This theory has been applied by a range of scholars seeking to understand how resilience is communicated in a variety of contexts ranging from communities comprised military spouses (Villagran et al., 2013) to the process of understanding psychological stress during the COVID-19 pandemic (Sherblom et al., 2022). Additionally, the *Communication Resilience Processes Scale* was developed and validated by Wilson et al. (2021) who reiterated that the enactment of these resilience processes often creates tensions between continuity and change. Buzzanell's (2018) theory embraces a range of tensions inherent to social life in that it focuses on "reactivity and proactivity, stability and change, disruption and reintegration, destabilization and re-stabilization" (p. 99). In their recent research devoted to U.S. Marines' experiences with end-of-life communication, for example, Mackenzie and Tenzek (2024) suggest that part of the resilience process for Marines who have engaged in final conversations entails acknowledging that the expected and unexpected elements of end-of-life contexts require knowing when to reveal *and* conceal emotions. A range of tensions associated with the CTR were explored throughout the course so as to remind students of Buzzanell's claim that resilience processes are often *tensional*, as opposed to exclusively beneficial.

Along with CTR, the approach for the pilot elective was also informed by Cacioppo et al.'s (2011) *Social Resilience: The Value of Social Fitness with an Application to the Military* who state that "social resilience refers to the capacity to foster, engage in, and sustain positive relationships, and to endure, recover from, and grow as a result of life stressors and social isolation" (p. 44). They go on to underscore the point that social resilience does not imply monolithic pressures toward uniformity nor an uncritically rosy view of the joys of relating. What is unique about social resilience is an appreciation for the key contributions of coordinated social activity and feelings of connectedness to human welfare. Social resilience emphasizes the role of connections with other individuals, groups, and large collectives as a means of fostering adaptation through new learning (including social learning) and growth (p. 44).

Additionally, the course drew heavily from Cross et al.'s (2021) research program which contends that thinking of resilience as a "team sport" requires the acknowledgment that resilience is deeply impacted by our connections to others. Their findings suggest that it is in the interactions themselves that we become resilient; Cross et al. offer a framework for capturing the ways in which we become more resilient through the strength of our relationships with others. With the increase in suicides by both active duty military and veteran populations (Perez, 2023), an emphasis on relational resources associated with resilience is particularly timely and relevant.

Before offering theory application excerpts from the 2024 pilot course, the context within which the course was offered will be discussed.

Context

This pilot course was offered during the winter of 2024 to students at the USMC Command & Staff College (CSC) in Quantico, VA where I have served as a faculty member since 2015. CSC is one of six colleges/schools at the Marine Corps University and offers a ten-month (August–June), resident master's degree program for both U.S. military officers, international officers, and civilians employed by various government agencies.

Throughout the past decade and a half, a range of publications devoted to teaching military students has suggested that they, like most adult learners, have a desire for immediate applicability and learn best when confronted with a particular problem that needs solving (Carter, 2010). Thus, I adapted many instructional processes to promote a discourse about a transferable mindset and skill set (i.e., skills that can be useful regardless of cultural context) rather than a memorized series of theoretical or conceptual facts (Steen et al., 2018). As discussed elsewhere (Mackenzie, 2021), I continue to try to involve Marines in the ongoing creation of their own education so as to render the content relevant across contexts and intercultural interactions.

As mentioned in endnote 2, there is a growing body of research devoted to the military scholarship of teaching and learning. This includes both the *Journal of Military Learning* [see, for example, Hamilton's (2019) discussion of the relatively recent turn toward active learning in military classrooms and how it might be usefully applied across various learning levels] as well as Air University's annual *Military Scholarship of Teaching & Learning* Forum (Air University, n.d.) which brings together scholars and practitioners dedicated to examining the unique challenges associated with teaching in a military context.

Pilot elective

In their seminal article, *Leadership: A Communicative Perspective*, Fairhurst and Connaughton (2014, p. 20) maintain that "culture influences how leadership is understood." This is certainly the case in military education contexts where officers are exposed to a substantial amount of leadership training and education from the moment they are commissioned as well as throughout their accessions. As such, many military officers tend to have a very clear idea of what good leadership is and is not, as well as what it should or should not entail. Resilience, like leadership, has commonly been thought of as an individual or stoic endeavor. There has been more of a communication-focused emphasis as of late that borrows from the old adage that *leadership happens in conversation*. The "Resilience and Leadership Communication" course aimed to leverage this acknowledgment as an opportunity to introduce and integrate communication theory into a curriculum that is otherwise primarily focused on military history and international relations. Drawing from Fairhurst and Connaughton's premise, this pilot class places communication at the center of both leadership and resilience processes. As noted by Buzzanell (2010), resilience isn't something we have, it's something we *do* – in and through communication. The course aims to bridge this communication perspective on leadership and the Communication Theory of Resilience via the two assignments described below.

For this new elective course, the student learning outcomes were as follows:

1 Assess the ways in which resilience can be practiced as a team sport
2 Apply a range of resilience theories to diverse leadership contexts
3 Analyze the ways in which social resilience can be used to enhance organizational cultures

During the winter of 2024, 14 graduate students from the Marine Corps, Army, Navy, Air Force Reserves, Department of State, and U.S. Agency for International Development were enrolled in and completed the course. There was a total of ten modules (all in person and conducted at Marine Corps University) which included the following:

a *Introduction: Social Resilience*
b *Know Thyself: Self-awareness, Reflection & Resilience*
c *Thinking Traps that Deplete Resilience*
d *Theory in Action: Emphasizing Relational Resilience*
e *Social Resilience: Connections as Resources*
f *Infographic Presentations*
g *Difficult Conversations: Conflict, Apologies & Feedback*
h *Building an Organizational Culture Designed to Promote Resilience*
i *Panel of Guest Speakers on Resilience & Leadership*
j *Final Presentations, Course Summary & the Way Ahead*

In the next section, I will review the ways in which the course was a vehicle for leadership professionals to engage with the various practical applications associated with the CTR.

Linking application

Along with course readings and seminar discussions, students had two opportunities (one graded and one ungraded) to apply CTR to their personal and professional leadership experiences. The first was the assignment to create an infographic (see Appendix A for assignment description) dedicated to a social/relational resilience concept or theory of their choice. Students were assigned a partner and provided with an infographic framework they would use to make an academic theory relevant and accessible to the young Marines/subordinates they will lead at their next assignment. The goal was to create a concise and relatable graphic depiction of a resilience-based concept/theory that they would present to the class. Students were evaluated based on the following criteria:

- *Content* (accurate and focused information is conveyed effectively so as to support the purpose of the infographic)
- *Visual organization* (information is systematically organized and supports the reader's comprehension of the main message)
- *Citations* (at least three scholarly citations are included on the back side or as endnotes)
- *Presentation* (7–10-minute presentation is well-rehearsed and clearly explains ways to apply your chosen resilience-related theory, research findings, data set, etc.)

Prior to student selection of the concept/theory they would bring to life via an infographic, I devoted a class seminar to the CTR. Students were asked to come to class having read Buzzanell's (2010) article and 2018 chapter and were then placed into small groups. They were given 20 minutes to address the following prompts in writing on the whiteboard:

- Explain the theory in your own words
- List one way it has been applied
- Write one quotation from the reading that made you stop and think

This set the foundation for them to think with their peers about how the theory could inform their leadership practices now and in the future. It offered a blend of theory definition reinforcement and practical application. One student noted, for example, that it was the "affirming or anchoring important identities during difficult times" that was most relevant to the way she was working to process and grow from the loss of a close family member. Buzzanell's (2010) story in which she describes leaving a place for her deceased father at the dinner table, helped the student make sense of why it was beneficial to do the same for her own father – and she offered that it will help inform how she hopes to support grieving members of her team moving forward. Another student mentioned that the *anchoring* of important identities was especially relevant for Marines who are struggling – given that their professional identities are closely tied to the "eagle, globe, and *anchor*" symbol of the U.S. Marine Corps. These brief anecdotes illustrate the role that communication can play for leaders in the resilience process – both their own and the team they are leading.

Although the basic purpose of an infographic assignment in the classroom is nothing new, the goal of creating graphic representations of complex theories/concepts so as to make them more accessible to junior audiences remains important for this particular group of students. With the vast majority of U.S. Marines being in their late teens/early 20s, the students in the "Resilience and Leadership Communication" course (mostly Majors in their mid-to-late 30s) were keenly aware of the value of condensing academic ideas for those across a range of learning levels. As such, the students used the infographic assignment to both *think back* on stressful/tragic experiences in their careers (to reflect on what they wish they had known then) as well as to *think ahead* in order to consider how they could use what they had learned in the course thus far to share some of the resources and knowledge in the future with the teams they will lead. In one infographic presentation devoted to mindfulness training, for example, the students illustrated the tensions associated with where to place one's attention during stressful experiences, noting that under stress, our attention gets pulled to the past by a memory or to the future with a worry. This tension can lead military personnel to lose focus on the present, and the students effectively captured this challenge through their "Own Your Attention: You are Missing 50% of Your Life" infographic. By listing several mindfulness techniques to help manage this challenge, they creatively addressed one of Buzzanell's resilience practices of *foregrounding productive action while backgrounding unproductive behaviors or negative feelings*. In doing so, the students offered succinct graphic depictions of various attention subsystems that were both accessible and, most importantly, actionable.

As stated previously, Buzzanell (2010) theorizes resilience as adaptive-transformative processes triggered by loss and involving five subprocesses: crafting a new normalcy, affirming or anchoring important identities during difficult times, using and/or maintaining salient communication networks, putting alternative logics to work, and foregrounding productive action while backgrounding unproductive behaviors or negative feelings. The second linking opportunity occurred during the class session after the infographic presentations were delivered. The following prompt was displayed for the students:

Scenario: *Your elective course requires that students deliver group presentations in front of the class. Each member gives part of the group's presentation, but all group members receive the same grade. This presentation is worth 40% of the final grade. The night before the presentation, you have* *a major argument with your best friend and don't sleep much. On the day of your group presentation, you're completely distracted, and everyone does well except you. Throughout the course, you had served as the leader of your group and took pride in that role, but you were not as prepared as you could have been and made several mistakes throughout your portion of the presentation. You know that your content was poorly delivered and that the whole group's grade will suffer as a result. After class, your co-presenter looks visibly annoyed and loudly asks you, "What happened?"*

Students were then asked to work in pairs to integrate an idea from one of Buzzanell's CTR subprocesses into their responses. This ungraded class activity provided students an opportunity to both (1) apply the theory to a communication response after a (fictional) disappointing class performance and (2) think through how the CTR subprocesses might usefully connect. The two most common subprocesses that were referred to in the student responses were "Putting alternative logics to work" and "foregrounding productive action while backgrounding unproductive behaviors or negative feelings." For example, one student stated that the military uses "family" as an object of unit culture and argued that there is value in "leaning on your family – wherever you find it." This point was connected to the scenario by noting the value of the "we are all in this together" mentality. When one member of the team or family is down, the others are there to lift him/her up and assist in offering a new logic/perspective on the challenge. It was also mentioned that the Marine Corps is a learning organization, and mistakes and failures are often required for growth. Re-framing the struggle in this way so as to integrate an aspect of the CTR into their response to the prompt gave students an opportunity to put the CTR into practice in a low-stakes classroom environment.

Conclusion

A central aim of this chapter was to offer an example of how the CTR could be usefully applied to a "Resilience and Leadership Communication" course for military students. An idea that was consistently reinforced throughout the ten seminars was that resilience processes – like leadership practices – do not happen in isolation. Although many military professionals find value in the concept of stoicism and prefer to look inward when confronting adversity, this course provided an array of scholarly and practical resources to underscore the point that resilience can be constructively viewed as a *team sport* (Cross et al., 2021) and that *we talk resilience into being* when recovering from loss and trauma (Buzzanell, 2010). Further, there was an undercurrent of the role of (potentially competing) tensions inherent to the resilience process throughout the course. Examples of how these tensions played out in both graded assignments and in-seminar groupwork were framed by the foundational assumptions of Buzzanell's CTR as well as the theory's various subprocesses (such as *affirming or anchoring important identities during difficult times* and *putting alternative logics to work).*

Although this course was a pilot and only 14 students completed it,[3] the Marine Corps CSC is making strides toward integrating a more communication-centered approach to its resilience core seminar (required of all 200 students enrolled at CSC) in the Leadership Department each fall. For example, in the fall of 2023, Cross et al.'s (2021) "Resilience as a Team Sport" article was a required reading, and I am working to integrate Buzzanell's work into forthcoming iterations of the course.

Despite this encouraging development, it should also be noted that military resilience programs, in general, are not without their critics. For example, Schott's (2021) chapter "Resilience as a Failed Concept: The Militarization of Intimate Lives" critiques the ways in which some programs have weaponized "resilience" to shame military personnel and their families when they haven't bounced back quickly enough after deployments. Although unpacking this critique is beyond the scope of the current chapter, it is acknowledged that resilience is not a one-size-fits-all process. Rather, as described in the introduction, this course offers students a chance to think of resilience not as something you *have* – but something you *do*. This certainly aligns with the "bias towards action" element associated with Marines' identities (Holmes-Eber, 2014) and offers a means for students to think about various communication practices that enable a relational perspective on resilience. Throughout the ten seminars of the course, students engaged constructively with the argument that social connections are a source of strength. These discussions extended the underlying premise woven throughout the course readings, in-class activities, and graded events that resilience is partly about "putting resources in place for the next stressor" (Ungar & Lustig, 2020). The pilot course that was described throughout this chapter is one such resource that military leaders can use both personally and professionally as they contend with unexpected challenges that lay ahead for them in an uncertain future security environment.

Suggested further readings

Buzzanell, P. (2010). Resilience: Talking, resisting, and imagining new normalcies into being. *Journal of Communication*, *60*, 1–14. https://doi.org/10.1111/j.1460-2466.2009.01469.x

Cross, R., Singer, J. & Dillon, K. (2021). Resilience is a team sport: The invisible ways networks create resilience for those who have invested well. *Connected*

Commons. https://irc4hr.org/wp-content/uploads/2021/06/Resilience-is-a-Team-Sport.pdf
Fairhurst, G. & Connaughton, S. (2014). Leadership: A communicative perspective. *Leadership*, *10*(1), 7–35. https://doi.org/10.1177/1742715013509396

Questions for further engagement

1 What are the five subprocesses (triggered by loss) that Buzzanell captures in the Communication Theory of Resilience?
2 If you were asked to add another process to this theory, what would you add?
3 How would you characterize the connection between leadership and resilience?

Notes

1 https://www.fitness.marines.mil/Resilience/Social-Fitness
2 For example, both the *Journal of Military Learning* and Hennessey's (2022) edited volume *Developing Military Learners' Communication Skills Using the Scholarship of Teaching & Learning* offer a variety of research-based and reflective pieces devoted to the challenges and opportunities associated with teaching in a military context.
3 It should be noted that the maximum number of students allowed to enroll in the electives program is 15.

References

Abilock, D. & Williams, C. (2014). Recipe for an infographic. *Knowledge Quest*, *43*(2), 46–55.
Air University. (n.d.) *Vector: The center of excellence for learning professionals*. https://www.airuniversity.af.edu/Vector/MSOTL/
Buzzanell, P. (2010). Resilience: Talking, resisting, and imagining new normalcies into being. *Journal of Communication*, *60*, 1–14. https://doi.org/10.1111/j.1460-2466.2009.01469.x
Buzzanell, P. (2018). Communication theory of resilience: Enacting adaptive-transformative processes when families experience loss and disruption. In D. Braithwaite, E. Suter & K. Floyd (Eds.), *Engaging theories in family communication* (2nd ed., pp. 98–109). Routledge.
Cacioppo, J., Reis, H. & Zautra, A. (2011). Social resilience: The value of social fitness with an application to the military. *American Psychologist*, *66*, 43–51. https://psycnet.apa.org/doi/10.1037/a0021419
Carter, B. (2010). No "holidays from history": Adult learning, professional military education, and teaching history. In D. Higbee (Ed.), *Military culture and education* (pp. 167–182). Routledge. https://doi.org/10.4324/9781315595405
Cross, R., Singer, J. & Dillon, K. (2021). Resilience is a team sport: The invisible ways networks create resilience for those who have invested well. *Connected Commons*. https://irc4hr.org/wp-content/uploads/2021/06/Resilience-is-a-Team-Sport.pdf

Fairhurst, G. & Connaughton, S. (2014). Leadership: A communicative perspective. *Leadership*, *10*(1), 7–35. https://doi.org/10.1177/1742715013509396

Hamilton, M. (2019, October). Prioritizing active learning in the classroom: Reflections for professional military education. *Journal of Military Learning*, 3–17. https://www.armyupress.army.mil/Journals/Journal-of-Military-Learning/Journal-of-Military-Learning-Archives/

Hennessey, M. (2022). *Developing military learners' communication skills using the scholarship of teaching & learning*. Air University Press. https://www.airuniversity.af.edu/Portals/10/AUPress/Books/B_177_Hennessy_Developing_Military_Leadership1.pdf

Holmes-Eber, P. (2014). *Culture in conflict: Irregular warfare, culture policy, and the Marine Corps*. Stanford University Press.

Knust, S. K., Booth, L. C., Toner, K. A., Novosel-Lingat, J. E. M. & Adrian, A. L. (2025). Master resilience trainer course quality improvement evaluation. *Military Psychology: The Official Journal of the Division of Military Psychology, American Psychological Association*, *37*(3), 220–230. https://doi.org/10.1080/08995605.2024.2346449

Mackenzie, L. (2021). On "becoming wise in the way of others": Lessons learned from integrating culture into professional military education. In K. Fosher & L. Mackenzie (Eds.), *The rise and decline of U.S. military culture programs 2004-20* (pp. 41–55). Marine Corps University Press. https://www.usmcu.edu/Outreach/Marine-Corps-University-Press/Books-by-topic/MCUP-Titles-A-Z/The-Rise-and-Decline-of-US-Military-Culture-Programs-2004-20/

Mackenzie, L. & Tenzek, K. (2024). Marines' reflections on end-of-life communication: Connecting resilience and difficult dialogue. *International Journal of Collaborative-Dialogic Practices*, *13*, 53–66. https://journal.lib.uoguelph.ca/index.php/ijcdp/article/view/8009

Perez, Z. (2023, July 03). Military suicide stats released: Army saw highest increase of deaths. *Military Times*. https://www.militarytimes.com/news/your-military/2023/07/03/military-suicide-stats-released-army-saw-highest-increase-of-deaths/

Reivich, K. & Shatte, A. (2002). *The resilience factor: 7 essential skills for overcoming life's inevitable obstacles*. Broadway Books.

Schott, R. (2021). Resilience as a failed concept: The militarization of intimate lives. In J. Bourke & R. Schott (Eds.), *Resilience: Militaries & militarization* (pp. 175–194). Palgrave-Macmillan.

Sherblom, J., Umphrey, L. & Swiatkowski, P. (2022). Resilience, identity tension, hope, social capital, and psychological stress during a pandemic. *Adversity and Resilience Science*, *3*(1), 37–51. https://doi.org/10.1007/s42844-021-00049-3

Steen, S., Mackenzie, L. & Buechner, B. (2018). Incorporating cosmopolitan communication into diverse teaching and training contexts: Considerations from our work with military students and veterans. In J. D. Wallace & D. Becker (Eds.), *Handbook of communication training: A best practices framework for assessing and developing competence* (pp. 401–413). Routledge. https://doi.org/10.4324/9781315185859

Ungar, M. & Lustig, S. (2020). *Building resilience: A framework for dealing with stress and adversity across the lifespan*. Cigna Resilience [White paper].

Villagran, M., Canzona, M. & Ledford, C. (2013). The milspouse battle rhythm: Communicating resilience throughout the deployment cycle. *Health Communication*, *28*(8), 778–788. https://doi.org/10.1080/10410236.2013.800441

Wilson, S., Kuang, K., Hintz, E. & Buzzanell, B. (2021). Developing and validating the communication resilience processes scale. *Journal of Communication*, *71*(3), 478–513. https://doi.org/10.1093/joc/jqab013

Appendix A

Resilience and Leadership Communication
2024 Elective Infographic Assignment

i *Purpose*
In assigned groups of 2–3, you will create an infographic to be presented to the class. Your infographic will offer a visual depiction of a theory, set of research findings, or specific skill associated with resilience for peers or subordinates at your next assignment.

ii *Definition of Infographic*

> An infographic is a claim expressed through a visual metaphor, conveying the fresh understanding of relationships, expressed through judicious selection and arrangement of visuals, evidence, and text acquired during inquiry research within a discipline.
>
> *(Abilock & Williams, 2014)*

iii *Deliverable*
Using the software of your choice (e.g., Canva, Piktochart, PowerPoint), you will create an infographic to communicate a complex idea about social resilience (e.g., research findings, theory, etc.) both efficiently and effectively. You will introduce the infographic to the class in a 7–10-minute presentation on 19th January. In order to avoid too much duplication in infographic topics, please note that topics must be approved by the instructors no later than 12 Jan.

iv *Grading Criteria*
This assignment is worth 20% of your final grade and will be graded according to the following criteria:

- **Content** (accurate and focused information is conveyed effectively so as to support the purpose of the infographic)
- **Visual organization** (information is systematically organized and supports the reader's comprehension of the main message)
- **Citations** (at least three scholarly citations are included on the back side or as endnotes)
- **Presentation** (7–10-minute presentation is well-rehearsed and clearly explains ways to apply your chosen resilience-related theory, research findings, data set, etc.)

19

COMMUNICATING MISSION COMMAND

A Four-Part Framework for Leaders*

John M. Hinck

Mission command

"Mission Command" in the context of military leadership is an important construct increasingly studied/discussed across numerous military venues. The US Joint Chiefs of Staff Focus Paper on Mission Command (January 2020) and the recent "mission command" Air Force Doctrine Publication 1–1 (US Air Force [USAF], 2023) are helpful, if not foundational, in elaborating the mission command construct. "Mission command" is a construct that continues to be challenging in military circles. It is foreign and sometimes dismissed by civilians with no military affiliation who think "mission command" is military jargon that simply means a uniformed boss issuing orders to subordinates. Formally, mission command is the conduct of military operations through decentralized execution based upon mission-type orders and has been studied for centuries as a hallmark of effective mission accomplishment within a commander's intent (Joint Chiefs of Staff [JCS], 2011; Leistenschneider, 2002; Moltke, 1911). Scholars have examined the concept of mission command in a historical context, to understand (1) military success/failure, (2) how leaders communicate, and (3) leadership development and organizational culture, yet there has been little application and bridging of communication and leadership theories that helps frame a holistic understanding of mission command as a leader-communication-centric

* Opinions, conclusions, and recommendations expressed or implied within are solely those of the author and do not necessarily represent the views of the Air University, the US Air Force, the Department of Defense, or any other US government agency.

DOI: 10.4324/9781003563662-23

concept (Shamir, 2011; Vandergriff, 2019; Vandergriff & Webber, 2017). While mission command is not a command authority nor is it a license to ignore a commander's intent or take unauthorized or unnecessary risk, it is "a philosophy of leadership that empowers Airmen to operate in uncertain, complex, and rapidly changing environments through trust, shared awareness, and understanding of commander's intent" (US Air Force [USAF], 2023, p. 4). The mission command principles are to clearly provide the commander's intent, create shared understanding, exercise discipline and initiative, build teams through mutual trust, accept prudent risk, and use mission-type orders when appropriate. Leaders need to develop the knowledge, skills, and attitudes to foster trust within their units. Trust is at the heart of organizational leadership. Not only is trust vital for an effective leader but represents "the bond that unifies leaders with their followers and commanders with their units" (Hinck & Hinck, 2023, p. 45).

Mission command culture can be understood as a network of relationships among attributes. These attributes of *character*, *competence*, *capability*, *cohesion*, and *capacity* constitute the individual and organizational attributes commanders should foster and reinforce to build the individual and organizational capacity. And among this constellation of attributes and their relationships, mission command is carried out through centralized command, distributed control, and decentralized execution; these remain hallmarks of mission command culture. (See the US Air Force's publication on mission command for a visual depiction of mission command culture, US Air Force [USAF], 2023.)

In examining the principles and attributes of mission command, two things must be noted. The first is an internal and external capacity. The internal capacity is around character and competence that are connected to an individual's duty. Cohesion and capacity are formed through trust and are foundational for a team or unit to accomplish their assigned mission. The second note is that those principles and attributes come alive through the words and actions of leaders and followers, through their communication and leadership. In other words, the culture of mission command is understood via the words, interactions, shared trust, and relationships between people. Character and trust are central to duty and mission execution. Air Force Doctrine Publication 1–2 (US Air Force [USAF], 2024) clarifies how Air Force personnel are warriors and innovators who must demonstrate character, competence, and trust, and underscores the importance of how a leader's actions and abilities are fundamental in how they communicate and exercise their leadership toward a common purpose of mission accomplishment.

This chapter focuses on the creation of the four-part framework outlining how leaders communicate mission command. The data-driven framework is grounded in relational leadership theory and discursive and relational communication theories, expands upon previous research, and links how mission command is communicated as a leadership practice in the military. Ideally, this chapter appeals to two audiences in ways that are both insightful and informative. The first audience is the conventional communication and leadership scholars who are inclined to follow lines of inquiry, and who appreciate relational theory, leadership/communication, and organizational purpose, but may not understand or have any appreciation of what's meant by "mission command." The second audience is the experienced military professionals who, at times, may be quick to dismiss conventional research/scholarship as peripheral, ivory towered exercises of marginal utility. They are also the ones who live in the integrity of honor and duty and are inclined to ask practical questions, trust their insights and experiences, and live by a code of conduct. In an attempt to reach both audiences as well as the universal audience of practitioners and scholars who are intrigued by the intersection of leadership and communication, this chapter expands an understanding of mission command across multiple organizational structures. The intersection is demonstrated in the development of leaders charged with operating in environments that require effective communication with their people to do their duty as part of a unit entrusted with a mission to get accomplished. It is through the lenses of communication and leadership theories and a newly developed four-part mission command framework that we can better understand how leaders communicate the concept of mission command.

Relational approaches in leadership and communication

Relational leadership emphasizes that relationships are key for effectiveness and includes a process that values purpose, inclusion and ethics, and empowering others to benefit the common good (Brower et al., 2000; Hunt & Dodge, 2000; Uhl-Bien, 2011). Followership is one of the newest leadership theories and is about how the actions of those in subordinate roles complement leadership through intentional and meaningful interchanges (Chaleff, 2009, 2015; Riggio et al., 2008; Uhl-Bien et al., 2014). Leader-member exchange (LMX) theory is a relationship-based approach to leadership that focuses on the dyadic (two-way) relationship between leaders and followers, characterized by in-groups and out-groups based on trust, emotion, respect, and benevolence toward each other (Dansereau et al., 1975; Graen & Cashman, 1975; Graen & Uhl-Bien, 1995; Hooper & Martin, 2008). Hence, it is the very interactions and relationships between people (leaders and followers) where trust is created that lies at the heart of mission command.

How leaders communicate internally (intrinsically) and externally (explicitly) has received due consideration (Ospina et al., 2020; Tourish, 2016) alongside the argument of the importance of cohesion and relational dynamics for successful duty and mission accomplishment by military organizations (Coleman, 2009; Duncan, 2022; Ekman, 2023). And, more recently, the emotional components have been studied as central to the power of language and the transmission of military ideology (mission command culture) in linguistically meaningful patterns (Fratila, 2022; US Air Force [USAF], 2024).

Previous literature on relational theory bridged communication and leadership elements but excluded examining the relationship with the organization's purpose or mission and the internal sense of performance obligation (Bylund et al., 2012; Parks, 1977). A consequence of communication among members in a team or organization is the nature of their relationship (Parks, 1977), especially at the interpersonal level, and how it impacts other relationships both internally and externally (Bylund et al., 2012). The levels are influenced by involvement, affiliation, and trust as manifested through interactions (Dillard et al., 1999) amid shared moral commitments and situational context (Barge & Little, 2008) and how participants socially construct the concepts of leadership and followership (Alvesson, 1996; Fairhurst, 2008).

Previous scholars either did not discuss or subordinated the relationship with self or character over relationship with others within an organization or unit that structured relational dynamics of empowerment, ethics, inclusion, purpose, and process between people (Dillard et al., 1999; Gale, 2010). While relational communication theory does account for systems of external relations, there is more to be known about the internal system of relations that focus on one's internal obligation or sense of duty to achieve a collective organizational purpose or mission (Coleman, 2009; Duncan, 2022; Ekman, 2023; Rogers, 2008).

Some discursive communication approaches to understanding leadership are limited in how they situate leader communication as primarily an external linear process and that leaders inherently use communication as manipulation or use concepts (e.g., entity or relational). Additionally, some approaches focus solely on individual attributes in relationships with others while excluding internal relationship with oneself and internal relational elements (Malik, 2019; Tourish, 2016; Uhl-Bien, 2006). While discursive elements of communication have been given adequate study, there is a lack of applying discursive theory involving mission command, which requires a reimagined framing of mission command (Clifton, 2012; Fratila, 2022; Kernic et al., 2023). A more expansive inclusion of intrapersonal (internal linear) communication with self and relationship with self is needed to understand how leaders communicate mission command to their individual subordinates and the larger unit or organization via trust at the collective level.

Methodological approach

To answer the aforementioned limitations, the research question of "How do leaders communicate mission command?" was explored through triangulation of data analysis from end-of-course surveys and discussion with instructors (n = 9,747) in two leadership development programs: the Leader Development Course for Squadron Command (LDC) and the US Air Force Officer Training School (OTS) (Air University, n.d.; US Air Force Officer Training School [USAF OTS], n.d.).[1] The Leader Development Course (LDC) is an initiative by the Chief of Staff for the US Air Force (CSAF) that "connects to a broader continuum of learning and closes gaps discovered during the squadron vitality study to prepare officers, civilian and enlisted leaders to thrive in command" (Air University, n.d.). Graduated squadron commanders, senior noncommissioned officers (SNCO), and civilian academic experts teach the eight-day seminar-based, experiential course. The LDC has been in existence since 2018 and has graduated over 5,000 leaders who have stronger human domain skills to better lead their people in accomplishing their mission. The OTS is an "8.5-week, five-module program designed for those with a college degree who are ready to take the next step as a leader" (USAF OTC, n.d.). The program comprises five modules that integrate acculturation, academics, and field exercises that focus on developing warrior-minded leaders of character. Modules 4 and 5 focus on mission command and mission command experiences (MCEs) both in the classroom and field environments. Using a cumulative coding process that developed codes, categories, and themes, the methodological approach analyzes data from both programs along with discussions and notes from 190 instructors that link the theories in the practice of how each program communicates mission command as a fundamental element and practice of leadership.

Honoring the voices of the participants

The voices of 8,557 participants from two different leader development programs provided the foundational data that examined how leaders communicate mission command. The author used a coding process that analyzed student responses and moved from codes to grouping of codes into categories supported with student quotations, followed by analysis of key words associated with mission command, and finally thematic analysis to produce themes aimed at helping to answer the research question. The findings from the data analysis are presented in four phases:

- Phase 1. Results from analyzing end-of-course surveys by participants (n = 5,331) in the Leader Development Course for Squadron Command (LDC) and developing categories.
- Phase 2. Results from analyzing end-of-module surveys (Modules 4 and 5) by participants (n = 3,226) in the USAF OTS and developing categories.
- Phase 3. Key word analysis on words and phrases (codes) related to mission command as discussed with and captured in notes by instructors (n = 190) from both programs.
- Phase 4. Thematic analysis of results from Phases 1 to 3.

Phase 1. Leader Development Course (LDC)

Data were collected on student responses to three questions in the end-of-course survey that related to the two lessons of clarity of purpose and leader communication on Day Three of the eight-day program.

Q6 – LDC spent time on many different areas of instruction. Please rate the value you found in these areas of instruction as they relate to your growth as a leader using the six-point scale of Strongly Agree, Agree, Slightly Agree, Slightly Disagree, Disagree, and Strongly Disagree.

Participants assessed the Clarity of Purpose lesson as #3 out of 22 content areas and the leader communication lesson as #4 out of 22 content areas.

Q7 – Please provide comments on the two or three most valuable areas of instruction.

Q13 – Please tell us how you plan on applying what you learned in this course.

Together, the two lessons provided content and application of how students and future leaders of USAF squadrons learn and practice communicating mission command. The two lessons were rated as highly valuable by participants with over 96% agreement that those lessons influenced their growth as a leader. Six categories emerged that encapsulated how participants learned and practiced communicating mission command. Categories are supported with student quotations.

1 Purpose and knowing my why.
   - "Clarity of purpose: I have to know my why... it's crucial I ensure my squadron has a why that everyone can buy in to."
   - "Clarity of purpose was also very helpful for me as I prepare to take command next summer. It helped me understand the importance of clearly articulating the message so it is perceived as intended."
2 Building trust with self and others.
   - "I not only increased my competence/confidence, I also strengthened trust in myself around communicating mission command; and maybe even trust with my peers."
   - "Clarity of purpose stuck out the most. Messaging matters and if we are not sending the message in an effective, understandable manner, how do we expect our organizations to have the buy-in and trust?"
3 Translating (communicating) the why into action through words and ideas.
   - "Clarity of purpose and telling the my story/unit story... focusing on the reason/why and how to communicate it."
4 Codifying approach to leading and trusting others.
   - "Clarity of purpose and leadership communication really forced me to evaluate how I approach my messaging."
   - "Clarity of purpose/Leader communication – the importance of communication is equal to that of developing a sense of purpose that requires trust."
5 Clarified how to think and talk like a leader/commander.
   - "Clarity of purpose was insightful to me. It highlighted a keen approach to bring understanding to the organization on the mission, line of effort, or specific task."
   - "Leader comm forced me to think about the clarity of purpose for my people and how to communicate in a clear way toward mission success."
6 Fostered my understanding of how to create, build, and strengthen myself and others for mission success and people success.
   - "I would like to go back and start thinking about who am I as a commander. I want to be more intentional with how I view a successful

unit and what things I can do to better get an organization to my dream squadron."

- "To better and more effectively communicate with unit members especially around duty and trust that are required for mission success. I also plan on sharing/teaching others some of the things I learned."

Phase 2. Officer Training School (OTS)

The answers to three questions related to mission command were used in this phase of the data analysis.

Q39 – Module 4's over-arching intent is focused on developing as a Warrior-Minded Leader of Character within the "Ideas" Foundational Competency Group. Please share your thoughts on what specific elements or activities in Module 4 you found most effective in achieving this goal.

Q40 – Regarding the over-arching intent of Module 4, which is focused on developing as a Warrior-Minded Leader of Character within the "Ideas" Foundational Competency Group, please share one specific improvement you believe would enhance our ability to achieve this goal.

Q54 – Module 5's over-arching intent is focused on developing as a Warrior-Minded Leader of Character within the "Teams" Foundational Competency Group. Please share your thoughts on what specific elements or activities in Module 5 you found most effective in achieving this goal.

After coding the responses using in vivo, descriptive, and values coding, the 68 codes were organized into categories. The six categories are supported with quotations on what OTS participants learned from the mission command-oriented lessons and MCEs undergone in the last two modules of leader development training.

1 Creativity, flexibility, and adaptability are key to achieving mission success.

  - "I was forced to get incredibly creative in order to complete the mission, in ways I did not think I could do. Flexibility is the cornerstone of airpower!"
  - "These events fostered creative ideas from my classmates where we did our individual duty to accomplish the mission together."

2 Brought everyone together and strengthened bonds through trust.

  - "I'm not a feeler, so these events caused me to step outside my comfort zone and really bond with others; I wanted to trust them and myself."

- "Really felt like we forged a strong bond together through the challenges; I trusted my instructors and my peers."

3 Fostered inclusion, teamwork, trust, unity, and an "us" mentality and "family" feeling.

- "Helped me grow a team, from people not particularly in my flight, showing through strong communication and leadership the way in which you can develop an effective team through trust and teamwork."
- "We all felt included and unified like in a good family."

4 Develop new, novel, creative, innovative ideas and ways of thinking to attack the problem.

- "I felt I was able to foster the creation of ideas of the people I lead and in the exercises I performed in."
- "MCEs taught me how to come up with plans on the fly. It also taught me the importance of clearly communicating that sense of duty that collectively leads to mission success."

5 Wanted more mindsets of good followership and skillsets of being a good follower and supporting leaders and the mission.

- "Needed more people to have the mindset of and skillset for followership."
- "We need to be professional followers and do our duty so that the mission can get done."

6 Wanted role models and key leaders to lead by example.

- "Want to observe others and learn from them."
- "Interactions with the wrong leaders or faculty just set the worst tone. We need a better model to follow; someone who leads by example."

Phase 3. Analysis of key words

Based on discussions with and notes from 190 instructors in LDC and OTS about what constitutes "mission command" to them, key words were generated that illuminated how they see mission command come alive in their programs. To them, mission command was about the relationship and trust with self and others in how they did their task and duty as a unit in accomplishing their assigned mission. For them, there was a consistent theme of an internal relationship to self (e.g., individual, leader, and follower) and the duty (i.e., individual task), and an external relationship

Character

LDC = 4106 (77%) OTS = 2613 (81%)

I	Self-aware	Leader	Develop
Me	Self-manage	Commander	Leadership style
Person	Know self	Role	Lead by example
Personal	Self-discovery	Values	Internal compass
Myself	Self-talk	Follower	Mindset
Individual	Identity	Ethics	Framing
Other(s)	Personality	Character	Warrior-minded

Trust

LDC = 4112 (77%) OTS = 2452 (76%)

Team	Family	Others	Dorms
Unit	Home	Identity	Rooms
Wing	Group	Culture	Seminars
Flight	Module	Environment	"Living with"
Us	My command	Climate	Organization
We	Collective	Talk(ing)	Trust
Squadron	Together	"Being with"	Communicate

Duty

LDC = 3253 (61%) OTS = 2258 (70%)

Act(ion)	Tools	Hone	Focused
Perform	Toolkit	Elevate	Responsibility
My job	Serve	Work	Effort
Get after it	Duty	Own	Practical
Do	First	Specific	Application
It	Practice	Task	Understanding
Clarity	Work	Purpose	"Be the example"

Mission

LDC = 3626 (78%) OTS = 2548 (79%)

Actions	Purpose	Change	Commander
Mission	Preparation	Adapt	Intent
"Go-do"	Courses of action	Flexible	Process
Decisions	Mission-type orders	Agile	Culture
Approach	Line of effort	Creativity	Teamwork
Execution	"Our task"	Innovate	Situation
Conducting	Plan of attack	Ready	Endstate

FIGURE 19.1 Structure of key word analysis

or trust with others (e.g., team, flight, and unit) and the mission (i.e., collective task). Based on those patterns identified via dialogue with the instructors and how they perceived the exchanges of their students and trainees, a more expansive word search was done across the 8,557 participants' responses. The results showed a collection of related key words associated with mission command and how they observed self and others communicating and practicing mission command during their programs. Figure 19.1 shows the structure of the key word analysis, including (1) the most common words that showed up 82 or more times in the analysis (the next cut line of words being used was at 56 and constituted a broader, yet not significantly wider, list of words), (2) the total number of words found from the participant responses (5,331 = LDC and OTS = 3,226), (3) the percentage of responses of the total participants from each program, and (4) how the words were organized or categorized into four constructs (character, duty, trust, and mission) based on the literature associated with mission command and leadership in the military.

Phase 4. Thematic analysis

The thematic analysis of the data from both programs reveals that participants found these lessons highly valuable for their leadership development. The focus on practical application, role-playing exercises, and immediate feedback contributed to their increased self-awareness and improved communication skills. The lessons and exercises were seen as essential for articulating the unit's mission, vision, and values, thereby enhancing team dynamics, trust, and overall leadership effectiveness. Based on the 12 categories and analysis of key words, eight key themes emerged. Those themes were further connected to the four concepts of character, duty, trust, and mission:

1 Knowing personal why and organizational why (people, character, duty, trust, and mission)
Knowing and articulating (communicating) the why or purpose of people and the organization are paramount for getting and trusting self and others on board to one's duty (or task) toward getting the mission done. Knowing one's why aids in seeing an approach to the future or end state of the mission and visioning success. Knowing the "why" helps translate one's character and duty with trust into action through words, ideas, and influence.
2 Clarity of purpose critical for leadership (duty and mission)
Many participants emphasized the significance of having clear objectives and mission-type orders. They found that clarity of purpose was fundamental in guiding their actions and decisions as leaders. The structure of the courses, where expectations and outcomes were explicitly communicated, greatly contributed to their understanding and focus.
Establishing and communicating a clear purpose was highlighted as crucial for leadership. Participants noted that understanding and articulating their mission, vision, and values helped them guide their teams more effectively and ensure that everyone was working toward the same goals.
3 Communication is a leader skill (character, duty, and mission)
Communication was a key focus, with many participants highlighting the improvement of their own communication skills as a crucial outcome of the course. This internal process is best captured as a person's character and to the extent each person internally understands their own mental and moral qualities as leaders. Practical exercises and scenarios were particularly effective in enhancing their ability to communicate effectively as leaders. Clear communication was repeatedly emphasized as a critical skill for leaders whether in the classroom or field environment conducting MCEs. Participants appreciated learning how to effectively communicate their vision and goals, which is essential for aligning their team's efforts with organizational objectives and achieving mission success.
4 Mission command mindset (duty, trust, and mission)
Having the right mission command mindset matters, which goes for both leaders and followers, as well as supporting the leader and group

to successfully accomplish the mission. Understanding the elements of mission command includes people and warrior-minded leaders of character, doing their duty (task) and being able to take a team (unit) that trusts each other and accomplish their assigned mission under challenging conditions of change and different environments.

5 Creativity, flexibility, and adaptability (mission and people/trust)
The interaction of the people with creativity that trust each other to adapt to the situation and environment was critical toward accomplishing the mission. The courses taught creativity, innovation, and new ways of thinking.

6 Practical application (duty and mission)
The emphasis on leader communication extended to practical applications, such as how to communicate values, expectations, and feedback within a team, all seen as doing one's duty. The courses provided opportunities for participants to practice these skills in realistic scenarios, e.g., mission command, clarity of purpose, and mission command exercises.

7 Peer interaction (team/trust and mission)
Peer-to-peer communication was also highlighted as a critical component. Participants valued the opportunity to hear different perspectives and learn from each other's experiences, which enriched their understanding and ability to communicate effectively in diverse situations, and to identify as a leader involved a relationship with others, peers, and followers. Teamwork was integral in bringing together diverse groups and strengthening bonds. The group exercises/events fostered inclusion, unity, camaraderie, and a "family" feeling and mentality largely due to trust in self and shared among others.

8 Leadership development and modeling the way (character and team/trust)
Participants noted that clarity of purpose and MCEs helped them in developing a coherent leadership philosophy. This included crafting personal missions and vision statements and understanding how to align their team's goals with organizational objectives, particularly during mission execution events. Having a role model and modeling the way for others were key elements of leadership and developing leadership capacity. Participants wanted to see shared values and principles represented in each other, which helped build trust in the team/unit.

The four-part framework

The four-part framework for communicating mission command, depicted in Figure 19.2, evolved from the findings, particularly the four concepts of character, duty, trust, and mission. Those concepts manifested via the

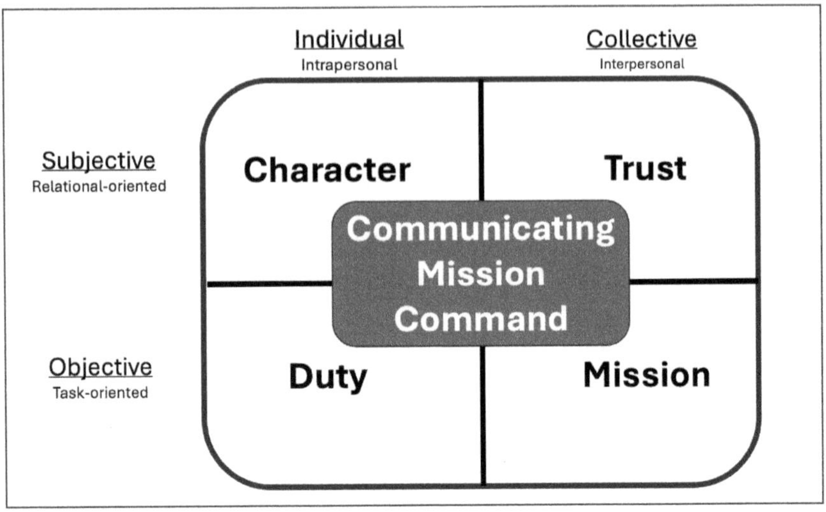

FIGURE 19.2 Four-part framework for communicating mission command

relational-discursive nature of how people (leaders and followers) communicated the concepts in their leadership roles. There exist four relationships:

- Internal individual subjective relationship with self (character)
- Internal individual objective relationship to task (duty)
- External collective subjective relationship with people (trust)
- External collective objective relationship to task (mission)

The four-part framework can be seen in how the concept of mission command is communicated internally and externally. An individual uses intrapersonal communication to understand the subjective, relational-oriented concept of Character and the objective, task-oriented concept of Duty. A unit, or collection of people, uses interpersonal communication to understand the subjective, relational-oriented concept of Trust and the objective, task-oriented concept of Mission.

Participants understood "character" as the manifestation of the internal and intersecting relationship of self and task via the relational self in intrapersonal communication with the discursive self in what people feel they need to do as their duty. The participants expressed the need and expectation to be the example of "character" through one's "duty" as much as they wanted and needed "the example to follow" of the right character and duty of others. In terms of the collective manifestation of people and tasks, participants expressed those external elements as having "trust" in each other to accomplish the "mission" via inter-relational discursive and interpersonal communication among self and others.

The framework bridges communication and leadership theories that help frame a holistic understanding of mission command as a leader-communication-centric concept (Shamir, 2011; Vandergriff, 2019; Vandergriff & Webber, 2017). The mission command attributes of character, cohesion, competence, capacity, and capability are expressed in how individuals and units exercise their duty to the mission, which aligns with the mission command culture, particularly building teams through mutual trust, expressed in joint military and USAF doctrine (Joint Chiefs of Staff [JCS], 2011; US Air Force [USAF], 2024) and reinforced in previous literature (Leistenschneider, 2002; Moltke, 1911; Shamir, 2011; Vandergriff, 2019; Vandergriff & Webber, 2017).

How someone communicates internally, or intrapersonal communication, now adds an element previously not discussed in relation to mission command or was otherwise subordinated in the literature to relationship with others within an organization (Dillard et al., 1999; Gale, 2010). Additionally, both internal elements of character and duty and external elements of trust and mission are now shown to be at greater play. They are integrated with the mission command systems of relationship that are connected to one's internal obligation or sense of duty with shared trust to achieve a collective mission (Coleman, 2009; Duncan, 2022; Ekman, 2023; Rogers, 2008). Hence, this four-part framework approaches communicating mission command as the manifestation of how people understand their own character and the character of others, and how they communicate and put into practice their duty as a unit of people who trust each other in achieving a mission, thus including both the internal and external communication practices with oneself and others (Malik, 2019; Tourish, 2016; Uhl-Bien, 2006). This reimagined framing of communicating mission command addresses some of the concerns expressed in the literature (Clifton, 2012; Fratila, 2022; Kernic et al., 2023). Additionally, this new framework adeptly shows a more expansive inclusion of intrapersonal communication with self and relationship with self that are needed to understand how leaders communicate mission command to their trusted individual subordinates and the larger unit or organization at the collective level. Duty and trust are the expressions of individuals and people who do their duty and accomplish their mission.

Mission command is now understood via the discursive and relational communicative elements embodied and expressed between people with emphasis on knowing their personal why and organizational why, having a shared clarity of purpose, with a mission command and warrior mindset, founded upon trust with self and trust with others, which includes creativity, flexibility, adaptability, and modeling the way.

Conclusion

With nearly 1,000 data points, the analysis of two programs focused on leader development provided a clear path to creating a new framework for understanding how leaders communicate mission command. The results are limited to the two programs and the USAF, yet have strong implications for both theory and practice: the inclusion of the discursive self and the intrapersonal self along with the duality of the internal and external relational elements at the individual and collective levels improve and deepen our understanding of how leaders communicate mission command to themselves and others.

This chapter showed the methodological development of the four-part framework called communicating mission command. Based on concerns, gaps, and limitations in the literature; how mission command is understood; and how leaders communicate mission command, data were collected from two military programs (n = 9,747). The collective voice of the participants showed the evolution from quotes, categorization, and thematic analysis that produced four constructs of character, duty, trust, and mission that comprise the four-part framework. It is through the manifestation (discursive and relational interactions of words and actions) of the internal relationships of people and tasks that character is enacted via one's duty. It is through the manifestation (discursive and relational interactions of words and actions) of the external relationships of the collective identity of people or unit who live and share trust with each other that mission is achieved. Duty can only be done with character. Mission can only be accomplished with trust. Leaders communicate mission command via their discursive and relational interactions that bring to life the four constructs of mission command: character, duty, trust, and mission.

Suggestions for further reading

Barge, J., & Little, M. (2008). A discursive approach to skillful activity. *Communication Theory*, *18*(4), 505–534, https://doi.org/10.1111/j.1468-2885.2008.00332.x

Brower, H. H., Schoorman, F. D., & Tan, H. H. (2000). A model of relational leadership: The integration of trust and leader–member exchange. *The Leadership Quarterly*, *11*(2), 227–250. https://doi.org/10.1016/S1048-9843(00)00040-0

Graen, G. B., & Uhl-Bien, M. (1995). Relationship-based approach to leadership: Development of leader-member exchange (LMX) theory of leadership over 25 years: Applying a multi-level, multi-domain perspective. *The Leadership Quarterly*, 6(2), 219–247. https://psycnet.apa.org/doi/10.1016/1048-9843(95)90036-5

Uhl-Bien, M. (2006). Relational leadership theory: Exploring the social processes of leadership and organizing. *The Leadership Quarterly*, *17*(6), 654–676. https://doi.org/10.1016/j.leaqua.2006.10.007

US Joint Chiefs of Staff (JCS). (January 2020). *JCS focus paper on mission command, insights and best practices focus paper*, Second Edition. https://www.jcs.mil/Portals/36/Documents/Doctrine/fp/missioncommand_fp_2nd_ed.pdf

Questions for discussion

1 What does "mission command" mean to you?
2 Is there a difference in how mission command is communicated in non-military environments, e.g., higher education, nonprofit, or for profit organizations?
3 What is the follower's role in communicating and exercising mission command?
4 Which of the four elements of mission command (character, duty, trust, and mission) could be replaced with a different word that would convey a similar meaning?
5 To what extent can mission command still be communicated without one of the four elements?
6 Where in your life do you see others communicating mission command?

Note

1 The data were collected from a larger study that was granted exemption by USAF IRB FWR20190084N with a determination of NHSR, Not Human Subjects Research.

References

Air University. (n.d.). *Leader development course for squadron command*. https://www.airuniversity.af.edu/Eaker-Center/CPDS/LDC/

Alvesson, M. (1996). Leadership studies: From procedure and abstraction to reflexivity and situation. *Leadership Quarterly*, *7*, 455–485. https://doi.org/10.1016/S1048-9843(96)90002-8

Barge, J., & Little, M. (2008). A discursive approach to skillful activity. *Communication Theory*, *18*(4), 505–534. https://doi.org/10.1111/j.1468-2885.2008.00332.x

Brower, H. H., Schoorman, F. D., & Tan, H. H. (2000). A model of relational leadership: The integration of trust and leader–member exchange. *The Leadership Quarterly*, *11*(2), 227–250. https://doi.org/10.1016/S1048-9843(00)00040-0

Bylund, C.L., Peterson, E. B., & Cameron, K. A. (2012). A practitioner's guide to interpersonal communication theory: An overview and exploration of selected theories. *Patient Education and Counseling*, *87*(3), 261–267. https://doi.org/10.1016/j.pec.2011.10.006

Chaleff, I. (2009). *The courageous follower: Standing up to and for our leaders*. Berrett-Koehler Publishers.

Chaleff, I. (2015). *Intelligent disobedience: Doing right when what you're told to do is wrong*. Berrett-Koehler Publishers.
Clifton, J. (2012). A discursive approach to leadership: Doing assessments and managing organizational meanings. *International Journal of Business Communication*, *49*(2). https://doi.org/10.1177/0021943612437762
Coleman, S. (2009). The problems of duty and loyalty. *Journal of Military Ethics*, *8*(2), 105–115. https://doi.org/10.1080/15027570903037892
Dansereau, F., Graen, G. B., & Haga, W. J. (1975). A vertical dyad linkage approach to leadership in formal organizations. *Organizational Behavior and Human Performance*, *13*, 46–78. http://dx.doi.org/10.1016/0030-5073(75)90005-7
Dillard, J. P., Solomon, D. H., & Palmer, M. T. (1999). Structuring the concept of relational communication. *Communications Monographs*, *66*(1), 49–65. https://psycnet.apa.org/doi/10.1080/03637759909376462
Duncan, C. J. (2022). Duty should not be an Army value, *Military Review*, 110–119. https://www.armyupress.army.mil/Portals/7/military-review/Archives/English/SO-22/Duncan/Duncan-2022-UA-v1.pdf
Ekman, L. (2023). Military duty during mission deployment: Exploring local relations and dynamics of cohesion—The case of Swedish troops. *Armed Forces & Society*, *50*(4), 1–25. https://doi.org/10.1177/0095327X231160424
Fairhurst, G. T. (2008). Discursive leadership: A communication alternative to leadership psychology. *Management Communication Quarterly*, *21*(4), 510–521. https://doi.org/10.1177/0893318907313714
Fratila, C.-B. (2022). On the power of language in military leadership. *Land Forces Academy Review*, *XXVII*(2), 106. https://doi.org/10.2478/raft-2022-0015
Gale, J. (2010). Discursive analysis: A research approach for studying the moment-to-moment construction of meaning in systemic practice. *Human Systems: The Journal of Therapy, Consultation & Training*, *21*(2), 7–37. https://www.taosinstitute.net/files/Content/5693709/Jerry_Gale_-discursive_analysis_paper_for_human_systems.pdf
Graen, G. B., & Cashman, J. F. (1975). A role-making model of leadership in formal organizations: A developmental approach. In J. G. Hunt, & L. L. Larson (Eds.), *Leadership frontiers* (pp. 143–166). Kent State University Press.
Graen, G. B., & Uhl-Bien, M. (1995). Relationship-based approach to leadership: Development of leader-member exchange (LMX) theory of leadership over 25 years: Applying a multi-level, multi-domain perspective. *The Leadership Quarterly*, *6*(2), 219–247. https://psycnet.apa.org/doi/10.1016/1048-9843(95)90036-5
Hinck R., & Hinck J. (2023). Strength through vulnerability: The role of trust formation in leader development programs. *Journal of Military Conflict Transformation*, *4*(1), 45–63. https://original-ufdc.uflib.ufl.edu/AA00086412/00005
Hooper, D. T., & Martin, R. (2008). Beyond personal leader–member exchange (LMX) quality: The effects of perceived LMX variability on employee reactions. *The Leadership Quarterly*, *19*(1), 20–30. https://doi.org/10.1016/j.leaqua.2007.12.002
Hunt, J. G., & Dodge, G. E. (2000). Leadership déjà vu all over again. *The Leadership Quarterly*, *11*(4), 435–458. https://doi.org/10.1016/S1048-9843(00)00058-8
Joint Chiefs of Staff (JCS). (2011). *Joint publication (JP) 3–0, joint operations*. https://www.jcs.mil/doctrine/joint-doctrine-pubs/3-0-operations-series/
Kernic, F., Elbe, M., & Richter, G. (2023). Military leadership: Concepts and theoretical approaches. In A. M. Sookermany (Ed.), *Handbook of military sciences* (pp. 1–22). Springer.

Leistenschneider, S. (2002). *Auftragstaktik im preußisch-deutschen Heer 1871 bis 1914* [Auftragstaktik in the Prussian-German army from 1871 to 1914]. E.S. Mittler & Sohn.
Malik, D. D. (2019). Leadership communication: Three model approaches. *Advances in Social Science, Education and Humanities Research*, *307*, 409–422. http://dx.doi.org/10.2991/sores-18.2019.95
Moltke, H. K. B. (1911). *Extracts from Moltke's military correspondence pertaining to the war of 1870–71* (H. Bell, Trans.). Fort Leavenworth Kansas Army Service. https://archive.org/details/extractsfrommolt00molt/page/n5/mode/2up
Ospina, S. M., Foldy, E. G., Fairhurst, G. T., & Jackson, B. (2020). Collective dimensions of leadership: Connecting theory and method. *Human Relations*, *73*(4), 441–463. https://doi.org/10.1177/0018726719899714
Parks, M. R. (1977). Relational communication: Theory and research. *Human Communication Research*, *3*(4), 372–381. https://doi.org/10.1111/j.1468-2958.1977.tb00541.x
Riggio, R. E., Chaleff, I., & Lipman-Blumen, J. L. (Eds.). (2008). *The art of followership: How great followers create great leaders and organizations*. Jossey-Bass.
Rogers, E. (2008). Relational communication theory. In L. A. Baxter, & D. O. Braithwaite (Eds.), *Engaging theories in interpersonal communication: Multiple perspectives* (pp. 335–347). Sage. https://doi.org/10.4135/9781483329529
Shamir, E. (2011). *Transforming command-The pursuit of mission command in the US, British, and Israeli armies*. Stanford University Press.
Tourish, D. (2016). Leadership from a communication perspective. In *Oxford research encyclopedia of communication*. Oxford Research Encyclopedias. https://oxfordre.com/communication/view/10.1093/acrefore/9780190228613.001.0001/acrefore-9780190228613-e-13.
Uhl-Bien, M. (2006). Relational leadership theory: Exploring the social processes of leadership and organizing. *The Leadership Quarterly*, *17*(6), 654–676. https://doi.org/10.1016/j.leaqua.2006.10.007
Uhl-Bien, M. (2011). Relational leadership theory: Exploring the social processes of leadership and organizing. In W. P. Painter, & M. Morland (Eds.), *Leadership, gender, and organization. Issues in business ethics* (pp. 65–74). Springer.
Uhl-Bien, M., Riggio, R. E., Lowe, K. B., & Carsten, M. K. (2014). Followership theory: A review and research agenda. *The Leadership Quarterly*, *25*(1), 83–104. https://doi.org/10.1016/j.leaqua.2013.11.007
US Joint Chiefs of Staff (JCS). (January 2020). *JCS focus paper on mission command, insights and best practices focus paper*, Second Edition. https://www.jcs.mil/Portals/36/Documents/Doctrine/fp/missioncommand_fp_2nd_ed.pdf
US Air Force (USAF). (August 2023). *Air Force doctrine publication 1–1, mission command*. https://www.doctrine.af.mil/Portals/61/documents/AFDP_1-1/AFDP%201-1%20Mission%20Command.pdf
US Air Force (USAF). (April 2024). *Air Force doctrine publication 1–2, leading airmen* [Unpublished manuscript].
US Air Force Officer Training School (USAF OTS). (n.d.). *Air Force Officer Training School*. U.S. Air Force. https://www.airforce.com/training/military-training/ots
Vandergriff, D. E. (2019). *Adopting mission command: Developing leaders for superior command culture*. Naval Institute Press.
Vandergriff, D. E., & Webber, S. (Eds.). (2017). *Mission command: The who, what, where, when, and why, an anthology*. CreateSpace Independent Publishing Platform.

20

AUTHENTICITY IN LEADERSHIP COMMUNICATION

Storytelling and Mission-Driven Messaging as Pedagogical Tools

Jacy King Gross

Effective communication is essential for leadership, yet few teaching strategies address present-day communication challenges. Competing for attention in media-saturated environments such as Zoom, TikTok, media interviews, and YouTube requires a skill set that differs from conventional public speaking. Digital audiences have short attention spans and are conditioned to receive information in small, succinct packages. The competition for attention in this media-soaked environment necessitates a paradigm shift in how we approach pedagogy and training in this domain. Modern communication demands a curated presence, a clear vision, and most importantly, authentic, personal messages.

Leaders face similar challenges. For example, artificial intelligence provides the workforce with instant access to information, requiring leaders to evolve in their leadership skills. No longer tasked with having all the answers, leaders must exhibit new qualities to inspire employee support. Leaders are also increasingly pressured to make choices that appease shareholders and offer short-term results (George, 2003). These short-term gains come at a cost, and it is usually felt by the employees. Both the organization and its leaders can experience entropy—the steady disintegration from within—causing a lack of trust in all parties (George, 2003). Rebuilding trust and relationships within organizations is the basis of authentic leadership.

This chapter explores the idea of authenticity and its increasingly important role in today's communication environment. I examine what it means to be authentic, the theoretical foundations of authentic communication and leadership, and pedagogical techniques leaders can use to incorporate authenticity into their communication and leadership styles.

DOI: 10.4324/9781003563662-24

Authentic communication tools allow learners to develop their own speaking and leading style, oftentimes breaking away from traditional practices mainly used by the dominant group. The idea of authenticity—knowing who we are, what we believe, and how we express these beliefs—is the backbone to creating communication practices and leadership styles that build trust. Learners are encouraged to develop communication tools that may be different from the norm but just as effective for contemporary communication and leadership.

I have chosen to focus on two communication elements that support the development of authentic leadership: storytelling and mission-driven messaging. These elements offer modern-day extensions of classical communication theory, providing relevant and impactful ways to connect more deeply with audiences in both physical and digital spaces.

Storytelling is a timeless tool that transcends cultures and disciplines—it allows leaders to share their values and experiences in ways that humanize their message and build emotional resonance. In many cases, a well-told personal story can cut through hierarchy and formality, creating stronger trust and clarity than traditional speech formats. It's also deeply aligned with authenticity, giving learners permission to share personal truth rather than mimic a "perfect" or traditional style of speaking.

I introduce mission-driven messaging (i.e., a "mission statement") not as a corporate marketing tool, but as a way for individuals to align their public expression with their values, vision, and purpose. It encourages learners to think critically about how they are perceived and how to align their messaging—visually, verbally, and behaviorally—with their core values. Rather than teaching learners to fit a mold, this chapter invites them to shape and share their own leadership identity in a way that is both strategic and personal.

Definitions

Defining authentic communication

The concept of authenticity is rooted in Greek philosophy with the saying "To thine own self be true" (Shakespeare, n.d., Act 1, Scene 3, Line 78). Self-exploration plays a vital role in the defining of "self." In order to communicate in a genuine way, one must first identify their own thoughts, emotions, beliefs, needs, and wants. For authentic communication to happen, one must then *act* in a way that is in accordance with those parameters. Authenticity is fundamental to the human experience because it enables us to build relationships with others out of similarities, interests, and most importantly, trust (Bull & Ebben, 2023).

The definition of authenticity can be hard to pin down. It usually involves self-reflection and ethical consideration, but authenticity is also ideologically driven and context dependent (Ebster, 2004). Maslow (1971) describes an authentic person as someone who is "in tune" with oneself. Psychologist Harter (2015) refers to owning one's personal experiences and then acting in a way that is consistent with those inner thoughts and feelings. A person who can accurately see themselves is less influenced by others' expectations of them and can therefore make clearer personal choices. In social media, for example, influencers and content creators take on a "face" that is edited and socially constructed. Knowing that editing tools and filters enable content manipulation and uniformity, it's understandable why audiences are drawn to honesty and genuine connections. Audiences aim to differentiate between influencers who exploit their attention and those who sincerely and authentically share their opinions and content.

Defining authentic leadership

A recent Gallup poll demonstrates how employee engagement in the U.S. has dropped to its lowest level in more than a decade (Harter, 2024). Employees report feeling less connected to their organization's purpose (George, 2003). Corruption scandals among top financial executives, criminal convictions of political leaders, and the dissemination of fake news on social media underscore why the public may seek alternative leadership styles. Business leaders must consider whether to redirect their focus from maximizing the physical and monetary output of their employees to actively engaging their employees' minds and hearts. The autocratic or directive leaders often can no longer keep up with the wealth of information available to those for whom they lead and do not blend with the increasing need for innovative employees (George, 2003). Authentic leadership has emerged as a way to navigate and unite an independent workforce.

There are many definitions of authentic leaders, but common themes focus around developing a personal leadership style that is consistent with a leader's vision and ethics, plus a genuine desire to serve others through leadership (Owolabi, 2020). Organizational behavior scholars Eilam and Shamir (2005) posit four characteristics of authentic leaders:

1 Leaders are true to themselves and do not conform to the expectations or pressures of others (they do not "fake" leadership skills).
2 Authentic leaders are motivated by personal convictions, rather than honors, status, or monetary compensations (e.g., shareholder reports).

3 Authentic leaders lead from their own point of view. Their self-knowledge is developed through continued self-reflection of their own experiences and narratives (originals, not copies).
4 Authentic leaders' actions are based on these personally developed values and narratives.

Leadership scholar George (2007) expands on this description by explaining that authentic leaders exhibit a passion for their purpose and consistently practice their values openly. Authentic leaders inspire others by example. They also work to establish long-term meaningful relationships with their employees and incorporate employee mental health and welfare as an integral part of company growth.

Authentic leadership can provide an answer to organizations looking for enhanced employee engagement, sustainable company performance, an environment that fosters employee innovation, and an overall more ethical work climate.

Theoretical foundations

Theoretical foundations provide a deeper understanding of the relationship between authentic communication and leadership. While communication theory offers insight into how messages are crafted, delivered, and received, leadership theory guides leaders in using those messages to inspire, connect with, and support their followers. This section explores how three specific theories—Classical Rhetoric, Narrative Paradigm, and Authentic Leadership Theory—intersect to form a strong foundation for effective, human-centered leadership.

Classical Rhetoric

Classical Rhetoric (Griffin et al., 2015) is rooted in the teachings of ancient Greek and Roman philosophers. As one of the oldest communication theories, it offers a foundational framework for persuasive speaking and writing. At its core, Classical Rhetoric is about understanding how to influence and move an audience through the strategic use of language, structure, and appeals. Aristotle's model, the most influential within this tradition, introduces three core persuasive appeals:

Ethos refers to the credibility or ethical character of the speaker. It involves building trust and establishing authority with the audience. A speaker with strong ethos is perceived as knowledgeable, honest, and reliable. In authentic leadership, ethos is essential—trust and credibility form the basis of effective influence. Personal stories can be a powerful tool for building ethos, as they reveal a leader's values, experiences, and integrity. By sharing meaningful narratives, leaders can foster trust and deepen their connection with followers. Ethos is especially important in digital mediums, where audiences are unlikely to engage with content they perceive as lacking credibility. Therefore, learning techniques to strengthen ethos in online communication is essential for contemporary leadership.

Pathos is the emotional appeal, focusing on creating an emotional connection with the audience. Through tone, storytelling, and vivid language, speakers can evoke feelings that inspire listeners to care, believe, or act. Vulnerability—a hallmark of authentic leadership—is expressed through pathos. Leaders who share personal challenges or heartfelt experiences invite empathy and trust, making their messages more impactful.

Logos is the logical appeal, relying on reasoning, evidence, and structure to persuade. Logos involves presenting clear arguments, relevant data, and sound logic to support a message. In authentic leadership, logos helps convey intentionality and competence. A well-articulated mission statement shows that a leader has thought deeply about their values and direction. This clarity not only builds trust but also signals a grounded sense of purpose and integrity.

Ultimately, Classical Rhetoric offers enduring communication frameworks that enhance the clarity and effectiveness of contemporary messages.

Narrative paradigm

Walter Fisher (1989), a philosopher and communication theorist, blends philosophy, storytelling, and public discourse to form his Narrative Paradigm. He proposes that humans are natural storytellers and that all meaningful communication happens through narrative, rather than solely through logical arguments. From Fisher's perspective, values are central to every story, and elements such as style and aesthetics influence how audiences judge a story's truth—not just logic. In contrast to classical philosophers, who believed that communication expertise must be cultivated through study and practice, Fisher argues that effective storytelling is an innate human capability, accessible to all rather than reserved for trained experts. This perspective parallels the principles of authentic leadership, which emphasize that leadership style should not be imitated but should instead emerge from personal reflection and genuine discourse.

Fisher (1989) proposes that we evaluate stories using narrative rationality, which consists of two key components: narrative coherence and narrative fidelity. Narrative coherence asks whether a story makes sense structurally—does it "hang together"? Narrative fidelity asks whether a story "rings true"—does it align with the audience's values and lived experiences? Fidelity is judged through five questions: (1) What values are embedded in the message? (2) Are those values relevant to the decisions at hand? (3) What are the consequences of following those values? (4) Do they align with the worldview of the audience? (5) Do they reflect what the audience believes is an "ideal basis for conduct"?

Storytelling is a powerful way for leaders to show vulnerability and authenticity without the need to logically dissect their emotions. Narrative Paradigm is particularly useful for leaders developing stories that build trust. By following Fisher's framework, anyone can become a compelling storyteller and a more authentic communicator.

Authentic leadership

While authentic leadership is grounded in research and theory, it is often not labeled as such in practice because it emphasizes lived experience, personal growth, and practical application over abstract frameworks. Rather than prescribing specific behaviors, it encourages leaders to reflect on their values and act with integrity, making authentic leadership feel more like a mindset or philosophy than a traditional leadership theory. Bill George (2003) is considered a pioneer in the development of Authentic Leadership Theory. His Authentic Leadership Model has played a significant role in shaping the modern understanding of authentic leadership.

Authentic Leadership Model

George's (2003) model is used as a map for leaders who want to incorporate purpose and principle into their leadership style. George prioritizes a leader's ethics and values, demonstrating their purpose and leading with empathy and compassion toward those they lead. He argues that a leader who leads with self-awareness, integrity, and consistent, clear values, provides a company with security and transparency, creating long-term positive growth environments both for the company and its shareholders.

George (2003) lays out five key dimensions to developing a personal leadership style. (1) Purpose—Having a clear sense of meaning behind your leadership. Why are you leading? What impact do you want to have? (2) Values—Staying true to your deeply held beliefs and principles, even under pressure. (3) Relationships—Building strong, genuine relationships with others based on trust and openness. (4) Self-Discipline—Staying focused, responsible, and consistent in your actions. (5) Heart—Leading with compassion and empathy, caring about the people you serve.

Leaders can use George's dimensions to shape their personal mission statement, fostering transparency and providing clear direction for their leadership style.

The praxiological combination of communication and leadership

Building on these theoretical foundations, the next step is to explore practical tools and strategies for applying these insights. Understanding the theories is just the beginning—leaders must also possess the skills to effectively communicate their messages in ways that resonate with and inspire their followers. The next section will focus on actionable techniques that can help leaders refine their communication practices and implement the principles of authentic communication in everyday leadership.

Pedagogical approaches to teaching authenticity

The personal nature of authenticity requires critical, action-based pedagogy. Learner-leaders (hereafter "learners") must be introduced to exercises that encourage self-discovery. In order to lead effectively, learners must first hone their authentic communication tools. This section provides action-based exercises in storytelling and mission-driven messaging. Learners can engage in these activities through various formats: classroom settings, in-person group training (outside of classroom settings), online asynchronous environments, or independently.

In-person group instruction is ideal for confident speakers who excel in traditional settings. In contrast, asynchronous, or independent self-recorded exercises at home can benefit shy learners, non-native speakers, or those with disabilities, offering them a comfortable environment to find their authentic voice. This setting also facilitates written discussions, as learners have time to prepare their comments. Additionally, closed captioning enhances comprehension for all participants. Asynchronous learners contribute to group presentations by recording and posting their presentations, allowing other members of the group to view and comment at their convenience.

Solo learners participate independently. Although they miss the opportunity for peer feedback, the simple act of pressing record on a camera or phone holds accountability and offers an excellent environment to learn and practice communication skills, whether in front of a group or alone.

Storytelling

Crafting personal stories provides a meaningful way to discover authentic communication narratives and learner perspectives. Everyone has a story to tell, and humans are natural communicators (Fisher, 1989). Through stories, learners practice speaking skills using self-created, familiar content, which makes it easier to uncover their natural communication style. Self-generated stories build confidence and help learners discover who they are and what they believe. In group settings, learners also benefit from each other's experiences and perspectives. These shared stories instill a sense of belonging, further enhancing a learner's security and confidence.

Story also plays a large part in dominant communication styles. Those in power have the means to control the stories told and the communication style with which they are presented (Adichie, 2009). Cultivating personal stories offers diverse communication experiences, changing the way learners view communication. Film director Peele (Giroux, 2017) talks about the power of story to change trenchant sociopolitical ideals. Peele describes how "we can discuss race all day long, but if you see a movie that successfully puts yourself in the shoes of somebody different than yourself, you see the world differently" (Giroux, 2017, p. 20). As both dominant and non-dominant groups gain a better understanding of their own communication styles and are exposed to others who communicate differently, dominant styles are softened and non-dominant styles are introduced with ease. The norm changes, and learners are further supported in their authenticity.

Using Bloom's Flipped Taxonomy for storytelling

Bloom's Flipped Taxonomy (Figure 20.1) is a pedagogical teaching structure that offers a solid instructional framework while encouraging innovation and personal reflection (Bergmann & Sams, 2012). By starting with a "creation," learners use communication styles and instincts they already possess and are unique to each learner. Working down the pyramid, learners use observation and reflection ("evaluation") to build on their skills, applying what they have observed to enhance their own authentic style. During the "analyze" step, learners study directive information available on performance and public speaking. This varies from the traditional public speaking curriculum, where established speaking practices are studied first and put into action last, often supporting the communication style of the dominant group and stifling non-dominant communication instincts. Learners then "apply" the knowledge they have gained by creating their own outline or toolkit for future communications. They conclude with a

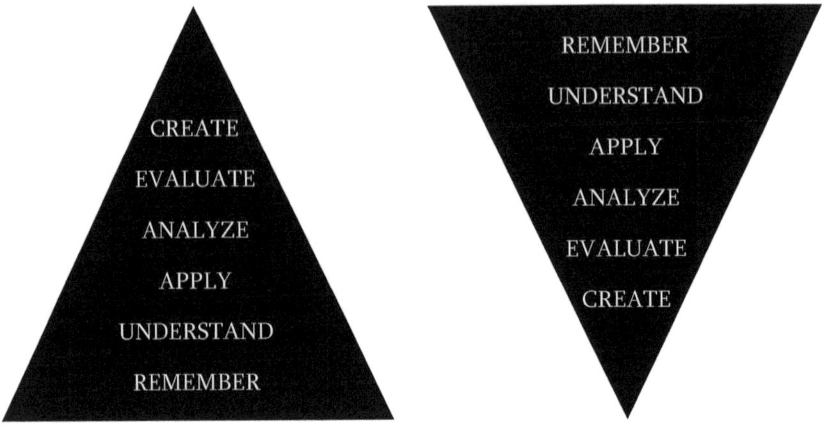

Bloom's Taxonomy   Bloom's Flipped Taxonomy

FIGURE 20.1 Flipping Bloom's Taxonomy for active learning

Source: Adapted from *Flip your classroom: Reaching every student in every class every day* (Bergmann & Sams, 2012)

final reflection to demonstrate their "understanding" of their authentic communication process and how they will use these tools in future assignments. This reflection solidifies their skills and helps them "remember" how to act in future communications, building their communication toolbox. This presentation-first, action-based learning is particularly effective for non-English speakers, speakers with disabilities, or any speaker from a non-dominant communication group with differing yet effective communication styles and instincts.

The following section contains specific examples of how this flipped taxonomy can be used to teach authentic communication.

Create

Beginning with the "create" level of the flipped taxonomy, the story assignment parameters are purposefully vague. This freedom encourages personal creativity and authenticity. Learners are encouraged to share a story about a significant event that has affected them in some way. A time limit (90 seconds to 3 minutes) gives a secure parameter to the assignment without stifling instinct or directing narrative. It also encourages practice. Even if learners are presenting to a group, they are advised to record their stories when they practice to establish a time measurement and begin the process of practice and observation.

EXAMPLE STORYTELLING "CREATE" ASSIGNMENT

Come up with a personal story to share with the group about a significant event in your life that affected you in some way.

- NO PRESSURE! This first story is just a chance for us to get to know each other and to see what works when we are communicating with others.
- The story needs to be at least 90 seconds but no more than 3 minutes. A period of 90 seconds is SHORT! Record yourself so you can get a sense of time.

Evaluate

After each learner shares their story, the group reflects on each presentation by sharing positive written comments with each presenter. (If the session is live, comments are written and submitted in person. If it is asynchronous, comments are written in the viewer's own time. Independent learners watch themselves and record comments as if they are viewers.) Written, versus verbal, comments encourage specificity and comprehension. The social activist Bordas (2007) describes a "we" culture where leadership and self-betterment do not come at a cost to others. As learners work together to better understand each other through these positive evaluations, this group learning is meant to strengthen the "we" culture. Learners realize their own public speaking strengths through the recognition of those strengths in others. Independent learners miss the opportunity for this group learning but can still identify their own effective communication strategies by reviewing and commenting on their own performances.

EXAMPLE "EVALUATE" PROMPT

Watch and comment on each presentation. We can each quickly identify our own negatives, so comments should concentrate on the presenter's positive communication attributes. The focus, as you watch each other, is to see what works and replicate those working elements. What effective tools did the speaker use to tell their story? What physical attributes worked? Did you like the organization of their material? Did they have good vocal inflection? Did they have natural body language? Write at least three positive comments for each presenter.

Analyze

The "analyze" component is where learners are finally introduced to established best practices and guidelines for public speaking. At this point, learners should have a good idea of their strengths, their authentic communication instincts, and where they would like to improve. This "analyze" step happens only after they have already recognized elements that are successful within their own speaking styles, particularly because they have received positive comments from their peers in the previous "evaluate" step. In the "analyze" step, then, the instructional material enhances communication rather than prescribes or directs. Showcasing a variety of learning sources, including traditional written instruction as well as videos and blog posts, appeals to different types of learners. Each information source offers guidelines in an alternative format. The variety of instruction is essential for continuing to cultivate diverse authentic communication tools.

A few specific examples of sources to ground this module are listed as follows, however, there is an enormous amount of public speaking instructional material available that can be catered to individual learning situations. An introduction to traditional written instruction, such as Aristotle's *The Rhetoric* (Griffin et al., 2015), offers solid historical rhetorical grounding. Duarte's (2011) *The Secret Structure of Great Talks* [Video] offers a more modern take on storytelling. Light-hearted YouTube videos, including *How to Organize and Structure a Presentation* (Ramanathan, 2019), aim to alleviate intimidation and spark creativity. Hasan's (2023) *Win Every Argument: The Art of Debating, Persuading, and Public Speaking* offers more perspectives on basic public speaking principles. Finally, Cutrara's (2019) article *If You Want to Write a Great Speech, Here's How to Do It* gives specific speech outline instructions.

Apply

During the "apply" level, learners are encouraged to merge the knowledge they have gained from the presentations, the various instructional resources, and their own personal observations. Assimilating the pieces of information they find most helpful, they then develop a personalized public speaking outline or storytelling blueprint that leverages their unique communication strengths. Moving beyond simply reading or observing, this exercise requires learners to select and apply concepts in a practical manner, resulting in the creation of an authentic communication tool for future use.

EXAMPLE "APPLY" PROMPT

Taking into account the presentations you watched this week, the comments from your peers, and the readings and video, think about your own speaking style. Develop a public speaking outline or storytelling blueprint based on your own communication strengths and weaknesses to use for future presentations.

Understand

The "understand" level offers students a chance to engage in reflective journaling. Learners are encouraged to identify the positive traits they have demonstrated when presenting in front of others, and critically evaluate areas where they would like to improve. Reflective journaling facilitates a deeper understanding of a learner's current abilities and challenges, fosters self-awareness, encourages authenticity, and lays the groundwork for targeted skill development in continued communication.

EXAMPLE "UNDERSTAND" PROMPT

Journal entry: Taking into account the presentations you watched this week, the comments from your peers, and the readings and video, reflect on your own personal public speaking strengths and weaknesses. What are the three positive traits you already exhibit when speaking in front of people? What are some ways in which you feel you can improve?

Remember

The "remember" stage asks learners to either revise their original story using the new parameters they have discovered, or move on to a new presentation activity where they can implement their new communication tools. Learners will also continue to refine their outlines and maintain a reflective journal as they participate in more presentations and speaking exercises. By consistently updating their tools, learners ensure they retain and refine their authentic communication style. Recalling and documenting details over time support ongoing learning, build confidence, and emphasize the growth in their public speaking skills.

Storytelling applied to authentic leadership

Authentic leaders can use storytelling as a tool to connect with and inspire others. When leaders share personal experiences in relatable and compelling ways, these stories humanize the leader, exposing vulnerabilities and strengths. This authenticity builds trust among those they lead. Through stories, leaders can also convey their values, vision, or purpose in a way that is engaging and memorable. This approach not only has the power to motivate and empower followers but also reinforces a leader's core beliefs and principles. Owolabi (2020) writes, "Leaders are, by default, story tellers. They tell stories of potential and possibility. They tell stories to motivate people to create the future. They help people interpret the past and move forward" (p. 70).

Dr. Martin Luther King Jr. (1963) was a masterful storyteller. In his *I Have a Dream* speech (1963), he used stories to personalize the moral and ethical dimensions of the civil rights struggle. He transformed the fight for equality into familiar narratives that resonated with both supporters and opponents. His stories humanized the movement and inspired a diversity of people to join the cause, demonstrating the profound impact of storytelling in authentic leadership.

Mission-driven messaging

Mission-driven messaging, or a "mission statement," defines a leader's identity, values, and vision. It builds trust and credibility by ensuring consistency between words and actions. A mission statement is the foundation of personal brand development, influencing further elements such as an elevator pitch, tagline, or logo.

The term *brand* originates from the idea of a mark of ownership (Henseler & Scheidt, 2018). A *personal brand* communicates what a leader uniquely "owns" about themselves, such as the qualities and purpose that define their leadership. A strong mission statement clarifies this identity, helping leaders define their unique value and more effectively influence and inspire others within and beyond their organizations.

Crafting a mission statement

Crafting a mission statement involves a structured approach to articulate your purpose, values, and goals. George (2007) discusses the concept of "finding your true north," or a deeply personal and authentic sense of direction that aligns with your ideals. A mission statement is a helpful way to articulate this "true north" concept. The following is a step-by-step guide to create an authentic mission statement:

- *Understand Your "Why."*: Determine the core reason for your existence of operation. Why do you do what you do? What motivates you? What impact do you want to make?
- *Identify Your "Who."*: Define who you serve or aim to impact. Who can gain the most from what you have to share? Who are your key stakeholders? Who are you trying to reach or inspire? How can you see yourself helping them?
- *Define Your "What."*: Outline what do you do to achieve your purpose. What services or products do you provide? What actions or processes do you undertake? What are your main activities? What do you do that makes you unique?
- *Articulate Your "How."*: Describe how you conduct your work. What values guide your actions? What principles are non-negotiable in your approach? How do you differentiate yourself?
- *Combine and Refine*: Consolidate your brainstorming from the previous steps into a concise, clear, and impactful mission statement. Aim for a few sentences that succinctly capture the essence of your mission.

MISSION STATEMENT TEMPLATE

Why: Start with your core purpose.
  Example: "To empower underserved communities…"
Who: Specify your audience or beneficiaries.
  Example: "…by providing high school graduates…"
What: State what you do to fulfill your purpose.
  Example: "…with the tools and resources…"
How: Explain how you achieve this, highlighting your values.
  Example: "…through innovative training programs and dedicated support."

Example Mission Statement

To empower underserved communities by providing high school graduates with the tools and resources they need to succeed, through innovative training programs and dedicated support, guided by our commitment to sustainability and integrity.

Summary

By integrating critical, action-based pedagogy, this chapter emphasizes the importance of self-discovery and practical application for authentic leadership. Whether through storytelling or mission-driven messaging, these activities are designed to enhance personal growth and leadership effectiveness across diverse learning environments. By engaging in these exercises, leaders will not only strengthen their communication tools but also foster deeper, more meaningful connections with their followers.

Discussion

Limitations

Authentic leadership, while praised for its focus on honesty, transparency, and ethical behavior, also faces several criticisms. The concept of authenticity in itself is subjective and can vary significantly from person to person. What one individual perceives as authentic may not resonate the same way with another. This can make it challenging to apply authentic leadership principles consistently across different organizations and cultures (Alvesson & Einola, 2019). There is also a potential for ethical dilemmas if a leader's authentic goals do not align with organizational goals or ethical standards, especially if accompanied by conservatism and inflexibility (Alvesson & Einola, 2019). Additionally, not all stories may be received equally because of cultural, gender, or racial differences. Relying too heavily on a leader's personal narratives may overshadow other diverse perspectives, leading to biased decision-making.

Authentic leaders are encouraged to be emotionally open and vulnerable. This vulnerability may backfire in cultures that value stoicism and decisiveness, especially if it distracts from what is required to align people and get tasks done (Alvesson & Einola, 2019). Authentic leaders might also be overly focused on staying true to their current vision, potentially resisting necessary changes and adaptation. This can hinder innovation and the ability to respond to evolving market conditions or organizational needs (Alvesson & Einola, 2019).

Conclusion

Authentic communication and leadership enhance a leader's ability to connect with and inspire their audience. By utilizing personal narratives and effective communication techniques, leaders can clearly articulate their values and vision. This transparency fosters strong employee connections and cultivates workplace trust. Classical Rhetoric emphasizes the importance of ethos, or credibility, in communication, reminding leaders that their words must align with their character to build trust, while also highlighting the roles of pathos (emotional appeal) and logos (logical argument) in creating a balanced and persuasive message. Similarly, Fisher's Narrative Paradigm underscores the power of storytelling, encouraging leaders to engage others through meaningful, relatable narratives that resonate with their values. George's Authentic Leadership Theory further supports this approach by advocating for leaders to remain true to themselves and lead from their personal beliefs and experiences. Together, these theories provide a cohesive framework for leaders to communicate authentically, fostering genuine rapport and honest, cooperative interactions.

Authentic leadership is not about oversharing but rather about building real connections and maintaining transparent, trustworthy relationships. In an increasingly cynical work environment, authentic leadership—supported by these communication principles—serves as a powerful strategy for fostering a successful, innovative, and cohesive workplace.

Suggested further readings

Cunningham, M., Crandall, H., & Dare, A. (2017). *Gender, communication, and the leadership gap*. Information Age Publishing, Inc.

George, B. (2003). *Authentic leadership: Rediscovering the secrets to creating lasting value*. Jossey-Bass.

Harvard Business Review Press. (2018). *Authentic leadership: Emotional intelligence*. Harvard Business School Publishing Corporation.

Owolabi, D. (2020). *Authentic leadership: How to lead with nothing to hide, nothing to prove & nothing to lose*. Green Onion Publishing.

Questions for engagement and discussion

1 How do Classical Rhetoric, Narrative Paradigm, and Authentic Leadership Theory complement each other in helping leaders communicate effectively? Which of these frameworks do you think is most critical in today's media-driven work environment, and why?

2 Considering the personal reflection required in authentic leadership, do you think artificial intelligence has influenced its popularity? Do AI tools enhance or challenge a leader's ability to be authentic?

3 As online communication becomes more common in meetings, how can you adapt authentic leadership strategies to build trust, connection, and influence in virtual settings?

4 What are the potential limitations or risks to practicing authentic leadership in diverse cultural, organizational, or digital settings? How might a leader balance authenticity with the need for adaptive or strategic decision-making?

References

Adichie, C. (2009, October 07). *The danger of a single story* [Video]. YouTube. https://www.ted.com/talks/chimamanda_ngozi_adichie_the_danger_of_a_single_story?language=en

Alvesson, M., & Einola, K. (2019). Excessive positivity: Authentic leadership and other traps in leadership studies. *The Leadership Quarterly*, *30*(3), 383–395. https://www.elsevier.com/locate/leaqua

Bergmann, J., & Sams, A. (2012). *Flip your classroom: Reaching every student in every class every day*. International Society for Technology in Education.

Bordas, J. (2007). *Salsa, soul, and spirit: Leadership for multicultural age*. Barret-Koehler Publishers, Inc.

Bull, E., & Ebben, M. (2023, September). Constructing authenticity: Social media influencers and the shaping of online identity. In *Online identity – An essential guide [Working title]*. ResearchGate. https://www.researchgate.net/publication/373956602_Constructing_Authenticity_Social_Media_Influencers_and_the_Shaping_of_Online_Identity

Cutrara, J. (2019, May 22). If you want to write a great speech, here's how to do it. *Grammerly.com*. https://www.grammarly.com/blog/how-to-write-a-speech/?gclid=CjwKCAiAlp2fBhBPEiwA2Q10D-Ahr6ooonXn63PChFsOhwKZEl8C-2NRSjTEoaX2cw4vPt9h8f5VkdRoC3ykQAvD_BwE&gclsrc=aw.ds

Duarte, N. (2011, November). *The secret structure of great talks* [Video]. Ted.com. https://www.ted.com/talks/nancy_duarte_the_secret_structure_of_great_talks?utm_campaign=tedspread&utm_medium=referral&utm_source=tedcomshare

Ebster, C. (2004). The role of authenticity in ethnic theme restaurants. *Journal of Foodservice Business Research*, 7(2), 41–52. https://doi.org/10.1300/J369v07n02_04

Eilam, G., & Shamir, B. (2005). "What's your story?" A life-stories approach to authentic leadership development. *The Leadership Quarterly*, *16*(3), 395–417. https://doi.org/10.1016/j.leaqua.2005.03.002

Fisher, W. R. (1989, March 1). *Human communication as narration: Toward a philosophy of reason, value, and action*. University of South Carolina Press. https://doi.org/10.2307/j.ctv1nwbqtk

George, B. (2003). *Authentic leadership: Rediscovering the secrets to creating lasting value*. Jossey-Bass.

George, B. (2007). *True north: Discover your authentic leadership*. Jossey-Bass.

Giroux, J. (2017, February 24). Interview: 'Get Out' director Jordan Peele on his filmmaking debut and the power of story. *SlashFilm.com*. https://www.slashfilm.com/549439/get-out-jordan-peeleinterview/

Griffin, E., Ledbetter, A., & Sparks, G. (2015). The rhetoric. In *A first look at communication theory* (9th ed., pp. 283–292). McGraw-Hill Education.

Harter, J. (2024). US engagement hits an 11-year low. *Gallup*. https://www.gallup.com/workplace/643286/engagement-hits-11-year-low.aspx#:~:text=In%20the%20latest%20reading%2C%20from,than%202020's%20high%20of%2036%25.

Harter, S. (2015). The development of self-representations. In M. R. Leary & J. P. Tangney (Eds.), *Handbook of self and identity* (2nd ed., pp. 610–642). Guilford Press.

Hasan, M. (2023). *Win every argument: The art of debating, persuading, and public speaking*. Henry Holt and Co.

Henseler, J., & Scheidt, S. (2018). Personal branding: A review on a contemporary phenomenon. *ResearchGate*. https://www.researchgate.net/publication/346914136_Personal_branding_A_review_on_a_contemporary_phenomenon
King, M. L., Jr. (1963). *I have a dream* [Speech]. Martin Luther King, Jr. Research and Education Institute. https://kinginstitute.stanford.edu/i-have-dream
Maslow, A. H. (1971). *The farther reaches of human nature* (vol. 19711). Viking Press.
Owolabi, D. (2020). *Authentic leadership: How to lead with nothing to hide, nothing to prove & nothing to lose*. Leek of Green Onion Publishing.
Ramanathan, A. (2019, July 24). *How to Organize and Structure a Presentation—Like a Hollywood movie!* [Video]. YouTube. https://www.youtube.com/watch?v=X3sR2OcIX2E
Shakespeare, W. (n.d.) *Hamlet*. In B. Mowat, P. Werstine, M. Poston, and R. Niles (Eds.), The Folger Shakespeare. https://www.folger.edu/explore/shakespeares-works/hamlet/read/
Tolliver, M., & Sass, J. (2024, June 17). Hybrid work has changed meetings forever. *Harvard Business Review*.

Appendix A

Virtual Authenticity

Virtual meetings have become a lasting part of professional life, even after the return to in-person work (Tolliver & Sass, 2024). For authentic leaders, a strong virtual presence can help build trust and connection. But how do we bring authenticity into a world that is physically removed?

In-person meetings offer opportunities for shared experiences—the walk to the conference room, the small talk before a meeting begins, or the informal follow-up as everyone packs up. Virtual meetings often eliminate these spontaneous, human moments. So how can leaders develop effective online strategies to lead with presence and purpose?

On-camera actors face a similar challenge: connecting emotionally through a screen. Drawing on my 25-year professional acting career, I've adapted an "actor's scene breakdown"—a series of questions actors use to define a character and create connected, authentic responses—to the virtual world. These guidelines help leaders uncover personal insights and communicate with greater authenticity online.

- *What Are the Facts of the Scene?*: Before a meeting begins, take a moment to write down the facts of the day beyond the agenda. Is it raining, is it Dean's birthday, is the team overworked to hit a deadline? Reminding yourself of these facts helps ground you in the virtual space and humanizes the meeting, often prompting stories or comments beyond your presentation or PowerPoint.

- *Who Are You Talking to? Who Are They to You Personally?*: Look at the list of attendees and quickly jot down one or two words about each person before the meeting starts. This helps you remember who you are speaking with and helps you to connect in a more authentic manner even when you can't see all the participants while you are presenting.
- *What Is the Moment before?*: What would the elevator conversation have been if you had met someone on the walk to the conference room? Do a vocal warm-up to get your articulators going. Set your mind, face, and energy into an open spot before the meeting begins.
- *What Are You Doing?*: Identify your action word. Are you working to inspire, to educate, to entertain? Clarifying your communicative intention establishes purpose and focus. Place a Post-it note near your computer's camera lens with your goal written on it. This serves as a visual cue to maintain eye contact with your audience through the lens. It also helps direct your energy outward, sustaining engagement and authenticity even without the natural feedback that comes from reading in-person body language.
- *Beginning–Middle–End*: Think of your presentation as a mini performance to keep the energy flowing and interest peaked. There should be a natural beginning–middle–end to keep you on track and interested.
- *Sum It Up in One Line*: What are you trying to accomplish in this meeting? Why did you schedule a Zoom instead of an email? Keeping your authentic message front of mind keeps the meeting on track and inspired.

21

#SWARMHUNGER

Mobilizing Feminist Communication Pedagogies and Adaptive Leadership to Combat Food Insecurity

Jasmine R. Linabary

Introduction

With significant and emerging challenges facing our communities (e.g., food insecurity, racial injustice, economic downturns, health crises, environmental threats, political polarization), it is imperative to cultivate leaders who have the capacity to tackle these complex problems that do not have clear or easy solutions (Iverson et al., 2019). Supporting college students in developing leadership knowledge and skills that allow them to respond to change and make progress on complicated and evolving challenges becomes an important responsibility of educators. In this chapter, I argue that *feminist communication pedagogies* can work in tandem with leadership theories, like *adaptive leadership*, to support meaningful transformative experiences for students as well as have the potential for broader impact. To do so, I offer as a case study a semester-long, community-based research project on food insecurity. Since everyone needs food to survive and thrive, food insecurity provides a unique opportunity for students to cultivate their leadership skills *and* make progress on an adaptive challenge. Through this case, I highlight the significant outcomes of the approach and project for students and communities.

Adaptive leadership

Adaptive leadership, largely developed by Heifetz and colleagues (e.g., Heifetz & Laurie, 2001; Heifetz & Linsky, 2017; Heifetz et al., 2009), recognizes the pressing problems and challenges faced by organizations

DOI: 10.4324/9781003563662-25

and societies and prepares individuals to make progress on them. As the name suggests, this approach is grounded in aiding individuals and organizations in *adapting* to change. As Heifetz et al. (2009) write, "adaptive leadership is the practice of mobilizing people to tackle tough challenges and thrive" (p. 14).

Unlike leadership approaches that focus on the position or traits of a leader, adaptive leadership focuses on behaviors that exhibit leadership (Northouse, 2019). Such a focus aligns with leadership communication scholarship that emphasizes leadership as constituted in and by communication (e.g., Fairhurst & Connaughton, 2014). Adaptive leadership centers interactions and relationships between leaders and followers. This focus is well suited to pedagogical practices, given leadership can be enacted by anyone regardless of position, enabling students to see themselves as enacting leadership even if they may not hold the title of "leader" in a traditional sense.

Adaptive leadership to date has been primarily prescriptive, outlining sets of behaviors leaders can put into practice (Northouse, 2019). Heifetz and Laurie (2001) discuss what they refer to as six principles for leading adaptive work. First, leaders must *get on the balcony*, which refers to the ability to zoom out and gain perspective. Adaptive leadership involves leaders taking steps to observe and reflect on what is happening with a broader and deeper view rather than merely being reactive to what is in front of them. Second, leaders need to be able to *identify adaptive challenges*. Adaptive leadership scholarship distinguishes between technical problems and adaptive challenges. While technical problems are easy to define and usually require singular solutions, adaptive challenges are complex, hard to define, and have no one, simple answer (Northouse, 2019). Leaders must be able to diagnose the adaptive challenges present to communicate about and effectively make progress on them. Third, leaders need to *regulate distress*. The need for change can lead to uncertainty and overwhelm. Leaders must support others and themselves in navigating these emotions productively. To do so, Heifetz and Laurie argue that a leader's role is to create a *holding environment*, or a "temporary 'place' in which a leader creates the conditions for diverse groups to talk to one another about the challenges facing them, to frame the debates and issues, and to clarify the assumptions behind competing perspectives and values." Fourth, leaders should *maintain disciplined attention*. When confronted with adaptive challenges, people often want to engage in avoidance or blame others. Leadership involves encouraging people to stay focused on the work that needs doing. Fifth, leaders should *give the work back to the people*. This recognizes everyone has something valuable to contribute and needs to be involved for progress to be made. Leaders can provide some structure but should support others to be active and full participants. Sixth, leaders need to *protect leadership voices from below*. This principle speaks to the importance of listening carefully to those who have been historically excluded and marginalized in the power structures, as well as alternative or deviating viewpoints. Leaders quick to quash such viewpoints risk creating groupthink. Adaptive leadership requires recognizing and valuing these perspectives and creating space for them to be heard.

Taken together, these principles illuminate how adaptive leadership calls on leaders to mobilize others to make progress on the difficult challenges before us. While adaptive leadership provides useful prescriptive strategies for mobilizing others, it has been critiqued for lacking a moral and ethical impetus for change and for the kinds of change it seeks to achieve (Northouse, 2019). This is where feminist communication pedagogies can provide both the imperative for social change and a set of values and practices that can enhance adaptive leadership.

Feminist communication pedagogies

Feminist scholars have long argued feminist epistemologies, theories, and pedagogical approaches can enhance and challenge students' understandings of organizational and leadership theories (e.g., Iverson et al., 2019; Trethewey, 1999). Pedagogies are, in essence, theoretical and ethical stances that shape how instructors engage in and beyond the classroom. While various theories and definitions of feminism exist, feminism is generally based on the assumption systems of gendered oppression exist—interlocking with systems of race, class, sexuality, ability, and nation (e.g., Buzzanell, 1994; hooks, 1994). Feminist theories interrogate these systems as well as seek transformation, given their activist roots (e.g., Buzzanell, 2016). As Briskin and Coulter (1992) explain, feminist pedagogy "acknowledges that the classroom is a site of gender, race, and class inequalities, and simultaneously a site of political struggle and change. It recognizes that teaching and learning have the potential to be about liberation" (pp. 250–251). As pedagogies, feminist approaches are less about teaching feminism and more about critiquing traditional hierarchical education models and seeking in contrast to embody alternative values such as equity, care, collectivity, reflexivity, and action through a variety of communication practices.

First, feminist communication pedagogies seek to *disrupt traditional hierarchies in the classroom and build more equitable relations*. Feminist communication pedagogies challenge assumptions that the instructor should be the all-knowing expert with ultimate authority and students should be passive receptacles for depositing knowledge (e.g., Freire, 2000;

hooks, 1994). In contrast, feminist pedagogies seek to reframe the relationship between students and instructors to one of mutual responsibility, where students are active participants in a co-learning community (Crabtree et al., 2009). As a result, classroom time may be spent engaging students in discussions and activities related to course content rather than the traditional one-way lecture format. Additionally, feminist educators recognize that historical exclusions and inequities are (re)produced in classroom spaces and seek to disrupt them (e.g., Walker & Muñoz Rojas, 2021). This may involve actively uncovering the "hidden curriculum"—taken-for-granted knowledge and practices about higher education that, in particular, first-generation students and students from other historically excluded groups may not otherwise know about (e.g., What are office hours? What does it mean to withdraw from a class? How do I get involved in research?).

Second, feminist communication pedagogies seek to exhibit *care*, seeing students as whole humans whose lived experiences shape their learning experiences (Buzzanell, 1993; Linabary & Rodriguez Carey, 2023). In contrast to approaches that treat students as universal subjects for whom standardized educational practices can be objectively applied, feminist educators see students as situated and embodied, recognizing the ways students' identities and lived experiences shape and constrain their participation. As a result, feminist pedagogies aim to respond to individual needs and personal growth journeys (Crabtree et al., 2009; Linabary et al., 2017). This may look like checking on students' well-being, sharing resources to support their needs, and developing flexible course policies.

Third, feminist communication pedagogies emphasize *collectivity*, recognizing the importance of relationships and our interconnectedness. Rather than a focus on competitive individualism, feminist pedagogies foreground cooperation and community (Buzzanell, 1993; Trethewey, 1999). In this sense, "relationships are sources of strength and self-knowledge" (Buzzanell, 1993, p. 533). This may look like fostering collaboration between students within the classroom but also between students and those within their broader communities through service learning and other forms of community engagement (e.g., Trethewey, 1999).

Fourth, given their attention to issues of power, feminist communication pedagogies also center *reflexivity* as central to their praxis. Reflexivity involves continuous critical reflection on taken-for-granted assumptions and power relations shaping our experiences (Hesse-Biber & Piatelli, 2012; Linabary et al., 2017; Stern, 2018). While reflexivity is central to the learning process generally, it is also key to the cultivation of critical consciousness in which students (and others) come to recognize the causes of inequities and act toward change (Freire, 2000; Watts et al., 2011).

Students may be encouraged to practice reflexivity through writing (e.g., journals, reflection papers) and in facilitated group discussions that foster critical thinking. Instructors who are informed by feminist communication pedagogies also regularly engage in reflexive practices themselves, recognizing teaching as an embodied praxis and seeing the need to continuously interrogate power relations in and beyond the classroom (e.g., Linabary et al., 2017; Stern, 2018).

Fifth, feminist communication pedagogies have an *orientation to action*. This requires moving beyond merely gaining new knowledge, to putting knowledge into action, and in ways that hold the potential for change. Feminist communication theories aim for *transformation* both at the individual (e.g., critical consciousness, empowerment) and collective levels (e.g., broader social change, imagining alternatives) (e.g., Crabtree et al., 2009; Meyer, 2004). In practice, this may take the form of projects that require students to mobilize knowledge and skills from a particular course to respond to community needs.

The above represent idealized values that inform feminist pedagogies, but these may be challenging to always live up to in practice. Feminist communication pedagogies specifically recognize the ways instructors, along with students, must navigate and embrace tensions involved with seeking to enact these values within particular institutional and socio-historical contexts to find new and creative possibilities (Linabary et al., 2017). Contradictions are an inherent part of organizational life requiring constant negotiation (e.g., Trethewey & Ashcraft, 2004). For example, in enacting feminist communication pedagogies, tensions between structure vs. ideology, power vs. voice, and justice vs. care are ever present as educators work within broader sociocultural and political systems that shape higher education (Linabary et al., 2017). Thus, feminist communication scholars argue that these tensions are "not problematic but are the means for gauging how to make change productively by transforming dualisms (either/or) into dialectics (both/and)" through reflection and dialogue (Linabary et al., 2017, p. 18). Thus, feminist pedagogical practices encourage cultivating skills to live within tension rather than to be immobilized by it. This can be especially important in the context of working on persistent challenges facing communities when putting adaptive leadership into action.

Putting leadership into action: EAT initiative

To explore the transformative possibilities of feminist communication pedagogies and adaptive leadership, I offer a case study of a semester-long, community-based research project that invited students to not only learn about leadership communication but also put what they were learning into practice. This project was part of the efforts of a larger collaborative and interdisciplinary effort called the EAT Initiative, standing for Emporia At the Table: Ending Hunger in Our Community. The EAT Initiative was founded at Emporia State University (ESU) in fall 2019 and involved classes taught by a dozen collaborating faculty and staff members across disciplines (e.g., art, economics, education, English, libraries and archives, sociology), as well as engagement with a variety of campus and community partners. In the reflections that follow, I draw specifically on the experiences of a class called Group Leadership, which played a central role in the launch and efforts of the initiative in fall 2019 and fall 2021. Group Leadership was an upper-division undergraduate major course that aimed to enhance students' theoretical and practical understanding of leadership communication. While the EAT Initiative may be a unique opportunity, I believe similar projects could be undertaken for other complex issues faced by communities either by a class on its own and/or in concert with colleagues and partners. Through this case, I highlight the significant outcomes for students and communities. To begin with, I identify the adaptive challenge—food insecurity—that is central to this case. I then discuss the ways students were mobilized to make progress on this challenge through the Group Leadership class and project, the significant outcomes for students and communities, and strategies for navigating tensions along the way.

Identifying the adaptive challenge

This case focuses on the adaptive challenge of food insecurity, or the lack of access to consistent, sufficient, nutritious, and culturally appropriate food. Food (in)security is a systems issue—involving complex interplays between processes of production, distribution, consumption, and waste—and shaped by a variety of interacting economic, sociocultural, contextual and environmental, and political forces (LeGreco & Douglas, 2021). Everyone needs food yet not everyone has access to the food they need or experiences barriers to food access in the same way, requiring critical attention to how these interacting forces shape what food access looks like, for whom, and to what effect (De Souza, 2019; LeGreco & Douglas, 2021). Food insecurity is thus a relevant context for students to cultivate and enhance their adaptive leadership skills.

Food insecurity in a rural Kansas county

Challenges related to food access are widespread across the United States, with people facing food insecurity in every county and congressional district. As of 2022, more than 44 million people in the United States were considered to be food insecure, or more than 1 in every 8 individuals (Feeding America, 2024b). Food insecurity is particularly prevalent in rural communities, with the majority of the counties with the highest hunger rates in rural areas (e.g., Feeding America, 2024b).

ESU is a regional public university located in Lyon County, Kansas, a rural county with a population of approximately 32,000 at the time of the 2020 U.S. Census (U.S. Census Bureau, 2022). At the time this project began in 2019, approximately 12.1% of residents were considered food insecure, including 16.3% of children (Feeding America, 2024a). In addition to common access challenges related to employment, high food costs, and stigma, specific challenges faced by the county included a food desert located on the south side of Emporia (the county seat and largest town) as well as in rural areas of the county. These particularly impacted Black and Hispanic residents, who are more likely to live on the south side as well as seniors who live in the rural areas.

Food insecurity among U.S. college students

Additionally, food insecurity is prevalent on U.S. college campuses at higher rates than among the general population (Willis, 2019), with estimates ranging from a quarter to more than half of all college students (e.g., Baker-Smith et al., 2020). Food-insecure students are likely to already be working, receiving financial aid, and/or enrolled in meal plans (Dubick et al., 2016). Food insecurity can have negative impacts on students' educational attainment, including impacting their grade point averages as well as their ability to stay enrolled and graduate (Leung et al., 2020). In addition to academic impacts, food insecurity can contribute to poor physical and mental health outcomes (Fortin et al., 2021).

Surveys conducted at ESU by the Hope Center for College, Community, and Justice during the time of this case found between 30 and 41% of ESU students had experienced food insecurity during 30 days before the survey (Basic Needs Coalition & EAT Initiative (BNC & EAT), 2021), similar to reports from other four-year institutions (Hope Center, 2021). Consistent with national data, students of color, LGBTQ+ students, first-generation students, and/or students with disabilities disproportionately experienced higher rates of food insecurity (Basic Needs Coalition & EAT Initiative (BNC & EAT), 2021).

While college campuses like ESU have responded by establishing campus food pantries, many students who are food insecure report not utilizing these and other basic needs resources (Baker-Smith et al., 2020). For many, this is due to lack of sufficient knowledge about the resources as well as stigma that keeps them from using them (El Zein et al., 2018; Hope Center, 2021).

Mobilizing for progress

To put what they were learning into action, students in the Group Leadership class enacted leadership through a community-based project on food insecurity. In this section, I will outline the project to illustrate the ways we mobilized both adaptive leadership and feminist communication pedagogies in tandem.

To respond to students' individual needs as well as cultivate mutual responsibility, students had the opportunity to identify where they were in their leadership journey and develop individualized plans to support their own growth. Students first wrote a leadership self-analysis paper reflecting on past experiences and outlining a leadership development plan. They then met with me individually and co-constructed leadership development contract related to their roles and responsibilities in the project and their teams. Students were encouraged to develop leadership goals to push them outside of their comfort zones. Examples of goals included "to learn how to better delegate to others and cultivate trust in teams," "to better live into my values especially when emotionally hooked," "to speak up more in group and class settings," and "to practice self-compassion."

Given that change requires mobilizing others, the project necessarily involved collaboration on multiple levels. First, we formed teams based on groupings of stakeholders (e.g., campus team, community team) as well as task areas (e.g., media and marketing team, event planning team, narrative team). Teams shared their goals and assigned roles as well as disclosed factors outside of class that could impact their groups and developed group contracts to guide their interactions with one another, including specific communication guidelines to create a holding environment. Additionally, we cultivated relationships with campus and community partners. Some partnerships I established in advance, while others were cultivated by or alongside students. Examples of campus partners included the campus pantry, student wellness center, libraries and archives, diversity student programs, and student government, while off-campus partners included the local food policy council, the county's history center, farmers markets, public libraries, and a variety of nonprofits, policy advocacy organizations, and other coalitions.

Reflexivity was central to the class and project. I provided content about practicing reflexivity at the beginning of the semester, and students had opportunities to engage in reflection on their own and with others both in writing and orally. In addition to their initial paper, students maintained leadership journals. At the end of the semester, students were asked to write a final reflection paper where they reflected on and analyzed their leadership development over the semester. Overall, the reflection papers and journals were how students made sense of their experiences, connected them to course concepts, and demonstrated their development as leaders. We also used class time for collaborative reflection and debriefing after events and activities such as the community action workshop, a key mechanism to practice "getting on the balcony." I also engaged in reflection alongside students to lead by example.

The project itself involved multiple phases leading to action designed to help us identify and deepen our understanding of the adaptive challenge, protect and amplify voices from below, create a holding environment, and give the work back to move toward collective action. During the design phase, students sought out background research, built relationships in the community and on campus, and gained first-hand experience through volunteering and/or observation. Following a stakeholder mapping activity, students were asked to each identify a specific stakeholder group on which to focus their individual research efforts, recognizing food insecurity impacts people in different ways. Examples of stakeholder groups students focused on included student-athletes, international students, students with dietary restrictions, rural communities, children, and food assistance programs, among others. To better understand the adaptive challenge, students completed an annotated bibliography of at least five scholarly sources related to food insecurity and their stakeholder group to enhance as well as performed a site visit by volunteering, participating, or observing at a site relevant to our project (e.g., visiting campus food pantry, riding the city bus to the grocery store, volunteering at the local soup kitchen) and writing a brief response paper about their experience.

During the second phase, we focused on deepening understanding by conducting in-depth interviews and/or focus groups with stakeholders, collecting narratives about food insecurity, and organizing and supporting events for education and action. Interviews enabled students to engage directly with those impacted by or impacting the issue to understand how food insecurity was experienced by their stakeholder group locally and to invite those who participated to consider what progress might look like and who needs to be involved. The teams during this phase also created preliminary reports that discussed what we knew based on the background research and what we learned from data collection to inform the design of the workshop in the final phase of the project.

The third phase of the project was centered on collaboration and action. At this point, students co-facilitated a community action workshop among stakeholders, hosted exhibits and events to reduce stigma related to food insecurity, and reported back the results. The project culminated in the execution of a workshop that brought multiple stakeholders together in a shared space to engage in dialogue to identify solutions and take action on food insecurity. Students, who had learned about and already practiced facilitation skills in class, served as co-facilitators of the workshop, applying what they learned to create a holding environment in real time. The workshop became one way to give the work back—inviting stakeholders to imagine futures without food insecurity, map out community assets and challenges, and identify action steps. After the workshop, students revised their preliminary reports and shared the findings in other ways as well. For example, one semester students decided to interview each other about what they learned and edit those interviews into videos that could be shared on social media.

Catalyzing transformation

Across the two semesters, students, alongside collaborating faculty, staff, and campus and community partners, accomplished a staggering amount. Collectively, the students conducted more than 100 semi-structured interviews as well as collected both written and art-based narratives. They co-facilitated three community action workshops, each bringing together between 25 and 40 stakeholders from the campus and community. We also organized guest speakers, a food giveaway, exhibits both on campus and in the community, an art and creativity contest, and workshops and training for specific student groups (e.g., student-athletes, TRIO students), among other activities. Students also produced reports and videos about what they learned. In this section, I highlight some of the key outcomes both for students and the community as a result of this approach.

Outcomes for students

By putting leadership into action, students (a) came to identify as leaders, (b) developed a greater sense of community and civic responsibility, and (c) shifted their own perspectives of food insecurity. As one student wrote in a final reflection paper, "We experienced what it felt like to be a leader day in and day out; the failing forward culture created in class is something that has been unmatched throughout my academic career." Students reported a sense of ownership and responsibility for the initiative and the work they were doing around it. In the class, students openly discussed not being concerned about their grade for this course, but rather being motivated by a sense of responsibility to make change happen. As one student stated,

> I loved the growth that I got out of this semester. I have gotten so much out of your classes and applied learning. It was not a class to me because you made us believe in the importance of what we were doing.

Many students talked about coming to see themselves as leaders, sometimes for the very first time. They discussed how the initiative pushed them out of their "comfort zone" in ways that fostered growth and encouraged their development as leaders. Another student wrote,

> This class has provided me with the most purposeful project I have ever been a part of and has provided me with takeaways from class lessons about leadership, the application of that in our project, and the development of my leadership through obstacles that I overcame or fell short on. I will continue to see myself as a leader from this point forward and recognize my strengths in that regard.

Students discussed how this project has instilled in them a greater sense of community and civic responsibility. They indicated the skills they developed would help them to "make a real and lasting change wherever [they] go." For several students, this was the first time Emporia felt like more than just a place they went to school. Many started seeing it as a "home" or "their" community. As one student wrote, "This course has inspired me to get more connected to Emporia. I have never thought of ESU as more than a school until this year. The EAT Initiative has given me a stake in the issue present in Emporia." For many students, this experience changed or shifted their career interests and goals, with several indicating they now hope to work for nonprofit organizations, go into higher education, or participate in politics.

Students reported shifts in their perspectives on food insecurity as they developed a critical consciousness of the issue. One student discussed how this project "changed how I view the world." Half of the students in this class had lived experience with food insecurity, including some who were food insecure while enrolled in the course. For these students, talking about and taking action on this issue not only gave them language to make sense of their experiences and a sense of purpose but also reduced the stigma related to food insecurity and made them more willing to ask for help and to encourage others to do the same. Several students continued to take action after the semester, interning with the EAT Initiative, volunteering with organizations, and/or pursuing related jobs.

Impacts for community

The project also had transformative impacts for the broader campus and Emporia community, including (a) reduced stigma and increased willingness to seek help, (b) increased usage of the on-campus food pantry, (c) co-created action plans with priorities, (d) increased connections between campus and the community, and (e) cultivated institutional buy-in.

Through the events we held, we contributed to reducing stigma and increased people's willingness to seek help. This was evidenced by students actually seeking out faculty members to ask for food when they needed it. Students and attendees also reported through reflections on public events and exhibits that they have come to recognize and name their own experiences of food insecurity and learned "it's OK to ask for help."

We helped increase usage of and donations to our own campus food pantry. The university decided to make the fall 2019 Day of Giving focused on the pantry. We also helped secure grants and funding to double the size of the pantry and furthered a relationship with campus dining services, to pursue strategies like donated meal swipes and repurposing food waste that would otherwise be discarded.

Through our community action workshops, we co-created community action plans with priorities that we then took steps to put into action. These also formed the basis of insights and recommendations incorporated into the Lyon County Food System Assessment, a major local policy report and document to which our research efforts contributed.

We also were able to build and enhance connections between the campus and community both by the students cultivating those relationships and also through the action workshops that often brought representatives of both into a shared space to find ways to work together. Some participants who had not had a chance to engage with each other before were able to spark new collaborations.

Most significantly, we cultivated institutional buy-in. ESU's then-president publicly signed the PUSH commitment, which stands for Presidents United to Solve Hunger, becoming one of more than 100 presidents worldwide who have signed on to this commitment to end hunger. Out of this commitment, we engaged in advocacy to institutionalize a university-wide basic needs coalition—composed of representatives of student affairs, faculty, students, and community members—tasked with addressing students' basic needs. This coalition went on to create further impacts by putting recommendations into action and succeeded in advocating for a new staff position to support student basic needs.

Navigating tensions

Even with these transformative outcomes, mobilizing others to make progress on issues like food insecurity is not without its own challenges. In this process, feminist communication pedagogies provided mechanisms for navigating the tensions experienced in the process when seeking to put adaptive leadership into action. Below I highlight two of the mechanisms by which we navigated these tensions.

Care as strategy for navigating the emotions of change work

Exercising care became a key mechanism to support students in regulating distress. While the students expressed that this was "more than a class" for them, that also meant some felt burdened by the weight of the responsibility of making a difference, which sometimes made them feel like they were letting down a whole lot more than themselves when they "failed" or fell behind. Students also felt discouraged at times by the challenges and roadblocks they encountered (e.g., non-responsiveness of potential partners or participants, institutional or governmental policies that limited or restricted what we were able to do, levels of commitment), the slowness of progress, and apathy of others once their consciousness was raised regarding the adaptive challenge. As previously indicated, a portion of the class had current or past lived experience with food insecurity, adding another layer of emotional labor. Taken collectively, these at times resulted in students feeling stuck or immobilized, requiring attention to how to maintain disciplined attention.

Given my commitments to feminist communication pedagogies, I adopted several care-based strategies to help students navigate these complex feelings while being able to move forward. First, I noted the potential for this project to bring up complicated emotions and past experiences and invited a representative of counseling services at the beginning of the semester to share about university services. I then provided reminders about these services at multiple time points. I also inserted content related to emotions, self-compassion, and resilience into class, recognizing these as important topics related to leadership communication. We had regular self-care check-ins in the class, inviting students to share strategies or commit to actions to care for themselves. Further, given the nature of the topic we were working on, I had snacks present in the classroom for those who needed it, regardless of why they needed it, and all of the students knew I had a filing cabinet drawer in my office filled with other food items. Most students ate the snacks throughout the semester and a few came to me in my office at times of need. While these strategies did not necessarily eliminate students' emotional distress, they did provide supportive structures to help them navigate those moments to continue their work toward change.

Critical reflexivity as strategy for navigating tensions in collective work

Critical reflexivity—practiced both individually and with others—became an important tool in navigating tensions in collective work. The adaptive leadership principle of "giving the work back" requires a level of trust and a willingness by leaders to release power and control. Doing so is also in line with the commitments within feminist communication pedagogy to disrupt hierarchies and embrace collectivity. In the context of the teams, students faced challenges typical of group work, including issues with willingness to delegate and experiences with social loafing (e.g., missed classes or meetings, lack of follow-through on tasks) that resulted at times in some carrying more of a load than others. These twin challenges—leaders' unwillingness to cede control by completing tasks themselves as well as others seemingly not stepping into their responsibility to the extent expected—can create vicious cycles that perpetuate both leading to resentment and further withdrawal from the group. Likewise, as their instructor, one of the key challenges to these kinds of community-engaged learning projects is the balancing act between letting students act on their own and "fail" so they learn from the experience, and wanting to ensure initiatives that affect real people in the campus and community are successful and outputs are useable.

Rather than being stuck in these vicious cycles, critical reflexivity was mobilized as a tool to help students (and myself as an instructor) navigate these tensions. For example, students had opportunities to reflect on group processes as well as their own contributions to them through their journals as well as other class activities. At the midpoint in the semester, students were also required to attend a learning conference with me where I provided individual coaching based on their reflections, encouraging them to dig deeper into the "problem," in some cases recognize their own role in it, and identify experiments to try. Student teams also engaged in debriefing meetings to talk about what was working well and what they needed to change to work together effectively going forward. Students were encouraged to interrogate the "why" behind their own and others' behaviors. For example, students were encouraged to consider that what might appear on the surface to reflect someone "not caring" about the project might rather reflect a hardship that person may be experiencing in their life (e.g., food insecurity or other basic needs issues, mental health, loss of a family member, caregiving). Doing so resulted in different kinds of responses toward group members (e.g., reaching out to check in individually to make sure the person was OK, offering support, becoming accountability buddies, changing structures to work better for the group, providing clearer task communication). I also engaged in critical reflexivity individually as well as alongside students, colleagues, and partners. This meant making adjustments along the way that were responsive to the needs of all parties. In some cases, this meant taking on certain tasks myself to ensure the success of an event *and* lighten the load and support emotional regulation for students. At other times, it meant embracing the messiness of the process and then debriefing afterward with students and partners to discuss what we would do differently in the future.

Critical reflexivity is not necessarily a panacea—it does not resolve the tensions as they often need constant navigation and (re)negotiation. Some students' experiments and groups' new strategies worked, while others did not. For example, one student who was experiencing basic needs issues herself ended up withdrawing in the latter half of the semester despite her group's (and my own) attempts to offer support. In some cases, a team's leader may have still struggled to relinquish control, leading to frustration for them and for their group. Recognizing the tensions though allows us to continue the practice of critical reflexivity and think again rather than giving up or giving in.

Conclusion

Increasingly, we as leaders are called to act upon the significant, complex, and evolving issues facing our organizations and communities. Given this, "the challenge, for developing leadership competencies, is how to develop people's adaptive capacity for tackling the complex problems that have no clear-cut solutions; knowing what to do when they don't know what to do" (Iverson et al., 2019, p. 185). In this chapter, I have argued that bringing together adaptive leadership alongside feminist communication pedagogies can support progress on these adaptive challenges, contributing to transformative outcomes for students developing leadership skills but also for communities. Feminist communication pedagogies bring to adaptive leadership both a moral and ethical impetus for change but also a set of values and practical mechanisms for navigating the tensions experienced when seeking to put adaptive leadership principles into action. Food insecurity is but one of many pressing needs facing our communities. I invite you to consider what adaptive challenges you see in your community and how you might mobilize leadership theories alongside communication pedagogies to mobilize others for change.

Suggested further readings

Heifetz, R. A., & Laurie, D. L. (2001, December). The work of leadership. *Harvard Business Review*. https://hbr.org/2001/12/the-work-of-leadership

hooks, b. (1994). *Teaching to transgress: Education as the practice of freedom*. Routledge. https://doi.org/10.4324/9780203700280

Linabary, J. R., Long, Z., Mouton, A., Rao, R. L., & Buzzanell, P. M. (2017). Embracing tensions in feminist organizational communication pedagogies. *Communication Education*, *66*, 257–279. https://doi.org/10.1080/03634523.2016.1257818

Northouse, P. G. (2019). *Leadership: Theory and practice* (8th ed.). Sage.

Questions for further engagement

- What adaptive challenges are present on your campus or in your community?
- How might a class guided by feminist communication pedagogies be different from one taking more traditional approaches to the classroom?
- What are the other potential outcomes of putting adaptive leadership principles and feminist communication pedagogies into action inside and beyond the classroom?
- What tensions do you anticipate experiencing when putting adaptive leadership principles into action? What strategies might you mobilize to navigate those tensions?
- What other communication pedagogies might be valuable companions to leadership theories and approaches like adaptive leadership?

References

Baker-Smith, C., Coca, V., Goldrick-Rab, S., Looker, E., Richardson, B., & Williams, T. (2020). #RealCollege 2020: Five years of evidence on campus basic needs insecurity. *Hope Center for College, Community, and Justice*. https://saragoldrickrab.com/wp-content/uploads/2023/06/2019_RealCollege_Survey_Report.pdf

Basic Needs Coalition & EAT Initiative (BNC & EAT). (2021, April). *2020 #RealCollege survey results—Emporia State University summary report*. Emporia State University.

Briskin, L., & Coulter, R. P. (1992). Introduction: Feminist pedagogy: Challenging the normative. *Canadian Journal of Education*, *17*(3), 247–263. https://www.jstor.org/stable/1495295

Buzzanell, P. M. (1993). Feminist approaches to organizational communication instruction. In C. Berryman-Fink, D. Ballard-Reisch, & L. H. Newman (Eds.), *Communication and sex role socialization* (pp. 525–553). Garland.

Buzzanell, P. M. (1994). Gaining a voice: Feminist organizational communication theorizing. *Management Communication Quarterly*, 7, 339–383. https://doi.org/10.1177/0893318994007004001

Buzzanell, P. M. (2016). Feminism. In R. T. Craig (Ed.), *International encyclopedia of communication theory and philosophy* (pp. 695–704). Wiley-Blackwell. https://doi.org/10.1002/9781118766804

Crabtree, R. D., Sapp, D. A., & Licona, A. C. (2009). *Feminist pedagogy: Looking back to move forward*. The Johns Hopkins University Press.

De Souza, R. T. (2019). *Feeding the other: Whiteness, Privilege, and neoliberal stigma in food pantries*. MIT Press.

Dubick, J., Matthews, B., & Cady, C. (2016, October). *Hunger on campus: The challenge of food insecurity for college students*. http://studentsagainsthunger.org/wp-content/uploads/2016/10/Hunger_On_Campus.pdf

El Zein, A., Mathews, A. E., House, L., & Shelnutt, K. P. (2018). Why are hungry college students not seeking help? Predictors of and barriers to using an on-campus food pantry. *Nutrients*, *10*(9). https://doi.org/10.3390/nu10091163

Fairhurst, G. T., & Connaughton, S. L. (2014). Leadership: A communicative perspective. *Leadership*, *10*(1), 7–35. https://doi.org/10.1177/1742715013509396

Feeding America. (2024a). *Map the meal gap*. https://map.feedingamerica.org/

Feeding America. (2024b, May). *Map the meal gap 2024: A report on county and congressional district food insecurity and county food costs in the United States in 2022*. https://www.feedingamerica.org/research/map-the-meal-gap/overall-executive-summary

Fortin, K., Harvey, S., & Swearingen White, S. (2021). Hidden hunger: Understanding the complexity of food insecurity among college students. *Journal of the American College of Nutrition*, *40*(3), 242–252. https://doi.org/10.1080/07315724.2020.1754304

Freire, P. (2000). *Pedagogy of the oppressed*. Continuum (Original work published 1970).

Heifetz, R. A., & Laurie, D. L. (2001, December). The work of leadership. *Harvard Business Review*. https://hbr.org/2001/12/the-work-of-leadership

Heifetz, R. A., & Linsky, M. (2017). *Leadership on the line: Staying alive through the dangers of change*. Harvard Business Review Press.

Heifetz, R. A., Linsky, M., & Grashow, A. (2009). *The practice of adaptive leadership: Tools and tactics for changing your organization and the world*. Harvard Business Press.

Hesse-Biber, S., & Piatelli, D. (2012). The feminist practice of holistic reflexivity. In S. Hesse-Biber (Ed.), *Handbook of feminist research: Theory and praxis* (pp. 557–582). Sage. https://doi.org/10.4135/9781483384740

hooks, b. (1994). *Teaching to transgress: Education as the practice of freedom*. Routledge. https://doi.org/10.4324/9780203700280

Hope Center for College, Community, and Justice. (2021, March 31). *The Hope Center Survey 2021: Basic needs insecurity during an ongoing pandemic*. https://hope.temple.edu/sites/hope/files/media/document/HopeSurveyReport2021.pdf

Iverson, S. V., McKenzie, B. L., & Halman, M. (2019). What can feminism offer student leadership education? *Journal of Leadership Education*, *18*(1), 183–199. https://doi.org/10.12806/V18/I1/T1

LeGreco, M., & Douglas, N. (2021). *Everybody eats: Communication and the paths to food justice*. University of California Press.

Leung, C. W., Farooqui, S., Wolfson, J. A., & Cohen, A. J. (2020). Understanding the cumulative burden of basic needs insecurities: Associations with health and academic achievement among college students. *American Journal of Health Promotion*, *34*(2), 275–278. https://doi.org/10.1177/0890117120946210

Linabary, J. R., Long, Z., Mouton, A., Rao, R. L., & Buzzanell, P. M. (2017). Embracing tensions in feminist organizational communication pedagogies. *Communication Education*, *66*, 257–279. https://doi.org/10.1080/03634523.2016.1257818

Linabary, J. R., & Rodriguez Carey, R. (2023). "I can't learn when I'm hungry": Responding to US college student basic needs insecurity in pedagogy and praxis. *Feminist Pedagogy*, *3*(4), 6. https://digitalcommons.calpoly.edu/feministpedagogy/vol3/iss4/6

Meyer, M. (2004). From transgression to transformation: Negotiating the opportunities and tensions of engaged pedagogy in the feminist organizational communication classroom. In P. M. Buzzanell, H. Sterk, & L. Turner (Eds.), *Gender in applied communication contexts* (p. 195214). Sage.

Northouse, P. G. (2019). *Leadership: Theory and practice* (8th ed.). Sage. https://doi.org/10.4135/9781452233123

Stern, D. M. (2018). Privileged pedagogy, vulnerable voice: Opening feminist doors in the communication classroom. *Journal of Communication Pedagogy*, *1*(1), 40–51. https://doi.org/10.31446/jcp.2018.09

Trethewey, A. (1999). Critical organizational communication theory, feminist research methods, and service-learning: Praxis as pedagogy. In D. A. Droge, & B. A. O. Murphy (Eds.), *Voices of strong democracy: Concepts and models for service-learning in communication studies* (pp. 177–189). Stylus Publishing. https://doi.org/10.4324/9781003448617

Trethewey, A., & Ashcraft, K. L. (2004). Practicing disorganization: The development of applied perspectives on living with tension. *Journal of Applied Communication Research*, *32*, 81–88. https://doi.org/10.1080/0090988042000210007

U.S. Census Bureau. (2022). *Quick facts—Lyon County*. Retrieved July 18, 2022, from https://www.census.gov/quickfacts/fact/table/US,KS,lyoncountykansas/PST045221

Walker, T. J., & Muñoz Rojas, L. A. (2021). Teaching and gaining a voice: A rhetorical intersectionality approach to pedagogy of feminist organizational communication. *Management Communication Quarterly*, *35*(1), 17–42. https://doi.org/10.1177/0893318920972692

Watts, R. J., Diemer, M. A., & Voight, A. M. (2011). Critical consciousness: Current status and future directions. *New Directions for Child and Adolescent Development*, *2011*(134), 43–57. https://doi.org/10.1002/cd.310

Willis, D. E. (2019). Feeding the student body: Unequal food insecurity among college students. *American Journal of Health Education*, *50*(3), 167–175. https://doi.org/10.1080/19325037.2019.1590261

22

ADVANCING SYSTEMS CHANGE THROUGH DOCTORAL EDUCATION

Leveraging Publicly Engaged Leadership Scholarship

Kerry L. Priest, Sean M. Eddington, Mac T. Benavides, and Saya Kakim

In the 2019 volume, *What's Wrong With Leadership*, Guthey et al. challenge leadership scholars and developers to consider *if and how* leadership research and development substantially contribute to society and provide meaningful support for collective efforts to address societal and global challenges. The idea of "leadership for the common good" has been advanced by numerous scholars (e.g., Chrislip & O'Malley, 2013; Crosby & Bryson, 2005; Grace, 2011; Komives & Wagner, 2016) and institutions (e.g., Harvard's Center for Public Leadership, the Kansas Leadership Center, and Humphrey Institute of Public Affairs). Across these people and platforms are insights into leadership practices needed to engage complex challenges: adaptive and systems thinking, collaboration with multiple stakeholders, empowerment, capacity building, attending to equity and inclusion, and mobilizing collective action.

Preparing individuals and groups to engage in this type of leadership is becoming increasingly important. Doctoral education can serve as a space where research, development, and meaningful impact intersect. By focusing on publicly engaged scholarship, doctoral education embodies a pedagogy of practice (Ganz & Lin, 2011), where learning activity transforms into leadership activity. From a learning perspective, doctoral education provides a framework, mentorship, and intellectual space for leadership learning and development, fostering systems-oriented scholars with the knowledge, skills, and critical perspectives necessary to navigate complex challenges. At the same time, doctoral education is a dynamic context where individuals collaborate with communities on leadership initiatives—conducting research, influencing practice, and mobilizing ideas

DOI: 10.4324/9781003563662-26

to promote systems change (Priest & Kliewer, 2017). Through this interplay, doctoral education is not merely a phase of preparation but an active site of leadership, where scholars help shape their fields and communities in real time.

Our chapter takes an integrative approach to bridge the concepts of publicly engaged scholarship and contemporary approaches to leadership communication practice, development, and research, emphasizing the potential of these approaches for fostering systems change. Then, we illustrate graduate leadership education's role in developing systems-oriented scholars and advancing systems change through engaged research activities. We offer a case example of the leadership communication doctoral program at Kansas State University, launched in 2018 in response to the need for interdisciplinary approaches to solving complex challenges. The research degree focuses on the theories and practices that lead to change locally and globally on complex public problems. The curriculum integrates experiential, theoretical, and applied approaches to understand leadership communication. The program began with an expectation that graduates of this program will "use community-engaged research to transform the academic, nonprofit, government, private, and civic sectors in which they live and work" (Tolar et al., 2017, p. 73). Finally, we offer critical questions for scholars and practitioners considering using community-engaged scholarship as a pedagogical tool for doctoral leadership education.

Engaged scholarship in higher education

We draw from concepts advanced by the engaged scholarship movement in U.S. American higher education, in which the terms "civic" or "community" are used synonymously with "public." Hartley and Saltmarsh (2016) describe the emergence of a civic engagement movement in pursuit of democratic purposes of higher education. The assumption of democratic purpose directs the core activities of higher education institutions—teaching and learning and knowledge generation—toward "addressing the pressing issues that face society locally, nationally, and globally" (pp. 34–35). *Civic* refers to reclaiming "the importance of political and democratic participation as a cornerstone of what being a citizen means and as a central purpose of higher education" (p. 34). At the heart of *engagement* is "authentic reciprocity"—or partnerships between those working at colleges and universities and those in the broader communities where non-academic expertise is equally valued in generating new knowledge to solve public problems (p. 34). Similarly, the Carnegie Foundation defines *community engagement* as "the collaboration between institutions of higher education and their larger communities (local, regional/state, national, and global) for the mutually beneficial exchange of knowledge and resources in a context of partnership and reciprocity" (Carnegie Classification, n.d.).

The Kettering Foundation & New England Resource Center for Higher Education *Democratic Engagement White Paper* (Saltmarsh et al., 2009) distinguishes democratic civic engagement as more than a focus on activity and place, but on purpose and process. In a democratic-centered framework, the university is part of an ecosystem of knowledge production addressing public problem-solving. Engagement is asset-based, inclusive, and collaborative. Democratic forms of collaborative engagement include deliberative dialogue, storytelling, participatory action research, and service-learning (Longo & Gibson, 2016). Community-based participatory research frameworks create the conditions for collaboration between academic and community partners across all stages of the research process (research done *with* versus done *for* the public). At the heart of community-engaged research are community-driven priorities, shared and equitable decision-making, co-creation of knowledge, and a purpose of social or cultural change (Jacquez et al., 2016).

Public research universities have over 150 years of experience spearheading scholarship and advancing the public interest. These universities were founded to serve the public through their education, research, and engagement work. They provide life-changing education to students, advance society-shaping innovations, and engage communities to tackle our most stubborn challenges (Aurbach et al., 2023). Against this backdrop of public engagement as a scholarly movement, we seek to illustrate the role of graduate leadership education in developing systems-oriented scholars *and* advancing systems change through engaged research activity.

The Association of Public and Land-Grant Universities (APLU) recently published key learnings from its *Modernizing Scholarship for the Public Good* initiative. The core lens for this initiative centered on public engagement and public impact research (PE&PIR) and diversity, equity, inclusion, and justice (DEIJ). Public engagement is "a variety of efforts connecting different public constituencies with university scholars" and includes community-engaged research. Public impact research describes university research as something that "improves lives and serves society—locally, regionally, nationally, and globally" (Aurbach et al., 2023, p. 10). DEIJ refers to efforts that "recognize, address, and support people and groups who have been historically marginalized based on identities including race, ethnicity, gender, social/economic class, geography, culture, sexual identity, ability, age, and relation, among others" (Aurbach et al., 2023, p. 10). Modernizing scholarship requires multiple approaches, including "formalizing curricular training and professional development opportunities for students" (Aurbach et al., 2023, p. 15).

Community-engaged scholarship invites systems thinking, innovation, and the development of more inclusive and participatory practices to develop and study leadership communication in higher education contexts like doctoral education. Across leadership and communication studies, scholars have been advancing theories, practices, and methods of inquiry rooted in democratic principles and collective, inclusive leadership practice. For example, Crosby and Bryson's (2005) leadership for the common good framework emphasizes creating the conditions for power-sharing practices to engage in ethical public problem-solving. Raelin (2011) suggests that the leadership-as-practice (LaP) framework lends itself to democratic practice through leaderful practice that privileges the co-creation of social organizations. Pares et al. (2017) advance a model of social innovation and democratic leadership that pursues and fosters social change, challenges hegemony, and co-emerges new frameworks and solutions. They emphasize practices of equality, inclusiveness, and transformation. Guthey et al. (2019) offer "collaboratories" as a model for multi-stakeholder leadership development and a co-created, collective experiment through which to address complex community and societal challenges. These participatory and equity-centered orientations are increasingly reflected in leadership and communication theories that embrace complexity, collaboration, and transformative action. Next, we will elaborate on how contemporary approaches to leadership communication perspectives offer a theoretical and practical foundation for community-engaged approaches to fostering systems change.

An integrative approach to leadership studies

We draw from three distinct perspectives of leadership theory—leadership as relational and collective, leadership as a constellation of practices and adaptation, and leadership as a social construction and discourse—to examine how these frameworks illuminate the diverse constellations of communication practices through which leadership is enacted, negotiated, and sustained. By integrating these theories, we aim to illuminate pathways for developing systems-oriented scholars—doctoral students and researchers who approach leadership and communication as interconnected, dynamic systems and who are prepared to analyze, engage with, and influence complex social structures through interdisciplinary, community-engaged scholarship capable of addressing pressing societal issues through community-engaged research and practice.

Leadership as relational and collective

First, we explore the role of relational and collective leadership approaches rooted in relational networks (e.g., Crevani, 2019; Cunliffe & Eriksen, 2011; Fairhurst, 2007; Ospina et al., 2020; Uhl-Bien, 2006; Uhl-Bien & Ospina, 2012). Unlike traditional leadership models focusing on individual authority and specific leader behaviors, relational and collective approaches advocate for a decentralized, socially constructed understanding of leadership. As Uhl-Bien (2006) argues, the essence of leadership is found not in individual traits or actions but in the interactional processes through which leadership is co-created. This reorientation dismantles the heroic, top-down leadership paradigm, emphasizing collective leadership structures' fluidity and shared responsibility (Raelin, 2016). Contrary to traditional, entitative approaches to leadership (e.g., focusing on what leaders *do*), relational approaches highlight how interactions between and amongst people constitute leadership (e.g., how leadership is co-created through communication; Fairhurst & Uhl-Bien, 2012).

The emphasis on social processes in relational leadership (Crevani, 2019) aligns closely with the collective approach's focus on shared leadership practices (Ospina et al., 2020). While relational leadership emphasizes leadership as a co-constructed process emerging from individual interactions, collective leadership expands this to a broader context, emphasizing leadership as a shared, distributed function within groups and collectives (Fairhurst et al., 2020). Both approaches dismantle hierarchical understandings of leadership by framing it as emerging from communication and participation rather than being the responsibility of a single leader. In contrast to fixed hierarchical structures, collective leadership is inherently dynamic and adaptable. As Yammarino and colleagues (2012) note, leadership is not the purview of a single individual but is continuously negotiated among multiple individuals who assume and relinquish leadership roles over time. This fluidity enables coalitional decision-making and fosters a collaborative culture where leadership responsibilities are shared and distributed across formal and informal relationships. Harrison (2017) aptly compares collective leadership to a jazz band, where leadership is dynamic, participatory, and reliant on the collective rather than an individual conductor. Just as jazz musicians must listen, adapt, and improvise to create harmonious music, members of a collective leadership structure work together, fluidly adjusting roles and responsibilities to respond to evolving circumstances. This improvisational nature of collective leadership allows for greater flexibility and innovation, fostering an environment where all voices contribute to the group's shared goals.

By emphasizing collaboration, shared responsibility, and non-hierarchical decision-making, relational and collective leadership gives researchers and communities the flexibility to navigate uncertainty and drive innovation effectively (Raelin, 2016; Škerlavaj, 2022). This shift from individual to collective leadership supports more inclusive and participatory organizational structures and fosters community-based research that integrates broader perspectives into leadership communication scholarship. As leadership processes are understood as inherently interconnected and co-constructed, we now examine how these principles are implemented through practice-based and adaptive leadership frameworks, which focus on practical, dynamic responses to complex and changing environments.

Leadership as practice and adaptation

LaP and adaptive leadership emphasize leadership as a collective and emergent phenomenon, where solutions are co-created in real time, responding fluidly to challenges as they arise. The emergent nature of LaP aligns with adaptive leadership's focus on collaboratively engaging with complexity and ambiguity. LaP is a growing movement in the study of leadership (Collinson, 2018; Raelin, 2011, 2017, 2020) that is interested in and focused on how leadership is done by shedding light on the constructionist and relational orientations of leadership as a form of discursive organizing—what Carroll and colleagues (2008) describe as uniting "the micro ('the situated doings of individual human beings') and the macro ('different socially defined practices')" (p. 366). Put differently, a practice perspective highlights "immanent collective action emerging from mutual, discursive, sometimes recurring and sometimes evolving patterns in the moment and over time among those engaged in the practice" (Raelin, 2017, p. 216). Leadership as practice views leadership as emergent. This view aligns with adaptive leadership's emphasis on responding to complex challenges.

Just as LaP views leadership as emergent and shaped by relational and discursive patterns, adaptive leadership emphasizes the importance of these evolving dynamics in responding to complex organizational challenges. Adaptive leadership frameworks underline the role of complexity and leadership practices that create environments ripe for learning, experimentation, and adaptability (Heifetz et al., 2009). In other words, adaptive leadership frameworks center on understanding the social, material, political, and cultural contexts through which change is possible (Lind & Ekwerike, 2022). Adaptive leadership frameworks recognize that most challenges contain both technical and adaptive elements, and they guide leaders in discerning and responding to these dimensions to facilitate meaningful change. Technical challenges have clear-cut solutions, whereas adaptive challenges are volatile, uncertain, complex, and ambiguous. Adaptive challenges require creative and innovative perspectives, practices, and leadership to adequately engage in problem-solving processes (Uhl-Bien & Arena, 2017).

In organizational[1] contexts, adaptive challenges emerge from tensions between the need to innovate and operational efficiency demands. Uhl-Bien and Arena (2017, 2018) argue that adaptability depends on fostering an adaptive leadership process wherein entrepreneurial leaders' ideas disrupt and interact with existing operational systems. Through this dynamic, adaptive leadership supports processes that enable individuals to connect, engage in productive conflict, and co-create innovative solutions. These interactions can be integrated into the organization to meet evolving needs. To produce adaptive outcomes, an "adaptive space" must be created to leverage the tension between innovation and operational demands. Adaptive spaces bridge the emergent nature of leadership, as described in LaP, and the structured demands of organizational systems. By intentionally fostering spaces where innovative ideas challenge operational routines, organizations can leverage the collective wisdom of their teams to adapt to evolving challenges.

Leadership as a social construction and discursive

As we have discussed, contemporary leadership communication theories increasingly highlight leadership not as a fixed trait but as a dynamic, co-constructed process shaped by interaction, context, and ethical negotiation. The final two key perspectives that reflect this shift are (1) leadership as a social construction and (2) leadership as a discursive construction. From a social constructionist standpoint, leadership emerges through collective sense-making and shared interpretation of experience within specific contexts (Fairhurst & Grant, 2010). Rather than residing in individuals, leadership is co-produced through relationships that foster power-sharing and participatory engagement (Uhl-Bien, 2006). This perspective highlights that leadership meanings are historically and culturally situated, influenced by sociopolitical narratives and structural power dynamics (Grint, 2011). As such, leadership communication must be responsive to these dynamics, calling for ethical reflection and inclusion of marginalized voices (Ospina & Foldy, 2010).

Building on this, the discursive construction of leadership emphasizes that leadership is enacted through language, dialogue, and the strategic framing of meaning (Fairhurst & Connaughton, 2014). From this view, leadership involves adaptive communication strategies that flex across shifting contexts and audiences. Leaders engage in discursive work—the ongoing negotiation of identities, meanings, and roles within everyday interactions (Wodak et al., 2011). These interactions occur in discursive spaces (Carroll & Simpson, 2012), where leadership is not imposed but collaboratively created through narrative, metaphor, and rhetorical framing (Schnurr, 2009). Critically, this view of leadership as co-constructed communication also foregrounds the ethical dilemmas leaders face in navigating diverse stakeholder interests, institutional pressures, and cultural narratives. Ethical leadership involves decision-making and cultivating inclusive spaces for dialogue, fostering transparency, and responding to complexity with humility and care.

These perspectives open up rich opportunities for engaged scholarship that partners academics with practitioners and communities in the co-production of leadership knowledge and practice. Researchers can collaborate with organizations to explore how power-sharing and collaborative meaning-making shape leadership outcomes. They can also help develop and evaluate adaptive communication tools for navigating change, uncertainty, and conflict. Finally, scholars can play a vital role in surfacing and addressing the ethical tensions embedded in leadership discourse, bringing critical reflection to how leadership is framed, practiced, and reproduced in diverse settings. By treating leadership as a communicative, cultural, and ethical practice, engaged scholars are uniquely positioned to foster more inclusive, context-sensitive, and socially responsible forms of leadership.

Advancing engaged graduate leadership education

To showcase the community-engaged potential of leadership communication research, we discussed two specific case studies, exemplars of former leadership communication doctoral studies. Both studies highlight community-engaged research encouraging systems thinking, innovation, and inclusive and participatory practices. We also share lessons learned as doctoral-engaged scholars and faculty mentors to students within the doctoral program.

Kansas State University Leadership Communication doctoral program interdisciplinary research degree

Since its establishment in 2018, the Leadership Communication doctoral program at Kansas State University has served as an interdisciplinary center for community-engaged scholarship, advancing the mission of "leading change, engaging community, and advancing communication" (Leadership Communication Doctorate at Kansas State University, n.d.). The program is collaborative among three academic units: the A.Q. Miller

School of Media and Communication, the Department of Agricultural Education and Communication, and the Staley School of Leadership.

Students develop expertise in community engagement, communication, and leadership theories through a multidisciplinary curriculum. They engage directly with community partners to identify needs, co-construct objectives, and make measurable progress toward addressing them through community-engaged scholarship. Throughout their coursework and research, students cultivate advanced competencies in research design, data analysis, interpretation, and the dissemination of findings to both academic and public audiences (Curriculum and Outcomes, n.d.). Our graduates' research significantly advances systemic change by fostering innovation and collaboration across diverse communities and organizational structures.

To support a diverse range of learners—including traditional and nontraditional students—the program offers courses in both in-person and hybrid formats, ensuring greater flexibility and accessibility. Central to the program's design and critical to the present chapter is the explicit expectation that students conduct engaged, participatory research that fosters reciprocal partnerships between the university and the communities it serves.

Publicly engaged leadership scholarship plays a crucial role in shaping practical strategies for power-sharing, ethical problem-solving, and co-creating social organizations to foster power-sharing, ethical public problem-solving, and the co-creation of social organizations. We will examine how these approaches can challenge existing hegemonies, promote social innovation, and foster equality, inclusivity, and transformative practices. Through this exploration, we seek to demonstrate the transformative potential of integrating leadership and communication theories by proposing innovations in doctoral education, such as interdisciplinary curriculum design, experiential pedagogical strategies, and methodologies that prioritize community engagement and systemic impact in doctoral education and research, ultimately contributing to meaningful systems change in academic, nonprofit, government, private, and civic sectors.

Building on this foundation, the following section showcases how Leadership Communication doctoral program graduates apply engaged scholarship to drive systems change. We present two case studies featuring the dissertations of two of the authors in this chapter, Drs. Saya Kakim and Mac Benavides. These dissertation projects advanced systemic transformation in two distinct contexts. These cases demonstrate the practical application of community engagement, leadership communication, and participatory research, offering tangible evidence of the program's commitment to collaborative, transformative scholarship.

Case 1: Engaged approaches to deliberative civic learning: Case study of a small urban middle school

The current political climate in the United States today is marked by polarization (Kakim, 2022). Thus, it is crucial to empower young people to participate actively in civic life and respectfully engage with one another. Creating a collaborative partnership between communities and universities to develop an innovative youth development curriculum is one way to achieve sustainable change. A new civic education intervention was implemented by collaborating with a Midwestern land-grant institution, a cooperative extension, a youth development program, a non-partisan organization for deliberation and dialogue, and a public middle school.

The doctoral community-engaged study aimed to explore the perceptions and learning experiences of gifted middle school students who participated in a new extracurricular program. The program incorporated deliberative pedagogy and art-based student-centered learning grounded in leadership and communication theories. Drawing on engaged approaches to education and research, the multidisciplinary study utilized a collaborative engagement research paradigm that emphasizes (1) community-driven priorities and (2) co-creation of knowledge as guiding principles (Horowitz et al., 2009; Jacquez et al., 2016; Ross et al., 2010), as well as participatory methods.

The engaged study provides evidence that deliberative pedagogy and art-based student-centered teaching methods can foster the building of capacity in gifted early adolescents for democratic citizenship. In particular, the research study demonstrates that youth gained a better understanding of leadership as practice and engaged in creative ways to practice leadership by facilitating community conversations (Kakim, 2022). This study contributed to advancing pedagogical practices that promote thinking that enables change.

The doctoral study's findings highlight the importance of forming collaborative partnerships for impactful educational interventions that empower middle school students to engage in their local and school communities. Furthermore, a community-engaged approach to dissemination efforts led to discussion of sustainable strategies for engaging youth in the curriculum, which expanded beyond middle school. By addressing real-world challenges, this community-engaged study provides findings that are both academically and practically relevant for K-12 educators and youth development workers (Alter, 2003; Post et al., 2016). The deliberative civic extra-curricular program for youth demonstrated the potential of engaged approaches to promote systems change.

Case 2: Hilos del mismo tejido: Weaving community perspectives into community-based global learning through critical micro-ethnographic testimonio

Across the globe, communities grapple with an interconnected web of complex challenges that (re)create injustice (Benavides, 2022). While many contemporary leadership frameworks recognize the need for boundary-spanning collective efforts, collaboration is often stifled by neoliberal commitments that promote resource scarcity and isolation. This dissertation explored the potential of higher education institutions to contribute to community-driven efforts, mainly through the practice of community-based global learning (CBGL) and commitments to co-constructing ethical and reciprocal partnerships.

An essential aspect of higher education's role in advancing the common good is understanding the contextual dependence of complex challenges. As a community-driven practice, CBGL should maintain a similar commitment to centering local priorities and interests (Hartman et al., 2018). However, the literature surrounding CBGL often prioritizes student learning outcomes and excludes community voices from the development of CBGL theory, practice, and pedagogy (Kennedy et al., 2020; Pisco, 2015).

Therefore, this study was grounded in the values and functions of engaged scholarship, a relational, participatory, and justice oriented approach to research that localizes knowledge production, dissemination, and application (Jacquez et al., 2016). Within Indigenous communities and/or communities with strong ties to Indigenous roots, engaged scholars must frame the research process through the community's values, knowledge, and cultural frameworks to promote sovereignty and self-determination (Smith, 2012). To bridge the knowledge systems of the local community and academic tradition, this project used a blend of methods to co-construct a critical narrative detailing the experiences of the Guatemalan community with foreign volunteers.

In theory, CBGL is well-positioned to make significant contributions to the civic mission of higher education and promote meaningful social transformation globally. In practice, however, a disconnect persists between established best practices and the experiences of host communities. The findings of this doctoral study illustrated that institutions must strengthen their commitment to reciprocity with community partners to design ethical learning experiences that align with community interests and needs for students (Benavides, 2022). Especially when partnerships are reframed as contributing to local change efforts, the dissertation findings demonstrated how sustainable systems change must be rooted in community-identified problems and interests. A framework for fostering reciprocal partnerships was offered, highlighting six distinct and iterative phases of program development with recommendations for how to do community-based learning *with* community. These recommendations focused on creating the conditions necessary for co-creating transformative systems-level change, including "overarching program design, decision-making at the institutional level, and engagement between university and community partners" (Benavides, 2022, p. 500). From a methodological perspective, this dissertation offers insights into managing rather than avoiding the creative tension of multiple ontological, epistemological, and methodological perspectives by leveraging integral methodological pluralism (Bailie et al., 2022) and indigenized research (Gaudry, 2011). Given that systems change requires strategy informed by complex understandings of the current reality, this dissertation successfully contributes a tangible example of managing paradox.

Conclusion

As detailed throughout this chapter, the Leadership Communication doctoral program is uniquely designed to foster movement and change across systems. Our program encounters tensions and growth opportunities in an era where higher education structures are evolving to serve residential and online learners and where public scholarship increasingly demands interdisciplinary and community-engaged approaches to address complex societal challenges. The shifting landscape of social problems and the turbulence of the academic labor market necessitate teaching and advising practices that extend beyond traditional mentorship. Faculty and administrators must engage in dynamic forms of emotional and care labor to support students conducting meaningful, transformative research. Moreover, they must remain responsive to emerging theories and innovative practices, even when such approaches challenge conventional doctoral success metrics, such as preliminary examinations, dissertations, and standardized career pathways.

These tensions foreground our work's ethical commitments: a sustained dedication to equity, inclusion, innovation, and authentic community engagement. They also highlight the urgency of preparing graduates who think critically across systems, work effectively within diverse and often polarized communities, and lead transformative change beyond traditional academic boundaries. Our program cultivates scholars who contribute not only to the research enterprise, a hallmark of the Ph.D., but also serve as catalysts for systemic transformation through leadership, collaboration, and strategic engagement across sectors. As public research universities renew their commitments to advancing the public good, programs like Leadership Communication are essential for preparing the next generation of scholar-practitioners poised to advance scholarship, shape practice, and drive meaningful systems change in an increasingly interconnected world.

Suggested further readings

Boyer, E. L. (1990). *Scholarship reconsidered: Priorities of the professoriate.* Princeton University Press.

Ganz, M., Lee Cunningham, J., Ben Ezer, I., & Segura, A. (2023). Crafting public narrative to enable collective action: A pedagogy for leadership development. *Academy of Management Learning & Education*, 22(2), 169–190. https://doi.org/10.5465/amle.2020.0224

Khalil, L., & Hartley, J. (2024). Public leadership to foster peacebuilding in violently divided societies. *Public Management Review*, 26(3), 724–745. https://doi.org/10.1080/14719037.2022.2116094

Kliewer, B. W., & Priest, K. L. (2019). Building collective leadership capacity: Lessons learned from a university-community partnership. *Collaborations: A Journal of Community-Based Research and Practice*, 2(1): 16, 1–10. https://doi.org/10.33596/coll.42

Ospina, S. M. (2017). Collective leadership and context in public administration: Bridging public leadership research and leadership studies. *Public Administration Review*, 77(2), 275–287. https://www.jstor.org/stable/26648243

Questions for further engagement

1 How can doctoral programs balance traditional academic expectations (such as dissertations and examinations) more effectively with the need to support community-engaged, systems-oriented scholarship? What tensions emerge from this balancing act, and what strategic approaches might programs adopt to address them?

2 In what ways does community-engaged scholarship challenge or reinforce traditional hierarchies of knowledge in higher education? How does recognizing and valuing alternative forms of expertise reshape research practices, academic norms, and scholarly outcomes?

3 What ethical responsibilities do leadership scholars have when conducting community-based or participatory research? How can scholars thoughtfully navigate power, cultural sovereignty, and reciprocity in their community partnerships?

4 How does framing leadership as relational, collective, and discursive shift how we prepare doctoral students to lead systemic change across diverse and complex contexts?

Note

1 Drawing on Schoeneborn et al. (2019), we adopt a broad definition of "organizational" to emphasize the fluid boundaries of what constitutes an organization. In doing so, this perspective suggests "that we study how social phenomena accomplish 'organizationality' in and through communication" (p. 490).

References

Alter, T. R. (2003). Where is extension scholarship falling short, and what can we do about it? *Journal of Extension*, *41*(6). https://open.clemson.edu/joe/vol41/iss6/3

Aurbach, E. L., Kennedy, H., Redd, K., Bennett, J., & Gobstein, H. (2023). *Modernizing scholarship for the public good: An action framework for public research universities*. Association of Public and Land-Grant Universities. https://doi.org/10.31219/osf.io/uekpb

Bailie, J., Cunningham, F., Abimbola, S., Laycock, A., Bainbridge, R., Bailie, R., Conte, K., Passey, M., & Peiris, D. (2022). Methodological pluralism for better evaluations of complex interventions: Lessons from evaluating an innovation platform in Australia. *Health Research Policy and Systems*, *20*(14). https://doi.org/10.1186/s12961-022-00814-5

Benavides, M. T. (2022). *Hilos del mismo tejido: Weaving community perspectives into community-based global learning through critical micro-ethnographic testimonio* (Publication No. 42167) [Doctoral dissertation, Kansas State University]. K-State Research Exchange. https://hdl.handle.net/2097/42167

Carnegie Classification of Institutions of Higher Education. (n.d.). *Elective classifications: Community engagement*. https://carnegieclassifications.acenet.edu/elective-classifications/community-engagement/

Carroll, B., Levy, L., & Richmond, D. (2008). Leadership as practice: Challenging the competency paradigm. *Leadership*, *4*(4), 363–379. https://doi.org/10.1177/1742715008095186

Carroll, B., & Simpson, B. (2012). Capturing sociality in the movement between frames: An illustration from leadership development. *Human Relations*, *65*(10), 1283–1309. https://doi.org/10.1177/0018726712451185

Chrislip, D., & O'Malley, E. (2013). *For the common good: Redefining civic leadership*. Lightning Source, Inc.

Collinson, M. (2018). What's new about leadership-as-practice? *Leadership*, *14*(3), 363–370. https://doi.org/10.1177/1742715017726879

Crevani, L. (2019). Relational leadership. In B. Carroll, J. Ford, & S. Taylor (Eds.), *Leadership: Contemporary critical perspectives* (2nd ed., pp. 223–247). Sage.

Crosby, B. C., & Bryson, J. M. (2005). *Leadership for the common good: Tackling public problems in shared power world*. Jossey-Bass.

Cunliffe, A. L., & Eriksen, M. (2011). Relational leadership. *Human Relations*, *64*(11), 1425–1449. https://doi.org/10.1177/0018726711418388

Curriculum and outcomes. (n.d.). *Leadership communication Ph.D.* https://www.k-state.edu/lead-comm/curriculum/

Fairhurst, G. T. (2007). Discursive leadership: A communication alternative to leadership psychology. *Management Communication Quarterly*, *21*(4), 510–521. https://doi.org/10.1177/0893318907313714

Fairhurst, G. T., & Connaughton, S. L. (2014). Leadership: A communicative perspective. *Leadership*, *10*(1), 7–35. https://doi.org/10.1177/1742715013509396

Fairhurst, G. T., & Grant, D. (2010). The social construction of leadership: A sailing guide. *Management Communication Quarterly*, *24*(2), 171–210. https://doi.org/10.1177/0893318909359697

Fairhurst, G. T., Jackson, B., Foldy, E. G., & Ospina, S. M. (2020). Studying collective leadership: The road ahead. *Human Relations*, *73*(4), 598–614. https://doi.org/10.1177/0018726719898736

Fairhurst, G. T., & Uhl-Bien, M. (2012). Organizational discourse analysis (ODA): Examining leadership as a relational process. *The Leadership Quarterly*, *23*(6), 1043–1062. https://doi.org/10.1016/j.leaqua.2012.10.005

Ganz, M., & Lin, E. (2011). Learning to lead: Pedagogy in practice. In S. Snook, N. Nohria, & R. Khurana (Eds.), *The SAGE handbook for teaching leadership* (pp. 353–366). Sage.

Gaudry, A. J. P. (2011). Insurgent research. *Wicazo Sa Review*, *26*(1), 113–136. https://dx.doi.org/10.1353/wic.2011.0006

Grace, B. (2011). *Sharing the rock: Shaping our future through leadership for the common good*. Common Good Works.

Grint, K. (2011). A history of leadership. In A. Bryman, D. Collinson, K. Grint, B. Jackson, & M. Uhl-Bien (Eds.), *The Sage handbook of leadership* (pp. 3–14). Sage.

Guthey, E., Kempster, S., & Remke, R. (2019). Leadership for what? In R. E. Riggio (Ed.), *What's wrong with leadership? Improving leadership research and practice* (pp. 277–298). Routledge. https://doi.org/10.4324/9781315163604

Harrison, R. T. (2017). Leadership, leadership development and all that jazz. *Leadership*, *13*(1), 81–89. https://doi.org/10.1177/1742715016681120

Hartley, M., & Saltmarsh, J. (2016). A brief history of a movement: Engagement and American higher education. In M. A. Post, E. Ward, N. V. Longo, & J. Saltmarsh (Eds.), *Publicly engaged scholars: Next-generation engagement and the future of higher education* (pp. 34–60). Stylus. https://doi.org/10.4324/9781003446583

Hartman, E., Kiely, R., Boettcher, C., & Friedrichs, J. (2018). *Community-based global learning: The theory and practice of ethical engagement at home and abroad*. Stylus. https://doi.org/10.4324/9781003443537

Heifetz, R., Grashow, A., & Linsky, M. (2009). *The practice of adaptive leadership: Tools and tactics for changing your organization and the world*. Harvard Business Press.

Horowitz, C., Robinson, M., & Seifer, S. (2009). Community-based participatory research from the margin to the mainstream: Are researchers prepared? *Circulation*, *119*(19), 2633–2642. https://doi.org/10.1161/CIRCULATIONAHA.107.729863

Jacquez, F., Ward, E., & Goguen, M. (2016). Collaborative engagement research and implications for institutional change. In M. A. Post, E. Ward, N. V. Longo, & J. Saltmarsh (Eds.), *Publicly engaged scholars: Next-generation engagement and the future of higher education* (pp. 76–95). Stylus. https://doi.org/10.4324/9781003446583

Kakim, S. (2022). *Engaged approaches to deliberative civic learning: Case study of a small urban middle school* (Publication No. 42154) [Doctoral dissertation, Kansas State University]. K-State Research Exchange. https://hdl.handle.net/2097/42154

Kennedy, A., McGowan, K., Lindstrom, G., Cook, C., Dean, Y., Stauch, J., Barnabe, C., & Price, S. (with Bear Chief, R., Spence, D., & Tagupa, K. F. D.). (2020). Relational learning with Indigenous communities: Elders' and students' perspectives on reconciling Indigenous service-learning. *International Journal of Research on Service-Learning & Community Engagement*, *8*(1). https://doi.org/10.37333/001c.18585

Komives, S., & Wagner, W. (2016). *Leadership for a better world: Understanding the Social Change Model of leadership development* (2nd ed.). Jossey-Bass.

Leadership communication doctorate at Kansas State University. (n.d.). https://www.k-state.edu/lead-comm/

Lind, C. J., & Ekwerike, O. (2022). Orientations toward community leadership. *Leadership*, *18*(4), 520–538. https://doi.org/10.1177/17427150221085134

Longo, N. V., & Gibson, C. M. (2016). The future of teaching and learning in higher education. In M. A. Post, E. Ward, N. V. Longo, & J. Saltmarsh (Eds.), *Publicly engaged scholars: Next generation engagement and the future of higher education* (pp. 61–75). Stylus. https://doi.org/10.4324/9781003446583

Ospina, S., & Foldy, E. (2010). Building bridges from the margins: The work of leadership in social change organizations. *The Leadership Quarterly*, *21*(2), 292–307. https://doi.org/10.1016/j.leaqua.2010.01.008

Ospina, S. M., Foldy, E., Fairhurst, G. T., & Jackson, B. (2020). Collective dimensions of leadership: Connecting theory and method. *Human Relations*, *73*(4), 441–463. https://doi.org/10.1177/0018726719899714

Pares, M., Ospina, S. M., & Subirats, J. (2017). *Social innovation and democratic leadership: Communities and social change from below*. Edward Elgar.

Pisco, K. (2015). Deepening service abroad: A call for reciprocal partnerships and ongoing support. *Michigan Journal of Community Service Learning*, *22*(1), 93–96. http://hdl.handle.net/2027/spo.3239521.0022.112

Post, M. A., Ward, E., Longo, N. V., & Saltmarsh, J. (Eds.). (2016). *Publicly engaged scholars: Next-generation engagement and the future of higher education*. Stylus. https://doi.org/10.4324/9781003446583

Priest, K. L., & Kliewer, B. W. (2017). Introduction: Advancing leadership education through community engagement. *Journal of Leadership Studies*, *11*(1), 36–39.

Raelin, J. (2011). From leadership-as-practice to leaderful practice. *Leadership*, *7*(2), 195–211. https://doi.org/10.1177/1742715010394808

Raelin, J. A. (Ed.). (2016). *Leadership-as-practice: Theory and application*. Routledge.

Raelin, J. A. (2017). Leadership-as-practice: Theory and application—An editor's reflection. *Leadership*, *13*(2), 215–221. https://doi.org/10.1177/1742715017702273

Raelin, J. A. (2020). Toward a methodology for studying leadership-as-practice. *Leadership*, *16*(4), 480–508. https://doi.org/10.1177/1742715019882831

Ross, L. F., Loup, A., Nelson, R. M., Botkin, J. R., Kost, R., Smith, G. R., & Gehlert, S. (2010). The challenges of collaboration for academic and community partners in a research partnership: Points to consider. *Journal of Empirical Research on Human Research Ethics*, *5*(1), 19–31. https://doi.org/10.1525/jer.2010.5.1.19

Saltmarsh, J., Hartley, M., & Clayton, P. (2009). Democratic engagement white paper. *New England Resource Center for Higher Education Publications*, *45*. https://scholarworks.umb.edu/nerche_pubs/45

Schnurr, S. (2009). *Leadership discourse at work: Interactions of humour, gender and workplace culture*. Palgrave Macmillan.

Schoeneborn, D., Kuhn, T. R., & Kärreman, D. (2019). The communicative constitution of organization, organizing, and organizationally. *Organization Studies*, *40*(4), 475–496. https://doi.org/10.1177/0170840618782284

Škerlavaj, M. (2022). *Post-heroic leadership: Context, process and outcomes*. Springer.

Smith, L. T. (2012). *Decolonizing methodologies: Research and Indigenous peoples*. Zed Books.

Tolar, M. H., Boone, K., Procter, D. E., & Steffensmeier, T. R. (2017). And now for something completely different. *Journal of Leadership Studies*, *11*(1), 71–74. https://doi.org/10.1002/jls.21516

Uhl-Bien, M. (2006). Relational leadership theory: Exploring the social processes of leadership and organizing. *The Leadership Quarterly*, *17*(6), 654–676. https://doi.org/10.1016/j.leaqua.2006.10.007

Uhl-Bien, M., & Arena, M. (2017). Complexity leadership: Enabling people and organizations for adaptability. *Organizational Dynamics*, *46*(1), 9–20. https://psycnet.apa.org/doi/10.1016/j.orgdyn.2016.12.001

Uhl-Bien, M., & Arena, M. (2018). Leadership for organizational adaptability: A theoretical synthesis and integrative framework. *The Leadership Quarterly*, *29*(1), 89–104. https://doi.org/10.1016/j.leaqua.2017.12.009

Uhl-Bien, M., & Ospina, S. M. (2012). *Advancing relational leadership research: A dialogue among perspectives*. Information Age Publishing.

Wodak, R., Kwon, W., & Clarke, I. (2011). 'Getting people on board': Discursive leadership for consensus building in team meetings. *Discourse & Society*, *22*(5), 592–644. https://doi.org/10.1177/0957926511405410

Yammarino, F. J., Salas, E., Serban, A., Shirreffs, K., & Shuffler, M. L. (2012). Collectivistic leadership approaches: Putting the "we" in leadership science and practice. *Industrial and Organizational Psychology*, *5*(4), 382–402. https://doi.org/10.1111/j.1754-9434.2012.01467.x

23

FREIRE'S REVOLUTIONARY LEADERSHIP AND CRITICAL COMMUNICATION PEDAGOGY

Sandra L. Pensoneau-Conway

Introduction

The world is in crisis.

The world is in crisis economically (witness the concentration of wealth at the top of the income bracket and the rising global poverty rates), meteorologically (global warming and other signs of climate change), politically (conflicts in nearly every sector of the globe and regular protests in the U.S. and other parts of the world), and socio-culturally (crises of identity permeate so many people's daily lives). Classrooms are just one context where these crises intersect. For example, many students enter classrooms with few resources at their disposal, some of them having to face discrimination or familial strife due to their ancestry, socioeconomic background, and/or concerns about food, clothing, and safety. To paint even more specific examples, transgender and gender non-conforming students are subject to harassment, misgendering, and harmful narratives (e.g., Republican politicians claiming that students identify as cats and demand to use litter boxes instead of bathrooms, leading to the idea that trans and gender non-conforming students have bizarre demands [Kingkade et al., 2022]). Across the U.S., students are seeing themselves and their families systemically erased from libraries and textbooks through book bans, restrictions on speech (such as the University of North Texas removing words like "race," "gender," and "equity" from course titles in anticipation of a state ban on diversity, equity, and inclusion (DEI) offices trickling down into curricular content [Davis, 2024]), and a general rhetoric of White supremacy and U.S. American exceptionalism. Schools

DOI: 10.4324/9781003563662-27

have taken to communicating with parents and community members how they will respond if (or when) U.S. Immigration and Customs Enforcement (aka ICE) comes knocking on their doors.

Certainly, such global and local crises necessitate a revolutionary leadership, one that looks beyond individual behavior to identify systemic conditions of oppression and social justice interventions. Importantly, classrooms are spaces of potential for such leadership to make an impact. Paulo Freire, a Brazilian educator and radical figure in the fight for global justice, may help to conceptualize such a leadership. In this chapter, I argue that Freirean revolutionary leadership, when understood through the lens of critical communication pedagogy (CCP), offers a communicative framework for enacting socially just and dialogically grounded leadership in educational contexts.

Freire's groundbreaking *Pedagogy of the Oppressed* (1970/2000) outlined a theory of leadership ("revolutionary leadership," sometimes referred to also as "transformative leadership" and "radical leadership") that relies upon, amongst other elements, dialogue, deep communion with those being led, co-intentionality, and humility, in the interest of social change toward justice. He refined his leadership theory in subsequent works. While the context in which Freire developed his revolutionary leadership is strikingly different than the current U.S. educational contexts, his theories of pedagogy and leadership are still relevant in many ways. In particular, the development of CCP (Fassett & Warren, 2007) both relies upon and extends Freirean pedagogy into more contemporary U.S. settings and entails a particular focus on communication processes, with a similar telos of social justice.

Freire's leadership has been examined in a variety of contexts, including hospital nurse training in Brazil (Amestoy et al., 2017); *horizontalidad*, or the Argentinian approach to social relationships that advocates for the equitable distribution of management (Watkins, 2012); and cultural invasion (Freire's antithesis of dialogue) in management education (Misoczky, 2024). However, less is understood about how CCP speaks to and with Freirean revolutionary *leadership* specifically.

In what follows, I first outline CCP as a specific approach that centers communication in critical processes, in the particular context of pedagogical environments (including, but not limited to, conventional classrooms). I then outline qualities of Freire's revolutionary leadership, identifying how each quality manifests in and is shaped by communication processes. Finally, I profile Rukia Rogers, founder of the Highlander School early childhood program in Atlanta, Georgia. I chose to focus on an early childhood education program to dispel the myth that children are too young or too innocent to understand complex issues and develop critical interventions.

A note on language

Within his oeuvre, Freire uses different terminology for the same referent in a number of instances. From the beginning of his work, he was deeply concerned about conditions of oppression and thus distinguished between *oppressor* and *oppressed*. He also referred to the *oppressed* as "the people," meaning those who are in subordinated positions and were objects of some type of violence. That violence can be as egregious as being arbitrarily targeted and forcibly removed from one's home due to perceptions of difference, to being denied the opportunity to participate in decision-making processes. This means that "the people" can refer to political refugees, students in classrooms, and so on. Thus, I often refer to "the people" in this chapter, in the way that Freire used the term. He also used various terms for leadership in transformative, revolutionary processes. These include "authentic leaders" and "revolutionary leaders." In this chapter, I maintain the terms "revolutionary leaders" and "revolutionary leadership."

Critical communication pedagogy

Freire's revolutionary pedagogical programs gave birth to the theoretical framework of critical pedagogy, developed primarily in the 1980s and 1990s by educational theorists such as Antonia Darder, Henry Giroux, Ira Shor, and Peter McLaren. Critical pedagogies positioned Freire's vision of education as a means to liberation and freedom in conversation with critical theory. In so doing, critical pedagogues name how education is a structure, amongst a constellation of other structures (such as religion, family, government, and identity), that participates in constituting a person as a subject in the context of culture and everyday life. This constitution process is always imbued with power dynamics that ebb and flow amongst objects within. Thus, the process is always also imbued with tensions that, when articulated and made known, show us the workings of the process itself. For example, when a teacher (i.e., classroom leader) makes available books such as *Love Makes a Family* (Beer, 2018), that teacher is using their power to mark legitimated knowledge content. When a parent does not believe that LGBTQ+ content should be available for students and complains to the school board, that teacher's ability to guide knowledge content is threatened. Even if the school board dismisses the parent's complaint, the question about representation is still present because it was articulated. It is now made possible. And when a case like this goes to the U.S. Supreme Court, and the court rules that schools should be required to inform parents of when "LGBTQ+-inclusive storybooks" (Quinn, 2025) are part of the curriculum so that parents can opt out on the basis of religious freedom and development, then the structure of the court (in this example) wields power. In a scenario like this, if the teacher were to hang a pride flag in the classroom, they would be exercising a different kind of power in the face of the structural power of the court and the familial power of the parents. Power is working in multiple flows at the same time, and critical pedagogy puts focus on these flows in the context of a commitment to democratic and liberatory education.

CCP, coined and developed in 2007 by scholars Fassett and Warren, draws heavily on Freire's pedagogy and is an extension of critical pedagogy with specific attention paid to the role of communication in the flow of power on micro-, meso-, and macro levels. CCP takes inspiration from several theorists such as Michel Foucault, Judith Butler, and Michel de Certeau. Specifically, Fassett and Warren draw upon Foucault's axes of power, which describe how individuals are controlled in space (e.g., desk arrangements), controlled in time (e.g., now is the time to read, now is the time to play, now is the time to eat), categorized (e.g., must be of a certain age in order to enter into public school), and forced to shift from individualistic to institutional thinking. "Foucault's four characteristics are not only communicative, but it is in and through communication that we come to see how they function and to what end" (Fassett & Warren, 2007, p. 68).

Fassett and Warren (2007) use Butler to show how bodies are disciplined in classrooms and educational spaces. Butler's (1990) performativity describes how "a *stylized repetition of acts*" (p. 270) constitutes identity structures. For example, there's nothing inherently biological in the marker of "woman," as evidenced by the changing ways we might understand "woman" over time. In a U.S. classroom, a common image is of a teacher standing in front of the room (the "front" being wherever the teacher's desk is, where the dry erase boards are located, etc.) and students sitting in desks in rows. This arrangement is not a requirement, nor is it the only way to learn or to do school. However, this arrangement has been repeated and repeated over time, both in actual classrooms and in representations of classrooms, such that it has become sedimented and expected. Thus, who is the "teacher" and who is the "student" can be generally surmised at a glance. Even still, this arrangement can be interrupted and done differently, as we see with some regularity in college classrooms. It's not uncommon in a collegiate context to see a group of people of varying ages sitting around a conference table, and at any given time, if someone were to walk in who is unfamiliar with the people around the table, that bystander wouldn't as easily be able to tell who is the teacher and who is the student. Thus, performatives (the repetition of acts over time) allow us to examine how certain constructs have been "naturalized," as well as how the naturalization process might be interrupted to speak truth to power. Communication is a powerful tool to enact these consequential interruptions.

Finally, de Certeau's strategies and tactics bring into relief how communication can craft powerful tactics with which to resist strategies. If strategies are used by those in positions of sanctioned power (such as the Supreme Court or other bodies of power mandating that schools warn parents if they are using a book with LGBTQ+ characters, as though such characters are harmful), then tactics are ways that those subject to power can speak back to and within the structure (such as a teacher hanging a pride flag in the classroom). Fassett and Warren (2007) argue that people aren't wholly dominated by strategies; strategies might work within people, but people are also capable of working back through tactics. Tactics and strategies exist in tension with one another, and both rely upon communication as their central mechanism.

Fassett and Warren (2007) identify ten commitments that undergird a CCP ethic. These commitments involve communication as it intersects with identity, power, culture, the interaction of mundane communication practices and larger structural systems, language, reflexivity, praxis, human subjectivity and agency, and dialogue. Atay and Pensoneau-Conway (2020)

> identify fundamental questions that a CCP perspective asks about any object of inquiry: practices, ideas, actions, processes, systems, and so on. From a phenomenological lens, CCP asks: What conditions have created the possibility of this object? From a critical theory lens, CCP asks: What power relations are at play in this object? From a philosophical lens, CCP asks: What are the fundamental assumptions about [knowledge-epistemology; values-axiology; being-ontology; action/reflection-praxiology] at work in this object? From a communicative lens, CCP asks: What communication acts are working in and on this object, and how might communication acts create change?
>
> *(p. 5)*

Thus, communication becomes a key factor in revolutionary change, and pedagogical contexts offer a heuristic environment for examining communication. Outside of the focus on communication, critical pedagogy and leadership have been put together in a number of inquiries, three of which I profile below.

In teaching transformational leadership theory, Harrison (2011) found that students often reacted with overwhelm, struggling to grasp the practicality of transformational leadership. Harrison identified a key conundrum in teaching such leadership, namely an "ambivalence about the role of power in developing and promoting a vision" (p. 127). The importance of addressing power and privilege in teaching transformational leadership can be aided by integrating critical pedagogy. Specifically, Harrison felt supported by "critical pedagogy's conceptual framework for interrogating systemic power" (p. 129) and rejection of the transactional model of education. However, conventional U.S. education is set up as a transaction. Thus, teaching transformational leadership in a transactional classroom poses a challenge. However, a classroom undergirded by Freire's and critical pedagogy's commitments to dialogue, collaboration, and agency funds the project of transformational leadership. A critical pedagogical orientation allowed Harrison to model the power critique important in transformational leadership. Further, students "understood now that transformational leadership asked much more of them than coming up with a convincing vision and getting people to follow it" (p. 134).

Also writing out of leadership education, Pendakur and Furr (2016) write specifically to leadership educators and those building leadership curriculum. They intended to provide such educators with the necessary critical tools to best support students of color. "When applied to leadership education, critical pedagogy opens possibilities for faculty and staff to work more effectively with various communities of students of color by centering issues of race, power, and identity as foundational to developing empowered leader identities" (p. 47). As a way to show how critical pedagogy can engage leadership theory specifically, they examine the social change model of leadership. While helpful with its focus on leadership development (as opposed to just the concept of leadership) and its understanding of personal, group, and service leadership, the social change model fails to "name or acknowledge how social identities such as race, gender, class, and so forth affect one's understanding of values or access to them, thus leaving out the varied experiences of students of color in particular" (p. 50).

Finally, Jeyaraj and Gandolfi (2019) turn their attention to servant leadership. They argue that critical pedagogy, with an emphasis on empowerment and ethics, has much in common with servant leadership. Specifically, they identify trust, dialogue, and empowerment as three concepts fundamental to critical pedagogy, which can speak to the ideals of servant leadership. After reviewing *how* these three concepts play out in critical pedagogy, they go on to show how and why servant leaders should also integrate trust, dialogue, and empowerment into their leadership approaches and practices. That is, a servant leader can engage in specific acts to build trust, which then creates the possibility for dialogue. In dialogue, "critical reflection and action are made possible" (p. 289), thus also creating the possibility for empowerment.

Missing from existing literature that combines critical pedagogy and leadership are two key points which I address in this chapter: specific attention to *Freirean leadership* and the role of *communication*. It is helpful, then, to put CCP into conversation with Freire's revolutionary leadership, in order to ask how such leadership might manifest in classroom environments undergirded by the commitments of CCP. Building upon CCP's emphasis on power, identity, and agency in educational spaces, Freirean revolutionary leadership provides an expanded theoretical map for understanding how leadership itself can function as a communicative and relational practice.

Freirean revolutionary leadership

Freire's ideas on the responsibility and role of revolutionary leaders were influenced by his personal experiences (e.g., sudden thrust into poverty as a child, exile as an adult), professional experiences (e.g., creating literacy programs, working with rural peasants), and sometimes volatile relationship with government and cultural leaders. In outlining the function of leaders, it's important to start with a fundamental claim of Freire: people (leaders themselves included) are incomplete when they are not full Subjects in the world. A full Subject in, as opposed to an object of, the world is one who experiences agency, who has the capacity for and opportunity to name their reality, critically reflect on it, and freely intervene to transform it. This, writes Freire, is our (leaders and the people) vocation—to be more fully human.

Rather than prescribing what leaders do, Freire identified various qualities and approaches of revolutionary leaders. In the next section, I expound upon these qualities and approaches of Freirean revolutionary leadership, beginning with a framework for critical pedagogy.

To name, to critically reflect, to act

Joan Wink (2005) provides a helpful heuristic for critical pedagogy: to name, to critically reflect, to act. This framework is evident in Freire's writings as a whole and undergirds his description of revolutionary leadership.

Naming one's reality becomes a first step in revolution, and this is done, in part, through organizing. Freire (1970/2000) argues that dominant elites seek only to organize themselves, so as to hold and wield more and more power over the people. However, revolutionary leaders organize *with* the people in naming the world, a categorically communicative act that engenders critical reflection and action. "Organizing the people is the process in which the revolutionary leaders, who are also prevented from saying their own word, initiate the experience of learning how to *name* the world" (p. 177–178). Further, "in the midst of reflective action on the world to be transformed, the people come to recognize that the world is indeed being transformed" (1970, p. 470). Thus, a circular process has begun—naming, critically reflecting, and acting happen in a continuous revolution. This heuristic sets a basis by which to examine additional elements of Freirean revolutionary leadership, which include dialogue, praxis, communal Subjecthood, a changed leadership, and humility.

Dialogue

In the framework of name-reflect-act, dialogue functions as a key context in which naming happens. This may also be the most obviously communicative component of revolutionary leadership. Dialogue is the process by which people and leaders come to make sense of their constructed world and by which they—together—name the conditions that created the present moment. In that sense, dialogue has a temporal character to it. Rather than simply conversation (which does not necessitate critical thinking), dialogue is a critical process by which people come to decode what's happening to and around them. It is an act of creation, "the encounter between [people], mediated by the world, in order to name the world" (Freire, 1970/2000, p. 88), and "in order to transform the world" (Freire, 1970/2000, p. 129).

Freire (1974/2005a) identified three primary modes of consciousness by which people move through the world: (1) naive consciousness, in which people feel like they have no power over their own lives, a sort of "what can I possibly do?" approach; (2) magical consciousness, in which people attribute their conditions and their situation to some divine or external providence, a sort of "this is what is meant to be for me" approach; and (3) critical consciousness, in which people identify their limiting situation as the result of a system of privileges and oppressions, a system in which they have the power to act and that can be transformed. The first two consciousnesses categorically strip autonomy away from people, while the third is fertile ground for liberation. Critical consciousness and dialogue exist in circularity: critical consciousness creates the possibility of dialogue, and within dialogue grows critical consciousness. A revolutionary leader cannot impose dialogue, or force dialogue, but rather can (and should) work to create the conditions that foster dialogue. Indeed, early and courageous dialogue is a condition for the revolution (1970/2000, p. 128) and is what Freire calls the "correct method for revolutionary leadership" (1970/2000, p. 67).

Praxis

In the name-reflect-act framework, praxis embodies the last two. It describes how revolutionary and transformative human activity should not be done outside of critical reflection; critical reflection comes alongside identified actions "directed at the structures to be transformed" (Freire, 1970/2000, p. 126). In other words, praxis, in revolutionary leadership, is a "theory of transforming [or transformative] action" (Freire, 1970/2000, p. 126). The revolution can only be achieved through praxis; it can't be considered that the leaders are thinkers and the oppressed are doers, but that both are both. "The leaders do bear the responsibility for coordination and, at times, direction—but leaders who deny praxis to the oppressed thereby invalidate their own praxis" (Freire, 1970/2000, p. 126). If leaders deny the oppressed the opportunity to engage in critical reflection and instead simply tell people what to do, then they deny their own praxis as well. Additionally, praxis is the space where "cultural action" becomes "cultural revolution" (Freire, 1970, p. 470)—action in the service of transformation. Dialogue, then, is the space where praxis grows.

Subjects, together, of and in revolutionary action

Such revolutionary action necessitates active participation by both leaders *and* people, together, in "unshakable solidarity" (Freire, 1970/2000, p. 129). In this sense, the people must enter into a Subject relationship with revolutionary action, not simply an object relationship. Oppressive conditions place the oppressed in a passive object position of being *acted upon* and *thought about*—the opposite of an active Subject. Freire (1970/2000) argues that the revolution cannot be carried out "'*by*' *the people for the leaders*" (p. 129), in the sense that leaders cannot set out an agenda and impose it on the people, then sit back and watch the people simply enact the will of the leader. Indeed, Freire (1970) is very specific in what revolutionary leadership cannot do, which includes "denounc[ing] reality without knowing reality" and "know[ing] reality without relying on the people as well as on objective facts for the source of its knowledge" (p. 468). He goes on to explain that revolutionary leadership is impossible when a leader imposes (or otherwise tries to garner conformity with) "a future that the leadership knows *a priori*" without being in communion with the people (1970, p. 468).

In other words, revolutionary leaders must think *with* the people, not *for* or *without* them (Freire, 1970/2000, p. 131). Leaders and people together determine action. Freire (1970/2000) establishes cultural synthesis as one element of the theory of dialogical action, in which leaders build genuine community with the people, and vice versa, through dialogue. In this synthetic process, the worldviews of leaders and people come together not in a way that further affirms their separate roles, but in such a way that honors the revolutionary transformation of reality and affirms one another's more fully human-ness (p. 181). In so doing, "leaders and the people become like one body" (1970, p. 477) but neither are the same as when they began. The people are "becoming more and more critically conscious" (1970, p. 473), and "leaders" are now "people."

A changed leadership

Being in communion with more critically conscious people is key in a changed leadership. In other words, revolutionary leaders can only be authentic if they renounce the more conventional vertical relationship between leaders and people, and if the people participate in the process of renunciation. Revolutionary leaders "must 'die,' in order to be reborn through and with the oppressed" (Freire, 1970/2000, p. 133). Such relational reciprocity is so foundational to revolution. Change cannot come from leaders, change cannot come from the people, but rather, change must come from the liberatory and dialogic relationship between people and leaders. For example, in naming reality, in articulating the world, "True leaders cannot say their word alone, they must say it with the people" (p. 178). In so doing, both leaders and the people are liberated.

This, in part, explains Freire's skepticism of traditional leadership training. (Freire passed away in 1997 and so did not comment on contemporary leadership training approaches, though certainly his critique could apply to some.) He surmised that leadership training courses tend to be alienating because they promote the parts rather than the whole (i.e., we only need to train the leaders, not the whole community). This "divide and rule" approach is a sure way to maintain the suppression of the people and the power of the leader and is wholly anti-dialogical (1970/2000, p. 142). He was of the belief that "modern business leaders accept, stimulate, and support technical training courses for their workers" (1998, p. 92) but fail to provide opportunities to reflect on what the content of such courses means for people's situations in the world. They fail to provide the resources by which the people/workers can examine the content in the context of a broader, connected understanding of how that content is part of a larger constellation of forces working in people's (and leaders') lives. But in unity, leaders and people collaborate with one another, and as a result, both are changed, both are better able to be Subjects of their worlds, and both create the power to intervene in reality.

Humility

Freire (2014) defines *humility* as being "that respect for the rights of others, that recognition that others can do things that we do not do" (p. 25), and is imperative for revolutionary leaders to adopt as an ethical posture. This entails a respect for and giving serious consideration to "the reasons for any attitude of mistrust on the part of the people" (1970/2000, p. 166). A humble leader is able to do so while not doubting "the utopia of democracy" (1997, p. 60). Revolutionary leaders must avoid the impulse to "invade" the people's culture with their own worldviews and values and, instead, approach leadership as an opportunity to learn (1970/2000, p. 180). A posture of humility involves a deep listening to others and "reveals an identification with democracy and not with elitism" (2005b, p. 72). When leaders have "convert[ed] to the cause of the oppressed," and when the people have committed to their own capacity to transform, then "both will have met the requirements to learning humility" (1997, p. 87).

I opened this chapter by establishing the theoretical foundation of CCP, with its emphasis on power, identity, and agency within educational spaces. I then profiled qualities of a Freirean revolutionary leader. I now turn to a concrete example of what it looks like when an educational leader embodies the principles of Freirean revolutionary leadership, undergirded by the commitments of CCP.

Rukia Rogers and the Highlander School

> I envision a world full of love, empathy, equity, and justice. A world here each human has agency over their body, freedom from harm and the "brutality of capitalism," access to health care, housing, food, and basic rights. Education creates connection between this envisioned world and our daily work and practices.
>
> *(Rukia Rogers [Mwenelupembe, 2023, p. 87])*

To better examine what revolutionary leadership might look like in practice, particularly in the context of education, I profile Highlander School early childhood program in Atlanta, GA, and its founder (a leader in early childhood education and a communication disruptor), Rukia Rogers.

In 2007, Rogers began concrete conversations about what would become the Highlander School, which opened its doors in 2013. The Highlander School was named to honor the Highlander Folk School, a movement and justice school founded by activist and educator Myles Horton in the early 1900s in Tennessee and still operating today. Even in the name of the school, Rogers adopts a stance of humility in honoring those who came before her. The mission of the Highlander Folk School (now the Highlander Research and Education Center) is and has always been to have strong grass roots in the communities it serves; to enact change grounded in the participation, reflection, and action of the community members (and thereby enact a critical pedagogical framework); and to draw upon collective power and knowledge in order to transform reality for the better. That mission informs the work of the Highlander School. While Rogers does not directly reference Freire's influence in her leadership and philosophy of education, there is a close indirect connection. Horton and Freire were familiars and engaged in many conversations about the convergences and divergences in their approaches to education as a liberatory practice. These conversations came together most notably in their book *We Make the Road by Walking: Conversations on Education and Social Change* (Horton & Freire, 1990). As such, the philosophy and practices behind Rogers's leadership very much align both with CCP and Freire's revolutionary leadership.

Even when the Highlander School was still in Rogers's dreamscape, she knew that she wanted to carry the legacy of Horton's Highlander Folk Center. The latter saw legendary change makers like Rosa Parks, Dr. Martin Luther King Jr., and John Lewis come through its doors as students, and Rogers wanted her early childhood center to emulate such a "safe haven for dialogue and nonviolent resistance to social injustices. Our hope and illuminating dream is that our Highlander School will embody this same spirit of freedom and cultivate a community of learners who are thirsty for knowledge" (Carter, 2013, p. 22). Thus, dialogue and participation are key components of the Highlander School's ethic. And as revolutionary leaders do, Rogers opened the Highlander School only after having sought the input and perspectives of others, especially the perspectives and dreams of the families. These proved particularly valuable to how the Highlander School approaches its relationship to food, nutrition, and the earth (Carter, 2013, p. 23).

As a leader in early childhood education, Rogers strives to create educational spaces grounded in decolonization, transparency, anti-capitalism, collaboration, connection, and interdependence—in other words, a meaningful engagement with issues of power and inequity becomes a key element of the Highlander School's world-building and world-engagement. She's deeply committed to children actively participating in their own lives, to learning from children, and to fostering a desire for relationship building and community thinking. Key values of her work, and of her leadership within the Highlander School, center on equity and justice in their many forms—cultural equity, environmental and social justice, food access and security, and so on. Informing her perspectives is a desire to "reclaim African and Indigenous values that were misunderstood and almost destroyed by centuries of global imperialism and colonization" (Rogers, 2022, p. 84). Such a commitment to epistemological justice rings throughout Roger's leadership. For Rogers (2022), social justice educators (or, as Freire might say, revolutionary pedagogical leaders) have a responsibility to foster an environment where children are able to see themselves "as a critical member of a wider community of living and not living, human and not human" (p. 84). She embodies these commitments through a number of communicative practices, including the physical arrangements of the Highlander School, rhetorical choices such as continually referring to children as "citizens," and a dialogic pattern of asking the children of the School to name and articulate what they see happening around them and how they are making sense of it. Thus, the children of the school learn the consequential quality of communication at a very early age, because they are invited to be agents within their own communicative practices, and they see themselves included in communicative processes.

At the Highlander School, "We believe children have the right to be treated with respect, dignity and to be a part of the decision-making process. Children are viewed not as passive participants, but as active discoverers and constructors of their own knowledge" (The Highlander School, n.d.b). Core values of the School include relationship building (with others and the environment), the rights of the child (to be taken seriously as a curious, competent, and capable human being), the rights of families (to be partners in school community and culture), the rights of teachers (as skilled professionals), democracy and a sense of belonging (empowerment to participate in decision-making), equity and social justice (early childhood education is a gateway for justice, and every child "has the right to attain his or her fullest potential through creative expression, thought, inquiry, collaboration and dissension"), the natural world and conservation (stewards of the honored earth), multiple perspectives (so as to challenge one's thinking and create deeper understandings of one another and one's surroundings), transparency, and joy (The Highlander School, n.d.a). These values directly stem from Rogers's leadership and vision of early childhood education.

The Highlander School has operated for over ten years now. Rogers's vision remains the same and is being actualized in informal and invisible ways (such as in the potential of the children who age out) and in ways that are visible, such as the community garden at the school (which the children agree is for those at the School, the animals, the unhoused in the community, and "for everyone who needs water and food" [Highlander School child Jace (Rogers, 2024, p. 164)]), the children's letters to the mayor of Atlanta asking that the laws regarding feeding unhoused populations be changed, and so on. Rogers (2024) stresses,

> We are compelled to reimagine a world full of love, justice, and equity. We are inspired to fashion a community of learners, where children are viewed as "citizens of today." We envision a world where every child is able to dream and to reach his or her full potential.
>
> *(p. 3)*

Conclusion

Seeds of change are often planted, cultivated, and grown in classrooms. Classrooms provide fertile ground for examining how individuals learn what place they have in the world, how they understand their capacity to act, and how they articulate possibilities for identifying and responding to issues as micro as communicating humanely with a classmate and as macro as election fraud or world poverty rates. Paulo Freire's work in critical pedagogy, cultural activism, world making, and revolution has much to teach us about leadership for change. Deanna Fassett and John Warren's work has much to teach us about the role of communication in developing revolutionary leadership within pedagogical contexts. And Rukia Rogers and the Highlander School's work demonstrates revolutionary leadership communication in action. She has built the Highlander School from a foundation of dialogue, praxis, collaboration as Subjects, a changed leadership, and humility.

> Highlander is motivated by the desire to facilitate young people's autonomy in a setting that promotes collective liberation, connection to the earth, and racial solidarity.... By creating a community and committing to the principles of abolitionist education, Rukia has helped to facilitate the advocacy of her young students and their parents.
>
> *(Abolitionist Teaching Network, 2022)*

The result is an early childhood education program that has respect for children, for the earth, and for the vocation of being more fully human, grounded in a spirit of revolution and transformation, guided by a revolutionary leader.

Suggested further readings

Darder, A. (n.d.) Revolutionary leadership for community empowerment: A Freirian approach. https://www.academia.edu/9322928/Revolutionary_Leadership_for_Community_Empowerment_A_Freirian_Approach

Dutta, M. J. (2015). Decolonizing communication for social change: A culture-centered approach. *Communication Theory*, 25(2), 123–143. https://doi.org/10.1111/comt.12067

Ford, D. (2021, September 17). Paulo Freire's centennial: Political pedagogy for revolutionary organizations. *Liberation School*. https://www.liberationschool.org/paulo-freire-and-revolutionary-leadership/

Rogers, R. M. (n.d.) *Our beloved community: Supporting children's compassion, kinship and activism* [video]. Exchange: Your Early Childhood Community. https://hub.exchangepress.com/video/9395/

Servaes, J. (2023). Communication for development and social change. In G. Gonçlaves & E. Oliveira (Eds.), *The Routledge handbook of nonprofit communication* (pp. 23–31). Routledge. https://doi.org/10.4324/9781003170563

Questions for further discussion

1 Discuss examples of revolutionary leadership that you've witnessed in your own schooling experiences. How would you describe the communication of such leaders? If you have trouble identifying revolutionary leadership examples, why might that be so?
2 How might teachers—from those in elementary education, through higher education, through community education—employ critical communication skills in the process of naming, reflecting, and acting? How might communication from revolutionary leaders be different from context to context and from group to group? What qualities of communication would be seemingly universal, regardless of context and group?

References

Abolitionist Teaching Network. (2022). *Rukia Rogers—The Highlander School Grantee Spotlight* [video]. YouTube. https://www.youtube.com/watch?v=1sEhCT6K5Bk

Amestoy, S. C., de Oliveira, A. F. L., Thofehrn, M. B., de Lima Trindade, L., dos Santos, B. P., & Bao, A. C. P. (2017). Contributions of Paulo Freire to understanding the dialogic leadership exercise of nurses in the hospital setting. Revista Gaúcha de Enfermagem, *38*(1). 1–7. http://dx.doi.org/10.1590/1983-1447.2017.01.64764

Atay, A., & Pensoneau-Conway, S. L. (2020). Introduction: Queering communication pedagogy. In A. Atay & S.L. Pensoneau-Conway (Eds.), *Queer communication pedagogy* (pp. 1–13). Routledge. https://doi.org/10.4324/9781315159164

Beer, S. (2018). *Love makes a family*. Dial Books.

Butler, J. (1990). *Gender trouble*. Routledge. https://doi.org/10.4324/9780203824979

Carter, M. (2013). Starting from scratch: Creating your dream center. *Exchange: The Early Childhood Leaders Magazine*, *214*, 22–25.

Davis, E. (2024, November 21). University of North Texas removes DEI language from course titles, descriptions. *Spectrum News 1*. https://spectrumlocalnews.com/tx/south-texas-el-paso/politics/2024/11/21/university-of-north-texas-removes-dei-language-from-course-names

Fassett, D. L., & Warren, J. T. (2007). *Critical communication pedagogy*. Sage. https://doi.org/10.4135/9781452225883

Freire, P. (1970). Cultural action and conscientization. *Harvard Educational Review*, *40*(3), 452–477. https://doi.org/10.17763/haer.40.3.h76250x720j43175

Freire, P. (1997). *Pedagogy of the heart*. Continuum.

Freire, P. (1998). *Pedagogy of freedom: Ethics, democracy, and civic courage*. Rowman & Littlefield.

Freire, P. (2000). *Pedagogy of the oppressed* (30th anniversary ed.). Continuum. (Original work published 1970.)

Freire, P. (2005a). *Education for critical consciousness*. Continuum. (Original work published 1974.)

Freire, P. (2005b). *Teachers as cultural workers: Letters to those who dare to teach*. (Expanded ed.). Westview Press. https://doi.org/10.4324/9780429496974

Freire, P. (2014). *Pedagogy of commitment*. Paradigm. https://doi.org/10.4324/9781315632919

Harrison, L. M. (2011). Using critical pedagogy to critique power issues in transformational leadership. In J. D. Barbour & G. R. Hickman (Eds.), *Leadership for transformation* (pp. 125–140). Jossey-Bass.

Horton, M., & Freire, P. (1990). *We make the road by walking: Conversations on education and social change*. B. Bell, J. Gaventa, & J. Peters (Eds.). Temple University Press.

Jeyaraj, J. J., & Gandolfi, F. (2019). Exploring trust, dialogue, and empowerment in servant leadership. *Journal of Management Research*, *19*(4), 285–290.

Kingkade, T., Goggin, B., Collins, B., & Zadrozny, B. (2022, October 14). How an urban myth about litter boxes in schools became a GOP talking point. *NBC News*. https://www.nbcnews.com/tech/misinformation/urban-myth-litter-boxes-schools-became-gop-talking-point-rcna51439

Misoczky, M. C. (2024). Paulo Freire and the praxis of liberation: Education, organization and ethics. *Management Learning*, *55*(1), 124–140.

Mwenelupembe, A. (2023). Passion: Rukia Monique Rogers. In *Stories of resistance: Learning from Black women in early care and education* (pp. 86–94). Exchange Press.

Pendakur, V., & Furr, S. C. (2016). Critical leadership pedagogy: Engaging power, identity, and culture in leadership education for college students of color. *New Directions for Higher Education*, *174*, 45–55. https://doi.org/10.1002/he.20188

Quinn, M. (2025, June 27). Supreme Court sides with parents who objected to kids' books on gender identity, sexuality. *CBS News*. https://www.cbsnews.com/news/supreme-court-parents-school-books-gender/

Rogers, R. M. (2022). Unpacking "child-centered": Reimagining early childhood through African and Indigenous lenses. *Exchange: The Early Childhood Leaders Magazine*, *263*, 82–85. https://hub.exchangepress.com/articles-on-demand/1891/

Rogers, R. M. (2024). *The many stories of our beloved community: Honoring young children's kinship and connections with the world*. Redleaf Press.

The Highlander School (n.d.a). *Our core values*. https://thehighlanderschool.com/our-approach/our-core-values/

The Highlander School (n.d.b). *Our philosophy*. https://thehighlanderschool.com/our-approach/our-philosophy/

Watkins, M. (2012). Revolutionary leadership: From Paulo Freire to the Occupy movement. *Journal for Social Action in Counseling and Psychology*, *4*(2), 1–22. https://doi.org/10.33043/JSACP.4.2.1-22

Wink, J. (2005). *Critical pedagogy: Notes from the real world* (3rd ed.). Pearson.

INDEX

Note: Page references in *italics* denote figures, in **bold** tables and with "n" endnotes.

For Product Safety Concerns and Information please contact our EU representative GPSR@taylorandfrancis.com
Taylor & Francis Verlag GmbH, Kaufingerstraße 24, 80331 München, Germany

www.ingramcontent.com/pod-product-compliance
Ingram Content Group UK Ltd.
Pitfield, Milton Keynes, MK11 3LW, UK
UKHW022346190926
475702UK00015B/2137

* 9 7 8 1 0 3 2 9 0 2 2 8 9 *